# U.S. Forces
# Travel Guide
## to U.S. Military Installations

Ann Crawford, Publisher
Military Living Publications, and
Executive Vice-President, Military Marketing Services, Inc.

William Roy Crawford, Sr., Ph.D., President
Military Living Publications, and
Military Marketing Services, Inc.

R.J. Crawford, Executive Vice President-Marketing

J.J. Caddell, Vice President-Editorial

Editor – J.J. Caddell

Project Editor – Deborah K. Harder

Cover Design – J.J. Caddell

Military Living Publications
P. O. Box 2347
Falls Church, Virginia 22042-0347


TEL: (703) 237-0203

FAX: (703) 237-2233

E-mail: milliving@aol.com

www.militaryliving.com

Printed in Canada

# NOTICE

The information in this book has been compiled and edited either from the activity/installation listed, its superior headquarters, or from other sources that may or may not be noted by the authors. Information about the facilities listed, including contact phone numbers and rate structures, could change. This book should be used as a guide to the listed facilities with this understanding. Please forward any corrections or additions by e-mail to editormlp@aol.com or by mail or phone to: **Military Living Publications, P. O. Box 2347, Falls Church, Virginia 22042-0347. TEL: 703-237-0203, FAX: 703-237-2233.**

This directory is published by Military Marketing Services, Inc., T/A Military Living Publications, a private business in no way connected with the U.S. Federal or any other government. This book is copyrighted by L. Ann and William Roy Crawford, Sr. Opinions expressed by the publisher and authors of this book are their own and are not to be considered an official expression by any government agency or official.

The information and statements contained in this directory have been compiled from sources believed to be reliable and to represent the best current opinion (at press time) on the subject. No warranty, guarantee, or representation is made by Military Marketing Services, Inc., as to the absolute correctness or sufficiency of any representation contained in this or other publications and we can assume no responsibility.

**Library of Congress Cataloging-in-Publication Data**

```
Crawford, Ann Caddell.
    U.S. forces travel guide to U.S. military installations / Ann Crawford, William Roy
  Crawford, Sr.
      p. cm.
    Includes index.
    ISBN: 0-914862-81-2
    1. Military bases, American--Directories. I. Crawford, William Roy, 1932-

  UA26.A2 C7323 1999
  355.7'0973--dc21                                                    99-056743
```

**ISBN 0-914862-81-2**

# HOW TO USE THIS DIRECTORY

Each listing has similar information, listed in the following order:

## Name of Installation (AL01R2)
Street/P.O. Box
City/APO/FPO, State, ZIP Code

**LOCATION IDENTIFIER:** Example (AL01R2). The first two characters (letters) are Country/State abbreviations used in Military Living's books (Appendix A). The next two characters are random numbers (00-99) assigned to a specific location. The fifth character is an R indicating region and the sixth character is the region number.

**TELEPHONE NUMBER INFORMATION: C-** This is the commercial telephone service for the installation's main or information/operator assistance number; the designation has also been used for other commercial numbers in this directory. Within the North American Area Code System, the first three digits are the area code. The next three digits are the area telephone exchange/switch number. The last four digits are usually the information or operator assistance number, or the line number of a specific telephone.

**D-** This is the Department of Defense, worldwide, Defense Switched Network (DSN). We have, at the request of our readers, included the DSN prefix with most numbers in each listing. In most cases, the number given is for information/operator assistance. *Note: The 312 CONUS area code on defense number is for calls made from areas outside CONUS. When calling within CONUS the 312 should not be used.*

**FAX:** Telefax numbers are listed when available.

**E-MAIL:** Electronic mail addresses for internet communication are listed when available.

**WEB:** Addresses for websites are listed when available.

**LOCATION:** Specific driving instructions to the installation from local major cities, interstate highways and routes are given. More than one routing may be provided. **USMRA:** is **MILITARY LIVING'S "United States Military Road Atlas"** reference to the location. **NMC:** is the nearest major city. The distance and direction from the installation to the NMC are given. This information is given for informational purposes only. As roads and exits are constantly undergoing construction and changes, we recommend you verify all information prior to travel.

**GENERAL:** Major activities, organizations, military units and special information concerning the installation, if any, are provided in this section.

**TEMPORARY MILITARY LODGING:** The billeting/lodging office or registration/check-in point, location and complete telephone/fax contact/reservation numbers are provided. Hours of operation are noted. Category of persons accommodated is specified and special contact

numbers for DV/VIP (Distinguished Visitor/Very Important Person, both officer and enlisted grades) are provided. **Detailed information at over 425 installations worldwide is contained in Military Living's all-time best-selling title, *Temporary Military Lodging Around the World*. See coupon in this book for ordering information.**

**LOGISTICAL SUPPORT**: The scope of support facilities available at the installation is specified and the telephone number for the facility is provided. Space limitations preclude listing all support numbers; however, the telephone numbers for facilities not listed are available through the information operator number in each listing.

**HEALTH & WELFARE:** The installation or nearest medical emergency information and/or appointment service numbers are listed. The installation or servicing medical inpatient numbers are provided as well. Chaplain support and chapel service contact numbers are specified.

**RECREATION:** The contact telephone number for most rest, recreation and athletic facilities are given for each installation. Information about camping and recreation areas on the installation, controlled by the installation, or near the installation is provided. **Complete camping and recreation area details are contained in *Military Living's Military RV, Camping and Rec Areas Around the World*. See coupons in this book for ordering information.**

**SPACE-A:** The numbers provided are the Space-A information numbers at specified departure locations. If no Space-A is available at the given installation, the name of the nearest installation with Space-A opportunities is provided. **Full Space-A information such as arrival/departure locations, aircraft used, schedules, terminal facilities, eligibility, rules, travel documents needed and more, are all contained in Military Living's best-selling book, *Military Space-A Air Opportunities Around the World*. See coupons in this book for ordering information.**

**ATTRACTIONS:** This section provides information to the traveler about attractions on the installation or in the surrounding area.

Please review the appendices for abbreviations used in this book and for other helpful information. **Address your questions regarding this title or other Military Living books to: Military Living Publications, P.O. Box 2347, Falls Church, Virginia 22042-0347. ATTN: Ann or Roy Crawford. You may telephone or fax us at 703-237-0203, FAX 703-237-2233 or E-mail: <milliving@aol.com>. No collect calls accepted. Visit our web site at www.militaryliving.com**

## SAMPLE MAP

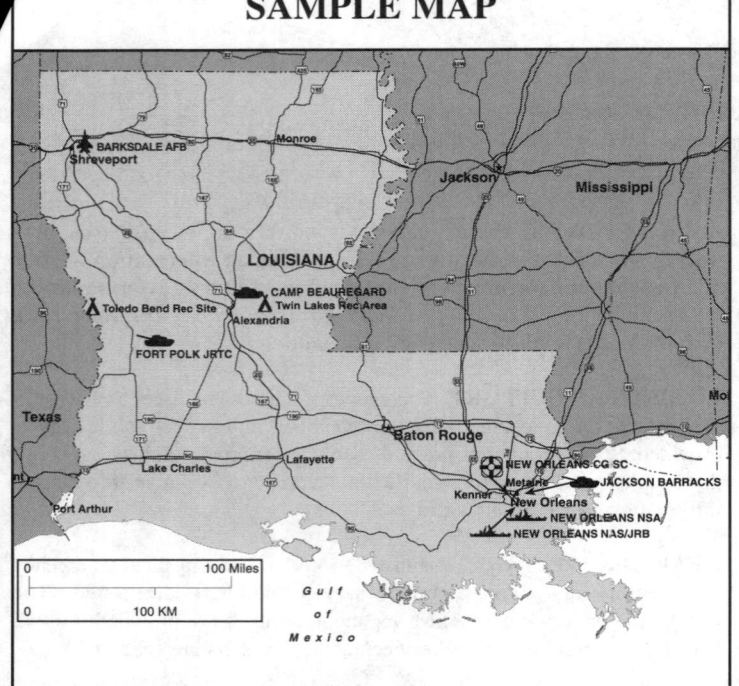

## MAP KEY

- 🛡 **Army** (Active, National Guard, Reserves)
- ⚓ **Navy** (Active, Reserves)
- **Marine Corps** (Active, Reserves)
- **Coast Guard** (Active, Reserves)
- ✈ **Air Force** (Active, Reserves, Air National Guard)
- ✈ **International Airport**
- Δ **Recreation Area**
- **Space Center**
- ⬟ **Defense Installation**

## BASE CLOSURES

The 1995 Defense Base Closure and Realignment Commission's Report was accepted by Congress and became Public Law on 28 September 1995.

The 1995 law, along with previous directed closures and realignments in the basic law in 1988, 1990, 1991 and 1993, complete the base closure and realignments which have been approved by Congress. These directed closures have been noted at the beginning of each listing affected with the DoD estimated date of final closure. Some bases have already closed and consequently have been deleted from this edition.

It should also be noted that final closure dates will be established for each installation. These dates could change as the DoD completes the final closure plans and as funding becomes available to effect the closures. Support facilities on the affected bases will normally decrease gradually, therefore it is best to check with each military installation scheduled for closure or realignment before you go.

Lastly, it should be noted that the 1995 Defense Base Closure and Realignment Law, along with previous base closure laws, only apply to domestic United States Bases and United States Bases located in United States possessions. There are very few bases remaining that have not closed.

## OUR CHANGING WORLD

The military is undergoing sweeping changes which have made this book both challenging and interesting to publish. Some installations are closing and others are realigning. We have included the dates of expected closure as provided to us at the beginning of each listing. We have not included installations which do not have support facilities and consequently are of limited value to our readers.

The information in this book is as accurate as we can make it. The information in this book has been provided by military installations in the Continental United States (CONUS), Alaska, Hawaii and US possessions overseas. However, as with all directories, there are changes that happen daily that cause inaccuracies.

**Military Living Publications** has always relied on its readers to write or call when information has become outdated. It is the secret of our success. Please do not hesitate to let us know when information is incorrect, or if we have missed an installation for your fellow travelers. Enjoy.

## PHOTO CREDITS

All photographs, including those on the cover and those located within the book, are provided courtesy of the facility shown unless otherwise noted.

# HOW TO SAVE MONEY ON YOUR TRAVEL

*Travel on less per day . . . the military way!*™

**STAY WITH "FAMILY"** - Right! Military families can stay with "family" as they travel around the United States and its territories. No matter where you go, there is probably a military installation en route! Our family always got that "back-home feeling" the minute they entered the front gate of a military installation. Does yours?

**MAKE EVERY MOVE A MINI-VACATION!** Military installations not only offer temporary military lodging to those military ID card holders on the road again. All kinds of facilities are available to help cut your cost on the way.

**EATING** - You have the added advantage of being able to pick up provisions at the commissary to make many of your meals while on the road. The savings are great - just like back home at your military post, base or station. Stop at a military fast-food outlet, a military club or at the golf course for a bite to eat and take a break. It's not good to keep moving without stopping - and the kids need a rest, too.

**GASOLINE & AUTO REPAIRS** - Stop at military exchange gas stations and save. Should you run into auto trouble, check and see if there is a military auto repair shop close by - these facilities are part of the military support facilities. You will know who you are dealing with and have someone to talk to if you are not satisfied!

**PICK UP NEEDED TRAVEL ITEMS** at your military exchange. Buy a telephone card to use instead of costly third-party dialing and collect calls. Cash checks. Use restrooms! Whatever was available to you at your home installation is almost always available to you when traveling.

**HAVE SOME FUN!** - Take a swim in a military pool, play a round of golf, or at some places on the water - take a sail! You are not limited to using morale, welfare and recreation (MWR) facilities or Services at your home base. Show the kids how the other Services live! The whole military network is yours!

**SPLURGE** - By saving on much of your travel, you may be able to make a special memory by stopping at amusement parks and other attractions. Their tickets are available at real savings at military ticket and tour offices. In addition, you may want to stay at civilian lodging sometimes - but don't forget to show your ID and ask for their military rates!

**STOP EARLY! USE MILITARY LODGING** - Play it safer and stop sooner in the afternoon to stay at a military lodging facility. All the military armed services offer lodging at reasonable rates. Here are three toll-free phone numbers to keep in mind for your next trip - 1-800-GO-ARMY-1 (1-800-462-7691), 1-800-NAVY INN (1-800-628-9466), and 1-888-AF LODGE (1-888-235-6343).

The Army Central Reservation Line offers reservations at many Army lodging facilities; the Air Force central line connects you to Air Force lodging facilities on the CONUS, including Hickam AFB, HI; and the Navy operates a fine Navy Lodge reservation system, as well. This book will give you the phone numbers for the direct dial to these military lodging facilities as well as to those not listed at the toll-free numbers.

The big news in savings is for our **Guard** and **Reserve** families. They can now use temporary military lodging and military RV, camping and recreation areas on the same basis as active duty personnel and their families.

**CAMP OUT** - Most military outdoor recreation offices offer camping gear, from tents to small mobile units, for rent. You will be surprised at how many military installations have on-base or nearby military RV, camping and rec areas.

**YES!** You can stay with family on your next move - your military family! Plan your trip to include staying at military installations and for shopping en route. You will find savings, familiar surroundings and more safety - no matter where you go. Let *U.S. Forces Travel Guide to U.S. Military Installations* be your guide to finding savings, fun and security on your next trip!

—by Ann Crawford
Publisher

# Travel Notes

## Travel Notes

# CONTENTS

ix

# UNITED STATES

## ALABAMA

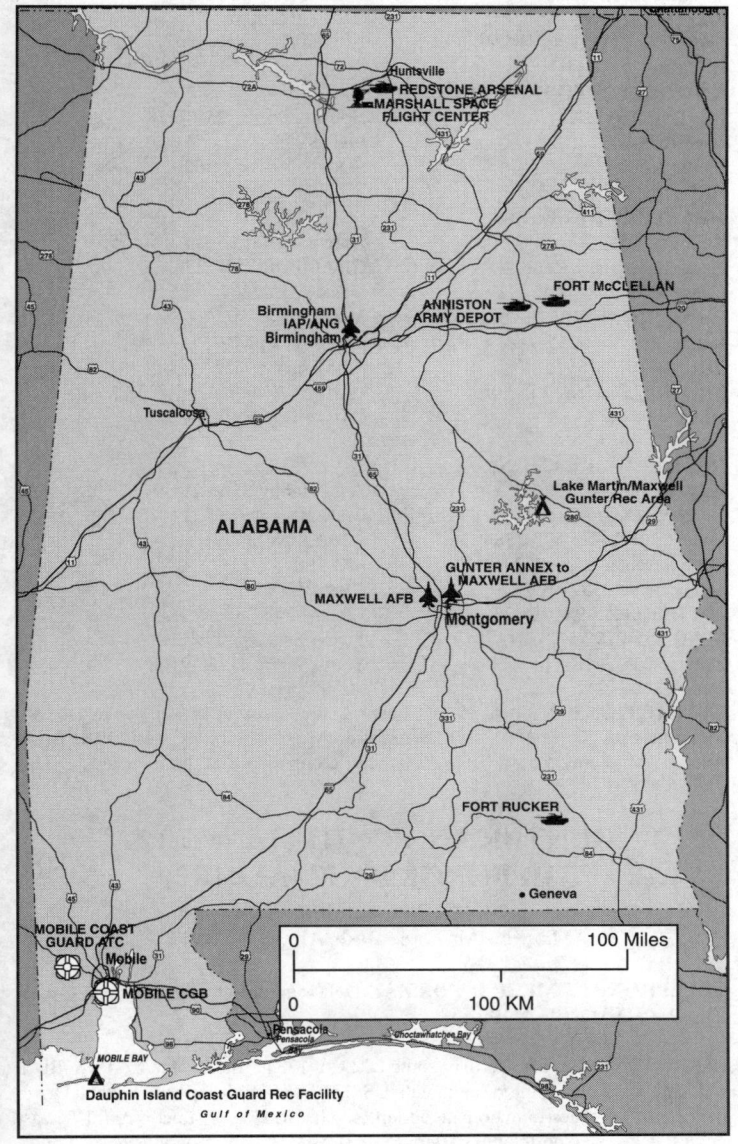

## ANNISTON ARMY DEPOT (AL13R2)

ATTN: SIOAN-CO
7 Frankford Avenue
Anniston, AL 36201-4199

**TELEPHONE NUMBER INFORMATION**: Main installation numbers: C-256-235-7501, D-312-571-1110.

**LOCATION:** From I-20 east or west take exit 185 (Oxford) north onto Highway US-78 west approximately 8 miles to state route 202 northeast and follow signs to the depot north of US-78. USMRA: Page 36 (F-3). NMC: Anniston, ten miles east.

**GENERAL INFORMATION:** Units at the Depot include the Defense Reutilization and Marketing Office, the TMDE Support Center, the CECOM Liaison Office, the Defense Logistics Agency and the Anniston Chemical Activity.

**TEMPORARY MILITARY LODGING:** None. Nearest facility is more than 100 miles away.

**RV, CAMPING/FAMCAMP:** None. Nearest facility is more than 100 miles away.

**SPACE-A:** None. See Birmingham IAP/Alabama ANGB listing.

**LOGISTICAL SUPPORT:**
Carlson Wagonlit Travel-820-3983     Exchange-237-9159

**ADMINISTRATIVE SUPPORT:**
Fire Department-235-6171     Legal-235-6334
Locator-235-7501     Public Affairs-235-6281

**HEALTH & WELFARE:**     Medical-235-7521

**REST & RECREATION:**
Camping Equipment-235-7170     Fitness Center-235-6385
MWR-235-7170     Recreation-235-6385

**ATTRACTIONS:** Anniston Museum of Natural History and the Berman Museum, also located in Anniston.

## BIRMINGHAM INTERNATIONAL AIRPORT/ AIR NATIONAL GUARD BASE (AL15R2)

5401 Eastlake Boulevard
Birmingham, AL 35217-3595

**TELEPHONE NUMBER INFORMATION:** Main installation numbers: C-205-714-2000, D-312-778-2000. WEB: www.arw117.ang.af.mil

**LOCATION:** From east or west on I-59/20 take exit 128 north onto Tallapoosa Street, then north for one-half mile to a right on Eastlake Blvd and follow the airfield fence for approximately two miles northeast to main gate on the right (southeast) side of street. USMRA: Page 36 (D,E-4). NMC: Birmingham, in city limits.

**GENERAL INFORMATION:** Home of the 117th Air Refueling Wing (KC-135R). The base is open Tue-Fri from 0700-1730 hours and some weekends.

**TEMPORARY MILITARY LODGING:** None. Nearest facility is more than 100 miles away.

**RV, CAMPING/FAMCAMP:** None. Nearest facility is more than 100 miles away.

**SPACE-A:** Pax Terminal: C-205-714-2208, D-312-778-2208. Fax: C-205-714-2610, D-312-778-2610. Some unscheduled flights available on MEDEVAC and KC-135s.

**LOGISTICAL SUPPORT:**
Exchange-714-2348     Gas Station-714-2294

**ADMINISTRATIVE SUPPORT:**
Legal-714-2305     Police-714-2240
Public Affairs-714-2527/2353

**HEALTH & WELFARE:**
Chapel-714-2215     Medical-714-2213

**REST & RECREATION:** None. Nearest facility is more than 100 miles away.

**ATTRACTIONS:** Vulcan (Iron Man Statue) on Red Mountain. The Riverchase Galleria, largest shopping mall in the Southeast, is located in Birmingham.

## DAUPHIN ISLAND COAST GUARD RECREATION FACILITY (AL07R2)

P.O. Box 436
Dauphin Island, AL 36528-0436

**TELEPHONE NUMBER INFORMATION:** Main installation number: C-334-861-7113. Police-861-5523.

**LOCATION:** On Gulf of Mexico approximately 40 miles south of Mobile. Take I-10 east or west to Highway 193 south (exit 17); south approximately 25 miles to Dauphin Island. Left (east) at dead end to east end of island. Follow signs to complex. USMRA: Page 36 (B-10). NMC: Mobile, 40 miles north. NMI: Mobile Coast Guard Group (Brookley), 40 miles north.

**GENERAL INFORMATION:**. Operated by Mobile Coast Guard Group, off base year round. Military personnel active, retired and DoD. Reservations: Required by phone, C-334-861-7113, then followed by reservation request form sent with payment.

**TEMPORARY MILITARY LODGING:** Three bedroom cottages-13

**RV, CAMPING/FAMCAMP:**

Camper spaces-5                     Camper/tent spaces-100

**ATTRACTIONS:** Explore old Fort Gaines, ancient Indian Shell mounds or Audubon Bird Sanctuary.

*For detailed information about this off-base recreation facility, as well as on-base recreation facilities, golf courses and marinas, consult Military Living's Military RV, Camping and Outdoor Recreation Around the World.*

# FORT McCLELLAN (AL01R2)

Building 51, Buckner Circle
ATTN: ATZN-GN
Fort McClellan, AL 36205-5000

**TELEPHONE NUMBER INFORMATION:** Main installation numbers: C-256-848-4611, D-312-865-1110.

**LOCATION:** From I-20 take AL-21 north nine miles to fort. From I-59 take US-431 25 miles southeast to fort. USMRA: Page 36 (F-3). NMC: Anniston, three miles southeast.

**GENERAL INFORMATION:** Scheduled to close 30 September 1999. Facilities will be turned over to community and National Guard. Commissary and Exchange scheduled to remain open.

**LOGISTICAL SUPPORT:**

Commissary-848-3130                     Exchange-820-9400

**ATTRACTIONS:**Natural History Museum located nearby. Fort adjacent to Talladega National Forest. Berman Museum (military artifacts) in nearby Anniston. Birmingham; 40 minute drive.

# FORT RUCKER (AL02R2)

Building 115
ATTN: ATZQ-GSC
Fort Rucker, AL 36362-5000

**TELEPHONE NUMBER INFORMATION:** Main installation numbers: C-334-255-1110, D-312-558-1110.

**LOCATION:** Eighty miles southeast of Montgomery, midway between the capital city and the Florida Gulf Coast, and seven miles south of Ozark, off US-231 on AL-249. Clearly marked. USMRA: Page 36 (F,G-8). NMC: Dothan, 26 miles southeast.

**GENERAL INFORMATION:** U.S. Army Aviation Center NCO Academy, First Aviation Brigade, Aviation Training Brigade, Army Air Traffic Control Activity, Army Aero-medical Center, Army Aero-medical Research Laboratory, Army Aviation Technical Test Center, U.S. Army Safety Center and U.S. Army School of Aviation Medicine.

**TEMPORARY MILITARY LODGING:** Lodging office, Building 308, 6th Avenue, 24 hours daily, C-334-598-5216, D-312-558-5780. All ranks. DV/VIP, Building 114, C-344-255-3100/3400.

**RV, CAMPING/FAMCAMP:** On-post recreation area at Lake Tholocco, year round (camping area closed November-February), Outdoor Rec C-334-255-4305, D-312-558-4305, 18 camper spaces with W/E hookups.

**SPACE-A:** Cairns Army Airfield, Building 30501, C-334-255-8563, D-312-558-8563, flights via executive aircraft to CONUS locations.

**LOGISTICAL SUPPORT:**

Bank-598-2401

Barber Shop-598-4484

Beauty Shop-598-4315
Car Rental-598-5401
Class Six-503-9044
Credit Union-598-4411
Education Office-255-3941
Gas Station-503-9044
Recycling-255-9505
Shoppette-503-9044

Carlson Wagonlit Travel-598-2167
Child Dev Center-255-2262
Commissary-255-3610
Dry Cleaner-503-9044
Exchange-503-9044
Postal Service-598-6446
SATO-255-9034

**ADMINISTRATIVE SUPPORT:**

Fire Dept-255-2511
Legal-255-3482
Public Affairs-255-2252

Housing Office-255-2318
Police-255-2222
SDO/NCO-255-3400

**HEALTH & WELFARE:**

ACS-255-9251
Army Emergency Relief-255-2341
Chapel-255-2989
Family Services-255-3898
Retiree Services-255-9124
TRICARE-598-6500
Veterinary Services-255-9061

American Red Cross-255-1055
CHAMPUS-255-7233
Dental-255-2367
Medical
  Central Appts-255-7000
  Emergency-255-7900
  Health Benefits-255-7233
  Hospital-255-7000

**REST & RECREATION:**

Arts & Crafts-255-9131
Bowling-255-9503
Equestrian Center-598-3384
Fitness Center-255-9567
Golf Course-255-9539
ITR Office-255-9517/2997
MWR-255-2292/598-5311
Theater-255-2408

Auto Hobby Shop-255-9725
Clubs
  NCO-598-2491
  O-598-2426
Gym-255-9539
Library-255-3885
Swimming-255-3998
Youth Services-255-9108

**ATTRACTIONS:** National Peanut Festival, first week of November in Dothan. Monument to the Boll Weevil, Enterprise, AL, seven miles west. U.S. Army Aviation Museum on post, 0900-1600 daily; group tours and library usage, C-334-255-3036.

# GUNTER ANNEX TO MAXWELL AIR FORCE BASE (AL04R2)

60 West Maxwell Boulevard
Maxwell Air Force Base, AL 36112-6307

**TELEPHONE NUMBER INFORMATION:** Main installation numbers: C-334-953-1110, D-312-493-1110.

**LOCATION:** From I-65 north or south take exit 173 northeast onto Northern Blvd. (AL-152) 6.1 miles to intersection with US-231. Take south exit onto Federal Drive, then south 1.5 miles to main gate on left (southeast) side of street. From I-85 east or west, take exit 6 north onto Eastern Blvd. (US-231 north). Continue north 4 miles to an exit south onto Federal Drive, then southwest 1.5 miles to main gate on left (south) side of street. USMRA: Page 36 (E,F-6). NMC: Montgomery, two miles southwest.

**GENERAL INFORMATION:** Standard Systems Group, Extension Course Institute, USAF Senior NCO Academy and educational activities.

**TEMPORARY MILITARY LODGING:** Lodging office, Building 826, 24 hours daily, C-334-416-3360, D-312-596-3360. Extensive facilities. DV/VIP call Maxwell AFB, C-334-253-2095, D-312-875-2095.

**RV, CAMPING/FAMCAMP:** Run by Maxwell AFB, Lake Martin Maxwell/Gunter Recreation Area and Lake Pippin Maxwell/Gunter Recreation Area C-334-953-3509, D-312-493-3509.

**SPACE-A:** None. See Maxwell AFB listing.

**LOGISTICAL SUPPORT:**

Commissary-416-4942
Gas Station-265-7773
Visitor Center-953-2014

Exchange-279-9776
SATO-263-5500

**ADMINISTRATIVE SUPPORT:**

| | |
|---|---|
| Fire Dept-953-7360 | Legal-953-2786 |
| Locator-953-5027 | Police-953-7222 |

**HEALTH & WELFARE:**

| | |
|---|---|
| CHAMPUS-953-7854 | Chapel-279-4131 |
| Child Care-953-6667 | Medical-953-6985 |

**REST & RECREATION:**

| | |
|---|---|
| Arts & Crafts-ext 3118 | Auto Hobby Shop-ext 3119 |
| Bowling-ext 3186 | Clubs |
| Family Services-953-3850 |  EM-953-6399 |
| Golf Course-263-7588 |  NCO-262-8364 |
| Gym-ext 3175 |  O-264-6423 |
| ITT Office-953-6168 | Library-ext 3179 |
| Picnic Area-ext 4888 | Rec Center-ext 4802 |
| Recreation-953-5675 | Theater-953-7411 |
| Wood Hobby Shop at Maxwell | Youth Activities-ext 4802 |

**ATTRACTIONS:** Alabama state capital, Alabama Shakespeare Festival, Coliseum, Montgomery Museum of Fine Arts, monument to powered flight at Maxwell AFB, First White House of the Confederacy, Civil Rights Memorial, and the new Alabama State Farmers Market–"largest in the southeastern U.S."

# LAKE MARTIN MAXWELL/GUNTER RECREATION AREA (AL05R2)

Maxwell Air Force Base
Maxwell AFB, AL 36112-5000

**TELEPHONE NUMBER INFORMATION:** Main installation numbers: C-334-953-3501, D-312-493-3509.

**LOCATION:** Off base. Located near Dadeville, southeast of Birmingham, northeast of Montgomery. From I-85 north of Montgomery take exit 32, north on AL-49 to Stillwaters Road (County Road 34) and proceed 2.5 miles to recreation area. USMRA: Page 36 (F-5). NMI: Maxwell AFB, 60 miles southwest. NMC: Montgomery, 60 miles southwest.

**GENERAL INFORMATION:** Operated by Maxwell AFB, off base, year round. Military personnel active, reservists, retired, DoD civilians at Maxwell/Gunter AFB. Reservations (required): Outdoor Recreation Reservations Office, 204 West Selfridge Street, Maxwell AFB, AL 36112-5000. C-334-953-3509/3510, D-312-493-3510. For information, C-256-825-6251. Recreation area includes areas for day picnicking and rough camping. Voted outstanding recreation area of the Air Force.

**RV, CAMPING/FAMCAMP:**

| | |
|---|---|
| Camper Spaces-61 | Mobile Homes-12 |
| Tent Spaces-15 | |

**ATTRACTIONS:** Located on Lake Martin Reservoir near dam. Excellent fishing; variety of water- and woods-oriented activities.

*For detailed information about this off-base recreation facility, as well as on-base recreation facilities, golf courses and marinas, consult Military Living's Military RV, Camping and Outdoor Recreation Around the World.*

# MARSHALL SPACE FLIGHT CENTER (AL17R2)

1 Tranquility Base
Huntsville, AL 35805-5000

**TELEPHONE NUMBER INFORMATION:** Main installation numbers: C-256-544-4230. WEB: www1.msfc.nasa.gov

**LOCATION:** From I-65 north or south take exit #340 east onto I-565 approximately 13 miles northeast to exit #14 south onto Rideout Road for 3.7 miles to center on east side of road. USMRA: Page 36 (D,E-1). NMC: Huntsville, 5 miles northeast.

**GENERAL INFORMATION:** NASA research and development center. U.S. Space & Rocket Center museum.

**LOGISTICAL SUPPORT:**   Visitor Center-544-2090

**ATTRACTIONS:** Nearby are Alabama Constitution Village, Burritt Museum and Park, Huntsville Depot Museum and Trolley, Huntsville Museum of Art, Early Works Museum, Huntsville/Madison County Botanical Garden, Old Town Historic District, Twickenham Historic District and the Tennessee River.

# MAXWELL AIR FORCE BASE (AL03R2)

50 LeMay Plaza South
Maxwell Air Force Base, AL 36112-6334

**TELEPHONE NUMBER INFORMATION:** Main installation numbers: C-334-953-1110, D-312-493-1110.

**LOCATION:** Take I-85 south to I-65 north to Herron Street (exit #172) west to right (north) on Dickerson Street two blocks to left (west) on Bell Street approximately 0.9 mile and follow signs to Bell Street Gate Visitor Center on right (north side of street). USMRA: Page 36 (E-6). NMC: Montgomery, 1.5 miles southeast.

**GENERAL INFORMATION:** Headquarters Air University (AETC), professional military education center for USAF.

**TEMPORARY MILITARY LODGING:** Lodging office, Building 157, 351 West Drive, 24 hours daily, C-334-953-2401/2430, D-312-493-2401/2430. Extensive facilities. DV/VIP C-334-953-2095.

**RV, CAMPING/FAMCAMP:** FAMCAMP on base, C-334-953-5161, year round, 31 camper spaces. Lake Martin Maxwell/Gunter Recreation Area, off base near Dadeville C-334-953-3509, D-312-493-3509, year round, 61 camper spaces, 12 mobile homes, 15 tent spaces; Lake Pippin Maxwell/Gunter Recreation Area near Niceville, FL, year round, C-334-953-3509, D-312-493-3509, 23 camper spaces, 10 tent spaces, and 8 mobile homes.

**SPACE-A:** Pax Term/Lounge, Building 844, 0700-1700 Mon-Fri, C-334-953-7372, D-312-493-7372, Rec: C-334-953-6760, D-312-493-6760; Fax: C-334-953-6114, D-312-493-6114; DV/VIP lounge C-334-953-5374. Flights scheduled 24 hours in advance, most via executive aircraft.

**LOGISTICAL SUPPORT:**

| | |
|---|---|
| Bank-953-8190 | Barber Shop-953-3444 |
| Beauty Shop-953-3010 | Cafeteria-953-6044 |
| Car Rental-264-7701 | Child Care-953-6667 |
| Commissary-953-6898 | Conv Store-265-7773 |
| Credit Union-953-2606 | Exchange-834-5946 |
| Dry Cleaner-953-7826 | Gas Station-265-7773 |
| Package Store-265-7472 | SATO-264-0076 |
| Visitor Center-953-4283 | |

**ADMINISTRATIVE SUPPORT:**

| | |
|---|---|
| Legal-953-2786 | Locator-953-5027 |
| Police-953-7222 | Public Affairs-953-2014 |
| SDO/NCO-953-2862 | |

**HEALTH & WELFARE:**

| | |
|---|---|
| CHAMPUS-953-7854 | Chapel-953-2109 |
| Family Services-953-5002 | Medical-953-2333 |
| Retiree Services-953-6725 | Hospital-953-7805 |

**REST & RECREATION:**

| | |
|---|---|
| Clubs | Golf Course-263-9587 |
|  Aero- ext 7342 | ITT Office-953-6351 |
|  EM-262-8364 | Library-ext 5947 |
|  NCO-262-8364 | Theater-953-7411 |
|  O-264-6423 | |

**ATTRACTIONS:** State capital, Shakespeare Theater, historic houses and buildings in Montgomery, including First White House of the Confederacy, Montgomery Museum of Fine Arts, Civil Rights Memorial Monument.

## MOBILE COAST GUARD AVIATION TRAINING CENTER (AL08R2)

USCG Aviation Training Center
85011 Tanner Williams Road
Mobile, AL 36608-9682

**TELEPHONE NUMBER INFORMATION:** Main installation numbers: C-334-441-6401, after hours C-334-441-6110.

**LOCATION:** From I-65 take Airport Boulevard (exit #3) west 5.8 miles, right (north) on Schillinger Road for 0.7 miles, to left (west) on Tanner Williams Road, 1 mile. Center in on left (south) side of road. Clearly marked. USMRA: Page 36 (B-9). NMC: Mobile, 2.5 miles east.

**GENERAL INFORMATION:** The Aviation Training Center for the U.S. Coast Guard and home for the Gulf Strike Team.

**TEMPORARY MILITARY LODGING:** Extremely limited. Usually filled by TDY students. C-334-441-6734. See Keesler AFB, MS.

**RV, CAMPING/FAMCAMP:** None. See Mobile CGB, Dauphin Island Recreational Complex.

**SPACE-A:** Extremely limited. Main hangar, 0800-1600 Mon-Fri, C-334-441-6401, D-312-436-3635, Fax: C-334-441-6435, flights to east and midwest.

**LOGISTICAL SUPPORT:**

| | |
|---|---|
| Barber Shop-441-6494 | Beauty Shop-441-6495 |
| Conv Store-441-6390 | Commissary-441-6390 |
| Credit Union-441-6325 | Dining Facilities-441-6744 |
| Education Office-441-6831 | Exchange-441-6390 |
| Gas Station-441-6496 | Package Store-441-6390 |

**ADMINISTRATIVE SUPPORT:**

| | |
|---|---|
| Housing Office-441-6326 | Locator-441-6724 |
| OOD-441-6110 | Pass/ID Office-441-6724 |
| Police-441-6100 | Public Affairs-441-6428 |
| Quarter Deck-441-6110 | |

**HEALTH & WELFARE:**

| | |
|---|---|
| American Red Cross-438-2571 | CHAMPUS-441-6038 |
| Chapel-441-6938 | Dental |
| Medical |   Central Appts-441-6404 |
|   Central Appts-441-6561 (AD) |   Clinic-441-6404 |
|   Health Benefits-441-6725 |   Emergency-441-5925 |
|   Information-6441-6560 | |
| TRICARE-441-6037 | |

**REST & RECREATION:**

| | |
|---|---|
| Auto Hobby Shop-441-6135 | Clubs |
| Fitness Center-441-6384 |   EM-441-6259 |
| MWR-441-6730 |   O-441-6358 |
| Outdoor Rec-441-6135 | |

**ATTRACTIONS:** Mobile is one of the largest commercial seaports in the country. Historic houses and beautiful flowers in the Mobile Bay area. Bellingrath Gardens (year round), USS *Alabama*, and Battleship Park.

## MOBILE COAST GUARD BASE (AL16R2)

South Broad Street
Brookley Complex Building 101
Mobile, AL 36615-1390

**TELEPHONE NUMBER INFORMATION:** Main installation numbers: C-334-441-6072.

**LOCATION:** From I-10 east or west, take exit #24 south onto Broad Street, go south approximately three quarters of a mile to base on left (east) side of street. NMI: Pensacola NAS, Pensacola, FL, 55 miles east. NMC: Mobile, one mile north.

**GENERAL INFORMATION:** U.S. Coast Guard Group activities.

**TEMPORARY MILITARY LODGING:** None. See Keesler AFB, MS listing.

**RV, CAMPING/FAMCAMP:** Operates Dauphin Island Recreation Area, 40 miles south of post. See Dauphin Island Recreation Area for more information.

**SPACE-A:** None. See Keesler AFB, MS listing.

**LOGISTICAL SUPPORT:**

| | |
|---|---|
| Barber Shop-441-5094 | Conv Store-441-5090 |
| Exchange-441-5090 | Gas Station-441-5097 |
| Package Store-441-5096 | |

**ADMINISTRATIVE SUPPORT:**

| | |
|---|---|
| Locator-441-6072 | Public Affairs-441-5419 |

**HEALTH & WELFARE:** None. See Keesler AFB, MS listing. Also see Pensacola Naval Hospital, FL listing.

**REST & RECREATION:**

| | |
|---|---|
| All Hands Club-441-5098/5099 | MWR-441-6198 |

**ATTRACTIONS:** Mobile Bay, Battleship Park, *USS Alabama* and other military displays, Bellingrath Gardens.

## REDSTONE ARSENAL (AL06R2)

Commander U.S. Army Aviation & Missile Command
Building 5300, ATTN: AMSMI-RA
Redstone Arsenal, AL 35898-5000

**TELEPHONE NUMBER INFORMATION:** Main installation numbers: C-256-876-2151, D-312-746-0011.

**LOCATION:** From I-565 east west take exit #14 south onto Rideout Road for 0.4 miles to gate #9. Or, from I-565 in city of Huntsville, exit south onto US-231 (Memorial Drive) for 4.5 miles to right (west) onto Martin Road to main gate (gate #1). Uniformed personnel may take I-565 to US-231 (Memorial Drive) south 1.0 mile to Drake exit west. Go west on Drake which becomes Goss Road to gate #8. USMRA: Page 36 (E-1). NMC Huntsville, adjacent.

**GENERAL INFORMATION:** Headquarters U.S. Army Aviation and Missile Command, U.S. Army Ordnance Missile & Munitions Center & School and NASA.

**TEMPORARY MILITARY LODGING:** Lodging office, Building 244, Goss Road, 24 hours daily, C-256-837-4130, D-312-746-5713/8028, Fax: C-256-876-2929; other SDO, Building 5300, C-256-876-3331. All ranks. DV/VIP call Billeting Office C-256-837-4130, D-312-746-5713/8028.

**RV, CAMPING/FAMCAMP:** C-256-876-6854, D-312-746-6854, Fax: C-256-842-9134, D-312-788-9134. Building 5132, 0930-1700 daily. Arsenal campground on post, year round, 23 camper spaces with W/E hookups; only electricity hookups during winter months. Outdoor Rec, Building 5132, C-256-876-6854.

**SPACE-A:** Redstone Arsenal Army Airfield, Building 4809, 0730-1630 Mon-Fri, C-256-876-1916, D-312-746-4290, Fax: C-256-842-0562, D-312-788-0562. Space available transit military air available periodically.

**LOGISTICAL SUPPORT:**

| | |
|---|---|
| Bank-535-0246 | Barber Shop-881-7409 |
| Beauty Shop-883-1450 | Cafeteria-876-8894 |
| Carlson Wagonlit Travel-880-3601 | Child Care-876-7880 |
| Child Dev Center-876-7952 | Class Six-883-0367 |
| Commissary-955-6627 | Credit Union-722-3740 |
| Dining Facilities-876-6743 | Dry Cleaner-882-3529 |
| Education Office-876-9761 | Exchange-883-6100 |
| Gas Station-883-0367 | Laundry-882-3529 |
| Postal Service-881-8883 | Shoppette-883-0367 |
| Snack Bar-881-7986 | Travel Office-880-3601 |

**ADMINISTRATIVE SUPPORT:**

| | |
|---|---|
| Fire Dept-911 | Housing-842-2449 |
| Legal-876-3405 | Locator-876-2151 |
| Police-876-2222 | Public Affairs-876-4161 |
| SDO/SNCO-876-3331 | |

## HEALTH & WELFARE:

ACS-876-5397
CHAMPUS-955-6497
Dental-876-2616/1643
Medical
  Central Appts-955-8888
  Emergency-876-8287
Retiree Services-876-2022
Veterinary Services-876-2441

Army Emergency Relief-876-5468
Chapel-876-5751
Family Services-876-2859

TRICARE-882-7404

## REST & RECREATION:

Arts & Crafts-876-1397
Bowling-876-6634
Fitness Center-313-6091
Golf Course-883-7977
Gym-876-2943
ITR-876-4531
Outdoor Rec-876-6854
Wood Hobby Shop-876-7974
Youth Services-876-5437

Auto Hobby Shop-955-7727
Clubs
  NCO-837-0750
  O-830-2582
Indoor Rec-876-4531
Library-876-4741
Wellness Center-955-6844
Youth Center-876-5437

**ATTRACTIONS:** Alabama Space and Rocket Center, Alabama Constitution Village, Burritt Museum and Park, Huntsville Depot Museum and Trolley, Huntsville Museum of Art, Early Works Museum, Huntsville/Madison County Botanical Garden, Old Town Historic District, Twickenham Historic District and the Tennessee River.

# BIRCH LAKE RECREATION AREA (AK01R5)

354 SVS/SVRO
3112 Broadway Street, U-6
Eielson AFB, AK 99702-1875

**TELEPHONE NUMBER INFORMATION:** Main installation numbers: C-907-488-6161, D-317-377-1232.

**LOCATION:** Off base. On Southwest side of Richardson Highway (AK-2) at mile post 305, 38 miles south of Eielson AFB. Turn southwest at Recreation Area sign; one mile to entrance. Check in at Boat Shop. NMI: Eielson AFB, 38 miles north. NMC: Fairbanks, 64 miles north.

**GENERAL INFORMATION:** Located on Birch Lake, which covers 804 acres, is spring-fed, and is stocked with rainbow trout and silver salmon. Operated by Eielson Air Force Base, off base, Memorial Day to Labor Day. (Over the winter season the Outdoor Adventure Program does weekend cabin rental on selected weekends along with ice fishing and snow mobile trips.) Military personnel active, reservists, retired, DoD civilians. Reservations (required): Address: 354 SVS/SVRO, 3112 Broadway Street, U-6, Eielson AFB, AK 99702-1875. C-907-488-6161, D-317-377-1232, 0900-1100 hours. Fax: C-907-377-2770. For information off-season, C-907-377-1839.

## RV, CAMPING/FAMCAMP:

Cabins-22
Tent Spaces-14

Camper Spaces-40

**ATTRACTIONS:** Harding Lake Recreation Area approximately ten miles north; Denali National Park, 130 miles southwest. Spectacular mountain scenery, unsurpassed fishing and hunting.
*For detailed information about this off-base recreation facility, as well as on-base recreation facilities, golf courses and marinas, consult Military Living's Military RV, Camping and Outdoor Recreation Around the World.*

# ALASKA

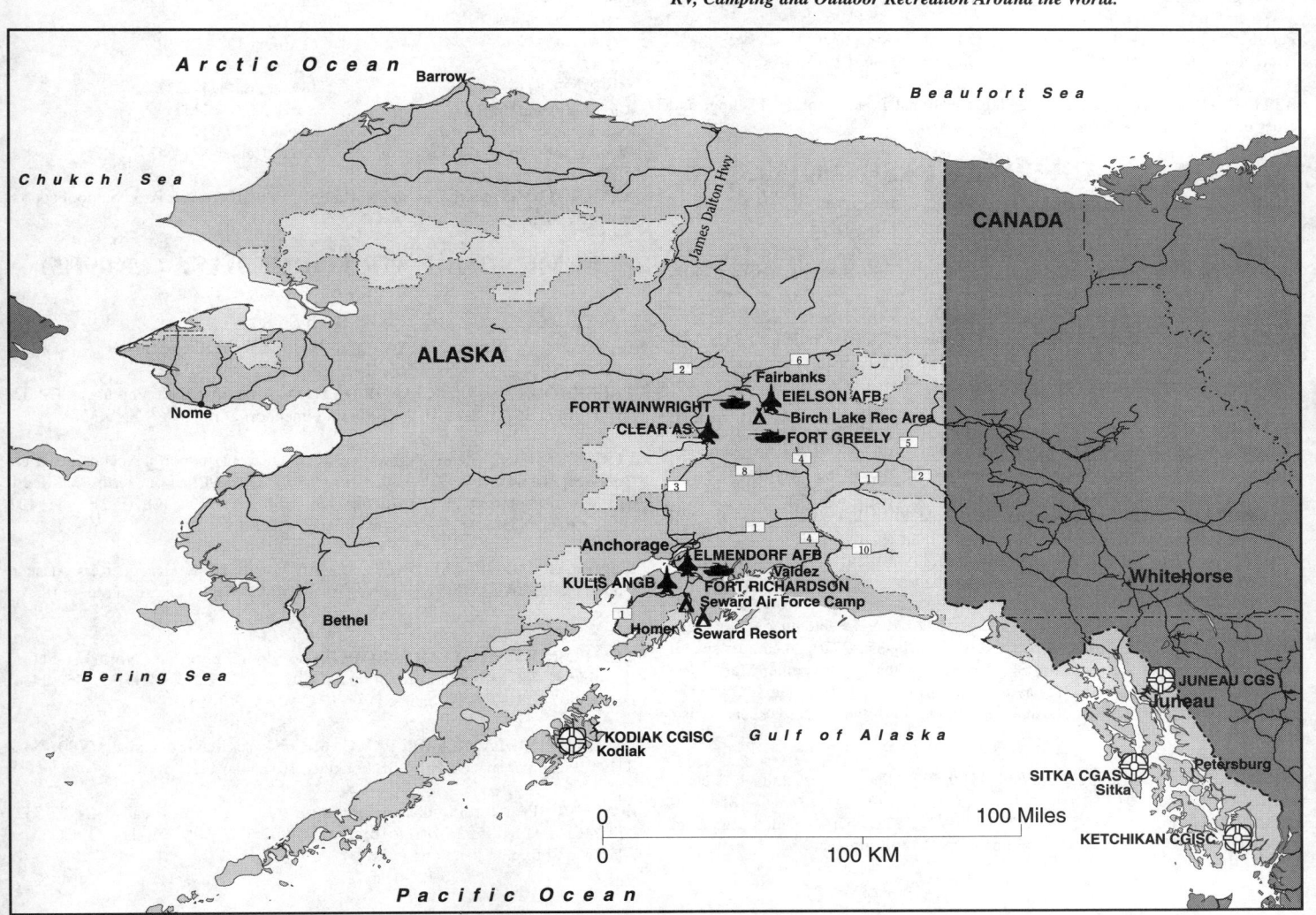

# CLEAR AIR STATION (AK18R5)

13 SWS, P.O. Box 40013
Clear Air Station, AK 99704-0013

**TELEPHONE NUMBER INFORMATION:** Main installation numbers: C-907-585-6409, D-317-585-6409/6416.

**LOCATION:** From Fairbanks, 80 miles southwest on Fairbanks/Anchorage Highway (AK-3). Located on east side of highway. NMC: Fairbanks: 80 miles northeast.

**GENERAL INFORMATION:** 13th Space Warning Squadron.
**TEMPORARY MILITARY LODGING:** Lodging office, Building 209, C-907-585-6224. All ranks.

**RV, CAMPING/FAMCAMP:** None. See Eielson AFB listing, Birch Lake Recreation Area.

**SPACE-A:** None. See Eielson Air Force Base listing.

**LOGISTICAL SUPPORT:**

| | |
|---|---|
| Exchange-585-6409 | Mail Room-585-6224 |
| Post Office-585-6268 | SATO-585-6364 |

**ADMINISTRATIVE SUPPORT:**

| | |
|---|---|
| Duty Manager-585-6224 | Fire Dept-585-6321/911 |
| Locator-585-1110 | NCO-585-6409 |
| Pass/ID Office-585-6293 | Police-585-6313 |

**HEALTH & WELFARE:**      Medical-585-6414

**REST & RECREATION:**

| | |
|---|---|
| Bowling-585-6546 | Clubs |
| MWR-585-6487 |   NCO/O-585-6536 |
| Public Affairs-585-6409 |   Polar Bar-585-6536 |
| Recreation Services-585-6576 | Services-585-6519 |

**ATTRACTIONS:** Near Mount McKinley National Park. Hunting, Fishing, and other outdoor activities.

# EIELSON AIR FORCE BASE (AK15R5)

3112 Broadway Avenue, Unit 15A
Eielson Air Force Base, AK 99702-1895

**TELEPHONE NUMBER INFORMATION:** Main installation numbers: C-907-377-1110, D-317-377-1110. WEB: www.eielson.af.mil

**LOCATION:** On east side of Richardson Highway (AK-2) at mile post 341. AFB is clearly marked. USMRA: Page 128 (F,G-4). NMC: Fairbanks, 26 miles northwest.

**GENERAL INFORMATION:** Home of the 354th Fighter Wing, and 168th Air Refueling Wing (ANG), Det 1, 210th Rescue Squadron (ANG), support activities. Major activity: COPE THUNDER-summer air combat training exercises.

**TEMPORARY MILITARY LODGING:** Gold Rush Inn, Bldg. 2270, Central Avenue, Eielson AFB, AK 99702-1885, 24 hours daily, C-907-377-1844, D-317-377-1844. Fax: C-907-377-2559. All ranks. DV/VIP: C-907-377-7686.

**RV, CAMPING/FAMCAMP:** FAMCAMP on base. 354 SVS/SVRO, 3112 Broadway U-6B, Eielson AFB, AK 99702-1885, 15 May-7 September, C-907-377-1232, D-317-377-1232. Fax: C-907-377-2770, D-317-377-2770, 24 camper spaces with full hookups; Ravenwood Ski Lodge, on base, November-March, C-907-377-1332, D-317-377-1232, day use only, snow skiing, rec room and support facilities; Birch Lake Recreation Area, 38 miles south of the AFB, see separate listing.

**SPACE-A:** Pax Term/Lounge, Building 1190, Flightline Avenue, Suite 1, Eielson AFB, AK 99702, 0730-1630 daily, or as required, C-907-377-1854, D-317-377-1854. Fax: C-907-377-2287, D-317-377-2287. Unscheduled flights to OCONUS, CONUS and Alaska locations via KC-135R aircraft.

**LOGISTICAL SUPPORT:**

| | |
|---|---|
| Barber Shop-372-2237 | Beauty Shop-372-3265 |
| Burger King- 372-4343 | Cafeteria-377-1341 |
| Child Care-377-3636 | Child Dev Center-377-3237 |
| Class Six-377-1231 | Commissary-377-5134 |
| Conv Store-377-2210 | Credit Union-372-6111 |
| Dining Facilities-377-2563 | Dry Cleaner-372-3541 |
| Education Office-377-3177 | Exchange-377-4154 |
| Laundry-372-3541 | Gas Station-377-1218 |
| Postal Service-377-2289 | SATO-377-2288 |
| Shoppette-377-2210 | Snack Bar-377-5154 |
| Visitor Center-377-3807 | |

**ADMINISTRATIVE SUPPORT:**

| | |
|---|---|
| Command Post-377-1500 | Fire Dept-377-4156 |
| Housing Office-377-1840 | Legal-377-4114 |
| Locator-377-1841 | Pass/ID Office-377-1033 |
|   Non Duty-377-7885 | Police-377-5130 |
| Public Affairs-377-2116 | |

**HEALTH & WELFARE:**

| | |
|---|---|
| Air Force Aid Society-377-3351 | American Red Cross-377-1855 |
| CHAMPUS-377-5155-ext 299 | Chapel-377-2130 |
| Dental | Family Services-377-2242 |
|   Central Appts-377-1846 ext 261 | Medical |
|   Clinic-377-1846-ext 261 |   Central Appts-377-1847 |
|   Emergency-377-2296 |   Clinic-377-2259 |
| Retiree Services-377-3192 |   Emergency-377-2296 |
| Veterinary Services-377-1146 |   Health Benefits-377-5155-ext 299 |

**REST & RECREATION:**

| | |
|---|---|
| Arts & Crafts-377-4880 | Auto Hobby Shop-377-3190 |
| Boat Shop-ext 1232 | Bowling-377-1129 |
| Clubs | Fitness Center-377-1231 |
|   NCO-377-2635 | Golf-377-1232 |
|   O-377-2051 | Gym-ext 1231 |
| ITT-377-2722 | Library-377-3174 |
| MWR-377-1839 | Recreation-377-1232 |
| Rec Equipment-ext 1232 | Services-377-2857 |
| Swimming-ext 1231 | Theater-377-1172 |
| Wood Hobby Shop-377-1168 | Youth Center-377-5437 |

**ATTRACTIONS:** Fairbanks and North Pole, Denali National Park, outdoor sports, and recreation.

# ELMENDORF AIR FORCE BASE (AK09R5)

3rd Wing/PA
6920 12th Street
Elmendorf Air Force Base, AK 99506-5000

**TELEPHONE NUMBER INFORMATION:** Main installation numbers: C-907-552-1110, D-317-552-1110. WEB: www.elmendorf.af.mil

**LOCATION:** Off Glenn Highway (AK-1) adjacent to north Anchorage. Take Boniface Parkway Exit. Take either Elmendorf Access Road or North Post Road. The base is adjacent to Fort Richardson. USMRA: Page 128 (F-5), page 131 (B,C,D,E-1). NMC: Anchorage, two miles southeast.

**GENERAL INFORMATION:** Pacific Air Forces Base. Headquarters Alaskan Command, 3rd Wing, Headquarters Alaska NORAD Region, Headquarters 11th Air Force.

**TEMPORARY MILITARY LODGING:** Lodging office, North Star Inn, Building 31-250, Acacia Street, 24 hours daily, C-907-552-2454, D-317-552-2454, Fax: C-907-552-8276. All ranks. DV/VIP C-907-552-3210.

**RV, CAMPING/FAMCAMP:** FAMCAMP, on base, May-September, C-907-552-3912; 39 camper spaces with W/E hookups, 10 tent spaces.

**SPACE-A:** Pax Term/Lounge, Building 32-233 24 hours daily, C-907-552-3781/4616, D-317-552-3781/4616, Fax: C-907-552-3996. Flights to CONUS, Alaska, and foreign locations.

**LOGISTICAL SUPPORT:**

| | |
|---|---|
| Bank-277-5577 | Cafeteria-753-2280/6146 |
| Child Care-753-5113 | Class Six-753-5151 |
| Commissary-552-4878/4425 | Conv Store-753-1291 |
| Dining Facilities-552-2253 | Exchange-753-4208 |
| Fast Food-753-4486 | Gas Station-753-7120 |
| SATO-753-0509 | Snack Bar-753-6146 |
| Visitors Center-552-5988 | |

*Note: Joint Military Mall opened October 1999.*

**ADMINISTRATIVE SUPPORT:**

| | |
|---|---|
| Legal-552-3046 | Locator-552-4860 |
| Police-552-3421 | Public Affairs-552-8151 |
| SDO/NCO-552-3013 | |

**HEALTH & WELFARE:**

| | |
|---|---|
| CHAMPUS-552-3430 | Chapel-552-4422 |
| Family Services-552-2694 | Medical |
| Retiree Services-552-2337 |    Central Appts-552-2778 |
| |    Emergency-552-5555 |

**REST & RECREATION:**

| | |
|---|---|
| Arts & Crafts-ext 2470 | Bowling-552-4108 |
| Clubs | Community Center-ext 8529 |
|   Aero-753-4167 | Field House-ext 5353/3504 |
|   EM-753-5190 | Golf Course-552-3821 |
|   Jogging -ext 5353/3504 | ITT-552-5191 |
|   NCO-753-5205 | Library-ext 3787 |
|   O-753-3131 | Racquetball-ext 5353 |
|   Riding-ext 4987 | Rec Equip-ext 2023 |
|  Riding Stables-ext 4987 | Services Squadron-ext 2468 |
| Ski Area-ext 4838 | Swimming-ext 3504 |
| Theater-753-2344 | Tennis-ext 8529/5353 |
| Youth Center-ext 2266 | |

**ATTRACTIONS:** Anchorage, outdoor sports and recreation, Portage Glacier, Earthquake Park.

# FORT GREELY (AK10R5)
### ATTN: APVR-GPC
### 502 2nd Street
### APO AP 96508-6050
### *Scheduled to close 2001*

**TELEPHONE NUMBER INFORMATION:** Main installation numbers: C-907-873-4720, D-317-873-4720.

**LOCATION:** West of AK-4 six miles south of junction of AK-2 and AK-4. Five miles south of Delta Junction. USMRA: Page 128 (F,G-4). NMC: Fairbanks, 105 miles northwest.

**GENERAL INFORMATION:** Army Northern Warfare Training Center, Army Cold Region Test Center and support units.

**TEMPORARY MILITARY LODGING:** Limited availability with TDY and new arrivals having priority. Lodging office, Building 663, First Street, 0730-1530 Mon, Tue, Thurs & Fri, 0730-1130 Wed, C-907-873-3285, D-317-873-3285, Fax: C-907-873-3003. Other hours, SDO, Building 501, C-907-873-4720. All ranks.

**RV, CAMPING/FAMCAMP:** None. See Eielson AFB, Birch Lake Recreation Area.

**SPACE-A:** None. See Elmendorf AFB listing.

**LOGISTICAL SUPPORT:**

| | |
|---|---|
| Child Care-873-4593 | Commissary-873-4404 |
| Exchange-869-3135 | Gas Station-869-3210 |
| SATO-873-3107 | Snack Bar-869-3110 |

**ADMINISTRATIVE SUPPORT:**

| | |
|---|---|
| Legal-873-3250 | Locator-873-3255 |
| SDO/NCO-873-4720 | |

**HEALTH & WELFARE:**

| | |
|---|---|
| Army Emergency Relief-873-3288 | Chapel-873-4610 |
| Emergency-911 | Family Services-873-3284/7 |
| Medical-873-4498 | Police-873-1111 |

**REST & RECREATION:**

| | |
|---|---|
| Arts & Crafts-873-3181 | Auto Crafts-873-3293 |
| Bowling-873-2695 | Com Club-895-3105 |
| Library-873-3217 | MWR-873-4207 |
| Outdoor Sports Center-873-3183/1115 | Rec Center-873-1115 |
| Theater-873-3283 | |

**ATTRACTIONS:** Outdoor sports and recreation.

# FORT RICHARDSON (AK03R5)
### 600 Richardson Drive, #5900
### Fort Richardson, AK 99505-5900

**TELEPHONE NUMBER INFORMATION:** Main installation numbers: C-907-384-1110, D-317-384-1110. WEB: www.usarak.army.mil

**LOCATION:** Main gate is on Glenn Highway, eight miles south of Eagle River. USMRA: Page 128 (F-5), page 131 (E-1). NMC: Anchorage, eight miles southwest.

**GENERAL INFORMATION:** Headquarters for U.S. Army, Alaska: Arctic Support Brigade; 1st Battalion (Airborne), 501st Infantry, and other support units.

**TEMPORARY MILITARY LODGING:** Lodging office, Building 600, Richardson Drive, 0600-2230 Mon-Fri, 1000-1730 Sat-Sun, C-907-384-0436, D-317-384-0436. All ranks.

**RV, CAMPING/FAMCAMP:** Black Spruce Travel Camp on post, 1 May-1 September, C-907-384-1476/1303; 22 camper spaces with W/E hookups, and 20 camper/tent spaces at Upper Otter Lake Campground; operates Seward Resort at Resurrection Bay near Seward, 133 miles south of post. See Seward Resort listing for more information.

**SPACE-A:** None. See Elmendorf AFB listing.

**LOGISTICAL SUPPORT:**

| | |
|---|---|
| Bank-563-4567 | Barber Shop-428-1811/1221 |
| Beauty Shop-428-1238 | Cafeteria-428-1314 |
| Child Care-384-0686 | Child Dev Center-384-1506 |
| Class Six-428-3190 | Commissary-384-1564* |
| Conv Store-428-3190 | Dining Facilities-384-1234 |
| Dry Cleaner-428-3828 | Exchange-428-1234* |
| Gas Station-428-1248 | SATO-428-1224 |
| Snack Bar-428-1926 | |

*\*Note: Commissary and Exchange facilities have moved to new Joint Military Mall at Elmendorf AFB, opened October 1999.*

**ADMINISTRATIVE SUPPORT:**

| | |
|---|---|
| Fire Dept-384-0774 | Housing-Legal-384-0309 |
| Legal-384-0371 | Locator-384-0306 |
| Police-384-0823 | Public Affairs-384-1538 |

**HEALTH & WELFARE:**

| | |
|---|---|
| ACS-384-1517 | Army Emergency Relief-384-7509 |
| CHAMPUS-552-3430 | Chapel-384-1468 |
| Dental-Clinic-384-2483 | Family Services-384-1513 |
| Medical-Clinic-384-0600 | Retiree Services-384-3500 |
|    Central Appointments-552-2748 | TRICARE-384-3600 |
|    Emergency-552-5556 | Veterinary Services-384-2865 |
|    Health Benefits Advisor-384-3600 | |

**REST & RECREATION:**

| | |
|---|---|
| Arts & Crafts-384-3717 | Auto Hobby Shop-384-3718 |
| Bowling-384-1840 | Fitness Center-384-1308 |
| Golf Course-428-0056 | ITR-384-1476 |
| Library-ext 1648 | MWR-384-1300 |
| Otter Lake Lodge-ext 6246 | Outdoor Rec Center-428-0001 |
| Recreation-384-1649/1480 | Rec Equipment-384-1476 |

Skeet Range-ext 1480
Swimming-ext 1301
Youth Center-384-1508/1516

Ski Slope/Lodge-ext 2975/6
Theater-428-1200

**ATTRACTIONS:** Great outdoors and Anchorage.

# FORT WAINWRIGHT (AK07R5)
## 1060 Gaffney Road, #5900
## Fort Wainwright, AK 99703-5900

**TELEPHONE NUMBER INFORMATION:** Main installation numbers: C-907-353-1110, D-317-353-1110. WEB: www.wainwright.army.mil

**LOCATION:** From Fairbanks, take Airport Way (AK-3) east which changes to Gaffney Road and leads to the Main Gate of the post. USMRA: Page 128 (F-4). NMC: Fairbanks, adjacent.

**GENERAL INFORMATION:** Infantry Brigade, Aviation Brigade and other support units.

**TEMPORARY MILITARY LODGING:** Lodging office, Building 1045 (Murphy Hall), Gaffney Road, 0730-1630 Mon-Fri, C-907-353-6294/7291, D-317-353-6294/7291, Fax: C-907-353-7409, D-317-353-7409. All ranks. DV/VIP: C-907-353-6671.

**RV, CAMPING/FAMCAMP:** Glass Park, on post, year round, C-907-353-6349, D-317-353-6349, camper spaces in open area, no hookups.

**SPACE-A:** Bldg 1558. C-907-353-6514/7212, D-317-353-6514/7212. Fax: 907-353-9941, D-317-353-9941.

**LOGISTICAL SUPPORT:**

| | |
|---|---|
| Barber Shop-356-1070 | Beauty Shop-356-2727 |
| Burger King-356-3130 | Child Care-353-7331 |
| Class Six-356-1044 | Commissary-353-7805 |
| Conv Store-356-7259 | Credit Union-356-1262 |
| Dry Cleaner-356-1359 | Education Office-353-7486 |
| Exchange-356-1345 | Gas Station-353-1263 |
| Postal Service-356-1980 | SATO-353-1166 |
| Shoppette-353-7529 | Snack Bar-356-3130 |

**ADMINISTRATIVE SUPPORT:**

| | |
|---|---|
| Fire Dept-353-6485 | Housing-353-1190 |
| Legal-353-6534 | Locator-353-6815 |
| Pass/ID Office-353-2243 | Police-353-7535 |
| Public Affairs-353-6701 | SDO/NCO-353-7500 |

**HEALTH & WELFARE:**

| | |
|---|---|
| American Red Cross-353-7234 | ACS-353-4227 |
| Army Emergency Relief-353-4237 | CHAMPUS-353-5340 |
| Chapel-353-9825 | Dental-353-5135 |
| Family Services-353-7331 | Medical-1-800-478-5172 or |
| Retiree Services-353-2102 | 353-5172/353-5112 |
| Veterinary Services-353-7179 | Central Appts-353-4000 |
| | Emergency-353-5143 |
| | Health Benefits-353-5340 |

**REST & RECREATION:**

| | |
|---|---|
| Arts & Crafts-ext 7520 | Auto Hobby Shop-ext 7436 |
| Boat Shop/Outdoor Equip-ext 6349 | Bowling-353-2654 |
| Clubs | Fitness Center-353-7272 |
| Arctic Oasis-353-1085 | Golf Course-353-6223 |
| Flying-ext 6671 | Gym-353-1994 |
| Last Frontier Club-353-1609 | ITR-353-2652 |
| Library-ext 7131 | Rec Center-ext 7882 |
| Recreation-353-3998 | Ski Lodge-ext 6780 |
| Swimming-ext 1993 | Theater-353-6792 |
| Wood Hobby Shop-353-7520 | Youth Center/Services-353-9661 |

**ATTRACTIONS:** Fairbanks, North Pole, Golden Days (mid-July), World Eskimo Indian Olympics, Tanana Valley State Fair, Jesse Owens Games, area tours, gold panning, riverboat tours, hiking, rafting, boating, hunting, fishing, camping, Alaskaland, Denali National Park, Mount McKinley (highest point in North

America), Northern Lights, Luge Run (Bobsled), skiing, hunting, ice fishing, Chena Hot Springs, Dog Sled Races, Eskimo Winter Olympics, Special Olympics, Nenana Ice Classic, Ice Festival. Continuous daylight in summer; two-three hours light in winter.

# JUNEAU COAST GUARD STATION (AK19R5)
## 345 Egan Drive
## Juneau, AK 99801-1701

**TELEPHONE NUMBER INFORMATION:** Main installation number: C-907-463-2365.

**LOCATION:** Accessible by air or boat. From ferry, right (southeast) on Eagan Drive (AK-7) 13 miles. Follow signs. USMRA: Page 128 (I-6). NMC: Juneau, in city limits.

**GENERAL INFORMATION:** Juneau is home to the Seventeenth Coast Guard District Offices, which has operational control over all Coast Guard units in Alaska.

**TEMPORARY MILITARY LODGING:** None. Nearest facility is more than 100 miles away.

**RV, CAMPING/FAMCAMP:** None. Nearest facility is more than 100 miles away.

**SPACE-A:** None. See Sitka Coast Guard Air Station listing.

**LOGISTICAL SUPPORT:**       Dining Facilities-463-2370

**ADMINISTRATIVE SUPPORT:**      Buoy Deck-463-2370

**HEALTH & WELFARE:**
Medical-463-2146
  Clinic-463-2140

**REST & RECREATION:**
Consol Club-463-2382              E M Club-463-2370

**ATTRACTIONS:** Beautiful Alaskan countryside. Hunting, fishing, and camping.

# KETCHIKAN COAST GUARD INTEGRATED SUPPORT COMMAND (AK21R5)
## 1300 Stedman Street
## Ketchikan, AK 99901-6698

**TELEPHONE NUMBER INFORMATION:** Main installation numbers: C-907-228-0222.

**LOCATION:** Accessible only via AK-7, also known as North and South Tongass. Located three miles south of the ferry terminals on AK-7. USMRA: Page 128 (J-7). NMC: Ketchikan, in the city.

**GENERAL INFORMATION:** Industrial Support Facility, responsible for area search-and-rescue and other Coast Guard operations. Also hosts The Cutter *Plane Tree*, the Cutter *Naushon* and Station Ketchikan.

**TEMPORARY MILITARY LODGING:** None. Nearest facility is more than 100 miles away.

**RV, CAMPING/FAMCAMP:** None. Nearest facility is more than 100 miles away.

**SPACE-A:** None. See Sitka Coast Guard Air Station listing.

**LOGISTICAL SUPPORT:**

| | |
|---|---|
| Cafeteria-228-0258 | Commissary-228-0250 |
| Exchange-225-4528 | Package Store-225-4528 |

**ADMINISTRATIVE SUPPORT:**

| | |
|---|---|
| OOD-228-0222 | Pass/ID Office-228-0311 |

**HEALTH & WELFARE:**

| | |
|---|---|
| CHAMPUS-228-0320 | Family Services-228-0211 |
| Medical-228-0320 | |

**REST & RECREATION:**

| | |
|---|---|
| Auto Hobby Shop-228-0330 | Camping/Rec Equip-ext 0389 |
| Clubs | Fitness Center-228-0211 |
| All Hands-228-0254 | Morale Boats-228-0389 |
| CPO/EM-228-0230 | MWR-228-0257 |
| Public Affairs-228-0344 | Recreation-228-0250 |

**ATTRACTIONS:** Sport fishing and hunting abundant.

## KODIAK COAST GUARD INTEGRATED SUPPORT COMMAND (AK08R5)
P.O. Box 190094
Kodiak, AK 99619-0094

**TELEPHONE NUMBER INFORMATION:** Main installation numbers: C-907-487-5760.

**LOCATION:** From Kodiak City, take Chiniak Highway southwest for seven miles. Base is on left (southeast) side. USMRA: Page 128 (E-7). NMC: Kodiak, seven miles northeast.

**GENERAL INFORMATION:** ISC, Air Station, Communication Station, LORAN station, Electronic Support Unit, North Pacific Regional Fisheries Training Center, Marine Safety Detachment and Public Affairs Detachment. Also home to three USCG Cutters: Storis, Ironwood and Firebush.

**TEMPORARY MILITARY LODGING:** Guest house, Building N-30, 0800-1700 daily, C-907-487-5446, D-317-487-5446. All ranks. PCS or official duty, all others Space-A. DV/VIP C-907-487-5265.

**RV, CAMPING/FAMCAMP:** None. Nearest facility is more than 100 miles away.

**SPACE-A:** Pax Term, Hangar #1, 0800-1600 Mon-Fri, C-907-487-5149, D-317-487-5149. Fax: C-907-487-5273. Flights to Alaska locations and Sacramento.

**LOGISTICAL SUPPORT:**

| | |
|---|---|
| Bank-487-4428 | Barber Shop-487-5847 |
| Beauty Shop-487-5432 | Cafeteria-487-5710 |
| Child Care-487-5922 | Child Dev Center-487-5481 |
| Commissary-487-5204 | Conv Store-487-5475 |
| Dining Facilities-487-5235 | Dry Cleaner-487-5450 |
| Education Office-487-5119 | Exchange-487-5370 |
| Gas Station-487-5107 | Laundry-487-5450 |
| Package Store-487-5475 | Postal Service-487-5263 |
| SATO-487-2500 | Snack Bar-487-5988 |

**ADMINISTRATIVE SUPPORT:**

| | |
|---|---|
| Fire Dept-487-5808 | Housing-487-5310, ext 141 |
| Legal-487-5474 | Locator-487-5267 |
| OOD-487-5267 | Pass/ID Office-487-5170, ext 157 |
| Police-487-5266, ext 010 | Public Affairs-487-5170, ext 186 |

**HEALTH & WELFARE:**

| | |
|---|---|
| American Red Cross-487-5200 | CHAMPUS-487-5757, ext 131 |
| Chapel-487-5730 | Dental-487-5757 |
| Family Services-487-5525 | Central Appts-487-5757, ext 115 |
| Medical-487-5757 | Retiree Services-487-5761 |
| Central Appts-487-5757, ext 125 | |
| Emergency-487-5222 | |
| Health Benefits-487-5757, ext 131 | |
| Information-487-5757, ext 125 | |

**REST & RECREATION:**

| | |
|---|---|
| Arts & Crafts-487-5493 | Auto Hobby Shop-487-5844 |
| Boat House-ext 5047 | Bowling-487-5401 |
| Clubs | Community Center-487-5250 |
| Com-487-5109 | Golf Course-486-7561 |
| Gym-487-5272 | Library-487-5661 |
| MWR-487-5108 | Outdoor Sports-ext 5272 |
| Racquetball-ext 5272 | Teen Center-ext 5271 |
| Theater-487-5884 | Weight Room-ext 5272 |
| Wood Hobby Shop-487-5550 | Youth Services-487-5457 |

**ATTRACTIONS:** Hunting and fishing paradise, National Wildlife Refuge-home of Kodiak brown bear, sightseeing and local museums displaying Alutiiq and Russian History.

## KULIS AIR NATIONAL GUARD BASE (AK24R5)
5005 Raspberry Road
Anchorage, AK 99502-1998

**TELEPHONE NUMBER INFORMATION:** Main installation numbers: C-907-249-1176, D-317-626-1176.

**LOCATION:** From downtown Anchorage, go south on Minnesota Thruway to right (west) on International Airport Road to left (south) on Jewel Lake Road, turn right onto Raspberry Road. Main gate is approximately one mile on right (north) side of road. USMRA: Page 128 (F-5), page 131 (A-4). NMC: Anchorage, in city limits.

**GENERAL INFORMATION:** Home of 176th Wing Air National Guard.

**TEMPORARY MILITARY LODGING:** None. See Elmendorf AFB listing.

**RV, CAMPING/FAMCAMP:** None. See Seward Resort listing.

**SPACE-A:** Base Ops, C-907-249-1000, D-317-626-1000, Fax: C-907-249-1648.

**LOGISTICAL SUPPORT:**

| | |
|---|---|
| Cafeteria-249-1454 | SATO-249-1206 |

**ADMINISTRATIVE SUPPORT:**

| | |
|---|---|
| Fire Department 249-1394 | Legal-249-1100 |
| Locator-249-1176 | Police-249-1271 |
| Public Affairs 249-1342 | SDO/NCO-249-1131 |

**HEALTH & WELFARE:**

| | |
|---|---|
| Chapel-249-1141* | Medical-249-1415* |

*Open only on unit training drill weekends.

**REST & RECREATION:**

| | |
|---|---|
| | NCO Club-249-1234 |

**ATTRACTIONS:** Great opportunity for skiing, hunting, fishing, camping, sightseeing, and bird watching.

## SEWARD AIR FORCE CAMP (AK05R5)
PO Box 915
Seward, AK 99664-5000

**TELEPHONE NUMBER INFORMATION:** Main installation numbers: Summer: C-907-552-5526; Winter: C-907-753-2378.

**LOCATION:** Off base. From Anchorage south on AK-1 to AK-9 south to mile post 2.1 of the Seward Highway. Camp is on right (west) side of AK-9 on Ressurection Bay. Follow signs. USMRA: Page 128 (F-6). NMC: Anchorage, 124 miles north.

**GENERAL INFORMATION:** Operated by Elmendorf AFB, off base, mid-May through mid-September. Closed during winter months. Off season address: 3 SVS/SVK, Bldg 6-920, 12th Street, Elmendorf AFB, AK 99506-2550. Summer: call C-907-552-5526, Fax: C-907-224-2279; Winter: call C-907-753-2378.

**TEMPORARY MILITARY LODGING:** Cabins-12

**RV, CAMPING/FAMCAMP:**

| | |
|---|---|
| RV/Trailer spaces-35 | Tent/Camper spaces-47 |

**ATTRACTIONS:** Scenic, heavily wooded area, with view of multiple glaciers. Excellent saltwater fishing.

*For detailed information about this off-base recreation facility, as well as on-base recreation facilities, golf courses and marinas, consult Military Living's Military RV, Camping and Outdoor Recreation Around the World.*

## SEWARD RESORT (AK06R5)

P.O. Box 329
Seward, AK 99664-5000

**TELEPHONE NUMBER INFORMATION:** Main installation numbers: C-907-224-2659/5559/2654 or for reservations call 1-800-770-1858, D-317-384-FISH (3474)/LINE (5463). WEB: www.usarak.army.mil/framwr/seward.htm

**LOCATION:** Off post, 125 miles south of Anchorage. Take Seward Highway (AK-1) south to AK-9. Continue south to Seward. Follow signs. USMRA: Page 128 (F-6). NMC: Anchorage, 124 miles north. NMI: Fort Richardson, 133 miles north.

**GENERAL INFORMATION:** Operated by Fort Richardson, off base 1 May-15 September 0600-2300, 16 September-30 April 1100-1900. Military personnel active, retired, reserve, DoD, NAF and contract civilians. Reservations: call for specific information 0600-2300 local time, seven days a week, C-907-224-2659/5559/2654 or for reservations call 1-800-770-1858, D-317-384-FISH (3474)/LINE (5463). No reservations may be made by mail.

**TEMPORARY MILITARY LODGING:**
Motel rooms-56                        Townhouses-14

**RV, CAMPING/FAMCAMP:**
RV/Trailer Spaces-40                  Tent spaces-10

**LOGISTICAL SUPPORT:**
Shoppette-224-7122 (seasonal)         Snack Bar-224-5425 (seasonal)

**ATTRACTIONS:** Superb fishing. Area is a photographer's dream. Late July to mid-August see active salmon spawning areas on drive to Seward.

*For detailed information about this off-base recreation facility, as well as on-base recreation facilities, golf courses and marinas, consult Military Living's Military RV, Camping and Outdoor Recreation Around the World.*

## SITKA COAST GUARD AIR STATION (AK25R5)

611 Airport Road
Sitka, AK 99835-6500

**TELEPHONE NUMBER INFORMATION:** Main installation numbers: C-907-966-5434.

**LOCATION:** Located at end of Airport Road on Japonski Island, five miles north of airport terminal. USMRA: Page 128 (I-7). NMC: Juneau, 90 miles by air or ferry.

**GENERAL INFORMATION:** Air Station Sitka primarily involved in search and rescue throughout southeast Alaska. Additionally, performs law enforcement, fisheries patrols and aids to navigation support.

**TEMPORARY MILITARY LODGING:** None. Nearest facility is more than 100 miles away.

**RV, CAMPING/FAMCAMP:** None. Nearest facility is more than 100 miles away.

**SPACE-A:** Very limited. C-907-966-5580, Fax: C-907-966-5428.

**LOGISTICAL SUPPORT**                Cafeteria-966-5546

**ADMINISTRATIVE SUPPORT:**
Locator-966-5431                      SDO/NCO-966-5420

**HEALTH & WELFARE:**
CHAMPUS-966-5438                      Emergency-911
Medical-966-5438

**REST & RECREATION:**
Com Club-966-5516                     Gym-ext 5518
MWR-966-5435

**ATTRACTIONS:** Sport fishing and hunting abundant. Sitka National Historical Park, totem poles and Sitka shoreline. Russian Bishop's House; St. Michael's Russian Orthodox Church, with many precious icons on display; Castle Hill, site of 1867 transfer of Alaska territory from Russia to the U.S.

# ARIZONA

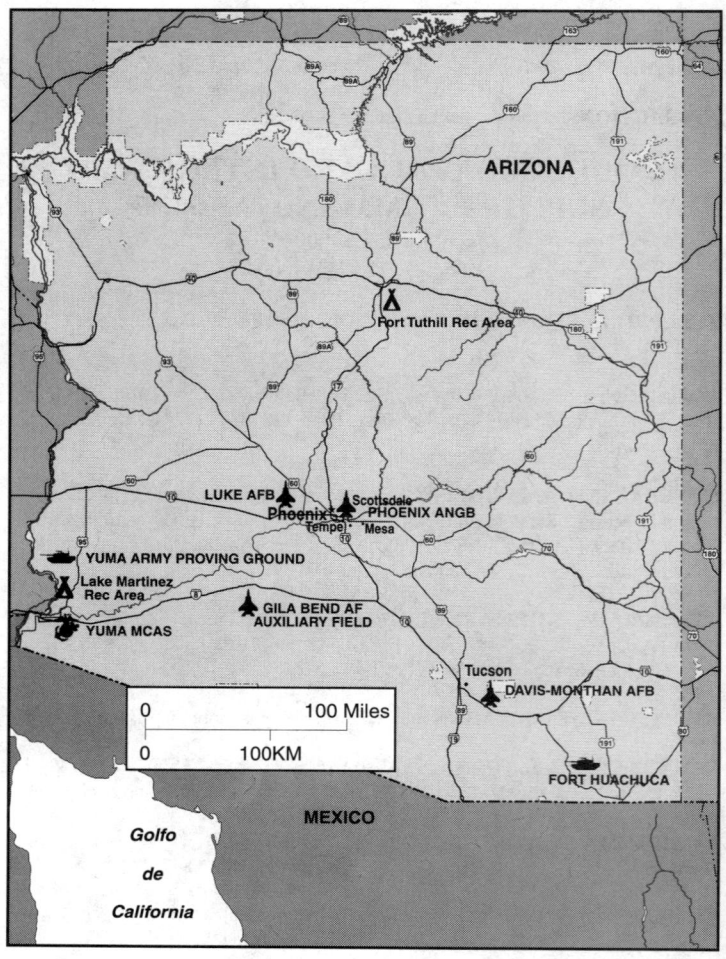

## DAVIS-MONTHAN AIR FORCE BASE (AZ01R4)

355th Wing, Hq 12th Air Force
5275 East Granite Street
Davis-Monthan Air Force Base, AZ 85707-3010

**TELEPHONE NUMBER INFORMATION:** Main installation numbers: C-520-228-3900, D-312-228-1110. WEB: www.dm.af.mil

**LOCATION:** From the east on I-10, exit #270 north onto Kolb Road, north 6 miles to Golf Links Road, left (west) to Craycroft Road, left (south) to main gate. From the west on I-10, exit #264 north onto Alvernon Way; turn left (north) following road to the main gate. (Alvernon Way turns into Golf Links Road at intersection with Ajo Way.) USMRA: Page 108 (F-9). NMC: Tucson, in city limits.

**GENERAL INFORMATION:** Air Combat Command Base, 355th Wing (host unit), HQ 12th Air Force, AAC Air Ops, and Aerospace Maintenance and Regeneration Center (AMARC) and 305th Rescue Squadron (AFRES).

**TEMPORARY MILITARY LODGING:** Lodging office, Building 2350, 10th Street, 24 hours daily, C-520-228-3230, D-312-228-3230. All ranks. DV/VIP 520-228-3600, D-312-228-3600.

**RV, CAMPING/FAMCAMP:** Davis-Monthan FAMCAMP on base, C-520-747-9144, year round, 73 camper spaces with full hookups, 35 overflow camper spaces without hookups.

**SPACE-A:** Pax Term/Ops in Building 4819, 0700-1600 Mon-Fri, C-520-228-3641, D-312-228-3641. Fax: C-520-228-7229, D-312-228-7229.

## LOGISTICAL SUPPORT:

Bank-792-7025
Beauty Shop-748-8334
Car Rental-571-0886
Child Dev Center-228-3336
Clothing & Sales-228-4408
Conv Store-748-8076
Dining Facilities-228-3072
Education Office-228-4813
Gas Station-748-8212
SATO-228-4841
Snack Bar-790-6150

Barber Shop-571-1604
Cafeteria-790-6150
Child Care-228-3336
Class Six-747-1365
Commissary-228-3116
Credit Union-298-7882
Dry Cleaner-790-1701
Exchange-748-7887
Postal Service-748-1651
Shoppette-745-3866
Visitor Center-228-4886

## ADMINISTRATIVE SUPPORT:

Fire Dept-228-4758
Legal-228-5242
Pass/ID Office-228-5246
Public Affairs-228-3204

Housing Office-228-3687
Locator-228-3347
Police-228-3200
SDO/NCO-750-3121

## HEALTH & WELFARE:

Air Force Aid Society-228-3891
CHAMPUS-228-2606
Dental-Hospital
   Central Appts-228-2652
   Clinic-228-2651
Retiree Services-228-5100
TRICARE-228-3835
Veterinary Services-228-3529

American Red Cross-228-3205
Chapel-228-5411
Family Services-228-3369
Medical-Hospital
   Central Appts-228-2778
   Emergency-228-2828
   Health Benefits-228-2606
   Information-228-2564

## REST & RECREATION:

Arts & Crafts-228-4385
Bowling-228-3461
Clubs
   Aero-ext 3603
   EM-228-3100
   NCO-228-3100
   O-228-3301
   Saddle-885-9049
Outdoor Rec-228-3736
Rec Center/Tickets-ext 3717
Theater-228-3623
Youth Center-228-4565

Auto Hobby Shop-228-3614
Ceramics-ext 4385/4028
Community Center-228-3717
Fitness Center-228-3714
Golf Course-228-3734
Gym-ext 3714
ITT-228-4491
Library-228-4381
Picnic Area-ext 3846
Swimming-ext 3579
Wood Hobby Shop-228-4385

**ATTRACTIONS:** Old Tucson, movie sets, Reid Park, zoo, Arizona-Sonora Desert, Pima Air and Space Museum, Titan Missile Museum, University of Arizona, Kitt Peak Observatory, Biosphere II, and Mount Lemon hiking and skiing. Also, twice weekly tours at AMARC.

# FORT HUACHUCA (AZ02R4)

USAIC & Fort Huachuca
ATTN: ATZS-CDR
Fort Huachuca, AZ 85613-6000

**TELEPHONE NUMBER INFORMATION:** Main installation numbers: C-520-538-7111, D-312-821-7111.

**LOCATION:** From I-10 take exit #302 south onto AZ-90 south approximately 28 miles to Sierra Vista and main gate to fort on right (west) side of road. USMRA: Page 108 (F,G-9,10). NMI: Davis-Monthan AFB, 75 miles northwest. NMC: Tucson, 75 miles northwest.

**GENERAL INFORMATION:** U.S. Army Intelligence Center and Fort Huachuca, U.S. Army Signal Command, U.S. Army Electronic Proving Ground, Joint Interoperability Test Command and 11th Signal Brigade.

**TEMPORARY MILITARY LODGING:** Lodging office, Building 43083, Service Road, 24 hours daily, C-520-533-2222, D-312-821-2222. Extensive facilities. All ranks. DV/VIP C-520-533-1231, D-312-821-1231.

**RV, CAMPING/FAMCAMP:** Apache Flats Campground on post, Building 15423, 1100-1900 hours Wed through Fri, 1000-1800 hours Sat and Sun, C-520-533-7085/6, D-312-821-7085/6. There are 24 camper spaces with W/E hookups, and a limited number of tent spaces.

**SPACE-A:** Limited flights from Libby Army Airfield on post via executive aircraft, C-520-538-2860.

## LOGISTICAL SUPPORT:

Barber Shop-459-1172
Carlson Wagonlit Travel-515-0914
Child Dev Center-533-5209
Commissary-533-5540
Dry Cleaner-458-2111
Gas Station-458-4022
Postal Service-458-4411
Snack Bar-533-5759

Beauty Shop-458-7140
Child Care-533-5209
Class Six-458-8389
Credit Union-459-1860
Exchange-458-7831
Laundry-533-2661
Shoppette-458-8389

## ADMINISTRATIVE SUPPORT:

Fire Dept-533-2116 or 911
Legal-533-2095
Pass/ID Office-533-1904
Public Affairs-533-3418

Housing Office-533-3083
Locator-533-7111
Police-533-2181 or 911
SDO/NCO-533-2291

## HEALTH & WELFARE:

American Red Cross-533-3883/3895
Army Emergency Relief-533-5972
Dental-533-3147
   Central Appts-533-5151
Retiree Services-533-5733
TRICARE-515-5840

ACS-533-3234
Chapel-533-5559
Family Services-533-2330
Medical
   Emergency-533-5132
Veterinary Services-533-2767

## REST & RECREATION:

Arts & Crafts-533-2015
Barnes Field House (Gym)-538-2022
Clubs
   EM (Ozone)-533-0861
   NCO (LaHacienta)-533-7322
   O/Civ (Lakeside)-533-2193
MWR-533-3107/1315
Picnic Reservations-538-7085
Swimming-533-3858/3853
Youth Center-533-3205

Auto Hobby Shop-538-1690
Bowling 533-2849
Eilfer Fitness Center-533-1723
Golf Course-533-7092
ITT/ITR-533-2404
Library-533-4101
Outdoor Rec-533-6706
Riding-533-5220
Theater-533-2950

**OTHER FACILITIES AVAILABLE:** Bank, cafeteria, community center, education office, civilian and military personnel offices and Defense Finance and Accounting Service.

**ATTRACTIONS:** Two post historical museum and original cantonment, now a national historical landmark. Tombstone, AZ, home of the famous OK Corral and the gun fight between the Earps, Doc Holiday and the Clantons, a 25 minute drive east on Charleston Road.

# FORT TUTHILL RECREATION AREA (AZ11R4)

HC 30, Box 5
Flagstaff, AZ 86001-8701

**TELEPHONE NUMBER INFORMATION:** Main installation numbers: C-800-552-6268, D-312-896-3401, Fax-C-602-856-7990.
*Ten digit dialing required for local calls.*

**LOCATION:** Located at an elevation of 7,000 feet at the base of the San Francisco Peaks. Four miles south of Flagstaff. Take I-17 north to exit #337 (Airport/Sedona). Enter park area at Fort Tuthill (adjoins Coconino County fairgrounds.) Take first road to left. USMRA: Page 108 (E-4). NMC: Flagstaff, four miles north. NMI: Luke AFB, 138 miles southwest.

**GENERAL INFORMATION:** Fort Tuthill Recreation Area was created in 1928 as a National Guard summer camp. It is operated by Luke Air Force Base and has off-base hotel, chalets, cabins and yurts that are open year round and a camping area open from May-October. Military personnel active, retired, reserve and DoD civilians. Check in after 1500, check out 1100; office open 24 hours. Reservations: Required, confirm with credit card or mail deposit. C-800-552-6268, D-312-896-3401, Fax C-602-856-7990. Reservations accepted at Fort Tuthill.

**TEMPORARY MILITARY LODGING:** A-Frames, Cabins, Hotel

**RV, CAMPING/FAMCAMP:**

Yurts                                   RV sites-33

**ATTRACTIONS:** Grand Canyon–90 miles, Sedona/Oak Creek Canyon–28 miles, Meteor Crater–40 miles, Wutpaki Indian ruins–30 miles, Lowell Observatory–Flagstaff, Museum of Northern Arizona–Flagstaff.

*For detailed information about this off-base recreation facility, as well as on-base recreation facilities, golf courses and marinas, consult Military Living's Military RV, Camping and Outdoor Recreation Around the World.*

# GILA BEND AIR FORCE AUXILIARY FIELD (AZ16R4)

3096 First Street
Gila Bend Air Force Auxiliary Field, AZ 85337-5000

**TELEPHONE NUMBER INFORMATION:** Main installation numbers: C-520-683-6224, D-312-896-6224.

**LOCATION:** From I-10 34 miles west of Phoenix, take exit 112 (Yuma/Gila Bend); south on AZ-85 through Gila Bend; right (west) at Gila Bend AFAF/Ajo sign, approximately three-and-a-half miles to the AFAF. Also take I-8 east or west, exit #116 north to left (west) at Gila Bend AAF/Ajo sign and 3.5 miles to base. USMRA: Page 108 (C-7,8). NMC: Phoenix, 69 miles northeast.

**GENERAL INFORMATION:** Primarily responsible for Barry M. Goldwater Air Force Gunnery Range, which covers 2.7 million acres.

**TEMPORARY MILITARY LODGING:** Lodging office, Building 4300, C-520-683-6238, D-312-896-5238.

**RV, CAMPING/FAMCAMP:** FAMCAMP on base, year round, C-520-683-6238, D-312-896-5238, 35 camper spaces with full hookups, various tent sites.

**SPACE-A:** Call 24 hours in advance for reservation. C-520-683-6238, D-312-896-5238.

**LOGISTICAL SUPPORT:**                    Police-683-6220

**ADMINISTRATIVE SUPPORT:** None. See Luke AFB listing.

**HEALTH & WELFARE:** None. See Luke AFB listing.

**REST & RECREATION:** None. See Luke AFB listing.

**ATTRACTIONS:** Pleasant winter weather. Mountain areas and Mexico within easy driving distance. Luke AFB, 65 miles away, has full support facilities.

# LAKE MARTINEZ RECREATION AREA (AZ12R4)

MWR Ticket & Tours, Bldg 693
P.O. Box 99119
Yuma, AZ 85369-9119

**TELEPHONE NUMBER INFORMATION:** Main installation numbers: C-520-341-2278, D-312-951-2278.

**LOCATION:** Off base. Located on the Colorado River 38 miles north of Yuma. From I-8, east or west, exit #2 to north on US-95 for 20 miles to left on Imperial Wildlife Refuge access road for approximately ten miles northwest. Turn right at sign for USMC Recreation area, follow road approximately two miles. USMRA: Page 108 (A-7). NMI: Yuma Army Proving Ground, 15 miles north. NMC: Phoenix, 20 miles east.

**GENERAL INFORMATION:** Operated by Yuma MCAS, off base, year round. Military personnel active, reservists, retired. Reservations: MWR Ticket & Tours, Bldg 693, P.O. Box 99119, Yuma, AZ 85369-9119. C-520-341-2278, D-312-951-2278 0900-1800 hours Mon-Fri. Recreation Area: Lake Martinez Recreation Area, P.O. Box 72202, Lake Martinez, AZ 85365-5000.

**RV, CAMPING/FAMCAMP:**

| | |
|---|---|
| Cabins-4 | Mobile Homes-8 |
| Camper Spaces-17 | Camper/Tent Spaces-3 |

**ATTRACTIONS:** Rustic semi-private fishing camp. Great for watersports.

*For detailed information about this off-base recreation facility, as well as on-base recreation facilities, golf courses and marinas, consult Military Living's Military RV, Camping and Outdoor Recreation Around the World.*

# LUKE AIR FORCE BASE (AZ03R4)

7131 North Litchfield Road
Luke Air Force Base, AZ 85309-1501

**TELEPHONE NUMBER INFORMATION:** Main installation numbers: C-623-856-7411, D-312-896-1110.
*Ten digit dialing required for local calls.*

**LOCATION:** From Phoenix, west on I-10 to Litchfield Road, exit 128, north on Litchfield Road approximately five miles. Also, from Phoenix, north on I-17 to Glendale Avenue exit #205 west on Glendale Avenue to intersection of Glendale Avenue and Litchfield Road approximately 10 miles. USMRA: Page 108 (D-6,7). NMC: Phoenix, 20 miles east.

**GENERAL INFORMATION:** Air Education Training Command Base. Largest fighter wing in world.

**TEMPORARY MILITARY LODGING:** Lodging office, Building 660, Bong Lane, 24 hours daily, C-602-856-3941. All ranks. DV/VIP: C-623-856-5840.

**RV, CAMPING/FAMCAMP:** Operates Fort Tuthill Rec Area, 150 miles north on I-17, four miles south of Flagstaff. See Fort Tuthill Recreation Area listing for more information. Gila Bend FAMCAMP at Auxiliary Field, on base year round, Lodging Office, HC01 Box 22, Gila Bend AFAF, AZ 85337-5000, C-520-683-6238, D-312-896-5238, 35 camper spaces with full hookups.

**SPACE-A:** Pax Term/Lounge, Building 439, 0630-2230 Mon-Fri, 0730-1800 Sat, Sun, Holidays, C-623-856-7131, D-312-896-7131. Flights to Midwest and West Coast.

**LOGISTICAL SUPPORT:**

| | |
|---|---|
| Car Rental-856-5005 | Child Care-856-6339 |
| Commissary-935-3821 | Conv Store-935-2414 |
| Exchange-935-2671 | Gas Station-935-4953 |
| SATO-856-6891 | Snack Bar-856-7102 |

**ADMINISTRATIVE SUPPORT:**

| | |
|---|---|
| Legal-856-6901 | Locator-856-6405 |
| Police-856-5970 | Public Affairs-856-6011 |
| SDO/NCO-856-5800 | |

**HEALTH & WELFARE:**

| | |
|---|---|
| CHAMPUS-856-7600 | Chapel-856-6211 |
| Medical-856-7506 | Retiree Services-856-6827 |

**REST & RECREATION:**

| | |
|---|---|
| Arts & Crafts-856-6502 | Auto Hobby Shop-856-6107 |
| Bowling-856-6946 | Clubs |
| Fitness Center-856-6241 |   EM-856-7136 |
| ITT Office-856-6000 |   O-856-6446 |
| Library-856-7191 | Rec Center-856-7152 |
| Theater-856-6461 | Wood Hobby Shop-856-6566 |
| Youth Center-856-6225 | |

**ATTRACTIONS:** Colorful Scottsdale nearby. Arizona state capital, fairgrounds and coliseum in Phoenix. ASU in Tempe. Lots of sunshine, hot summers, cool winters.

# PHOENIX AIR NATIONAL GUARD BASE (AZ06R4)

161 Air Refueling Wing (ANG)
3200 East Old Tower Road
Phoenix, AZ 85034-6098

**TELEPHONE NUMBER INFORMATION:** Main installation numbers: C-602-302-9000.
*Ten digit dialing required for local calls.*

**LOCATION:** From I-10 in Phoenix, take the 24th street exit; go north one-quarter mile, turn east on Old Tower Road; follow Old Tower Road to the front gate of post. NMI: Luke AFB, 30 miles west. NMC: Phoenix, five miles west.

**GENERAL INFORMATION:** Home to 161st ARW (ANG), direct connection to Sky Harbor IAP.

**TEMPORARY MILITARY LODGING:** None. See Luke AFB listing.

**RV, CAMPING/FAMCAMP:** None. See Luke AFB listing.

**SPACE-A:** Sky Harbor IAP, Pax Term, 0630-1600 Tue-Fri, C-602-302-9000 ext 1, D-312-853-9000 ext 1. Fax: C-602-302-9288, D-312-853-9288. Flights via KC-135 Aerial Refuelers, CONUS and OCONUS year round.

**LOGISTICAL SUPPORT:** None. See Luke AFB listing.

**ADMINISTRATIVE SUPPORT:**     Public Affairs-302-9235

**HEALTH & WELFARE:** None. See Luke AFB listing.

**REST & RECREATION:** Fitness Center, Gym, Phoenix ANG Club, Swimming Pool.

**ATTRACTIONS:** Located in downtown Phoenix, warm weather year round offers every opportunity for sightseeing, Phoenix Suns basketball, NFL Arizona Cardinals and Arizona State University.

## YUMA ARMY PROVING GROUND (AZ05R4)
ATTN: STEYP-CO
Building 2100
Yuma Army Proving Ground, AZ 85365-9100

**TELEPHONE NUMBER INFORMATION:** Main installation numbers: C-520-328-2151, D-312-899-2151. WEB: www.yuma.army.mil

**LOCATION:** Northeast of I-8, turn right (north) on US-95 which bisects the post. Southwest of I-10 turn left (south) on US-95. US-95 bisects Army Proving Ground. USMRA: Page 108 (A-6,7,8; B-7,8). NMC: Yuma, 27 miles southwest.

**GENERAL INFORMATION:** Army Materiel Test Facility with instrumented ranges.

**TEMPORARY MILITARY LODGING:** Lodging office, Building 1003, 5th Street & Barranca Road, 0700-1800 daily, C-520-328-2127/2129, D-312-899-2127/2129. All ranks. DV/VIP C-520-328-2020.

**RV, CAMPING/FAMCAMP:** Desert Breeze Travel Camp on post, C-520-329-8710, 42 camper spaces with full hookups.

**SPACE-A:** None. See Yuma MCAS listing.

**LOGISTICAL SUPPORT:**
Child Care-328-2588
Gas Station-343-1365
Commissary-328-2240Conv Store-328-2252
Exchange-328-2252
Leisure Travel Office-ext 2/3/4586

**ADMINISTRATIVE SUPPORT:**
Fire Dept-328-2949
Locator-328-2151/2430
Public Affairs-328-6189/6533
Legal-328-2608
Police-328-2720

**HEALTH & WELFARE:**
ACS-328-2513
Chapel-328-3465
Medical-328-2502
  Central Appts-328-2502
  Emergency-328-2911
CHAMPUS-328-2502
Family Services-328-2711

**REST & RECREATION:**
Bowling-ext 2790
Fitness Center-ext 2400
Swimming-ext 2209
Outdoor Rec-ext 4586
Com Club-328-2097
MWR-328-2223
Tennis Courts-ext 2400

**ATTRACTIONS:** Isolated post, next to Kofa National Wildlife Refuge and the Colorado River; boating on the Colorado River.

## YUMA MARINE CORPS AIR STATION (AZ04R4)
Box 99131
Yuma Marine Corps Air Station, AZ 85369-9131

**TELEPHONE NUMBER INFORMATION:** Main installation numbers: C-520-341-2011, D-312-951-2011.

**LOCATION:** From I-8 east or west take exit #3 onto Avenue 3E south for one mile to base on right, adjacent to Yuma IAP. USMRA: Page 108 (A-8). NMC: Yuma, three miles northwest.

**GENERAL INFORMATION:** The premier Marine Corps Combat Air Training Base. Near perfect flying conditions and range facilities are available.

**TEMPORARY MILITARY LODGING:** Lodging office, Sta S-4, Billeting fund, Building 1058, Martini Avenue, 24 hours daily, C-520-341-2262, D-312-951-2262. All ranks.

**RV, CAMPING/FAMCAMP:** Operates Lake Martinez Rec Area year round, on the Colorado River, 38 miles north of Yuma MCAS off US-95. See separate listing for details.

**SPACE-A:** Pax Term/Lounge and Ops, Building 151, 0700-1530 daily, C-520-341-2729, D-312-951-2729. Fax: C-520-341-3667, D-312-951-3667.

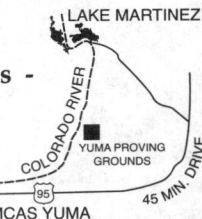

**Fishing at Lake Martinez Recreation Area**

Photo courtesy of Lake Martinez Recreation Area

**LOGISTICAL SUPPORT:**

Child Care-341-2350

Conv Store-341-3567

Gas Station-341-2110

SATO-341-5782

Commissary-341-2248

Exchange-341-2256

Package Store-341-3567

**ADMINISTRATIVE SUPPORT:**

Legal-341-2481

Police-341-2205/2361

SDO/NCO-341-2253

Locator-341-2011

Public Affairs-341-2275

**HEALTH & WELFARE:**

CHAMPUS-341-2916

Family Services-341-5615

Chapel-341-2371

Medical-341-2772

   Emergency-341-2111

**REST & RECREATION:**

Athletic/Picnic Facilities-ext 2278

Bowling-341-5585

Clubs

   EM-341-2457

   O-341-2711

   SNCO-341-2711

Swimming

   EM-ext 2926

   O-ext 3474

Auto Hobby Shop-ext 2395

Camping Equipment-ext 2848

Gym-ext 2727

ITT-341-2278

Library-ext 2785

Services-ext 2278

Theater-341-2358

**ATTRACTIONS:** Desert type climate, Colorado River.

# ARKANSAS

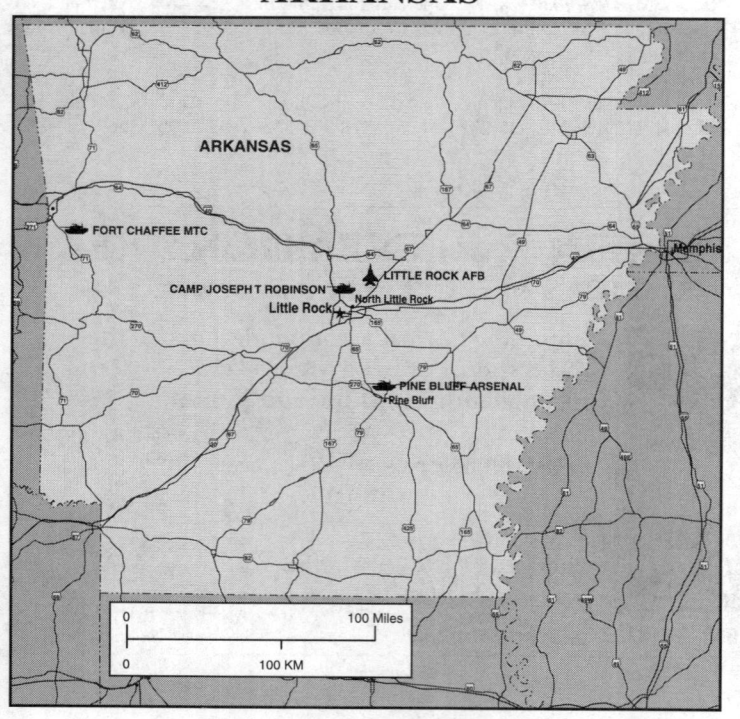

## CAMP JOSEPH T. ROBINSON (AR07R2)

ATTN: TAG-AR-PR

Building 6000

North Little Rock, AR 72199-9600

**TELEPHONE NUMBER INFORMATION:** Main installation numbers: C-501-212-5100, D-312-962-5100.

**LOCATION:** From east or west on I-40, take Burns Park exit 150 to Military Drive, follow signs to camp (two miles). USMRA: Page 76 (D-5). NMC: North Little Rock, one mile south.

**GENERAL INFORMATION:** Headquarters Arkansas National Guard, 90th Regional Support Command U.S. Army Reserve Center.

**TEMPORARY MILITARY LODGING:** Lodging office, Building 5130, Phillips Armory, Arkansas Avenue, 0700-1530 Mon-Thu, 0700-2000 Fri, 0700-1630 Sat, 0600-1530 Sun, C-501-212-5274.

**RV, CAMPING/FAMCAMP:** Sixteen sites. Call C-501-212-5274, D-312-962-5274. Fax: C-501-212-5271, Fax D-312-962-5271.

**SPACE-A:** None. See Little Rock AFB listing.

**LOGISTICAL SUPPORT:**

Exchange-753-9017

Snack Bar-758-8468

**ADMINISTRATIVE SUPPORT:**

Fire Dept-212-5280

Locator-212-5100

Public Affairs-212-5020

Legal-212-5030

Police-212-5280

**HEALTH & WELFARE:**

Chapel-212-5926

Medical-212-5262

**REST & RECREATION:**

All Ranks Club-758-5076

Gym-212-4661

Rec Equipment-212-4661

MWR-753-9017

Golf Course-791-8592

Fitness Center-212-4661

Swimming Pool-753-9017

**ATTRACTIONS:** State Capital, Burns Park, Wild River Country, Quapaw District, Little Rock Zoo, Arkansas Arts Center, Governor's Mansion, Old Mill, Pinnacle Mountain, War Memorial Park, Arkansas Travelers baseball.

## FORT CHAFFEE MANEUVER TRAINING CENTER (AR04R2)

1370 Fort Smith Boulevard

Fort Chaffee, AR 72905-1370

**TELEPHONE NUMBER INFORMATION:** Main installation numbers: C-501-484-4230, D-312-962-2111.

**LOCATION:** From I-40, take the I-540 exit 7 southwest in Fort Smith. From I-540, exit 8 onto AR-22 southeast (Rogers Avenue) and continue through the town of Barling to Fort Chaffee, one mile east of Barling. USMRA: Page 76 (A,B-4,5). NMC: Fort Smith, six miles northwest.

**GENERAL INFORMATION:** Active Army and Reserve Component training support, USAR NCO Academy, Regional Training Brigade.

**TEMPORARY MILITARY LODGING:** Lodging office, Building 1370, Fort Smith Blvd, 0730-1630 Mon-Fri, 0700-1600 Sat & Sun, C-501-484-2252/2917, D-312-962-2252. After duty hours contact SDO C-501-484-2666.

**RV, CAMPING/FAMCAMP:** Chaffee Trailer Park on post, C-501-484-2252, D-312-962-2252, 39 camper spaces with full hookups.

**SPACE-A:** None. See Little Rock AFB, listing.

**LOGISTICAL SUPPORT:**

Barber Shop-484-2256

Shoppette-478-6141

Dry Cleaner-452-1127

Snack Bar-484-2843

**ADMINISTRATIVE SUPPORT:**

CDO/OOD-484-2666
Locator-484-2610
Police-414-3788
SDO/NCO-719-1414

Fire Dept-484-2212
Pass/ID Office-414-3788
Public Affairs-484-2610

**HEALTH & WELFARE:**

Medical-484-2488
  Emergency-484-6241
  Information-484-6100

Retiree Services-484-3130
TRICARE-478-1515

**REST & RECREATION:**

Golf Course-484-2326
Library-ext 2550
Rec Equipment-ext 2550

Fitness Center-484-2550
MWR-452-5385
Rec Center-ext 2550

**ATTRACTIONS:** Ouachita and Ozark National Forests, city of Fort Smith, Arkansas River. Fayetteville, home of the University of Arkansas Razorbacks, offers great opportunity for sporting events.

# LITTLE ROCK AIR FORCE BASE (AR02R2)

314 AW/PA
1250 Thomas Avenue, Suite 154
Little Rock Air Force Base, AR 72099-4940

**TELEPHONE NUMBER INFORMATION:** Main installation numbers: C-501-987-3131, D-312-731-1110. E-mail: 314aw.pa@littlerock.af.mil. WEB: www.little-rock.af.mil

**LOCATION:** From I-40 take exit 55 north on US-67/167 to Jacksonville, take exit 11 west to Vandenberg Blvd. Follow signs to main gate west of US-67/167. USMRA: Page 76 (D,E-5). NMC: Little Rock, 18 miles southwest.

**GENERAL INFORMATION:** Air Education and Training Command Base Group with two AMC tenant units, C-130 Training, USAF Combat Aerial Delivery School, Headquarters Arkansas Air National Guard, and other missions.

**TEMPORARY MILITARY LODGING:** P.O. Box 1192, Building 1024, Cannon Drive, 24 hours daily, C-501-987-3067, D-312-731-3067, Fax: C-501-987-7769, D-312-731-7769. DV/VIP 501-987-6828.

**RV, CAMPING/FAMCAMP:** On base. Little Rock FAMCAMP, year round, C-501-987-3365, D-312-731-3365. Fax: C-501-987-6164, D-312-731-6164; 23 camper spaces with W/E hookups, six tent spaces.

**SPACE-A:** Pax Term/Lounge, Building 430, 0730-1630 Mon-Fri, C-501-987-3342/3393, D-312-731-3342/3393, Rec: C-501-987-3684. Fax: C-501-987-6726, D-312-731-6726. Flights to CONUS, OCONUS and foreign locations.

**LOGISTICAL SUPPORT:**

Bank-985-4025
Beauty Shop-987-1900
Child Dev Center-987-3373
Commissary-987-3203
Dining Facilities-987-3072
Education Office-987-3417
Gas Station-987-2301
SATO-988-2771
Snack Bar-988-4412
Visitor Center-987-3425

Barber Shop-987-1160
Child Care-987-6139
Class Six-987-1374
Conv Store-987-4841
Dry Cleaner-988-4834
Exchange-987-1180
Postal Service-987-3695
Shoppette-988-4841
Travel Office-988-4116

**ADMINISTRATIVE SUPPORT:**

CDO/OOD 988-3200
Housing Office-987-7654
Locator-987-6025
Police-987-3221

Fire Dept-987-3228
Legal-987-7886
Pass/ID Office-987-6831
Public Affairs-987-3601

**HEALTH & WELFARE:**

Air Force Aid Society-987-6801
CHAMPUS-987-7458
Dental Clinic-987-7304

American Red Cross-987-3428
Chapel-987-6014
Family Services-987-6801

Medical Clinic-987-7362
Retiree Services-987-6095
Veterinary Services-987-7250

Medical Central Appts-987-8811
TRICARE-988-2057

**REST & RECREATION:**

Auto Hobby Shop-987-6761
Clubs
  EM-987-3760
  O-987-1111
ITT-987-3216
MWR-987-3365
Theater-987-6461
Youth Center-987-6355

Bowling-ext 3793
Community Center-987-6720
Fitness Center-987-3283
Golf Course-987-6199
Library-987-6817
Outdoor Rec-987-3365
Wood Hobby Shop-987-6504

**ATTRACTIONS:** Little Rock, Governor's Mansion, State Capital, Old State House, River Market, Quapaw Quarter, Museum of Science and History, Little Rock Zoo, Children's Museum, Pinnacle and Petit Jean Mountains, Burns Park, War Memorial Stadium, Arkansas River, and Lake Conway.

# PINE BLUFF ARSENAL (AR03R2)

ATTN: SIOPB-CO
10020 Kambrich Circle
Pine Bluff Arsenal, AR 71602-9500

**TELEPHONE NUMBER INFORMATION:** Main installation numbers: C-870-540-3000, D-312-966-3000.

**LOCATION:** Southeast of Little Rock, take US-65 south to exit 32, then east to AR-256 to main gate. Off US-65 northwest of Pine Bluff. Take AR-256, cross AR-365 into main gate of arsenal. USMRA: Page 76 (E-6). NMC: Pine Bluff, eight miles southeast. NMI: Little Rock Air Force Base, 32 miles northwest.

**GENERAL INFORMATION:** Design, development, manufacture and disposal of chemical defenses, 52nd Explosive Detachment, Technical Escort Unit, Test Management and Diagnostic Equipment Support Center, USA Health Clinic and Pine Bluff Chemical Activity.

**TEMPORARY MILITARY LODGING:** Lodging office, Building 15-390, Sibert Road, 0730-1400 daily, C-870-540-3008, D-312-966-3008. DV/VIP facilities available.

**RV, CAMPING/FAMCAMP:** None. See Little Rock AFB listing.

**SPACE-A:** None. See Little Rock AFB listing.

**LOGISTICAL SUPPORT:**

Child Care-540-3612
Commissary-540-3474
Dining Facilities-540-3620
Exchange-535-1707

Child Dev Center-540-3612
Credit Union-535-2441
Education Office-540-3092
Travel Office-540-3611

**ADMINISTRATIVE SUPPORT:**

Fire Dept-540-3507
Legal-540-3131
Pass/ID Office-540-3491
Public Affairs-540-3421

Housing Office-540-3008
Locator-540-3000
Police-540-3505
SDO/NCO-540-3505

**HEALTH & WELFARE:**

Army Community Services-540-3217
CHAMPUS-540-3410

Army Emergency Relief-540-3031
Medical-540-3409
  Health Benefits-540-3814

**REST & RECREATION:**

Bowling-540-3779
Fitness Center-540-3779
MWR-540-3620

Community Club-540-3620
Golf Course-540-3028
Youth Center-540-3602

**ATTRACTIONS:** Hot Springs National Park, Ozarks Mountains, University of Arkansas at Pine Bluff and the Arkansas River.

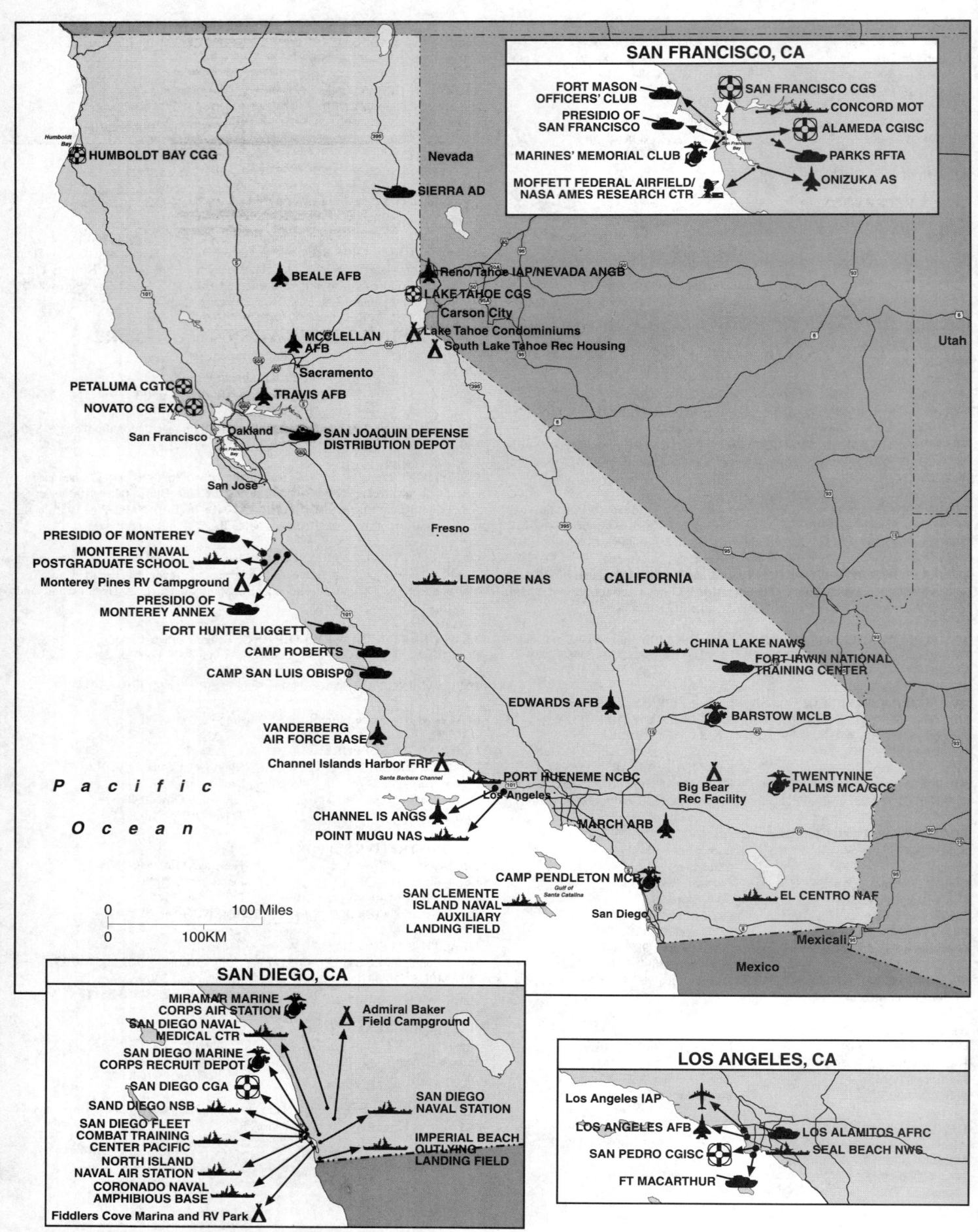

## SAN FRANCISCO, CA

FORT MASON OFFICERS' CLUB

PRESIDIO OF SAN FRANCISCO

MARINES' MEMORIAL CLUB

MOFFETT FEDERAL AIRFIELD/ NASA AMES RESEARCH CTR

SAN FRANCISCO CGS

CONCORD MOT

ALAMEDA CGISC

PARKS RFTA

ONIZUKA AS

HUMBOLDT BAY CGG

SIERRA AD

Nevada

Utah

BEALE AFB

Reno/Tahoe IAP/NEVADA ANGB

LAKE TAHOE CGS

Carson City

Lake Tahoe Condominiums

South Lake Tahoe Rec Housing

MCCLELLAN AFB

Sacramento

PETALUMA CGTC

NOVATO CG EXC

TRAVIS AFB

San Francisco

Oakland

SAN JOAQUIN DEFENSE DISTRIBUTION DEPOT

San Jose

PRESIDIO OF MONTEREY

MONTEREY NAVAL POSTGRADUATE SCHOOL

Monterey Pines RV Campground

PRESIDIO OF MONTEREY ANNEX

FORT HUNTER LIGGETT

CAMP ROBERTS

CAMP SAN LUIS OBISPO

Fresno

LEMOORE NAS

CALIFORNIA

CHINA LAKE NAWS

FORT IRWIN NATIONAL TRAINING CENTER

EDWARDS AFB

BARSTOW MCLB

VANDERBERG AIR FORCE BASE

Channel Islands Harbor FRF

Santa Barbara Channel

PORT HUENEME NCBC

Los Angeles

Big Bear Rec Facility

TWENTYNINE PALMS MCA/GCC

CHANNEL IS ANGS

POINT MUGU NAS

MARCH ARB

Pacific

Ocean

CAMP PENDLETON MCB

SAN CLEMENTE ISLAND NAVAL AUXILIARY LANDING FIELD

Gulf of Santa Catalina

San Diego

EL CENTRO NAF

Mexicali

Mexico

0        100 Miles

0      100KM

## SAN DIEGO, CA

MIRAMAR MARINE CORPS AIR STATION

SAN DIEGO NAVAL MEDICAL CTR

SAN DIEGO MARINE CORPS RECRUIT DEPOT

SAN DIEGO CGA

SAND DIEGO NSB

SAN DIEGO FLEET COMBAT TRAINING CENTER PACIFIC

NORTH ISLAND NAVAL AIR STATION

CORONADO NAVAL AMPHIBIOUS BASE

Fiddlers Cove Marina and RV Park

Admiral Baker Field Campground

SAN DIEGO NAVAL STATION

IMPERIAL BEACH OUTLYING LANDING FIELD

## LOS ANGELES, CA

Los Angeles IAP

LOS ANGELES AFB

SAN PEDRO CGISC

FT MACARTHUR

LOS ALAMITOS AFRC

SEAL BEACH NWS

# CALIFORNIA

## ADMIRAL BAKER FIELD CAMPGROUND
### (CA64R4)

San Diego Naval Station
San Diego, CA 92136-5000

**TELEPHONE NUMBER INFORMATION:** Main installation numbers: C-619-556-5525. Police for campground: C-619-556-5555.

**LOCATION:** Off Base. From north or south on I-15 approximately 0.75 miles north of intersection with I-8, exit east onto Friar's Road for approximately 0.5 miles to left (north) on Santo Road and an immediate right (northeast) onto Admiral Baker Road. USMRA: Page 118 (D-4). NMI: San Diego NS, 11 miles southwest. NMC: San Diego, 4 miles southwest.

**GENERAL INFORMATION:** Operated by San Diego Naval Station, off base, year round. Military personnel active, reservists, retired, DoD civilians. Reservations: Mission Gorge RV Park, c/o Navy Golf Course, Friar's Road and Santo Road, San Diego, CA 92120-5000. Call: C-619-556-5525. Fax: C-619-556-5501.

**RV, CAMPING/FAMCAMP:** Camper Spaces-39

**ATTRACTIONS:** San Diego sights include downtown Gaslamp District, Horton Plaza Shopping Center, San Diego Bay Area, Seaport Village, San Diego Zoo, Balboa Park, Sea World, and Wild Animal Park.

*For detailed information about this off-base recreation facility, as well as on-base recreation facilities, golf courses and marinas, consult Military Living's Military RV, Camping and Outdoor Recreation Around the World.*

## ALAMEDA COAST GUARD INTEGRATED SUPPORT COMMAND (CA28R4)

Coast Guard Island, Building 21
Alameda, CA 94501-5100

**TELEPHONE NUMBER INFORMATION:** Main installation numbers: C-510-437-2905.

**LOCATION:** From the north on I-880 exit at 16th Street/Embarcadero; left (south) on Embarcadero approximately 0.3 mile to right (west) on Dennison Street Follow signs to causeway and island. Signs posted. From the south on I-880 exit onto 29th Street north, Make left U-turn at first left cross overpass onto southbound 29th Street, then first right through the light, follow signs around to causeway and island. USMRA: Page 119 (D-5). NMC: Oakland, one mile northwest

**GENERAL INFORMATION:** Major Coast Guard Support Base in San Francisco area.

**TEMPORARY MILITARY LODGING:** Housing office, Building 21, McCullough Drive, 0730-1530 daily, C-510-437-3180; other hours OOD, Building 3, C-510-437-3304. Limited facilities. DV/VIP: C-510-437-3303. Duty personnel only. Also operates two condominiums at Lake Tahoe. See Lake Tahoe Condominiums listing for details.

**RV, CAMPING/FAMCAMP:** None.

**SPACE-A:** None. See Travis AFB.

**LOGISTICAL SUPPORT:**
| | |
|---|---|
| Carlson Wagonlit Travel-437-3686 | Child Care-437-2740 |
| Class Six-437-3165 | Conv Store-437-3165 |
| Dining Facilities-437-3303 | Exchange-437-3165 |
| Gas Station-437-3165 | Postal Service-437-3161 |
| Special Services-437-3577 | |

**ADMINISTRATIVE SUPPORT:**
| | |
|---|---|
| CDO-437-3151 | Housing Office-437-5936 |
| Legal-437-3330 | Locator-437-2904 |
| Police-437-3156 | Public Affairs-437-3325 |

**HEALTH & WELFARE:**
| | |
|---|---|
| Chapel-437-3067 | Dental-437-3582/3 |
| Medical | |
|    Central Appts-437-3582 | |
|    Clinic-437-3581 | |

**REST & RECREATION:**
| | |
|---|---|
| Auto Hobby Shop-437-3883 | Gym-437-3580 |
| Marina-437-3285 | MWR-437-3545 |

**OTHER FACILITIES AVAILABLE:** Balboa Travel, outdoor rec, racquetball, swimming, tennis, ticket Office.

**ATTRACTIONS:** San Francisco and the exciting San Francisco Bay Area nearby.

## BARSTOW MARINE CORPS LOGISTICS BASE
### (CA13R4)

Command Headquarters, Box 110100
Barstow Marine Corps Logistics Base, CA 92311-5001

**TELEPHONE NUMBER INFORMATION:** Main installation numbers: C-760-577-6211, D-312-282-6211.

**LOCATION:** On I-40, one and a half miles east of Barstow. Take I-15 northeast from San Bernardino, or west from Las Vegas, NV exit East Main Street east to I-40 east, exit to Josep L. Boll Avenue and Main Gate. Signs mark direction to MCLB. USMRA: Page 111 (G-12,13). NMC: San Bernardino, 75 miles southwest.

**GENERAL INFORMATION:** The Marine Corps Logistics Base serving the western part of the U.S.

**TEMPORARY MILITARY LODGING:** Lodging office, Building 171, 0700-1530 daily, C-760-577-6418, D-312-282-6418, Fax: C-760-577-6542. Other hours OD, Building 30, Room 8, ext 6611. All ranks. DV/VIP C-760-577-6555, D-312-282-6555. Oasis ext 6550 Active Duty, Retired Military and guests of the same.

**RV, CAMPING/FAMCAMP:** C-760-577-6418, D-312-282-6418.

**SPACE-A:** None. See Travis AFB listing.

**LOGISTICAL SUPPORT:**
| | |
|---|---|
| Bank-256-8713 | Barber Shop-577-6446 |
| Cafeteria-577-6428 | Child Care-577-6287 |
| Commissary-577-6403 | Conv Store-256-8974 |
| Exchange-256-8974 | Gas Station-256-9411 |
| Package Store-256-8974 | Postal Service-577-6254 |
| SATO-577-6258 | Snack Bar-577-6629 |

**ADMINISTRATIVE SUPPORT:**
| | |
|---|---|
| CDO/OOD-577-6611 | Fire Dept-577-6731 |
| Housing Office-577-6707 | Legal-577-6418 |
| Locator-577-6675 | OOD-577-6611 |
| Pass/ID Office-577-6457 | Police-577-6669 |
| Public Affairs-577-6430 | |

**HEALTH & WELFARE:**
| | |
|---|---|
| CHAMPUS-577-6593 | Chapel-577-5402/6846 |
| Dental-Clinic-577-6597 | Family Services-577-6533 |
| Medical | Navy-MC Relief-256-1378 |
|    Central Appts-577-6591 | Retiree Services-577-6755 |
|    Health Benefits Advisor-577-6583 | TRICARE-577-6593 |
|    Hospital-577-6593 | Veterinary Services-577-6929 |

**REST & RECREATION:**
| | |
|---|---|
| Auto Hobby Shop-577-6441 | Bowling-577-6264 |
| Ceramics-577-6228 | Clubs |
| Golf Course-577-6431 |    EM/NCO-577-6495 |
| Gym-577-6899 | ITT-577-6541 |
| Library-577-6395 | Rec Equipment-577-6898 |
| Wood/Rock Hobby-577-6441 | Youth Services-577-6499 |

**ATTRACTIONS:** Calico Ghost Town, Solar One, Lake Dolores.

# BEALE AIR FORCE BASE (CA47R4)
5900 C Street
Beale Air Force Base, CA 95903-1221

**TELEPHONE NUMBER INFORMATION:** Main installation numbers: C-530-634-3000, D-312-368-3000. E-mail: learyc@cs9.beale.af.mil. WEB: www.beale.af.mil

**LOCATION:** From CA-70 north or south, take Feather River Blvd. exit east (south of Marysville), follow to North Beale Road, take right (east), (follow signs to Beale), continue for 7 miles until road dead ends at main gate of AFB. USMRA: Page 110 (C,D-5,6). NMC: Sacramento, 35 miles southwest.

**GENERAL INFORMATION:** Air Combat Command Base, home of the 9th Reconnaissance Wing and high-altitude reconnaissance aircraft training, 7th Space Warning Squadron and AF Combat and Munitions Center (AFCOMAC) training school.

**TEMPORARY MILITARY LODGING:** Lodging office, 5786 A Street, 24 hours daily, C-530-634-2953, D-312-368-2953. Fax: C-530-634-2755, D-312-368-2755. All ranks. DV/VIP: C-530-788-0216.

**RV, CAMPING/FAMCAMP:** Beale FAMCAMP on base, year round, 9 SVS/SVRO, 17630 Doolittle Drive, 0900-2200 daily, C-530-634-3382, D-312-368-3382. Fax: C-530-634-2269, D-312-368-2269. Forty-three camper spaces with full hookups.

**SPACE-A:** Beale Terminal, C-530-634-2569/8386, D-312-368-2589/8386; Recording: C-530-634-8494, D-312-368-8494; Fax: C-530-634-2571, D-312-368-2571.

**LOGISTICAL SUPPORT:**

| | |
|---|---|
| Barber Shop-634-3437 | Beauty Shop-788-0053 |
| Cafeteria-788-2270 | Child Care-634-4717 |
| Child Dev Center-634-4717 | Class Six-788-0224 |
| Commissary-634-2421 | Conv Store-788-1915 |
| Credit Union-788-0265 | Dining Facilities-634-2537 |
| Dry Cleaner-788-0300 | Education Office-634-2525 |
| Exchange-634-2987 | Gas Station-788-0214 |
| Omega (official)-634-2940 | Postal Service-788-2401 |
| (leisure)-634-2264 | Shoppette-788-1271 |
| Snack Bar-788-1320/2517 | |

**ADMINISTRATIVE SUPPORT:**

| | |
|---|---|
| Fire Dept-634-8675 | Housing Office-634-2792 |
| Legal-634-2928 | Locator-634-2113 |
| Pass/ID Office-634-3154 | Police-634-2131 |
| Public Affairs-634-8890 | |

**HEALTH & WELFARE:**

| | |
|---|---|
| Air Force Aid Society-ext 4-2843 | American Red Cross-ext 4-2078 |
| Chapel-634-4701 | Dental |
| Family Services-634-2863 | Central Appts-ext 4-4781 |
| Medical | Clinic-ext 4-4782 |
| Central Appts-ext 4-2941 | Emergency-ext 4-4444 |
| Emergency-ext 4-4444 | Retiree Services-634-2157 |
| Health Benefits-788-1160 | TRICARE-1-800-242-6788 |
| Information-ext 4-4849 | Veterinary Services-ext 4-2104 |

**REST & RECREATION:**

| | |
|---|---|
| Arts & Crafts-ext 4-2294 | Auto Hobby Shop-ext 4-2296 |
| Bowling-ext 4-2299 | Clubs |
| Community Center-ext 4-2275 | Aero-ext 4-9011 |
| Fitness Center Annex-634-2260 | Consol-788-7266/0286 |
| Golf Course-634-2124 | Rod/Gun-788-2473 |
| Gym-ext 4-2259 | ITT-ext 4-3942 |
| Library-ext 4-2314 | MWR-634-3140 |
| Rec Center-ext 4-2264 | Rec Equip-ext 4-3340 |
| Services-ext 4-2273 | Swimming-contact clubs |
| Theater-634-2520 | Youth Center-ext 4-4953 |
| Youth Services-ext 4-3543 | |

**ATTRACTIONS:** WW II German POW site-National Historical Landmark. Within a two-hour drive: Lake Tahoe and Reno, Nevada, Sacramento, Sutter's Fort, Zoo, Grass Valley and Nevada City nearby. Napa Valley Wineries and San Francisco is less than three hours south.

# BIG BEAR RECREATION FACILITY (CA05R4)
Miramar Marine Corps Air Station
San Diego, CA 92145-2008

**TELEPHONE NUMBER INFORMATION:** Main installation numbers: C-858-577-4126/4141.

**LOCATION:** Off base. Located at Big Bear Lake. From I-10 at Redlands, take CA-30 north to CA-330. Go north on CA-330 to CA-18 at Running Springs. Take CA-18 east to Big Bear. At the Big Bear Dam, bear right. This is still CA-18 but also called Big Bear Blvd. Take Big Bear Blvd. to right on Moonridge Road to right on Elm Street to right on Switzerland Drive and then take an immediate left. Facility is approximately a 0.25 miles down the dirt road. *Note: Don't be tempted to take a shortcut through Snow Summit Ski Area as many people have been stuck in snow and mud on the forestry service road over which you must travel.* USMRA: Page 111 (G-13). NMI: March ARB, approximately 30 miles southwest. NMC: San Bernardino, 50 miles southwest.

**GENERAL INFORMATION:** Operated by MCAS Miramar, off base, cabins: Year round; RV campsites: May-October. Military personnel active, reservists, retired, DoD civilians. For cabin reservations (required): MWR Department, ITT-Big Bear, MCAS Miramar, P.O. Box 452008, San Diego, CA 92145-2008. C-858-577-4141/4126. For Recreation Facility general information and campsite reservations (required): Big Bear Recreation Facility, P.O. Box 1664, Big Bear Lake, CA 92315-1664. C-909-866-3965. Fax: C-909-866-4069.

**RV, CAMPING/FAMCAMP:**

| | |
|---|---|
| Cabins-8 | Camper/Tent Spaces-5 |

**ATTRACTIONS:** Centrally located 7,000 feet above sea level between Snow Summit and Bear Mountain ski resorts in the San Bernardino National Forest, area offers excellent fishing, boating, hiking and skiing.

*For detailed information about this off-base recreation facility, as well as on-base recreation facilities, golf courses and marinas, consult Military Living's Military RV, Camping and Outdoor Recreation Around the World.*

# CAMP PENDLETON MARINE CORPS BASE (CA30R4)
Box 555019
Camp Pendleton, CA 92055-5019

**TELEPHONE NUMBER INFORMATION:** Main installation numbers: C-760-725-4111, D-312-365-4111. WEB: www.cpp.usmc.mil

**LOCATION:** From north or south of Oceanside, take I-5 which is adjacent to Camp Pendleton along the Pacific Ocean. From I-5 north or south take the "Camp Pendleton Only" off ramp from I-5 at Oceanside to Vandegraft Blvd. USMRA: Page 111 (F-14,15). NMC: Oceanside, adjacent to base southeast.

**GENERAL INFORMATION:** The only Marine Corps Amphibious Training Base on the West Coast.

**TEMPORARY MILITARY LODGING:** Lodging office, Building 1310 (Mainside), 24 hours daily, C-760-725-5304, D-312-365-5304. All ranks. DV/VIP C-760-725-5194.

**RV, CAMPING/FAMCAMP:** Operates three camping facilities on base, year round: Lake O'Neill Recreation Park, C-760-725-4241, D-312-365-4241, five camper spaces with full hookups, 40 camper spaces with W/E hookups, 20 camper spaces with W only, 52 camper/tent spaces without hookups; Del Mar Beach Cottages, C-760-725-2134, 84 camper spaces with W/E hookups; 8 mobile homes; San Onofre Recreation Beach on base, year round, C-760-725-7935 (campsites), C-760-725-7629 (cottages), D-312-365-7935, 36 mobile homes/cottages, 80 camper spaces with W/E hookups, 26 camper spaces without hookups, 42 camper/tent spaces with W only.

**SPACE-A:** None. See March ARB listing.

**LOGISTICAL SUPPORT:**

| | |
|---|---|
| Barber Shop-725-5773 | Beauty Shop-725-5938 |
| Child Care-725-6112 | Child Dev Center-725-6112 |
| Commissary-725-4012 | Conv Store-725-3585 |
| Credit Union-725-4491 | Dry Cleaner-725-5581 |
| Education Office-725-6593 | Exchange-725-6233 |
| Gas Station-725-6815/6080 | Laundry-725-5581 |
| Package Store-725-3585 | Postal Service-725-5832 |
| SATO-725-4396 | |

**ADMINISTRATIVE SUPPORT:**

| | |
|---|---|
| CDO/OOD-725-5617 | Fire Department-725-3377 |
| Housing Office-725-6246 | Legal-725-6172 |
| Locator-725-5171 | Pass/ID Office-725-2768 |
| Police-725-3888 | Public Affairs-725-5011 |
| SDO/NCO-725-5617 | |

**HEALTH & WELFARE:**

| | |
|---|---|
| American Red Cross-725-6877 | CHAMPUS-725-1616 |
| Chapel-725-3518 | Dental-725-5992 |
| Family Services-725-5361 | Central Appts-725-5782 |
| Medical | N-MC Relief Society-725-5337 |
| Central Appts-725-1288 | Retiree Services-725-9052 |
| Clinic-725-1507 | Veterinary Services-725-3439 |
| Emergency-725-3258 | |
| Health Benefits-725-1616 | |
| Hospital-725-1437 | |

**REST & RECREATION:**

| | |
|---|---|
| Archery-ext 6288 | Arts & Crafts-725-4880 |
| Auto Hobby Shop-725-5963 | Bowling-725-6784 |
| Beach Info-ext 2463/7935 | Clubs |
| Community Center-725-9717 | EM-725-4894/7633/4896 |
| Equipment Rental-ext 5296 | Flying-ext 4910 |
| Fitness Center-723-5331 | O-725-6571/2828 |
| Golf Course-725-5331 | Gym-725-5205 |
| Indoor Rec-725-5945 | ITT-725-5864 |
| ITR-725-7447 | Library-725-5669 |
| Marinas-725-2802 | MWR-725-5355 |
| Outdoor Rec-725-6722 | Riding Stables-ext 5094 |
| Services-ext 6288 | Skeet/Trap-ext 4832 |
| Swimming Pool-ext 4344/5084 | Theater-725-7735 |
| Youth Center-725-5374 | Youth Services-725-6614 |

**ATTRACTIONS:** Sandy beaches, Old California Missions, Disneyland, Knott's Berry Farm, Magic Mountain, Sea World, Wild Animal Park, Lion Country Safari, San Diego Zoo, Balboa Park, Maritime Museum, Carlsbad Raceway, Palomar Observatory; race tracks at Hollywood Park, Del Mar, Santa Anita or Los Alamitos.

## CAMP ROBERTS (CA98R4)

California Army National Guard
Western Mobilization and Training Complex Installation
Headquarters, Building 109
Camp Roberts, CA 93451-5000

**TELEPHONE NUMBER INFORMATION:** Main installation numbers: C-805-238-3100, D-312-949-8210.

**LOCATION:** On U.S 101, halfway between Los Angeles and San Francisco, 13 miles north of Paso Robles. Use Bradley Blvd exit west. USMRA: Page 111 (C-10). NMC: Paso Robles, 13 miles south.

**GENERAL INFORMATION:** Army National Guard training site.

**TEMPORARY MILITARY LODGING:** Camp Roberts, Billeting Office, Building 6038, 0800-1630 Mon to Fri, C-805-238-8304, D-312-949-8304, Fax C-805-238-8384.

**RV, CAMPING/FAMCAMP:** Camp Roberts, on base year round, Billeting, Building 6038, Camp Roberts, CA 93451-5000, C-805-238-8312, D-312-949-8312, Fax C-805-238-8384. 12 camper spaces with full hookups.

**SPACE-A:** None. See Lemoore NAS listing.

**LOGISTICAL SUPPORT:**

| | |
|---|---|
| Consol Mess-238-8237 | Exchange-238-8195 |
| Postal Service-238-8209 | Snack Bar-238-8120 |

**ADMINISTRATIVE SUPPORT:**

| | |
|---|---|
| Fire Dept-238-8220 | Housing Office-238-8312 |
| Locator-238-8390 | Public Affairs-238-8203 |

**HEALTH & WELFARE:** Chapel-238-8185

**REST & RECREATION:** MWR-238-8203

**OTHER FACILITIES AVAILABLE:** Athletic field/track, fitness center, gym, recreation center, pizza pub, laundry.

**ATTRACTIONS:** A short drive to the Hearst Castle and the Pacific Ocean, hunting, fishing, military museum, California Missions nearby.

## CAMP SAN LUIS OBISPO (CA83R4)

California Army National Guard
Western Mobilization and Training Complex Installation
P.O. Box 4360, Highway 1, Headquarters Building 738
San Luis Obispo, CA 93403-4360

**TELEPHONE NUMBER INFORMATION:** Main installation numbers: C-805-594-6500/1, D-312-594-6500/1.

**LOCATION:** From US-101 north or south to San Luis Obispo, then northwest on CA-1 (Cabrillo Highway) for approximately 5 miles toward Morro Bay to Camp San Luis Obispo on southwest side of CA-1. USMRA: Page 111 (C-11). NMC: San Luis Obispo, 5 miles southeast.

**GENERAL INFORMATION:** Permanent tenant facilities include USPFO for California, National Interagency Counter Drug Institute, California Special Training Institute, California Conservation Corps, Federal Youth Program and 223rd Infantry Regiment.

**TEMPORARY MILITARY LODGING:** Lodging office, Building 738, 0800-1630 Mon-Fri, C-805-594-6500, D-312-630-9800.

**RV, CAMPING/FAMCAMP:** Camp San Luis Obispo RV Park, on post year round, Billeting Office, Camp San Luis Obispo, P.O. Box 4360, San Luis Obispo, CA 93403-4360, C-805-594-6500. Four camper spaces with full hookups, eight camper spaces with W/E hookups, primitive tent spaces with no hookups.

**SPACE-A:** None. Travis AFB listing.

**LOGISTICAL SUPPORT:** Exchange-549-3912

**ADMINISTRATIVE SUPPORT:**

| | |
|---|---|
| Locator-549-6500 | Public Affairs-594-6501 |

**HEALTH & WELFARE:** None. See Edwards AFB listing.

**REST & RECREATION:**

| | |
|---|---|
| MWR-594-6501 | O Club-541-6168 |

**ATTRACTIONS:** Twelve miles from Pacific Ocean and scenic central coast of California; thirty-five miles from Hearst Castle, midway between Los Angeles and San Francisco.

## CHANNEL ISLANDS AIR NATIONAL GUARD STATION (CA93R4)

Point Mugu, CA 93041-4001

**TELEPHONE NUMBER INFORMATION:** Main installation numbers: C-805-986-8000, D-312-893-7000.

**LOCATION:** From US-101 north or south to Camarillo, go south on S. Las Posas Road to East Port Hueneme Road past CA-1, then left (southeast) on Navalair Road.

ANG Station entrance is 200 yards on right (southwest) side of road. USMRA: Page 111 (D,E-13). NMC: Oxnard,3.5 miles northwest. NMI: Point Mugu NAS, adjacent.

**GENERAL INFORMATION:** Home of the 146th Airlift Wing.

**SPACE-A:** Information: C-805-986-7577, D-312-893-7577.

**ATTRACTIONS:** Beaches, Los Angeles, Disneyland within three hour drive.

## CHANNEL ISLANDS HARBOR FAMILY RECREATIONAL FACILITY (CA88R4)

11 Coast Guard District
4201 Victoria Avenue
Oxnard, CA 93035-4366

**TELEPHONE NUMBER INFORMATION:** Main installation numbers: C-805-982-4392/6123.

**LOCATION:** On Coast Guard base. Northwest of Los Angeles. From US-101 at Oxnard take Victoria Avenue exit south past Channel Islands Blvd. to Coast Guard Station on right (west side of street). USMRA: Page 111 (D-13). NMI: Port Hueneme Naval Construction Battalion Center, adjacent. NMC: Los Angeles, 50 miles southeast.

**GENERAL INFORMATION:** Operated by Port Hueneme NCBC, off base, year round. Military personnel active, reservist, retired. Reservations: RV Park, Naval Base Ventura County CBC, Code MW300, Bldg 1362, 1000 23rd Avenue, Port Hueneme, CA 93043-4301. C-805-982-4392/6123.

**RV, CAMPING/FAMCAMP:**     Camper Spaces-7

**ATTRACTIONS:** Located near the southern coast of California at Channel Islands Harbor, minutes away from water sports, charter boat fishing, shopping and bicycle touring and within easy driving distance of world-famous tourist attractions in the Los Angeles area.

*For detailed information about this recreation facility, as well as other recreation facilities, golf courses and marinas, consult Military Living's Military RV, Camping and Outdoor Recreation Around the World.*

## CHINA LAKE NAVAL AIR WEAPONS STATION (CA34R4)

1 Administration Circle, Building 00001
China Lake, CA 93555-6001

**TELEPHONE NUMBER INFORMATION:** Main installation numbers: C-760-939-2303, D-312-437-2303.

**LOCATION:** From north or south on US-395 or CA-14, go east on CA-178 to Ridgecrest to the main gate on Inyokern Road. USMRA: Page 111 (G-10,11,12; H-11) NMC: Los Angeles, 130 miles south.

**GENERAL INFORMATION:** A major Navy Research, Development, and Test Center for Naval Weapons Systems principally for air warfare. Located in the upper Mojave Desert.

**TEMPORARY MILITARY LODGING:** Lodging office, CD 823620D CBO, 24 hours daily, C-760-939-3146, D-312-437-3146, Fax: C-760-939-2789. All ranks. DV/VIP C-760-939-3039/2338, Fax: C-760-939-3152.

**RV, CAMPING/FAMCAMP:** None. See Edwards AFB listing.

**SPACE-A:** Armitage Air Field at Center for test flights. Very limited. C-760-939-2303, D-312-437-5308, Fax: C-616-446-7204.

**LOGISTICAL SUPPORT:**

| | |
|---|---|
| Barber Shop-446-8862 | Beauty Shop-446-8822 |
| Child Care-939-6683 | Child Dev Center-939-3171 |
| Class Six-446-2078 | Commissary-939-3138 |
| Credit Union-371-7130 | Education Office-939-3649 |
| Exchange-446-2586 | Gas Station-446-5044 |

| | |
|---|---|
| Postal Service-446-5251 | Shoppette-446-2078 |
| SATO-446-9047 | Snack Bar-446-2415 |
| Visitor Center-939-3105 | |

**ADMINISTRATIVE SUPPORT:**

| | |
|---|---|
| Fire Dept-939-2085 | Housing Office-939-4449 |
| Legal-939-2203 | Locator-939-9011 |
| Police-939-3323 | Public Affairs-939-3511 |
| Quarter Deck-939-2303 | SDO/NCO-939-2303 |

**HEALTH & WELFARE:**

| | |
|---|---|
| American Red Cross-678-5441 | CHAMPUS-939-8019 |
| Chapel-939-3506 | Dental-939-8040 |
| Family Services-939-4545 | Medical |
| N-MC Relief-939-2921 |    Central Appts-939-8000 |
| Retiree Services-678-5441 |    Clinic-939-8000 (duty) |
| |       939-2911 (after hours) |
| |    Health Benefits-939-8019 |

**REST & RECREATION:**

| | |
|---|---|
| Arts & Crafts-939-3252 | Auto Hobby Shop-939-2346 |
| Bowling-939-3471 | Ceramics-ext 3252 |
| Clubs | Fitness Center-939-2334 |
|   Com-939-8660 | Golf Course-939-2990 |
|   NCO-939-8661 | Gym-939-2334 |
|   O-939-3116 | ITT-939-8660 |
| Library-939-2595 | MWR-932-2010 |
| Swimming-ext 2334 | Wood Hobby Shop-939-3252 |
| Youth Services-939-2909 | |

**ATTRACTIONS:** Weapons Exhibit Facility for air-launched Navy & Marine Corps weaponry. Desert type attractions and recreation, isolated area.

## CONCORD MILITARY OCEAN TERMINAL (CA58R4)

10 Delta Street
Concord Military Ocean Terminal, CA 94520-5100

**TELEPHONE NUMBER INFORMATION:** Main installation numbers: C-510-246-2000.

**LOCATION:** From north or south on I-680 take exit in Concord to CA-4 east. Continue east on CA-4 approximately 2.7 miles to Port Chicago Highway exit north. Clearly marked. USMRA: Page 119 (F-2,3). NMC: San Francisco, 35 miles southwest.

**GENERAL INFORMATION:** Formerly a Naval Weapons Station, now a contingency installation operated by the Army. The MWR ticket office will remain open until September 2000.

**REST & RECREATION:** MWR-246-5341

**ATTRACTIONS:** San Francisco is 35 miles southwest.

## CORONADO NAVAL AMPHIBIOUS BASE (CA38R4)

Bldg 650
Box 357033
San Diego, CA 92135-7033

**TELEPHONE NUMBER INFORMATION:** Main installation numbers: C-619-545-8123, D-312-735-8123. WEB: www.nasni.navy.mil

**LOCATION:** From San Diego, take I-5 south to CA-75 across Coronado-San Diego Bay Bridge ($1 toll for non-carpool, free to motorcycles and carpools). Left (south) on Orange Avenue which becomes Silver Strand Blvd.) for 2.2 miles. Pass Hotel del Coronado and watch for signs to base. Left (northeast) turn at fourth light after hotel. USMRA: Page 118 (C,D-7,8). NMI: North Island Naval Air Station, three miles northwest. NMC: San Diego, five miles north.

**GENERAL INFORMATION:** West Coast Naval Amphibious Training Base, Naval Surface, Expeditionary Warfare Training Group Pacific, Special Warfare Group, and 27 Tenant Commands.

**TEMPORARY MILITARY LODGING:** Lodging office, Building 500, Tulagi Street, 24 hours daily, C-619-437-3494, D-312-577-3494. BOQ C-619-437-3473/5432, D-312-577-3473/5432; BEQ C-619-437-3494; Fax: C-619-577-3475. Navy Lodge: C-619-435-0191.

**RV, CAMPING/FAMCAMP:** Fiddlers Cove, one-and-a-half miles south of base, year round, C-619-435-8788, Fax: C-619-437-1389, 50 camper spaces with W/E hookups.

**SPACE-A:** None. See North Island NAS listing.

**LOGISTICAL SUPPORT:**

| | |
|---|---|
| Barber Shop-522-7404/18 | Child Care-437-2119 |
| Child Dev Center-437-2119 | Conv Store-522-7267 |
| Credit Union-1-800-220-1872 | Dining Facilities-437-3040 |
| -ext 431 | Dry Cleaner-522-7416 |
| Education Office-437-2651 | Exchange-522-7215 |
| Gas Station-522-7415 | Laundry-522-7416 |
| Postal Service-437-2470 | SATO-435-4414 |
| Shoppette-522-7414 | Snack Bar-437-2188 |
| Visitor Center-437-8788 | |

**ADMINISTRATIVE SUPPORT:**

| | |
|---|---|
| CDO-545-8123 | Fire Dept-437-2931 |
| Housing Office-556-8027 | Legal-437-2080 |
| Locator-437-2011 | Pass/ID Office-437-3021 |
| Police-437-3432 | Public Affairs-545-8167 |
| SDO/NCO/OOD-437-3432 | |

**HEALTH & WELFARE:**

| | |
|---|---|
| Chapel-437-2070 | Dental-437-2954 |
| Medical-437-3047 | Retiree Services-437-2780/2107 |
| Central Appts-437-2981 | TRICARE-437-2526 |
| Clinic-437-3048 | |
| Health Benefits-437-3048 | |

**REST & RECREATION:**

| | |
|---|---|
| Athletics-ext 2185/86 | Auto Hobby Shop-437-3834 |
| Bowling-437-3016 | Catering-437-2181 |
| Clubs | Fitness Center-437-3066 |
| All Hands-437-3171 | Gym-437-3066 |
| EM-437-3171 | Indoor Rec (Q-Zone)-437-5135 |
| Restaurant-437-3040 | ITT-437-3018 |
| Library-437-3026 | Marina-435-8788 |
| MWR-437-0993 | Outdoor Rec-437-3028 |
| Rec Center-437-5135 | Camping Gear |
| Theater-437-3027 | Youth Center-435-5056 |

**ATTRACTIONS:** Downtown Gaslamp District, Horton Plaza Shopping Center, San Diego Bay Area, Seaport Village, San Diego Zoo, Balboa Park, Sea World, and Wild Animal Park.

# EDWARDS AIR FORCE BASE (CA48R4)

1 South Rosamond Boulevard
Edwards Air Force Base, CA 93524-1225

**TELEPHONE NUMBER INFORMATION:** Main installation numbers: C-661-277-1110, D-312-527-1110. WEB: www.edwards.af.mil

**LOCATION:** From north or south on CA-14, to Rosamond (11 miles north of Lancaster). Exit east onto Rosamond Blvd., then east approximately 16 miles to Edwards AFB. Also, from east or west on CA-58, exit at Mojave south onto CA-14, then approximately 12 miles south to Rosamond, then east on Rosamond Avenue approximately 16 miles to air base. USMRA: Page 111 (F,G-12). NMC: Los Angeles, 90 miles southwest. NMI: China Lake Naval Air Weapons Station, 40 miles north.

**GENERAL INFORMATION:** Major Units: 412 Test Wing, Benefield Anechoic Chamber. Base Conducts a full range of flight and system testing. NASA Dryden Flight Research Facility located on base. Alternate landing field for the space

shuttle. Home of the world's premiere flight test facility. Air Force Materiel Command Base. Air Force Flight Test Center, and USAF Test Pilot School and Air Force Research Laboratory, Propulsion Directorate.

**TEMPORARY MILITARY LODGING:** Lodging office, Building 5602, 24 hours daily, C-661-277-3394, D-312-527-3394. All ranks. DV/VIP C-661-277-3326.

**RV, CAMPING/FAMCAMP:** FAMCAMP on base, year round, C-661-277-3394, D-312-527-3394, 26 camper spaces with full hookups, 10 without hookups.

**SPACE-A:** None. See Travis AFB listing.

**LOGISTICAL SUPPORT:**

| | |
|---|---|
| Barber Shop-277-2946 | Beauty Shop-258-5371 |
| Cafeteria-277-1040 | Car Rental-258-1586 |
| Child Care-258-2883 | Child Dev Center-258-2883 |
| Class Six-277-3768 | Commissary-277-2334 |
| Conv Store-258-8131 | Credit Union-258-4407 |
| Dining Facilities-277-3489 | Dry Cleaner-258-4606 |
| Education Office-277-2713 | Exchange-258-1078 |
| Gas Station-258-5037 | Laundry-258-4606 |
| Postal Service-277-4315 | Shoppette-258-8131 |
| Snack Bar-277-5054 | Travel Office-277-7777 |

**ADMINISTRATIVE SUPPORT:**

| | |
|---|---|
| Fire Dept-277-4540 | Housing Office-277-4506 |
| Legal-277-4310 | Locator-277-2777 |
| OOD-277-7964 | Pass/ID Office-277-7964 |
| Police-277-3340 | Public Affairs-277-3510 |
| SDO/NCO-277-3040 | |

**HEALTH & WELFARE:**

| | |
|---|---|
| Air Force Aid Society-277-0723 | CHAMPUS-277-2662 |
| Chapel-277-6976 | Dental-277-2872 |
| Family Services-277-2246 | Retiree Services-277-4931 |
| Medical | TRICARE-277-7118 |
| Central Appts-277-7118 | Veterinary Services-277-3205 |
| Emergency-277-2331 | |
| Health Benefits-277-8480 | |
| Hospital-277-4386 | |
| Information-277-6955 | |

**REST & RECREATION:**

| | |
|---|---|
| Arts & Crafts-277-4275 | Auto Hobby Shop-277-4275 |
| Bowling-277-2590 | Ceramics-277-4171 |
| Clubs | Community Center-277-7488 |
| Aero-275-8321 | Fitness Center-277-3077 |
| Com-277-2830 | Golf Course-277-3469 |
| EM-277-0810 | Gym-277-3077 |
| Rod/Gun-277-3182 | Horse Stables-277-2898 |
| Indoor Rec-277-3546 | Library-277-2375 |
| Outdoor Rec-277-2895 | Services-277-4240 |
| Theater-277-4178 | Wood Hobby Shop-277-3139 |
| Youth Services-277-3004 | |

**ATTRACTIONS:** Mojave Desert area. Adjacent to mountain and winter sports areas; two hours from beaches; historic mining and ghost towns nearby, 150 miles from Disneyland, 70 miles from Magic Mountain.

# EL CENTRO NAVAL AIR FACILITY (CA09R4)

Naval Air Facility Command
El Centro, CA 92243-5001

**TELEPHONE NUMBER INFORMATION:** Main installation numbers: C-760-339-2524, D-312-958-2524.

**LOCATION:** From east or west on I-8, two miles west of El Centro, to Forrester Road (S-30) exit, north one and a half miles to Evan Hewes Highway (S-80) left (west) for four miles, right on Bennet Road to main gate. USMRA: Page 111 (H-15,16). NMC: El Centro, seven miles east.

**GENERAL INFORMATION:** Winter training camp of the Blue Angels. Air Show third weekend every March. Operates bombing and gunnery ranges in support of fleet operations. Ideal flying conditions.

**TEMPORARY MILITARY LODGING:** Lodging office, Building 270, B & 2nd Streets, 24 hours daily, DV/VIP Officers, C-760-339-8535, Fax: C-760-353-1492. Navy Lodge: C-760-339-2341, D-312-958-8341.

**RV, CAMPING/FAMCAMP:** Campground on base, year round, C-760-339-2486, D-312-958-8486, 59 camper spaces with full hookups.

**SPACE-A:** Pax Term, Building 519, 0700-2300 Mon-Sat, C-760-339-2426, D-312-958-8426, limited Space-A flights to CONUS and OCONUS locations.

**LOGISTICAL SUPPORT:**

| | |
|---|---|
| Barber Shop-339-2597 | Child Care-339-2327 |
| Commissary-339-2558/337-5253 | Conv Store-339-2670 |
| Exchange-339-2341 | Gas Station-339-2339 |
| Package Store-339-2339 | |

**ADMINISTRATIVE SUPPORT:**

| | |
|---|---|
| Fire Dept-339-2232 | Housing Office-337-4920 |
| Legal-339-2594 | Pass/ID Office-339-2681 |
| Police-339-2585 | Public Affairs-339-2519 |
| SDO/NCO-339-2699 | |

**HEALTH & WELFARE:**

| | |
|---|---|
| CHAMPUS-339-2674 | Chapel-339-2520 |
| Medical-339-2674 | Navy-MC Relief-339-2454 |

**REST & RECREATION:**

| | |
|---|---|
| Auto Hobby Shop-339-2689 | Bowling-339-2575 |
| Consol-339-2330 | Fitness Center-339-2489 |
| ITT-339-2575 | MWR-339-2481 |
| Theater-339-2440 | Youth Center-339-2644 |

**ATTRACTIONS:** Winter (January-March) home of the Navy Blue Angels. Imperial Valley, near Mexico.

## FIDDLER'S COVE MARINA & RV PARK (CA87R4)

NASNI MWR Dept Code 92, Bldg 650
Box 357081
San Diego, CA 92155-7081

**TELEPHONE NUMBER INFORMATION:** Main installation numbers: C-619-435-4770, D-312-735-4770. Police for RV park, C-619-545-7423.

**LOCATION:** Off base. From north or south on I-5 in San Diego, take San Diego-Coronado Bay Bridge (CA-75) exit; cross bridge and go south (left) on Orange Avenue which becomes Silver Strand. Continue south on CA-75 past Amphibious Base gate for approximately1.5 miles . RV Park is next to Naval Amphibious Base Marina (Navy Yacht Club) and Aquatic Sports Center. USMRA: Page 118 (D-8). NMI: Coronado Naval Amphibious Base, 1.5 miles north. NMC: San Diego, 6.5 miles northeast.

**GENERAL INFORMATION:** Operated by North Island Naval Air Station, off base, year round. Military personnel active, reservists, retired, DoD civilians. Reservations (accepted up to 90 days in advance): Fiddler's Cove RV Park, c/o NASNI MWR, Dept Code 92, Box 357081, San Diego, CA 92135-7081. C-619-435-8788/4700, 1000-1830 hours Mon-Fri, 0830-1830 hours Sat-Sun. Fax: C-619-437-1389.

**RV, CAMPING/FAMCAMP:** Camper Spaces-50

**ATTRACTIONS:** Within half a mile of the Pacific Ocean and state beach. Popular activities include tours of historic sites, shopping in Tijuana, and attractions in San Diego.

*For detailed information about this off-base recreation facility, as well as on-base recreation facilities, golf courses and marinas, consult Military Living's Military RV, Camping and Outdoor Recreation Around the World.*

## FORT HUNTER LIGGETT (CA37R4)

US Army Garrison, Building 205
ATTN: AFRC-FMH-PAD, P.O. Box 7000
Fort Hunter Liggett, CA 93928-7000

**TELEPHONE NUMBER INFORMATION:** Main installation numbers: C-831-386-3000, D-312-686-2291.

**LOCATION:** From US-101 north or south, exit approximately one mile southwest of King City onto G-14 (Jolon Road), then south approximately 19 miles to main gate. USMRA: Page 111 (C-10). NMC: King City, approximately 20 miles north.

**GENERAL INFORMATION:** Sub-Installation of Fort McCoy. Western training center for the Army Reserve Command.

**TEMPORARY MILITARY LODGING:** Lodging office, Building 229, 0800-1630 daily, C-831-386-2511, D-312-686-2511. All ranks. DV/VIP C-831-386-2025.

**RV, CAMPING/FAMCAMP:** Fort Hunter Liggett Primitive Campground, on post year round C-831-386-3310, 20 graded camper/tent spaces with central W.

**SPACE-A:** None. See Lemoore NAS listing.

**LOGISTICAL SUPPORT:**

| | |
|---|---|
| Commissary-386-2190 | Exchange-385-4585 |
| Gas Station-386-6032 | Snack Bar-386-2645 |
| Theater-386-2645 | |

**ADMINISTRATIVE SUPPORT:**

| | |
|---|---|
| Fire Dept-386-2527 | Police-386-2613 |
| Public Affairs-386-2605 | |

**HEALTH & WELFARE:**

| | |
|---|---|
| ACS-386-2605 | Chapel-386-4363 |

**REST & RECREATION:**

| | |
|---|---|
| Com Club-386-2588 | ITT-386-2406 |
| MWR-386-2762 | Rec Center-ext 2406 |

**OTHER FACILITIES AVAILABLE:** Bowling, craft shops, gym, hunting and fishing, library.

**ATTRACTIONS:** Old California, hacienda formerly owned by the Hearst family, San Antonio Mission, prime hunting and fishing area.

## FORT IRWIN NATIONAL TRAINING CENTER (CA01R4)

ATTN: AFZJ-GC
Innerloop Road, Building 983
Fort Irwin National Training Center, CA 92310-5000

**TELEPHONE NUMBER INFORMATION:** Main installation numbers: C-760-380-4111, D-312-470-4111.

**LOCATION:** From east or west on I-15, exit onto CA-58 at Barstow (approximately 2.5 miles northeast of junction with I-40). Go west on CA-58 approximately 2.6 miles to intersection with Irwin Road. Go north on Irwin Road, which becomes Fort Irwin Road, approximately 36 miles to fort. Watch for signs. USMRA: Page 111 (G,H-11,12). NMC: San Bernardino, 70 miles southwest.

**GENERAL INFORMATION:** The U.S. Army National Training Center, Home of the 11th Armored Cavalry Regiment, NTC Support Battalion & Operations Group.

**TEMPORARY MILITARY LODGING:** Lodging office, Building 109, 1st Avenue 0800-1630 daily, C-760-380-4599, D-312-470-4599. All ranks. DV/VIP C-760-380-3000. Very limited.

**RV, CAMPING/FAMCAMP:** None. See Edwards AFB listing.

**SPACE-A:** None. See China Lake NAWS listing.

**LOGISTICAL SUPPORT:**

| | |
|---|---|
| Child Care-380-1029 | Commissary-380-3422 |
| Conv Store-380-2417 | Exchange-386-2060 |
| Gas Station-386-2417 | Package Store-386-2417 |
| Travel Office-380-3652 (official) | |

**ADMINISTRATIVE SUPPORT:**

| | |
|---|---|
| Legal-380-6359 | Locator-380-3369 |
| IG-380-3038 | Police-380-4444/3474 |
| SDO/NCO-380-3750 | |

**HEALTH & WELFARE:**

| | |
|---|---|
| Chapel-380-3562 | Dental-380-3166 |
| Family Services-380-3513 | Medical |
| Veterinary Clinic-380-3025 | Central Appts-380-3124 |
| | Emergency-380-3777 |

**REST & RECREATION:**

| | |
|---|---|
| Arts & Crafts-ext 3431 | Auto Hobby Shop-ext 3531 |
| Batting Cages-ext 4653 | Bowling-ext 4249 |
| Clubs | Golf Course-ext 4653 |
| Outer Limits (all ranks)-380-8646 | Gym-ext 3810 |
| Leaders/Reggie's (all ranks)-380-3293 | ITT-380-4767 |
| Library-ext 3462 | Mini-Golf Course-ext 4653 |
| Morale Support Hq-ext 3582 | Rec Center-ext 3585 |
| Rec Equip-ext 3434 | Riding Stables-ext 4796 |
| Swimming-ext 4951/ 3046 | Teen Center-ext 5685 |
| Theater-380-3490 | Youth Activities-ext 4163 |

**ATTRACTIONS:** Goldstone Deep Space Station. Painted Rock, Opposing Force Display Yard, Rainbow Basin, Calico Ghost Town, and NTC/11th ACR Museum.

## FORT MacARTHUR (CA46R4)

2400 South Pacific Avenue, Building 37
San Pedro, CA 90731-2960

**TELEPHONE NUMBER INFORMATION:** Main installation numbers: C-310-363-8296, D-312-833-8296. WEB: www.laafb.af.mil
*Ten digit dialing required for local calls.*

**LOCATION:** From I-110 (Harbor Freeway) go south toward San Pedro. Keep left to Gaffney Street, continue south approximately 1.5 miles to 19th Street, then left (east) to Pacific Avenue and right (south) approximately 0.25 miles to main gate on left (east) side of street. USMRA: Page 117 (C-7). NMI: Los Angeles AFB, 18 miles north. NMC: Los Angeles, in city limits.

**GENERAL INFORMATION:** Military family housing annex, located 18 miles from Los Angeles AFB.

**TEMPORARY MILITARY LODGING:** Billeting Manager, Building 37, Patton Quadrangle, 24 hours daily, C-310-363-8296. DV/VIP C-310-363-3751.

**RV, CAMPING/FAMCAMP:** None. See Los Angeles AFB listing.

**SPACE-A:** None. See Los Angeles AFB listing.

**LOGISTICAL SUPPORT:**      Exchange-832-9611

**ADMINISTRATIVE SUPPORT:**      Police-363-8385

**HEALTH & WELFARE:**      Medical-363-8301

**REST & RECREATION:** None. See Los Angeles AFB listing.

**ATTRACTIONS:** Hollywood and beaches within easy driving distance, major league sports attractions; Los Angeles Dodgers, Los Angeles Lakers, Los Angeles Clippers, and the Los Angeles Kings.

Visit Military Living online at
www.militaryliving.com

## FORT MASON OFFICERS' CLUB (CA45R4)

Bldg 1, Bay and Franklin Streets
San Francisco, CA 94123-5000

**TELEPHONE NUMBER INFORMATION:** Main installation numbers: C-415-441-7700.

**LOCATION:** Entrance on Bay and Franklin Streets, three blocks north of US-101 (Lombard Street). USMRA: Page 119 (C-5). NMC: San Francisco, in the city.

**GENERAL INFORMATION:** Older Victorian structure, remodeled 1990. Officers all ranks, active duty, reservist, retirees or GS-7 DoD employees. Reservations (up to six months in advance): Bldg #1, Bay and Franklin Streets, San Francisco, CA 94123-5000. C-415-441-7700, Fax: C-415-441-2680, 0900-1700 hours Tue.-Sat.

**TEMPORARY MILITARY LODGING:** Guest Quarters-5

**ATTRACTIONS:** Fort Mason is a National Park, offering a magnificent view of Alcatraz Island and San Francisco Bay. Close to North Beach, Fisherman's Wharf and Chinatown. Convenient location, good public transportation.

*For detailed information about this off-base lodging facility, as well as other on- and off-base facilities, consult Military Living's Temporary Military Lodging Around the World.*

## HUMBOLDT BAY COAST GUARD GROUP (CA02R4)

1001 Lycoming Way
McKinleyville, CA 95519-5000

**TELEPHONE NUMBER INFORMATION:** Main installation numbers: C-707-839-6123.

**LOCATION:** From Eureka, take US-101 north approximately 14 miles to Airport Road exit east. Go east on Airport Road to first left onto Coast Guard Road, then left at "T." Follow road to gate. USMRA: Page 110 (A-2,3). NMC: Eureka, 15 miles south.

**GENERAL INFORMATION:** Small Group/Air Station, three helicopters, 150 people. Small Boat Station in Eureka with TML-1 unit; call for reservations and priority.

**TEMPORARY MILITARY LODGING:** None. Nearest facility is more than 100 miles away.

**RV, CAMPING/FAMCAMP:** None. Nearest facility is more than 100 miles away.

**SPACE-A:** None. Nearest facility is more than 100 miles away.

**LOGISTICAL SUPPORT:**      Exchange-443-7796

**ADMINISTRATIVE SUPPORT:**      Public Affairs-839-6114/6113

**HEALTH & WELFARE:**      Medical Clinic-839-6176

**REST & RECREATION:** None. Nearest facility is more than 100 miles away.

**ATTRACTIONS:** Northern California beaches, scenery, redwood forests.

## IMPERIAL BEACH OUTLYING LANDING FIELD (CA04R4)

1498 13th Street
Imperial Beach, CA 91932-5000

**TELEPHONE NUMBER INFORMATION:** Main installation numbers: C-619-437-2011, D-312-577-2011.

**LOCATION:** From San Diego, take I-5 south to Palm Avenue exit. Go west on Palm Avenue approximately 0.9 mile, then left (south) on 13th Street to base. Watch for signs. USMRA: Page 118 (D,E-10). NMC: San Diego, 9 miles north.

**TEMPORARY MILITARY LODGING:** None. See Coronado NAB listing.

**RV, CAMPING/FAMCAMP:** None. See Coronado NAB listing, Fiddlers Cove RV Park.

**SPACE-A:** None. See North Island listing.

**LOGISTICAL SUPPORT:**
Commissary-437-9481/2          Exchange-424-2900
Service Station-424-2938/8

**ADMINISTRATIVE SUPPORT:**
Locator-437-2011          Police-524-2001
Public Affairs-437-8167

**HEALTH & WELFARE:** None. See Coronado NAB listing.

**REST & RECREATION:** None. See Coronado NAB listing.

**ATTRACTIONS:** San Diego Bay area, San Diego Zoo, Mexico approximately two miles south.

# LAKE TAHOE COAST GUARD STATION (CA24R4)

P.O. Box 882, 2500 Lake Forest Road
Tahoe City, CA 96145-0882

**TELEPHONE NUMBER INFORMATION:** Main installation numbers: C-530-583-7438. E-mail: admin/statahoe@internet.uscg.mil

**LOCATION:** From I-80 east or west to Truckee; exit onto CA-89 south (approximately 1.5 miles west of Truckee). Go 12 miles south to Tahoe City. At intersection with CA-28 (to Kings Beach), continue straight through stoplight onto CA-28 northeast approximately 1.5 miles. Turn right (southeast) on Lake Forest Road and right (south) at entrance. USMRA: Page 110 (E-6). NMI: McClellan AFB, CA, 80 miles southwest. NMC: Reno, NV, 45 miles northeast.

**GENERAL INFORMATION:** Located at Lake Tahoe, this is an operational Search and Rescue and Law Enforcement Unit. Open year round. Military personnel active, reservists, retired, CG NAF and other federal civilians. Reservations (required): A-Frame Coordinator, Coast Guard Station Lake Tahoe, 2500 Lake Forest Road, P.O. Box 882, Tahoe City, CA 96145-0882. Or call C-530-583-7438, leave message.

**RV, CAMPING/FAMCAMP:**          A-Frame Cottages-4

**ATTRACTIONS:** Much to do and see in nearby cities of Reno and Carson City. Many recreational activities available on Lake Tahoe and surrounding Sierra Nevada mountains.

*For detailed information about this recreation facility, as well as other recreation facilities, golf courses and marinas, consult Military Living's Military RV, Camping and Outdoor Recreation Around the World.*

# LAKE TAHOE CONDOMINIUMS (CA49R4)

MWR, Bldg 16, Coast Guard Island
Alameda Coast Guard Integrated Support Command
Alameda, CA 94501-5100

**TELEPHONE NUMBER INFORMATION:** Main installation numbers: C-510-437-3573.

**LOCATION:** Off base. Two condos, located at Lake Tahoe. To Lake Forest Glen (North Shore Condo): Take I-80 to Hwy 89 (to Tahoe City). Hwy 89 becomes Hwy 28 (North Lake Blvd). Go through Tahoe City, turn right on Lake Forest Road. Turn left on Bristlecone. To Tahoe Keys (South Shore Condo): Take I-80 to Hwy 50 toward Placerville to South Shore Lake Tahoe. Follow Hwy 50 toward Nevada state line. Turn left on Tahoe Keys Blvd. USMRA: Page 110 (E-6). NMI: McClellan AFB, Sacramento CA, 110 miles southwest. NMC: Carson City NV, 30 miles southeast.

**GENERAL INFORMATION:** Operated by Alameda Coast Guard Integrated Support Command, off base, year round. Military personnel active, reservists,

retired. Reservations may be made up to six months in advance: MWR, Bldg 16, Coast Guard Island, Alameda, CA 94501-5100. Or call C-510-437-3573. These two condos provide every amenity except linens.

**RV, CAMPING/FAMCAMP:**
Lake Forest Glen (North Shore Condo)-sleeps 10
Tahoe Keys (South Shore Condo)-sleeps 8

**ATTRACTIONS:** Lake Tahoe offers a wide range of mountain and water-oriented recreational activities. Casinos are located within a few miles.

*For detailed information about this off-base recreation facility, as well as on-base recreation facilities, golf courses and marinas, consult Military Living's Military RV, Camping and Outdoor Recreation Around the World.*

# LEMOORE NAVAL AIR STATION (CA06R4)

700 Avenger Avenue
Lemoore Naval Air Station, CA 93246-5001

**TELEPHONE NUMBER INFORMATION:** Main installation numbers: C-559-998-0100, D-312-949-0100. WEB: www.lemoore.navy.mil

**LOCATION:** In south central part of state. From north or south on I-5, exit onto CA-198 east for approximately 24 miles to main gate on north (left) side of highway. Or, from north or south on CA-99, exit onto CA-198 west for approximately 27 miles to main gate on right (north) side of CA-198. USMRA: Page 111 (D-10). NMC: Fresno, 40 miles north.

**GENERAL INFORMATION:** Navy's newest and largest master jet air station.

**TEMPORARY MILITARY LODGING:** Lodging office, Building 852, Hancock Circle, 24 hours daily, C-559-998-4784, D-312-949-4784. All ranks. BOQ, C-559-998-4609, D-312-949-4609. DV/VIP - E7-E9, C-559-998-3344. Fax: C-559-998-4587. Navy Lodge: C-559-998-5791, 1-800-NAVY INN.

**RV, CAMPING/FAMCAMP:** Twelve spaces–four long-term, eight day-to-day. Call C-559-998-4895/7.

**SPACE-A:** Pax Term/Lounge, Building 180, 24 hours daily, C-559-998-1680/1/3, D-312-949-1680/1/3, Fax: C-559-998-3046, D-312-949-3046. Flights to CONUS Naval Air Stations and other locations.

**LOGISTICAL SUPPORT:**
Barber Shop-998-4644          Beauty Shop-998-4644
Child Care-998-4919          Child Dev Center-998-4919
Commissary-998-4669          Conv Store-998-4939
Credit Union-998-4578          Dining Facilities-998-4812
Dry Cleaner-998-4703          Education Office-998-3857
Exchange-998-4722          Gas Station-998-4729
Postal Service-998-1850          PSO Travel-998-3993
Snack Bar-997-8960

**ADMINISTRATIVE SUPPORT:**
CDO-998-3301          Fire Dept-998-4507
Housing Office-998-2000          Legal-998-3873
OOD/Locator-998-3300          Pass/ID Office-998-3386
Police-998-4749          Public Affairs-998-3394
Quarter Deck-998-3300

**HEALTH & WELFARE:**
American Red Cross-998-3383          CHAMPUS-998-4490
Chapel-998-4618          Dental
Family Services-998-4042              Central Appts-998-4219
Medical-998-4481              Clinic-998-4300
    Central Appts-998-4448          Emergency-998-4220
    Emergency-998-4435          Navy-MC Relief-998-4045
    Health Benefits-998-4490          Veterinary Services-998-5195
    Hospital-998-4481
    Information-998-4481

**REST & RECREATION:**
Arts & Crafts-997-8904          Auto Hobby Shop-998-4908
Bowling-998-4647          Clubs
Electronics Hobby-ext 4904              Combined-997-8963

| | |
|---|---|
| Fitness Center-998-4141 | CPO-998-4858 |
| Gym-998-4141 | EM(Tailgates)-998-4877 |
| ITT-997-8905 | Flying-ext 3526 |
| Library-998-4633 | O-998-4857 |
| MWR-998-4886 | Outdoor Rec-998-4897 |
| Rec Center-ext 4804 | Services-998-4898 |
| Theater-998-4643 | Youth Center-998-4936 |

**ATTRACTIONS:** Sequoia National Park. Ski areas within a 200 mile radius.

# LOS ALAMITOS ARMED FORCES RESERVE CENTER (CA39R4)

Building 15, Post Headquarters
Los Alamitos, CA 90720-5001

**TELEPHONE NUMBER INFORMATION:** Main installation numbers: C-562-795-2000, D-312-972-2011.

**LOCATION:** From I-405 (San Diego Freeway) north or south, take exit to I-605 (San Gabriel River Freeway) north approximately 1.5 miles to exit east onto East Katella Avenue, then east 1.7 miles to right (south) on Lexington Drive and proceed to main gate. Clearly marked. USMRA: Page 117 (E-6,7). NMC: Los Angeles, 15 miles northwest.

**GENERAL INFORMATION:** Armed Forces Reserve Center (AFRC), supporting all active military and reservists from all branches of the Armed Forces, including retired military, DoD personnel, certain state active duty and civil service personnel and quasi-military personnel.

**TEMPORARY MILITARY LODGING:** Transient Quarters, Building 19, Hq AFRC, 0800-1630 hours, C-562-795-2124, D-312-972-2124; Fax: C-562-795-2125.

**RV, CAMPING/FAMCAMP:** None. See Los Angeles AFB listing.

**SPACE-A:** C-562-795-2571, D-312-972-2571, Fax: C-562-795-2566.

**LOGISTICAL SUPPORT:**

| | |
|---|---|
| Beauty Shop-430-3698 | Carlson Wagonlit Travel-430-4936 |
| Clothing Sales-795-2059 | Dry Cleaners-594-5503 |
| Exchange-430-1076 | Package Store-795-1076 |

**ADMINISTRATIVE SUPPORT:**

| | |
|---|---|
| Fire Dept-795-2144 | Police-795-2100 |
| SDO/NCO-795-2090 | |

**HEALTH & WELFARE:** None. See Los Angeles AFB listing.

**REST & RECREATION:** Golf Course-430-9913

**ATTRACTIONS:** Los Angeles, Hollywood and Orange County.

# LOS ANGELES AIR FORCE BASE (CA75R4)

2430 East El Segundo Boulevard, Suite 4049
Los Angeles Air Force Base, CA 90045-4687

**TELEPHONE NUMBER INFORMATION:** Main installation numbers: C-310-363-1110, D-312-833-1110.
*Ten digit dialing required for local calls.*

**LOCATION:** From I-405 (San Diego Freeway) north or south, take El Segundo Blvd exit and go west for 0.25 miles. Base is on both sides of street. USMRA: Page 117 (B-5). NMC: Los Angeles, 10 miles northeast.

**GENERAL INFORMATION:** Space and Missile Systems Center, manages research, development and acquisition of DoD space systems; 61st Air Base Group.

**TEMPORARY MILITARY LODGING:** Limited. Fort MacArthur Inn. C-310-363-8296, D-312-833-8296.

**RV, CAMPING/FAMCAMP:** FAMCAMP on base, year round, C-310-363-2081, D-312-833-2081, 15 camper spaces with W/E hookups.

**SPACE-A:** Available at Los Angeles IAP, 0730-2030 daily, C-310-363-0714, D-312-833-0714, Fax: C-310-216-2670. Limited number of flights to CONUS and foreign locations via Air Force contract commercial aircraft.

**LOGISTICAL SUPPORT:**

| | |
|---|---|
| Child Care-363-1792 | Commissary-833-6148 |
| Exchange-640-0129 | Gas Station-615-0295 |
| Package Store-322-7533 | SATO-363-1130 |

**ADMINISTRATIVE SUPPORT:**

| | |
|---|---|
| Legal-363-2483 | Locator-363-1876 |
| Police-363-2123 | Public Affairs-363-0030 |

**HEALTH & WELFARE:**

| | |
|---|---|
| Chapel-514-3558 | Family Services-363-1121 |
| Medical-363-5029 | Retiree Services-363-5120 |
| Clinic-363-0263 | |

**REST & RECREATION:**

| | |
|---|---|
| Auto Skills Center-363-1705 | Consol Club-363-2230 |
| Equipment Rental-363-2081 | Fitness Center-363-2269 |
| Swimming Pool-363-8260 | Tickets & Tours-363-2190 |

**ATTRACTIONS:** Disneyland, Universal Studios and City Walk, Magic Mountain, and Chinatown. Numerous attractions are available within the Los Angeles, Hollywood, and Orange County area.

# LOS ANGELES INTERNATIONAL AIRPORT (CA61R4)

200 World Way, Box 2
Los Angeles, CA 90045-5810

**TELEPHONE NUMBER INFORMATION:** Main installation numbers: C-310-363-1110, D-312-833-1110.
*Ten digit dialing required for local calls.*

**LOCATION:** From north or south on I-405 take Century Boulevard exit west, then drive 1.5 miles west to Terminal 2. Or, from I-105 east or west, take Sepulveda Blvd. exit north, the continue north one mile to Century Blvd. and turn left (west) to airport. Clearly marked. USMRA: Page 117 (B-5). NMC: Los Angeles, in the city. NMI: Los Angeles Air Force Base, 3 miles south.

**GENERAL INFORMATION:** Provides facilities of an international airport.

**TEMPORARY MILITARY LODGING:** None. See Los Angeles AFB listing.

**SPACE-A:** From 0730-2030 daily, C-310-363-0714, D-312-833-0714, Fax: C-310-216-2670.

**LOGISTICAL SUPPORT:**

| | |
|---|---|
| Barber Shop-640-0379 | Cafeteria-363-0715 |
| Car Rental-646-4861/645-1880 | Dry Cleaner-322-1333 |
| Exchange-640-0129 | |

**ADMINISTRATIVE SUPPORT:** Police-363-2122/3

**HEALTH & WELFARE:** See Los Angeles AFB listing.

**ATTRACTIONS:** Disneyland, Universal Studios and City Walk, Magic Mountain, and Chinatown. Numerous attractions are available within the Los Angeles, Hollywood, and Orange County area.

# MARCH AIR RESERVE BASE (CA08R4)

452 AMW/PA
2145 Graeber Street, Suite 211
March Air Reserve Base, CA 92518-1671

**TELEPHONE NUMBER INFORMATION:** C-909-655-1110, D-312-947-1110.
E-mail: pa452@tecnet2.jcte.jcs
WEB: www.airforce-reserve.org/marchfield

**LOCATION:** From north or south on I-215/CA-215 use March AFRB exit east onto Cactus Avenue. Continue east approximately 1.5 miles to traffic light at main gate on right (south) side of road. USMRA: Page 111 (G-14). NMC: Riverside, nine miles northwest.

**GENERAL INFORMATION:** Air Force Reserve Base, 452nd Air Mobility Wing (AFRES host); Home of the 163rd Air Refueling Wing (CA, ANG); 119th Fighter Group (ND, ANG); Armed Forces Radio and Television Services; Defense Visual Info Center; Air Force Audit Agency; U.S. Customs Service; Domestic Air Interdiction Coordination Center; Base activated 1918, named after 2nd Lt Peyton C. March, Jr. who died in Texas in a crash, 19 February 1918. Base converted to ARB, 1 April 1996.

**TEMPORARY MILITARY LODGING:** The March Inn, C-909-655-3347/653-3174, Fax: C-909-655-4574.

**RV, CAMPING/FAMCAMP:** Outdoor Rec, 452 SVS/SVRO, Bldg 803, March ARB, CA 92518. C-909-655-2816, Fax: C-909-655-5221. Twelve sites with W/E/S.

**SPACE-A:** Pax Terminal: C-909-655-2397/3214, D-312-947-2397/3214 between 0730-1600, Mon-Fri. Rec: C-909-655-2913, D-312-947-2913. Fax: C-909-655-3887, D-312-947-3887. Sign up also via web site listed above.

**LOGISTICAL SUPPORT:**

| | |
|---|---|
| Bank-656-4111 | Commissary-655-3967 |
| Exchange-655-3111 | Snack bar-655-3663 |

**ADMINISTRATIVE SUPPORT:**     Public Affairs-655-4137

**HEALTH & WELFARE:** None. See Camp Pendleton MCB.

**REST & RECREATION:**

| | |
|---|---|
| Fitness Center 655-2284 | Hap Arnold Club-655-2121 |
| ITT-655-4123 | MWR-655-4303 |
| Outdoor Rec-655-2816 | |

**ATTRACTIONS:** Southern California offers many sights and activities – Disneyland, Universal Studios, Magic Mountain, Chinatown, skiing in the mountains, water activities at the beaches.

# MARINES' MEMORIAL CLUB (CA20R4)
### 609 Sutter Street
### San Francisco, CA 94102-1022

**TELEPHONE NUMBER INFORMATION:** Main installation numbers: C-415-673-6672. Reservations: 1-800-5-MARINE. E-mail: resv@marineclub.com WEB: www.marineclub.com

**LOCATION:** From north or south on I-580, exit onto I-80 west and cross the San Francisco-Oakland Bay Bridge. Take 5th Street exit northwest approximately 0.75 miles to O'Farrell Street, right (east) one block to Powell Street, left (north) three blocks to west on Sutter Street one block to club entrance on left (south) side of street. USMRA: Page 119 (C-5). NMC: San Francisco, in city limits.

**GENERAL INFORMATION:** The Marines' Memorial Club is a club/hotel exclusively for uniformed services personnel, active duty and retirees and their guests. **The club is not a part of the government but is a private, non-profit organization and is completely self supporting.** This club/hotel is a living memorial to Marines who lost their lives in the Pacific during WW II. It opened on the Marine Corps' Birthday, November 10, 1946, and chose as its motto "A tribute to those Marines who have gone before; and a service to those who carry on."

**TEMPORARY MILITARY LODGING:** Hotel, all ranks, leave or official duty. Guest rooms (137); deluxe suites (11); family suites (3). Reservations required. C-1-800-5-MARINE or 415-673-6672 (direct).

**RV, CAMPING/FAMCAMP:** None. See Travis AFB listing.

**SPACE-A:** None. See Travis AFB listing.

**LOGISTICAL SUPPORT:** Club facilities include coin-operated launderette, valet, exchange store, package store, rooms for private parties, and a dining room and lounge in the Skyroom on the 12th floor, overlooking San Francisco. Convenience store/news stand and coffee shop outside hotel adjacent to entrance.

Hotel discount parking on Sutter Street, ask at desk. *Military Living books, maps and atlases are sold in the Club exchange, first floor.*

**ADMINISTRATIVE SUPPORT:** None. See Travis AFB listing.

**HEALTH AND WELFARE:** None. See Travis AFB listing.

**REST & RECREATION:** Theater, library/museum, swimming, gym.

**ATTRACTIONS:** In the heart of San Francisco, within walking distance of Cable Cars; Union Square is just one-and-a-half blocks away. Many major attractions.

# McCLELLAN AIR FORCE BASE (CA35R4)
### 3237 Peacekeeper Way, Suite 5
### McClellan Air Force Base, CA 95652-1048
### *Scheduled to close July 2001*

**TELEPHONE NUMBER INFORMATION:** Main installation numbers: C-916-643-2111, D-312-633-2111.

**LOCATION:** From west on I-80 take exit onto Watt Avenue north for approximately 1.25 miles. Main Gate and Visitor's Gate are on left (west) side of street. Or, from northeast on I-80, take exit onto Madison Avenue west for approximately 1.25 miles to intersection with Watt Avenue, then right (north) 0.25 miles to Main Gate and Visitor's Gates on left (west) side of street. Clearly marked. USMRA: Page 110 (C-6). NMC: Sacramento, 9 miles Southwest.

**GENERAL INFORMATION:** Air Force Materiel Command Base. Headquarters Sacramento Air Logistics Center. U.S. Coast Guard Station McClellan. Also AMC, ACC AFCC, and AFRES units.

**TEMPORARY MILITARY LODGING:** Lodging office, Building 89, 54 O'Malley Avenue, 24 hours daily, C-916-643-3267, D-312-633-6223. DV/VIP C-916-643-4311. All ranks.

**RV, CAMPING/FAMCAMP:** None. See Beale AFB listing, C-530-634-3382, D-312-368-3382.

**SPACE-A:** None. See Travis Air Force Base-1-800-787-2534.

**LOGISTICAL SUPPORT:**

| | |
|---|---|
| Cafeteria-643-3598 | Child Care-643-3611 |
| Commissary-925-8541* | Conv Store-332-3872 |
| Exchange-920-0537* | Gas Station-922-8868 |
| Package Store-643-3080 | SATO-643-4410 |
| Snack Bar-920-9394 | |

*\* Facility will remain open after base closure.*

**ADMINISTRATIVE SUPPORT:**

| | |
|---|---|
| CDO/OOD-643-2751 | Legal-643-3150 |
| Locator-643-4113 | Police-643-6160 |
| Public Affairs-643-6127 | |

**HEALTH & WELFARE:**

| | |
|---|---|
| CHAMPUS-800-930-2929 | Chapel-643-6021 |
| Family Services-643-1106 | Medical-643-7212 |
| Retiree Services-643-2207 | |

**REST & RECREATION:**

| | |
|---|---|
| Arts & Crafts-ext 3004 | Bowling-ext 5752 |
| Consol Club-643-3526 | Gym-643-2596 |
| Golf Course-643-3313 | Hobby Shop-ext 2323 |
| ITT-643-2259 | Library-ext 4640 |
| MWR-643-6660 | Outdoor Rec-ext 2738 |
| Picnic Area-ext 2596 | Rec Center-ext 2259 |
| Rec Equipment-ext 6034 | Rec News-ext 5311 |
| Swimming-ext 2259 | Theater-643-8706 |
| Youth Center-ext 3946 | |

**ATTRACTIONS:** Lake Tahoe and Reno, NV, San Francisco Bay Area. Air Museum on base, C-916-643-3192, 0900-1500 Mon-Sat, closed Sun and federal holidays.

# MIRAMAR MARINE CORPS AIR STATION (CA14R4)

Commanding Officer
Headquarters & Headquarters Squadron
P.O. Box 452013
Miramar Marine Corps Air Station, CA 92145-2013

**TELEPHONE NUMBER INFORMATION:** Main installation numbers: C-858-577-1011, D-312-267-1011. WEB: www.miramar.usmc.mil

**LOCATION:** From I-15 north of San Diego, take Miramar Way exit west which leads directly to the main gate. USMRA: Page 118 (C,D-2,3,4; E,F-2,3). NMC: San Diego, 10 miles southwest.

**GENERAL INFORMATION:** Commander Airborne Early Warning Wing Pacific, Commander 3rd Marine Air Wing, Commander Marine Air Group 11, Commander Air Group 46.

**TEMPORARY MILITARY LODGING:** Lodging office, Building 4312, 24 hours daily, C-858-577-4235, D-312-267-4235; Fax: C-858-577-4243, D-312-267-4243. DV/VIP C-858-577-1221. Miramar Lodge, Building 516, C-858-271-7111 or 1-800-NAVY-INN.

**RV, CAMPING/FAMCAMP:** RV Park on base, year round, C-858-577-4149, D-312-577-4149, 36 camper spaces with full hookups, 12 camper spaces with with E.

**SPACE-A:** Limited. C-858-577-4285, D-312-577-4285, Fax: C-858-577-4261/1721.

**LOGISTICAL SUPPORT:**

| | |
|---|---|
| Barber Shop-695-7312 | Beauty Shop-695-7227 |
| Cafeteria-695-7278 | Car Rental-695-7349 |
| Child Care-577-4144 | Commissary-577-4523 |
| Credit Union-547-8656 | Dining Facilities-577-1382 |
| Dry Cleaner-577-7238 | Exchange-695-7200 |
| Gas Station-695-7252 | Package Store-695-7315 |
| Postal Service-577-4578 | SATO-577-4396 |
| Shoppette-695-7315 | Visitor Center-577-1421 |

**ADMINISTRATIVE SUPPORT:**

| | |
|---|---|
| Housing Office-577-1121 | Legal-577-1656 |
| OOD-577-1227 | Public Affairs-577-6000 |

**HEALTH & WELFARE:**

| | |
|---|---|
| American Red Cross-577-4107 | CHAMPUS-577-4630 |
| Chapel-577-1333 | Community Services-577-4099 |
| Dental-Clinic-577-1824 | Family Services-577-4103 |
| Medical | Navy-MC Relief-577-1807 |
| Central Appts-577-4656 | Retiree Services-577-4103 |
| Health Benefits Advisor-577-4630 | TRICARE-577-4630 |
| Emergency-911 | Veterinary Services-577-6552 |

**REST & RECREATION:**

| | |
|---|---|
| Arts & Crafts-ext 4134 | Auto Hobby Shop-577-1215 |
| Bowling-577-4131 | Clubs |
| Golf Course-577-4155 | EM-577-4820 |
| Gym-577-4128 | O-577-4808 |
| Library-577-1261 | Picnic Area-577-3526 |
| Rec Supply-577-4149 | Services-577-4117 |
| Swimming-577-4140 | Theater-577-4143 |
| Tickets-577-4126 | Wood Hobby Shop-577-4134 |
| Youth Center-577-4136 | |

**ATTRACTIONS:** Old Town San Diego, Sea World, San Diego Zoo, Wild Animal Park, beautiful beaches and boardwalk, Mission Blvd.

# MOFFETT FEDERAL AIRFIELD NASA/AMES RESEARCH CENTER (CA15R4)

P.O. Box 0128
Moffett Federal Airfield, CA 94035-0128

**TELEPHONE NUMBER INFORMATION:** Main installation numbers: C-650-604-5000, D-312-359-5000. WEB: ccf.arc.nasa.gov/jf/mfa

**LOCATION:** On north side of US-101 (Bayshore Freeway), 35 miles south of San Francisco. Take Moffett Federal Airfield exit north onto Moffett Boulevard which leads directly to main gate. USMRA: Page 119 (F-9). San Jose, seven miles south, San Francisco, 35 miles north.

**GENERAL INFORMATION:** NASA/Ames Research Center. Onizuka AS Annex is a tenant. Santa Clara NAR is a fomer tenant recently disestablished but having left behind some support facilities. At press time, Moffett was undergoing a great deal of reorganization.

**TEMPORARY MILITARY LODGING:** Navy Lodge: C-650-962-1542 or 800-NAVY-INN. All ranks.

**RV, CAMPING/FAMCAMP:** None. See San Joaquin Defense Distribution Depot.

**SPACE-A:** None. See Travis AFB listing.

**LOGISTICAL SUPPORT:**

| | |
|---|---|
| Barber Shop-603-9917 | Cafeteria-604-5969 |
| Child Dev Center-940-1554 | Dry Cleaner-603-9929 |
| Class Six-603-9927 | Commissary-603-9976 |
| Exchange-603-9907 | SATO-604-1686 |
| Visitor Center-604-6274 | |

**ADMINISTRATIVE SUPPORT:**

| | |
|---|---|
| Housing Office-603-8100 | Locator-604-5000 |
| Police-604-5461 | Public Affairs-604-9000 |

**HEALTH & WELFARE:**

| | |
|---|---|
| Chapel-603-8073 | TRICARE-800-242-6788 |

**REST & RECREATION:**

| | |
|---|---|
| Auto Hobby Shop-603-9717 | Golf Course-603-8026 |
| Gym-ext 4697 | Moffett Club-604-1680 |
| Swimming-ext 4712 | ITT-ext 4757 |
| Youth Center-691-1216 | |

**ATTRACTIONS:** Paramount Great America Park is five miles south. Located in the heart of the "Silicon Valley." San Jose and Santa Cruz are nearby.

# MONTEREY NAVAL POSTGRADUATE SCHOOL (CA16R4)

1 University Circle
Monterey, CA 93943-5000

**TELEPHONE NUMBER INFORMATION:** Main installation numbers: C-831-656-2441, D-312-878-2441.

**LOCATION:** Take CA-1 south to central Monterey exit, right (west) at light onto Camino Aguajito. Then first right (right fork) (east) onto 10th street, turn left (north) at stop sign onto Sloat Avenue, and right at 9th Street gate. Or north on CA-1, use Aguajito Road exit to Mark Thomas Drive north, to left (north) on Sloat Avenue, right (east) at 9th Street gate. USMRA: Page 111 (B-9). NMC: Monterey, in city limits.

**GENERAL INFORMATION:** Naval Postgraduate School, Defense Resource Management Institute, Fleet Numerical Oceanography Center, and Naval Support Activity-Monterey Bay.

**TEMPORARY MILITARY LODGING:** Lodging office, Building 220, Herrmann Hall, 1 University Circle, 24 hours daily, C-831-656-2060, D-312-878-2060, Fax: C-831-646-3024.

**RV, CAMPING/FAMCAMP:** Off base. Monterey Pines RV Campground, year round, MWR Department NSAMB, 1 University Circle, P.O. Box 8688, Monterey, CA 93943-5000. C-831-656-4029, D-312-878-4029. Thirty sites.

**SPACE-A:** None. See Lemoore NAS listing.

**LOGISTICAL SUPPORT:**

| | |
|---|---|
| Child Care-656-2734 | Commissary-242-3418 |
| Conv Store-375-0959 | Exchange-375-3737 |
| Gas Station-373-7271 | Package Store-373-7511 |
| SATO-656-3357 | Snack Bar-373-0557 |

**ADMINISTRATIVE SUPPORT:**

| | |
|---|---|
| CDO/OOD-656-2441 | Fire Dept-656-2334 |
| Legal-656-2506 | Locator-656-2441 |
| Police-656-2555 | Public Affairs-656-2023 |

**HEALTH & WELFARE:**

| | |
|---|---|
| Chapel-656-2241 | Family Services-656-3141 |
| Medical | Retiree Services-242-5595 |
| Central Appts-242-5741 | |
| Emergency-242-5234 | |

**REST & RECREATION:**

| | |
|---|---|
| Clubs | Golf Course-656-2167 |
| O-656-2170 | Gym-ext 2167 |
| MWR-656-3223 | Recreation-656-2275 |
| Rec Equipment-ext 3118 | Rec Office-ext 2467 |
| Swimming-ext 2275 | |

**ATTRACTIONS:** Beaches, seafood, Carmel Valley, Carmel-By-The-Sea, Pebble Beach, Big Sur coastline, Salinas Valley. Beautiful area, Monterey Bay Aquarium and Cannery Row.

# MONTEREY PINES RV CAMPGROUND (CX05R4)

MWR Department NSAMB
1 University Circle, P.O. Box 8688
Monterey, CA 93943-5001

**TELEPHONE NUMBER INFORMATION:** Main installation numbers: C-831-656-4029, D-312-656-2167.

**LOCATION:** Off base. From north or south on CA-1, in Monterey, exit at Casa Verde Way and turn south at the stop sign. Proceed straight south through the traffic light at Fremont Street and turn right (west) on Fairgrounds Road. At the next light, turn left (south) on Garden Road, make an immediate left (east) at entrance to the Monterey Fairgrounds/Navy Golf Course. (Campground is in the middle of golf course.) USMRA: Page 111 (B-9). NMC: Monterey, 0.5 miles north.

**GENERAL INFORMATION:** Operated by Monterey Bay Naval Support Activity, off base, year round. Eligibility: Military personnel active, reservists, retired, immediate family members and bona fide guests, Monterey Bay NSA and Naval Postgraduate School, DoD civilians. Reservations (accepted under certain conditions): Monterey Pines RV Campground/Golf Course, MWR Department NSAMB, 1 University Circle, P.O. Box 8688, Monterey, CA 93943-5000. C-831-656-4029, D-312-878-4029.

**RV, CAMPING/FAMCAMP:**  Camper Spaces-30

**ATTRACTIONS:** Located in a nature sanctuary which is situated between the 13th hole of the golf course and picnic grounds amongst Monterey pine trees on the historic grounds of the old premier coast resort, the Del Monte Hotel.

*For detailed information about this off-base recreation facility, as well as on-base recreation facilities, golf courses and marinas, consult Military Living's Military RV, Camping and Outdoor Recreation Around the World.*

# NORTH ISLAND NAVAL AIR STATION (CA43R4)

Building 605, McCain Boulevard
P.O. Box 357033
North Island Naval Air Station, CA 92135-7033

**TELEPHONE NUMBER INFORMATION:** Main installation numbers: C-619-545-8123, D-312-735-8123. WEB: www.nasni.navy.mil

**LOCATION:** From San Diego, take I-5 north or south to CA-75 across Coronado-San Diego Bay Bridge (toll) to CA-282 northwest directly to main gate. Also, take CA-75 north from Imperial Beach to downtown Coronado, then left (northwest) on CA-28 directly to main gate. Adjacent to Coronado. USMRA: Page 118 (B,C-6,7). NMC; San Diego, four miles northeast.

**GENERAL INFORMATION:** Largest Naval Industrial Complex on the West Coast.

**TEMPORARY MILITARY LODGING:** Lodging office, Building I (BOQ), 24 hours daily, BEQ, C-619-545-9551, D-312-735-9551. Fax: C-619-545-9042, BOQ, C-619-545-7545, D-312-735-7545. Navy Lodge, Building 1402, 24 hours daily, C-619-435-0191, D-312-735-0191. DV/VIP EM C-619-545-9551, Officers C-619-545-7545, Fax: C-619-545-9072. All ranks.

**RV, CAMPING/FAMCAMP:** None. See Coronado NAB listing, Fiddlers Cove RV Park.

**SPACE-A:** Pax Term/Lounge, Building 700, 24 hours daily, C-619-545-9567, D-312-735-9567, flights to CONUS. Some to foreign locations.

**LOGISTICAL SUPPORT:**

| | |
|---|---|
| Barber Shop-522-7230 | Beauty Shop-522-7229 |
| Cafeteria-522-7267 | Child Care-545-7226 |
| Commissary-545-8396 | Conv Store-522-7277 |
| Credit Union-656-1600 | Dry Cleaner-522-7231 |
| Education Office-545-7923 | Exchange-522-7215 |
| Gas Station-522-7282 | Laundry-522-7231 |
| Package Store-545-7279 | Postal Service-545-4380 |
| SATO-545-7937 | Snack Bar-522-7266/69 |

**ADMINISTRATIVE SUPPORT:**

| | |
|---|---|
| CDO/OOD-545-8123 | Fire Dept-524-6250 |
| Legal-545-8141 | Locator-524-0444 |
| Pass/ID Office-525-7916 | Police-545-6122 |
| Public Affairs-545-8167 | Quarter Deck-545-8123 |

**HEALTH & WELFARE:**

| | |
|---|---|
| American Red Cross-435-4285 | ACS-232-1133 |
| CHAMPUS-545-4319 | Chapel-545-8213 |
| Dental | Family Services-545-6071 |
| Central Appts-545-6938 | Medical |
| Clinic-545-6397 | Central Appts-545-4263 |
| Emergency-545-6397 | Clinic-545-4268 |
| N-MC Relief-545-7202 | Emergency-9-911 |
| | Hospital-532-6400 |
| | Information-545-4265 |

**REST & RECREATION:**

| | |
|---|---|
| Auto Hobby Shop-545-7237 | Bowling-545-7240 |
| Clubs | Fitness Center-ext 2876 |
| CPO-545-7223 | Golf Course-545-9659 |
| EM-545-7205 | Gym-522-2877 |
| O-545-6945 | ITT-545-9576 |
| Library-ext 5-8230 | MWR-545-8032 |
| Outdoor Rec-545-7237 | Pool |
| Recreation-545-9206 | Crew-ext 2880 |
| Skeet/Trap Range-ext 7225 | Officers-ext 7228 |
| Theater-545-9479 | Women's Spa-522-2871 |
| Wood Hobby Shop-545-7236 | |

**ATTRACTIONS:** Beaches, sport fishing, Old San Diego, Sea World, Bay Area, San Diego Zoo, and Mexico nearby.

## NOVATO COAST GUARD EXCHANGE
### (CA89R4)
583 Crescent Drive, Hamilton Field
Novato, CA 94949-5000

**TELEPHONE NUMBER INFORMATION:** Main installation numbers: C-415-883-3006.

**LOCATION:** Southbound on US-101 take exit onto Bel Marin Keys Blvd./Hamilton Field, go east on Bel Marin Keys Blvd. to right (south) on Nave Drive to left (east) on Main Gate Road for approximately 0.4 mile to right (south) on Crescent Drive to CGEX on right (west) side of street. Northbound on US-101 take exit onto Nave Drive/Hamilton Field, go (north) to Main Gate Road, then turn east (right) to Crescent Drive and (right) south to CGEX. USMRA: Page 110 (B-7). NMC: San Francisco, 20 miles south.

**LOGISTICAL SUPPORT:**              Exchange-883-3006

**ATTRACTIONS:** Point Reyes National Seashore. Nearby San Francisco and Bay area.

## ONIZUKA AIR STATION (CA96R4)
1080 Lockheed Way, Box 053
Sunnyvale, CA 94089-1236
*Scheduled to close 2001*

**TELEPHONE NUMBER INFORMATION:** Main installation numbers: C-408-752-3000, D-312-561-3000. WEB: www.onizuka.af.mil
*Ten digit dialing required for local calls.*

**LOCATION:** On northeast side of US-101 (Bayshore Freeway) and north on CA-237, 35 miles south of San Francisco. Located on Moffett Federal Airfield. From US-101 north or south take Moffett Federal Airfield exit north onto Moffett Boulevard which leads directly to airfield main gate. Ask at gate for directions to Air Station. USMRA: Page 119 (F-9), San Jose, seven miles south, San Francisco, 35 miles north.

**GENERAL INFORMATION:** Maintenance for AF Satellite Control network, 21st Space Operations Squadron, tenant of Moffett Federal Airfield/NASA Ames.

**TEMPORARY MILITARY LODGING:** None. See Moffett Federal Airfield/NASA Ames listing.

**RV, CAMPING/FAMCAMP:** None. See San Joaquin Defense Distribution Depot.

**SPACE-A:** None. See Travis AFB listing.

**LOGISTICAL SUPPORT:**              Conv Store-752-4601

**ADMINISTRATIVE SUPPORT:**         Public Affairs-752-3234

**HEALTH & WELFARE:** None. See Travis AFB listing.

**REST & RECREATION:** None. See Moffett Federal Airfield/NASA Ames listing.

**ATTRACTIONS:** San Francisco, a one hour drive. Monterey (south) and Napa Valley (north), under two hour drives. Day trips to Lake Tahoe, Yosemite National Park.

*Note: Most of Onizuka AS support is located at Moffett Federal Airfield/NASA Ames, just two miles away.*

## PARKS RESERVE FORCES TRAINING AREA
### (CA97R4)
Building 790
Dublin, CA 94568-5000

**TELEPHONE NUMBER INFORMATION:** Main installation numbers: C-925-803-5648.

**LOCATION:** East Bay area, east of Dublin. From east or west on I-580, exit north onto Dougherty Road (0.8 miles east of I-680 interchange) Main entrance is on right (east) side of Dougherty Road, clearly marked. USMRA: Page 119 (G-6). NMC: San Francisco, 30 miles west.

**TEMPORARY MILITARY LODGING:** Call C-925-803-5607.

**RV, CAMPING/FAMCAMP:** None.

**SPACE-A:** None. See Travis AFB listing.

**LOGISTICAL SUPPORT:**              Exchange-829-7780

**ADMINISTRATIVE SUPPORT:**
Fire Dept-803-5613                   Police-803-5604
Public Affairs-803-5636

**HEALTH & WELFARE:**               Medical-803-5606

**REST & RECREATION:**
Com Club-803-5615                    Recreation-803-5618

**ATTRACTIONS:** San Francisco and Bay Area. Many exciting things to see and do in and around Oakland. Jack London Square shopping area at the foot of Broadway in Oakland is a waterfront promenade lined with stores, restaurants and entertainment.

## PETALUMA COAST GUARD TRAINING CENTER (CA23R4)
599 Tomales Road
Petaluma, CA 94952-5000

**TELEPHONE NUMBER INFORMATION:** Main installation numbers: C-707-765-7212/7215.

**LOCATION:** From north or south on US-101 exit at Petaluma onto East Washington Street southwest through city of Petaluma, Washington Street becomes Bodega Avenue. Continue west following signs to Coast Guard Training Center a total of about 11 miles. Turn left (southwest) onto Tomales Road. A flashing amber light marks the main gate. USMRA: Page 110 (B-6,7). NMC: San Francisco, approximately 58 miles south.

**GENERAL INFORMATION:** The major Coast Guard Training Center on the West Coast.

**TEMPORARY MILITARY LODGING:** Guest Housing, Building T-134, Nevada Avenue, 0730-1600, C-707-765-7248. All ranks.

**RV, CAMPING/FAMCAMP:** Petaluma Lake Area Campsites, on base, year round, C-707-765-7348. Six camper spaces without hookups, 25 tent spaces.

**SPACE-A:** None. See Travis AFB listing, C-707-424-1854, D-312-837-1854, Fax: C-707-424-2048.

**LOGISTICAL SUPPORT:**
Barber Shop-762-8026                 Cafeteria-765-7168
Child Care-765-7334                  Conv Store-765-7252
Credit Union-765-1075                Education Center-765-7360
Exchange-765-7258                    Gas Station-765-7254
Package Store-765-7252               SATO-765-7362
Travel Office-765-7550

**ADMINISTRATIVE SUPPORT:**
CDO/OOD-765-7212                     Fire Dept-765-7355
Locator-765-7212                     Police-765-7215
Public Affairs-765-7145

**HEALTH & WELFARE:**
CHAMPUS-765-7563                     Chapel-765-7330
Dental Clinic-765-7234               Family Services-765-7326
Medical-765-7200
   Emergency-765-7333
   Health Benefits Advisor-765-7564

**REST & RECREATION:**

Bowling Center-765-7351
Driving Range-765-7348
ITT-765-7340
MWR-765-7340
Theater-765-7346

Consol Club-765-7248
Gym-765-7348
Library-765-7580
Swimming-765-7176

**ATTRACTIONS:** The base is a federal game preserve.

# POINT MUGU NAVAL AIR STATION (CA40R4)

Naval Station Ventura County
521 9th Street, Building 1, Room 117
Point Mugu, CA 93042-5001

**TELEPHONE NUMBER INFORMATION:** Main installation numbers: C-805-989-1110, D-312-351-1110. WEB: www.naspm.navy.mil

**LOCATION:** Eight miles south of Oxnard and 40 miles north of Santa Monica on CA-1 (Pacific Coast Highway). From north or south on CA-1 take exit at Los Posas Road south onto Pacific Road directly to Gate 3 (Los Posas Gate). Take Frontage Road parallel to CA-1 northwest to Gate 1 and Main Gate (Gate 2). Or take exit onto Wood Drive southwest to Frontage Road and all three gates which will be on southwest (Right) side of road. USMRA: Page 111 (E-13). NMC: Oxnard, seven miles north.

**GENERAL INFORMATION:** Naval Air Warfare Center Weapons Division, Naval Air Weapons Station, Navy Weapons Test Squadron, Air Test & Evaluation Squadron 9 Detachment, Antarctic Development Squadron 6, Explosive Ordnance Disposal MU 3 Detachment, Helicopter Combat Support Squadron 5, Marine Aviation Detachment, Naval Satellite Operations Center, Naval Air Reserve Forces, Patrol Squadron 5, Naval Air Reserve. No general visits permitted.

**TEMPORARY MILITARY LODGING:** Protocol Code 08AE00E, NAWCWP-NS, 521 9th Street, Point Mugu, CA 93042-5001, Protocol office, Building 36, Mon-Thurs 0730-1630 hours, C-805-989-7532/8672, D-312-351-8672, Fax: C-805-939-4358, D-312-351-4358. All ranks. VIP EM/Officers C-805-989-8672, Fax: C-805-989-7470.

**RV, CAMPING/FAMCAMP:** Point Mugu Recreation Facilities on base, year round, MWR Beach Motel, Code 860000E, NAWS, 521 9th Street, Point Mugu, CA 93042-5001, C-805-989-8407, D-312-351-8407, 51 camper spaces with full hookups, six camper spaces without hookups, 24 motel units, beach motel located in Building 774 on 18th street.

**SPACE-A:** Pax Terminal, Building 339, Mon-Thurs 0600-1800, every other Fri 0600-1800, C-805-989-7731/7305, D-312-351-7731/7305. Fax: C-805-989-4085, D-312-351-4085. Flights to CONUS and foreign locations. (Note: In person sign-up only.)

**LOGISTICAL SUPPORT:**

Bank-989-8787
Beauty Shop-989-8701
Child Care-989-8375
Commissary-989-7891
Dining Facilities
   Mugu's Pizza-989-7747
   The Point-989-8570
Laundry-989-5111
Postal Service-989-8707
Travel Office-488-1084 (leisure)

Barber Shop-989-7271
Cafeteria-989-8898
Child Dev Center-989-7481
Dry Cleaner-989-5111
Education Office-989-8457
Exchange-989-8896
Gas Station-488-0161
Package Store-989-8896
SATO-989-8378 (official)

**ADMINISTRATIVE SUPPORT:**

CDO/OOD-989-7209
Housing Office-989-7250
Locator-703-614-9221 (off base)
Police-989-7058
Quarter Deck-989-7209

Fire Dept-989-7034/7035
Legal-989-7309
Pass/ID Office-989-7670/7648
Public Affairs-989-8094/95

**HEALTH & WELFARE:**

American Red Cross-989-7393 or
   982-3074

CHAMPUS-982-6322
Chapel-989-7967

Dental
   Central Appts-989-7126/7603
   Clinic-989-7126/7603
   Emergency-989-7126/7603
Navy-MC Relief-989-8918
TRICARE-981-2819

Family Services-989-8146
Medical
   Central Appts-989-8932
   Clinic-989-8815/16
   Emergency-911

**REST & RECREATION:**

Auto Hobby Shop-989-7353
Clubs
   CPO-989-8570
   EM-989-7747
   O-989-8849
ITT-989-7628
Library-989-7771
Swimming-ext 7788
Youth Center-989-7580

Bowling-989-7667
Community Center-989-7580
Fitness Center-989-7728
Golf Course-989-7109
Gym-989-7728
ITT Recording-989-8349
MWR-989-7509
Theater-989-8249

**ATTRACTIONS:** Beautiful beaches and Los Angeles area nearby. Annual Point Mugu Air Show in the Fall. Disneyland, Marineland, Movieland, Universal Studios, Queen Mary, Spruce Goose, Lion Country Safari and more. Ronald Reagan Presidential Library in Simi Valley (C-805-522-8444).

# PORT HUENEME NAVAL CONSTRUCTION BATTALION CENTER (CA32R4)

Naval Station Ventura County
1000 23rd Avenue
Port Hueneme, CA 93043-4301

**TELEPHONE NUMBER INFORMATION:** Main installation numbers: C-805-982-4711, D-312-551-4711. WEB: www.cbcph.navy.mil

**LOCATION:** From east or west on US-101 (Ventura Freeway) exit onto Wagon Wheel Road which leads into South Bank Drive southwest into Ventura Road for total of approximately 6.25 miles to right on Pleasant Valley Road directly to Main Gate. USMRA: Page 111 (D,E-13). NMC: Los Angeles, approximately 50 miles southeast.

**GENERAL INFORMATION:** Major units include Naval Mobile Construction Battalions 3, 4, 5 and 40 and Underwater Construction Team 2, 31st Naval Construction Regiment; Naval Construction Training Center, Engineering Duty Officers School; Port Hueneme Naval Reserve Center; Naval School, Civil Engineer Corps Officers; Naval Facilities Engineering Services Center; Air Force Detachment 1, 345 TRS, Vehicle Maintenance Training School.

**TEMPORARY MILITARY LODGING:** Central reservation number (officer and enlisted) C-805-982-4115. Navy Lodge, Building 1172, C-805-985-2624.

**RV, CAMPING/FAMCAMP:** On base, year round. C-805-982-4392/6123. RV Park, Naval Base Ventura County CBC, Bldg 1362, 1000 23rd Avenue, Port Hueneme, CA 93043-4301. Check in at Bldg 805. Thirty-seven pull-through spaces with full hookups including phone/TV.

**SPACE-A:** None. See Point Mugu NAWS listing.

**LOGISTICAL SUPPORT:**

Barber/Beauty Shop-982-9420
Commissary-982-4711/6864
Education Office-982-2913
Gas Station-982-4768
Mini Mart-982-9400
Travel Office (leisure)-982-4276

Child Dev Center-982-4849
Credit Union-982-3405
Exchange-982-4711
Laundry-982-9421
Postal Service-982-4761
Travel Office (official)-982-3536

**ADMINISTRATIVE SUPPORT:**

CDO/OOD-982-2007
Housing Office-982-4321
Locator-982-5333 (Mil)
       982-4711 (Civ)
Public Affairs-982-4493

Fire Dept-982-4595
Legal-982-3124
Pass/ID Office-982-2018
Police-982-4494
Quarter Deck-982-4576

**HEALTH & WELFARE:**

American Red Cross-982-3074
Chapel-982-4358
Family Services-982-5037
Medical-982-6301
  Central Appts-984-8433
  1-800-446-5271
Emergency-911

CHAMPUS-982-6322
Dental-982-5584
Navy-MC Relief-982-4409
Retiree Services-982-5037
TRICARE-982-6322

**REST & RECREATION:**

Auto Hobby Shop-982-6123/4399
Clubs
  EM-982-2872
  O-982-2754
ITT-982-4284
Museum-982-5163
Rec Equip-982-4285
Theater-982-5491

Bowling-982-2619
Community Center-982-4282
Golf Course-982-2620
Gym-982-5173
Library-982-4743
MWR-982-4287
Swimming-982-4752
Youth Center-982-4218

**ATTRACTIONS:** CEC/Seabee Museum, the Navy's second oldest museum. Annual open house - Seabee Days, local attractions with beautiful beaches, two marinas, Channel Islands, historic sites. Santa Barbara and Los Angeles nearby. Attractions include zoo, Disneyland, Universal Studios, Knott's Berry Farm, waterparks and museums.

## PRESIDIO OF MONTEREY (CA74R4)
Building 1759, Room 142
Presidio of Monterey, CA 93944-5006

**TELEPHONE NUMBER INFORMATION:** Main installation numbers: C-831-242-5000, D-312-878-5000. WEB: pom-www.army.mil

**LOCATION:** From north or south on CA-I in Monterey, exit to Del Monte Blvd. and go west approximately 1.75 miles onto Lighthouse Avenue. Continue northwest and enter post from Lighthouse Avenue. Watch for signs. USMRA: Page 111 (B-9). NMC: Monterey, in city limits.

**GENERAL INFORMATION:** Defense Language Institute, Foreign Language Center.

**TEMPORARY MILITARY LODGING:** C-831-242-5091, Fax: C-831-242-5298.

**RV, CAMPING/FAMCAMP:** South Lake Tahoe Recreation Housing off post, year round, C-831-242-5506, D-312-878-5506, one A-Frame chalet, one cabin, two condominiums and motel lodgings.

**SPACE-A:** None. See Lemoore NAS, CA listing.

**LOGISTICAL SUPPORT:**

Commissary-242-7671
Dining Facilities-242-5384/5008
Gas Station-394-8219
SATO-648-8045

Child Care-242-1058
Exchange-242-9602
Package Store-899-2336
Snack Bar-647-9606

**ADMINISTRATIVE SUPPORT:**

Fire Dept-242-7701
Legal-242-5083/84
Police-242-5634
SDO/SNCO-242-5119

Housing Office-656-2321
Locator-242-5119
Public Affairs-242-5104

**HEALTH & WELFARE:**

ACS-242-7650/60
Chapel-242-5281
Community Services-242-7661

CHAMPUS-242-0304
Chaplain-242-7620
Medical-242-5741

**REST & RECREATION:**

Consol Club-649-1823
Golf Course-899-2351
MWR-242-6995
Sports Arena-ext 5295
Youth Center-ext 5277

Fitness Center-ext 5641
ITT-242-5377
Rec Center-242-5447
Theater-373-2234

**ATTRACTIONS:** Beaches, seafood, Carmel Valley, Carmel-by-the-Sea, Salinas Valley. Beautiful location on a hill above the bay.

## PRESIDIO OF MONTEREY ANNEX (CA36R4)
Building 614, Room 142
Presidio of Monterey, CA 93944-5006

**TELEPHONE NUMBER INFORMATION:** Main installation numbers: C-831-242-5104/5184, D-312-929-5104/5184.

**LOCATION:** From north or south on CA-1 use Fort Ord exit east directly to main gate of post. USMRA: Page 111 (B,C-9). NMC: Monterey, seven miles south.

**TEMPORARY MILITARY LODGING:** None. See Presidio of Monterey listing.

**RV, CAMPING/FAMCAMP:** None. See Presidio of Monterey listing.

**SPACE-A:** None. See Lemoore NAS, CA listing.

**LOGISTICAL SUPPORT:**

Barber Shop-899-3198
Child Care-583-1059
Credit Union-393-3480
Gas Station-394-8219

Beauty Shop-899-3198
Commissary-242-7671
Exchange-899-2336

**ADMINISTRATIVE SUPPORT:**

Locator-242-2271
Public Affairs-242-5555/5104

Police-242-7851

**HEALTH & WELFARE:**

Army Community Service-242-7652/7660

**REST & RECREATION:**

Outdoor Rec-242-5700

Youth Services-242-7823

**ATTRACTIONS:** Beaches, seafood, Carmel Valley, Carmel-by-the-Sea, Salinas Valley. Beautiful location on a hill above the bay.

## PRESIDIO OF SAN FRANCISCO (CA19R4)
Mason Street
Presidio of San Francisco, CA 94129-7000

**TELEPHONE NUMBER INFORMATION:** Only Exchange and Commissary at this facility. See numbers below.

**LOCATION:** Off US-101 near Golden Gate Bridge. From east or west on Lombard Street (US-101) go north five blocks on Laguna Street to left (west) on Beach Street one block to right (northwest) onto Marina Blvd. and west for 0.75 miles. At fork in road keep right (west) onto Mason Street directly to entrance. USMRA: Page 119 (C-5). NMC: San Francisco, in the city.

**LOGISTICAL SUPPORT:**

Commissary-415-561-2382

Exchange-415-922-4591

**ATTRACTIONS:** Golden Gate Park and Bridge nearby. Bus service to downtown and Fisherman's Wharf.

## SAN CLEMENTE ISLAND NAVAL AUXILIARY LANDING FIELD (CA53R4)
P.O. Box 357054
San Diego, CA 92135-7054

**TELEPHONE NUMBER INFORMATION:** Main installation numbers: C-619-524-9214, D-312-524-9214.

**LOCATION:** This is a closed island accessible by air or boat only. Visitors must be sponsored by military stationed on the island. USMRA: Page 111 (E-15). NMC: Los Angeles, 50 miles east.

**GENERAL INFORMATION:** Visitors must be sponsored by military stationed on the island.

**TEMPORARY MILITARY LODGING:** Billeting Office: C-619-524-9202.

**RV, CAMPING/FAMCAMP:** None. See Camp Pendleton MCB listing.

**SPACE-A:** None. See Los Angeles AFB listing.

**LOGISTICAL SUPPORT:**       Exchange-524-9147

**ADMINISTRATIVE SUPPORT:**
CDO/OOD-524-9214                Fire Dept-524-9212
Police-524-9214

**HEALTH & WELFARE:** None. See Camp Pendleton listing.

**REST & RECREATION:**        Consol Club-524-9227

**ATTRACTIONS:** Beaches and wildlife.

# SAN DIEGO COAST GUARD ACTIVITIES (CA77R4)

2710 North Harbor Drive
San Diego, CA 92101-1079

**TELEPHONE NUMBER INFORMATION:** Main installation numbers: C-619-683-6333.

**LOCATION:** From south on I-5, take exit south onto North Hawthorn Street which becomes N. Kettner Road. Continue southeast on N. Kettner Road to a right (west) on W. Laurel Street, which runs into N. Harbor Drive. Main entrance is approximately 0.1 mile on left (south) side of road. From north on I-5, exit west onto W. Hawthorn Street, continue southwest on for 0.9 miles to right (northwest) on N. Harbor Drive for 1.1 miles to gate on left (south) side of road. USMRA: Page 118 (C-6), NMC: San Diego, in city limits.

**GENERAL INFORMATION:** Responsible for search and rescue missions, law enforcement, marine environment protection and providing aids to navigation. Marine Safety Office, ATON unit, and Coast Guard Station.

**TEMPORARY MILITARY LODGING:** None. See San Diego NSB listing.

**RV, CAMPING/FAMCAMP:** None. See Camp Pendleton MCB listing.

**SPACE-A:** CG Hangar, C-619-557-6510. Fixed wing Space-A opportunities extremely limited, also see North Island Naval Air Station listing.

**LOGISTICAL SUPPORT:**       Exchange-557-6388

**ADMINISTRATIVE SUPPORT:**
CDO/OOD-683-6470               Locator-683-6333
Public Affairs-683-6320        SDO/NCO-683-6470

**HEALTH & WELFARE:**
CHAMPUS-532-8329              Family Services-683-6336
Medical-683-6380
  Emergency-532-8275
  Information-532-6400

**REST & RECREATION:** None. See San Diego MCRD listing.

**ATTRACTIONS:** City of San Diego, Del Mar Racetrack, San Diego Zoo, Balboa Park, Sea World, Mission San Luis Rey.

# SAN DIEGO FLEET COMBAT TRAINING CENTER, PACIFIC (CA90R4)

53690 Tomahawk Drive, Suite 144
San Diego, CA 92147-5000

**TELEPHONE NUMBER INFORMATION:** Main installation numbers: C-619-553-8123, D-312-533-8123.

**LOCATION:** Southwest on Rosecrans Street (CA-209) to right (northwest) on Canon Street, then northwest curving around to southwest on Canon St. to south on Catalina Blvd. to entrance. Watch for signs. USMRA: Page 118 (A,B-6). NMC: San Diego, 10 miles east.

**GENERAL INFORMATION:** Naval Command Control & Ocean Surveillance Center (NCCCSC, Navy Center for Tactical Systems Inter-operability (NCTSI) & Det 1 Tactical Training Group, Pacific (TATRAGRUPAC).

**TEMPORARY MILITARY LODGING:** None. See San Diego NSB listing.

**RV, CAMPING/FAMCAMP:** None. See Camp Pendleton MCB listing.

**SPACE-A:** None. See North Island NAS listing.

**LOGISTICAL SUPPORT:**
Barber Shop-221-2056           Cafeteria-221-2054
Conv Store-221-2053            Dry Cleaner-221-2653
Education Office-553-8176      Exchange-221-2053
Postal Service-553-8121

**ADMINISTRATIVE SUPPORT:**
CDO/OOD-553-8225              Legal-553-8110
Pass/ID Office-553-8328       Police-553-8329
Public Affairs-553-8110

**HEALTH & WELFARE:** None. See San Diego NMC listing.

**REST & RECREATION:** None. See San Diego NS listing.

**OTHER FACILITIES AVAILABLE:** Fitness center.

**ATTRACTIONS:** Sea World, San Diego Zoo, Balboa Park, city of San Diego.

# SAN DIEGO MARINE CORPS RECRUIT DEPOT (CA57R4)

1600 Henderson Avenue, Suite 120
San Diego, CA 92140-5093

**TELEPHONE NUMBER INFORMATION:** Main installation numbers: C-619-524-1011, D-312-524-1268.

**LOCATION:** On the west side of I-5. From north or south on I-5 use Old Town Avenue exit south to Hancock Street, then southeast one block to Witherby Street, then southwest directly to main gate and follow signs. USMRA: Page 118 (C-6). NMC: San Diego, two miles southeast; adjacent to San Diego International Airport (Lindbergh Field).

**GENERAL INFORMATION:** Recruit Training Regiment, Headquarters and Service Battalion, Drill Instructor School, Recruiters School, Headquarters 12th Marine Corps Recruiting District, USCG Pacific Area Tactical Law Enforcement Team.

**TEMPORARY MILITARY LODGING:** Lodging office, Building 625, 0700-2230 daily, C-619-524-4401. All ranks.

**RV, CAMPING/FAMCAMP:** None. See Camp Pendleton MCB listing.

**SPACE-A:** None. See North Island NAS listing.

**LOGISTICAL SUPPORT:**
Barber Shop-524-4432           Child Care-524-4430
Child Dev Center-524-4430      Conv Store-524-4435
Credit Union-524-9400          Dining Facilities-524-6878
Dry Cleaner-524-1958           Education Office-524-6865
Exchange-297-2500              Gas Station-296-3987
Package Store-524-4435 ext 651 Postal Service-524-4398
SATO-295-7286                  Travel Office-295-7286
Visitor Center-524-6038

**ADMINISTRATIVE SUPPORT:**
Fire Dept-524-4222             Housing Office-524-4401
Legal-524-4110/1               Locator-524-1719
OOD-524-8700 (after 1600 hours) Pass/ID Office-524-4200
Police-524-4202                Public Affairs-524-8727

*[handwritten: (619) Miramar Beauty Shop (858) 577-1011 Information]*

**HEALTH & WELFARE:**

American Red Cross- 524-5727
Chapel-524-8820
Family Services-524-5728
Medical
  Central Appts-524-4036
  Clinic-524-4036
  Emergency-9-911

CHAMPUS-557-7500
Dental-524-4008
  Central Appts-524-4005
  Clinic-524-4005
Navy-MC Relief-524-5734

**REST & RECREATION:**

Auto Hobby Shop-524-5240
Camping Equipment-524-6180
Fitness Center-524-4428
Gym-524-4428
ITT-524-6772
Marina-524-5269
  Boat Rental
Outdoor Rec-524-6769
Visitor Center-524-6038

Bowling-524-4446
Clubs
  Combined-524-6878
  NCO-524-4448
Library-524-1850
Museum-524-6038
MWR-524-4435
Services-524-5055

**ATTRACTIONS:** Sea World, San Diego Zoo, Balboa Park, city of San Diego, Wild Animal Park, Command Museum, Mexico nearby.

# SAN DIEGO NAVAL MEDICAL CENTER
## (CA59R4)

34800 Bob Wilson Drive
San Diego, CA 92134-5000

**TELEPHONE NUMBER INFORMATION:** Main installation numbers: C-619-532-6400, D-312-522-6400. WEB: www-nmcsd.med.navy.mil

**LOCATION:** From north or south on I-5, exit northeast onto Pershing Drive north for approximately 0.3 miles, then left (west) on Florida Canyon Drive to entrance on left (west) side of road. USMRA: Page 118 (D-6). NMC: San Diego, in city limits.

**GENERAL INFORMATION:** Large Naval medical treatment facility serving the San Diego area.

**TEMPORARY MILITARY LODGING:** None. See San Diego NS listing.

**RV, CAMPING/FAMCAMP:** None. See Camp Pendleton MCB listing.

**SPACE-A:** None. See North Island NAS listing.

**LOGISTICAL SUPPORT:**

Child Care-532-6665
SATO-532-6607

Exchange-525-1502

**ADMINISTRATIVE SUPPORT:**

CDO/OOD-532-6400
Public Affairs-532-9380

Fire Dept-911

**HEALTH & WELFARE:**

CHAMPUS-532-8328
TRICARE-1-800-242-6788

Medical
  Emergency-532-8275

**REST & RECREATION:**

Fitness Center-532-7260
MWR-532-7245
Swimming Pool-532-8516

Library-532-7950
Rec Services Office-532-7245
Tickets-532-7255

**ATTRACTIONS:** Zoo, Sea World, Balboa Park, city of San Diego, Wild Animal Park, Mexico nearby.

# SAN DIEGO NAVAL STATION (CA26R4)

3445 Surface Navy Boulevard
San Diego, CA 92136-5000

**TELEPHONE NUMBER INFORMATION:** Main installation numbers: C-619-556-1011, D-312-526-1011.

**LOCATION:** From north or south on I-5, seven miles south of San Diego, take 28th Street exit south to Main Street. Station is at 28th & Main Streets. Continue southwest on 28th Street and south to main gate at 32nd Street. USMRA: Page 118 (D-7,8). NMC: San Diego, in the city.

**GENERAL INFORMATION:** Pacific Fleet Training Center, Public Works Center, and home port for major ships of the Pacific Fleet.

**TEMPORARY MILITARY LODGING:** Lodging office, 0730-1630 daily, Building 3362 (BEQ) C-619-556-8144; and Building 254 (BOQ) C-619-556-8162. DV/VIP C-619-556-8672/8163, Fax: C-619-556-9325. Navy Lodge near Harbor Dr, 24 hours daily, C-619-234-6142, D-312-958-6142. Reservations: 1-800-628-9466. All ranks.

**RV, CAMPING/FAMCAMP:** Admiral Baker Field Campground off base, year round, C-619-556-5525, 27 camper spaces with W/E hookups, 12 camper spaces without hookups.

**SPACE-A:** None. See North Island NAS listing.

*[handwritten: 1-(858) 695-7260 Beauty Shop. 12:00 N]*

**LOGISTICAL SUPPORT:**

Barber Shop-544-2229
Cafeteria-544-2228
Commissary-556-7200
Credit Union-234-7448
Education Office-556-4920
Gas Station-544-2289
SATO-231-7361

Beauty Shop-544-2232
Child Care-556-7475
Convenience Store-544-2195
Dining Facilities-556-5502
Exchange-544-2111/2100
Package Store-544-2252
Travel Office-556-1055/1091

**ADMINISTRATIVE SUPPORT:**

CDO/OOD-556-1246/47
Locator-556-1011
Police-556-1527

Fire Dept-524-6250
Pass/ID Office-556-9248
Public Affairs-556-7356

**HEALTH & WELFARE:**

American Red Cross-556-7061
Chapel-556-1921/6025
Medical-556-8114
  Emergency-556-8114

CHAMPUS-557-7505
Family Services-556-7404
Navy-MC Relief-556-8283
Retiree Services-556-7404

**REST & RECREATION:**

Admiral Robinson Center-556-7486
Auto Hobby Shop-556-7031
Clubs
  CPO-556-7050
  EM-556-1915
  O-556-7948/556-3113
MWR-556-7455/8906
Rec Equipment-556-7493
Sports Director-556-7444
Theater-556-5568

Arts & Crafts-556-7030
Bowling-556-7486
Fitness Center-556-8471
Golf Course-556-7502/5520
Gym-556-7450
ITT-556-7498
Rec Center-556-5706/7550
Rec Services-556-7029/7455
Swimming-556-8659/5504

**ATTRACTIONS:** Zoo, Sea World, Balboa Park, City of San Diego, Wild Animal Park, Mexico nearby.

# SAN DIEGO NAVAL SUBMARINE BASE
## (CA79R4)

140 Sylvester Road
San Diego, CA 92106-3521

**TELEPHONE NUMBER INFORMATION:** Main installation numbers: C-619-553-7533, D-312-553-7533.

**LOCATION:** Southwest on Rosecrans Street (CA-209) directly to main gate. USMRA: Page 118 (B-6). NMC: San Diego, five miles southeast.

**GENERAL INFORMATION:** Submarine Training Facility, Submarine Development Group One.

**TEMPORARY MILITARY LODGING:** Lodging office, Building 601, 24 hours daily, BEQ C-619-553-7533, D-312-553-7533, BOQ C-619-553-9381, D-312-553-9381. DV/VIP C-619-553-9381, D-312-553-9381, Fax: C-619-553-0613.

**RV, CAMPING/FAMCAMP:** None. See Camp Pendleton MCB listing.

**SPACE-A:** None. See North Island Naval Air Station listing.

**LOGISTICAL SUPPORT:**
| | |
|---|---|
| Conv Store-221-2011 | Exchange-221-2011 |
| Gas Station-221-1095 | SATO-222-3632 |

**ADMINISTRATIVE SUPPORT:**
| | |
|---|---|
| Legal-553-8594 | Police-553-7070 |
| Public Affairs-553-8644 | SDO/NCO-553-7533 |

**HEALTH & WELFARE:**
| | |
|---|---|
| CHAMPUS-532-8300 | Chapel-553-7201 |
| Family Services-553-7505 | |

**REST & RECREATION:**
| | |
|---|---|
| Archery-ext 7549 | Arts & Crafts-ext 7162 |
| Auto Hobby Shop-ext7162 | Bowling-ext 7521 |
| Camping Equipment-ext 7549 | Ceramics-ext 7545 |
| Clubs | Gym-ext 7552 |
| CPO-553-7597 | Hobby Shop-ext 7549 |
| EM-553-7519 | Library-ext 9851 |
| O-553-9384 | ITT-553-7162 |
| Rec Center-ext 7552 | Services-ext 7162 |
| Swimming-ext 7552 | |

**ATTRACTIONS:** City of San Diego, San Diego Zoo, Balboa Park, Sea World, Mission San Luis Rey. Pacific Ocean, mountains, and deserts within a short driving distance.

# SAN FRANCISCO COAST GUARD STATION (CA94R4)

Yerba Buena Island
San Francisco, CA 94130-9309

**TELEPHONE NUMBER INFORMATION:** Main installation numbers: C-415-399-3400.

**LOCATION:** On Yerba Buena Island, just south of where the east span of the San Francisco-Oakland Bay Bridge crosses the island. From I-80 east or west take Treasure Island exit. Follow signs. USMRA: Page 119 (C-5). NMC: San Francisco, one mile west

**GENERAL INFORMATION:** Part of Eleventh District U.S. Coast Guard.

**LOGISTICAL SUPPORT:**          Exchange-399-3478

**ATTRACTIONS:** Treasure Island Museum, San Francisco sights.

# SAN JOAQUIN DEFENSE DISTRIBUTION DEPOT (CA52R4)

700 East Roth Road, Building 205
Stockton, CA 95296-0002

**TELEPHONE NUMBER INFORMATION:** Main installation numbers: C-209-982-2000.

**LOCATION:** From north or south on I-5, exit east onto E. Roth Road to main entrance on right (south) side of road. Or from north or south on CA-99, exit west onto CA-120 approximately 3.5 miles west to north (right) on Airport Way approximately 5.1 miles to left (west) on E. Roth Road to main entrance on left (south) side of road. USMRA: Page 110 (C-7,8). NMC: Stockton, seven miles north.

**GENERAL INFORMATION:** Joint Service Command under the Defense Logistics Agency flag to continue the unified mission of supply and support to the military services.

**TEMPORARY MILITARY LODGING:** None. See Travis AFB listing.

**RV, CAMPING/FAMCAMP:** Travel Camp on post, year round, C-209-982-2232, D-312-462-2232; 12 camper spaces with full hookups.

**SPACE-A:** None. See Travis AFB.

**LOGISTICAL SUPPORT:**
| | |
|---|---|
| Exchange-982-3886 | SATO-982-2233 |

**ADMINISTRATIVE SUPPORT:**
| | |
|---|---|
| Locator-982-2000 | Police-982-2560 |
| Post Rest-982-2262 | |

**HEALTH & WELFARE:**
| | |
|---|---|
| CHAMPUS-982-3836 | Medical-982-3831 |
| Retiree Services-982-2213 | |

**REST & RECREATION:**
| | |
|---|---|
| Consol Club-982-2265 | Services-ext 2237 |

**OTHER FACILITIES AVAILABLE:** Arts & crafts, library, racquetball and tennis courts, swimming, youth center.

**ATTRACTIONS:** San Joaquin and Sacramento Valleys. San Francisco and Bay Area, 90 miles west. Reno/Tahoe to north; Yosemite National Park to south.

# SAN PEDRO COAST GUARD INTEGRATED SUPPORT COMMAND (CA25R4)

Commanding Officer
P.O. Box 8, Terminal Island Station
San Pedro, CA 90731-0208

**TELEPHONE NUMBER INFORMATION:** Main installation numbers: C-310-732-7400.
*Ten digit dialing required for local calls.*

**LOCATION:** On southwest end of Terminal Island. From San Pedro go east on CA-47 across Vincent Thomas Bridge to south on S. Ferry Street to right (west) on E. Terminal Way which becomes S. Seaside Avenue. Follow Coast Guard and Federal Corrections signs south to end of S. Seaside Avenue. Or from Long Beach, go west on Ocean Blvd. to south on S. Ferry Street and follow above directions. USMRA: Page 117 (C-7). NMC: Long Beach, six miles northeast.

**GENERAL INFORMATION:** Integrated Support Command for the Los Angeles area.

**TEMPORARY MILITARY LODGING:** Local Housing Authority, PCS, Base PO Box 8, Terminal Island Station, San Pedro, 0700-1530 daily, C-310-732-7560. BEQ only at CG ISC San Pedro. All ranks. DV/VIP 310-732-7400.

**RV, CAMPING/FAMCAMP:** None. See Big Bear Recreation Facility.

**SPACE-A:** Available at Los Angeles IAP; see Los Angeles AFB listing.

**LOGISTICAL SUPPORT:**          Exchange-732-7555

**ADMINISTRATIVE SUPPORT:**
| | |
|---|---|
| Housing Office-ext 7560 | OOD-ext 7400 |
| Pass/ID Office-ext 7420 | Public Affairs-ext 7354 |

**HEALTH & WELFARE:**
| | |
|---|---|
| CHAMPUS-ext 7500 | Dental-ext 7511 |
| Family Services-ext 7583 | |

**REST & RECREATION:** None. See Los Angeles AFB listing.

**OTHER FACILITIES AVAILABLE:** Barber shop, convenience store, dining facilities, laundry, education office, postal service.

**ATTRACTIONS:** Greater Los Angeles area.

# SEAL BEACH NAVAL WEAPONS STATION
## (CA80R4)
800 Seal Beach Boulevard
Seal Beach, CA 90740-5050

**TELEPHONE NUMBER INFORMATION:** Main installation numbers: C-562-626-7011, D-312-873-7011. WEB: www.sbeach.navy.mil

**LOCATION:** From east or west on I-405, take exit to Seal Beach Blvd. south. Continue south approximately 2.2 miles to main gate on left (east) side of street. USMRA: Page 117 (E-7). NMC: Long Beach, adjacent.

**GENERAL INFORMATION:** Home of the Seal Beach National Wildlife Refuge.

**TEMPORARY MILITARY LODGING:** BOQ: C-562-626-7227.

**RV, CAMPING/FAMCAMP:** None. See Los Angeles AFB listing.

**SPACE-A:** None. See Los Angeles AFB listing.

**LOGISTICAL SUPPORT:**
| | |
|---|---|
| Credit Union-626-7335 | Shoppette-431-8983 |
| Snack Bar-626-7555 | |

**ADMINISTRATIVE SUPPORT:**
| | |
|---|---|
| CDO/OOD-626-7229 | Fire Dept-626-7280 |
| Legal-626-7603 | Locator-626-7692 |
| Pass/ID Office-626-7230 | Police-626-7210 |
| Public Affairs-626-7215 | |

**HEALTH & WELFARE:**
| | |
|---|---|
| Chapel-626-7784 | Medical-626-7322 |

**REST & RECREATION:**
| | |
|---|---|
| All Hands Club-626-7105 | Camping Equip-ext 7555/7576 |
| Golf Course-430-9913 | Gym-ext 7278 |
| MWR-626-7106 | Rec Center/Equip-ext 7278 |
| Youth Activities-ext 7278 | |

**ATTRACTIONS:** Greater Los Angeles area, Hollywood.

# SIERRA ARMY DEPOT (CA44R4)
ATTN: SIOSI-CO
First Street, Building P-1
Herlong, CA 96113-5000

**TELEPHONE NUMBER INFORMATION:** Main installation numbers: C-530-827-2111, D-312-855-4910. E-mail: siosi-pa@sierra-emh.army.mil

**LOCATION:** Fifty-five miles northwest of Reno, NV, northeast of US-395. Northbound on US-395 from Reno, turn right (north) on CA-A26 (Garnier Road). When traveling south on US-395, turn left (northeast) on CA-A-25 (Herlong Access Road). Watch for signs. USMRA: Page 110 (E-4). NMC: Reno, NV, 55 miles southeast.

**GENERAL INFORMATION:** Major Army Materiel Command Depot, maintenance and storage activities.

**TEMPORARY MILITARY LODGING:** Lodging office, Building P-144, Mon-Thurs 0630-1700; other hours, Building P-100, C-530-827-4544/4345. All ranks.

**RV, CAMPING/FAMCAMP:** None. See Travis AFB listing.

**SPACE-A:** None. See Travis AFB listing.

**LOGISTICAL SUPPORT:**
| | |
|---|---|
| Conv Store-827-3292 | Commercial Travel-827-4175 |
| Commissary-827-4480 | Credit Union-827-2191 |
| Gas Station-827-3292 | Postal Service-827-3074 |
| Snack Bar-827-4442 | |

**ADMINISTRATIVE SUPPORT:**
| | |
|---|---|
| Fire Dept-827-4323 | Housing Office-827-5350 |
| Legal-827-4548 | Locator-827-4407 |
| Pass/ID Office-827-4108 | Police-827-4345 |
| Public Affairs-827-4343 | SDO/NCO-827-4345 |

**HEALTH & WELFARE:**
| | |
|---|---|
| ACS-827-4425 | Army Emergency Relief-827-4570 |
| CHAMPUS-827-4141 | Family Services-827-4425 |
| Medical-827-4575 | |
|   Emergency-827-4911 | |

**REST & RECREATION:**
| | |
|---|---|
| Bowling-827-4442 | Community Club-827-4360 |
| Gym-827-4497 | Library-827-4157 |
| MWR-827-4563 | Outdoor Rec-827-4354 |
| Swimming-827-4295 | Youth Services-827-4696 |
| *summer only* | |

**ATTRACTIONS:** Reno for entertainment, casinos. Lake Tahoe is a one-and-a-half hour drive south.

# SOUTH LAKE TAHOE
# RECREATION HOUSING (CA17R4)
228 Lewis Hall
Presidio of Monterey, CA 93944-5006

**TELEPHONE NUMBER INFORMATION:** Main installation numbers: C-831-242-5506, D-312-878-5506. E-mail: macksa@pom-emh1.army.mil WEB: pom-www.army.mil

**LOCATION:** Off post. Located at Lake Tahoe. Specific directions will be furnished when reservation is made. To Presidio of Monterey: From north or south on CA-I in Monterey, exit to Del Monte Blvd. and go west approximately 1.75 miles onto Lighthouse Avenue. Continue northwest and enter post from Lighthouse Avenue. Watch for signs. USMRA: Page 111 (B-9) .NMC: Monterey, in city limits.

**GENERAL INFORMATION:** Leased lodging facilities on the south shore of Lake Tahoe, operated by the Presidio of Monterey, year round. Military personnel active, reservists, retired, U.S. government civilian employees. Reservations (required, up to six months in advance): Outdoor Recreation Equipment Center, Bldg 228, Lewis Hall, Presidio of Monterey, CA 93944-5000. C-831-242-5506/6132/3, D-312-878-5506/6132, 1030-1400 hours and 1500-1800 hours, Mon-Fri.

**RV, CAMPING/FAMCAMP:**
| | |
|---|---|
| A-Frame Chalet-1 | Cabin-1 |
| Condos-2 | |

**ATTRACTIONS:** Located in Heavenly Resort Valley near a wide range of mountain and water-oriented recreational activities. Casinos located within a few miles.

*For detailed information about this off-base recreation facility, as well as on-base recreation facilities, golf courses and marinas, consult Military Living's Military RV, Camping and Outdoor Recreation Around the World.*

# TRAVIS AIR FORCE BASE (CA50R4)
400 Brennan Circle, Bldg 51
Travis Air Force Base, CA 94535-2712

**TELEPHONE NUMBER INFORMATION:** Main installation numbers: C-707-424-1110, D-312-837-1110. WEB: www.travis.af.mil

**LOCATION:** Halfway between San Francisco and Sacramento, off I-80. From north or south on I-80 take Airbase Parkway exit east at Fairfield directly to main gate. Clearly marked. USMRA: Page 110 (B,C-7). NMC: San Francisco, 45 miles southwest.

**GENERAL INFORMATION:** Air Mobility Command Base, 60th Air Mobility Wing, Headquarters 15th Air Force, 349th Air Mobility Wing (AFRES).

**TEMPORARY MILITARY LODGING:** Lodging office, Building 404, Sevedge Drive, 24 hours daily, C-707-437-0700. D-312-837-2987. All ranks. DV/VIP 707-424-3185.

**RV, CAMPING/FAMCAMP:** Travis FAMCAMP on base, year round, C-707-424-3583, D-312-837-3583, 70 camper spaces with full hookups, eight camper/tent spaces without hookups.

**SPACE-A:** Pax Term/Lounge, Building P-3, 24 hours daily, C-707-424-5703; Rec:C-707-424-1854 or 1-800-787-2534, D-312-837-1854; Fax: C-707-424-2048, D-312-837-2048. Flights to CONUS, OCONUS, and foreign locations.

**LOGISTICAL SUPPORT:**

| | |
|---|---|
| Car Rental-437-7300 | Child Care-424-0341 |
| Commissary-437-9211 | Dining Facilities-424-0906/2155 |
| Exchange-437-4634 | Gas Station-437-2232 |
| Package Store-437-3692 | Postal Service-437-2889 |
| SATO-437-7380 | Shoppette-437-6606 |

**ADMINISTRATIVE SUPPORT:**

| | |
|---|---|
| Legal-424-3251 | Locator-424-2798 |
| Police-424-3293 | |

**HEALTH & WELFARE:**

| | |
|---|---|
| Air Force Aid Society-424-4349 | American Red Cross-424-2262 |
| CHAMPUS-437-7100 | Chapel-424-3217 |
| Family Services-424-2486 | Medical |
| Retiree Services-424-3904 |   Central Appts-423-3000 |
| |   Emergency-423-3826 |

**REST & RECREATION:**

| | |
|---|---|
| Bowling-ext 5048 | Clubs |
| Fitness Center-ext 5680 |   Aero-437-3470 |
| Golf Course-ext 5797 |   EM-424-5071 |
| Hobby Shops-ext 1338 |   O-424-3711 |
| Library-ext 3279 |   Saddle-437-9060 |
| Museum-ext 5605 | Rec Center-424-5659 |
| Youth Center-ext 5392 | Theater-437-3855 |

**ATTRACTIONS:** Travis Air Museum, San Francisco 55 miles southwest, Sacramento 45 miles northeast, discount outlet stores in Vacaville, Solano Mall in Fairfield, Busch Brewery, Western Railway Museum, Jelly-Belly Factory.

# TWENTYNINE PALMS MARINE CORPS AIR/GROUND COMBAT CENTER (CA27R4)

Box 788101
Twentynine Palms, CA 92278-8101

**TELEPHONE NUMBER INFORMATION:** Main installation numbers: C-760-830-6000, D-312-957-6000. WEB: www.29palms.usmc.mil

**LOCATION:** East or west on I-10 to CA-62 (exit to Twentynine Palms/Yucca Valley). Take CA-62 (29 Palms Highway) east approximately 46 miles to town of Twentynine Palms. Once in town take Adobe Road north (left) to main gate of base, approximately five miles. USMRA: Page 111 (H,I-13,14). NMC: Palm Springs, 60 miles northwest.

**GENERAL INFORMATION:** Headquarters Battalion, Marine Corps Communication-Electronics School, 7th Marine Regiment, Combat Service Support Group-1, Aviation Ground Support Element, Marine Unmanned Aerial Vehicle Squadron-1, "D" Company, 3rd Assault Amphibian Battalion, 1st Tank Battalion, 3rd Battalion, 11th Marines, 3rd Light Armored Reconnaissance Battalion.

**TEMPORARY MILITARY LODGING:** Building 1565, 5th Street, 24 hours daily, C-760-830-6583, D-312-957-6583. All ranks. DV/VIP C-760-830-6109.

**RV, CAMPING/FAMCAMP:** See Big Bear Rec Facility.

**SPACE-A:** None. See Los Angeles AFB listing.

**LOGISTICAL SUPPORT:**

| | |
|---|---|
| Bank-830-6103 | Barber Shop-830-6163 |
| Beauty Shop-830-6163 | Cafeteria-830-6989 |
| Car Rental-830-6752 | Child Care-830-6269 |
| Child Dev Center-830-5589 | Conv Store-830-6138 |
| Commissary-830-7572 | Dry Cleaner-830-6163 |
| Education Office-830-4702 | Exchange-830-6163 |
| Gas Station-830-6693 | Package Store-830-6860 |
| SATO-830-6622 | Snack Bar-830-6163 |
| Visitor Center-830-5453 | |

**ADMINISTRATIVE SUPPORT:**

| | |
|---|---|
| CDO/OOD-830-7200 | Fire Dept-830-5239 |
| Housing Office-830-6075 | Legal-830-5270 |
| Locator-830-6000 | Pass/ID Office-830-7440 |
| Police-830-5457 | Public Affairs-830-6213 |
| Quarter Deck-830-2037 | |

**HEALTH & WELFARE:**

| | |
|---|---|
| American Red Cross-830-6685 | CHAMPUS-830-2572 |
| Chapel-830-6464 | Dental-830-7663 |
| Community Services-830-6540 |   Central Appts-830-7053 |
| Medical-830-2037 |   Clinic-830-7664 |
|   Central Appts-830-2286 |   Emergency-830-7043 |
|   Emergency-830-2398 | Navy-MC Relief-830-7451 |
|   Health Benefits-830-2572 | Retiree Services-830-7550 |
|   Information-830-2872 | TRICARE-830-2572 |
| Veterinary Services-830-7521 | |

**REST & RECREATION:**

| | |
|---|---|
| Auto Hobby Shop-830-4179 | Bowling-830-6422 |
| Clubs | Fitness Center-830-6451 |
|   Combined-830-4138 | Golf Course-830-6132 |
|   NCO-830-4140 | Gym-830-6440 |
|   O-830-6610 | ITT Office-830-6163 ext 264 |
| Library-830-6875 | MWR-830-6163 |
| Outdoor Rec-830-7235 | Services-830-6163 |
| Theater-830-5236 ext 264 |   Hunting |
| Wood Hobby Shop-830-7214 |   Riding Stables |
| Youth Center-830-6269 |   Skeet Range |
| Youth Services-830-6269 |   Swimming |

**ATTRACTIONS:** Joshua Tree National Monument. Locale is in the center of Southern California's attraction areas: Two-and-a-half hours to Los Angeles, three-and-a-half hours to San Diego, one-and-a-half hours to Palm Springs, three hours to Las Vegas, NV and one-and-a-half hours to Laughlin, NV.

# VANDENBERG AIR FORCE BASE (CA29R4)

30 SW/PA
747 Nebraska Avenue, Suite A 103, Building 10577
Vandenberg Air Force Base, CA 93437-6267

**TELEPHONE NUMBER INFORMATION:** Main installation numbers: C-805-606-1110, D-312-276-1110. For extension numbers below: call main installation number and wait for recording, then dial extension or "0" for operator assistance. E-mail: pubaffairs@plans.vafb.af.mil

**LOCATION:** From the north on US-101, exit westbound at Santa Maria onto Clark Avenue, then go west approximately 2.3 miles to left (south) on CA-135 which merges into CA-1. Continue southbound on CA-1 directly to main gate. Or, from the south, take US-101 north to Buelton. Exit northwest onto CA-246. Just before Lompoc, bear right on Purisima Road which runs into CA-1. Follow CA-1 northwest to the main gate on left. USMRA: Page 111. (C-12). NMC: Santa Barbara, 55 miles southeast.

**GENERAL INFORMATION:** Air Force Space Command, 30th Space Wing.

**TEMPORARY MILITARY LODGING:** Lodging office, Building 13005, 24 hours daily, C-805-734-1111, ext 2802; D-312-276-1844. All ranks. Two suites for handicapped. DV/VIP C-805-734-3711.

**RV, CAMPING/FAMCAMP:** FAMCAMP on base, year round, Building 10122, C-805-606-8579, D-312-276-8579; 20 camper spaces with full hookups, 30 camper spaces with W/E, 19 camper spaces without hookups, 15 tent spaces.

**SPACE-A:** Pax Term: Building 1749, 0800-1700 daily, C-805-606-1854/7742, D-312-276-1854/7742.

## LOGISTICAL SUPPORT:

| | |
|---|---|
| Barber Shop-734-1259 | Beauty Shop-734-1264 |
| Cafeteria-606-3330 | Child Care-606-4639 |
| Child Dev Center-606-1555 | Class Six-605-8269 |
| Commissary-605-8812 | Conv Store-605-8269 |
| Credit Union-734-8550 | Dining Facilities-606-7540 |
| Dry Cleaner-734-3039 | Education Office-606-5936 |
| Exchange-734-5521 | Gas Station-734-3566 |
| Laundry-734-3039 | Postal Service-606-3766 |
| SATO-734-4381 | Shoppette-734-2250 |
| Visitor Center-606-7662 | |

## ADMINISTRATIVE SUPPORT:

| | |
|---|---|
| Fire Dept-ext 6-4680 | Housing Office-ext 6-3434 |
| Legal-605-6207 | Locator-606-1841 |
| Pass/ID Office-606-1853 | Police-606-3911 |
| Public Affairs-606-3595 | |

## HEALTH & WELFARE:

| | |
|---|---|
| Air Force Aid Society-605-8551 | American Red Cross-800-660-4272 |
| CHAMPUS-734-1878 | Chapel-606-5773 |
| Dental-606-1846 | Family Services-606-5484 |
| Medical-606-3011/6-3875 | Retiree Services-606-5474 |
| TRICARE-734-1878 | Veterinary Services-606-3019 |

## REST & RECREATION:

| | |
|---|---|
| Arts & Crafts-606-6438 | Auto Hobby Shop-606-6014 |
| Bowling-734-1310 | Ceramics-606-5209 |
| Clubs | Community Center-606-7976 |
|   Aero-734-2733 | Fitness Center-606-3832 |
|   Co-located-734-4376 | Fitness Center Annex-606-4699 |
|   Rod & Gun-606-4560 | Golf Course-606-6262 |
| Gym-606-3832 | ITT-606-7976 |
| Library-606-6414 | MWR-606-0960 |
| Outdoor Rec-606-8579 | Rec Center-606-7976 |
| Services-606-5031 | Swimming-606-3581 |
| Theater-734-1315 | Wood Hobby Shop-606-4567 |
| Youth Center-606-0035 | |

**ATTRACTIONS:** Great beaches, historic missions, Hearst Castle, north of AFB.

# COLORADO

## BUCKLEY AIR NATIONAL GUARD BASE (CO11R3)

18500 East Sixth Street
Buckley ANGB, CO 80011-9599

**TELEPHONE NUMBER INFORMATION:** Main installation numbers: C-303-677-9011, D-312-877-9011.
*Ten digit dialing required for local calls.*

**LOCATION:** From north or south on I-225, take Exit #9 east onto East 6th Avenue (CO-30) 2.5 miles east to main gate on south (right) side of road. Clearly marked. USMRA: Page 109 (G-3), Page 116 (C,D-3,4). NMC: Denver, 21 miles west,

**GENERAL INFORMATION:** 140th Wing, 200th Airlift Squadron, 2nd Space Warning Squadron, 821st Space Group, Navy/Marine Reserve Training Center, Army Aviation Support Facility, 743rd Military Intelligence Battalion, 566th Operations Support Squadron.

**TEMPORARY MILITARY LODGING:** None. See Peterson AFB listing.

**RV, CAMPING/FAMCAMP:** None. See USAF Academy listing, Farish Rec Area.

**SPACE-A:** None. See Peterson AFB listing.

## LOGISTICAL SUPPORT:

| | |
|---|---|
| Barber Shop-677-6898 | Child Dev Center-677-6174 |
| Class Six-677-6898 | Credit Union-677-9829 |
| Education Office-677-6675 | Laundry-677-6898 |
| Shoppette-677-6898 | |

## ADMINISTRATIVE SUPPORT:

| | |
|---|---|
| Fire Dept-677-9924 (non emergency) | Housing Office-677-6361 |
| Pass/Registration Office-677-9935 | Police-677-9930 |
| Public Affairs-677-9431 | |

## HEALTH & WELFARE:

| | |
|---|---|
| Air Force Aid Society-677-6694 | Dental-Clinic-367-3360 |
| Family Services-677-6693 | Medical-677-6458 |
| Retiree Services-677-6693/6694 | |

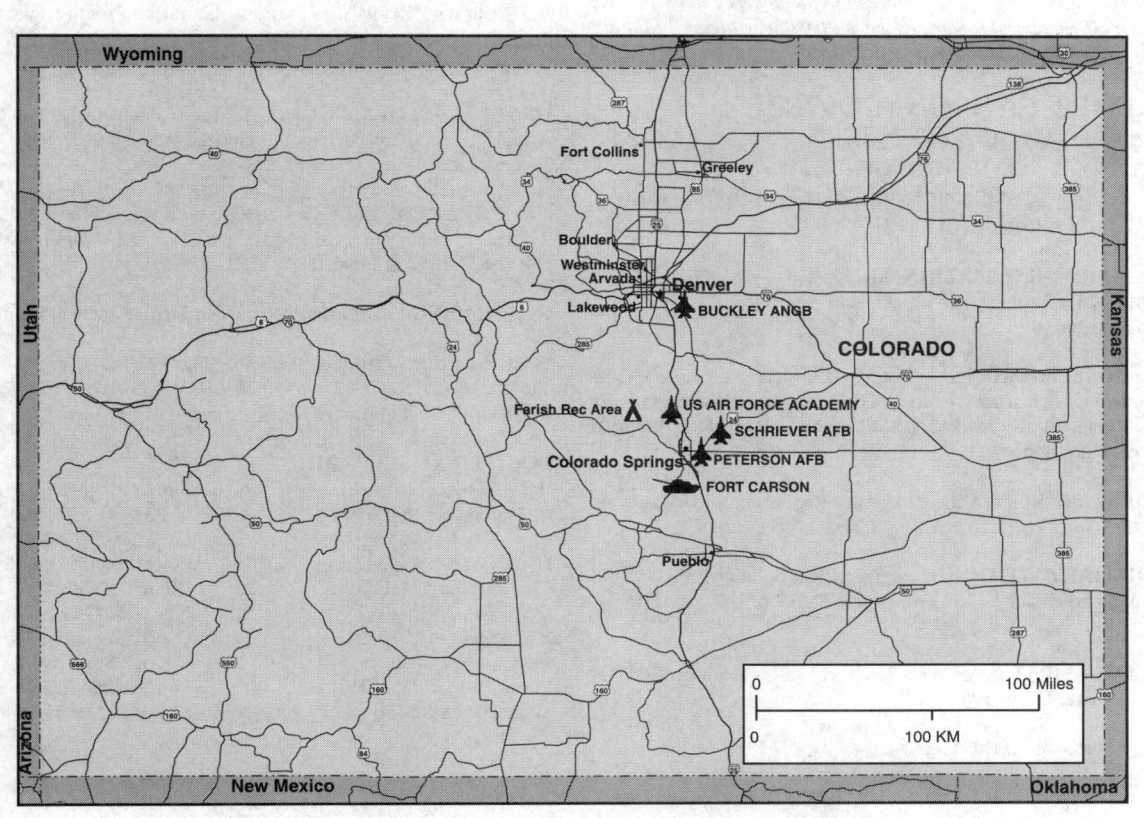

**REST & RECREATION:**

All Ranks Club-677-9840          Community Center-677-6693
Fitness Center-677-6679          ITT-677-6853

**ATTRACTIONS:** Denver nearby. Snow sports, Pro sports teams, National Western Stock Show and Rodeo in January.

# FARISH RECREATION AREA (CO01R3)

P.O. Box 146
Woodland Park, CO 80866-0146

**TELEPHONE NUMBER INFORMATION:** Main installation numbers: C-719-687-9098, D-312-259-9098.

**LOCATION:** From north or south on I-25 at Colorado Springs, take exit #141 onto US-24 west for 18 miles to Woodland Park. At second stoplight near McDonalds, turn right (north) onto Baldwin Street. (County Road 22) which changes to Rampart Range Road. Follow road through four stop signs. Road forks just past water treatment facility; keep left and follow Farish signs. Approx. 0.2 mile after road changes from asphalt to dirt, turn right onto Forest Service Road 312 which dead ends into facility. USMRA: Page 109 (F-4). NMI: U.S. Air Force Academy, 35 miles east; Peterson AFB and Fort Carson, 40 miles southeast. NMC: Colorado Springs, 30 miles southeast.

**GENERAL INFORMATION:** Operated by U.S. Air Force Academy, off base year round for lodge and cottage and day use; campsites closed during the winter. Call for conditions during winter months. Military personnel active, retired, reserve, DoD civilians and retired/NAF civilians. Questions may be addressed to Farish Management, C-719-687-9098. Reservations (required): C-719-687-9098/9306, Fax C-719-686-1437.

**TEMPORARY MILITARY LODGING:**

Cottage-1                        Duplexes-6
Sleeping Lodge-4 rooms

**RV, CAMPING/FAMCAMP:**

Camper spaces-15                 Camper space pavilion-3
Camper cabins-4                  Primitive tent spaces-unlimited

**ATTRACTIONS:** Abundant wildlife and three fishing lakes. Enjoy a mountain getaway with a real backwoods feel within driving distance of area attractions.

*For detailed information about this off-base recreation facility, as well as on-base recreation facilities, golf courses and marinas, consult Military Living's Military RV, Camping and Outdoor Recreation Around the World.*

# FORT CARSON (CO02R3)

4TH ID & Fort Carson
ATTN: AFZC-GC
Building 1544
Fort Carson, CO 80913-5000

**TELEPHONE NUMBER INFORMATION:** Main installation numbers: C-719-526-5811, D-312-691-5811. E-mail: pao@carson-ctch1.army.mil WEB: www.carson.army.mil

**LOCATION:** From north or south on I-25, take exit #135 west onto CO-83 (Academy Blvd. for two miles to a left (south) on Co-115 for two miles to main gate on left (east) side of road. Clearly marked. USMRA: Page 109 (C,D-6,7). NMC: Colorado Springs, six miles north.

**GENERAL INFORMATION:** 3rd Armored Cavalry Regiment; 3rd Brigade, 4th Infantry Division; 43rd Support Group and 10th Special Forces Group.

**TEMPORARY MILITARY LODGING:** Lodging office, Building 731, Woodfill Road, Colorado Inn, 24 hours daily, C-719-526-4832, D-312-691-4832. All ranks. DV/VIP C-719-526-5811.

**RV, CAMPING/FAMCAMP:** Turkey Creek Ranch, 12 miles south on CO-115, Rec Area and Ranch House, C-719-526-3905.

**SPACE-A:** None. See Peterson AFB listing.

**LOGISTICAL SUPPORT:**

Bank-526-6601                    Carlson Wagonlit Travel-576-5404
Child Care-526-4188              Class Six-576-6531
Commissary-526-5644              Conv Store-576-1803
Exchange-576-6313                Gas Station-576-4096

**ADMINISTRATIVE SUPPORT:**

Fire Dept-526-5615               Legal-526-5572
Locator-526-0227                 Police-526-2333
Public Affairs-526-1269          SDO/SNCO-526-3400

**HEALTH & WELFARE:**

ACS-526-4590                     Chapel-526-0480
Family Services-526-4590         Medical-526-7298
TRICARE-526-7256                   Central Appts-264-5000
                                   Emergency-526-7111

**REST & RECREATION:**

Arts & Crafts-526-0900           Auto Hobby Shop-526-2147
Bowling-526-5542                 All Ranks Club-576-7540
Events Center-576-6646           Fitness Center-526-2597
Golf Course-526-4122             ITT-526-5366
Library-526-2350                 MWR-526-1992
Outdoor Rec-526-2083             Rec Equipment-526-1992/3
Swimming                         Wood Hobby Shop-526-3487
  Indoor-526-5739                Youth Activities-526-2680
  Outdoor-526-4456

**ATTRACTIONS:** USAF Academy, guided tours, Colorado Springs, Pikes Peak, museums, Seven Falls.

# PETERSON AIR FORCE BASE (CO06R3)

21 Space Wing
775 Loring Avenue, Suite 241
Peterson Air Force Base, CO 80914-1294

**TELEPHONE NUMBER INFORMATION:** Main installation numbers: C-719-556-4020, D-312-834-4020. WEB: www.spacecom.af.mil

**LOCATION:** Off US-24 (Platte Avenue) east of Colorado Springs. Eastbound from Colorado Springs on US-24, keep right onto CO-94 for 0.2 miles to right (south) on Peterson Blvd. directly to main gate. Clearly marked. Or, westbound on US-24, take exit south onto CO-94 then west for 0.2 miles to south (right) on Peterson Blvd. directly to main gate. USMRA: Page 109 (G-5); page 116 (D,E-5,6). NMC: Colorado Springs, six miles west.

**GENERAL INFORMATION:** U.S. Space Command, Air Force Space Command, Army Space Command, North American Aerospace Defense Command, 302nd Tactical Airlift Wing (Reserve), 21st Space Wing.

**TEMPORARY MILITARY LODGING:** Lodging office, Building 1042, Stewart Avenue, 24 hours daily, C-719-556-8048, D-312-834-8048, Fax: C-719-556-7852, D-312-834-7852. All ranks. DV/VIP C-719-556-5007.

**RV, CAMPING/FAMCAMP:** None. See USAF Academy listing, Farish Rec Area.

**SPACE-A:** Pax Term/Lounge, Building 123, C-719-556-4521/4707, D-312-834-4521/4707; Rec: C-719-556-4707, D-312-834-4707; Fax: C-719-556-4979, D-312-834-4979. Flights to CONUS locations.

**LOGISTICAL SUPPORT:**

Bank-574-2777                    Barber Shop-597-8307
Beauty Shop-596-0579             Child Care-556-7460
Child Dev Center-556-7460        Class Six-597-5041
Commissary-556-4247              Conv Store-597-5041
Credit Union-574-1100            Dining Facilities-556-4180
Dry Cleaner-597-3050             Education Office-556-4064
Exchange-596-7270                Gas Station-597-0360
Laundry-597-3050                 Package Store-597-5685
Postal Service-556-4596          Professional Travel-556-4199
Shoppette-597-5041               Visitor Center-556-6406

**ADMINISTRATIVE SUPPORT:**

Fire Dept-556-4790

Legal-556-4871

Pass/ID Office-556-7577

Public Affairs-556-4696

Housing Office-556-4364

Locator-556-4020

Police-556-4805

**HEALTH & WELFARE:**

Air Force Aid Society-556-6141

CHAMPUS-556-1057

Dental-556-1000

Medical-556-1000

   Health Benefits-556-1657

American Red Cross-556-7570

Chapel-556-4442

Family Services-556-7614

Retiree Services-556-7153

TRICARE-556-1053

**REST & RECREATION:**

Auto Hobby Shop-556-4481

Clubs

   Aero-ext 4310

   NCO-556-4194

   O-576-4181

   Rod/Gun-ext 7688

Library-556-7462

Outdoor Rec-556-4867

   Camping Equipment

Skeet/Trap-ext 7688

Swimming-ext 4608

Youth Services-556-7220

Bowling-556-4607

Community Center-556-7671

Fitness Center-556-8069

Golf Course-556-7414

ITT-556-7671

   Hobby Shops

Museum-556-4915

Rec Center-ext 7941

Rec Equipment-ext 7751

Ski Shop-ext 4487

Youth Center-ext 7413

**ATTRACTIONS:** Fine Arts Center, Seven Falls, Museums, Pikes Peak, Royal Gorge, Railway in Manitou Springs, ski resorts, U.S. Olympic Training Center.

## SCHRIEVER AIR FORCE BASE (CO13R3)

300 O'Malley Avenue

Schriever Air Force Base, CO 80912-3024

**TELEPHONE NUMBER INFORMATION:** Main installation numbers: C-719-567-1110, D-560-1110.

**LOCATION:** From Colorado Springs, go east on US-94 to intersection with CO-94. Keep right and continue east on CO-94 approximately 8.9 miles beyond intersection to a right (south) turn on Enoch Road. Facility is located on west side of Enoch Road. USMRA: Page 109 (G-5). NMC Colorado Springs, 10 miles west.

**GENERAL INFORMATION:** This is a closed security base, home of 50th Space Wing, Ballistic Missile Defense Organization, Space Warfare Center.

**TEMPORARY MILITARY LODGING:** None. See Peterson AFB listing.

**RV, CAMPING/FAMCAMP:** None. See USAF Academy listing, Farish Rec Area listing.

**SPACE-A:** None. See Peterson AFB listing.

**LOGISTICAL SUPPORT:**

Cafeteria-567-8752

Visitor Center-567-5643/5620

**ADMINISTRATIVE SUPPORT:**

Fire Dept-567-3370

Locator-567-5305

Police-567-5643

Legal-567-5050

Pass/ID Office-567-5620

Public Affairs-567-5040

**HEALTH & WELFARE:**

Chapel-567-3705

Medical-567-6666

Dental-567-5065

**REST & RECREATION:**

Fitness Center-567-2666

ITT-567-6050

**ATTRACTIONS:** Pikes Peak, ski resorts, Colorado Springs.

## UNITED STATES AIR FORCE ACADEMY (CO07R3)

2304 Cadet Drive, Suite 316

United States Air Force Academy, CO 80840-5001

**TELEPHONE NUMBER INFORMATION:** Main installation numbers: C-719-333-1110, D-312-333-1110.

**LOCATION:** West of I-25, north of Colorado Springs. From I-25 north or south, use Exit #150B northwest onto Southgate Blvd. which leads to main visitors' entrance. Or take exit #150A west onto Northgate Blvd. which leads to Stadium Blvd. on the left (south ) side of the road. Clearly marked. NMC: USMRA: Page 109 (F-4,5), page 115 (A,B-1,2; C-1,2,3). NMC: Colorado Springs, eight miles south.

**GENERAL INFORMATION:** U.S. Air Force Academy, education of future Air Force officers, and other tenant units.

**TEMPORARY MILITARY LODGING:** Lodging office, Building 3130, Academy Drive, C-719-333-3061. All ranks. DV/VIP C-719-472-3540.

**RV, CAMPING/FAMCAMP:** Operates Farish Recreation Area off base, 35 miles west of post. See Farish Recreation Area listing for more information. Peregrine Pines FAMCAMP on base, year-round, C-719-333-4356/4980, 53 camping sites, including 40 sites with with E/S, picnic tables, barbecue grills, and 13 other sites for tent camping, 45 camper spaces with full hookups, 33 camper spaces without hookups.

**SPACE-A:** None. See Peterson AFB listing.

**LOGISTICAL SUPPORT:**

Barber Shop-472-1369

Child Care-333-4733

Class Six-472-0554

Conv Store-472-0395

Dining Facilities

   Airmen's Dining Hall-333-4730

Education Office-333-2269

Gas Station-472-0395

Package Store-472-0554

Professional Travel-472-6644

Visitor Center-333-2555

Beauty Shop-472-1495

Child Dev Center-333-4166

Commissary-333-3610

Credit Union-472-1090

Dry Cleaning-472-6216

Exchange-472-0861

Laundry-472-6216

Postal Service-333-3505

Snack Bar-472-1321

**ADMINISTRATIVE SUPPORT:**

Housing Office-333-2100

Locator-333-4262

Public Affairs-333-4050

Legal-333-3642

Police-333-2000

**HEALTH & WELFARE:**

CHAMPUS-333-4983

Family Services-333-3444

Chapel-333-3300

Medical

   Central Appts-264-5000

   Emergency-333-5000

**REST & RECREATION:**

Arts & Crafts-333-4579

Bowling-333-4709

Golf Course-333-4735

Gym-333-4522

ITT-333-3241

Pool-333-4430

Sports Tickets-472-1895

Auto Hobby Shop-333-4752

Clubs

   EM-472-0061/333-4377

   O-333-4253

Library-333-4665

Sports Info-800-666-8723

Stables-333-4607

**ATTRACTIONS:** Pikes Peak, snow skiing, ghost towns, Colorado Springs.

# CONNECTICUT

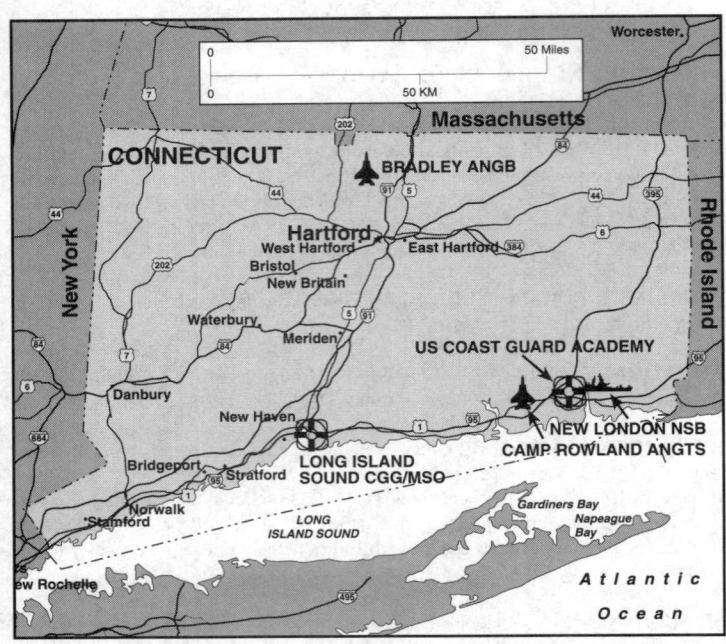

## BRADLEY AIR NATIONAL GUARD BASE (CT03R1)

100 Nicholson Road
East Granby, CT 06026-9390

**TELEPHONE NUMBER INFORMATION:** Main installation numbers: C-860-292-8356, D-312-636-8356.
*Ten digit dialing required for local calls.*

**LOCATION:** Take I-91 north or south, exit to 40 west. Follow signs to route 20 (East Granby) and base. USMRA: Page 16 (E-5,6). NMC: Hartford, 10 miles south.

**GENERAL INFORMATION:** 103rd Fighter Wing, "The Flying Yankees," 118th Tactical Fighter Squadron and other support units and facilities.

**TEMPORARY MILITARY LODGING:** None. See Westover ARB, MA listing.

**RV, CAMPING/FAMCAMP:** None. See United States Coast Guard Academy listing.

**SPACE-A:** None. See Westover ARB, MA listing.

**LOGISTICAL SUPPORT:**      Exchange-653-6994

**ADMINISTRATIVE SUPPORT:**
Legal-292-2478                    Police-292-2312
Public Affairs-292-2506

**HEALTH & WELFARE:**      Chapel-292-2445

**REST & RECREATION:** None. See New London NSB listing.

**ATTRACTIONS:** Historic Newgate Prison and the homes of Mark Twain and Harriet Beecher Stowe located within one hour's drive. New England Air Museum adjacent to Bradley IAP.

## CAMP ROWLAND ARMY NATIONAL GUARD TRAINING SITE (CT05R1)

38 Smith Street
Niantic, CT 06357-2597

**TELEPHONE NUMBER INFORMATION:** Main installation numbers: C-860-691-6000, D-312-636-6000.

**LOCATION:** From I-95 north or south, exit 74 south, follow Route 161 toward Niantic Center, turn right onto Smith Street. USMRA: Page 16 (F,G-9). NMC: New London, 11 miles north.

**GENERAL INFORMATION:** Tenant activities: Northeast Leadership Training Regiment; Co C 280th Signal Battalion; 208th Personnel Detachment, Detachment 5 Medical Detachment.

**TEMPORARY MILITARY LODGING:** 38 Smith Street, 0800-1600 Mon-Fri, C-860-691-6001, D-312-636-6000. Two cottages.

**RV, CAMPING/FAMCAMP:** None. See Newport NS, RI listing.

**SPACE-A:** None. See Bradley ANG listing.

**LOGISTICAL SUPPORT:**
Exchange-739-9672                    Visitor Center-691-6001

**ADMINISTRATIVE SUPPORT:**      Police-691-6008

**HEALTH & WELFARE:** None. See United States Coast Guard Academy listing.

**REST & RECREATION:** Fitness center, outdoor rec available.

**OTHER FACILITIES AVAILABLE:** Laundry, locator, outdoor rec (basketball, baseball, soccer) available.

**ATTRACTIONS:** State parks, beaches, casinos.

## LONG ISLAND SOUND COAST GUARD GROUP/MARINE SAFETY OFFICE (CT04R1)

120 Woodward Avenue
New Haven, CT 06512-3698

**TELEPHONE NUMBER INFORMATION:** Main installation numbers: C-203-468-4400.

**LOCATION:** Take I-95 north to exit 50, right at light. Unit is one mile on right. Take I-95 south to the New Haven Airport exit 51 (Frontage Road). Pass shopping center, left at second light. Unit is one mile on the right. USMRA: Page 16 (E-9). NMC: New Haven, in city limits.

**GENERAL INFORMATION:** MSO, Long Island Sound, Aid to Navigation Team, Long Island Sound, USCGC Bollard and CGSTA New Haven.

**TEMPORARY MILITARY LODGING:** None. See New London NSB listing.

**RV, CAMPING/FAMCAMP:** None. See Newport NS, RI listing.

**SPACE-A:** None. See Stewart ANGB, NY listing.

**LOGISTICAL SUPPORT:**      Exchange-468-2712

**ADMINISTRATIVE SUPPORT:**
CDO-468-4401                    OOD-468-4455
Pass/ID Office-468-4450            Public Affairs-468-4464

**HEALTH & WELFARE:**      CHAMPUS-468-4415

**REST & RECREATION:** None. See New London NSB listing.

**ATTRACTIONS:** New Haven: Yale University, museums, boating, shopping.

# NEW LONDON NAVAL SUBMARINE BASE
## (CT01R1)
Route 12 and Crystal Lake Road
Groton, CT 06349-5044

**TELEPHONE NUMBER INFORMATION:** Main installation numbers: C-860-694-4636, D-312-694-4500.

**LOCATION:** From I-95 north or south, take exit 86 to CT-12. Turn left on Crystal Lake Road. Main gate on right. Base clearly marked. USMRA: Page 16 (G,H-8), page 25 (C,D-1). NMC: Hartford, 50 miles northwest.

**GENERAL INFORMATION:** Naval Submarine School, Naval Underwater Medical Institute, Naval Ambulatory Care Clinic, Commander Submarine Group Two, Submarine Group Four, Naval Submarine Support Facility, Submarine Squadrons Two and Twelve.

**TEMPORARY MILITARY LODGING:** Navy Lodge, Building CT-380, 77 Dewey Avenue, 0700-2300 daily, Check in 1500-1800, Check out 1200, C-860-446-1160, D-312-241-1160. All ranks, BEQ C-860-694-2408, BOQ C-860-694-2105. DV/VIP C-860-694-2105.

**RV, CAMPING/FAMCAMP:** None. See Newport NS, RI listing.

**SPACE-A:** None. See Stewart ANGB, NY listing.

**LOGISTICAL SUPPORT:**

| | |
|---|---|
| Child Care-694-3519 | Commissary-694-3911 |
| Conv Store-446-8593 | Dining Facilities |
| Exchange-694-3811 |   Enlisted Galley-694-3679 |
| Package Store-694-3535 | SATO-694-3404 |

**ADMINISTRATIVE SUPPORT:**

| | |
|---|---|
| CDO/OOD-694-3777 | Fire Dept-694-3333 |
| Legal-694-3741 | Locator-694-3087 |
| Pass/ID Office-694-3224 | Police-694-3222 |
| Public Affairs-694-3889 | |

**HEALTH & WELFARE:**

| | |
|---|---|
| CHAMPUS-694-4968 | Chapel-694-3232 |
| Family Services-694-3383 | Medical-694-3428 |
| Retiree Services-694-3284 |   Central Appts-694-4877 |
| |   Emergency-694-3333 |

**REST & RECREATION:**

| | |
|---|---|
| Auto Hobby Shop-ext 3582 | Bowling-ext-3477 |
| Clubs | Golf Course-694-3763 |
|   CPO-694-3721 | Gym-ext 4205 |
|   EM-694-3050 | Hobby Shops-ext 3217 |
| ITT-694-3238 | Library-ext 3723 |
| Marina-ext 3164 | MWR-694-3238 |
| Recreation-694-3238 | Services-ext 3687 |
| Swimming-ext 3562 | Theater-694-3358 |

**ATTRACTIONS:** USCG Academy, Nautilus Memorial/Submarine Library and Museum.

# UNITED STATES COAST GUARD ACADEMY
## (CT02R1)
15 Mohegan Avenue
New London, CT 06320-4195

**TELEPHONE NUMBER INFORMATION:** Main installation numbers: C-860-444-8474, or 860-444-8474. WEB: www.cga.edu/

**LOCATION:** From southbound I-95 take exit 83 in New London. From northbound I-95 take exit 82-A. Follow signs, CT-32, Mohegan Drive, clearly marked. USMRA: Page 16 (G-8,9), page 25 (C-2). NMI: New London NSB, across the Thames. NMC: New Haven, 40 miles west.

**GENERAL INFORMATION:** The Officer Education and Training Academy for the U.S. Coast Guard.

**TEMPORARY MILITARY LODGING:** Billeting Office, Building 3130, Academy Drive, 24 hours daily, C-860-446-1160. Guest Quarters: C-860-444-8325. VIP Quarters: C-860-444-8499.

**RV, CAMPING/FAMCAMP:** None. See Newport NS, RI listing.

**SPACE-A:** None. See Stewart ANGB, NY listing.

**LOGISTICAL SUPPORT:**

| | |
|---|---|
| Barber Shop-444-8306/8454 | Bookstore-444-8308 |
| Cafeteria-444-8148 | Child Dev Center-444-8329 |
| Conv Store-444-8491 | Credit Union-439-0780 |
| Dining Facilities-444-8148 | Dry Cleaner-437-1212 |
| Exchange-444-8488/87 | Gas Station-444-8494 |
| Main Gate-444-8614 | Package Store-444-8491 |
| Personnel Support Center-444-8689 | Postal Service-444-6752 |
| Snack Bar-444-8473 | Travel Office-440-0696 |
| Visitor Center-444-8611 | |

**ADMINISTRATIVE SUPPORT:**

| | |
|---|---|
| Housing Office-444-8211 | Legal-701-6795 |
| OOD-444-8452 | Pass/ID Office-444-8208 |
| Police-444-8597 | Public Affairs-444-8270 |
| SDO/NCO-444-8450/1 | |

**HEALTH & WELFARE:**

| | |
|---|---|
| American Red Cross-444-8400 | CHAMPUS-444-8432 |
| Chapel-444-8480 | Dental-444-8424 |
| Medical | |
|   Central Appts-444-8401 | |
|   Health Benefits-444-8408 | |

**REST & RECREATION:**

| | |
|---|---|
| Bowling-444-8470 | Clubs |
| Equipment Rental-ext 8476 |   EM-444-8456 |
| Events Recording-442-1092 |   O-444-8458 |
| Fitness Center/Gym-ext 8600 | Hobby Shop-ext 8489 |
| Library-444-8510 | Musical Activities-ext 8471 |
| MWR Office-444-8476 | Ticket Office-ext 8154 |
| Visitors Center (May-Oct)-444-8611 | |

**ATTRACTIONS:** Self-guided tours of the Academy; Visitor's Pavilion (May-October); Museum (year round); when in port, the barque *EAGLE* is open to the public; formal reviews by the Corps of Cadets are held on the Washington parade ground on Fridays (fall & spring); Mystic Seaport; Casinos.

# DELAWARE

# DELAWARE ARMY NATIONAL GUARD
## (DE03R1)
Bethany Beach Training Site, Route 1
Bethany Beach, DE 19930-5000

**TELEPHONE NUMBER INFORMATION:** Main installation numbers: C-302-854-7902, D-312-440-7902.

**LOCATION:** Located on west side of DE-1, half a mile north of DE-26 and US-1 intersection in Bethany Beach. USMRA: Page 42 (J-6). NMC: Bethany Beach, in city limits.

**GENERAL INFORMATION:** Delaware Army National Guard training site.

**TEMPORARY MILITARY LODGING:** For info call C-302-854-7902.

**RV, CAMPING/FAMCAMP:** C-302-854-7902, D-312-440-7902, Fax: C-302-854-7999, D-312-440-7999. Twenty-three mobile homes, four apartments and 10 campsites.

**SPACE-A:** None. See Dover AFB listing.

**LOGISTICAL SUPPORT:**      Exchange-854-7900 (seasonal)

**ADMINISTRATIVE SUPPORT:** None. See Dover AFB listing.

**HEALTH & WELFARE:** None. See Dover AFB listing.

**REST & RECREATION:**      Fitness center-854-7902

**ATTRACTIONS:** Beach resorts, amusement parks, beaches.

## DOVER AIR FORCE BASE (DE01R1)
201 Eagle Way
Dover Air Force Base, DE 19902-7209

**TELEPHONE NUMBER INFORMATION:** Main installation numbers: C-302-677-3000, D-312-445-3000. WEB: www.dover.af.mil/~airlift

**LOCATION:** From Philadelphia, take I-95 south to Route 13 south. Base is five miles south of Dover, on east side of DE-1 toll or US-13. Follow signs to base. Clearly marked. USMRA: Page 42 (I-3,4). NMC: Dover, five miles northwest.

**GENERAL INFORMATION:** 436th Airlift Wing is host unit; 512th Airlift Wing is Reserve Wing (Associate); East Coast Port Mortuary, Air Mobility Command Base. Largest air cargo port on the East Coast. AFRES units.

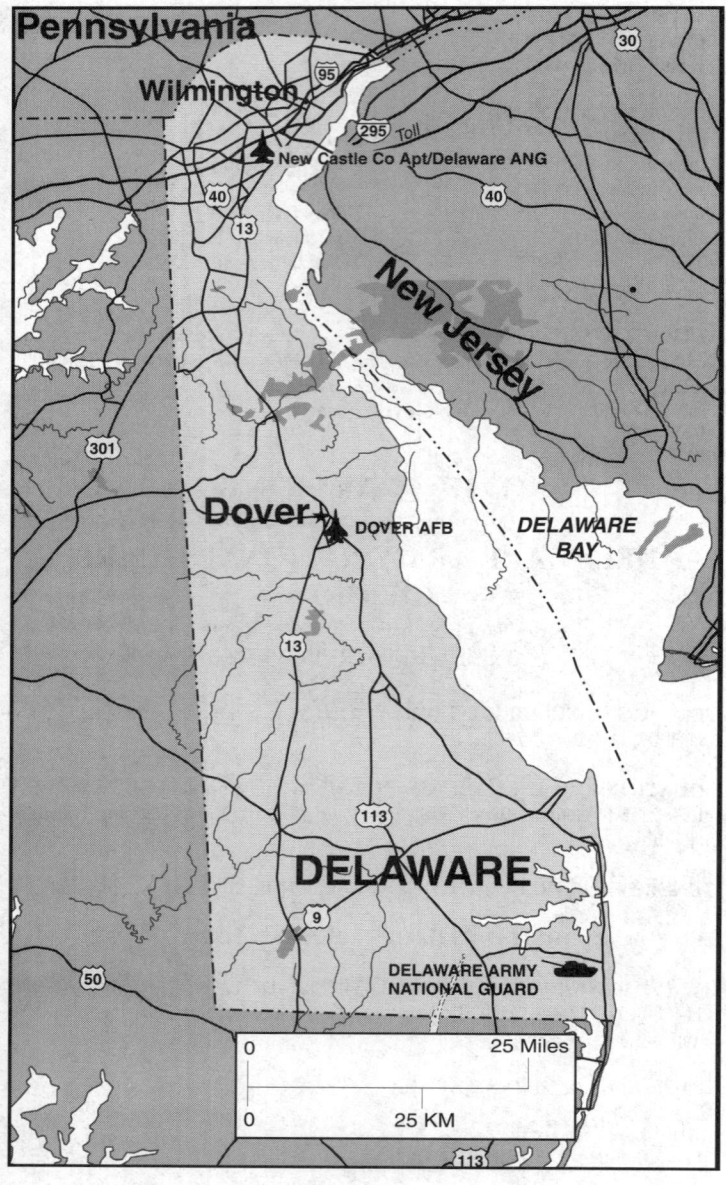

**TEMPORARY MILITARY LODGING:** Lodging office, Building 846, 14th Street, 24 hours daily, C-302-677-2841, D-312-445-2841. All ranks. DV/VIP C-302-677-6649.

**RV, CAMPING/FAMCAMP:** Dover AFB Famcamp: C-302-677-3959.

**SPACE-A:** Pax Term, Building 500, 24 hours, C-302-677-4088, D-312-445-4088, Rec: 302-677-2854, D-312-445-2854, Fax: C-302-677-2953, D-312-445-2853, Fax: C-302-677-2953. Flights to CONUS and overseas.

**LOGISTICAL SUPPORT:**

| | |
|---|---|
| Barber Shop-677-6344 | Beauty Shop-734-8262 |
| Car Rental-677-3000 | Child Care-677-3716 |
| Child Dev Center-677-3716 | Class Six-677-6301 |
| Commissary-674-4189 | Conv Store-674-3551 |
| Credit Union-678-8000 | Dining Facilities-677-3925 |
| Dry Cleaner-678-3069 | Education Office-677-4619 |
| Exchange-674-4862 | Gas Station-674-4228 |
| Postal Service-677-6198 | Rogers Travel-736-1668 |
| Services Squadron-677-6901 | Shoppette-674-3551 |
| Snack Bar-674-3380 | Visitor Center-677-3921 |

**ADMINISTRATIVE SUPPORT:**

| | |
|---|---|
| Fire Dept-677-4401 | Housing Office-677-6969 |
| Legal-677-3300 | Locator-677-3000 |
| Pass/ID Office-677-2853 | Police-677-6666 |
| Public Affairs-677-3372 | |

**HEALTH & WELFARE:**

| | |
|---|---|
| Air Force Aid Society-677-6930 | American Red Cross-677-2855 |
| CHAMPUS-677-2530 | Chapel-677-3932 |
| Dental | Family Services-677-6941 |
|   Central Appts-677-2846 | Medical-677-2525 |
|   Emergency-677-2600 | Retiree Services-677-4612 |
| TRICARE-677-2486 | Veterinary Services-677-5252 |

**REST & RECREATION:**

| | |
|---|---|
| Arts & Crafts-677-3245 | Auto Skills Center-677-3249 |
| Bowling-ext 3946 | Clubs |
| Community Center-677-6899 |   EM-677-6351 |
| Equipment Rental-ext 3959 |   O-677-6022 |
| Fitness Center-677-3962 |   "The Club"-677-6024 |
| Golf Course-677-6039 | ITT-677-3955 |
| Library-677-3992 | Outdoor Rec-677-5553 |
| Skeet-ext 6380 | Swimming-ext 3963 |
| Tennis-ext 3963 | Theater-678-8711 |
| Youth Activities-ext 6376 | Youth Center-677-6379 |

**ATTRACTIONS:** State capital, Dover Air Force Base Museum, great beaches and the Delaware Bay, Dover Downs racing and gambling.

## NEW CASTLE COUNTY AIRPORT/ DELAWARE AIR NATIONAL GUARD (DE02R1)
2600 Spruance Drive, Corporate Commons
New Castle, DE 19720-1615

**TELEPHONE NUMBER INFORMATION:** Main installation numbers: C-302-323-3525, D-312-445-7525.

**LOCATION:** From I-95 take exit 5 to DE-141 south for one mile to intersection of DE-37 (Corporate Commons Blvd). Turn right into Corporate Commons Blvd, then left onto Spruance Drive and follow to gate entrance. USMRA: Page 42 (I-2). NMC: Wilmington, seven miles northeast.

**GENERAL INFORMATION:** Delaware Air National Guard Base.

**TEMPORARY MILITARY LODGING:** None. See Aberdeen Proving Ground, MD listing.

**RV, CAMPING/FAMCAMP:** None. See Aberdeen Proving Ground, MD listing.

**SPACE-A:** Pax Term, Building 2812, C-302-323-3525, D-312-445-3525, Fax: C-302-323-3330. Flights to CONUS and overseas. 0800-1630, ANG units.

**LOGISTICAL SUPPORT:**     Exchange-322-5988

**ADMINISTRATIVE SUPPORT:**
Fire Dept-323-3450     Police-323-3440

**HEALTH & WELFARE:**     Medical-323-3385
    Clinic-445-7418/9

**REST & RECREATION:** None. See Aberdeen Proving Ground, MD listing.

**ATTRACTIONS:** State parks and the Chesapeake and Delaware Canal.

# DISTRICT OF COLUMBIA

## BOLLING AIR FORCE BASE (DC01R1)
20 MacDill Boulevard, Suite 230
Bolling Air Force Base, Washington, D.C. 20332-5100

**TELEPHONE NUMBER INFORMATION:** Main installation numbers: C-202-767-1110, D-312-297-4080. WEB: www.bolling.af.mil

**LOCATION:** Take I-95 (east portion of Capital Beltway, I-495), exit 22 to I-295 south, exit to Portland Street, and main entrance to AFB. Also, I-395 north, exit South Capitol Street, main entrance to AFB on right. Visitors entrance is at south gate, one mile south of main gate. Clearly marked. USMRA: Page 54 (F-6). NMC: Washington, D.C., in southeast section of city.

**GENERAL INFORMATION:** 11th Wing. Support for Air Force activities of the National Capital Region.

**TEMPORARY MILITARY LODGING:** Bolling Inn, Building 602, Thiesen Street, 24 hours, C-202-767-5316, D-312-297-5316/5741. All ranks. DV/VIP C-202-767-5316, Officer retirees Space-A.

**RV, CAMPING/FAMCAMP:** None. See Andrews AFB, MD listing.

**SPACE-A:** None. See Andrews AFB, MD listing.

**LOGISTICAL SUPPORT:**
Cafeteria-562-4419     Child Care-767-2890
Child Dev Center-ext 3047     Command Post-767-1111
Commissary-767-4695     Conv Store-563-6490
Credit Union-562-5300     Exchange-562-3000
SATO     Gas Station-563-6490
    Official-574-5182     Visitor Center-767-5505
    Leisure-574-0120

**ADMINISTRATIVE SUPPORT:**
Fire Dept-767-5777     Housing Office-404-1838
Legal-767-5297
Locator-703-767-4522     Police-767-5000
Public Affairs-767-4781

**HEALTH & WELFARE:**
CHAMPUS-767-5540     Chapel-767-5900
Family Services-767-4464     Medical
Retiree Services-767-5244        Central Appts-767-5520
      Clinic-767-5534

**REST & RECREATION:**
Arts & Crafts-767-4422     Auto Hobby Shop-767-5471
Bowling-563-4054     Camping Equipment-767-9135

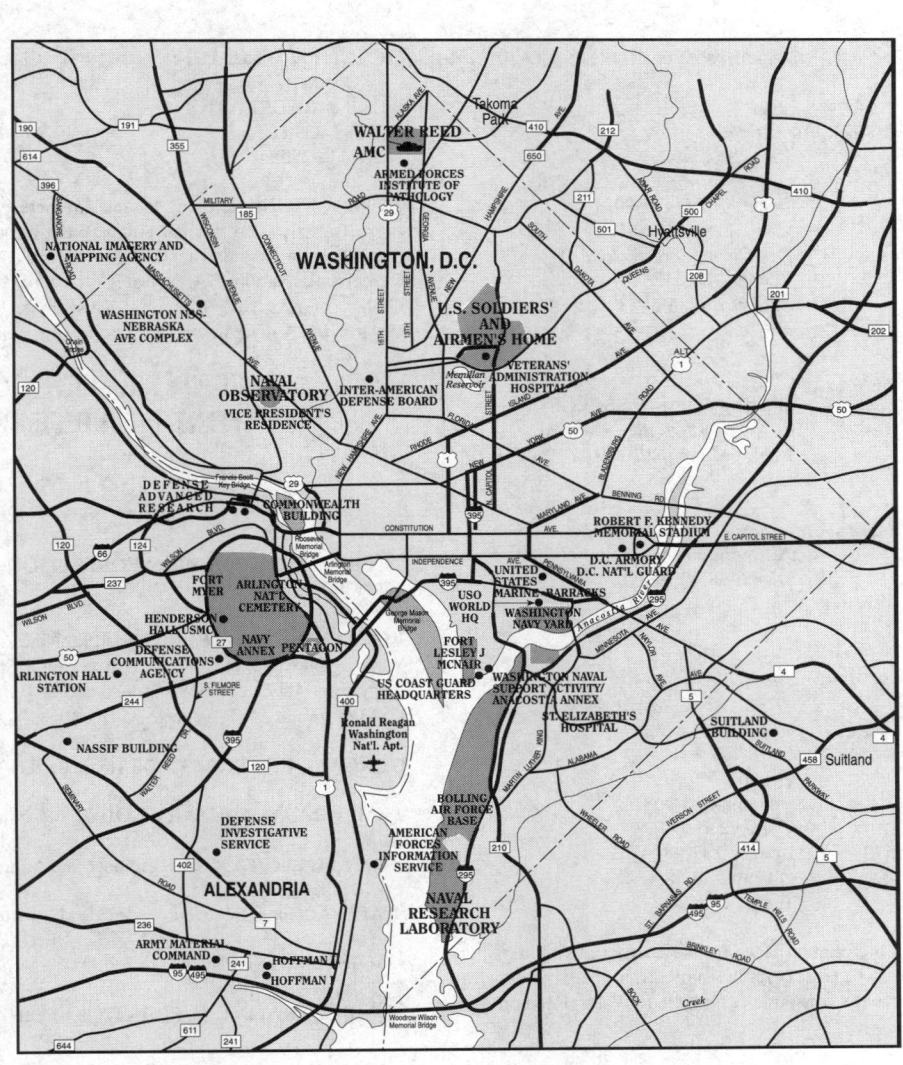

Clubs
  NCO-563-1400
  O-563-2072
Marina-767-9136
Rec Center-767-3847
Swimming Pool-767-4942

Fitness Center-767-5895
ITT-767-6211
Library-767-6067
Outdoor Rec-767-9136
Rec Equipment-767-9136
Youth Center-767-4575

**ATTRACTIONS:** Washington, D.C., with its many museums, galleries, monuments and other attractions. Kennedy Center for the Performing Arts.

## FORT LESLEY J. McNAIR (DC05R1)
103 3rd Avenue
Washington, D.C. 20319-5058

**TELEPHONE NUMBER INFORMATION:** Main installation numbers: C-703-545-6700, D-312-227-0101 (7 am-7 pm EST). E-mail: anpa@mcnair-emh2.army.mil

**LOCATION:** At confluence of Anacostia River and Washington Channel, southwest. Enter on P-Street, SW. Take Maine Avenue, SW, to right on 4th Street, SW, to dead end at P-Street. Left and then immediate right onto the main gate. USMRA: Page 54 (F-5), page 55 (E-4). NMC: Washington, D.C., in southwest section of city.

**GENERAL INFORMATION:** Headquarters U.S. Army Military District of Washington, Co A, 3rd U.S. Infantry (The Old Guard) "Commander in Chief's Guard," home to the National Defense University, consisting of the National War College (NWC) and the Industrial College of the Armed Forces (ICAF); home to the Inter-American Defense College (IADC).

**TEMPORARY MILITARY LODGING:** Lodging office, Fort Myer, Building 50, Johnson Lane, 24 hours daily, C-703-696-3576/3577. Limited VOQ facilities (Building 54, 24 hours daily) at Fort McNair. DV/VIP C-703-697-7051, D-312-297-7051.

**RV, CAMPING/FAMCAMP:** None. See Andrews AFB, MD listing, C-301-981-4109.

**SPACE-A:** None. See Andrews AFB, MD listing.

**LOGISTICAL SUPPORT:**

Barber Shop-863-1130
Child Care-696-3095
Credit Union-(703) 706-5126
Gas Station-484-5823
Package Store-484-5833
Snack Bar-685-3038

Beauty Shop-484-0921
Conv Store-484-5823
Dry Cleaner-863-1251
Laundry-863-1251
Shoppette-484-5823

**ADMINISTRATIVE SUPPORT:**

Fire Dept-911
Legal-696-0762
Police-685-3139
SDO/NCO-475-0918

Housing Office-696-3576
Locator-475-2005
Public Affairs-685-2892

**HEALTH & WELFARE:**

ACS-696-3510
CHAMPUS-696-3030
Medical
  Central Appts-685-3100
  Clinic-685-3100
  Emergency-911
  Health Benefits-685-3100
  Information-685-3100

Army Emergency Relief-696-8435
Dental-685-3388/3100

**REST & RECREATION:**

Ball Field-ext 1964
Fitness Center-685-3117
Golf Course-685-3138/3415/3570
Multi Craft Shop-ext 2000
Swimming-ext 0504

Bowling-685-3038
Gym-ext 1964
Library-287-9490
O Club-484-5800
Tennis-ext 1964

**ATTRACTIONS:** Included in the original plans for the District of Columbia, and nearly 200 years old. Second only to West Point in length of service. Site of the trial and execution of President Lincoln's conspirators and where Walter Reed did his

research work. Washington waterfront with restaurants, seafood markets, monuments and scenic Potomac River nearby.

## MARINE BARRACKS (DC09R1)
8th and I Streets, SE
Washington, D.C. 20390-5000

**TELEPHONE NUMBER INFORMATION:** Main installation numbers: C-202-433-4073, D-312-288-4073.

**LOCATION:** At 8th & I Streets, SE. From I-395 north, take 6th Street exit, drive east two blocks to 8th Street, turn left. From I-295/I-395 north interchange area, continue to follow I-295 north, 6th Street exit, follow as above. From I-295 south take exit 13, U.S. Naval Station/Suitland Parkway exit, follow exit ramp around to reenter I-295 north. From I-495 (Capital Beltway), take Pennsylvania Avenue west exit, follow Pennsylvania Avenue to 8th Street, turn left and follow to I Street. USMRA: Page 54 (F,G-5). NMC: Washington D.C., in SE section of the city.

**GENERAL INFORMATION:** USMC light infantry battalion. *Note: the Marine Barracks is a closed post for all practical purposes. Facilities are not available unless user, if not permanently stationed at barracks, is escorted by a Marine stationed there.*

**TEMPORARY MILITARY LODGING:** None. See Bolling AFB listing.

**RV, CAMPING/FAMCAMP:** None. See Andrews AFB, MD listing.

**SPACE-A:** None. See Andrews AFB, MD listing.

**LOGISTICAL SUPPORT:**              Exchange-433-4961

**ADMINISTRATIVE SUPPORT:**
Legal-433-3180                        Public Affairs-433-4173

**HEALTH & WELFARE:**               Chaplain-433-6201

**REST & RECREATION:**
ITT-433-2338                          MWR-433-2338
NCO-433-2528

**ATTRACTIONS:** Evening Parades are held every Friday. Sunset Parades are held every Tuesday (May through August). For information and reservations call C-202-433-4073. Smithsonian Institution, Lincoln and Jefferson Memorials, Washington Monument, National Archives, Library of Congress, the U.S. Mint, National Gallery of Art, Navy Memorial Museum and the Marine Corps Museum at the Washington Navy Yard and many other attractions.

## UNITED STATES COAST GUARD HEADQUARTERS (DC08R1)

2100 2nd Street, SW
Washington, D.C. 20593-0001

**TELEPHONE NUMBER INFORMATION:** Main installation numbers: C-202-267-1340.

**LOCATION:** Next to Fort Lesley J. McNair. At confluence of Anacostia River and Washington Channel, southwest. Enter on P Street, SW. Take Maine Avenue, SW, to right on 4th Street, SW, to dead end at P Street left, then right into main gate. USMRA: Page 54 (F-5), page 55 (F-4).

**GENERAL INFORMATION:** Headquarters U.S. Coast Guard.

**TEMPORARY MILITARY LODGING:** None. See Bolling AFB listing.

**RV, CAMPING/FAMCAMP:**None. See Andrews AFB, MD listing.

**SPACE-A:** None. See Andrews AFB, MD listing.

**LOGISTICAL SUPPORT:**              Exchange-267-2372

**ADMINISTRATIVE SUPPORT:**          Public Affairs-267-1587

**HEALTH & WELFARE:**          Medical-366-0892

**ATTRACTIONS:** Smithsonian Institution, Lincoln and Jefferson Memorials, Washington Monument, National Archives, Library of Congress, the U.S. Mint, National Gallery of Art and many other attractions.

# USO WORLD HEADQUARTERS (DC06R1)

7008 Eberle Place, SE Suite 301
Washington Navy Yard
Washington, D.C. 20374-5096

**TELEPHONE NUMBER INFORMATION:** Main installation numbers: C-202-610-5700. E-mail: info@uso.org  WEB: www.USO.org
*For a list of USOs worldwide, see Appendix C.*

**LOCATION:** In the Washington Navy Yard, Building 220. The offices of the USO World Headquarters are on the third floor. See receptionist on third floor. USMRA: Page 54 (F,G-5).

**GENERAL INFORMATION:** The administrative branch of the USO network worldwide; there are more than 125 USO centers worldwide.

**RECREATION:** Free tickets for shows and sporting events. Ticket and information hot line: 703-696-2551. USO Metro Washington's Service. There are nine outreach locations of the USO in the greater Washington, D.C. area serving uniformed personnel and their families. See Appendix C in this book for addresses and telephone numbers.

# UNITED STATES SOLDIERS' AND AIRMEN'S HOME (DC10R1)

3700 N Capitol Street, NW
Washington, D.C. 20317-5000

**TELEPHONE NUMBER INFORMATION:** Main installation number: C-800-422-9988, 202-722-3556/3337. WEB: www.afrh.com

**LOCATION:** Two and one-half miles north of the Capitol. Enter from North Capitol Street. Across the street from VA Hospital and Shrine of the Immaculate Conception. USMRA: Page 54 (F-3). NMI: Walter Reed Army Medical Center. NMC: Washington, D.C., in city limits.

**LOGISTICAL SUPPORT:**          Exchange-291-6252

**ADMINISTRATIVE SUPPORT:**
Locator-722-3111                Police-722-3111
Public Affairs-722-3556

**OTHER FACILITIES AVAILABLE:** Arts & crafts, auto hobby shop, bank, barber shop, beauty shop, bowling, cafeteria, chapel, conv store, credit union, dental, dining facilities, dry cleaner, fitness center, golf course, gym, indoor rec, library, medical, outdoor rec, postal, retiree services, services, shoppette, snack bar, theater, wood hobby shop.

**ATTRACTIONS:** Smithsonian, Capitol, Washington Monument, National Archives, Library of Congress, the U.S. Mint, National Gallery of Art.

# WALTER REED ARMY MEDICAL CENTER (DC03R1)

6900 Georgia Avenue
Washington, D.C. 20307-5001

**TELEPHONE NUMBER INFORMATION:** Main installation numbers: C-202-782-3501, D-312-662-3501.

**LOCATION:** From I-495 (Capital Beltway) take Georgia Avenue/SilverSpring exit south to Medical Center. To reach the Forest Glen support facilities from Georgia Avenue south, right turn onto Linden Lane, cross over B&O railroad bridge. Support facilities on left (three-quarter miles from Georgia Avenue). USMRA: Page 54 (F-2). NMC: Washington, D.C., in city limits.

**GENERAL INFORMATION:** The major Army medical research, teaching, and treatment facility; Armed Forces Institute of Pathology (AFIP) located on main post. Forest Glen Annex, located in Silver Spring, MD, has a large commissary and exchange. Walter Reed Institute of Research to be completed by year 2000.

**TEMPORARY MILITARY LODGING:** Fisher House I, Forest Glen Annex, (for families of critically ill patients), C-301-295-7374. Fisher House II, C-202-356-7564. Guest House, Building 17, priority to PCS, members of immediate family of seriously ill patients and MEDEVAC/AIRVAC, C-202-782-4600. Mologne House Hotel, P.O. Box 59728, Washington, D.C. 20012, 24 hours daily, C-202-782-0443.

**RV, CAMPING/FAMCAMP:** None. See Andrews AFB, MD listing.

**SPACE-A:** None. See Andrews AFB, MD listing.

**LOGISTICAL SUPPORT:**
Barber Shop-722-2209                Carlson Wagonlit Travel
Child Dev Center-782-5024              Official-882-0303
Exchange-882-0802/0369                Leisure-882-1919
Snack Bar-423-5401/565-0900

**ADMINISTRATIVE SUPPORT:**
Fire Dept-782-3318                   Legal-782-1550/5810
Locator                              Police-782-3325
  Civilian-782-0546                  Public Affairs-782-7177
  Military-782-1150                  SDO-782-7309

**HEALTH & WELFARE:**
ACS-782-3412                         CHAMPUS-782-6136/1336
Chapel-782-6308                      Family Services-782-3412
Medical                              Retiree Services-782-3412
  Central Appts-782-7761

**REST & RECREATION:**
Auto Crafts-782-4972/7433            Clubs
DPCA-782-4946                          Abrams Lounge-782-3383
Fitness Center-782-7324/7022           Patients Lounge-782-6359
ITR-782-0600                         Library-782-6314/5
MWR-782-7034/7377                    Swimming-ext 2324
Tennis-ext 2324

**ATTRACTIONS:** Washington, D.C., White House, Capitol, National Zoo, Washington National Cathedral, Arlington Cemetery, Smithsonian.

# WALTER REED ARMY MEDICAL CENTER FOREST GLEN ANNEX (DC11R1)

Brookville Road
Silver Spring, MD 20307-5001

**TELEPHONE NUMBER INFORMATION:** Main installation numbers:C-202-782-3501/3412, D-312-622-3501/3412.

**LOCATION:** Located seven miles from WRAMC. From main post, exit onto 16th Street. Go one mile and turn left onto East West Hwy. Turn right on Grubbs Road, then left on Lytonsville Road. At the stop sign turn right on Brookville Road to Annex. From WRAMC, go west on Georgia Avenue to left on Seminary Place to left (south) on Brookville Road to right on Steven Sitter Avenue and the Annex. USMRA: Page 54 (E-1).

**GENERAL INFORMATION:** Forest Glen Annex, located in Silver Spring, MD, has a large commissary and exchange. Walter Reed Institute of Research to be completed by year 2000.

**TEMPORARY MILITARY LODGING:** Fisher House I, Forest Glen Annex, (for families of critically ill patients), C-301-295-7374.

**LOGISTICAL SUPPORT:**
Commissary-295-8041                  Exchange-565-0900/0028
Gas Station-588-1602

**ADMINISTRATIVE SUPPORT:**
Locator-301-295-7542                 P-301-295-7554/5

**HEALTH & WELFARE:** See Walter Reed AMC.

**REST & RECREATION:**          Bowling-295-8011

**ATTRACTIONS:** Washington, D.C., White House, Capitol, National Zoo, Washington National Cathedral, Arlington Cemetery, Smithsonian.

## WASHINGTON NAVAL SECURITY STATION-NEBRASKA AVENUE COMPLEX(DC07R1)

3801 Nebraska Avenue, NW
Washington, D.C. 20393-5440

**TELEPHONE NUMBER INFORMATION:** Main installation numbers: C-202-764-0211, D-312-764-0211. WEB: www.ndw.navy.mil

**LOCATION:** From Virginia cross the Key Bridge, turn left onto Foxhall Road. Go approximately two and a half miles to Nebraska Avenue and turn right. Station is half a mile on your right. USMRA: Page 54 (D,E-3,4). NMC: Washington, D.C., in the city.

**GENERAL INFORMATION:** Naval Security Station, and assigned units.

**TEMPORARY MILITARY LODGING:** BEQ C-202-764-0254, D-202-764-0211. Navy Lodge in Bellevue Navy Housing area, Building 4412, C-202-563-6950 or 1-800-NAVY-INN.

**RV, CAMPING/FAMCAMP:** None. See Andrews AFB, MD listing.

**SPACE-A:** None. See Andrews AFB, MD listing.

**LOGISTICAL SUPPORT:**
Barber Shop-764-0249          Credit Union-255-8440
Visitor Center-764-0211

**ADMINISTRATIVE SUPPORT:**
CDO-764-0220                  Locator-764-2296
OOD-764-0211                  Police-764-0294
Quarter Deck-764-0211

**HEALTH & WELFARE:**
Chapel-764-0313               Dental-764-0204
Medical-764-0224

**REST & RECREATION:**        Gym-764-0295

**ATTRACTIONS:** Washington, D.C., with its many museums, galleries, monuments and other attractions. Kennedy Center for the Performing Arts.

## WASHINGTON NAVAL SUPPORT ACTIVITY-ANACOSTIA ANNEX (DC02R1)

2770 Enterprise Way SW Suite 106
Washington, D.C. 20373-5823

**TELEPHONE NUMBER INFORMATION:** Main installation numbers: C-703-545-6700, D-312-227-0101. (Note: The area code for the following numbers is 202.) WEB: www.ndw.navy.mil

**LOCATION:** From I-395, exit South Capitol Street, cross South Capitol Street Bridge, main entrance is on right, before Bolling AFB. USMRA: Page 54, (F,G-5). NMC: Washington, D.C., in southeast section.

**GENERAL INFORMATION:** Naval Media Center, White House Communications Agency, U.S. Navy Ceremonial Guard.

**TEMPORARY MILITARY LODGING:** Limited transient billeting, C-202-433-8796/0806, D-312-288-8796/0806. Navy Lodge in Bellevue Navy Housing area, Building 4412, C-202-563-6950 or 1-800-NAVY-INN.

**RV, CAMPING/FAMCAMP:** None. See Andrews AFB, MD listing.

**SPACE-A:** None. See Andrews AFB, MD listing.

**LOGISTICAL SUPPORT:**
Child Care-433-0771           Dining-433-2391

**ADMINISTRATIVE SUPPORT:**
CDO/OOD-433-2231/32           Locator-545-6700
Fire Dept-433-3334            Police-433-2411
PSD Anacostia-685-0667        Public Affairs-433-2218
SDO/SNCO-433-2231/32

**HEALTH & WELFARE:**
Chapel-433-2058               Family Services-433-6150
Retiree Services-433-6150

**REST & RECREATION:**
All Hands Club-433-4070       Fitness Center-433-3041/2062
MWR-433-3005                  Outdoor Recreation-433-2269

**ATTRACTIONS:** On the Potomac, and in sight of the Capitol and many famous monuments. Museums, and professional sports.

## WASHINGTON NAVY YARD/NAVAL STATION (DC04R1)

901 M Street SE
Washington, D.C. 20374-5000

**TELEPHONE NUMBER INFORMATION:** Main installation numbers: C-703-545-6700, D-312-277-0101. (Note: The area code for the following numbers is 202.) WEB: www.ndw.navy.mil

**LOCATION:** Exit I-395 north at 6th Street SE/Navy Yard, proceed to 8th Street, turn right to M Street, turn left to Main Gate at 9th and M Streets, SE. USMRA: Page 54 (F,G-5), page 55 (F-4). NMC: Washington, D.C., in southeast section.

**GENERAL INFORMATION:** Headquarters Naval District Washington, Military Sealift Command, Naval Criminal Investigative Service, and the Navy Band.

**TEMPORARY MILITARY LODGING:** Lodging office, in the Anacostia complex adjacent to Bolling AFB. From I-95 (Beltway east) take I-295 north, exit at South Capitol Street NDW Anacostia is clearly marked. C-202-433-8796/0806, D-312-288-8796/0806, 0730-1600 daily, other hours-ext 2193. Navy Lodge in Bellevue Navy Housing area, 24 hours daily, C-202-563-6950.

**RV, CAMPING/FAMCAMP:** None. See Andrews AFB, MD listing.

**SPACE-A:** None. See Andrews AFB, MD listing.

**LOGISTICAL SUPPORT:**
Child Care-433-0771           Credit Union-(703) 255-8055
Exchange-889-7534

**ADMINISTRATIVE SUPPORT:**
CDO/OOD-433-0960              Family Housing-685-1187
Fire Dept-433-3334           Legal-433-4331
Pass/ID Office-433-3017       Police-433-2411
PSD Anacostia-685-0667        Public Affairs-433-2218

**HEALTH & WELFARE:**
Chapel-433-2058               Dental-433-3115
Family Services-433-6150      Medical-433-6529/3976/3407
Navy-MC Relief-433-3365        Emergency-433-3269
Retiree Services-433-6150

**REST & RECREATION:**
Clubs/Conference/Tickets-433-3041    Fitness Center-433-2829/5340
Library 433-4132              Marinas-433-2269
MWR-433-3005                  O Club-433-3041
Outdoor Recreation-433-2269   Tennis 433-2829

**ATTRACTIONS:** Navy Memorial Museum, Navy Art Gallery, Display Ship *Barry*, Marine Corps Museum. *Concerts on the Avenue* at the U.S. Navy Memorial located at 701 Pennsylvania Avenue, NW, on Tuesday evenings beginning at 8 pm. The summer concerts, performed weekly between June and August by the U.S. Navy Band specialty groups, are free and open to the public and no reservations are required. Call 202-433-2525 for more information.

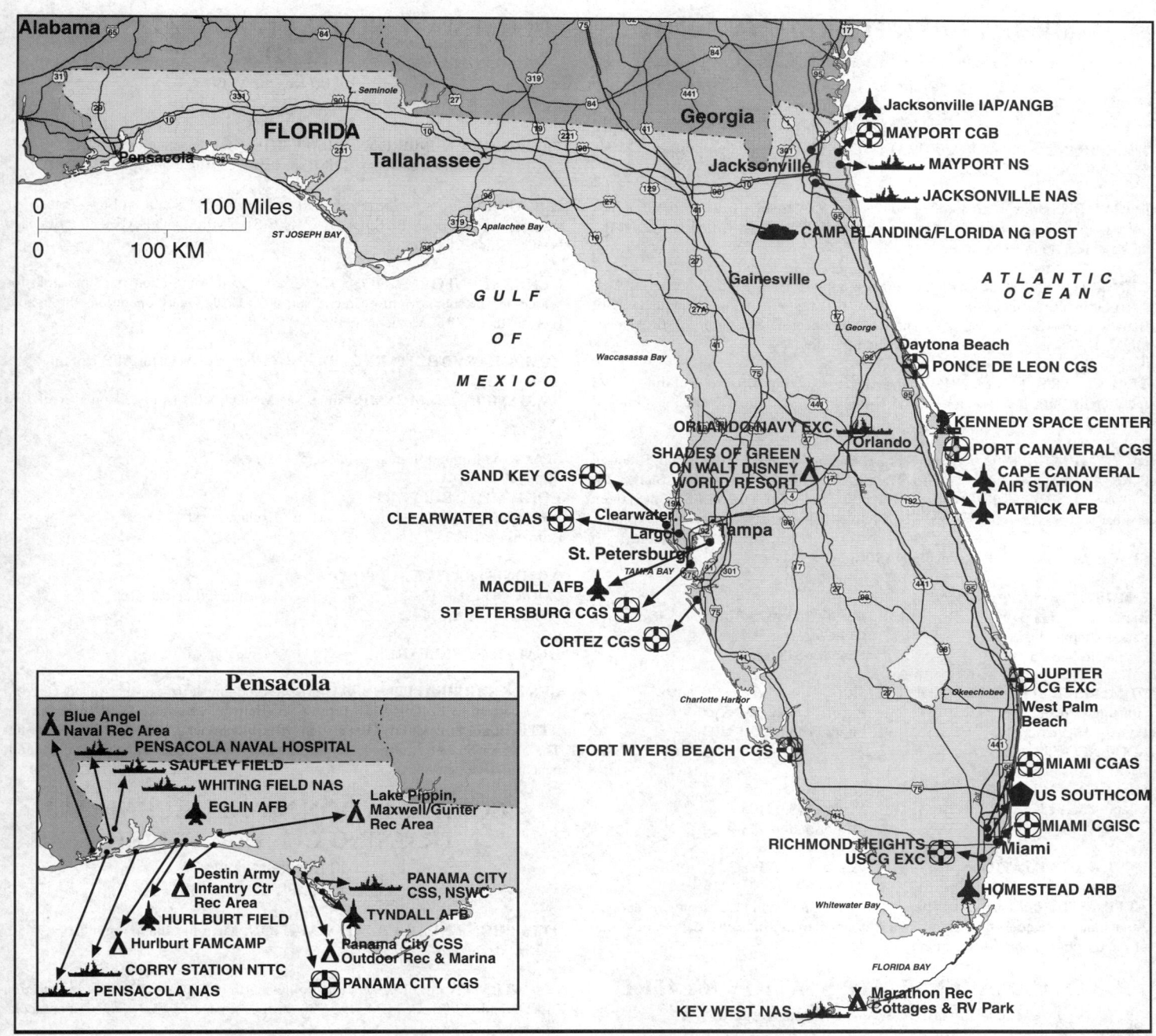

# FLORIDA

## BLUE ANGEL NAVAL RECREATION AREA (FL36R1)

2100 Bronson Road
Pensacola, FL 32506-5000

**TELEPHONE NUMBER INFORMATION:** Main installation numbers: C-850-452-2000, D-312-922-0111. Police-453-2030/4530

**LOCATION:** From I-10 west of Pensacola, take exit 2 (FL-297/Pine Forest Road) south approximately one-and-a-half miles to Blue Angel Parkway; south eight miles, then west on US-98 for three miles. Watch for sign to Blue Angel Recreation Area on the left. USMRA: Page 39 (A-13). NMC: Pensacola, eight miles east. NMI: Corry Station, eight miles northeast.

**GENERAL INFORMATION:** Operated by Corry Station Naval Technical Training Center, off base year round. E-mail: nttc-pen.mwr-0720@nttc-pen.navy.mil. Military personnel active, retired, DoD civilians and guests. Check in 1400, check out 0800-1100. Reservations: Recommended for rental campers, C-850-453-9435, Fax C-850-453-1147.

**RV, CAMPING/FAMCAMP:**
Rental campers-17                    Camper/RV spaces-138
Primitive tent spaces-unlimited

**ATTRACTIONS:** The park offers spectacular camping, boating, swimming and picnic areas.

*For detailed information about this off-base recreation facility, as well as on-base recreation facilities, golf courses and marinas, consult Military Living's Military RV, Camping and Outdoor Recreation Around the World.*

## CAMP BLANDING/FLORIDA NATIONAL GUARD POST (FL42R1)
Route 1, Box 465
Starke, FL 32091-9703

**TELEPHONE NUMBER INFORMATION:** Main installation number: C-904-533-2268, D-312-960-3100.

**LOCATION:** From I-95 north or south, exit 95A to FL-16 west for 31 miles. Follow exit signs to support activities. USMRA: Page 38 (F,G-4). NMC: Jacksonville, 30 miles north.

**GENERAL INFORMATION:** Installation Support Unit, 653rd Engineering Det, 221st Ordnance Detachment, Florida Regional Training Institute, Headquarters 3rd Battalion, 20th Special Forces, 202nd Civil Engineering Squadron, 159th Weather Flight, 159 Weather School, and other support units.

**TEMPORARY MILITARY LODGING:** Lodging office, Building 2392 Jacksonville Road, 0800-1630 daily, C-904-533-3381, D-312-960-3381 (closed Sundays).

**RV, CAMPING/FAMCAMP:** RV Park & Campsites on post year round, Billeting Office Campsites, Camp Blanding Training Site, Route 1, Box 465, Starke, FL 32091-9703, C-904-533-3104, D-312-970-3104, Fax-904-533-6123. Sixteen camper spaces with full hookups, 32 primitive camper/tent spaces with W hookups.

**SPACE-A:** None. See Jacksonville NAS listing.

**LOGISTICAL SUPPORT:**

| | |
|---|---|
| Barber Shop-533-3195 | Beauty Shop-533-3195 |
| Credit Union-533-2184 | Dry Cleaner-533-3369 |
| Exchange-533-3513 | Laundry-533-3369 |

**ADMINISTRATIVE SUPPORT:**

| | |
|---|---|
| Housing Office-533-3381/2 | Pass/ID Office-533-3566 |
| Police-533-3526 | Public Affairs-533-3407 |
| SDO/SNCO-533-3462 | |

**HEALTH & WELFARE:**

| | |
|---|---|
| Chapel-533-3231 | Medical-533-3105 |
| | Information-533-3514 |

**REST & RECREATION:**          Consol Club-533-3320

**ATTRACTIONS:** Under one hour drives to Gainesville, Jacksonville and St. Augustine, three hours to Disney and the Orlando area. Kingsley Lakes on post; one of the best bass fishing lakes in area.

## CAPE CANAVERAL AIR STATION (FL45R1)
1201 Edward H. White II Street, Suite C
Patrick Air Force Base, FL 32925-5000

**TELEPHONE NUMBER INFORMATION:** Main installation numbers: C-407-494-1110, D-312-854-1110.
*Ten digit dialing required for local calls.*

**LOCATION:** From I-95 take FL-528 east, exit 401 north to AFS. USMRA: Page 38 (I-7). NMC: Cocoa Beach, two miles north.

**GENERAL INFORMATION:** Home of space shuttle launches.

**LOGISTICAL SUPPORT:**

| | |
|---|---|
| Commissary-853-3196 | Exchange-853-3196 |
| Visitor Center-494-2659 | |

**ATTRACTIONS:** Shuttle launches. At Patrick AFB, Air Force Space Museum, John F. Kennedy Space Center, Disney World, Daytona Beach, Epcot Center, Spaceport USA, Sea World.

## CLEARWATER COAST GUARD AIR STATION (FL32R1)
15100 Rescue Way
Clearwater, FL 33762-2990

**TELEPHONE NUMBER INFORMATION:** Main installation numbers: C-727-535-1437 (ask for extensions). E-mail: pado/asclearwater@internet.uscg.mil

**LOCATION:** From I-275, take FL-60 west to FL-611 south. Follow signs to air station. USMRA: Page 38 (E-8), page 56 (C-3). NMI: MacDill AFB, 30 miles east. NMC: Tampa, 20 miles east.

**GENERAL INFORMATION:** The Coast Guard Air Station is responsible for search-and-rescue, law enforcement, and other Coast Guard operations throughout Florida, the Gulf of Mexico and the Caribbean.

**TEMPORARY MILITARY LODGING:** None. See MacDill AFB listing.

**RV, CAMPING/FAMCAMP:** None. See MacDill AFB listing, Coon's Creek Rec Area.

**SPACE-A:** Limited flights. C-727-535-1437, ext 1223.

**LOGISTICAL SUPPORT:**

| | |
|---|---|
| Barber Shop-ext 1712 | Exchange-ext 1710 |
| Cafeteria-ext.1725 | |

**ADMINISTRATIVE SUPPORT:**

| | |
|---|---|
| CDO/OOD-ext 1210 | Housing Office-ext 1160 |
| Public Affairs-ext 1145 | |

**HEALTH & WELFARE:**          Medical-ext 1606

**REST & RECREATION:**          MWR-ext 1180

**ATTRACTIONS:** Busch Gardens–the Dark Continent, Salvador Dali Museum, The Pier in St. Petersburg, Adventure Island Water Park, Tampa's Latin Quarter, beaches, water sports.

## CORRY STATION NAVAL TECHNICAL TRAINING CENTER (FL19R1)
640 Roberts Avenue
Pensacola, FL 32511-5138

**TELEPHONE NUMBER INFORMATION:** Main installation numbers: C-850-452-2000, D-312-922-0111.

**LOCATION:** North of US-98, three miles north of Pensacola NAS at intersection FL-295 and US-98. USMRA: Page 38 (A,B-13), page 53 (B-4). NMC: Pensacola, five miles northeast.

**GENERAL INFORMATION:** Home of the Naval Technical Training Center.

**TEMPORARY MILITARY LODGING:** BQ: C-850-452-6609, D-312-922-6609.

**RV, CAMPING/FAMCAMP:** See Blue Angel Naval Recreation Area listing.

**SPACE-A:** None. See Pensacola NAS listing.

**LOGISTICAL SUPPORT:**

| | |
|---|---|
| Child Care-452-6286 | Conv Store-453-5311 |
| Exchange-453-5311 | SATO-452-6291 |

**ADMINISTRATIVE SUPPORT:**

| | |
|---|---|
| Legal-452-6334 | Locator-452-6512 |
| Police-452-6130 | Public Affairs-452-6318 |
| SDO/NCO-452-6512 | |

**HEALTH & WELFARE:**

| | |
|---|---|
| CHAMPUS-452-6709 | Chapel-452-6376 |
| Medical-452-5242 | Retiree Services-452-6529 |

**REST & RECREATION:**

| | |
|---|---|
| Clubs | ITT-452-6143 |
| CPO-452-6330 | MWR-452-6568 |
| EM-452-6347 | Recreation-453-2129 |
| Rec Center 452-6520 | RV/Camping-453-2129 |

**OTHER FACILITIES AVAILABLE:** Bowling, hobby shop, swimming, tennis.

**ATTRACTIONS:** Visit the historic section of Pensacola, beaches. Naval Aviation Museum at NAS Pensacola.

## CORTEZ COAST GUARD STATION (FL46R1)

4530 124th Street, Court West
Cortez, FL 34215-9999

**TELEPHONE NUMBER INFORMATION:** Main installation numbers: C-941-794-1262.

**LOCATION:** I-75 south to SR-64 west (Manatee Avenue), left on 75th Street, right on Cortez Road, left on 124th Street West. Station is at end of street on right. USMRA: Page 39 (E,F-9). NMC: Tampa, 60 miles north.

**GENERAL INFORMATION:** Part of Seventh Coast Guard District.

**LOGISTICAL SUPPORT:** Exchange-795-2805

**ADMINISTRATIVE SUPPORT:** OOD-764-1607

**ATTRACTIONS:** Beaches, fishing, boating.

## DESTIN ARMY INFANTRY CENTER RECREATION AREA (FL01R1)

557 Calhoun Avenue
Destin, FL 32541-5000

**TELEPHONE NUMBER INFORMATION:** Main installation numbers: C-850-837-6423. Police-651-7400/911.

**LOCATION:** Located on 15-acre site on Choctawhatchee Bay in Destin, FL. US-231 south to I-10, west exit 19 to US-331, south exit 14 to US-98, west to Benning Drive, right to area. Or I-10 to FL-85; south to Fort Walton Beach; US-98 east to Destin, left at Benning Drive to area. USMRA: Page 39 (C-13). NMC: Pensacola, 45 miles west. NMI: Eglin AFB, 17 miles north.

**GENERAL INFORMATION:** Operated by Fort Benning, GA, off post year round. Military personnel active, retired, National Guard, reserves and DoD civilians. Check in at office 1600-2000, check out 1100. Reservations: Required for cabins, motel and charter boat, C-850-837-2725; not accepted for camper spaces. Call C-1-800-642-0466. Reservations may also be made at Fort Benning, C-706-545-5600. Information only, C-850-837-6423, Fax: C-850-837-5706.

**TEMPORARY MILITARY LODGING:**

| | |
|---|---|
| Duplexes-22 | Motel rooms-54 |

**RV, CAMPING/FAMCAMP:**

| | |
|---|---|
| Camper spaces-48 | Primitive camper/tent spaces-23 |

**ATTRACTIONS:** Enjoy sparkling sugar-white quartz sands of Emerald Coast. Gulf of Mexico fishing and swimming areas approximately two miles from recreation area. Area also offers golf at six public courses, two greyhound race tracks within 45 miles, Destin Fishing Museum, Gulfariam, Zoo, and Indian Temple Mound Museum.

*For detailed information about this off-base recreation facility, as well as on-base recreation facilities, golf courses and marinas, consult Military Living's Military RV, Camping and Outdoor Recreation Around the World.*

## EGLIN AIR FORCE BASE (FL27R1)

101 West D Avenue, Suite 110
Eglin Air Force Base, FL 32542-5498

**TELEPHONE NUMBER INFORMATION:** Main installation numbers: C-850-882-1110, D-312-872-1110. WEB: www.eglin.af.mil

**LOCATION:** Exit I-10 at Crestview. Follow signs to Niceville and Valparaiso (Eglin AFB). USMRA: Page 39 (B,C,D-13), page 53 (E-2,3; F-1,2,3; G,H-1,2,3,4). NMC: Fort Walton Beach, seven miles south.

**GENERAL INFORMATION:** Air Force Materiel Command Base. Largest AFB in the DoD, Air Armament Center, 53rd Wing, 33rd Fighter Wing, Navy School Explosive Ordnance Disposal, 919 SOW (AFRC), USA Camp J.E. Rudder.

**TEMPORARY MILITARY LODGING:** Lodging office, Building 11001, Boatner Road, 24 hours daily, C-850-882-8761, D-312-872-8761, Fax: C-850-882-2708. All ranks. DV/VIP C-850-882-3011. Navy CBQ (Officers & E M) C-850-882-5683, D-312-872-5683.

**RV, CAMPING/FAMCAMP:** FAMCAMP on base, year round, C-850-882-5058; 22 camper spaces with W/E hookups, 20 tent spaces.

**SPACE-A:** Pax Term/Lounge, Building 60, 0700-1800 Mon-Fri, 0800-1600 Sat-Sun, C-850-882-3332/4757/2636, D-312-872-3332/4757/2636; Fax: C-850-882-1461, D-312-872-1461. Frequent flights to CONUS and OCONUS locations.

**LOGISTICAL SUPPORT:**

| | |
|---|---|
| Bank-651-1112 | Barber Shop-651-5122 |
| Beauty Shop-651-5224 | Child Care-882-9048 |
| Commissary-882-3172/2677 | Dry Cleaner-651-4924 |
| Exchange-651-1839 | Gas Station-678-7222 |
| Postal Service-882-3548 | SATO-882-8016 |

**ADMINISTRATIVE SUPPORT:**

| | |
|---|---|
| Legal-882-4611 | Locator-882-1110 |
| Police-882-2502 | |

**HEALTH & WELFARE:**

| | |
|---|---|
| CHAMPUS-882-7249 | Chapel-882-4426/2111 |
| Family Services-882-9060 | Medical-883-8221 |
| Retiree Services-882-5916 | Appts-883-8614 |
| | Emergency-883-8600 |

**REST & RECREATION:**

| | |
|---|---|
| Clubs | Golf-882-2949 |
| NCO-678-5127 | Hobby Shops-882-3570 |
| O-651-1010 | ITT-882-5930 |
| Library-882-2460 | Theater-882-3813 |
| Youth Activities-882-8212 | |

**OTHER FACILITIES AVAILABLE:** Bowling, gym, fishing, large and small game hunting on the AFB, skeet and swimming.

**ATTRACTIONS:** Air Force Armament Museum, Fort Walton Beach and beach areas, sport fishing, deep sea fishing, dog races, Pensacola, 60 miles west.

## FORT MYERS BEACH COAST GUARD STATION (FL47R1)

719 San Carlos Drive
Fort Myers, FL 33931-2221

**TELEPHONE NUMBER INFORMATION:** Main installation numbers: C-941-463-5754.

**LOCATION:** South on 75 exit 21, get on Daniels Pkwy. Take a left on Cypress, left on Summerlin Road, left on San Carlos Blvd, right on Main Street, left on San Carlos Drive. USMRA: Page 39 (F-11). NMC: Fort Myers, 15 miles north.

**GENERAL INFORMATION:** Part of the U.S. Coast Guard Seventh District.

**LOGISTICAL SUPPORT:** Exchange-437-0090

**ATTRACTIONS:** Beaches, water activities.

# HOMESTEAD AIR RESERVE BASE (FL17R1)
29050 Coral Sea Boulevard
Homestead ARB, FL 33039-1299

**TELEPHONE NUMBER INFORMATION:** Main installation numbers: C-305-224-7000, D-312-791-7000. WEB: www.homestead.af.mil/

**LOCATION:** Exit 5 (Biscayne Blvd/288th Street) off Florida Turnpike, left at bottom of ramp. Road leads straight to base. Or take exit 6 (Speedway Blvd) off Florida Turnpike, left at bottom of ramp. At first light take a left. Road leads straight to base. USMRA: Page 39 (I-14), page 51 (A,B-10). NMC: Miami, 40 miles northeast.

**GENERAL INFORMATION:** Home of the 482nd Fighter Wing and other federal agencies.

**TEMPORARY MILITARY LODGING:** Lodging Office, Homestead Inn, 0700-2100 hours daily; holiday hours are 0900-1800 hours, C-305-224-7168, D-312-791-7168, Fax: C-305-224-7290, D-312-224-7290.

**RV, CAMPING/FAMCAMP:** Accommodations possible. Contact Outdoor Recreation at ext 7092, Mon-Fri 0900-1700 hours, Sat-Sun 0900-1300 hours.

**SPACE-A:** Pax Terminal/lounge Building 701, C-305-224-7518, D-312-791-7518, flights to CONUS locations.

**LOGISTICAL SUPPORT:**

| | |
|---|---|
| Bank-224-1800 | Barber Shop-224-7362 |
| Conv Store-224-7464 | Commissary-258-3881 |
| Dry Cleaner-224-7095 | Exchange-258-3881 |
| Laundry-224-7095 | Package Store-258-3881 |
| Omega World Travel-224-7051 | SATO-224-7051 |

**ADMINISTRATIVE SUPPORT:**

| | |
|---|---|
| CDO/OOD-224-7023 | Fire Dept-224-7117 |
| Legal-224-7063 | Locator-224-7000 |
| Pass/ID Office-224-7058/7222 | Police-224-7115 |
| Public Affairs-224-7303 | |

**HEALTH & WELFARE:**

| | |
|---|---|
| CHAMPUS/TRICARE-1-800-444-5445 | Chapel-224-7093 |
| Family Services-224-7329 | Retiree Services-224-7580 |

**REST & RECREATION:**

| | |
|---|---|
| Consol Club-224-7485 | Fitness Center-224-7091 |
| Outdoor Rec-224-7092 | |

**ATTRACTIONS:** Key West, Biscayne Bay, deep sea fishing, Everglades National Park, Metro Zoo, Monkey Jungle, seaquarium, horse and dog racing, boating, and water sports.

# HURLBURT FAMCAMP (FL51R1)
16 SVS/SVRO, 345 Tully Street
Bldg 90505
Hurlburt Field, FL 32544-5272

**TELEPHONE NUMBER INFORMATION:** Main installation numbers: C-850-884-6939, D-312-579-6939.

**LOCATION:** Off Base. US-98 east of main gate to Hulburt Air Force Base, north of US-98, 100 yards on left. USMRA: Page 39 (C-13). NMC: Pensacola, 40 miles west.

**GENERAL INFORMATION:** Operated by Hurlburt Field, off base, year round. Military personnel active, reservists, retired, DoD civilians. Reservations (accepted with restrictions): 16 SVS/SVRO, 345 Tully Street, Bldg 90505, Hurlburt Field, FL 32544-5000. C-850-884-6939, D-312-579-6939.

**RV, CAMPING/FAMCAMP:**

| | |
|---|---|
| Camper Spaces-25 | Tent Spaces-10 |

**ATTRACTIONS:** Located on the Gulf of Mexico with the Gulf on south side and US-98 on the other; excellent bird-watching location.

*For detailed information about this off-base recreation facility, as well as on-base recreation facilities, golf courses and marinas, consult Military Living's Military RV, Camping and Outdoor Recreation Around the World.*

# HURLBURT FIELD (FL18R1)
424 Cody Avenue, Bldg 90229
Hurlburt Field, FL 32544-5000

**TELEPHONE NUMBER INFORMATION:** Main installation numbers: C-850-884-1110 (Eglin Base info), D-312-579-1110, ask for Hurlburt.

**LOCATION:** Off US-98, five miles west of Fort Walton Beach, north of US-98. Clearly marked. USMRA: Page 39 (C-13), page 53 (H-4). NMC: Pensacola, 35 miles west.

**GENERAL INFORMATION:** Air Force Special Operations Command Base, on the Eglin AFB reservation, U.S. Special Operations Command AF Component, 16th Special Operations Wing, Air Force Air Ground Operations School, USAF Special Operations School.

**TEMPORARY MILITARY LODGING:** Billeting Office, Building 90509, 24 hours daily, C-850-884-6245/7115, D-312-579-6245/7115, Fax: C-850-884-5043, D-312-579-5043. All ranks. DV/VIP C-850-884-2308.

**RV, CAMPING/FAMCAMP:** Hurlburt FAMCAMP off base year round, 345 Tully Street, Bldg 90505, Hurlburt Field, FL 32544-5000, C-850-884-6939. Twenty-five camp spaces with full hookups, 10 tent spaces with no hookups.

**SPACE-A:** Base Ops, C-850-884-5781, D-312-579-5781. Recording: C-850-884-5783. Fax: C-850-884-2448, D-312-579-2448. Bldg 90761. Hours: 0730-1630. Also see Eglin AFB listing.

**LOGISTICAL SUPPORT:**

| | |
|---|---|
| Bank-581-2222 | Bay Area Travel-884-4771 |
| Beauty Shop-581-3524 | Child Care-884-6937 |
| Child Dev Center-884-6937 | Class Six-581-0488 |
| Commissary-881-2139 | Credit Union-862-0111 |
| Dining Facilities-884-6935/1276 | Dry Cleaner-581-3614 |
| Education Office-884-6724 | Exchange-581-0030 |
| Laundry-581-3614 | Gas Station-581-2224 |
| Postal Service-884-7646 | SATO-884-6344 |
| Shoppette-581-0488 | |

**ADMINISTRATIVE SUPPORT:**

| | |
|---|---|
| Fire Dept-884-1357/911 | Housing Office-884-7505 |
| Legal-884-7821 | Locator-882-3300 |
| Pass/ID Office-884-5125 | Police-884-6423 |
| Public Affairs-884-7464 | Command Post-884-7774 |

**HEALTH & WELFARE:**

| | |
|---|---|
| Air Force Aid Society-884-5441 | American Red Cross-884-6107/6246 |
| CHAMPUS-881-3912 | Chapel-884-7795 |
| Dental-884-7881 | Family Services-884-6201 |
| Medical | TRICARE-881-3912 |
|   Central Appts-884-7882 | |
|   Clinic-881-5177 | |
|   Emergency-911 | |
|   *or* Eglin ER-883-8227 | |
|   Health Benefits-881-3912 | |
|   Information-883-8242 | |

**REST & RECREATION:**

| | |
|---|---|
| Arts & Crafts-884-6942/7405 | Auto Hobby Shop-884-6674 |
| Bowling-884-6941 | Clubs |
| Community Center-884-6105 |   Consol-884-6469 |
| Fitness Center-884-6949 |   O-884-7507 |
| Golf Course-884-6940/581-0007 |   Soundside-581-3110/3111 |
| Gym-884-6884/6905 | Indoor Rec-884-6105 |
| Library-884-6947/7143 | Marina-884-4097 |
| MWR-884-4099 | Outdoor Rec-884-6939 |
| Recreation-884-7397 |   Equipment Rental |

Services-884-4684
Theater-884-7648
Wood Hobby Shop-884-7244

Swimming-884-6866
Tickets & Tours-884-7848
Youth Center-884-6355

**ATTRACTIONS:** Zoo, Gulf Islands National Seashore, Pensacola Historical Museum, Naval Air Museum, Air Force Armament Museum, Navaree Beach Campgrounds, Gulfarium, Ft. Walton Beach Art Museum, numerous golf courses, sport fishing, boating, water sports, beaches, shopping, Indian Temple Mound Museum, Pensacola (west) and Panama City (east), both short drives.

# JACKSONVILLE INTERNATIONAL AIRPORT/AIR NATIONAL GUARD BASE (FL55R1)

159th Fighter Squadron
Jacksonville, FL 32229-5000

**TELEPHONE NUMBER INFORMATION:** Main installation numbers: C-904-741-7150, D-312-460-7150.

**LOCATION:** Take 95 south, exit 127 on FL-102 west, Airport Road, into airport. USMRA: Page 38 (G-2,3).

**GENERAL INFORMATION:** Home of 125th Fighter Wing.

**LOGISTICAL SUPPORT:**                Exchange-741-7150

**HEALTH & WELFARE:**                Medical-741-7150

**ATTRACTIONS:** Golfing, beaches, deep sea fishing, St. Augustine, Orlando. Museum of Science and History in Jacksonville, art museums, planetarium.

# JACKSONVILLE NAVAL AIR STATION (FL08R1)

Box 2, PAO, Naval Air Station
Jacksonville, FL 32212-5000

**TELEPHONE NUMBER INFORMATION:** Main installation numbers: C-904-542-2345/2346, D-312-942-2345/2346.
E-mail: doolingp@jaxm.navy.mil. WEB: www.nasjax.org

**LOCATION:** Access from US-17 south, Roosevelt Blvd. Clearly marked. USMRA: Page 38 (G-3), page 50 (B,C-6,7). NMC: Jacksonville, nine miles northeast.

**GENERAL INFORMATION:** Fixed and rotary wing anti-submarine warfare aircraft support and training, Naval Hospital, Naval Aviation Depot, Naval Supply Center.

**TEMPORARY MILITARY LODGING:** Lodging office, Building 11, 24 hours daily, C-904-542-3138 (EM), 904-542-3537 (Officer). DV/VIP C-904-542-3147/3427. Navy Lodge: C-904-772-6000, D-312-942-6000 or 1-800-NAVY-INN, Fax: 904-777-1736.

**RV, CAMPING/FAMCAMP:** RV Park on base, year round, C-904-542-3227, D-312-942-3227, eight camper spaces with full hookups, four camper spaces with W/E, 14 camper/tent spaces without hookups.

**SPACE-A:** Pax Term/Lounge, Building 118, 24 hours daily, C-904-542-3956, D-312-942-3956; Fax: C-904-542-3257. Flights to CONUS and Caribbean area.

**LOGISTICAL SUPPORT:**

Child Care-542-5529
Conv Store-777-7285
Gas Station-778-7142
SATO-1-800-949-7286

Commissary-573-5010
Exchange-777-7200
Navy Campus-542-2477
Snack Bar-542-2936

**ADMINISTRATIVE SUPPORT:**

CDO/OOD-542-2338
Legal-542-3481
Police-542-2661

Fire Dept-542-2451
Locator-542-2340
Public Affairs-542-4032

**HEALTH & WELFARE:**

CHAMPUS-573-3300
Family Services-542-2766
Retiree Services-542-5783
Health Benefits Advisor-542-9164
Navy-MC Relief-542-3515
Veterinary Services-542-3786

Chapel-542-3051/3440
Medical-Clinic-542-3500
  Central Appts-542-4677
  Emergency-911
  Health Benefits Advisor-542-9164
  Information-542-7300

**REST & RECREATION:**

Archery-542-3111
Auto Hobby Shop-542-3227
Clubs
  EM-542-3521
  O-542-3041
Library-542-3415
MWR-542-3112
Storage-542-3227
Wood Hobby Shop-542-3681

Athletic Director-542-3239
Bowling-542-3403
Fitness Center-542-3518
Golf Course-542-3249
ITT-542-3318
Marina-542-3260
Recreation-542-3112
Swimming-542-2930

**ATTRACTIONS:** Golfing, beaches, deep sea fishing, St. Augustine, Orlando. Museum of Science and History in Jacksonville, art museums, planetarium.

# JUPITER COAST GUARD EXCHANGE (FL48R1)

US-1, Lighthouse Park
Jupiter, FL 33469-5000.

**TELEPHONE NUMBER INFORMATION:** Main installation numbers: C-561-746-5402.

**LOCATION:** From US-1 south, turn right on FL-707, take first right onto station. USMRA: Page 39 (J-10). NMC: West Palm Beach, 15 miles south.

**LOGISTICAL SUPPORT:**                Exchange-746-5402

# KENNEDY SPACE CENTER (FL56R1)

Kennedy Space Center, FL 32899-0001

**TELEPHONE NUMBER INFORMATION:** Main installation numbers: C-407-452-2121. WEB: www.kennedyspacecenter.com
*Ten digit dialing required for local calls.*

**LOCATION:** From I-95 exit 77, take 528 east to FL-3 (Kennedy Pkwy) north to center on east and west of FL-3. Follow signs, clearly marked. USMRA: Page 38 (I-7). NMC: Cocoa Beach, two miles north.

**GENERAL INFORMATION:** This NASA space center offers tours and exhibits to the public. Open 0900 to dusk daily.

**LOGISTICAL SUPPORT:**

Gift Shop-452-2121                Visitor Center-452-2121

# KEY WEST NAVAL AIR STATION (FL15R1)

Code 01J, P.O. Box 9001
Key West Naval Air Station, FL 33040-9001

**TELEPHONE NUMBER INFORMATION:** Main installation numbers: C-305-293-2268, D-312-483-2268. E-mail: naskwpao@norfolk.navy.mil

**LOCATION:** Take Florida Turnpike, US-1 south to exit signs east for Key West Naval Air Station on Boca Chica Key, seven miles north of Key West. USMRA: Page 39 (G-16). NMC: Miami, 150 miles north.

**GENERAL INFORMATION:** Search and Rescue helicopters, Tactical Aircrew Combat Training (TACTS), Joint Interagency Task Force East (JIATF East), USCGG Key West, Caribbean Regional Operations Center (CARIBROC), U.S. Army Special Forces Underwater Operations School, tactical aircraft and rescue aircraft operations; pilot training, Coast Guard, reserve and other services support detachments.

**TEMPORARY MILITARY LODGING:** Consolidated Bachelor Quarters, P.O. Box 9058, 24 hours daily, C-305-293-4143, D-312-483-4143, Fax: C-305-293-4302, D-312-483-4302. (BOQ) C-305-293-5571, BEQ: C-305-293-2488. Navy Lodge: C-305-292-7556 or 1-800-NAVY-INN.

**RV, CAMPING/FAMCAMP:** Sigsbee RV Park on base, year round, C-305-293-4432, 70 camper spaces with full hookups, 200 camper spaces with W, unlimited tent spaces.

**SPACE-A:** Check at Control Tower, Boca Chica Annex, 0730-1630 daily, C-305-293-2769, D-312-483-2769, Fax: C-305-293-2755, D-312-483-2416, flights to CONUS locations.

**LOGISTICAL SUPPORT:**

| | |
|---|---|
| Barber Shop-292-7223 | Beauty Shop-292-7223 |
| Child Care-293-4376 | Child Dev Center-293-4376 |
| Commissary-293-4402 | Conv Store-292-7226 |
| Credit Union-294-6622 | Dining Facilities-293-2435 |
| Dry Cleaner-292-7229 | Education Office-293-2705 |
| Exchange-292-7210 | Laundry-292-7229 |
| Gas Station-292-7219 | Mini Mart-293-7216 |
| Package Store-292-7226 | Postal Service-293-2406 |
| SATO-294-8470 | Shoppette-293-7216 |
| Travel Office-293-4434 | |

**ADMINISTRATIVE SUPPORT:**

| | |
|---|---|
| CDO/OOD-293-2268 | Fire Dept-293-3145 |
| Housing Office-293-4417 | Legal-293-4310 |
| Pass/ID Office-293-2803 | Police-293-2531 |
| Public Affairs-293-2627 | Quarter Deck-293-2268 |

**HEALTH & WELFARE:**

| | |
|---|---|
| Chapel-293-2318 | Dental-293-2309 |
| Family Service-293-4408 | Medical |
| Navy-MC Relief-293-2169 |   Central Appts-293-4500 |
| TRICARE-293-4543 |   Clinic-293-2444 |
| Veterinary Services-293-2364 |   Emergency-293-2337 |
| |   Health Benefits-293-4543 |
| |   Hospital-293-4500 |
| |   Information-293-4500 |

**REST & RECREATION:**

| | |
|---|---|
| Auto Hobby Shop-293-2615 | Bowling-293-2976 |
| Clubs | Community Center-293-4432 |
|   CPO-293-2407 | Fitness Center-293-2480 |
|   Consol-293-2495 | Gym-293-2480 |
|   EM-293-2495 | ITT-293-4433 |
|   NCO-293-2495 | Marina-293-4434 |
|   O-293-2480 | MWR-293-2112 |
| Outdoor Rec-293-2682 | Rec Center-ext 2112 |
| Water Rec-293-2468 | Youth Center-293-4437 |

**ATTRACTIONS:** Audubon House, Aquarium, Looe Key Reef, Ernest Hemingway Home and Museum, Harry Truman Little White House, Mel Fischer's Maritime Museum, Shipwreck Historium, boating, diving, snorkeling, sport fishing, water sports.

## LAKE PIPPIN, MAXWELL/GUNTER RECREATION AREA (FL12R1)

801 White Point Road
Niceville, FL 32578-5000

**TELEPHONE NUMBER INFORMATION:** Main installation numbers: C-850-897-2411. Police (Eglin AFB) for recreation area, C-850-882-2502.

**LOCATION:** From I-10 at Crestview take Fl-85 south to Niceville. Take Fl-20 east approximately 6.5 miles to sign for Maxwell/Gunter Recreation Area. Mid-Bay Bridge (toll) FL-293 makes area easily accessible from both FL-20 and US-98. USMRA: Page 39 (C,D-13). NMI: Eglin AFB, FL, five miles west. NMC: Fort Walton Beach, FL, eight miles west.

**GENERAL INFORMATION:** Operated by Maxwell AFB, AL, off base, year round. Military personnel active, reservists, retired, DoD civilians. Reservations

(mobile homes only): Outdoor Recreation Reservations Office, 204 West Selfridge Street, Maxwell AFB, AL 36112-5000. C-334-953-3509/3510, D-312-493-3509.

**RV, CAMPING/FAMCAMP:**

| | |
|---|---|
| Mobile Homes-5 | Camper Spaces-39 |
| Tent Spaces-10 | |

**ATTRACTIONS:** Located on Choctawhatchee Bay on northern coast of Gulf of Mexico. Lovely wooded site on beach, within driving distance of Pensacola, Panama City, Fort Walton Beach and fishing attractions.

*For detailed information about this off-base recreation facility, as well as on-base recreation facilities, golf courses and marinas, consult Military Living's Military RV, Camping and Outdoor Recreation Around the World.*

## MacDILL AIR FORCE BASE (FL02R1)

8208 Hangar Loop Drive, Suite 14
MacDill Air Force Base, FL 33621-5502

**TELEPHONE NUMBER INFORMATION:** Main installation numbers: C-813-828-1110, D-312-968-1110. WEB: www.macdill.af.mil

**LOCATION:** From I-75 north or south exit 57 to I-275 south, exit 23 at Dale Mabry Highway (US-92/573), south five miles to MacDill AFB main gate. USMRA: Page 38 (E,F-8), page 56 (E,F-3,4). NMC: Tampa, five miles north.

**GENERAL INFORMATION:** Air Mobility Command Base. Headquarters U.S. Special Operations Command, U.S. Central Command and 6th Air Refueling Wing.

**TEMPORARY MILITARY LODGING:** Lodging office, Building 411, corner Garden Drive & Tampa Blvd, 24 hours daily, C-813-828-2617/4259/2661, D-312-968-2617/4259/2661. All ranks. DV/VIP C-813-828-2056.

**RV, CAMPING/FAMCAMP:** Coon's Creek Recreation Area on base, year round, C-813-840-6919 or 1-800-821-4982, D-312-968-4982, Fax: C-813-828-7507; 199 camper spaces with full hookups, 57 camper spaces with W/E hookups, 33 spaces without hookups, and 34 tent spaces without hookups.

**SPACE-A:** Pax Term/Lounges, Hangar 4, 0730-1630 Mon-Fri, C-813-828-2485, D-312-968-2485, Rec: C-813-828-2310, D-312-968-2310; Fax: C-813-828-7844, D-312-968-7844. Flights to CONUS locations and MEDEVAC.

**LOGISTICAL SUPPORT:**

| | |
|---|---|
| Bank-837-2451 | Barber Shop-840-2154 |
| Beauty Shop-840-0525 | Cafeteria-840-0511 |
| Car Rental-840-2613 | Child Care-828-3332 |
| Commissary-828-4832 | Conv Store-840-2077 |
| Dry Cleaner-840-2329 | Education Center-828-3115 |
| Exchange-840-0511 | Fast Food-840-2992 |
| Gas Station-840-0448 | Package Store-840-2323 |
| Post Office-840-4438 | SATO-843-4327 |
| Snack Bar-840-2211 | Travel Office |
| |   Leisure-840-1338 |
| |   Official-828-5409 |

**ADMINISTRATIVE SUPPORT:**

| | |
|---|---|
| Fire Dept-828-3438 | Legal-828-4421 |
| Locator-828-2444 | Police-828-3322 |
| Public Affairs-828-2215 | |

**HEALTH & WELFARE:**

| | |
|---|---|
| ACS-828-4413 | CHAMPUS-828-5220 |
| Chapel-828-3621 | Family Services-828-2721 |
| Medical | Retiree Services-828-4555 |
|   Central Appts-828-2778/6738 | Veterinary Services-828-3537 |
|   Emergency-828-2334 | |

**REST & RECREATION:**

| | |
|---|---|
| Arts & Crafts-828-4413 | Auto Hobby Shop-ext 4553 |
| Bowling-840-3008 | Clubs |
| Fitness Center-828-4648 |   E M-840-6900 |
| Golf Course-840-6904 |   NCO-828-3357 |
| Gym-ext 4496 |   O-837-1031 |
| ITT-828-2478 | Library-828-3607 |

Marina-ext 4983
Outdoor Rec-840-6919
Theater-828-3973

MWR-ext 4983
Rec Center-ext 4518
Youth Activities-828-6757

**ATTRACTIONS:** Busch Gardens, Disney World, Sea World, professional sports (football, hockey, baseball (spring training), sport fishing, water sports.

# MARATHON RECREATION COTTAGES & RV PARK (FL28R1)

US Coast Guard Station
1800 Overseas Highway MM48
Marathon, FL 33050-2199

**TELEPHONE NUMBER INFORMATION:** Main installation number: C-305-743-3549.

**LOCATION:** Situated on Marathon Key in the heart of the Florida Keys on US-1 (Overseas Highway) at mile marker 48 at Marathon. Enter recreation area from US-1. USMRA: Page 39 (H-15). NMC: Miami, 111 miles northeast. NMI: Key West Naval Air Station on Boca Chica Key, 40 miles south.

**GENERAL INFORMATION:** Topography is similar to that of islands in the eastern Caribbean. Beaches on Atlantic and Gulf sides. Operated by Miami CG Integrated Support Command, on base year round. Military personnel active, retired and reserve. Check in between 1400-1800 hours with OOD, Coast Guard Station Marathon, 1800 Overseas Highway. Phone: C-305-743-3549. Reservations for RV spaces, call C-305-743-3549, Fax: C-305-743-4988. Reservations for cottages, write to: Commanding Officer, U.S. Coast Guard Integrated Support Command Miami, 100 MacArthur Causeway, Miami Beach, FL 33139-5101 or call C-305-535-4565, Fax: C-305-535-4566. E-mail: csova@iscmiami.uscg.mil

**TEMPORARY MILITARY LODGING:** Cottages-4

**RV, CAMPING/FAMCAMP:** RV Spaces-4

**ATTRACTIONS:** The Florida Keys, beautiful beaches and the Florida sun.

*For detailed information about this off-base recreation facility, as well as on-base recreation facilities, golf courses and marinas, consult Military Living's Military RV, Camping and Outdoor Recreation Around the World.*

# MAYPORT COAST GUARD BASE (FL44R1)

4200 Ocean Street
Mayport, FL 32267-0385.

**TELEPHONE NUMBER INFORMATION:** Main installation numbers: C-904-247-7301.

**LOCATION:** From Jacksonville, take Atlantic Boulevard (FL-10) to Mayport Road (FL-A1A). Base is east of FL-A1A. USMRA: Page 38 (H-3), page 50 (F-3). NMC: Jacksonville, eight miles west.

**GENERAL INFORMATION:** Part of Seventh District, U.S. Coast Guard. Two miles from Mayport Naval Station and its many support facilities.

**LOGISTICAL SUPPORT:** Exchange-247-8740/38

**ATTRACTIONS:** Beaches, water activities.

# MAYPORT NAVAL STATION (FL13R1)

Box 32
Mayport Naval Station, FL 32228-0032

**TELEPHONE NUMBER INFORMATION:** Main installation numbers: C-904-270-5011, D-312-960-5011.

**LOCATION:** From Jacksonville take Atlantic Boulevard (FL-10) east to Mayport Road (FL-A1A), left to Naval Station, east of FL-A1A. USMRA: Page 38 (H-3), page 50 (G-3,4). NMC: Jacksonville, 10 miles west.

**GENERAL INFORMATION:** Homeport for 20 ships. Major commands include Commander, Western Hemisphere Group, Commander Carrier Group Six, Commander Cruiser Destroyer Group Twelve.

**TEMPORARY MILITARY LODGING:** Lodging office, Building 1586, Bailey Avenue, 24 hours daily, C-904-247-3964, D-312-960-5707; BEQ: C-904-270-5575, D-312-960-5575; BOQ: C-904-270-5423, D-312-960-5423. All ranks. DV/VIP (EM) C-904-270-5707, D-312-960-5707; (Officers) C-904-247-3964. Navy Lodge, 1-800-NAVY-INN.

**RV, CAMPING/FAMCAMP:** None. See Jacksonville NAS listing.

**SPACE-A:** Information: C-904-270-6023, D-312-960-6023. Flights to CONUS locations. U.S. Customs Service Airport.

**LOGISTICAL SUPPORT:**

| | |
|---|---|
| Barber Shop-247-5203 | Beauty Shop-247-5203 |
| Car Rental-249-0955 | Child Care-270-5339 |
| Child Dev Center-270-5339 | Commissary-249-7362 |
| Conv Store-270-5449 | Credit Union-270-5358 |
| Dry Cleaner-247-5301 | Exchange-247-5752 |
| Gas Station-270-5619 | Postal Service-270-5560 |
| SATO-270-5605 | Snack Bar-270-5143 |

**ADMINISTRATIVE SUPPORT:**

| | |
|---|---|
| CDO/OOD-270-5401 | Fire Dept-270-5334 |
| Housing Office-270-5730 | Legal-270-5647 |
| Locator-270-5401 | Pass/ID Office-270-5585 |
| Police-270-5583 | Public Affairs-270-5226 |
| Quarter Deck-270-5401 | SDO/NCO-270-5401 |

**HEALTH & WELFARE:**

| | |
|---|---|
| American Red Cross-270-5241 | CHAMPUS-270-5763 |
| Chapel-270-5212 | Dental-270-5351 |
| Family Services-270-5392 | Medical |
| Navy-MC Relief-270-5418 | Clinic-270-5675 |
| Retiree Services-270-5783 | Hospital-777-7300 |
| TRICARE-270-5763 | Veterinary Services-270-7004 |

**REST & RECREATION:**

| | |
|---|---|
| Auto Hobby Shop-270-5392 | Bowling-270-5377 |
| Clubs | Golf Course-270-5380 |
| CPO-270-5432 | Gym-270-5451 |
| Beach Club-270-7197 | Intramural Sports-ext 5451 |
| Ocean Breeze Conf Cntr-270-5313 | ITT-270-5145 |
| Library-270-5393 | Rec Center-ext 5680 |
| Swimming-ext 5425 | Tennis-ext 5717 |
| Youth Services-270-5680 | |

**ATTRACTIONS:** Zoo, beaches, deep sea fishing. Three-hour drive to Orlando.

# MIAMI COAST GUARD AIR STATION (FL30R1)

Opa Locka Airport
ATTN: PAO
Opa Locka, FL 33054-2397

**TELEPHONE NUMBER INFORMATION:** Main installation number: C-305-953-2100.

**LOCATION:** Take exit 14 from I-95 onto NW 135th Street (Opa Locka Blvd., also FL-916) west to Lejeune Road, then north to the airport. Turn left on Wright. Air Station is at the end of the road. USMRA: Page 39 (J-13), page 51 (B-4,5). NMC: Miami, 10 miles southeast.

**GENERAL INFORMATION:** A Coast Guard Air Station with regional search-and-rescue and drug-interdiction responsibilities.

**TEMPORARY MILITARY LODGING:** None. See Key West NAS listing.

**RV, CAMPING/FAMCAMP:** None. See Marathon Rec Cottages listing.

**SPACE-A:** No regularly scheduled flights from the Air Station. See Key West NAS listing.

**LOGISTICAL SUPPORT:**
Commissary-953-2290
Package Store-953-2290
Exchange-685-1661-ext 42

**ADMINISTRATIVE SUPPORT:**
CDO/OOD-953-2280
SDO/NCO-953-2130/2140
Public Affairs-953-2151

**HEALTH & WELFARE:**
CHAMPUS-953-2265/2266
Family Services-953-2110
Dental-953-2265
Medical-953-2266

**REST & RECREATION:**
All Hands Club-953-2291
MWR-953-2115
Auto Hobby Shop-953-2115

**OTHER FACILITIES AVAILABLE:** Barber shop, beauty shop, dining facilities, police.

**ATTRACTIONS:** Hollywood/Rembroke Pines Area, city of Miami, Gratigny Park, Spanish Monastery, Vizcaya Art Museum, Hialeah Park, Miami Seaquarium, Miami Serpentarium, Dade City Art Museum, beaches.

## MIAMI COAST GUARD INTEGRATED SUPPORT COMMAND (FL31R1)

100 MacArthur Causeway
Miami Beach, FL 33139-5119

**TELEPHONE NUMBER INFORMATION:** Main installation number: C-305-535-4300.

**LOCATION:** Take I-95 to MacArthur Causeway (also I-359) east. USMRA: Page 39 (J-13), page 51 (D-6). NMC: Miami Beach, in city limits.

**GENERAL INFORMATION:** The Coast Guard Base in Miami is responsible for regional search-and-rescue, drug-interdiction missions and aids to navigation.

**TEMPORARY MILITARY LODGING:** None. See Homestead ARB listing.

**RV, CAMPING/FAMCAMP:** Operates Marathon Rec Cottages and RV Park. C-305-743-3549, Fax-305-743-4988. See Marathon Rec Cottages listing for more information.

**SPACE-A:** None. See Key West NAS listing.

**LOGISTICAL SUPPORT:**
Barber Shop-535-4477
Credit Union-373-5801
Exchange-535-4354/4410
Commissary-305-953-2115
Dining Facilities-535-4460

**ADMINISTRATIVE SUPPORT:**
CDO-535-4377
Legal-536-5610
Pass/ID Office-535-4598
Public Affairs-536-5642
SDO/NCO-535-4361
Housing Office-535-4570
OOD-535-4377
Security-535-4167

**HEALTH & WELFARE:**
CHAMPUS-535-4350
Medical-535-4350

**REST & RECREATION:** None. See Miami CGAS listing.

**ATTRACTIONS:** City of Miami (tours available), Gratigny Park, Spanish Monastery, Vizcaya Art Museum, beaches, water sports.

## ORLANDO NAVY EXCHANGE (FL11R1)

7151 Earhart Drive
Orlando, FL 32827-5000

**TELEPHONE NUMBER INFORMATION:** Main installation numbers: C-407-646-4111, D-312-791-4111.
*Ten digit dialing required for local calls.*

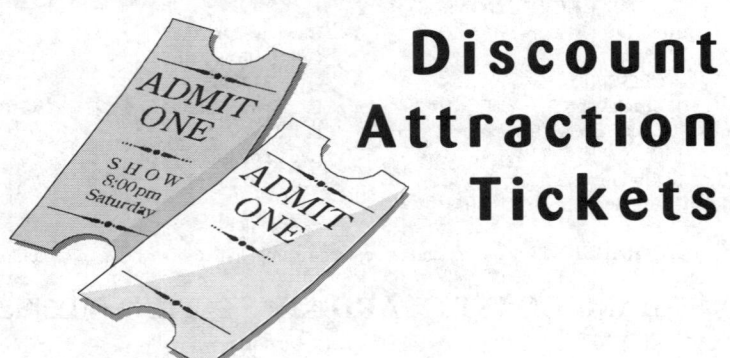

**LOCATION:** From I-4 in Orlando take FL-50 (Colonial Drive) east about three miles; then north on Maguire for one-half mile to NTC. USMRA: Page 38 (H-7), page 53 (D-1). NMI: Patrick AFB, on hour near Cocoa Beach. NMC: Orlando, three miles from downtown.

**GENERAL INFORMATION:** Formerly Naval Training Center.

**LOGISTICAL SUPPORT:**        Navy Exchange-857-3550

**REST & RECREATION:**         MWR-tickets-855-0116

**ATTRACTIONS:** The playground of Florida, Disney World, Busch Gardens, Cypress Gardens, Sea World, Epcot Center, Universal Studios, Church Street Station.

## PANAMA CITY COAST GUARD STATION (FL43R1)

1700 Thomas Drive, Panama City, FL 32407-5898.

**TELEPHONE NUMBER INFORMATION:** Main installation numbers: C-850-234-2475.

**LOCATION:** From the north, take Hwy 231 to 98 west, to south on Thomas Drive. Located 0.25 miles on left on Navy Base (Coastal Systems Station). USMRA: Page 39 (D,E-14). NMC: Panama City, adjacent.

**GENERAL INFORMATION:** Part of Seventh District, U.S. Coast Guard. See Panama City Coastal Systems Station for full range of support.

**LOGISTICAL SUPPORT:**        Exchange-235-5880

**ATTRACTIONS:** Beaches, water sports.

## PANAMA CITY COASTAL SYSTEMS STATION, NAVAL SURFACE WARFARE CENTER (FL35R1)

6703 West Highway 98
Panama City, FL 32407-7001

**TELEPHONE NUMBER INFORMATION:** Main installation numbers: C-850-234-4100, D-312-436-4100. WEB: www.ncsc.navy.mil

**LOCATION:** Located on US-98 at the west foot of the Hathaway Bridge in Panama City Beach. USMRA: Page 39 (D,E-14). NMC: Panama City, adjacent.

**GENERAL INFORMATION:** The Station is a Navy Research and Development Laboratory responsible for coastal and harbor defense activities.

**TEMPORARY MILITARY LODGING:** Central lodging number: C-850-236-2500, D-312-436-2500. Seashore Inn- reservations only: C-850-234-4217, D-312-436-4217, 24 hours daily. DV/VIP (Officers): C-850-234-2500, D-312-436-2500. Transient Family Units: C-850-236-2960.

**RV, CAMPING/FAMCAMP:** Operates Panama City CSS Outdoor Rec/Marina on base; see listing for more information.

**SPACE-A:** None. See Pensacola NAS listing.

**LOGISTICAL SUPPORT:**
Barber Shop-234-4630            Dining Facilities-235-5020
Exchange-235-2407

**ADMINISTRATIVE SUPPORT:**        Police-234-4332

**HEALTH & WELFARE:**
Family Services-235-5800         Medical-234-4177

**REST & RECREATION:**
Auto Hobby Shop-234-4300        Bowling-234-4589
Consol Club-235-5502            Fitness Center-234-4370
ITT-234-4374                    MWR-235-5900
Swimming-235-5921

**ATTRACTIONS:** Beaches, water sports.

## PANAMA CITY COASTAL SYSTEMS STATION OUTDOOR RECREATION/MARINA (FL07R1)

MWR, 6703 W Highway 98
Panama City Coastal Systems Station, FL 32408-5000

**TELEPHONE NUMBER INFORMATION:** Main installation numbers: C-850-234-4100, D-312-436-4100. Police-234-4373.

**LOCATION:** On Base. Located on US-98 at the west foot of the Hathaway Bridge in Panama City Beach. USMRA: Page 39 (D,E-14). NMC: Panama City, adjacent.

**GENERAL INFORMATION:** Reservations: C-850-324-4217. Operated by Panama City Coastal Systems Station, Naval Surface Warfare Center, on base 1 April-31 October, Mon-Thu, 0900-1800; Fri-Sun, Holidays, 0700-1900; 1 November-31 March, Mon-Fri, 0900-1700. Military personnel active, retired, reserve, DoD civilians at Coastal Systems Station. Reservations: For campers/boats, call the Marina, C-850-234-4402 or write to address above. Fax: C-850-234-4334. *Note: As of 1 February 2000, condos on the beach will no longer be available.*

**TEMPORARY MILITARY LODGING:** Mobile homes-3

**RV, CAMPING/FAMCAMP:** Camper spaces-29

**ATTRACTIONS:** Water sports (jet skiing, sailing, boating, swimming, etc).

*For detailed information about this off-base recreation facility, as well as on-base recreation facilities, golf courses and marinas, consult Military Living's Military RV, Camping and Outdoor Recreation Around the World.*

## PATRICK AIR FORCE BASE (FL03R1)

1201 Edward H. White Street, Suite C-129
Patrick Air Force Base, FL 32925-3237

**TELEPHONE NUMBER INFORMATION:** Main installation numbers: C-407-494-1110, D-312-854-1110.
*Ten digit dialing required for local calls.*

**LOCATION:** Take I-95 south to exit 73 east (Wickham Road), three miles to FL-404 (Pineda Causeway), left on South Patrick Drive, to Patrick AFB. USMRA: Page 38 (I-8). NMC: Orlando, 45 miles northwest.

**GENERAL INFORMATION:** Air Force Space Command Base, 45th Space Wing, support to DoD and NASA.

**TEMPORARY MILITARY LODGING:** Billeting Office, Building 720, 820 Falcon Avenue, 24 hours daily, C-407-494-6590, D-312-854-6590. Fax: C-407-494-7597. All ranks. DV/VIP-407-494-4511.

**RV, CAMPING/FAMCAMP:** Manatee Cove Campground on base, year round, C-407-494-4787, D-312-854-4787, 56 camper spaces with W/E, five spaces without hookups.

**SPACE-A:** Pax Term/Lounge, Building 800, 0730-1630 Mon-Fri, C-407-494-5631, D-312-854-5631; Fax: C-407-494-7991, D-312-854-7991. Flights to CONUS and Caribbean locations.

**LOGISTICAL SUPPORT:**
Bank-633-1100                   Barber Shop-784-2781
Beauty Shop-784-1241            Car Rental-783-2424
Child Care-494-7028             Commissary-494-4060
Conv Store-494-4555             Dinette-494-4248
Dry Cleaner-783-3625            Exchange-799-1300
Gas Station-494-2655            Package Store-494-6686
SATO-494-4155                   Snack Bar-494-5614
Visitor Center-494-2659

**ADMINISTRATIVE SUPPORT:**
Fire Department-494-7642        Legal-494-7357
Locator-494-4542                Police-494-2008
Public Affairs-494-5933         SDO/NCO-494-7001/7491

**HEALTH & WELFARE:**
CHAMPUS-494-8112
Family Services-494-4907
Retiree Services-494-5464

Chapel-494-4073
Medical-494-8229
  Central Appts-494-8134
  Emergency-494-8134

**REST & RECREATION:**
Auto Hobby Shop-ext 2537
Clubs
  Aero-ext 4356
  EM-494-7491
  NCO-494-7491
  O-494-4011
MWR-494-8382
Rec Center-ext 5523
Swimming-ext 6796
Youth Center-ext 4747

Bowling-ext 2958
Golf Course-494-7856
Gym-ext 6697
Hobby Shops-ext 2482
ITT-494-5158
Library-ext 6881
Recreation-853-1287
Skeet-ext 4787
Theater-494-2057

**ATTRACTIONS:** Air Force Space Museum, John F. Kennedy Space Center, Disney World, Daytona Beach, Epcot Center, Spaceport USA, Sea World.

# PENSACOLA NAVAL AIR STATION (FL14R1)

190 Radford Boulevard
Pensacola Naval Air Station, FL 32508-5217

**TELEPHONE NUMBER INFORMATION:** Main installation numbers: C-850-452-0111, D-312-922-0111.

**LOCATION:** Four miles south of US-98, and 12 miles south of I-10. Take Navy Blvd from US-98 or US-29 directly to NAS. USMRA: Page 39 (A,B-13,14), page 53 (A,B-4,5). NMC: Pensacola, eight miles north.

**GENERAL INFORMATION:** Chief of Naval Education & Training, Naval Aviation Schools Command, home of Navy Blue Angels, Navy Public Works Center, Naval Air Technical Training Center.

**TEMPORARY MILITARY LODGING:** Lodging office, 24 hours daily, Building 600, C-850-452-2756, D-312-922-2756, Fax: C-850-452-3188. Navy Lodge C-1-800-628-9466.

**RV, CAMPING/FAMCAMP:** Oak Grove Park on base, year round, C-850-452-2535, D-312-922-2535, 0800-1630 (winter), 0830-1700 (summer), 12 cabins, 42 camper spaces with W/E hookups, 15 tent sites.

**SPACE-A:** Pax Term/Lounge, Building 1852, 0600-2100 daily, C-850-452-3311, D-312-922-3311, Fax: C-850-452-2512, flights to CONUS locations.

**LOGISTICAL SUPPORT:**
Bank-453-3411/2311
Beauty Shop-458-3328
Chapel-452-2341
Child Dev Center-452-2211
Commissary-452-6889
Conv Store-453-3356
Credit Union-453-4341
Dining Facilities-452-3859
Exchange-458-3317
Laundry-458-3275
Postal Service-452-2627
Shoppette-458-3356
Travel Office-452-2481

Barber Shop-458-3339
Cafeteria-458-3271
Child Care-452-4569
Clubs
  E M-452-4357
  O-455-2276
Dry Cleaner-458-3275
Education Office-452-4119
Gas Station-458-3220
Package Store-455-3356
SATO-452-2589
Snack Bar-452-3899
Visitor Center-452-4412

**ADMINISTRATIVE SUPPORT:**
CDO/OOD-452-3100 ext 0
Housing Office-452-4412
Locator-452-4693
Police-452-2453
Quarter Deck-452-3100 ext 0

Fire Dept-452-2896
Legal-452-3730
Pass/ID Office-452-4153
Public Affairs-452-2311

**HEALTH & WELFARE:**
American Red Cross-452-2492
Chapel-452-2341
Family Services-452-5990
Navy-MC Relief-455-8574
Retiree Services-452-5990
TRICARE-457-7878
Veterinary Services-452-3530

CHAMPUS-452-6711
Dental-452-5600
Medical-452-5662
  Central Appts-452-5242
  Clinic-452-5242
  Emergency-452-4138
  Health Benefits-452-6711
  Hospital-452-5242
  Information-452-5242

**REST & RECREATION:**
Auto Hobby Shop-452-7815
Bowling-ext 4630
Fitness Center-452-2317
Golf Course-452-2454
Gym-452-2317
Indoor Rec-452-2317
Library-452-4362
MWR-452-3806
Sailing452-3369
Wood Hobby Shop-452-6489
Youth Center-452-2417

Beach-ext 4391
Clubs
  EM-452-4357
  NCO-452-2443
  O-455-2276/8860
ITT-452-4229/6354
Marinas-452-3369
Outdoor Rec-452-4931
Services-458-3356
Swimming 452-4391
Youth Services-452-2417

**ATTRACTIONS:** Sport fishing, water sports, golf, National Museum of Naval Aviation, Fiesta of Five Flags, Fort Pickens, Fort Barrancas, annual Blue Angels Marathon, annual Blue Angels Homecoming Air Show (Nov).

# PENSACOLA NAVAL HOSPITAL (FL20R1)

6000 West Highway 98
Pensacola, FL 32512-0003

**TELEPHONE NUMBER INFORMATION:** Main installation numbers: C-850-505-6601, D-312-534-6601.

**LOCATION:** On US-98 between Navy Blvd and Fairfield Drive, west of Corry Station and north of US-98, in Pensacola. USMRA: Page 39 (A,B-13), page 53 (B-4). NMC: Pensacola, in city limits.

**GENERAL INFORMATION:** The Naval Hospital, built in 1976, supports four naval training bases and has four branch medical clinics in the area. It also supports four other branch medical clinics at Panama City, Florida, Pascagoula, Gulfport and Meridian, Mississippi.

**TEMPORARY MILITARY LODGING:** None. See Pensacola NAS listing, and Whiting Field NAS.

**RV, CAMPING/FAMCAMP:** None. See Pensacola NAS listing, Oak Grove Trailer Park.

**SPACE-A:** None. See Pensacola NAS listing.

**LOGISTICAL SUPPORT:**
Conv Store-455-9649
Snack Bar-455-6267

Exchange-505-6601

**ADMINISTRATIVE SUPPORT:**
CDO-505-6601
Public Affairs-505-6796

OOD-505-6604
Quarter Deck-505-6601

**HEALTH & WELFARE:**
CHAMPUS-505-6709
Medical
  Emergency-505-6730/1/88
  Health Benefits-505-6709
  Information-505-6601

Chapel-505-6844
TRICARE-457-7878

**REST & RECREATION:** None. See Pensacola NAS and Corry NTTC listings.

Visit Military Living's helpful site and online order store on the world wide web at
# w w w . m i l i t a r y l i v i n g . c o m

**OTHER FACILITIES AVAILABLE:** Dining facilities, postal service.

**ATTRACTIONS:** The Blue Angels, beaches, fishing.

## PONCE DE LEON COAST GUARD STATION (FL50R1)

2999 North Peninsula Avenue
New Smyrna Beach, FL 32169-0370

**TELEPHONE NUMBER INFORMATION:** Main installation numbers: C-904-428-9085.

**LOCATION:** From 95 South exit 84, or I-4 exit at FL-44 east, across two bridges, turn left at the first light onto Peninsula Avenue. USMRA: Page 38 (I-6). NMC: Orlando, 50 miles southwest.

**GENERAL INFORMATION:** Part of Seventh District U.S. Coast Guard.

**LOGISTICAL SUPPORT:**              Exchange-427-2786

**ADMINISTRATIVE SUPPORT:**         OOD-428-9085

**ATTRACTIONS:** Beautiful beaches, Ponce Inlet Lighthouse, fishing, Turnbull Ruins, Turtle Mound.

## PORT CANAVERAL COAST GUARD STATION (FL58R1)

9235 Grouper Road
Cape Canaveral, FL 32920-4402

**TELEPHONE NUMBER INFORMATION:** Main installation numbers: C-407-868-7769.
*Ten digit dialing required for local calls.*

**LOCATION:** From I-95 north or south, exit 77, take Route 528 east to Bennett Causeway. Take a left on Cape Road to a right on Grouper Street. USMRA: Page 38 (I-7). NMC: Orlando, 60 miles east.

**GENERAL INFORMATION:** Part of Seventh District, missions include maritime law enforcement, search and rescue, security for Space Shuttle and rocket launches from Cape Canaveral Air Station and Kennedy Space Center. Homeport of several cutters, Electronics Support Detachment and Marine Safety Detachment.

**LOGISTICAL SUPPORT:**              Exchange-868-7769

**ATTRACTIONS:** Tours of Kennedy Space Center, fantastic beaches, fishing, camping, parks.

## RICHMOND HEIGHTS COAST GUARD EXCHANGE (FL57R1)

Richmond Heights, 15298 SW 121st Avenue
Miami, FL 33177-5000

**TELEPHONE NUMBER INFORMATION:** Main installation numbers: C-305-234-2479.
*Ten digit dialing required for local calls.*

**LOCATION:** On 21st Avenue, west of I-826, exit 16 (152nd Street) off of Florida Turnpike, west to 121st Avenue, right near Miami's Metro Zoo. USMRA: Page 51 (A-9).

**GENERAL INFORMATION:** One of several branch stores run by USCG Air Station Miami.

**LOGISTICAL SUPPORT:**              Exchange-305-234-2479

**ATTRACTIONS:** City of Miami (tours available), Gratigny Park, Spanish Monastery, Vizcaya Art Museum, beaches, water sports.

## ST. PETERSBURG COAST GUARD GROUP (FL33R1)

600 8th Avenue SE
St. Petersburg, FL 33701-5099

**TELEPHONE NUMBER INFORMATION:** Main installation numbers: C-727-824-7506, 1-800-732-6864.

**LOCATION:** Take I-275 to I-175 east and south, exit 9 east, go three blocks, make a right to CG Group. Located adjacent to Albert Whitted Airport. USMRA: Page 38 (E-8), page 56 (D-5). NMC: St. Petersburg, in city limits. NMI: MacDill AFB.

**TEMPORARY MILITARY LODGING:** None. See MacDill AFB listing.

**RV, CAMPING/FAMCAMP:** None. See MacDill AFB listing, Coon's Creek Rec Area.

**SPACE-A:** None. See MacDill AFB listing.

**LOGISTICAL SUPPORT:**
Barber Shop-896-2816 ext. 37          Dining Facilities-824-7651
Exchange-896-2816                     Minimart-824-7667
Package Store-896-2816                SDO/NCO-824-7501

**ADMINISTRATIVE SUPPORT:**
CDO/OOD-824-7627                      Locator-824-7506
Police-825-7599                       Public Affairs-824-7564

**HEALTH & WELFARE:**
CHAMPUS-824-7579                      Chapel-823-3454
Family Services-824-7684             Medical-824-7579
Retiree Services-824-7504             Emergency-824-7579

**REST & RECREATION:**
Clubs                                 MWR-824-7598
  Consol-824-7658

**OTHER FACILITIES AVAILABLE:** Swimming pool with picnic area.

**ATTRACTIONS:** Close to beaches, boating, fishing, skin diving, scuba diving, snorkeling, water skiing, St. Petersburg sights, professional sports, MLB spring training, Salvador Dali Museum.

## SAND KEY COAST GUARD STATION (FL16R1)

1375 Gulf Boulevard
Clearwater, FL 34630-5000

**TELEPHONE NUMBER INFORMATION:** Main installation numbers: C-727-596-8540.

**LOCATION:** From CG Group St. Petersburg, west on I-175, north on I-275, west on 686 (Roosevelt), to Gulf Blvd North. Station is three miles on right. USMRA: Page 38 (E-8), page 56 (A-2). NMC: St. Petersburg, 10 miles south.

**GENERAL INFORMATION:** Part of Seventh District U.S. Coast Guard.

**LOGISTICAL SUPPORT:**              Exchange-596-8744

**ADMINISTRATIVE SUPPORT:**         OOD-596-8666

**ATTRACTIONS:** Wonderful beaches, water activities.

## SAUFLEY FIELD (FL34R1)

NETPDTC
6490 Saufley Field Road
Pensacola, FL 32509-5237

**TELEPHONE NUMBER INFORMATION:** Main installation numbers: C-850-452-1628, D-312-922-1628. WEB: www.cnet.navy.mil

**LOCATION:** From I-10 take exit 2 to FL-297 (Pine Forest Road) south to a right onto Blue Angel Parkway south, then take a right onto Saufley Field Road to main gate of base. USMRA: Page 39 (A,B-13), page 53 (A,B-3). NMC: Pensacola, in the city.

**GENERAL INFORMATION:** Host unit at Saufley Field is the Naval Education and Training Professional Development and Technology Center (NETPDTC). Tenant units include the Defense Activity for Non-Traditional Education Support (DANTES), Federal Prison Camp, Finance and Accounting Service Center, Naval Reserve Center, and other minor units.

**TEMPORARY MILITARY LODGING:** None. See Pensacola NAS listing.

**RV, CAMPING/FAMCAMP:** None. See Pensacola NAS listing, Oak Grove Trailer Park.

**SPACE-A:** None. See Pensacola NAS listing.

**LOGISTICAL SUPPORT:**               Exchange-456-3526

**ADMINISTRATIVE SUPPORT:**
CDO-452-1628                          MSO-452-1519
Postal Service-452-1002

**HEALTH & WELFARE:**
Chapel-452-1655                       Dental-452-5600
Medical
   Emergency-452-3333

**REST & RECREATION:**
CMO Club-452-1556                     Golf Course-452-1097
Gym-ext 1071                          Services-452-1071 (Corry Annex)

**ATTRACTIONS:** Gulf Islands National Seashore (Fort Pickens, Fort Barrancas, Fort Barrancas Advanced Redoubt), Naval Museum of Aviation.

# SHADES OF GREEN™ ON WALT DISNEY WORLD® RESORT (FL49R1)
P.O. Box 22789
Lake Buena Vista, FL 32830-2789

**TELEPHONE NUMBER INFORMATION:** Main installation number: C-407-824-3400.
*Ten digit dialing required for local calls.*

**LOCATION:** From Orlando take I-4 west, exit 26-B. Walt Disney World, follow Magic Kingdom Resort signs, go through Magic Kingdom toll booth, stay in far right lane following signs to resort and hotels, at first light turn left, Seven Seas Drive past Polynesian Resort, come to three way stop, turn right on Floridian Way. Driveway is first road to the left, Magnolia Palm Drive. USMRA: Page 38 (G-7), page 53 (A-2). NMC: Orlando, 15 miles northeast.

**GENERAL INFORMATION:** Operated by the Army as an Armed Forces Rec Center (AFRC). Season of Operation: Year round. Military personnel, active, retired, guard & reserve, family members and DoD employees. Reservations (required): call C-407-824-3600, or Fax C-407-824-3665. You may also write for reservation and information packet.

**TEMPORARY MILITARY LODGING:**
Rooms-287                             Suite-1

**LOGISTICAL SUPPORT:**
Car Rental-824-3600                   Dining Facility-824-3574
Gift Shop-824-3400                    Garden Gallery Restaurant/
Travel Office-824-3600                  Evergreens Sport Bar & Grill

**ATTRACTIONS:** A child's dream come true, a visit to Walt Disney World®, Epcot Center and Disney MGM Studios Theme Park. Located on the Magic Kingdom Resort area with transportation available to all Walt Disney World® attractions. Shades of Green™ lies directly adjacent to two PGA Championship Golf Courses, home of the Walt Disney World®/Oldsmobile Golf Classic. If that is not enough to keep you busy, there is golf, swimming, and tennis all without leaving the resort.

*For detailed information about this off-base lodging facility, as well as on-base lodging facilities, consult Military Living's Temporary Military Lodging Around the World.*

# TYNDALL AIR FORCE BASE (FL04R1)
445 Suwannee Road, Building 662, Suite 101
Tyndall Air Force Base, FL 32403-5541

**TELEPHONE NUMBER INFORMATION:** Main installation number: C-850-283-1110, D-312-523-1110. E-mail: 325fw/pa@tyndall.af.mil
WEB: www.tyndall.af.mil

**LOCATION:** Take I-10, exit to US-231 south to US-98 east. Tyndall AFB is southeast of US-98. Clearly marked. USMRA: Page 39 (E-14). NMC: Panama City, 10 miles northwest.

**GENERAL INFORMATION:** Air Education and Training Command Base, 325th Fighter Wing, 1st Air Force Headquarters Southeast Air Defense Sector, Headquarters USAF Civil Engineering Support Agency, 475th Weapons Evaluation Group.

**TEMPORARY MILITARY LODGING:** Billeting Office, Building 1329, C-850-283-4210/4211. All ranks. DV/VIP C-850-283-2232.

**RV, CAMPING/FAMCAMP:** FAMCAMP on base, year round, C-850-283-2798, D-312-523-2798, three cottages, 76 camper spaces with full hookups, 14 camper spaces with W/E, eight tent spaces.

**SPACE-A:** Base Ops, Building 149, C-850-283-4360, D-312-523-4360. Also see Pensacola NAS listing.

**LOGISTICAL SUPPORT:**
Barber Shop-286-4300                  Child Care-283-2266
Child Dev Center-283-4747             Commissary-283-4825
Conv Store-286-5804                   Credit Union-769-9999
Dining Facilities-283-2239            Education Office-283-4285
Exchange-283-4110                     Gas Station-286-5826
Package Store-286-5886                Postal Service-283-2366
SATO-283-2581                         Shoppette-286-5852
Snack Bar-283-2814                    Travel Office-283-3177
Visitor Center-283-3860

**ADMINISTRATIVE SUPPORT:**
Command Post-283-2115                 Fire Dept-283-4777
Housing Office-283-2706               Legal-283-4681
Locator-283-2138/4210                 Pass/ID Office-283-4191
Police-283-2254                       Public Affairs-283-2983
SDO/NCO-283-4145

**HEALTH & WELFARE:**
Air Force Aid Society-283-4205        American Red Cross-283-2770
CHAMPUS-283-3883                      Chapel-283-2925
Dental                               Family Services-283-4204
   Central Appts-283-7572             Medical
   Clinic-283-7579                       Central Appts-283-2778
Retiree Services-283-2737               Emergency-911
TRICARE-283-7168                        Hospital-283-7515
Veterinary Services-283-2434            Information-283-7583

**REST & RECREATION:**
Arts & Crafts-283-4511                Auto Hobby Shop-283-4542
Bowling-283-2380                      Clubs
Community Center-283-2495                Flying-283-2495
Golf Course-286-2565                     NCO/EM-283-4146
Gym-283-2631                             O-286-5171
ITT-283-2499                          Library-283-4287
Marinas-286-9911                      MWR-283-2501
Outdoor Rec-283-4473                  Swimming-283-2495
Tennis-283-2495                       Theater-283-2594
Wood Hobby Shop-283-2594              Youth Center-283-4366
Youth Services-283-2517

**ATTRACTIONS:** Panama City and beautiful white sand beaches.

# UNITED STATES SOUTHERN COMMAND (FL59R1)

3511 NW 91st Avenue
Miami, FL 33172-5000

**TELEPHONE NUMBER INFORMATION:** Main installation numbers: C-888-547-4025. WEB: www.ussouthcom.com/mrc/indexmia.htm

**LOCATION:** From 95 north or south, take the NW 36th Street exit. Turn right onto NW 36th Street, left on NW 87th Street, right on 33rd Street. Follow signs. USMRA: Page 51 (B-5). NMC: Miami, in city limits.

**GENERAL INFORMATION:** Operational command and control for all U.S. land, sea, and air activities in the Southern Hemisphere and the Caribbean.

**TEMPORARY MILITARY LODGING:** None. See Homestead ARB listing.

**RV, CAMPING/FAMCAMP:** None. See Homestead ARB listing.

**SPACE-A:** None. See Homestead ARB listing.

**LOGISTICAL SUPPORT:**
Barber Shop-437-1128        Dry Cleaning-437-1930
Shoppette-437-1856

**ADMINISTRATIVE SUPPORT:**
Family Services-437-2665/888-547-4025-ext 2665
Public Affairs-1-888-547-4025 ext-1208

**HEALTH & WELFARE:**
Dental-                      Medical-
  Appointments-437-1148/3559    Appointments-437-3559/1148
                                Health Benefits-437-1394/ 3559

**REST & RECREATION:**       MWR-438-1737

**ATTRACTIONS:** Miami museums, fine beaches, water activities.

# WHITING FIELD NAVAL AIR STATION (FL05R1)

7550 USS Essex Street
Milton, FL 32570-6155

**TELEPHONE NUMBER INFORMATION:** Main installation numbers: C-850-623-7011, D-312-868-7011. E-mail: naswf.00b1@smtp.cnet.navy.mil WEB: www.cnet.navy.mil/tw5

**LOCATION:** From US-90 east exit, FL-87 north for eight miles to NAS on east side of FL-87. USMRA: Page 39 (B-13). NMC: Pensacola, 30 miles southwest.

**GENERAL INFORMATION:** Naval Aviation Training, fixed- and rotary-wing aircraft.

**TEMPORARY MILITARY LODGING:** Lodging office, Building 2942, 24 hours daily, C-850-623-7605/6, D-312-868-7605/6. All ranks. DV/VIP C-850-623-7201/7605.

**RV, CAMPING/FAMCAMP:** None. See Pensacola NAS listing, Oak Grove Trailer Park.

**SPACE-A:** None. See Pensacola NAS listing.

**LOGISTICAL SUPPORT:**
Bank-623-5489               Child Care-623-7472
Commissary-623-7131         Credit Union-623-6649
Education Office-452-4510    Exchange-623-8066
Gas Station-623-8088        Package Store-623-7198

**ADMINISTRATIVE SUPPORT:**
CDO/OOD-623-7437           Fire Dept-623-7331
Legal-623-7231             Locator-623-7437
Navy-MC Relief-623-7261     Police-623-7431/2

Public Affairs-623-7651

**HEALTH & WELFARE:**
CHAMPUS-623-7657           Chapel-623-7211
Chapel-623-7395            Family Services-623-7177
Medical-623-7151           Retiree Services-623-7177

**REST & RECREATION:**
Boat Dock-623-2383         Bowling-623-7313
Consol Club-623-7311       Fitness Center-623-7798
Golf Course/Pro Shop-623-7348   Gym-623-7798
Hobby Shop-623-7445        ITT-623-7313
Indoor Rec-623-7283        Library-623-7274
MWR-623-7221               Outdoor Rec Equip-623-7533
Racquetball-623-7412       Recreation-623-7502

**ATTRACTIONS:** Deep sea fishing, hunting, water sports, golf, dog races, stock car racing, Pensacola Symphony Orchestra.

# GEORGIA

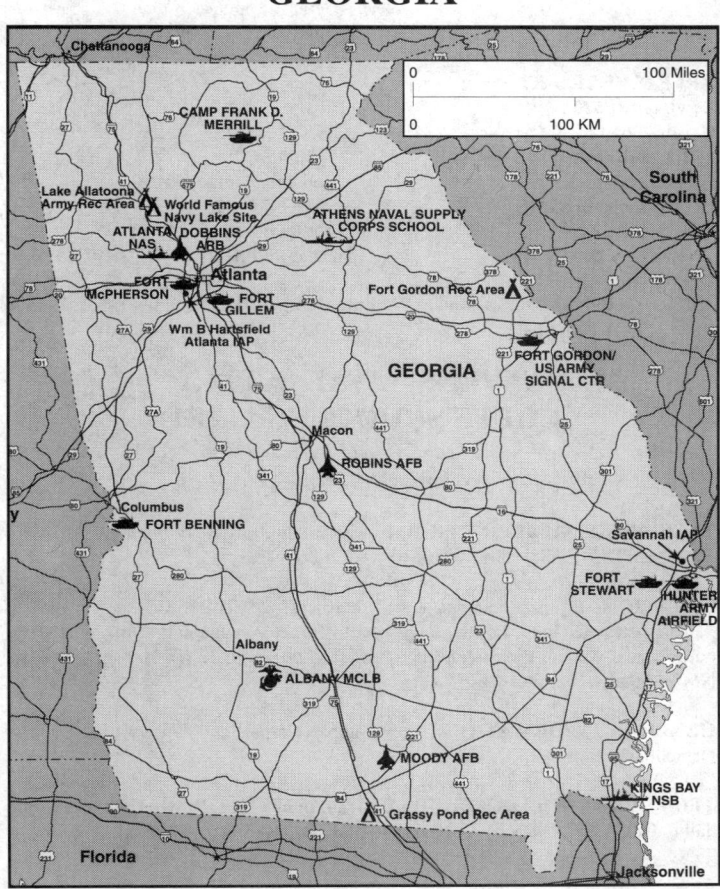

# ALBANY MARINE CORPS LOGISTICS BASE (GA17R1)

814 Radford Boulevard
Albany, GA 31704-1128

**TELEPHONE NUMBER INFORMATION:** Main installation numbers: C-912-439-5000, D-312-567-5000.

**LOCATION:** Off US-82 east of Albany, take Mock Road south from 5-Points to Fleming Road. Go east to main gate. USMRA: Page 37 (C-8). NMC: Albany, three miles west.

**GENERAL INFORMATION:** The East Coast main Marine Corps Logistics Base.

**TEMPORARY MILITARY LODGING:** Housing office, Building 3600, 0800-1630 daily. C-912-439-5614, D-312-567-5614.

**RV, CAMPING/FAMCAMP:** None. See Moody AFB listing, Grassy Pond Rec Area.

**SPACE-A:** None. See Moody AFB listing.

**LOGISTICAL SUPPORT:**

| | |
|---|---|
| Child Care-439-5247 | Commissary-435-1721 |
| Conv Store-435-8352 | Exchange-888-6801 |
| Gas Station-436-8352 | Package Store-888-6801 |
| Omega Travel-435-1946 | Snack Bar-432-2759 |

**ADMINISTRATIVE SUPPORT:**

| | |
|---|---|
| Legal-439-5212 | Locator-439-5000/5206 |
| Police-439-5181 | SDO/NCO-439-5206 |

**HEALTH & WELFARE:**

| | |
|---|---|
| CHAMPUS-435-5544 | Chapel-439-5282 |
| Family Services-439-5276 | Medical |
| | Central Appts-435-5984 |
| | Emergency-439-5911 |

**REST & RECREATION:**

| | |
|---|---|
| Bowling-ext 5233 | Clubs |
| Covella Pond Picnic Area-ext 5234 | NCO-439-5223 |
| Golf Course-ext 5211 | O-439-5239 |
| Gym-ext 5246 | Rod/Gun Club-ext 5000 |
| Hobby Shops-ext 5226 | SNCO-439-5197 |
| Library-ext 5242 | Skeet Range-ext 5234 |
| Swimming-ext 5234 | Theater-439-5166 |

**ATTRACTIONS:** MCLB Band, Wildlife Refuge, Tallahassee, FL, easy drive south.

## ATHENS NAVAL SUPPLY CORPS SCHOOL (GA12R1)

1425 Prince Avenue
Athens, GA 30606-2205

**TELEPHONE NUMBER INFORMATION:** Main installation numbers: C-706-354-1500, D-312-588-1500. WEB: www.nscs.com

**LOCATION:** From Atlanta, take I-85 northeast to GA-316/US-29. Go east to Athens perimeter loop. Follow loop west to Prince Avenue exit. Turn left (north) onto Prince Avenue. Base is on the right. USMRA: Page 37 (D-3), page 49 (A-1). NMC: Atlanta, 70 miles west.

**GENERAL INFORMATION:** Navy Supply Corps School, Personnel Support Detachment.

**TEMPORARY MILITARY LODGING:** Lodging office, Brown Hall, 0800-1600 daily, BEQ/BOQ/DV/VIP C-706-354-7360, D-312-588-7360, Fax: C-706-354-7360.

**RV, CAMPING/FAMCAMP:** None. See Fort Gordon listing.

**SPACE-A:** None. See Atlanta NAS listing.

**LOGISTICAL SUPPORT:**

| | |
|---|---|
| Barber Shop-354-7388 | Car Rental-354-3850 |
| Child Care-543-6113 | Child Development-548-4832 |
| Commissary-354-7371 | Conv Store-354-8761 |
| Credit Union-549-4438 | Dining Facilities-354-7380 |
| Dry Cleaner-354-3850 | Exchange-354-3850 |
| Gas Station-354-8761 | Laundry-354-3850 |
| Package Store-354-3850 | Postal Service-354-7306 |
| Travel Office-354-7345 | |

**ADMINISTRATIVE SUPPORT:**

| | |
|---|---|
| CDO/OOD-354-1500 | Police-354-7355 |
| Housing Office-354-7302 | Legal-354-7203 |
| OOD-354-1500 | Pass/ID Office-354-7336 |
| Public Affairs-354-7316 | Quarter Deck-354-1500 |

**HEALTH & WELFARE:**

| | |
|---|---|
| CHAMPUS-354-7321 | Chapel-354-7208 |
| Dental-354-7324 | Medical-354-7320 |
| Navy-MC Relief-354-7324/7486 | Retiree Services-354-7335 |

**REST & RECREATION:**

| | |
|---|---|
| Consol Club-354-7381 | Fitness Center-354-7374 |
| Library-354-7217 | MWR-354-7374 |

**ATTRACTIONS:** Athens, University of Georgia, Naval Supply Corps Museum, many parks.

## ATLANTA NAVAL AIR STATION (GA16R1)

1000 Halsey Avenue
Marietta, GA 30060-5099

**TELEPHONE NUMBER INFORMATION:** Main installation numbers: C-770-919-6392, D-312-925-6392.
*Ten digit dialing required for local calls.*

**LOCATION:** From I-75 north or south, take exit 110 to GA-280 west. Proceed west on Windy Hill to Atlanta Road. Take right, north on Atlanta Road to Richardson Road. Take right, east. Main gate on left. USMRA: Page 37 (B-3), page 49 (A-1). NMC: Atlanta, 15 miles southeast.

**GENERAL INFORMATION:** Navy and Marine Corps tactical aircraft and crew training, training and administration of Naval Reservists.

**RV, CAMPING/FAMCAMP:** World Famous Navy Lake Site, off base, C-770-974-6309, nine cabins, one camper with W/E, ten camper spaces with W/E hookups, two camper spaces without hookups, three tent spaces.

**TEMPORARY MILITARY LODGING:** Lodging office, Building 54, 24 hours daily. Very limited. BEQ/BOQ/DV/VIP C-770-919-6393, D-312-925-6393.

**SPACE-A:** C-770-919-6359, D-312-925-6359.

**LOGISTICAL SUPPORT:**

| | |
|---|---|
| Barber Shop-919-6592 | Child Care-919-6590 |
| Credit Union-422-4469 | Exchange-428-1274 |
| Gas Station-427-4400 | Package Store-419-0776 |
| SATO-424-3909 | Shoppette-428-4711 |
| Snack Bar-919-6493 | Travel Office-919-6341 |
| Visitor Center-919-6735 | |

**ADMINISTRATIVE SUPPORT:**

| | |
|---|---|
| CDO/OOD-919-6392 | Legal-919-6237/8 |
| Police-919-6394 | Public Affairs-919-6419/6415 |
| Quarter Deck-919-6392 | |

**HEALTH & WELFARE:**

| | |
|---|---|
| CHAMPUS-919-5314 | Chapel-919-6472 |
| Family Services-919-6735 | Medical-919-5300 |
| Navy-MC Relief-919-6622 | Central Appts-919-5302 |
| Retiree Services-919-6735 | Emergency-919-5304 |

**REST & RECREATION:**

| | |
|---|---|
| Bowling-919-6101 | Clubs |
| Fitness Center-919-6785 | CPO-919-6508 |
| ITT-919-6502 | NCO-919-6508 |
| MWR/QOL-919-6498 | O-919-6508 |

**ATTRACTIONS:** Atlanta, Stone Mountain State Park, Six Flags Over Georgia, and other attractions are within 30 miles of NAS.

# CAMP FRANK D. MERRILL (GA23R1)

Wahsega Road
Dahlonega, GA 30533-9499

**TELEPHONE NUMBER INFORMATION:** Main installation numbers: C-706-864-3327, D-312-797-5770.

**LOCATION:** From GA 400 north from Atlanta, take Highway 60 north to Dahlonega, follow 60 and US 19 approximately three miles. Take left on Wahsega Road. Camp is approximately nine miles. USMRA: Page 37 (C-2). NMC: Gainesville, 25 miles south.

**GENERAL INFORMATION:** Mountain training phase of Ranger School.

**TEMPORARY MILITARY LODGING:** Small lodging facility (two units), C-706-864-3327 ext-187. All ranks. (Can be bumped by incoming assigned duty status personnel.)

**RV, CAMPING/FAMCAMP:** None. See Dobbins ARB listing.

**SPACE-A:** See Dobbins ARB listing.

**LOGISTICAL SUPPORT:**

| | |
|---|---|
| Commissary-ext-109 | Exchange-ext-188 |

**ADMINISTRATIVE SUPPORT:**

| | |
|---|---|
| Fire Dept-ext-130 | Public Affairs-ext-106 |
| SDO-864-3327 | |

**HEALTH & WELFARE:**

| | |
|---|---|
| CHAMPUS-ext-189 | Medical-ext-189 |
| | Clinic-864-3327 |
| | Emergency-864-6136 |

**REST & RECREATION:**

| | |
|---|---|
| All Ranks Club-ext-158 | Sauna-ext 126 |

**OTHER FACILITIES AVAILABLE:** Gym, horseshoe pit, outdoor grills, picnic areas, racquetball, swimming pool.

**ATTRACTIONS:** Old gold mining town of Dahlonega-site of first gold rush, Blue Ridge Mountains, State parks, Appalachian Trail, North Georgia College-formerly a military college-built in 1873, abundant opportunity for hunting and fishing. One hour drive to Atlanta.

# DOBBINS AIR RESERVE BASE (GA13R1)

1430 First Street
Dobbins Air Reserve Base, GA 30069-5009

**TELEPHONE NUMBER INFORMATION:** Main installation numbers: C-770-919-5000, D-312-915-1110.
*Ten digit dialing required for local calls.*

**LOCATION:** From Atlanta take I-75 north to Lockheed/Dobbins Exit (#110 west). Turn right (north) onto Highway 41. Follow signs to Dobbins main gate. USMRA: Page 37 (B-3), page 49 (A-1). NMC: Atlanta, 16 miles northeast.

**GENERAL INFORMATION:** Air Reserve Training Base, Headquarters 22nd Air Force (AFRES), 94th Airlift Wing (AFRES).

**TEMPORARY MILITARY LODGING:** Lodging Office, Dobbins Inn, Building 800, 1295 Barracks Court, 24 hours daily. Reservations: C-770-919-4745, D-312-925-4745. Lodging switchboard: C-770-424-1352, Fax: C-770-919-5185. All ranks. DV/VIP 770-919-4520.

**RV, CAMPING/FAMCAMP:** Lakeside FAMCAMP on base, year round, C-770-919-4870, D-312-925-4870, 16 camping spaces with W/E hookups.

**SPACE-A:** Pax Term/Lounge, Building 737, 0700-2300 daily, C-770-919-4903/6559, D-312-925-4903/6359; Fax: C-770-919-5105. Flights to CONUS locations.

**LOGISTICAL SUPPORT:**

| | |
|---|---|
| Bank-422-4469 | Barber Shop-425-3092 |
| Class Six-428-1122 | Credit Union-422-4469 |
| Education Office-919-5043 | Exchange-428-1274 |
| Postal Service-919-5049 | SATO-919-4848 |
| Shoppette-428-1122 | Travel Office-919-4850/5788 |

**ADMINISTRATIVE SUPPORT:**

| | |
|---|---|
| Fire Dept-919-4839 | Legal-919-5199 |
| Locator-919-5000 | Pass/ID Office-919-5738 |
| Police-919-4908 | Public Affairs-919-5055 |
| SDO/NCO-919-5000 | |

**HEALTH & WELFARE:**

| | |
|---|---|
| CHAMPUS-919-5305/5314 | Chapel-919-4955 |
| Family Services-919-5004 | Medical-919-5300 |
| | Emergency-919-5302 |

**REST & RECREATION:**

| | |
|---|---|
| Clubs | Fitness Center-919-4872 |
| Consol-919-4594 | ITT-919-6502 (NAS Atlanta) |
| Flying-919-4870 | Gym-919-4872 |
| MWR-919-4870 | |

**ATTRACTIONS:** Jimmy Carter Presidential Library, Stone Mountain, Six Flags, Metro Atlanta, Underground Atlanta, Atlanta Braves baseball, Piedmont Park, The Fox Theater, Hight Museum of Art, Atlanta Art Gallery.

# FORT BENNING (GA11R1)

U.S. Army Infantry Center
ATTN: ATZB-GC
Fort Benning, GA 31905-5065

**TELEPHONE NUMBER INFORMATION:** Main installation numbers: C-706-545-2011, D-312-835-2011.

**LOCATION:** Off I-85 north or south and US-27/280 east or west. South to Benning Blvd and main gate. USMRA: Page 37 (B-6). NMC: Columbus, five miles northwest.

**GENERAL INFORMATION:** Army Infantry Center and School, Army Infantry Training Brigade, School of the Americas, 75th Ranger Regiment, 29th Infantry Regiment, 36th Engineer Group, 11th Infantry Regiment, 3rd Brigade, 3rd Infantry Division, Ranger Training Brigade, U.S. Army Marksmanship Unit, U.S. Physical Fitness School, Basic Combat Training Brigade.

**TEMPORARY MILITARY LODGING:** Lodging office, Building 399, 24 hours daily. C-706-689-0067, D-312-835-3146. All ranks. DV/VIP 706-545-5724.

**RV, CAMPING/FAMCAMP:** Uchee Creek Rec Area on post, year round, C-706-545-4053, D-312-835-4053, 22 cabins, 38 camper spaces with full hookups, 27 camper spaces with W/E hookups. Also, operates Destin Army Infantry Center Recreation Area, FL, on Choctawatchee Bay. See Destin Army Infantry Center Recreation Area listing for more information.

**SPACE-A:** Lawson Army Airfield on post, limited flights via executive Army aircraft, C-706-545-3524, D-312-835-3524. Fax: C-706-545-7249, D-312-835-7249.

**LOGISTICAL SUPPORT:**

| | |
|---|---|
| Car Rental-686-0896 | Child Care-689-8698 |
| Commissary-544-3663 | Conv Store-682-0473 |
| Exchange-682-0826 | Gas Station-687-6520 |
| Package Store-687-9674 | SATO-682-0622 |
| Snack Bar-687-0349 | |

**ADMINISTRATIVE SUPPORT:**

| | |
|---|---|
| Legal-545-3281 | Locator-545-5217 |
| Police-545-5222 | |

**HEALTH & WELFARE:**

| | |
|---|---|
| CHAMPUS-544-3401 | Chapel-545-2288 |
| Family Services-545-1169 | Medical |
| Retiree Services-545-2715 | Central Appts-544-2041 |
| SDO/NCO-545-2218 | Emergency-544-1502 |

**REST & RECREATION:**

| | |
|---|---|
| Arts & Crafts-545-4436/3677 | Bowling-545-4436/3677 |
| Clubs | Golf Course-687-1940 |
| EM-689-0887 | Gym-545-4436/3677 |
| NCO-687-1232 | Hobby Shops-545-4436/3677 |
| O-682-1861 | Intramural Sports-545-4436/3677 |
| Rod/Gun-545-4436/3677 | Library-545-4436/3677 |
| Pool-545-4436/3677 | Rec Center-545-4436/3677 |
| Tennis-545-4436/3677 | Theater-682-0562 |
| Youth Center-545-4436/3677 | |

**ATTRACTIONS:** National Infantry Museum on post, Springer Opera House, Columbus, Callaway Gardens, Pine Mountain, Roosevelt Little White House.

## FORT GILLEM (GA21R1)

4705 North Wheeler Drive
Forest Park, GA 30297-5000

**TELEPHONE NUMBER INFORMATION:** Main installation numbers: C-404-362-7311, D-312-797-7311.
WEB: www.mcpherson.army.mil/Fort_Gillem.htm
*Ten digit dialing required for local calls.*

**LOCATION:** From I-75 north or south, go east on I-285 to I-675, south to Fort Gillem exit, right to Anvil Block Road, go one-half mile to light at main gate. Also from I-75 to east on I-285 to GA-54 south, three miles to main gate. East gate is located west of US-23, south of I-285. Fort is five miles from the William Hartsfield (Atlanta) IAP. USMRA: Page 37 (C-4), page 49 (C-4). NMC: Atlanta, 10 miles northwest.

**GENERAL INFORMATION:** Subpost of Fort McPherson. Headquarters 1st U.S. Army, 2nd U.S. Army Recruiting Brigade (SW), 3rd CID Region, Army CID Lab, Army and Air Force Exchange Distribution Region, and other tenant agencies.

**TEMPORARY MILITARY LODGING:** Lodging office, Building 816, Hood Avenue, 0730-1600 Mon-Fri, C-404-363-5431/5810, D-312-797-5431/5810. All ranks. DV/VIP 404-363-5431/5810.

**RV, CAMPING/FAMCAMP:** None. See Dobbins ARB listing, Lakeside FAM-CAMP.

**SPACE-A:** None. See Dobbins ARB listing.

**LOGISTICAL SUPPORT:**

| | |
|---|---|
| Barber Shop-363-4808 | Beauty Shop-363-8798 |
| Class Six-363-9047 | Commissary-363-5148 |
| Credit Union-448-8200/3060 | Dry Cleaner-366-0931 |
| Fast Food-361-4844 | Exchange-363-5483 |

**ADMINISTRATIVE SUPPORT:**

| | |
|---|---|
| Fire Dept-363-5532 | Police-363-5981 |
| Public Affairs-464-2446 | |

**HEALTH & WELFARE:**

| | |
|---|---|
| Chapel-362-7395 | Family Services-362-7764 |

**REST & RECREATION:**

| | |
|---|---|
| Bowling-363-5460 | Com Club-363-3830 |
| Fitness Center-362-3276 | Gym-363-5854 |
| Tennis-363-5853 | Youth Center-363-5520 |

**ATTRACTIONS:** Atlanta Braves, Six Flags, Stone Mountain.

## FORT GORDON RECREATION AREA (GA04R1)

P.O. Box 67
Appling, GA 30802-5000

**TELEPHONE NUMBER INFORMATION:** Main installation numbers: C-706-541-1057. Police for recreation area, C-706-541-1057 ext 131.

**LOCATION:** Off post. From I-20 east or west if Augusta, take exit 61 north on US-221 to GA-47 north to end (Washington Road). Left on Washington Road to recre-

ation area. USMRA: Page 37 (F-4). NMI: Fort Gordon, 25 miles south. NMC: Augusta, 25 miles southeast.

**GENERAL INFORMATION:** Operated by Fort Gordon, off base, year round. Military personnel active, reservists, retired, DoD civilians. Reservations (usually required for mobile homes, cabins): Fort Gordon Recreation Area, P.O. Box 67, Appling, GA 30802-5000. C-706-541-1057. Fax: C-706-541-1963.

**RV, CAMPING/FAMCAMP:**

| | |
|---|---|
| Cabins-9 | Mobile Homes-8 |
| Bunk House-sleeps 24 | Camper Spaces-90 |
| Tent Spaces-50 | |

**ATTRACTIONS:** Located on 904-acre site with a 1200 mile shoreline along Thurmond Lake (formerly Clarks Hill Lake) on Georgia/South Carolina line, ideal for wide range of outdoor activities in fresh-water lakes and rivers of the area.

*For detailed information about this off-base recreation facility, as well as on-base recreation facilities, golf courses and marinas, consult Military Living's Military RV, Camping and Outdoor Recreation Around the World.*

## FORT GORDON/U.S. ARMY SIGNAL CENTER (GA09R1)

U.S. Army Signal Center
Building 29808, Chamberlain Avenue
Fort Gordon, GA 30905-5000

**TELEPHONE NUMBER INFORMATION:** Main installation numbers: C-706-791-0110, D-312-780-0110. WEB: www.gordon.army.mil

**LOCATION:** From I-20 east or west, exit 61 south, between US-78/278 and US-1. Gates are on both US-78 and US-1. Gate 2 and Gate 1 (McKenna Gate) on US-78 east-west. USMRA: Page 37 (F-4). NMC: Augusta, 12 miles northeast.

**GENERAL INFORMATION:** Home of 15th Regimental Signal Brigade, Regimental Noncommissioned Officer Academy, Dwight David Eisenhower Army Medical Center, 63rd Signal Battalion, 67th Signal Battalion, 73rd Ordnance Battalion, 513th Military Intelligence Brigade, Regional Signal Intelligence Operations Center.

**TEMPORARY MILITARY LODGING:** Lodging office, Griffith Hall, Building 250, Chamberlain Avenue, 0730-2400 daily, C-706-791-2277/3103, D-312-780-2277. Stinson Guest House C-706-793-7160.

**RV, CAMPING/FAMCAMP:** Recreation Area off base, year round, C-706-541-1057, Fax: C-706-541-1963. Nine cabins, eight mobile homes, one bunk house, 60 camper spaces with full hookups, 30 camper spaces with E, 50 tent spaces.

**SPACE-A:** May be obtained through the Fort Gordon Operational Support Airlift. C-706-791-5811.

**LOGISTICAL SUPPORT:**

| | |
|---|---|
| Bank-771-5960 | Barber Shop-787-7282/791-6516 |
| Beauty Shop | Book Store-791-7019 |
| 793-0185/793-5070 | Cafeteria-771-6921 |
| 793-0230/791-8015 | Carlson Wagonlit Travel-798-0990 |
| Car Rental-798-6006 | Child Care-791-6494 |
| Child Dev Center-791-6494 | Class Six-793-5366 |
| Commissary-791-2354 | Conv Store-793-1160 |
| Credit Union | Dining Facilities-791-4507 |
| Dry Cleaner-798-1888/793-0818 | 798-9869 (on post) |
| Education Office-791-2000 | 793-0012 (off post) |
| Exchange-793-7171 | Anthony's-798-1947 |
| Gas Station-793-8363 | Burger King-793-8542 |
| Laundry-798-1888/7100/9999 | Burger King-798-1947 |
| Postal Service-790-3651 | Food Court-772-9742 |
| Shoppette-793-7177 | Snack Bar-798-2190 |
| Travel Office-798-7966 | Visitor Center-791-3579 |

**ADMINISTRATIVE SUPPORT:**

| | |
|---|---|
| CDO-791-4517 | Fire Dept-791-1201 |
| Housing Office-791-5116 | ID Office-791-1927 |
| Legal-791-7812 | Police-791-4380 |

Public Affairs-791-7003

SDO/NCO-791-4517

**HEALTH & WELFARE:**

American Red Cross-791-3169
Army Emergency Relief-791-4525
Chapel-791-4683
Family Services-791-6967
Retiree Services-791-2654
TRICARE-1-800-444-5445

ACS-791-3579
CHAMPUS-791-6261
Dental-787-5304
Medical-787-5811
    Family Practice Appts-791-7300
    Health Benefits-787-6346
    Hospital-787-5811
    Information-787-5811
    Patient Rep-787-4656

**REST & RECREATION:**

Auto Hobby Shop-791-2390
Clubs
    Cafe-771-6921
    EM-791-6780
    NCO-791-6780
    O-791-2205
Gyms
    791-2849/2864/3692
    791-7370/791-6872
Libraries
    Eisenhower-787-6763
    Woodworth-791-2449
Riding Stables-ext 4864
Theaters
    Musical-791-4603
    Signal-791-3982

Bowling-791-3446
Community Activities-791-6491
Fish & Wildlife-ext 5025
Fitness Center-791-6872
Golf Courses
    Center-791-8319
    Gordon Lakes-791-2433
Indoor Pool-791-3034
ITR-798-7956
MWR-791-4140
Outdoor Rec-791-2390
Rec Center-341-1057
Services-791-2013/2887

Youth Services-791-5104

**ATTRACTIONS:** Augusta Masters Golf Tournament, many golf courses, and historical sites in old Augusta.

## FORT McPHERSON (GA08R1)

1386 Troop Row, SW
Fort McPherson, GA 30330-1069

**TELEPHONE NUMBER INFORMATION:** Main installation numbers: C-404-464-3113, D-312-367-3113. E-mail: ID then @ftmcphsn.army.mil. WEB: www.mcpherson.army.mil
*Ten digit dialing required for local calls.*

**LOCATION:** Off I-75 north or south, take Lakewood Freeway (GA-154/GA-166), exit 88 west past MARTA Station to north on Lee Street (US-29) and main gate west of Lee Street. USMRA: Page 49 (B-3). NMC: Atlanta, in city limits.

**GENERAL INFORMATION:** Headquarters Forces Command, Headquarters Third Army, U.S. Army Reserve Command.

**TEMPORARY MILITARY LODGING:** Billeting Office, Lodging T-22, 0630-2330 daily. C-404-464-3833/2253, D-312-367-2253/3833. DVQ: C-707-669-6196. All ranks. DV/VIP 404-464-4145.

**RV, CAMPING/FAMCAMP:** Operates Lake Allatoona Army Recreation Area off post. See Lake Allatoona Army Recreation Area listing for more information.

**SPACE-A:** None. See Dobbins ARB listing.

**LOGISTICAL SUPPORT:**

Barber Shop-753-8880
Cafeteria-753-4575
Class Six-753-4537
Credit Union-753-4585/753-4592
Dry Cleaner-755-3161
Gas Station-753-2114

Beauty Shop-752-8078
Child Care-464-3945
Commissary-464-3663
Dining-753-4520
Exchange-753-6258

**ADMINISTRATIVE SUPPORT:**

Legal-464-2626/3394
SDO/NCO-464-2980/3602

Police-464-2282
Public Affairs-464-2204

**HEALTH & WELFARE:**

American Red Cross-753-8315
CHAMPUS-464-2044

ACS-464-2968
Chapel-464-2616/2004

Dental-464-0361/2
Retiree Services-464-3219

Medical-464-2778
    Army Clinic-464-3139
    Appts-464-2778
    Appts-464-2183 (Ret)

**REST & RECREATION:**

Arts & Crafts-464-2221
Bowling-464-2479
Fitness Center-464-2121
Gym-464-2409
Rec Center-464-3677
Youth Center-464-2763

Auto Hobby Shop-464-2070
Community Club-464-3828
Golf Course-464-2178/2078
Library-464-2665
Tickets-464-3677/4392

**ATTRACTIONS:** Six Flags, Cyclorama, pro sports, Stone Mountain.

## FORT STEWART (GA15R1)

3rd Infantry Division (Mech) & Fort Stewart
ATTN: AFZP-GC
Fort Stewart, GA 31314-5000

**TELEPHONE NUMBER INFORMATION:** Main installation numbers: C-912-767-1110, D-312-870-1110.

**LOCATION:** On US-84. Accessible from US-17 or I-95. Also GA-119 or GA-144 crosses the post but may be closed occasionally. From I-95 north or south, exit 15 to GA-144 west and east. From I-16 east or west exit 29 to GA-119 south. USMRA: Page 37 (G-7). NMC: Savannah, 35 miles northeast.

**GENERAL INFORMATION:** Hq 3rd Infantry Division (mechanized).

**TEMPORARY MILITARY LODGING:** Billeting Office, Building 4951, 0730-2400 daily, C-912-767-8384, D-312-870-8384. Other hours, SDO, Building1, C-912-767-8666. All ranks. DV/VIP 912-767-8610.

**RV, CAMPING/FAMCAMP:** Holbrook Pond Recreation Area and Campground on post, year round, C-912-767-2717, D-312-870-2717, 20 camper spaces with W/E hookups, 20 camper spaces with W hookups.

**SPACE-A:** None. See Savannah IAP listing.

**LOGISTICAL SUPPORT:**

Bank-368-3332
Beauty Shop-876-2663
Child Dev Center-767-3202
Conv Store-876-8434
Dry Cleaner-876-9820
Exchange-876-2850
Laundry-876-7275
Postal Service-368-3380
Shoppette-876-2785
Visitor Center-767-5058

Barber Shop-876-3060
Child Care-767-2311
Commissary-767-1392
Credit Union-876-2785
Education Office-767-8331
Gas Station-876-8434
Package Store-368-5080
SATO-767-3642
Snack Bar-876-2782

**ADMINISTRATIVE SUPPORT:**

Fire Dept-767-1711/8118/8320/911
ID Office-767-2277
Locator-767-2862/5058
Police-767-2822
SDO/NCO-767-8666

Housing Office-767-3280
Legal-767-8809
Pass/Permit Office-767-5032
Public Affairs-767-5457

**HEALTH & WELFARE:**

ACS/AER-767-5058/9
Chapel-767-8801/8549
Medical-767-5551
    Central Appts-767-6633/09
    Emergency-767-6666
    Health Benefits-767-6015
    Hospital-767-6557

American Red Cross-767-2197
CHAMPUS-767-6015
Retiree Services-767-5013
TRICARE-767-6015
Veterinary Services-767-2842

**REST & RECREATION:**

Arts & Crafts-767-2515
Auto Hobby Shop-767-3527
Clubs
    Consol-767-2212
    Teen-ext 2815

Archery/Rifle Range-ext 5032
Bowling-767-4273/4127
Community Center-767-2191
Fitness Center-767-3031
Golf Course-368-2370

Gym-368-9074
MWR-767-3319
Performing Arts-ext 3410
Skeet-ext 3519
Theater-767-7083
Wood Hobby Shop-767-2515
Youth Center-767-4491

Library-767-2828
Outdoor Rec-767-2717
Rec Equip-ext 2988
Swimming
  Indoor-ext 3034
  Outdoor-ext 8575
Youth Services-767-4491

**ATTRACTIONS:** Tybee, Jekyll, and St. Catherines Islands off coast of Georgia; fishing, beaches, and boating; Savannah and other historic sites; Cumberland Island National Seashore; Okefenokee Swamp National Wildlife Refuge. Hunting and fishing on Fort Stewart.

## GRASSY POND RECREATION AREA (GA06R1)

Recreation Services, Grassy Pond
5360 Grassy Pond Road
Lake Park, GA 31636-5000

**TELEPHONE NUMBER INFORMATION:** Main installation numbers: C-912-257-4211, D-312-460-1110. Police, C-912-333-5133 (sheriff's office).

**LOCATION:** Off base. From I-75 north or south of Valdosta, take exit 2, to west on GA-376 (Clyattville Road). Immediately watch for signs and left turn to recreation area. USMRA: Page 37 (D-9). NMI: Moody AFB, 25 miles north. NMC: Valdosta, 12 miles north.

**GENERAL INFORMATION:** Operated by Moody AFB, off base, year round. Military personnel active, reservists, retired, DoD and NAF civilians. Reservations (required for cabins): Recreation Services, Grassy Pond, 5360 Grassy Pond Road, Lake Park, GA 31636-5000. C-912-559-5840, D-312-460-1110 ext 559-5840.

**RV, CAMPING/FAMCAMP:**

Cabins-13
Tent Spaces-numerous

Camper Spaces-18

**ATTRACTIONS:** Located along a 275-acre pond surrounded by 500 acres of rolling, wooded terrain near Georgia/Florida line, Grassy Pond is a major fishing area offering a variety of facilities and activities.

*For detailed information about this off-base recreation facility, as well as on-base recreation facilities, golf courses and marinas, consult Military Living's Military RV, Camping and Outdoor Recreation Around the World.*

## HUNTER ARMY AIRFIELD (GA10R1)

Army Community Services
ATTN: AFZP-GC, Building 1201
Hunter Army Airfield, GA 31409-5000

**TELEPHONE NUMBER INFORMATION:** Main installation numbers: C-912-767-1411, D-312-870-1110. E-mail: afzp-pah@emh5.stewart-army.mil.

**LOCATION:** From I-95 north or south exit 16 to GA-204 east for 13 miles to Savannah. Turn left (north) onto Stephenson Avenue, proceed to Wilson Avenue gate to installation. USMRA: Page 37 (H-7). NMC: Savannah, in southwest part of city.

**GENERAL INFORMATION:** Aviation Brigade, 3rd Infantry Division (Mechanized), 603rd Support Battalion (Aviation), 559th Quartermaster Battalion, 3/160th Special Operations Aviation Regiment, 1st Battalion, 1/75th Ranger Regiment, 260th Quartermaster Battalion, 224th Military Intelligence Battalion, USCG Air Station Savannah.

**TEMPORARY MILITARY LODGING:** Lodging office, Building 6010, Duncan & Leonard Street, 0730-2400 Mon-Fri, 0800-1700 Sat, Sun, Holidays, C-912-352-5910/5834, D-312-971-5910/5834, other hours, Building 1201, C-912-352-5140. All ranks. DV/VIP C-912-355-8610, D-312-870-8610.

**RV, CAMPING/FAMCAMP:** Lotts Island Army/Air Field Travel Camp on post year round, Community Recreation Division (AFZP-PAR), Outdoor Recreation, Building 8454, Hunter Army Airfield, Savannah, GA 31409-5000, C-912-352-5916/5722, D-312-971-5722, 15 camper/tent spaces with W hookups.

**SPACE-A:** Very Limited. Army Ops, Hunter AAF, C-912-352-5110, D-312-971-5110. Also, Savannah CGAS at Hunter AAF Ops, Very limited flights, C-912-352-6035.

**LOGISTICAL SUPPORT:**

Barber Shop-354-9214
Carlson Wagonlit Travel-353-9295
Child Dev Center-352-6064
Commissary-352-5007
Credit Union-354-6420
Dry Cleaner-352-5251
Exchange-352-5336
Postal Service-355-3217

Beauty Shop-354-9214
Child Care-368-2212
Class Six-354-8752
Conv Store-354-0075
Dining Facility-352-6209
Education Office-352-6130
Laundry-352-5251
Shoppette-354-0075

**ADMINISTRATIVE SUPPORT:**

CDO-352-5425
Housing Office-352-5268
Locator-767-2862
Police-352-6133
SDO/NCO-352-5000

Fire Dept-352-5684
Legal-352-5115
Pass/ID Office-352-6133
Public Affairs-352-5994

**HEALTH & WELFARE:**

American Red Cross-352-5410
Army Emergency Relief-352-6801
Chapel-352-5111

ACS-352-6816
CHAMPUS-352-5552
Medical-352-5551
  Central Appts-352-6100
  Emergency-233-5700

**REST & RECREATION:**

Auto Hobby Shop-352-6244
Combined Club-912-368-2212
Gym-352-5078
Marina-352-5722
Theater-352-5556
Youth Services-352-5708-5005

Bowling-352-6279
Golf Course-352-5622
ITT-353-9295
Outdoor Rec-352-5722
Youth Center-352-5708/5005

**ATTRACTIONS:** Historic Savannah, period homes, General Sherman's headquarters, Cotton Exchange, Fort Pulaski and Fort McAllister.

## KINGS BAY NAVAL SUBMARINE BASE (GA03R1)

1063 USS Tennessee Avenue
Kings Bay, GA 31547-2606

**TELEPHONE NUMBER INFORMATION:** Main installation numbers: C-912-673-2000, D-312-573-2111. E-mail: pao@subasekb.navy.mil

**LOCATION:** Off I-95 north or south, of GA/FL border. Take exit 1 east, which leads right into base, or exit 2A or 2B, east to Kings Bay Road and follow the road north to base. USMRA: Page 37 (G-9). NMC: Jacksonville, Fl, 40 miles south.

**GENERAL INFORMATION:** East Coast Submarine Base, Headquarters Submarine Squadron 20. Home of the East Coast Trident submarines and headquarters of Submarine Group 10 Commander.

**TEMPORARY MILITARY LODGING:** Lodging office, Building 1051-N, James Madison Road, 0800-1630 Mon-Fri, C-912-673-2163, D-312-573-2163. DV/VIP 912-673-2165, Fax: C-912-673-2752. Navy Lodge, Building 0158, C-912-882-6868.

**RV, CAMPING/FAMCAMP:** None. See Jacksonville NAS, FL listing.

**SPACE-A:** None. See Jacksonville NAS, FL listing.

**LOGISTICAL SUPPORT:**

Cafeteria-882-6229
Commissary-673-9586
Exchange-882-6098
Package Store-882-9586
Snack Bar-882-6229

Child Care* ext 2043
Conv Store-882-6944
Gas Station-882-9586
SATO* ext 2230
Visitor Center* ext 2272

**ADMINISTRATIVE SUPPORT:**

CDO/OOD-673-2020

Fire Dept-673-2263

Legal-673-2025
Police-673-2265

Locator* ext 3980
Public Affairs-673-4714

**HEALTH & WELFARE:**

CHAMPUS-673-2928-ext 4228
Dental-673-4262
Medical-673-4247/4212
  Emergency-673-4262

Chapel-673-4501
Family Services-673-4513
Retiree Services* ext 4517

**REST & RECREATION:**

Bowling* ext 9492
Fitness Center* ext 8972/ext 2485
Golf Course* ext 8476
TT* ext 2289
MWR* ext 2041
Outdoor Recreation* ext 8103

Clubs
CPO* ext 8999
EM* ext 8999
NCO* ext 8999
O* ext 8999

*Dial 673-2001 then the number listed.*

**ATTRACTIONS:** Beautiful beaches, sport fishing, hunting, Cumberland Island, and Jekyll and St. Simons Islands are one hour drives north.

# LAKE ALLATOONA ARMY RECREATION AREA (GA05R1)

Army Recreation Area
40 Old Sandtown Road S.E.
Cartersville, GA 30121-7678

**TELEPHONE NUMBER INFORMATION:** Main installation numbers: C-770-974-3413. Fax; C-770-974-1278. Police for rec area, C-770-464-3712.

**LOCATION:** Located on 85-acre site at Lake Allatoona reservoir. From I-75 north or south of Atlanta, take exit 122 east (Emerson exit). Turn right off exit, travel 2.7 miles, turn left on Old Sandtown Road. Travel one block and bear left into park; follow signs to office. USMRA: Page 37 (B-3). NMC: Atlanta. NMI: Dobbins ARB, 28 miles southeast.

**GENERAL INFORMATION:** Full range of beach and water activities. Operated by Fort McPherson, off post year round. Military personnel active, retired, reserve, NG, and DoD civilians at Fort McPherson and Fort Gillem. Check in 1700 to closing. Reservations: Required for lodging. Active duty at Forts McPherson and Gillem have priority to make reservations during first 10 days of any month and three succeeding months; all others may make reservations for same period after 10th day. C-770-974-3413/9420, Fax: C-770-974-1278.

**TEMPORARY MILITARY LODGING:**

Three bedroom apartments-3
Two bedroom cabin-12
Efficiencies-2

Two bedroom deluxe cabins-5
One bedroom cabin-8

**RV, CAMPING/FAMCAMP:**

RV spaces-12

Tent spaces-15

**REST & RECREATION:**

Marina-974-3413

Outdoor Recreation-974-3413

**ATTRACTIONS:** Conveniently situated for sightseeing in Atlanta and surrounding area, including Stone Mountain Memorial State Park and Six Flags.

*For detailed information about this off-base recreation facility, as well as on-base recreation facilities, golf courses and marinas, consult Military Living's Military RV, Camping and Outdoor Recreation Around the World.*

# MOODY AIR FORCE BASE (GA02R1)

5113 Austin Ellipse Suite 6
Moody Air Force Base, GA 31699-1599

**TELEPHONE NUMBER INFORMATION:** Main installation numbers: C-912-257-4211, D-312-460-1110. WEB: www.moody.af.mil
*Ten digit dialing required for local calls.*

**LOCATION:** On GA-125, 10 miles north of Valdosta, east of GA-125. Also, can be reached from I-75 north or south via GA-122 east to GA-125 south. USMRA: Page 37 (D,E-9). NMC: Valdosta, 10 miles south.

**GENERAL INFORMATION:** Air Combat Command Base, 69th Fighter Squadron, 68th Fighter Squadron, 70th Fighter Squadron, 71st Air Control Squadron, 71st Reserve Squadron and 41st Reserve Squadron.

**TEMPORARY MILITARY LODGING:** Billeting Office, Building 3131, Cooney St, 24 hours daily, C-912-257-3893, D-312-460-3893, Fax: C-912-257-4971, D-312-466-4771 All ranks. DV/VIP 912-257-4144.

**RV, CAMPING/FAMCAMP:** Grassy Pond Rec Area off base, year round, C-912-559-5840, D-312-460-5840, 13 cabins, 18 camper spaces with full hookups, many tent spaces.

**SPACE-A:** Pax Term, Building 8153, 0700-2300 Mon-Fri, 0800-1600 Sat, Sun, Holidays. C-912-257-1776, D-312-460-1776; Rec: C-912-257-1776, D-312-460-1776. Fax: C-912-257-4112, D-312-460-4112. Unscheduled flights to CONUS locations. Also see Jacksonville NAS, FL listing.

**LOGISTICAL SUPPORT:**

Bank 244-7761
Commissary-257-3365
Class VI-257-4166
Exchange-257-3431
Gas Station-257-3451
SATO-257-3307
Shoppette-257-3876
Visitor Center-257-4443

Child Care 257-3935
Conv Store-257-3876
Dining-257-3031
Fast Food-245-8296
Package Store-257-4166
Snack Bar-257-3093
Theater-257-3557

**ADMINISTRATIVE SUPPORT:**

Command Post-257-3503
Locator-257-3585/3516

Legal-257-3414
Police-257-3200/3108

**HEALTH & WELFARE:**

CHAMPUS-257-3799
Family Services-257-3333
Retiree Services-257-3315

Chapel-257-3211/3646
Medical-257-2778
  Central Appts-257-3816
  Clinic-257-3232

**REST & RECREATION:**

Auto Hobby Shop-ext 3056
Ceramics-ext 3452
Fitness Center-ext 3348
Golf-257 3297
Library-ext 3539
Swimming-ext 3560/3864
Wood Hobby Shop-ext 3452

Bowling-257-3872
Clubs
  NCO-257-3794
  O-257-3792
Rec Center-ext 3280
Services-257-3280
Youth Center-ext 3067

**ATTRACTIONS:** Historic homes in Valdosta, Crystal Lake, 40 miles north and Wild Adventures, 20 miles south.

# ROBINS AIR FORCE BASE (GA14R1)

215 Page Road, Suite 106
Robins Air Force Base, GA 31098-1662

**TELEPHONE NUMBER INFORMATION:** Main installation numbers: C-912-926-2137, D-312-468-1110. WEB: www.robins.af.mil

**LOCATION:** Off US-129 on GA-247 at Warner Robins. Go south on I-75. Get off exit 46. Go east on Hwy 247 (Watson Blvd) until dead-end at Robins AFB, east of US-129. USMRA: Page 37 (D-6). NMC: Macon, 15 miles northwest.

**GENERAL INFORMATION:** Air Force Materiel Command Base. Warner Robins Air Logistics Center and AFRC headquarters stationed here.

**TEMPORARY MILITARY LODGING:** Lodging office, Building 557, Club Drive, 24 hours daily, C-912-926-2100, D-312-468-2100. All ranks. DV/VIP 912-926-2761.

**RV, CAMPING/FAMCAMP:** FAMCAMP on base at Luna Lake, year round, C-912-926-4500, D-312-468-4500, 16 camper spaces with W/E hookups, 12 tent spaces.

**SPACE-A:** Pax Term/Lounge, Building 127, 0700-1700 hours daily, C-912-926-3166, D-312-468-3166 Fax: C-912-926-4355, flights to CONUS locations.

**LOGISTICAL SUPPORT:**

Bank-923-3773
Beauty Shop-923-7027
Child Care-923-6349
Class Six-923-5085
Conv Store-923-5085
Exchange-923-5536
Postal Service-926-2127
Shoppette-922-3851
Visitor Center-926-4208

Barber Shop-923-7027
Cafeteria-922-8635
Child Dev Center-926-6349
Commissary-926-2126
Dining Facilities-926-6596
Gas Station-923-7292
Bay Area Travel-926-3101
Snack Bar-922-0136

**ADMINISTRATIVE SUPPORT:**

CDO-327-2612
Housing Office-926-5035
Locator-926-6027
Police-926-2187/1025

Fire Dept-926-5323/911
Legal-926-3931
Pass Office-926-3583
Public Affairs-926-2137

**HEALTH & WELFARE:**

Air Force Aid Society-926-1256
CHAMPUS-926-5004
Dental-926-2691
Medical
    Central Appts-926-0195
    Emergency-926-3845
    Health Benefits-926-5004

American Red Cross-926-5493
Chapel-926-2821
Family Services-926-1256
Retiree Services-926-2019
TRICARE-926-5004
Veterinary Services-926-6116

**REST & RECREATION:**

Arts & Crafts-926-5282
Bowling Center-926-5240
19th Hole-923-1717
Clubs
    Aero-ext 4867
    NCO-923-5581
    O-922-3011
MWR-927-0217
Swimming-ext 2105
Youth Center-926-2356

Bowling-926-2112
Rec Center-922-0136
Community Center-ext 2105
Golf Course-926-4103
Indoor Rec-926-2208
Library-926-5378
ITT-926-2945
Services-926-3135
Theater-926-2919

**ATTRACTIONS:** Macon, 4th largest city in Georgia, Andersonville Trail, Ocmulgee National Park, Robins AFB Museum of Aviation.

## SAVANNAH INTERNATIONAL AIRPORT (GA24R1)

165th (ANG)/P.O. Box 7568
Garden City, GA 31402-5000

**TELEPHONE NUMBER INFORMATION:** C-912-966-1941/8201, D-312-860-8201

**LOCATION:** From I-95 north or south, exit 18A east to Airways Avenue to IAP. USMRA: Page 37 (H-7). NMC: Savannah, four miles southeast.

**GENERAL INFORMATION:** Home of the 165th Airlift Wing.

**SPACE-A:** C-912-964-1941, D-312-860-8201. Fax: C-912-966-8200.

**LOGISTICAL SUPPORT:**      Exchange-964-6842

**HEALTH & WELFARE:**      Medical-966-8221/2

**ATTRACTIONS:** Historic Savannah, museums, parks, wildlife refuge.

## WILLIAM B. HARTSFIELD ATLANTA INTERNATIONAL AIRPORT (GA26R1)

AMC, 437 APS/TRG, Charleston IAP
5500 International Blvd, Suite 124
Charleston, SC 29418-0308

**TELEPHONE NUMBER INFORMATION:** Main installation numbers: C-843-963-5794, D-312-673-5794.

**LOCATION:** Off I-285 east or west, exit 42, follow signs. USMRA: Page 37 (B,C-4). NMC: Atlanta, in city limits. NMI: For McPherson, 4.5 miles north.

**GENERAL INFORMATION:** The AMC Counter is located in the South Terminal of the William B. Hartsfield Atlanta, IAP in Atlanta, GA (near baggage claim).

**SPACE-A:** C-843-963-5794, D-312-673-5794. Recording: C-843-963-3082, D-312-673-3082. Fax: C-843-963-3845, D-312-673-3845.

**LOGISTICAL SUPPORT:** Chapels, post office, foreign currency exchange, duty free shops, food services are available in the airport.

**ATTRACTIONS:** Six Flags over Georgia and the Atlanta area.

## WORLD FAMOUS NAVY LAKE SITE (GA01R1)

166 Sandtown Road
Cartersville, GA 30121

**TELEPHONE NUMBER INFORMATION:** Main installation numbers: C-770-974-6309. Police for recreation site, C-770-919-6394.
*Ten digit dialing required for local calls.*

**LOCATION:** Off base. From I-75 north or south of Atlanta, take exit 122 east. Turn right on Sandtown Road going east for approximately three miles to marked entrance on the left. USMRA: Page 37 (B-3). NMI: Atlanta NAS, Marietta, 20 miles east. NMC: Atlanta, 40 miles southeast.

**GENERAL INFORMATION:** Operated by Atlanta Naval Air Station, off base, year round. Military personnel active, reservists, retired, DoD civilians. Reservations (required for cabins): 166 Sandtown Road, Cartersville, GA 30121. Call C-770-974-6309.

**RV, CAMPING/FAMCAMP:**

Cabins-9
Tent Spaces-13

RV Camper Spaces-14

**ATTRACTIONS:** Located in a 25 acre park on Lake Allatoona reservoir, ideal spot for many outdoor recreational activities.

*For detailed information about this off-base recreation facility, as well as on-base recreation facilities, golf courses and marinas, consult Military Living's Military RV, Camping and Outdoor Recreation Around the World.*

Look for Military Living's full line of books, maps and atlases at your local military exchange and *$AVE,*

*or you may use the order coupon at the end of this book. Visit us online at www.militaryliving.com for more information.*

# HAWAII

## ALIAMANU MILITARY RESERVATION (HI04R6)

1875 Aliamanu Drive
Aliamanu, HI 96854-5000

**TELEPHONE NUMBER INFORMATION:** Main installation numbers: C-808-833-1185.

**LOCATION:** From Honolulu take HI-78 northwest to Exit 2 (Red Hill) and go left over freeway straight to reservation. Or, from Ewa take exit 2 (Red Hill) and make a right to enter reservation. Make a left onto Aliamanu Drive after guard shack. USMRA: Page 131 (C-2). NMC: Honolulu, 8 miles southeast.

**GENERAL INFORMATION:** Housing area.

**TEMPORARY MILITARY LODGING:** None. See Hickam AFB listing.

**RV, CAMPING/FAMCAMP:** None. See Hickam AFB listing.

**SPACE-A:** None. See Hickam AFB listing.

**LOGISTICAL SUPPORT:**
Child Care 438-7074
Dry Cleaning 833-5033
Child Development Center 833-5570
Shoppette/Service Station-833-6997

**ADMINISTRATIVE SUPPORT:** See Hickam AFB listing.

**HEALTH & WELFARE:**
Chapel-836-4599
Medical-633-7116

**REST & RECREATION:**
Gym-836-0338
MWR-836-0338
Library-833-4851
Youth Activities-833-4932/0920

**ATTRACTIONS:** Honolulu, beaches. island tours.

## BARBERS POINT COAST GUARD AIR STATION (HI24R6)

Barbers Point, HI 96862-5800

**TELEPHONE NUMBER INFORMATION:** Main installation numbers: C-808-682-2621.

**LOCATION:** From airport, take H-1 west toward Waianae; take NAS Barbers Point exit, left (south) on Fort Barrette Road to main NAS gate. Take immediate left on Roosevelt Avenue, right on Coral Sea Road to CGAS. USMRA: Page 129 (C-7). NMC: Honolulu 25 miles east.

**GENERAL INFORMATION:** See Barbers Point NAS for most support facilities.

**LOGISTICAL SUPPORT:**
Exchange-682-2731

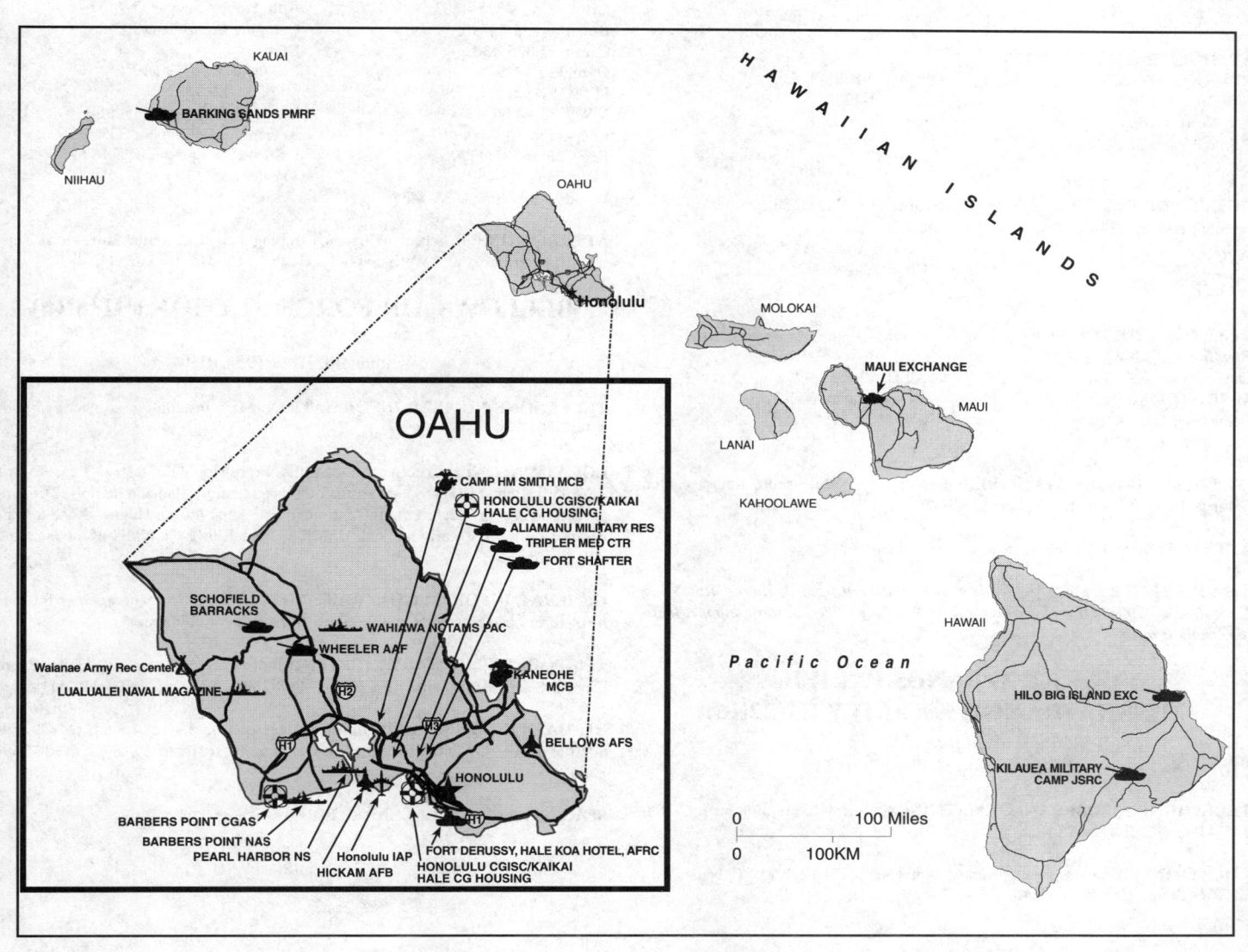

# BARBERS POINT NAVAL AIR STATION
## (HI10R6)
Building 1
Barbers Point Naval Air Station, HI 96862-5050

**TELEPHONE NUMBER INFORMATION:** Main installation numbers: C-808-449-7110. E-mail:berwin@bptnas.navy.mil

**LOCATION:** Take H-1 west (toward Waianae) to Barbers Point NAS/Makakilo/Kadolei exit. Turn left (south) at light on off-ramp, go south on Fort Barrette Road for a mile to main gate. USMRA: Page 129 (C-7). NMC: Honolulu, 15 miles east. NMI: Hickam Air Force Base.

**GENERAL INFORMATION:** As of 1 July 1999 this base is considered closed in terms of military operations, but many support facilities have remained open.

**TEMPORARY MILITARY LODGING:** None. See Pearl Harbor NS listing.

**RV, CAMPING/FAMCAMP:** Recreation Area on base, year round, C-808-682-2019, 24 two-bedroom cottages, 21 camper spaces with water faucet only.

**SPACE-A:** None. See Hickam AFB listing.

**LOGISTICAL SUPPORT:**
| | |
|---|---|
| Bank 681-3116 | Cafeteria 684-4173 |
| Child Care-682-0013 | Commissary-684-0702 |
| Conv Store-682-3074 | Credit Union 682-4511 |
| Dining Facilities 684-4173 | Exchange-682-7330 |
| Gas Station-682-3074 | Package Store 682-3074 |
| SATO-682-4551 | Shoppette 682-3074 |
| Snack Bar 673-4600 | Visitor Center 684-6262 |

**ADMINISTRATIVE SUPPORT:**
| | |
|---|---|
| CDO/OOD-684-6266 | OFC/CPO-682-4925 |
| Fire Dept-471-7117 | Legal-684-4202 |
| Locator-684-1005 | Police-684-6222 |
| Public Affairs-684-7101 | |

**HEALTH & WELFARE:**
| | |
|---|---|
| CHAMPUS-474-4406 | Chapel-684-3111/3188 |
| Family Services-684-7290 | Medical |
| | Central Appts-684-6201/0642 |
| | Clinic-684-4300 |
| | Emergency-684-8244 |

**REST & RECREATION:**
| | |
|---|---|
| Bowling 682-5146 | Clubs |
| Golf Course-682-1911 | All Hands-682-4925 |
| MWR-684-8283 | CG Hideaway-682-2731 |
| Recreation-682-2010/19 | EM-682-5243 |
| Rec Center 684-8281 | |

**OTHER FACILITIES AVAILABLE:** International sports shop, fitness center, library, picnic area, swimming, tennis.

**ATTRACTIONS:** Honolulu, beaches, island tours.

*Note: P-3 and Helicopter Squadrons were transferred from Barbers Point NS to Kaneohe Bay MCB, HI and the base "closed" 1 July 1999, but most support facilities remain open.*

# BARKING SANDS PACIFIC MISSILE RANGE FACILITY (HI22R6)
P.O. Box 128
Kekaha, Kauai, HI 96752-0128

**TELEPHONE NUMBER INFORMATION:** Main installation numbers: C-808-335-4254, D-315-471-6254.

**LOCATION:** Six miles west of Kekaha on Kaumualii Highway (HI-50 west). USMRA: Page 129 (B-2). NMC: Lihue, 30 miles east.

**GENERAL INFORMATION:** Naval Base with the following tenant activities: 154th Composite Group, 115th Aircraft Warning Squadron Hawaii ANG, National Bureau of Standards, Naval Undersea Warfare Engineering Station, Sandia National Laboratories, Dept of Agriculture. Operations and maintenance.

**TEMPORARY MILITARY LODGING:** Lodging office, Building 1261, Tartar Drive, 0730-1600 daily, C-808-335-4383, D-315-471-6383, Fax: C-808-335-4194; Beach cottages C-808-335-4446.

**RV, CAMPING/FAMCAMP:** Beach cottages on base, year round, C-808-335-4446, D-312-471-6446, 10 two-bedroom cottages.

**SPACE-A:** Air Ops, Building 300, C-808-335-4310, D-315-471-6310.

**LOGISTICAL SUPPORT:**
| | |
|---|---|
| Barber Shop 335-4450 | Cafeteria-335-4249 |
| Child Care-335-4453 | Dining 335-4249 |
| Exchange-335-4300 | Gas Station-335-4347 |
| Package Store-335-4202 | Snack Bar-335-4708 |
| Visitor Center-335-4221 | |

**ADMINISTRATIVE SUPPORT:**
| | |
|---|---|
| CDO/OOD-335-4254/4743 | Fire Dept-335-4372 |
| Legal-335-4732 | Locator-335-4254 |
| Police-335-4523/4525 | Public Affairs-335-4742 |

**HEALTH & WELFARE:**
| | |
|---|---|
| CHAMPUS Advisor-944-2281 | Medical-335-4203 |
| | Hospital-338-9431 |

**REST & RECREATION:**
| | |
|---|---|
| Arts & Crafts 335-4303 | Auto Hobby Shop-335-4439 |
| Bowling-335-4379 | Camping Equipment-335-4379 |
| Ceramics-335-4303 | Clubs |
| Gym-335-4379 | Consol-335-4780/09 |
| ITT-335-4195 | O-335-4219 |
| MWR-335-4446 | Racquetball/Tennis-335-4446 |
| Recreation-335-4446 | Recreation Equipment-335-4379 |
| Rec Center-335-4379 | Off-Post Camping 335-6061 |
| Swimming335-4391 | Theater-335-4210 |
| Wood Hobby Shop-335-4438 | |

**ATTRACTIONS:** Beaches, hiking and camping; beautiful countryside, views, sunsets, Kalalau Lookout, "Wettest spot on Earth," "The Garden Island."

# BELLOWS AIR FORCE STATION (HI18R6)
220 Tinker Road
Waimanalo, HI 96795-1010

**TELEPHONE NUMBER INFORMATION:** Main installation numbers: C-808-259-8080.

**LOCATION:** On the eastern shore of Oahu. From Honolulu, take H-1 east to exit 21-A Pali Highway (HI-61), go north. Take a right onto Kalanianaole (HI-72), south to AFS on east at beach. Off HI-72 to main gate, then left on Hughes Road to registration on right. Clearly marked. USMRA: Page 129 (E-7). NMC: Kaneohe, nine miles northwest.

**GENERAL INFORMATION:** Pacific Air Force Base, recreation center for uniformed services personnel and families, and Marine training area.

**TEMPORARY MILITARY LODGING:** Bellows Rec Center, 220 Tinker Road. From U.S. mainland 1-800-437-2607, C-808-259-8080, Fax: C-808-259-4119.

**RV, CAMPING/FAMCAMP:** Beach cottages on base, year round, C-808-259-8080 or 1-800-437-2607, 97 cottages. Camping, year round, 52 sites, C-808-259-8080.

**SPACE-A:** None. See Hickam AFB listing.

**LOGISTICAL SUPPORT:**
Class Six-259-5913                          Dining Facilities-259-4210
Exchange-259-5913                          Gas Station-259-5913
Shoppette-259-5913

**ADMINISTRATIVE SUPPORT:**
Police-259-4200                            Public Affairs-259-4210

**HEALTH & WELFARE:** None. See Kaneohe Bay MCB listing.

**REST & RECREATION:**
Golf Driving Range-ext 4121                Indoor Rec-259-8080
Recreation-ext 4121
  Miniature Golf
  Equipment Rental

**ATTRACTIONS:** Great beaches on windward side of Island of Oahu. Watch out for the strong undertow. Blow Hole is nearby, and beautiful Kaneohe Bay.

# CAMP H.M. SMITH MARINE CORPS BASE (HI15R6)
P.O. Box 64124, Building 1B
Camp H.M. Smith, HI 96861-5001

**TELEPHONE NUMBER INFORMATION:** Main installation numbers: C-800-445-1708.

**LOCATION:** Off H-1 west in Halawa Heights. Take Halawa Heights Road to Elrod Road to main gate on right (east). Clearly marked. USMRA: Page 129 (D-7), page 131 (C-1). NMI: Pearl Harbor Navy Base, five miles southwest. NMC: Honolulu, 10 miles southeast.

**GENERAL INFORMATION:** Headquarters U.S. Pacific Command, Headquarters Commander Marine Forces Pacific and support units.

**TEMPORARY MILITARY LODGING:** None, see Fort Shafter listing.

**RV, CAMPING/FAMCAMP:** Camp Hawkins Campground/Camp Smith Stables, year round, C-808-477-6382, Fax: C-808-477-0506. Twenty five units without hookups.

**SPACE-A:** None. See Hickam AFB listing.

**LOGISTICAL SUPPORT:**
Barber Shop-486-8018                        Dry Cleaner-488-1695
Education Office-477-0412                   Exchange-488-1233
Gas Station-484-9321                        Postal Service-477-8408
SATO-487-1567                               Snack Bar-484-9419
Travel Office-487-1567

**ADMINISTRATIVE SUPPORT:**
Housing Office-977-8690                     Legal-477-8505
Locator-477-0344                            OOD-477-8363
Pass/ID Office-477-8735                     Police-477-8745
Public Affairs-477-8309                     SDO/NCO-477-8363

**HEALTH & WELFARE:**
American Red Cross-471-3155                 CHAMPUS-474-4406
Chapel-477-8529                             Dental-477-5016
Medical-477-0629                            Navy-MC Relief-422-9742
  Clinic-477-3773                           Retiree Services-471-3345
  Emergency-477-7116
**REST & RECREATION:**
Auto Hobby Shop-477-6335                    Consol Club-484-9322
Fitness Center-477-5197                     Gym-477-5197
ITT-477-5143                                Library-477-6963
MWR-477-0498                                Pool-477-5067
Stables-484-9417

**ATTRACTIONS:** Beautiful view of Honolulu and Pearl Harbor.

# FORT DeRUSSY HALE KOA HOTEL ARMED FORCES RECREATION CENTER (HI08R6)
2055 Kalia Road
Honolulu, HI 96815-1998

**TELEPHONE NUMBER INFORMATION:** Main installation numbers: C-808-955-0555; C-1-800-367-6027 from CONUS (0800-1600 hours daily HI time except holidays). Fax: C-808-955-9670
E-mail: information@halekoa.com   WEB: www.halekoa.com

**LOCATION:** On Fort DeRussy at 2055 Kalia Road, on the beach at Waikiki, Oahu. Fort DeRussy is between Ala Moana Blvd, Kalakaua Avenue, and Saratoga Road, nine miles east of Honolulu IAP. USMRA: Page 129 (D,E-7,8), page 131 (F-4). NMC: Honolulu, in city limits.

**GENERAL INFORMATION:** Hale Koa Hotel and Armed Forces Rec Center, Fort DeRussy Military Museum.

**TEMPORARY MILITARY LODGING:** The Hale Koa Hotel, two towers with 817 guest rooms, A/C and all modern resort hotel facilities. First class beachfront resort built by and run for active duty and retired uniformed personnel of all services, including DOD civilians. Reservations may be made up to one year in advance.

**LOGISTICAL SUPPORT:**
Exchange-955-0060                          Dining-955-0555

**HEALTH & WELFARE:** Chapel located on Fort DeRussy, one-half block from Hale Koa Hotel. Medical-955-0555

**OTHER FACILITIES AVAILABLE:** For info call hotel operator C-808-955-0555. Coffee house, dining room, lounge, snack bar, activity desk, tour office, athletic fields, fitness center, handball, racquetball, swimming, tennis, volleyball.

**ATTRACTIONS:** Diamond Head Crater, Famous Waikiki, Punch Bowl Crater, Honolulu Zoo, resort hotels, entertainment, beaches, water sports, military museum.

*For detailed information about this off-base recreation facility, as well as on-base recreation facilities, golf courses, marinas and lodging facilities consult Military Living's Temporary Military Lodging Around The World or Military RV, Camping & Rec Areas Around The World.*

# FORT SHAFTER (HI09R6)
Building 5-380
ATTN: APVG-GF
Fort Shafter, HI 96858-5100

**TELEPHONE NUMBER INFORMATION:** Main installation numbers: C-808-449-7110, D-315-449-7110.

**LOCATION:** Take H-1 east or west, exit at Fort Shafter on middle street to main gate. Clearly marked. USMRA: Page 129 (D-7), page 131 (D,E-1,2). NMC: Honolulu, seven miles east.

**GENERAL INFORMATION:** U.S. Army Pacific Command (USARPAC).

**TEMPORARY MILITARY LODGING:** Lodging office, Building 453B, Burr Road, 24 hours Mon-Fri, 0745-1145 Sat, Sun & holidays. C-808-839-2336, D-315-839-2336. All ranks. DV/VIP ext 1577.

**RV, CAMPING/FAMCAMP:** Off base. Waianae Army Rec Center, year round. C-1-800-333-4158, D-315-333-4158, 0900-1600 Mon-Fri. Studio, two and three bedroom beach cabins.

**SPACE-A:** None. See Hickam AFB listing.

**LOGISTICAL SUPPORT:**
Barber Shop-847-3141                       Beauty Shop-845-9666
Carlson Wagonlit Travel-847-0329           Child Care-438-1151
Child Dev Center-438-1960                  Class VI-845-9655
Commissary-438-1367                        Credit Union-841-0181
Dining-438-1974                            Dry Cleaner-848-0466

Education Office-438-9217
Gas Station-848-0404
Shoppette-845-9626/624-3316/9825
Visitor Center-438-6996

Exchange-845-9626
Laundry-848-0466
Travel Office-438-9309

**ADMINISTRATIVE SUPPORT:**

Fire Dept-471-7117
Legal-438-2845
Pass & ID Office-438-1757
Public Affairs-655-2918

Housing Office-438-9205
Locator-655-2299
Police-438-7114

**HEALTH & WELFARE:**

American Red Cross-433-6631
CHAMPUS-1-800-2929
Dental
    Clinic-433-9868
    Emergency-433-5700
Retiree Services-438-2798
TRICARE-1-800-930-2929

ACS-438-9285
Chapel-438-1939
Family Services-438-9285
Medical
    Central Appts-433-2778
    Emergency-433-8850
Veterinary Services-438-2271

**REST & RECREATION:**

Arts & Crafts-438-1071
Bowling-438-6733
Fitness Center-438-1152
Gym-438-1152
ITR-438-1985
MWR-438-8768
Theater-438-4480
Youth Center-438-8762

Auto Hobby Shop-438-9402
Com Club-438-1974
Golf Course-438-9587
Indoor Rec-438-6733
Library-438-9521
Services-655-4806
Wood Hobby Shop-438-1071
Youth Services-438-1159

**ATTRACTIONS:** Honolulu, USS Arizona National Memorial, National Memorial Cemetery of the Pacific (Punch Bowl), Pearl Harbor.

# HICKAM AIR FORCE BASE (HI11R6)

800 Scott Circle
Hickam Air Force Base, HI 96853-5328

**TELEPHONE NUMBER INFORMATION:** Main installation numbers: C-808-449-7110, D-315-449-7110. E-mail: 635amss.trps@hickam.af.mil WEB: www2.hickam.af.mil

**LOCATION:** Adjacent to the Honolulu International Airport. Accessible from H-1 eixt 5 or Nimitz Highway south. Main gate on Vandenberg Blvd. Clearly marked. USMRA: Page 129 (D-7), page 131 (B,C-2,3,4).

**GENERAL INFORMATION:** Pacific Air Force Base. Headquarters PACAF, Air Mobility Command, 635th Airlift Squadron, 15th Air Base Wing Support Units.

**TEMPORARY MILITARY LODGING:** Lodging office, Building 1153, 24 hours daily, C-808-449-2603, D-315-449-2603. Fax: C-808-449-3572. All ranks.

**RV, CAMPING/FAMCAMP:** Hickam Harbor Recreation Area, on base year round, Recreation Services, 15 SVS/SVRO, 900 Hangar Avenue, Hickam AFB, HI 96853-5246, C-808-449-5215, D-312-430-5215. Day use (1000-2200) of cabanas; no overnight facilities.

**SPACE-A:** Pax Term/Lounge, Building 2028, 24 hours daily. C-808-449-6833/1854, D-315-449-6833/1854. Fax: C-808-448-1503. Flights to CONUS and overseas locations.

**LOGISTICAL SUPPORT:**

Bank-422-2781
Beauty Shop-422-6121
Class Six-422-4533
Credit Union-423-1391
Dry Cleaner-422-5821
Exchange-423-1304
Postal Service-422-6435
Shoppette-422-8404
Travel Office-422-2729

Barber Shop-422-4045
Car Rental-422-6915
Commissary-449-7692
Dining Facilities-449-1666
Education Office-449-6363
Gas Station-422-8744
SATO-422-2729
Snack Bar-422-8008
Visitor Center-449-1083

**ADMINISTRATIVE SUPPORT:**

Fire Protection-449-7117
Legal-449-1737

Housing Office-449-0317
Locator-449-0165

Pass/ID Office-449-9394
Public Affairs-449-2490

Police-449-2200
Q-Deck-474-6249

**HEALTH & WELFARE:**

Air Force Aid Society-449-2494
Chapel-449-1754/6562
Family Services-449-1550
Retiree Services-449-9896
TRICARE-448-6124
Veterinary Services-449-6481

American Red Cross-471-3155
Dental-448-6371
Medical
    Central Appts-448-6000
    Clinic-448-6110
    Emergency-448-6189

**REST & RECREATION:**

Bowling-449-2702
Community Center-449-2361
Fitness Center-449-1044
Golf-449-2047
Gym-449-6711

Clubs
    NCO-449-1188
    OC-449-1998/1592
Library-449-2831
Theater-449-2239

**ATTRACTIONS:** Honolulu, Waikiki Beaches and Pearl Harbor.

# HILO BIG ISLAND EXCHANGE (HI06R6)

1300 Kekuanaoa Street, Building 505
Hilo, HI 96720-5000

**TELEPHONE NUMBER INFORMATION:** Main installation numbers: C-808-935-3449.

**LOCATION:** Cross Street, Hwy 11. Connects to Hilo IAP Airport Access Road. USMRA: Page 129 (J-6). NMC: Hilo, in city limits.

**LOGISTICAL SUPPORT:**                    Exchange-935-3449

**ATTRACTIONS:** The Big Island, volcanic formations, beaches.

# HONOLULU COAST GUARD INTEGRATED SUPPORT COMMAND/KAIKAI HALE COAST GUARD HOUSING (HI21R6)

400 Sand Island Access Road
Honolulu, HI 96819-4398

**TELEPHONE NUMBER INFORMATION:** Main installation numbers: C-808-541-2490/1, D-315-430-0111. WEB: www.ischon.net
*Note: Prefix of 833 or 839 indicates activity is located at Red Hill.*

**LOCATION:** Take Nimitz Hwy east or west (HI-92) and exit at HI-64 south to Sand Island Access Road east to base. USMRA: Page 129 (D-7), page 131 (C,D-1,2). NMC: Honolulu, in city limits.

**GENERAL INFORMATION:** The largest operating unit in the 14th Coast Guard District is located at Sand Island. Personnel perform all Coast Guard functions with the exception of ice-breaking.

**TEMPORARY MILITARY LODGING:** None. See Hickam Air Force Base listing.

**RV, CAMPING/FAMCAMP:** None. See Hickam AFB listing.

**SPACE-A:** None. See Hickam AFB listing.

**LOGISTICAL SUPPORT:**

Exchange-541-2469
Package Store-541-2499

Gas Station-833-2448/72
SATO-541-2468

**ADMINISTRATIVE SUPPORT:**

OOD-541-2490

Public Affairs-541-2170

**HEALTH & WELFARE:** None. See Pearl Harbor Naval Base listing.

**REST & RECREATION:**

Athletic Field-ext 2413
Consol Club-541-2475
MWR-541-2414

Auto Hobby Shop-ext 2416
Gym/Weight Room-ext-2415
Racquet Courts-833-9632

Special Services-833-9632
Tennis-833-9632 or ext 2415
Youth Center-833-7850

Swimming-833-9632
Tickets-ext 2413

**ATTRACTIONS:** Honolulu, island tours, helicopter tours, USS Arizona Memorial and USS Bowfin Submarine Exhibit, USS Missouri, Waikiki Beach, Diamond Head, National Memorial Cemetery of the Pacific.

## KANEOHE BAY MARINE CORPS BASE (HI12R6)

4th Street, Building 216, Base Headquarters
Box 63002
Kaneohe Bay, HI 96863-3002

**TELEPHONE NUMBER INFORMATION:** Main installation numbers: C-808-449-7110, D-315-430-7110. E-mail: littlec@mfp.usmc.mil
WEB: www.mcbh.usmc.mil

**LOCATION:** At the end of H-3 on the Windward (east) side of Oahu. From Honolulu IAP: Take H-1 west to H-3 interchange. Take H-3 east to Kaneohe, continue to main gate. Off Mokapu Blvd and Kaneohe Bay Drive. Clearly marked. USMRA: Page 129 (E-6). NMC: Honolulu, 14 miles southwest.

**GENERAL INFORMATION:** 3rd Marine Regiment, Combat Service Support Group-3, 1st Marine Aircraft Wing, Aviation Support Element and other units.

**TEMPORARY MILITARY LODGING:** Lodging office, Building 3038, 0630-1800 Mon-Fri, 0900-1800 Sat-Sun, Holidays, C-808-254-2806/2716; BOQ: 24 hours daily, C-808-257-1317, D-312-457-1317; BEQ: 24 hours daily C-808-257-3470, D-312-457-3470. Beach cottages-C-808-254-2716.

**RV, CAMPING/FAMCAMP:** Campsites on base, year round, C-808-254-7667/2719, D-315-457-7666, 24 studio units, 11 cottages, four camper spaces with W hookups.

**SPACE-A:** Information: C-808-257-2121, D-315-457-2121. Frequent unscheduled flights to CONUS and OCONUS locations.

**LOGISTICAL SUPPORT:**

| | |
|---|---|
| Bank-254-1551 | Barber Shop-254-6588/6586 |
| Beauty Shop-254-6585 | Book Store-254-7586 |
| Cafeteria-257-1310 | Car Rental-254-0808 |
| Child Care-254-1593 | Child Dev Center-257-1388 |
| Commissary-257-1452/63 | Conv Store-254-7644 |
| Credit Union-254-6455 | Dining Facilities-257-1004 |
| Dry Cleaner-254-3392 | Education Office-257-2158 |
| Exchange-254-7616 | Gas Station-254-0516 |
| Laundry-254-3392 | Package Store-254-7670 |
| Postal Service-257-2008 | Snack Bar-254-7585 |
| Travel Office-254-3581 | |

**ADMINISTRATIVE SUPPORT:**

| | |
|---|---|
| Fire Dept-257-2022 | Housing Office-257-2705 |
| Legal-257-0074/2110 | Locator-257-1294 |
| OOD-257-1824 | Pass/ID Office-257-2047 |
| Police-257-2103 | Public Affairs-257-2728 |
| SDO/NCO-257-2494 | |

**HEALTH & WELFARE:**

| | |
|---|---|
| American Red Cross-257-3150 | CHAMPUS-257-1701 |
| Chapel-257-3552 | Dental-257-3100 |
| Family Services-257-7787 | Medical-257-2145 |
| Navy-MC Relief-254-1327 | Central Appts-257-2131 |
| Retiree Services-257-3135 | Clinic-257-2145 |
| TRICARE-257-1701 | Emergency-254-3133 |
| Veterinary Services-257-3643 | Health Benefits-257-1701 |

**REST & RECREATION:**

| | |
|---|---|
| Auto Hobby Shop-254-7674 | Bowling-254-7665 |
| Clubs | Fitness Center-254-7659 |
| EM-254-7660 | Golf Course-254-1745 |
| NCO-254-5592 | Gym-254-7597 |
| SNCO-254-5592 | ITT-254-7562 |

Officer-254-7649
Marina-254-7666/7667
MWR-254-7500/15
Theater-254-7642
Youth Center-254-7610

Library-254-7623
Outdoor Rec-254-7695
Services-254-7501
Youth Services-254-7610

**ATTRACTIONS:** Kaneohe Bay, beaches, outdoor sports, historical sites, and wildlife refuges.

## KILAUEA MILITARY CAMP JOINT SERVICES RECREATION CENTER (HI17R6)

Building 40
Hawaii Volcanoes National Park, HI 96718-5000

**TELEPHONE NUMBER INFORMATION:** Main installation number: C-808-967-8333/34.

**LOCATION:** On island of Hawaii, 216 air miles southeast of Honolulu, 32 miles southwest off HI-11 from Hilo International Airport. Scheduled bus transportation to camp: reservations required 48 hours prior. Hilo to Kilauea Military Camp (KMC). USMRA: Page 129 (I,J-6,7). NMC: Hilo, 32 miles northeast.

**GENERAL INFORMATION:** Kilauea Military Camp (KMC) Joint Services Rec Center. A resort for uniformed services personnel, retirees, DoD civilians and their families.

**TEMPORARY MILITARY LODGING:** Lodging office, 0800-1630 Mon-Thu, 0800-1830 Fri, C-808-967-8333/34; direct from Oahu C-438-6707. All ranks. Seventy-five units plus a dormitory (for large groups). Reservations required.

**RV, CAMPING/FAMCAMP:** Kilauea Military Camp AFRC, on post year round, 62 cabins. C-808-438-6707 (from Oahu), C-808-967-8333/34. Fax: C-808-967-8343.

**SPACE-A:** None. See Hickam AFB listing.

**LOGISTICAL SUPPORT:**

| | |
|---|---|
| Cafeteria-967-8356 | Country Store-967-8364 |
| Gas Station-967-8362 | Shoppette-967-8364 |
| Snack Bar-967-8350 | Visitor Center-985-6000 |

**ADMINISTRATIVE SUPPORT:** SDO/NCOIC-967-7315

**HEALTH & WELFARE:** Medical Clinic-967-8368

**REST & RECREATION:**

| | |
|---|---|
| Bowling-967-8350 | Consol Club-967-8363 |
| Golf-967-7331 | |

Tours–check with registration desk. Call C-438-6707/967-8333.

**OTHER FACILITIES AVAILABLE:** Bicycle rental, mini health center, multi-purpose court, rental equipment, tennis.

**ATTRACTIONS:** Tours of the Big Island–Hawaii, Hilo, Black Sands Beach, Kona, Hawaii Volcanoes National Park, active lava flows. Hula shows. Helicopter rides.

## LUALUALEI NAVAL MAGAZINE (HI23R6)

3 Constellation Street
Waianae, HI 96792-4301

**TELEPHONE NUMBER INFORMATION:** Main installation numbers: C-808-474-4341 or C-808-449-7110. E-mail: enost@navmagiii.navy.mil

**LOCATION:** Follow H-I west to Fort Weaver Road south. Turn left at intersection of Fort Weaver and North Road. Follow North Road to intersection of Iroquois Drive. Turn right. Lualualei Naval Magazine West Loch Branch gate is on left. USMRA: Page 129 (B,C-7), page 131 (A,B-3,4). NMC: Honolulu, 20 miles southeast. NMI: Pearl Harbor Naval Base, 18 miles southeast.

**GENERAL INFORMATION:** NUWC, SUBASE Pearl Harbor MK48 Torpedo Shop, USAO, DIO, Munitions Branch, Cruise Missile Shop, MR 46 Torpedo shop.

**TEMPORARY MILITARY LODGING:** Lodging office, Building 600, 0600-2200 hours daily, C-808-474-7908, Fax: C-808-474-7919.

**RV, CAMPING/FAMCAMP:** None. See Barbers Point NAS listing.

**SPACE-A:** None. See Hickam AFB listing.

**LOGISTICAL SUPPORT:**

| | |
|---|---|
| Exchange-668-3386 LB | Galley-474-7846 |
| Snack Bar | |
| LB-668-3586 | |
| WB-474-1381 | |

*Note: LB = Lualualei Branch, WB = West Loch Branch.*

**ADMINISTRATIVE SUPPORT:**

| | |
|---|---|
| CDO/OOD-474-4541 | Fire Dept-474-7829 |
| Legal-474-4515 | Pass/ID Office-474-4341 |
| Police-668-3261 LB | Public Affairs-474-4315 |
| Quarter Deck-474-4341 | |

**HEALTH & WELFARE:** None. See Barbers Point NAS or Tripler Medical Center listing.

**REST & RECREATION:**

| | |
|---|---|
| Auto Hobby Shop-499-2421 | CMO Club-474-7928 |
| MWR-668-3347 | Rec Equip-ext 7933 |
| Special Services-ext 7933 | Swimming-ext 7933 |

**ATTRACTIONS:** Beaches, outdoor rec activities, tourist attractions.

# MAUI EXCHANGE (HI07R6)

1686 Kaahumanu Avenue
Wailuku, HI 96793-5000

**TELEPHONE NUMBER INFORMATION:** Main installation numbers: C-808-244-3006.

**LOCATION:** Off I-30 in the northwest section of Maui Island. USMRA: Page 129 (G-4). NMC: Wailuku, in city limits.

**LOGISTICAL SUPPORT:**      Exchange-244-3006

# PEARL HARBOR NAVAL STATION (HI20R6)

Commander Navy Region Hawaii
517 Russell Avenue, Suite 110
Pearl Harbor, HI 96860-4884

**TELEPHONE NUMBER INFORMATION:** Main installation number: C-808-449-7110, D-315-449-7110. E-mail: publicity@mwrph.navy.mil
WEB: www.hawaii.navy.mil

**LOCATION:** From Honolulu IAP, take H-1 west. Follow signs for Pearl Harbor/Hickam AFB. Take exit 15 north on Kamehameha Hwy to Makalapa gate on North Road. USMRA: Page 129 (C-7). NMC: Honolulu, five miles east.

**GENERAL INFORMATION:** Headquarters Pacific Fleet, Headquarters Submarine Force Pacific, Naval Shipyard, support units and home port for approximately 36 ships and submarines.

**TEMPORARY MILITARY LODGING:** Central lodging office BEQ: USS Arizona Hall, Building 1623, 24 hours daily, C-808-473-5983, D-315-474-5210. BOQ Naval Station: C-808-473-4165, D-315-473-4165. BOQ Lockwood Hall: C-808-791-8300 ext 1000. BOQ Makalapa: C-808-421-4911. DV/VIP: C-808-473-4165, Fax: C-808-491-2944.

**RV, CAMPING/FAMCAMP:** None. See Hickam AFB listing.

**SPACE-A:** None. See Hickam AFB listing.

**LOGISTICAL SUPPORT:**

| | |
|---|---|
| Barber Shop-423-3395/3387 | Beauty Shop-423-3397 |
| Child Care-422-7133 | Commissary-471-0263 |
| Conv Store-423-3250 | Credit Union-423-3508 |
| Dining Facilities-474-3114/471-9171 | Education Center-474-4077 |
| Exchange-423-3344 | Gas Station-423-3229 |
| Package Store-423-3254 | SATO-423-8770 |
| Shoppette-423-3517 | Snack Bar-471-1746 |
| Visitor Center-471-3627 | |

**ADMINISTRATIVE SUPPORT:**

| | |
|---|---|
| CDO/OOD-473-1222 | Fire Dept-471-7117 |
| Legal-473-3300 | Locator-449-7110 |
| Police-474-7182 | Public Affairs-471-0281 |
| Quarterdeck-473-3646 | |

**HEALTH & WELFARE:**

| | |
|---|---|
| American Red Cross-471-3155 | Chapel-473-3971 |
| Dental-471-3911 | Family Services-473-4222 |
| Medical | Navy-MC Relief-423-1314 |
| Central Appts-473-9541 | Retiree Services-449-9896 |
| Clinic-473-1880 | TRICARE-1-800-242-6788 |
| Emergency-471-7116 | |

**REST & RECREATION:**

| | |
|---|---|
| Auto Hobby Shop-471-9072 | Bowling-473-2162/471-9212 |
| Camping/Rec Equip-474-1198 | Community Center-471-0392 |
| Clubs-Combined-471-8456/474-7235 | Dive Shop-422-5551 |
| CPO-473-1583 | Golf Course-471-0142 |
| EM-Club Pearl-473-0841 | Gym-474-0793/473-0784 |
| Beeman Center-471-2581 | ITT-473-1190 |
| Library-471-8238 | Marina-471-9680 |
| MWR-474-0787/1190 | Swimming Pool-474-5149 |
| Tennis/Racquetball-471-0610 | Theater-471-0726 |
| YMCA-471-3398 | Youth Activities-474-3501/3071 |

**ATTRACTIONS:** Diamond Head, beaches, island tours, Polynesian Cultural Center.

# SCHOFIELD BARRACKS (HI13R6)

25th Infantry Division (Light) & U.S. Army, Hawaii
Building 580, Room 229
Schofield Barracks, HI 96857-6000

**TELEPHONE NUMBER INFORMATION:** Main installation numbers: C-808-449-7110, D-315-449-7110.

**LOCATION:** Off H-2 or HI-99, west on HI-750 to gates, in the center of the island of Oahu. Clearly marked. USMRA: Page 129 (C-6). NMC: Honolulu, 20 miles southeast.

**GENERAL INFORMATION:** 25th Infantry Division (Light) and U.S. Army, Hawaii, U.S. Army Garrison, Hawaii.

**TEMPORARY MILITARY LODGING:** The Inn at Schofield Barracks: C-808-624-9650, 1-800-490-9638, D-315-624-9650, Fax: C-808-624-5606, 24 hours daily, 190 guest rooms.

**RV, CAMPING/FAMCAMP:** None. See Fort Shafter Listing.

**SPACE-A:** None. See Hickam AFB listing.

**LOGISTICAL SUPPORT:**

| | |
|---|---|
| Bank-623-8616 | Barber Shop-624-5541 |
| Beauty Shop-624-5144 | Carlson Wagonlit Travel-624-1700 |
| Car Rental-624-2324 | Child Care-655-5293 |
| Child Dev Center-655-7106 | Commissary-655-5066 |
| Conv Store-624-3316 | Credit Union-624-9883 |
| Dry Cleaner-621-8088 | Dining-624-5600 |
| Education Office-655-0805 | Exchange-622-1773 |
| Gas Station-624-9857 | Laundry-621-8088 |
| Package Store-624-2692 | Shoppette-624-9825 |
| Travel Office-655-2248 | Visitor Center-655-0216 |

## ADMINISTRATIVE SUPPORT:

Fire Dept-471-7117
Legal-655-4884
Pass/ID Office-655-4104
Public Affairs-655-2918

Housing Office-474-2343
Locator-655-2299
Police-655-0911

## HEALTH & WELFARE:

American Red Cross-655-4927
Army Emergency Relief-656-1900
Chapel-655-93071
Family Services-656-1900
Medical
   Central Appts-433-2778
   Clinic-433-2778
   Emergency-655-7116
   Health Benefits-433-2778
   Hospital-433-6661
   Information-433-6661

ACS-656-1900
CHAMPUS-1-800-930-2929
Dental
   Clinic-433-8903
   Emergency-433-8814
Retiree Services-438-2798
TRICARE-1-800-930-2929
Veterinary Services-655-4041

## REST & RECREATION:

Arts & Crafts-655-4202
Auto Hobby Shop-655-9368
Clubs
   Combined-624-5600
   NCO-655-2251
   Sports Dome-624-2230
Indoor Rec-655-8522
Library-655-0145
Outdoor Rec-655-0143
Rec Equip-ext 0143
Services-655-4804
Tennis-624-7366
Wood Hobby Shop-655-4202
Youth Services-655-4641

Athletic Fields-ext 0900
Bowling-655-0573
Community Center-655-8522
Fitness Center-655-0900
Golf Course-655-9833/4653
Gym-655-8007
ITR-655-9971
MWR-655-0002
Rec Center-ext 0968
Scuba-ext 0143
Swimming-655-9698
Theater-251-4583
Youth Center-655-4641

**ATTRACTIONS:** Sugar cane and pineapple fields. Tropic Lightning Museum.

## TRIPLER MEDICAL CENTER (HI03R6)

1 Jarrett White Road
Tripler Medical Center, HI 96859-5000

**TELEPHONE NUMBER INFORMATION:** Main installation numbers: C-808-433-6662, D-315-433-6662.
E-mail: web-tamc@smtplink.tamc.amedd.army.mil
WEB: www.tamc.amedd.army.mil

**LOCATION:** Take H-1 west to Tripler exit. Turn right on Jarret White Road to Tripler Medical Center. USMRA: Page 129 (D-7), page 131 (D-1,2). NMC: Honolulu, three miles southeast.

**GENERAL INFORMATION:** Tripler Medical Center is the largest military medical center in the Pacific area of operations. Tripler treats service members from all branches of the military.

**TEMPORARY MILITARY LODGING:** Lodging office, Building 228B, Jarrett White Road, 0630-2300 Sun-Sat, Holiday hours: 0800-1700-Fri, C-808-839-2336. All ranks. DV/VIP 433-2336.

**RV, CAMPING/FAMCAMP:** None. See Bellows AFS listing.

**SPACE-A:** None. See Hickam AFB listing.

## LOGISTICAL SUPPORT:

Barber Shop-839-6810
Commissary-438-6164
Credit Union-833-1257
Exchange-433-1267
Snack Bar-833-1259

Carlson Wagonlit Travel-834-7499
Cafeteria-433-2365
Dining-433-6067
Shoppette-433-1267

The Aliamanu Military Reservation, a nearby housing area, has a large Shoppette/Gas Station 833-6997.

## ADMINISTRATIVE SUPPORT:

Legal-433-5311

AOD/SDNCO-433-6661

## HEALTH & WELFARE:

CHAMPUS-1-800-242-6788
Medical-433-6661
   Central Appts-433-2778
   Emergency-433-6629

Chapel-433-5727
Patient Rep-433-6336

## REST & RECREATION:

Gym-ext 6443
Library-ext 6968
Special Services-ext 5772
Tennis-ext 6443

ITR-438-1985
Racquet/Handball-ext 6443
Swimming-ext 5257

**ATTRACTIONS:** USS Arizona National Memorial, Pearl Harbor. Great view of Honolulu.

## WAHIAWA NAVAL COMPUTER AND TELECOMMUNICATIONS AREA MASTER STATION, PACIFIC [NCTAMS PAC] (HI16R6)

500 Center Street
Wahiawa, HI 96786-3050

**TELEPHONE NUMBER INFORMATION:** Main installation numbers: C-808-653-5385, D-315-453-5385. WEB: www.nctamspac.navy.mil

**LOCATION:** Take H-1 west approximately seven miles to H-2 north interchange.Take H-2 to Wahiawa exit, proceed through town of Wahiawa; cross the trestle bridge. At next traffic light, take a right onto Whitmore Avenue, continue four miles straight ahead to main gate. USMRA: Page 129 (C-6). NMC: Honolulu, 20 miles southeast.

**GENERAL INFORMATION:** Naval Communications for Pacific area, provides operational direction and management to all Pacific Naval telecommunications system users.

**TEMPORARY MILITARY LODGING:** BEQ C-808-622-1792, D-315-453-1792, Fax: C-808-653-4600.

**RV, CAMPING/FAMCAMP:** None. See Waianae Army Rec Center listing.

**SPACE-A:** None. See Hickam AFB listing.

## LOGISTICAL SUPPORT:

Barber Shop-653-5527
Child Care-653-5305
Exchange-653-5364
Mini-Mart-653-5364

Beauty Shop-653-5527
Education Office-653-7700
Gas Station-653-5451
SATO-621-0733

## ADMINISTRATIVE SUPPORT:

CDO/OOD-653-5385
Legal-653-5397
Police-653-0234
Quarter Deck-653-5385

Fire Dept-653-5479
Locator-653-5385
Public Affairs-299-2423

## HEALTH & WELFARE:

CHAMPUS-474-4406
Dental-653-5475
Medical-653-5340

Chapel-653-5577
Family Services-653-0203

## REST & RECREATION:

Arts & Crafts-653-5574
Bowling-653-5576
Gym-653-5542
Library-653-5420
Racquet Sports-ext 5542
Special Services-ext 0191
Youth Center-653-0220

Auto Hobby Shop-653-5485
EM Club-653-5470
Indoor Rec-653-5470
MWR-653-5485
Rec Equip-ext 5542
Swimming-ext 5306
Youth Services-653-0220

**ATTRACTIONS:** Short drive to Honolulu, beach areas.

## WAIANAE ARMY RECREATION CENTER
### (HI05R6)
85-010 Army Street
Waianae, HI 96792-5000

**TELEPHONE NUMBER INFORMATION:** Main installation numbers: C-808-696-4158, 1-800-333-4158 (from mainland), or 1-800-847-6771 (from outer islands).

**LOCATION:** On the west coast of Oahu. Take H-1 west to HI-93 north (Farrington Highway) to Waianae. Look for the Aloha gas station on your left (west); turn left at Army Street. USMRA: Page 129 (B-6). NMC: Honolulu, 35 miles southeast. NMI: Schofield Barracks, 20 miles northeast.

**GENERAL INFORMATION:** Located along beach of Pokai Bay in once-quiet fishing and plantation village. One of the favorite swimming and fishing spots on Oahu. Operated by Fort Shafter, off post year round. Military personnel active, retired, reserve, DoD civilians, other federal employees. Reservations required: C-808-696-4158, 1-800-333-4158 (from mainland), or 1-800-847-6771 (from outer islands), 0900-1600 M-F, Hawaiian time.

**TEMPORARY MILITARY LODGING:**  Cabins-4

**LOGISTICAL SUPPORT:**

| | |
|---|---|
| Dining-696-6783 | Package Store-696-2886 |
| SATO-624-9513 | Shoppette-696-2886 |

**ADMINISTRATIVE SUPPORT:**  Police-696-2811

**HEALTH & WELFARE:**  CHAMPUS-433-6330

**REST & RECREATION:**

| | |
|---|---|
| Beach Club-696-4778 | Equipment Rental-696-3442 |
| ITT-655-9971 | MWR-655-9971 |

**ATTRACTIONS:** Beautiful beaches, swimming, surfing, kayaking, snorkeling and fishing.
*For detailed information about this off-base recreation facility, as well as on-base recreation facilities, golf courses and marinas, consult Military Living's Military RV, Camping and Outdoor Recreation Around the World.*

## WHEELER ARMY AIRFIELD (HI14R6)
25th ID, Building 580, Room 229
Schofield Barracks, HI 96857-6000

**TELEPHONE NUMBER INFORMATION:** Main installation numbers: C-808-449-7110, D-315-449-7110.

**LOCATION:** Off H-2 or HI-99 in the center of the island of Oahu. Adjacent to and south of Schofield Barracks. Kunra Gate from HI-750. USMRA: Page 129 (C-6). NMC: Honolulu, 20 miles southeast.

**GENERAL INFORMATION:** Aviation Support for 25th INF DIV (Light), Air National Guard Aircraft Control and Warning Squadron and support units, Garrison Support Activities.

**TEMPORARY MILITARY LODGING:** None. See Schofield Barracks listing, the Inn at Schofield Barracks.

**RV, CAMPING/FAMCAMP:** None. See Fort Shafter Listing.

**SPACE-A:** None. See Hickam AFB listing.

**LOGISTICAL SUPPORT:**

| | |
|---|---|
| Bank-623-8616 | Barber Shop-624-5818 |
| Beauty Shop-624-5144 | Car Rental-624-2324 |
| Carlson Wagonlit Travel-624-1700 | Child Care-656-1900 |
| Child Dev Center-656-1900 | Commissary-655-2360 |
| Conv Store-624-9818 | Dry Cleaner-624-3271 |
| Education Office-655-0800 | Exchange-624-9818 |
| Gas Station-624-3451 | Laundry-624-3271 |
| Shoppette-624-9817 | Snack Bar-656-1745 |
| Travel Office-655-2248 | Visitor Center-655-0216 |

**ADMINISTRATIVE SUPPORT:**

| | |
|---|---|
| Fire Dept-471-7117 | Housing Office-474-2343 |
| Legal-655-4884 | Locator-655-2299 |
| Pass/ID Office-655-4104 | Police-655-7114 |
| Public Affairs-655-2918 | |

**HEALTH & WELFARE:**

| | |
|---|---|
| American Red Cross-655-4927 | ACS-656-1900 |
| Army Emergency Relief-656-1900 | CHAMPUS-1-800-930-2929 |
| Chapel-655-9207 | Dental |
| Family Services-656-1900 |   Clinic-433-8903 |
| Medical |   Emergency-433-8814 |
|   Central Appts-433-2778 | Retiree Services-438-2798 |
|   Emergency-433-8850 | TRICARE-1-800-930-2929 |
|   Health Benefits-433-2778 | Veterinary Services-655-4041 |
|   Hospital-433-2778 | |
|   Information-433-2778 | |

**REST & RECREATION:**

| | |
|---|---|
| Arts & Crafts-655-4202 | Auto Hobby Shop-655-9368 |
| Bowling-656-1745 | Clubs |
| Community Center-655-8522 |   Com-624-5600 |
| Fitness Center-655-0900 |   NCO-655-2251 |
| Golf Course-655-9833 | Gym-655-8007 |
| Indoor Rec-655-8522 | ITR-655-9971 |
| Library-655-0145 | MWR-438-8768 |
| Outdoor Rec-655-0143 | Services-655-4806 |
| Theater-251-4583 | Wood Hobby Shop-655-4202 |
| Youth Center-656-1601 | Youth Services-655-4641 |

**ATTRACTIONS:** Numerous activities on Oahu and other islands. Pineapple and sugar cane fields.

# IDAHO

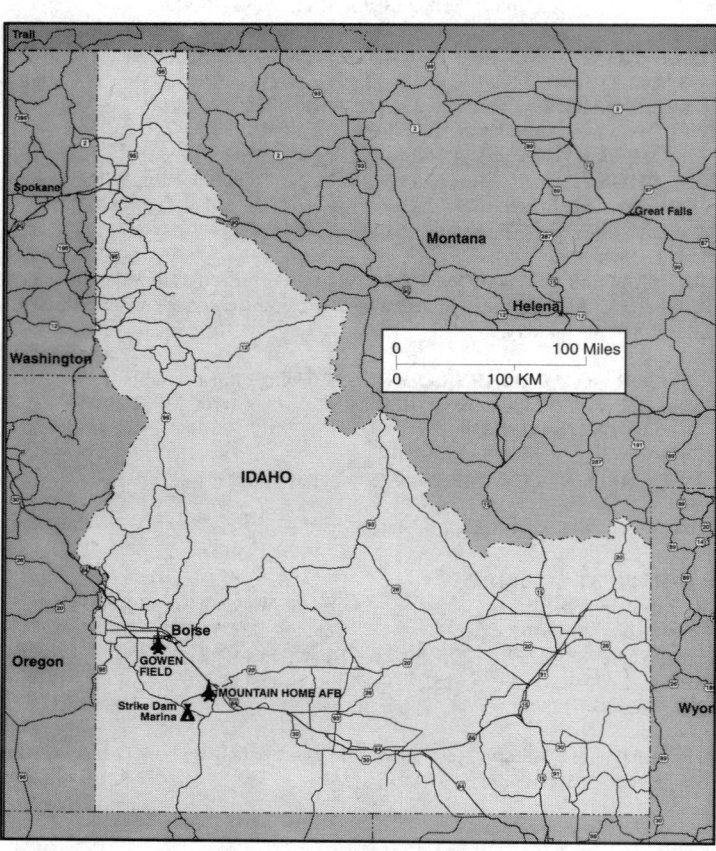

## GOWEN FIELD (ID04R4)
4040 Guard Street
Boise, ID 83705-5004

**TELEPHONE NUMBER INFORMATION:** Main installation numbers: C-208-422-5011, D-312-941-5011.

**LOCATION:** From I-84 east or west, take Orchard Street exit (exit 52 south). Turn left and remain on Gowen road as it goes behind the airport. Watch for "Gowen Field" sign near tanks. Turn left into Main Gate. USMRA: Page 98 (B-8). NMC: Boise, five miles north.

**GENERAL INFORMATION:** Headquarters, Idaho Army and Air National Guard, U.S. Naval , Marine and Army Reserves, Headquarters, 1/204th Regiment Armor Training, Headquarters, 2/204th Ordnance Training, 124th Wing, Headquarters, 321st Combat Engineer Battalion, 116th Cavalry Brigade.

**TEMPORARY MILITARY LODGING:** Lodging office, Building 669, 0800-1700 daily, C-208-422-4451, D-312-422-4451, Fax: C-208-422-4452, D-312-422-4452.

**RV, CAMPING/FAMCAMP:** None. See Mountain Home AFB listing.

**SPACE-A:** C-208-422-5989, D-312-422-5989. Fax: 208-422-6410, D-312-422-6410. Frequent flights to CONUS and OCONUS locations.

**LOGISTICAL SUPPORT:**

| | |
|---|---|
| Conv Store-422-5676 | Exchange-422-5676 |
| SATO-422-5000 | Snack Bar-422-5674 |

**ADMINISTRATIVE SUPPORT:**

| | |
|---|---|
| Fire Dept-422-5867 | Legal-422-5474 |
| Locator-422-5011 | Police-422-5366 |
| Public Affairs-422-5268 | |

**HEALTH AND WELFARE:**

| | |
|---|---|
| CHAMPUS-422-5027 | Chapel-422-6467/5394 |
| Family Services-422-5067 | Medical-422-5369 |
| Retiree Services-422-5817 | |

**REST & RECREATION:**

| | |
|---|---|
| Clubs | Fitness Center-422-6046 |
| NCO-422-5674 | MWR-422-6703 |
| O-422-5667/5668 | Recreation-422-5381 |
| Theater-422-6245 | |

**ATTRACTIONS:** Boise River: trout and bass fishing, swimming, waterskiing, windsurfing, skin diving, tubing, City of Trees, with five large parks along the river. Zoo, Rose Garden, State Historical Museum, Art Museum. Bogus Basin Ski Resort (both nordic and alpine skiing), snowmobiling, rodeos and fairs.

## MOUNTAIN HOME AIR FORCE BASE (ID01R4)
366 Gunfighter Avenue, Suite 152
Mountain Home Air Force Base, ID 83648-5000

**TELEPHONE NUMBER INFORMATION:** Main installation numbers: C-208-828-2111, D-312-728-1110.

**LOCATION:** From Boise, take I-84 southeast, 39 miles to Mountain Home, exit 95 west, follow road through town to Airbase Road, (ID- 67 west), 10 miles to main gate on left. USMRA: Page 98 (C-9). NMC: Boise, 51 miles northwest.

**GENERAL INFORMATION:** Air Combat Command Base. B-1B, F-15C, F-15E, F-16, & KC-135R Air intervention aircraft composite wing. Air-to-ground and air-to-air combat.

**TEMPORARY MILITARY LODGING:** Lodging office, 366 SVS/SVMH, Building 2604, Falcon Street, 24 hours daily, C-208-828-5200/5352, D-312-728-5200/5352. Fax: C-208-828-4797. All ranks. DV/VIP C-208-828-4536, D-312-728-4536.

**RV, CAMPING/FAMCAMP:** FAMCAMP on base, year round, 366 SVS/SVML, 445 Falcon Street, 24 hours daily, C-208-828-6333, D-312-728-6333, 22 camper spaces with full hookups, 10 tent spaces. Operates Strike Dam Marina off base (see listing), and Yellowstone Country Trailers off base (see listing).

**SPACE-A:** Pax Term/Lounge, Building 262, 0730-1630 Mon-Fri. C-208-828-4747, D-312-728-4747. Fax: C-208-828-4128, D-312-728-4128. Flights to CONUS locations. Also, Boise Air Terminal, limited Space-A, Reserve Units.

**LOGISTICAL SUPPORT:**

| | |
|---|---|
| Bank-832-4202 | Barber Shop-832-7191 |
| Beauty Shop-832-4090 | Child Care-828-2443 |
| Child Dev Center-828-2443 | Commissary-828-2286 |
| Conv Store-828-6921 | Credit Union-832-4675 |
| Dining Facilities-828-6420 | Dry Cleaner-832-7465 |
| Education Office-828-6363 | Exchange-832-4353 |
| Gas Station-832-4459 | Laundry-832-7893 |
| N&N Travel-832-2276 | Package Store-828-4459 |
| Postal Service-832-7008 | Shoppette-828-4459 |
| Snack Bar-828-6546 | |

**ADMINISTRATIVE SUPPORT:**

| | |
|---|---|
| Fire Dept-828-6292 | Housing Office-828-2781 |
| Legal-828-2238 | Locator-828-1110 |
| Pass/ID Office-828-2371 | Police-828-2256 |
| Public Affairs-828-6800 | SDO/NCO-828-2071 |

**HEALTH & WELFARE:**

| | |
|---|---|
| Air Force Aid Society-828-2458 | American Red Cross-828-6622 |
| CHAMPUS-828-7800 | Chapel-828-6417 |
| Dental-828-7300 | Family Services-828-2272 |
| Medical-828-7600 | Retiree Services-828-4878 |
| Central Appts-832-1560 | TRICARE-828-7460 |
| Emergency-828-7100 | Veterinary Services-828-2221 |
| Hospital-828-7460 | |

**REST & RECREATION:**

| | |
|---|---|
| Arts & Crafts-828-6229 | Auto Hobby Shop-828-2295 |
| Bowling-828-6329 | Clubs |
| Community Center-828-2246 | Com-828-2105 |
| Golf Course-828-6151 | O-828-2597 |
| Gym-828-2381 | Library-828-2326 |
| Marinas-834-2723 | MWR-828-6080 |
| Outdoor Recreation-828-6333 | Rec Center-ext 2246 |
| Rec Equip-ext 2237 | Services-828-6081 |
| Skeet/Trap-ext 6093 | Stables-ext 4093 |
| Swimming-ext 6620 | Theater-828-6184 |
| Wood Hobby Shop-828-6338 | Youth Center-828-2501 |

**ATTRACTIONS:** Snow skiing, hunting, and fishing. Boise, capital city of Idaho.

## STRIKE DAM MARINA (ID02R4)
366 SVS/SVRM
Attn: Strike Dam Marina, Bldg 2800
Mountain Home AFB, ID 83648-5125

**TELEPHONE NUMBER INFORMATION:** Main installation numbers: C-208-834-2723, D-312-728-1110. Police for marina area, C-208-828-2256, D-312-728-2256.

**LOCATION:** Off base. From I-84 east of Boise, follow signs to Mountain Home AFB (on ID-67), exit 95 southwest and onto C.J. Strike Reservoir. USMRA: Page 98 (B-9). NMI: Mountain Home AFB, 27 miles northeast. NMC: Boise, 60 miles north.

**GENERAL INFORMATION:** Operated by Mountain Home AFB, off base, open 15 April-Labor Day. Military Personnel active, reservists, retired, DoD civilians. Reservations: 366 SVS/SVRM, Attn: Strike Dam Marina, Bldg 2800, Mountain Home AFB, ID 83648-5125. C-208-828-6333 (Outdoor Adventure Program Info available year round).

**RV, CAMPING/FAMCAMP:** Unlimited space

**ATTRACTIONS:** Situated along Snake River and surrounded by mountains. Full support for water sports and picnic activities.

*For detailed information about this off-base recreation facility, as well as on-base recreation facilities, golf courses and marinas, consult Military Living's Military RV, Camping and Outdoor Recreation Around the World.*

## YELLOWSTONE COUNTRY TRAILERS (ID05R4)

SVS/SVRO Outdoor Recreation
655 Pine Street, Bldg 2800
Mountain Home AFB, ID 83648-5237

**TELEPHONE NUMBER INFORMATION:** Main installation numbers: C-208-828-6333, D-312-728-6333.

**LOCATION:** Off base. Trailers are placed at commercial RV parks around Yellowstone National Park both in Idaho and Wyoming. USMRA: Page 98 (H-6,7). NMI: Malmstrom AFB, 254 miles north. NMC: Idaho Falls, 80 miles south.

**GENERAL INFORMATION:** Travel trailers are positioned at three different locations around Yellowstone National Park. One unit is at Henry's Lake, which is nationally known for its trophy cutthroat and brook trout, and is 15 miles from the west entrance to the park. Four units are at Lionshead Resort which is only eight miles from the west entrance and four miles from Hebgen Lake. Six units are at Flagg Ranch, Grand Teton National Park, two miles from the south entrance of Yellowstone National Park. Operated by Mountain Home AFB, off-base, Memorial Day-Labor Day. Military personnel active, reservists, retired, DoD civilians. Reservations (required): Outdoor Recreation, 655 Pine Street, Mountain Home AFB, ID 83648-5125. C-208-828-6333, D-312-728-6333. Reservations may not be made by mail.

**RV, CAMPING/FAMCAMP:**     Travel Trailers-11

**ATTRACTIONS:** Yellowstone National Park.

*For detailed information about this off-base recreation facility, as well as on-base recreation facilities, golf courses and marinas, consult Military Living's Military RV, Camping and Outdoor Recreation Around the World.*

# ILLINOIS

## CAMP LINCOLN EXCHANGE (IL05R2)

Ima Building 10, 1301 North MacArthur Boulevard
Springfield, IL 62702-5000

**TELEPHONE NUMBER INFORMATION:** Main installation numbers: C-217-524-1758.

**LOCATION:** From the north, take I-55 to exit 100 (Sangamon Avenue) to a left on 5th Street. Turn right on North Grand Avenue, 15 blocks to camp. USMRA: Page 64 (E-6). NMC: Decatur, 32 miles east.

**GENERAL INFORMATION:** Training location and home of the Illinois National Guard State Headquarters and the Illinois Military Academy.

**LOGISTICAL SUPPORT:**     Exchange-217-524-1758

## CAPITAL AIRPORT/AIR NATIONAL GUARD BASE (IL12R2)

183 Fighter Wing (ANG), 3101 J. David Jones Parkway
Springfield, IL 63707-5000

**TELEPHONE NUMBER INFORMATION:** Main installation numbers: C-217-753-8850, D-312-892-8210.

**LOCATION:** From I-55 exit to Sangamon Avenue, west on 5th Street, approximately one-half mile and left to Browning Road, right on David Jones Parkway. Follow signs on the left. USMRA: Page 64 (D-5). NMC: Springfield, in city limits.

**GENERAL INFORMATION:** Home of the 183d Fighter Wing.

**TEMPORARY MILITARY LODGING:** None. See Scott AFB listing.

**RV, CAMPING/FAMCAMP:** None. See Scott AFB listing.

**SPACE-A:** None. See Greater Peoria Regional Airport or Scott AFB listings.

**LOGISTICAL SUPPORT:**     Exchange at Camp Lincoln

**HEALTH & WELFARE:**     Medical-757-1221/2

## CHARLES MELVIN PRICE SUPPORT CENTER (IL04R2)

Army Community Service
Granite City, IL 62040-1801

**TELEPHONE NUMBER INFORMATION:** Main installation numbers: C-618-452-4212, D-892-4212.

**LOCATION:** From I-70 north take McKinley Bridge exit east, cross Mississippi River, IL-3 north, follow signs to Center. From I-270 east, cross river bridges and take first Granite City exit (Route 3 south) to Center. USMRA: Page 64 IC,D-7). NMC: St. Louis, seven miles west.

**GENERAL INFORMATION:** Army Area Support Center, Army Materiel Command aviation and other materiel procurement and logistical activities. Military Traffic Management Command POV processing center (nearby).

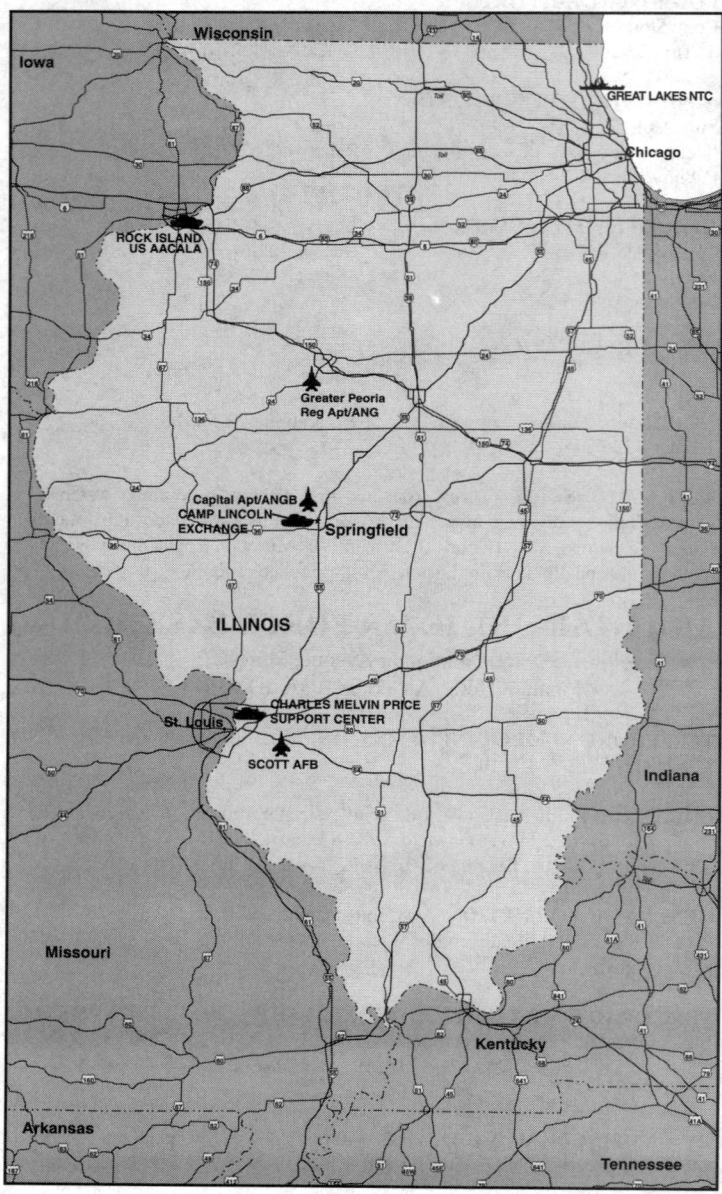

**TEMPORARY MILITARY LODGING:** Lodging office, Building 102, Niedringhaus Street, 0730-1615 daily, C-618-452-4287, D-312-892-4287. Other hours, Security Office, Building 221, C-618-452-4224. All ranks.

**RV, CAMPING/FAMCAMP:** None. See Scott AFB listing.

**SPACE-A:** None. See Scott AFB listing.

**LOGISTICAL SUPPORT:**

| | |
|---|---|
| Child Care-452-4480 | Commissary-452-4227 |
| Credit Union-451-7596 | Class VI-452-6112 |
| Exchange-452-5230 | Package Store-452-6112 |
| POV Center-452-4650/4651 | SATO-452-4375 |
| Snack Bar-452-4444 | |

**ADMINISTRATIVE SUPPORT:**  Police-452-4224

**HEALTH & WELFARE:**

| | |
|---|---|
| ACS-452-4550 | CHAMPUS-314-425-4851 |
| Chapel-452-4277 | Family Services-452-4260 |
| Medical-331-4851 | Retiree Services-452-4472 |

**REST & RECREATION:**

| | |
|---|---|
| Auto Hobby-ext 4279 | Bowling- 452-4319 |
| C C-452-4425 | Golf-452-4444 |
| Gym-ext 4209 | Library-ext 4322 |
| MWR-452-4632 | Rec Services 4632 |
| Swimming-ext 4221 | |

**ATTRACTIONS:** Gateway Arch, Mississippi River Tours, St. Louis, Lacledes Landing, Grants Farm, Busch Stadium, Six Flags, Kiel Aud, VP Fair (July), Fox Theater, Soulard Market area, museums, USS Inaugural Minesweeper.

# GREAT LAKES NAVAL TRAINING CENTER (IL07R2)

2701 Sheridan Road
Great Lakes, IL 60088-5001

**TELEPHONE NUMBER INFORMATION:** Main installation numbers: C-847-688-3500, D-312-792-3500. E-mail: ntc-grl.n1e@smtp.cnet.navy.mil. WEB: www.ntcpao.com

**LOCATION:** From I-94 north or US-41 north of Chicago, exit to IL-137 east to Sheridan Road north, turn right into the gate. Clearly marked. USMRA: Page 64 (G-1). NMC: Chicago, 30 miles south.

**GENERAL INFORMATION:** Naval Training Center, Service School Command, Recruit Training Command, Naval Hospital, Hospital Corps School, Hq U.S. Military Entrance Processing Command, Personnel Support Activity.

**TEMPORARY MILITARY LODGING:** Lodging office, (BEQ) Building 834, 0700-1530 daily, C-847-688-2170, D-312-792-2710, Fax: C-847-688-4736. Navy Lodge, Building 2500, C-847-689-1485, Fax: C-708-689-1489. (BOQ) Building 62, 24 hours daily, C-847-688-3777, D-312-792-3777, Fax: C-847-688-5815.

**RV, CAMPING/FAMCAMP:** Great Lakes Naval Training Center, on base year round, 0800-1600 Tue-Sun, MWR, Building 160-NTC, C-847-688-5417, D-312-792-5417, Fax: C-847-688-5421, D-312-792-5421, eight camper spaces without hookups.

**SPACE-A:** None. See Greater Peoria Regional Airport/ANG listing.

**LOGISTICAL SUPPORT:**

| | |
|---|---|
| Barber Shop-578-6169 | Beauty Shop-578-6211 |
| Cafeteria-578-6120 | Child Care-688-1291 |
| Child Dev Center-688-2845 | Commissary-688-2644 |
| Conv Store-578-6247 | Credit Union-578-7000 |
| Dining Facilities-688-6946 | Dry Cleaner-578-6218 |
| Education Office-688-4681 | Exchange-578-6100 |
| Gas Station-578-6247 | Laundry-578-6218 |
| Package Store-578-6271 | Postal Service-688-5392 |
| SATO-689-1884 | Snack Bar-578-6120 |
| Travel Office-473-5775 | Visitor Center-688-5670 |

**ADMINISTRATIVE SUPPORT:**

| | |
|---|---|
| CDO/OOD-688-3939/3300 | Fire Dept-688-3333 |
| Housing Office-688-3391 | Legal-688-3805 |
| Locator-688-2445 (recruits) | Locator-688-3536 (service school) |
| Pass/ID Office-688-5550, ext 393 | Police-688-3430 |
| Public Affairs-688-2430 | SDO/SNCO-688-3500 |

**HEALTH & WELFARE:**

| | |
|---|---|
| American Red Cross-847-688-5676 | CHAMPUS-688-5457 |
| Chapel-688-2384 | Dental |
| Family Services-688-3603 | Central Appts-688-2423 |
| Medical-688-3444 | Clinic-688-2424 |
| Central Appts-688-5600 | Emergency-688-2424 |
| Clinic-688-5600 | Navy-MC Relief-689-2228 |
| Emergency-688-5618 | Retiree Services-688-5434 |
| Health Benefits-688-5457 | Veterinary Services-688-5740 |
| Hospital-688-4560 | |

**REST & RECREATION:**

| | |
|---|---|
| Auto Hobby Shop-688-5612 | Bowling-688-5612 |
| Clubs | Fitness Center-688-3994 |
| Com-688-6946 | Golf Course-688-4593 |
| EM-688-4641 | Gym-688-3419 |
| Indoor Rec-688-3419 | ITT-688-3537 |
| Library-688-4617 | Marina-688-5417 |
| Outdoor Rec-688-6978 | Services-688-2110, ext 697 |
| Theater-688-6763 | Travel (TSG)-473-7045 |
| Youth Center-688-5573 | Youth Services-688-5581 |
| Wood Crafts-688-4813 | |

**ATTRACTIONS:** Six Flags Great America, Gurnee Mills Shopping Mall, Milwaukee Zoo, Chicago Museum of Science and Industry. Excellent seasonal recreation available on Lake Michigan and in the Chain O'Lakes area.

# GREATER PEORIA REGIONAL AIRPORT/ AIR NATIONAL GUARD (IL13R2)

182nd Airlift Wing (ANG)
2416 S. Falcon Blvd
Peoria, IL 61607-5000

**TELEPHONE NUMBER INFORMATION:** C-309-633-5216, D-312-724-5216.

**LOCATION:** rom I-474 north or south, take exit at 5 southwest to airport. Left on Airport Road to right on Smithville Road. Approximately three miles to base on right. USMRA: Page 64, (D-4). NMC: Peoria, seven miles northeast.

**GENERAL INFORMATION:** Home of the 182nd Airlift Wing.

**SPACE-A:** C-309-633-5216, D-312-724-5216. Fax: C-309-633-5306. Frequent flights via ANG C-130A-H aircraft to CONUS and OCONUS locations.

**ATTRACTIONS:** Peoria has many golf courses, museums, Illinois riverfront.

# ROCK ISLAND U.S. ARMY ARMAMENT & CHEMICAL ACQUISITION & LOGISTICS ACTIVITY (IL08R2)

ATTN: AMSTA-AC-AP
Rock Island Arsenal, IL 61299-5000

**TELEPHONE NUMBER INFORMATION:** Main installation numbers: C-309-782-6001, D-312-793-6001. E-mail: stoutr@ria.army.mil WEB: www.acala1.ria.army.mil

**LOCATION:** From I-74 north in Moline, exit 1 to 4th Avenue west and follow signs to Arsenal Island, located in middle of Mississippi River. USMRA: Page 64 (C-2). NMC: Quad Cities of Rock Island, Moline, Davenport and Bettendorf.

**GENERAL INFORMATION:** Headquarters Rock Island Arsenal and Industrial Operations Command.

**TEMPORARY MILITARY LODGING:** Housing Office, Building 102, C-309-782-2376, D-312-793-2376, Fax: C-309-782-2550.

**RV, CAMPING/FAMCAMP:** None. See Great Lakes NTC listing.

**SPACE-A:** None. See Greater Peoria Airport listing.

**LOGISTICAL SUPPORT:**

| | |
|---|---|
| Cafeteria-793-4337 | Child Care-782-2828 |
| Commissary-782-4798 | Exchange-788-4940 |

**ADMINISTRATIVE SUPPORT:**

| | |
|---|---|
| Legal-782-8432 | Locator-782-3004 |
| Police-782-2846 | |

**HEALTH & WELFARE:**

| | |
|---|---|
| Chapel-782-4736 | Family Services-782-3828 |
| Medical-782-0805/0801 | |

**REST & RECREATION:**

| | |
|---|---|
| Arsenal Club-788-4860 | Auto Hobby Shop 782-4950 |
| Fitness Center-782-6787 | Gym-782-6787 |
| Outdoor Rec-782-8630 | Skeet-782-2014 |

**ATTRACTIONS:** Rock Island Arsenal Museum, National Cemetery, Confederate Cemetery, Colonel Davenport House.

## SCOTT AIR FORCE BASE (IL02R2)

101 Heritage Drive, Room 28
Scott Air Force Base, IL 62225-5000

**TELEPHONE NUMBER INFORMATION:** Main installation numbers: C-618-256-1110, D-312-576-1110.

**LOCATION:** From I-64 east or west, take exit 19 east or 19-A west to IL-158 south, two miles and watch for signs to AFB entry. USMRA: Page 64 (D-8). NMC: St. Louis, 25 miles west.

**GENERAL INFORMATION:** Headquarters for U.S. Transportation Command; Air Mobility Command; Air Force Communications Agency; Air Weather Service; Defense Information Technology Contracting Office, USAF Medical Center Scott, 932rd. Airlift Wing (AFRES) and 126th Air Refueling Wing (ANG).

**TEMPORARY MILITARY LODGING:** Scott Inn, Building 1510, 24 hours daily, C-618-256-2045, D-312-576-2045. All ranks. DV/VIP 256-5555.

**RV, CAMPING/FAMCAMP:** FAMCAMP on base, year round, C-618-256-2067, D-312-576-2067, 24 camper spaces with W/E hookups.

**SPACE-A:** Pax Term, Building P-8, C-618-256-3017, D-312-576-3017; Rec: C-618-256-1854, D-312-576-1854. Fax: C-618-256-1946, D-312-576-1946.

**LOGISTICAL SUPPORT:**

| | |
|---|---|
| Bank-256-1144 | Barber Shop-256-2899 |
| Beauty Shop-256-1544 | Cafeteria-256-4199 |
| Car Rental-800-325-8007 | Child Care-576-2405 |
| Class VI-256-0237 | Commissary-256-2783 |
| Dry Cleaner-256-2417 | Exchange-256-0888 |
| Gas Station-256-2184 | Postal Service-256-5942 |
| Snack Bar-256-3921 | Rogers Travel-256-5397 |

**ADMINISTRATIVE SUPPORT:**

| | |
|---|---|
| Fire Dept-256-5130 | Legal-256-2358 |
| Locator-256-1841 | Housing Office-256-3430 |
| Police-256-2223 | Public Affairs-256-4241 |

**HEALTH & WELFARE:**

| | |
|---|---|
| CHAMPUS-256-7521 | Chapel-256-3303 |
| Family Services-256-3616 | Medical |
| Retiree Services-256-5092 | Central Appts-256-1847 |
| | Emergency-256-7595/911 |

**REST & RECREATION:**

| | |
|---|---|
| Auto Hobby Shop-256-4566 | Bowling-256-4054 |

| | |
|---|---|
| Clubs | Fitness Center-256-2086 |
| Aero-256-2170 | Library-256-5100 |
| EM-256-1777 | Golf Course-256-2385 |
| O-256-1333 | Gym-256-4524 |
| Community Center-256-5919 | Outdoor Rec-256-2067 |
| Skills Dev Center-256-3839 | Swimming-256-2579 |
| Theater-256-5177 | Youth Center-256-2115 |

**ATTRACTIONS:** St. Louis and the Arch are nearby, Mississippi River, Six Flags Amusement Park, Cahokia Mounds and numerous caves.

# INDIANA

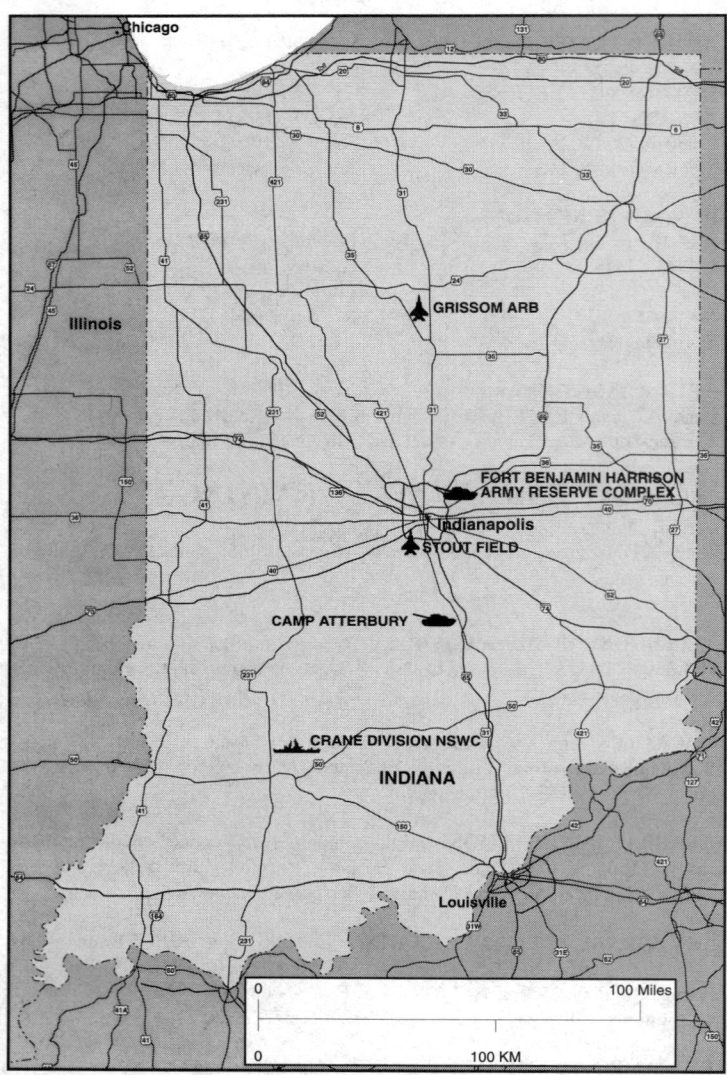

## CAMP ATTERBURY (IN05R2)

Army National Guard
Building 708
Edinburg, IN 46124-1096

**TELEPHONE NUMBER INFORMATION:** Main installation numbers: C-812-526-9711, D-312-569-2348.

**LOCATION:** From I-65 north or south, take exit 76 (31 north), left at Hospital Road. Enter post on Eggleston Street at Main Gate. USMRA: Page 65 (E-6,7). NMC: Indianapolis, 45 miles north.

**GENERAL INFORMATION:** Indiana Army National Guard Maneuver Training Center.

**TEMPORARY MILITARY LODGING:** Contract Quarters, Post Billeting Office, C-812-526-1128.

**RV, CAMPING/FAMCAMP:** Campgrounds, on post year round, Building 1, MWR, Camp Atterbury, C-812-526-1149, D-312-569-2149, 16 camper spaces with full hookups, unlimited tent spaces.

**SPACE-A:** None. See Grissom ARB listing.

**LOGISTICAL SUPPORT:**                 Exchange-526-1140

**ADMINISTRATIVE SUPPORT:**
Pass/ID Office-526-1111                 Public Affairs-526-1306

**HEALTH & WELFARE:** None. See Crane Division NSWC listing.

**REST & RECREATION:**
Clubs                                   MWR-526-1101
  Kings Hall-526-1141
  NCO-526-1143
  O-526-1141

**ATTRACTIONS:** Indianapolis, 45 miles north, Camp Atterbury Veteran's Memorial Park, Camp Atterbury Prisoner of War Chapel.

## CRANE DIVISION, NAVAL SURFACE WARFARE CENTER (IN03R2)
ATTN: N00164
300 Highway 361
Crane, IN 47522-5001

**TELEPHONE NUMBER INFORMATION:** Main installation numbers: C-812-854-1222, D-312-482-1222. WEB: www.crane.navy.mil

**LOCATION:** From Indianapolis, take Highway 465 south to 37 south to Bloomington, exit right on 45 southwest. Follow to Crane. Or from US-231 east, IN-645 to gate. USMRA: Page 65 (D-8). NMC: Bloomington, 30 miles northeast.

**GENERAL INFORMATION:** A major Naval Weapons and Ammunition Support Center, Army Ammunition Activity (tenant) and Explosive Ordnance Disposal Unit (tenant) located on station.

**TEMPORARY MILITARY LODGING:** Limited lodging, Building 2682, Code QL4, NAVSURFWARCEN Division, BEQ/BOQ/DV/VIP, C-812-854-1176, D-312-482-1176, Fax: C-812-854-4416, D-312-482-4416, 0700-1500 Mon-Fri. All ranks.

**RV, CAMPING/FAMCAMP:** Crane MWR Campgrounds on base, 1 April-31 Oct, MWR Campgrounds, NAVSURFWARCENDIV, C-812-854-1368, D-312-482-1368, 52 camper spaces with full hookups, 20 tent spaces.

**SPACE-A:** None. See Scott AFB, IL listing.

**LOGISTICAL SUPPORT:**
| | |
|---|---|
| Bank-854-1583 | Barber Shop-854-1392 |
| Cafeteria-854-1519 | Commissary-854-1297 |
| Conv Store-854-1392 | Credit Union-854-3414 |
| Dining Facilities | Education Office-854-3262 |
|   Consol Mess-854-3435 | Exchange-854-1392 |
| Gas Station-854-1864 | Package Store-854-1392 |
| Postal Service-854-3400 | SATO-854-1244 |
| Travel Office-854-1232 | Visitor Center-854-4521 |

**ADMINISTRATIVE SUPPORT:**
| | |
|---|---|
| CDO/OOD-854-1225 | Fire Dept-854-5606 |
| Housing Office-854-3510 | Legal-854-1130 |
| Locator-854-2511 | Pass/ID Office-854-1213 |
| Police-854-1640 | Public Affairs-854-1640 |
| Quarter Deck-854-1225 | SDO/NCO-854-5621 |

**HEALTH & WELFARE:**
| | |
|---|---|
| CHAMPUS-854-1220 | Medical-854-1220 |
| Retiree Services-854-1222 | Emergency-854-1333 |

**REST & RECREATION:**
| | |
|---|---|
| Bowling-854-6057 | Community Center-854-1501 |
| Fitness Center-854-6057 | Golf Course-854-1242 |
| Gym-854-1586 | ITT-854-6059 |
| Library-854-1526 | Marinas-854-1368 |
| MWR-854-2241 | Outdoor Rec-854-3947 |

**ATTRACTIONS:** Indiana University, Bloomington, and Lake Greenwood Nature Trail.

## FORT BENJAMIN HARRISON ARMY RESERVE COMPLEX (IN02R2)
ATTN: ATZI-CDR
Indianapolis, IN 46216-5005

**TELEPHONE NUMBER INFORMATION:** C-317-510-2297, D-312-699-2297.

**LOCATION:** Take I-165 east to Fort Harrison exit 40, east on 56th Street, or take Pendleton Pike (IN-67/US-36) exit 42 to Post Road and north to Fort Harrison. USMRA: Page 65 (E-5).

**GENERAL INFORMATION:** U.S. Army Transition Activity, subinstallation of Fort Knox.

**TEMPORARY MILITARY LODGING:** None. See Camp Atterbury listing.

**RV, CAMPING/FAMCAMP:** None. See Camp Atterbury listing.

**SPACE-A:** None. See Grissom ARB listing.

**LOGISTICAL SUPPORT:**
| | |
|---|---|
| Commissary-549-5293 | Exchange-542-5698/2163 |

**ADMINISTRATIVE SUPPORT:**        Locator-317-542-4537

**HEALTH & WELFARE:** None. See Camp Atterbury listing.

**REST & RECREATION:** None. See Camp Atterbury listing.

**ATTRACTIONS:** Indianapolis, thirteen miles southwest.

## GRISSOM AIR RESERVE BASE (IN01R2)
Grissom ARB, IN 46971-5000

**TELEPHONE NUMBER INFORMATION:** C-765-688-5211.D-312-928-1110.

**LOCATION:** On US-31, 15 miles north of Kokomo and 7 miles south of Peru. Turn at Grisson Aeroplex, proceed on Hoosier Blvd west of US-31 to main gate. Take a left onto Warthog Drive and proceed to Bldg 600. USMRA: Page 65 (E-3). NMC: Indianapolis, 64 miles south.

**GENERAL INFORMATION:** Home of the 434th Air Refueling Wing

**TEMPORARY MILITARY LODGING:** Grissom Inn: C-765-688-2596. Fax: C-765-688-8751, D-312-928-8571; DV/VIP: C-765-688-2844.

**RV, CAMPING/FAMCAMP:** None. See Camp Atterbury listing.

**SPACE-A:** Information: C-765-688-2861, D-312-928-2861. Fax: 765-688-3643, D-312-928-3643. Hours: 0700-2300 daily. Limited flights to CONUS, OCONUS and foreign country locations.

**LOGISTICAL SUPPORT:**
| | |
|---|---|
| Car Rental-457-4980 | Com Club-689-9151 |
| Credit Union-689-9181 | Fast Food-689-8776 |
| Shoppette-689-5270 | |

**ADMINISTRATIVE SUPPORT:**
| | |
|---|---|
| Police (Security)-688-2503 | Public Affairs-688-3348 |

**HEALTH & WELFARE:** None. See Camp Atterbury listing.

**REST & RECREATION:**                 MWR-688-2414/8362

**ATTRACTIONS:** Grissom Air Museum, City of Peru, Circus Hall of Fame Indianapolis Motor Speedway, 72 miles south.

# STOUT FIELD (IN08R2)

2002 South Holt Road
Indianapolis, IN 46241-4839

**TELEPHONE NUMBER INFORMATION:** C-317-247-3300, D-312-369-2300. E-mail:mdipa@sourc.isd.state.in.us WEB: www.state.in.us/guard

**LOCATION:** From I-495 bypass northbound, exit 11 at Airport Expressway, east approximately two miles, north on Holt Road entrance. USMRA: Page 65 (E-6). NMC: Indianapolis, in city limits.

**GENERAL INFORMATION:** Indiana National Guard site.

**TEMPORARY MILITARY LODGING:** None. See Camp Atterbury listing.

**RV, CAMPING/FAMCAMP:** None. See Camp Atterbury listing.

**SPACE-A:** None. See Grissom ARB listing.

**LOGISTICAL SUPPORT:**
SATO-247-3333                     Education Center-247-3224

**ADMINISTRATIVE SUPPORT:**
Pass/ID Office-247-3225           Public Affairs-247-3222

**HEALTH & WELFARE:** None. See Camp Atterbury listing.

**REST & RECREATION:** None. See Camp Atterbury listing.

**ATTRACTIONS:** Indianapolis offers museums, restaurants, Indianapolis 500.

# IOWA

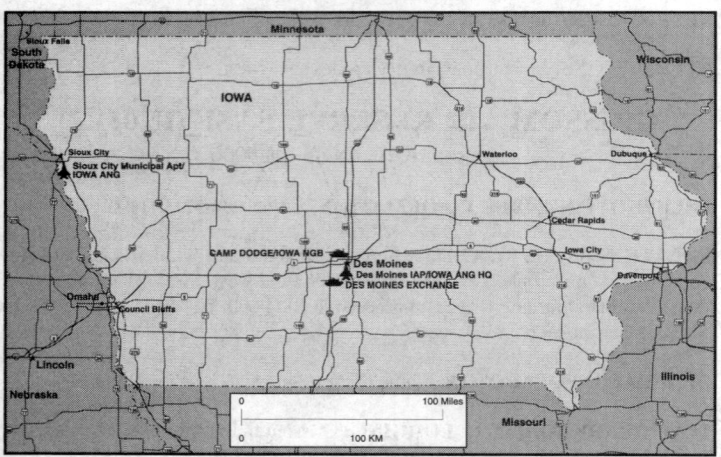

# CAMP DODGE/IOWA NATIONAL GUARD BASE (IA02R2)

Headquarters, Iowa National Guard
7700 Northwest Beaver Drive
Johnston, IA 50131-1902

**TELEPHONE NUMBER INFORMATION:** Main installation numbers: C-515-252-4011, D-312-946-2011. E-mail: kingr@ia-arng.ngb.army.mil WEB: www.guard.state.ia.us

**LOCATION:** From I-35/I-80 east or west, take Merle Hay Road/Camp Dodge exit 131 north on Iowa 401 (Merle Hay Road) to northwest Beaver Drive, left to Camp Dodge. Clearly marked. USMRA: Page 77 (E-5). NMC: Des Moines, eight miles southeast.

**GENERAL INFORMATION:** State Headquarters Iowa National Guard, Iowa Law Enforcement Academy, Iowa Communications Network, National Maintenance Training Center.

**TEMPORARY MILITARY LODGING:** Lodging office, Building A-8 (facilities), 7th Street and Des Moines Avenue, 24 hours daily, C-515-252-4238, D-312-946-2238. 1630-0800, call Security C-515-240-3742.

**RV, CAMPING/FAMCAMP:** None. See Offutt AFB, NE listing.

**SPACE-A:** None. See Offutt AFB, NE listing.

**LOGISTICAL SUPPORT:**
Exchange-252-4382                 SATO-270-2445

**ADMINISTRATIVE SUPPORT:**
Fire Dept-911                     Housing Office-252-4238
Legal-252-4259                    Locator-252-4413
Pass/ID Office-252-4413           Police-250-3742
Public Affairs-252-4582           SDO-971-6383

**HEALTH AND WELFARE:**
CHAMPUS-252-4679                  Chapel-252-4378*
Medical-252-4265*                 Retiree Services-252-4413

**REST & RECREATION:**
ITT-270-2445                      Museum-252-4531*
Swimming 276-1106

*These facilities are not manned by full-time personnel, call Public Affairs at 252-4582 for information.*

**OTHER FACILITIES AVAILABLE:** Class Six, credit union, education office, ball fields.

**ATTRACTIONS:** Camp Dodge is adjacent to the Saylorville Recreational Area, which provides boating, fishing, camping, hiking, and bicycling. Des Moines, with full cultural and entertainment activities. Adventureland Theme Park, White Water University Park, aquarium, zoo, State Fairgrounds.

# DES MOINES EXCHANGE (IA01R2)

Building 106, 217 E Army Post Road
Des Moines, IA 50315-5000

**TELEPHONE NUMBER INFORMATION:** Main installation numbers: C-515-287-7671.

**LOCATION:** From I-35 north or south to airport exit 68 east, to Army Post Road to entance on Union Street. USMRA: Page 77 (E-5). NMC: Des Moines, in city limits.

**LOGISTICAL SUPPORT:**                 Exchange C-515-287-7671

# DES MOINES INTERNATIONAL AIRPORT/IOWA AIR NATIONAL GUARD HEADQUARTERS (IA04R2)

132 Fighter Wing
3100 McKinley Avenue
Des Moines, IA 50321-5000

**TELEPHONE NUMBER INFORMATION:** Main installation numbers: C-515-256-8210.

**LOCATION:** From north, take I-35 south. Get off at the Army Post exit (68 east). Go east to Fleur Drive North, to west on McKinley Avenue and follow to 31st Street. USMRA: Page 77 (E-5). NMC: Des Moines, in city limits.

**GENERAL INFORMATION:** Home of the 132d Fighter Wing. Extremely limited support facilities. See Offutt AFB listing for nearest facilities.

**LOGISTICAL SUPPORT:**
Exchange-256-8550 (annex of Des Moines Exchange)

## SIOUX CITY MUNICIPAL AIRPORT/ IOWA AIR NATIONAL GUARD (IA03R2)

185 Fighter Wing
2920 Headquarters Avenue
Sioux City, IA 51111-1300

**TELEPHONE NUMBER INFORMATION:** Main installation numbers: C-712-233-0200, D-312-585-0200. WEB: www.185fw.ang.af.mil

**LOCATION:** From I-29 north or south to Sergeant Bluff airport exit (exit 141), west toward airport exit to F-16 airplane, south to gate. USMRA: Page 77 (A-4). NMC: Sioux City, ten miles north.

**GENERAL INFORMATION:** Home of the 185th Fighter Wing.

**TEMPORARY MILITARY LODGING:** None. See Camp Dodge/Iowa NGB.

**RV, CAMPING/FAMCAMP:** None. See Offutt AFB, NE listing.

**SPACE-A:** None. See Offutt AFB, NE listing.

**LOGISTICAL SUPPORT:**
Credit Union-279-0055/233-0742      Exchange-277-2042/233-0759

**ADMINISTRATIVE SUPPORT:**
Legal-233-0737      Public Affairs-233-0733

**HEALTH & WELFARE:**
American Red Cross-252-4081      Chapel-233-0744
Family Services-233-0534      Medical-255-3511

**REST & RECREATION:** None. See Camp Dodge/Iowa NGB.

**ATTRACTIONS:** Sioux City's Art Center, museums, Missouri River.

# KANSAS

## FORBES FIELD KANSAS AIR NATIONAL GUARD BASE (KS01R3)

Forbes Field Air National Guard Base
5920 SE Coyote Drive
Topeka, KS 66619-5370

**TELEPHONE NUMBER INFORMATION:** Main installation numbers: C-785-861-4210, D-312-720-4210.

**LOCATION:** From I-70 east or west, exit 361A, take US-75 south. Main gate located at second stoplight on US-75. Base is east of US-75 south. USMRA: Page 78 (I-4). NMC: Topeka, three miles north.

**GENERAL INFORMATION:** 190th Air Refueling Wing, 117th Air Refueling Squadron, 127th Weather Flight.

**TEMPORARY MILITARY LODGING:** None. See Fort Riley listing.

**RV, CAMPING/FAMCAMP:** None. Nearest facility is over 100 miles away.

**SPACE-A:** Limited, infrequent flights. Call C-785-861-4210, D-312-720-4210, Fax: C-785-861-4555, D-312-720-4555.

**LOGISTICAL SUPPORT:**      Exchange-861-4962

**ADMINISTRATIVE SUPPORT:**
Fire Dept-861-4501      Legal-861-4002
Locator-861-4210      Police-861-4195
Public Affairs-861-4395

**HEALTH & WELFARE:**
CHAMPUS-861-4130      Chapel-861-4001
Medical-861-4522

**REST & RECREATION:**
Museum 862-3303      MWR-861-0144

**ATTRACTIONS:** Combat Air Museum on post. Lake Shawnee, Topeka, Heartland Park Race Track, Kansas Expocenter, Topeka Zoo, Kansas Museum of History.

## FORT LEAVENWORTH (KS04R3)

USACAC & Fort Leavenworth
ATTN: ATZL-GC
600 Thomas Avenue
Fort Leavenworth, KS 66027-1399

**TELEPHONE NUMBER INFORMATION:** Main installation numbers: C-913-684-4021, D-312-552-4021. E-mail: pao@leav-emh1.army.mil
WEB: leav-www.army.mil

**LOCATION:** From I-70 east or west, exit 223 to US-73 north to Leavenworth. From I-29 north or south, exit 19, KS-92 west to Leavenworth. Fort is adjacent to

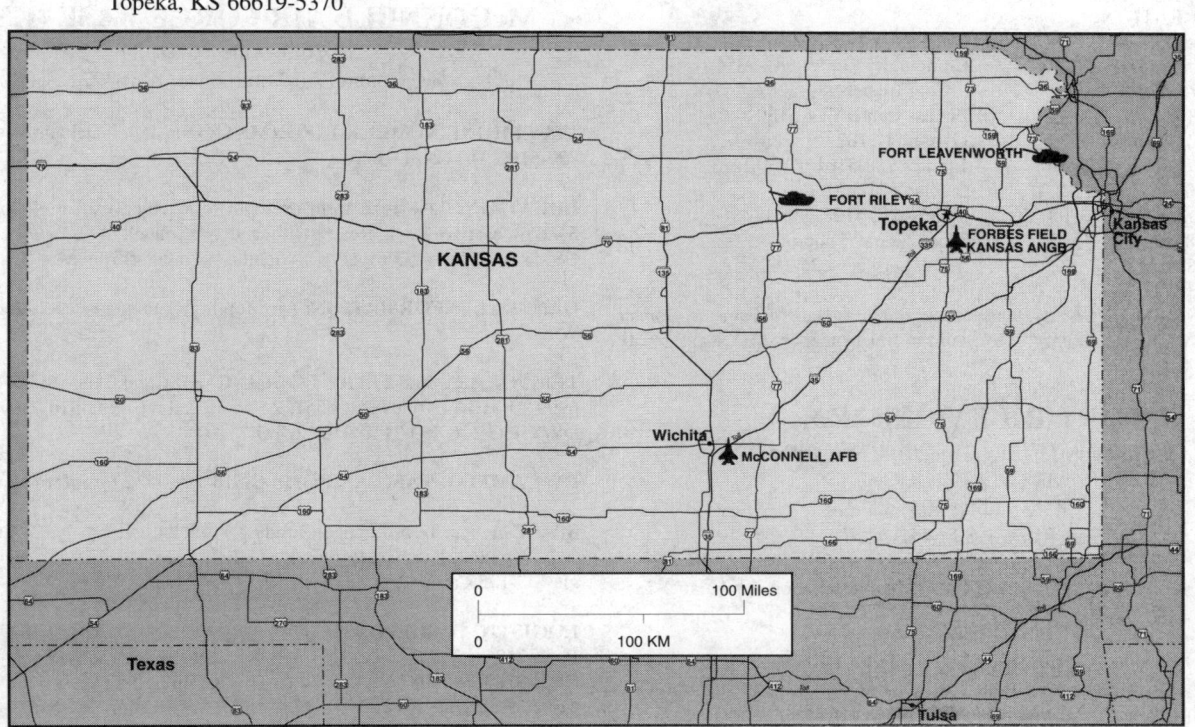

city of Leavenworth. Main gate on US-73 (Metropolitan Avenue). USMRA: Page 78 (J-3). NMC: Kansas City, 30 miles southeast.

**GENERAL INFORMATION:** Combined Arms Center, U.S. Disciplinary Barracks, Command and General Staff College, Headquarters 35th Infantry Division (Mech).

**TEMPORARY MILITARY LODGING:** Lodging office, Building 695, 214 Grant Avenue, 24 hours daily, C-913-684-4091, D-312-552-4091, Fax: C-913-684-4397. All ranks. DV/VIP C-913-684-4063.

**RV, CAMPING/FAMCAMP:** None. Nearest facility is over 100 miles away.

**SPACE-A:** Sherman Army Airfield, VIP/Lounge, Building 132, 0730-1630 Mon-Fri. C-913-684-2396, D-312-552-2396, flights to CONUS locations.

**LOGISTICAL SUPPORT:**

| | |
|---|---|
| Bank-682-9090 | Barber Shop-651-3815 |
| Beauty Shop-651-6753 | Book Store-651-6552 |
| Cafeteria-651-6573 | Carlson Wagonlit Travel-682-5455 |
| Child Care-684-9350 | Child Dev Center-684-9354 |
| Class VI 651-7186 | Commissary-684-4903 |
| Conv Store-651-7186 | Credit Union-651-6575 |
| Dry Cleaner-651-3923 | Education Office-684-2496 |
| Exchange-651-7271 | Gas Station-651-6541 |
| Laundry-651-3923 | Package Store-651-7186 |
| Postal Service-682-0052 | SATO-682-5455 |
| Snack Bar-651-6573 | |

**ADMINISTRATIVE SUPPORT:**

| | |
|---|---|
| Fire Dept-684-4172 | Housing Office-684-4921 |
| Legal-684-4944 | Locator-684-7889 |
| Pass/ID Office-684-4452 | Police-684-2111 |
| Public Affairs-684-5604 | SDO/SNCO-684-4154 |

**HEALTH & WELFARE:**

| | |
|---|---|
| American Red Cross-684-6356 | ACS-684-2800 |
| Army Emergency Relief-684-4357 | Chapel-684-2210 |
| Dental | Family Services-684-4357 |
| Central Appts-684-5516 | Retiree Services-684-2425 |
| Medical (Active duty only) | TRICARE-684-4000 |
| Central Appts-684-4000 | Veterinary Services-684-6510 |
| Clinic -684-6600 | |
| Health Benefits-684-6105 | |
| Information-684-6000 | |

**REST & RECREATION:**

| | |
|---|---|
| Arts & Crafts-684-3373 | Bowling-651-2195 |
| Clubs | Community Center-684-9354 |
| EM-684-1707 | Conf Center-684-2287 |
| Flying-651-6808 | Fitness Center-684-5120 |
| Golf Course-651-7176 | Gym-684-2187 |
| ITR-684-2580 | Library-758-3101 |
| MWR-684-1666 | Stables-651-7307 |
| Swimming-684-2187/3088/3998 | Tennis-684-5128 |
| Theater-684-4683 | Wood Hobby Shop-684-3378 |
| Youth Center-684-5115 | Youth Services-684-1653 |

**ATTRACTIONS:** Frontier Army Museum, Agriculture Hall of Fame in Bonner Springs, Harry S. Truman Library & Museum in Independence, MO, Kansas City Royals, Kansas City Chiefs.

## FORT RILEY (KS02R3)

1st Infantry Division (Mech) & Fort Riley
ATTN: AFZN-GC
Building 405
Fort Riley, KS 66442-5007

**TELEPHONE NUMBER INFORMATION:** Main installation numbers: C-785-239-3911, D-312-856-1110.

**LOCATION:** Near Junction City. From east or west on I-70, take exit #301 north-west onto Henry Drive directly to Main Post. Or take exit #296 at Junction City north onto Washington Street. Continue north through Junction City across

Republican River to post. Follow signs. USMRA: Page 78 (G,H-3,4). NMC: Topeka, 50 miles east.

**GENERAL INFORMATION:** Home of America's Army.

**TEMPORARY MILITARY LODGING:** Lodging office, Building 45, Barry Avenue, 24 hours daily, C-1-800-643-8991 or C-785-239-2830/3525, D-312-856-2830. Fax: C-785-239-8882. All ranks. DV/VIP C-785-239-3926/3037.

**RV, CAMPING/FAMCAMP:** None. Nearest facility is over 100 miles away.

**SPACE-A:** None. See Forbes Field listing.

**LOGISTICAL SUPPORT:**

| | |
|---|---|
| Carlson Wagonlit | Child Care-239-4847 |
| Leisure travel-784-2223/2285 | Class Six-784-5182 |
| Official travel-784-2002/2218 | Commissary-239-2921 |
| Conv Store-784-6037 | Credit Union-784-3100 |
| Exchange-784-4672 | Gas Station-784-5081 |
| Snack Bar-784-2231 | Travel-239-2586 |
| Visitor Center-239-2672 | |

**ADMINISTRATIVE SUPPORT:**

| | |
|---|---|
| Fire Dept-239-4257 | Legal-239-3117 |
| Locator-239-9867/9868 | Police-239-2431 |
| Public Affairs-239-3032 | SDO/EOC-239-2222 |

**HEALTH & WELFARE:**

| | |
|---|---|
| ACS-239-9435 | CHAMPUS-239-7727 |
| Chapel-239-3359/2694 | Family Services-239-9435 |
| Medical-239-7777 | Retiree Services-239-3667 |
| TRICARE-784-1200 | |

**REST & RECREATION:**

| | |
|---|---|
| Auto Hobby Shop-239-9764 | Clubs |
| Crafts-239-9205 | Leaders'-784-5999 |
| Golf Course-239-5412 | Riding-239-6651 |
| Gyms-239-3868/5562/5771/4683 | ITR-239-5614 |
| Library-239-5305 | MWR-239-3467 |
| Outdoor Rec-239-6363 | Skating Rink-239-2243 |
| Swimming-239-9441 | Theater-239-9454 |
| Wood Hobby Shop-239-9328 | Youth Center-239-9224 |

**ATTRACTIONS:** Moon Lake Rec Area on post, 239-6189, no camping facilities. Custer House, U.S. Cavalry Museum, and First Territorial Capital.

## McCONNELL AIR FORCE BASE (KS03R3)

57837 Coffeyville Street, Suite 240
McConnell Air Force Base, KS 67221-3504

**TELEPHONE NUMBER INFORMATION:** Main installation numbers: C-316-759-6100, D-312-743-1110.

**LOCATION:** Take I-35 north or south to Wichita, exit at Kellogg Street (US-54/400) east to Rock Road south and McConnell AFB, west of Rock Road. USMRA: Page 78 (G-6). NMC: Wichita, six miles northwest.

**GENERAL INFORMATION:** Air Mobility Command Base, 22nd Air Refueling Wing.

**TEMPORARY MILITARY LODGING:** Air Capital Inn, Bldg 196, C-316-612-6999, D-312-743-6999, ext 5551, 24 hours daily. Fax: C-316-759-4190 All ranks. DV/VIP C-316-759-3110, D-312-743-3110.

**RV, CAMPING/FAMCAMP:** Call C-316-759-4432 for information.

**SPACE-A:** Pax Term/Lounge, Building 1112, 24 hours daily, C-316-759-3840, D-312-743-3840, Fax: C-316-652-4957, flights to CONUS, OCONUS and overseas via KC-135R aircraft.

**LOGISTICAL SUPPORT:**

| | |
|---|---|
| Bank-759-5450/57 | Child Care-759-4223 |
| Class Six-759-5198 | Clothing Store-759-4171 |
| Commissary-759-5692 | Credit Union-759-5457 |

Exchange-685-0231
Food Services-759-6185
Gas Station-759-5215
Shoppette-685-0291

Family Day Care-759-5783
Fast Food-759-4272
N & N Travel-759-5263
Visitor Center-759-4713

**ADMINISTRATIVE SUPPORT:**

Fire-117
Locator-759-3555
Public Affairs-759-3141

Legal-759-3590
Police-759-3976
CDO-759-3251

**HEALTH & WELFARE:**

CHAMPUS-759-5017
Family Services-759-3729
TRICARE-691-6300

Chapel-759-3562
Family Support Center-759-6020

**REST & RECREATION:**

Arts & Crafts-759-4084
Clubs
  EM-759-6183
  O-759-6182
Library-759-4207
Rec Equip-759-4432
Youth Center-759-4071

Bowling-759-6189
Fitness Center-759-4009
Golf Course-759-4038
Indoor Pool-759-6066
Rec Center-759-4432
Tickets & Tours-759-6038

**ATTRACTIONS:** Rebuilt downtown core area has resulted in an outstanding civic and cultural complex, zoo, museums of art and history, botanical garden.

# KENTUCKY

## FORT CAMPBELL (KY02R2)

101st Airborne Division & Fort Campbell
ATTN: AFZB-GC
39 26th Street
Fort Campbell, KY 42223-5628

**TELEPHONE NUMBER INFORMATION:** Main installation numbers: C-502-798-2151, D-312-635-1110. E-mail: afzb-po@campbell-emh1.army
WEB: www.campbell.army.mil

**LOCATION:** In the southwest part of Kentucky, four miles south of intersection of US-41A and I-24, exit 86 on I-24, 10 miles northwest of Clarksville, TN. USMRA: Page 40 (E,F-7). NMC: Hopkinsville, 15 miles north.

**GENERAL INFORMATION:** 101st Airborne Division (Air Assault), Air Assault School, 5th SFG (A), 101st Corps Support Group Regiment, 160th Special Operation Aviation Regiment.

**TEMPORARY MILITARY LODGING:** Turner Guest House, Building 82, Texas Avenue & Indiana, C-502-439-2229. Fax: C-502-439-7758. All ranks. DV/VIP C-615-431-8924.

**RV, CAMPING/FAMCAMP:** Destiny Parks & Pavilion (Army Travel Camp) on post, year round, Bldg. 6615 Lafayette, C-502-798-3126, D-312-635-3126. Also available 75 camper spaces with W&E hookups, four cabins.

**SPACE-A:** Campbell Army Airfield, Pax Term, Zone H/I, 24 hours daily, Bldg 2301, 18th and Indiana, C-502-798-7146, D-312-635-7146. Fax: C-502-798-9288, D-502-798-9288. AMC Medevac flights, C009A available on Fridays.

**LOGISTICAL SUPPORT:**

Bank-502-439-4141
Beauty Shop-502-439-3155
Carlson Wagonlit-931-431-6664
Child Care-798-3643
Class VI-931-431-3622
Conv Store-439-1914
Dry Cleaner-502-439-1768
Exchange-439-1841/6
Postal Service-502-439-4114
Shoppette-502-439-1924

Barber Shop-502-439-0198
Cafeteria-631-3779
Car Rental-439-9988
Child Development Center-798-4180
Commissary-798-4104/4206
Credit Union-931-431-3800
Education Center-502-798-4918
Gas Station-431-3399/3415
SATO-431-5660
Visitor Center-798-5047/5049

**ADMINISTRATIVE SUPPORT:**

Fire Dept-798-3922
Legal-798-4927
Police-798-7111
SDO-798-9793

Housing Office-798-6154/6155
Pass/ID Office-798-4838
Public Affairs-798-3025

**HEALTH & WELFARE:**

ACS-798-9516
Chapel-798-6124
Family Services-798-5127
Medical
  Central Appts-1-800-941-4501
  Emergency-1-800-941-4501
  Hospital-798-8400

CHAMPUS-1-800-941-4501
Dental-502-798-8751
Health Benefits-1-800-941-4501
Retiree Services-798-5680
Veterinary Services-798-4749

**REST & RECREATION:**

Arts & Crafts-502-798-6693
Bowling-502-798-5887/4993
Golf Course-798-4906
ITR-798-7436
Library-798-7466
Outdoor Rec-798-3126/5590
Rec Center-ext 6383/4616/5818
Rec Equip-ext 3919/6806

Auto Hobby Shop-502-798-6693
Clubs
  EM-439-3897
  NCO-431-5188
  O-431-5603
MWR-798-9953
Recreation-798-7466
Show Center-ext 6087

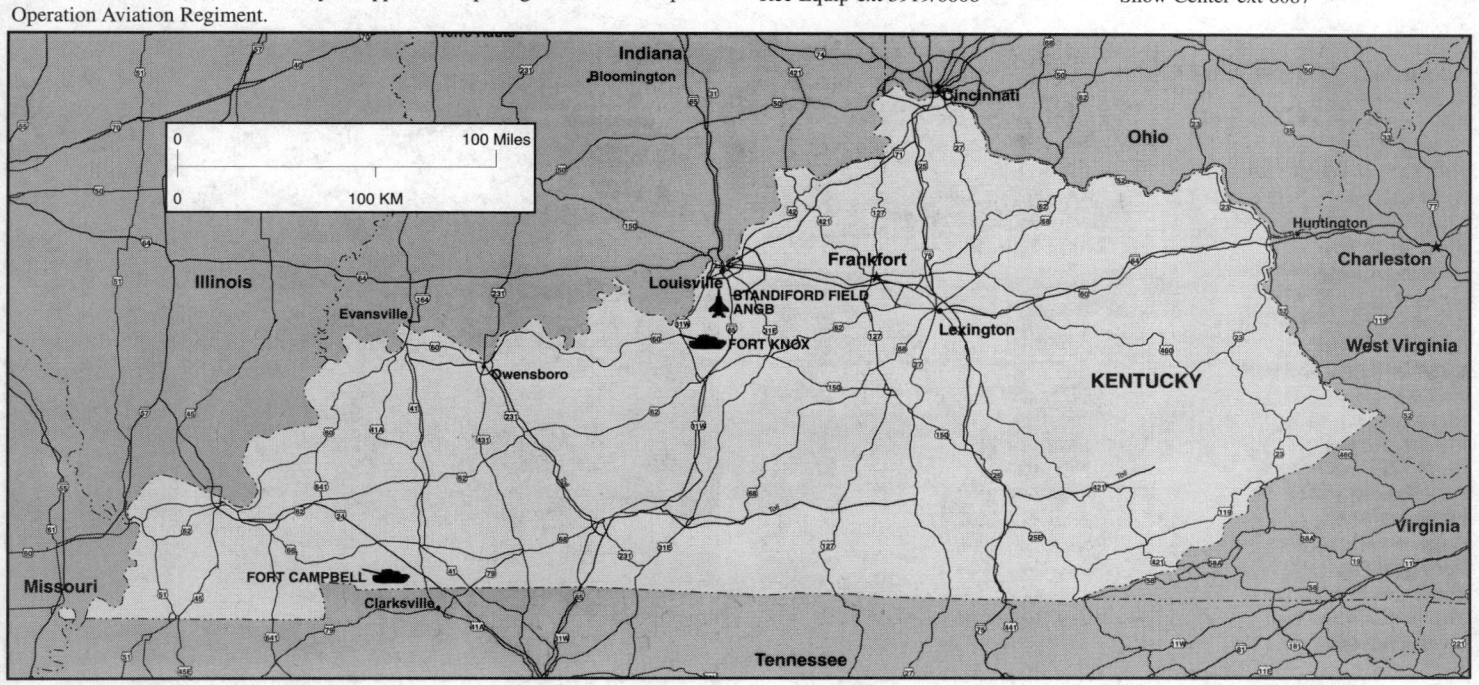

Stables-ext 2629/2487
Tennis-ext 6973/5225
Youth Center-798-6317

Swimming-ext 6290
Theater-798-3636
Woody Hobby Shop -798-6317

**ATTRACTIONS:** A growing recreational area in Nashville–"Home of the Grand Ole Opry," Land Between the Lakes (170,000-acre national recreational and environmental education area).

## FORT KNOX (KY01R2)

US Army Airmen Center & Fort Knox
ATTN: ATZK-GC
P.O. Box 995
Fort Knox, KY 40121-5000

**TELEPHONE NUMBER INFORMATION:** Main installation numbers: C-502-624-1000/1181, D-312-464-1000/1181.

**LOCATION:** From I-65 north or south, in Louisville, exit Gene Snyder Expressway west to US-31 west, go south to Fort Knox. From I-64, exit I-264 (Waterson Expressway west) to US-31 west, south to Fort Knox. Or from I-71, exit I-65 south to Gene Snyder Expressway to US-31 west then south to Fort Knox. USMRA: Page 40, 41 (H,I-3,4). NMC: Louisville, 25 miles north.

**GENERAL INFORMATION:** Army Armor Center, Training Brigades, HQ USAREC, and HQ, 2 ROTC Region.

**TEMPORARY MILITARY LODGING:** Lodging office, Building 4770 (Newgarden Tower), Dixie Highway 31 west, 24 hours daily, C-502-942-0490 or 502-943-1000, D-312-464-3491. All ranks. DV/VIP C-502-624-6951.

**RV, CAMPING/FAMCAMP:** Camp Carlson Army Travel Camp, on post, year round, C-502-624-4836, D-312-464-4836, seven camper spaces with W/E/S hookups, 18 camper spaces with W/E hookups, four family cabins, four youth cabins, 25 tent spaces.

**SPACE-A:** Godman Army Airfield, Pax Term, Building 5220, 24 hours daily, C-502-624-5545, D-312-464-5545, Fax: C-502-624-2421, D-312-464-2421 flights via executive aircraft to CONUS locations.

**LOGISTICAL SUPPORT:**

Cafeteria-942-0805/0230
Child Care-624-8320
Commissary-624-5355
Dining Facilities
  Burger King-942-4281
  Food Court-942-4269
Package Store-942-4208
Shoppette-942-4262

Carlson Wagonlit-942-3191
Child Development-624-6707
Credit Union-942-0254
Education Center-624-4114
Exchange-942-0067/4300
Gas Station-942-4256
SATO-942-2509

**ADMINISTRATIVE SUPPORT:**

Legal-624-2771
Police-624-2111/112

Locator-624-1141
SDO/NCO-624-4481/4421

**HEALTH & WELFARE:**

Army Community Service-624-6291
Chapel-624-4524
Medical
  Central Appts-624-9148
  Emergency-624-9000
  Hospital-624-9333/9759

CHAMPUS-624-9050
Family Services-624-6291
Retiree Services-624-4315

**REST & RECREATION:**

Arts & Crafts-624-4725/1552
Bowling-624-1651
Field House-624-2214
Golf Course-624-1548
Gym-624-3316/3641
ITT-624-5030/8254
Outdoor Rec-624-7754
Rec Equip-624-2314
Swimming-624-6217
Theater-624-4284/3048
Youth Center-624-6442

Auto Hobby Shop-624-5410/5338
Clubs
  EM-942-0305
  NCO-942-0409
  O-942-0959
Library-624-1232/4723
Rec Center-624-8254
Skeet-624-7754
Tennis-624-2214/4033
Wood Hobby Shop-624-3540

**ATTRACTIONS:** Mammoth Cave, Louisville, Hodgenville–"Birthplace of Abraham Lincoln," and Bardstown–site of "My Old Kentucky Home," all within 50 miles. Patton Museum at Chaffee Avenue entrance to Fort Knox opens at 0900 to 1630 Mon-Fri year round, with special hours: 1 May through 30 Sept 1000-1800, 1000-1430 on Sat, Sun and holidays.

## STANDIFORD FIELD/AIR NATIONAL GUARD BASE (KY05R2)

123 Airlift, 1019 Grade Lane
Louisville, KY 40213-2678

**TELEPHONE NUMBER INFORMATION:** Main installation numbers: C-502-364-9400, D-312-989-4400. WEB: www.kyang.win.net

**LOCATION:** I-65 north or south, south of Louiville, Grade Lane exit west, turn right. Main gate is on right. USMRA: Page 41 (I-3). NMC: Louisville, in city limits.

**GENERAL INFORMATION:** Home of the 123d Airlift Wing and 223d Communications Squadron.

**TEMPORARY MILITARY LODGING:** None. See Fort Knox listing.

**RV, CAMPING/FAMCAMP:** None. See Fort Knox listing.

**SPACE-A:** C-502-364-9459, D-312-989-4459.

**LOGISTICAL SUPPORT:** None. See Fort Knox listing.

**ADMINISTRATIVE SUPPORT:**    Locator-364-9400

**HEALTH & WELFARE:** None. See Fort Knox listing.

**REST & RECREATION:** None. See Fort Knox listing.

**ATTRACTIONS:** Louisville, Kentucky Derby.

# LOUISIANA

## BARKSDALE AIR FORCE BASE (LA01R2)

841 Fairchild Avenue, Suite 103
Barksdale Air Force Base, LA 71110-2270

**TELEPHONE NUMBER INFORMATION:** Main installation numbers: C-318-456-1110, D-312-781-1110.

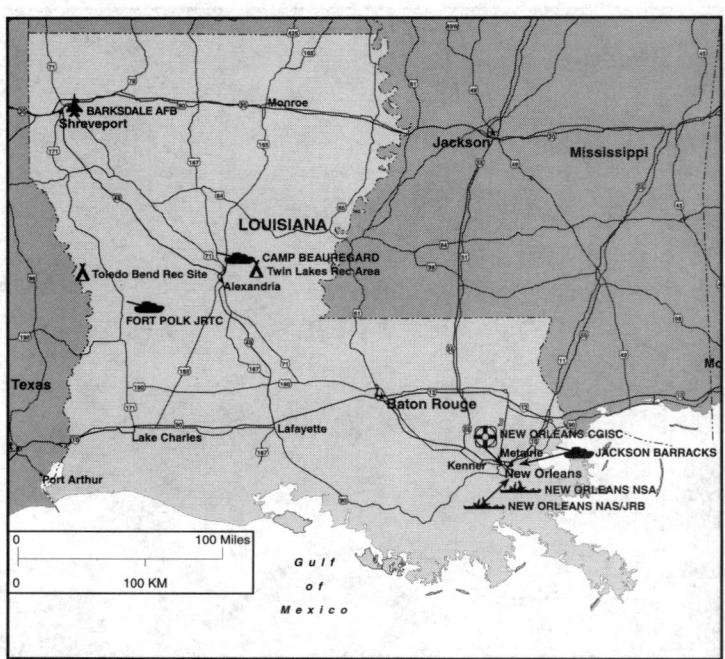

**LOCATION:** Exit I-20 east or west, at Airline Drive exit 22, go south to Old Minden Road (one quarter mile), left on Old Minden Road (one block), then right on North Gate Drive (one mile) to North Gate of AFB. USMRA: Page 79 (B-2). NMC: Shreveport, one mile west. Co-located with Bossier City and Shreveport.

**GENERAL INFORMATION:** Air Combat Command Base, Headquarters 8th Air Force, 2d Bomb Wing, B-52, 917th Wing AFRES units with B52 and A-10.

**TEMPORARY MILITARY LODGING:** Building 5155, Davis Avenue, 24 hours daily, C-318-747-4708, D-312-781-3091. All ranks. DV/VIP C-318-456-2151.

**RV, CAMPING/FAMCAMP:** FAMCAMP on base, year round, C-318-456-2679, D-312-781-2679, 18 camper spaces with W&E hookups, four without hookups.

**SPACE-A:** Building 6402, C-318-456-3226/5630, D-312-781-3226/5630, Fax: C-318-456-4989/3800, D-312-781-4989/3800.

**LOGISTICAL SUPPORT:**
| | |
|---|---|
| Bank-226-2722 | Barber Shop-741-3114 |
| Beauty Shop-746-5930 | Credit Union 456-4773 |
| Child Dev Center-456-4139 | Class Six-746-5662 |
| Commissary-456-8263 | Conv Store-746-5662 |
| Dining Facilities-456-8367 | Dry Cleaner-742-0133 |
| Exchange-746-2554 | Education Office-456-2615 |
| Gas Station-746-5662 | Postal Service-456-3950 |
| SATO-741-3095 | Snack Bar-741-3394 |
| Travel Office-456-4901 | Visitor Center-456-3587 |

**ADMINISTRATIVE SUPPORT:**
| | |
|---|---|
| Fire Dept-117 | Housing Office-456-4740 |
| Legal-456-2561 | Locator-456-3555 |
| Pass/ID Office-456-3561 | Police-456-2551 |
| Public Affairs-456-3065 | |

**HEALTH & WELFARE:**
| | |
|---|---|
| AF Aid-456-8400 | American Red Cross-456-8073 |
| CHAMPUS-456-6572 | Chapel-456-2111 |
| Dental-456-4017 | Family Services-456-8331 |
| Medical | Retiree Services-456-4480 |
| Central Appts-456-6555 | TRICARE-456-6572 |
| Clinic-456-6538 | Veterinary Services-456-4172 |
| Emergency-911 | |
| Health Benefits-456-6572 | |
| Information-456-6084 | |

**REST & RECREATION:**
| | |
|---|---|
| Arts & Crafts-456-3140 | Auto Hobby Shop-456-4695 |
| Bowling-456-4133 | Clubs |
| | EM-456-4467 |
| Fitness Center-456-4135 | O-456-4926 |
| Golf Course-456-2263 | Library-456-4101 |
| Outdoor Rec-456-2679 | Theater-456-3666 |
| Wood Hobby Shop-456-3409 | Youth Center-456-3448 |

**ATTRACTIONS:** Moderate climate. Great water sports. Horse racing (Louisiana Downs) April-November, NCAA sanctioned Independence Bowl late in December, Riverboard Casinos open 24 hours daily.

## CAMP BEAUREGARD (LA12R2)

Training Site, Detachment 1 HQ STARC
409 F Street
Pineville, LA 71360-3737

**TELEPHONE NUMBER INFORMATION:** Main installation numbers: C-318-640-2080, D-312-435-5600.

**LOCATION:** West off US-165, seven miles south of Pollock. USMRA: Page 79 (D-4). NMC: Alexandria, five miles southwest.

**GENERAL INFORMATION:** National Guard Training Site with Modified Record Fire Range, M203 Range, 9MM Range. HQ, 225th Engineer Group. NGB Region VI NCO Academy at Camp Ball, five miles north of Camp Beauregard on US-165.

**TEMPORARY MILITARY LODGING:** Building 1111, 0730-1600, C-318-641-8269, D-312-485-8222, Fax: C-318-641-3341. After hours C-318-640-2080.

**RV, CAMPING/FAMCAMP:** Twin Lakes Recreation Area off base. C-318-640-2080 ext 269, 4 camper spaces with W&E hookups, 10 primitive sites with W hookups, 3 mobile homes.

**SPACE-A:** None. See Fort Polk listing.

**LOGISTICAL SUPPORT:**
| | |
|---|---|
| Barber Shop-640-2938 | Credit Union-641-8308 |
| Exchange-641-9661 | Tailor-641-1362 |

**ADMINISTRATIVE SUPPORT:**
| | |
|---|---|
| Fire Dept-ext 2080 | Housing Office-641-8269 |
| Locator-640-2080 | Police-641-8266 |

**HEALTH & WELFARE:** None. See Fort Polk listing.

**REST & RECREATION:**
| | |
|---|---|
| Clubs | Gym/Pool-641-2080 |
| EM-640-8219 | |
| O-641-8277 | |

**OTHER FACILITIES AVAILABLE:** Shoppette.

**ATTRACTIONS:** Alexandria Zoo, Kent House Plantation, Historic Natchatiches 50 miles north, Baton Rouge, state capital, approximately 100 miles southeast. New Orleans, approximately 150 miles southeast. Hunting and fishing opportunities available.

## FORT POLK/JOINT READINESS TRAINING CENTER(LA07R2)

ATTN: AFZX-PO
7073 Radio Road, Building 411
Fort Polk, LA 71459-5342

**TELEPHONE NUMBER INFORMATION:** Main installation numbers: C-318-531-2911, D-312-863-2911. E-mail: afzxpo@polk-emh2.army.mil. WEB: www.jrtc-polk.army.mil

**LOCATION:** Off US-171 north or south, nine miles south of Leesville. East of US-171 south. USMRA: Page 79 (C-4). NMC: Alexandria, 60 miles southwest.

**GENERAL INFORMATION:** Headquarters Joint Readiness Training Center, 2d Armored Cavalry Regiment, Warrior Brigade and 519th Military Police Battalion.

**TEMPORARY MILITARY LODGING:** Lodging office, Magnolia House, Building 522, Utah Avenue, 24 hours daily, C-318-531-2941, D-312-863-2941, Fax: C-318-535-0968. All ranks.

**RV, CAMPING/FAMCAMP:** Toledo Bend Recreation Site off post, year round, C-318-565-4235, 15 camper spaces with W&E hookups, 12 mobile homes. South Fort RV Park on post, year round, C-318-531-2941/4822, 10 camper spaces with full hookups.

**SPACE-A:** Polk Army Airfield, Base Ops, 0700-2200 Mon-Fri, during JRTC rotations 24 hours a day. C-318-531-4831/7328, D-312-863-4831/7328.

**LOGISTICAL SUPPORT:**
| | |
|---|---|
| Bank-537-3421 | Barber Shop-537-7921 |
| Beauty Shop-537-3102 | Car Rental-537-8694 |
| Carlson Wagonlit Travel-537-0658 | Child Care-531-2149 |
| Child Dev Center-531-2149 | Class Six-531-0456 |
| Commissary-531-2088 | Credit Union-531-2991/2992 |
| Dry Cleaner-537-2233 | Education Office-531-5401 |
| Exchange-537-1001 | Gas Station-537-8269 |
| Postal Service-531-2795/8676 | Shoppette-537-1050 |
| Snack Bar-537-0251 | Travel-531-1905/1934 |
| Visitor Center-531-6812/6339 | |

**ADMINISTRATIVE SUPPORT:**

| | |
|---|---|
| Fire Dept-531-2026 | Housing Office-531-2762 |
| Legal-531-2580 | Locator-531-1272/1273 |
| Pass/ID Office-531-1839/1430 | Police-531-2677 |
| Public Affairs-531-2714 | SDO-531-1726 |

**HEALTH & WELFARE:**

| | |
|---|---|
| American Red Cross-531-1927/1929 | ACS-531-2840 |
| Army Emergency Relief-531-1957 | CHAMPUS-531-3176 |
| Chapel-531-4228/2332 | Dental-531-2603/2327 |
| Medical-531-3118 | Retiree Services-531-4515 |
| Central Appts-531-3000 | TRICARE-1-800-406-2833 |
| Emergency-531-3368/3361 | Veterinary Services-531-1322 |

**REST & RECREATION:**

| | |
|---|---|
| Arts & Crafts-531-1980 | Auto Hobby Shop-531-6169 |
| Bowling-531-6273 | Fitness Center-531-6795 |
| Golf Course-531-4661 | ITR-531-1794 |
| Library-531-1986/1987 | O Club-531-4440/6695 |
| Outdoor Rec-531-5332 | Youth Services-531-6907/6917 |

**ATTRACTIONS:** Fort Polk Military Museum, 5th Infantry Division Memorial Park at Fort Polk; Baton Rouge, state capital, 155 miles southeast. New Orleans, 232 miles southeast.

## JACKSON BARRACKS (LA13R2)
Louisiana National Guard Base
Jackson Barracks,
Bldg. 35, Room 213
New Orleans, LA 70146-0330

**TELEPHONE NUMBER INFORMATION:** Main installation numbers: C-504-271-6262, D-312-485-8460.

**LOCATION:** From Baton Rouge, take I-10 east to I-10/I-610 east to exit 2. Go straight over an overpass, then cross a drawbridge. Entrance to Jackson Barracks is about two miles past drawbridge. Claiborne Avenue will go through Jackson Barracks. USMRA: Page 90 (F-3,4). NMC: New Orleans, in city limits.

**TEMPORARY MILITARY LODGING:** Building 57, Area A, 0730-1600. C-504-278-8364, D-312-485-6207.

**RV, CAMPING/FAMCAMP:** None. See New Orleans NSA listing, Magnolia Shade RV Park.

**SPACE-A:** None. See New Orleans NAS listing.

**LOGISTICAL SUPPORT:**

| | |
|---|---|
| Carlson Wagonlit Travel-278-8409 | Credit Union-277-0288 |
| Exchange-278-8245 | |

**ADMINISTRATIVE SUPPORT:**

| | |
|---|---|
| Police-278-8460 | Public Affairs-278-8281 |
| SDO-278-8460 | |

**HEALTH & WELFARE:** None. See New Orleans NSA listing.

**REST & RECREATION:**
Clubs
  EM-278-8490
  NCO-278-8490 *(Only open drill weekends)*

**OTHER FACILITIES AVAILABLE:** Fitness center, gym, basketball court, jogging track, picnic area, softball field, tennis court, volleyball court, weight rooms, military library and military museum.

**ATTRACTIONS:** Officer quarters comprise largest collection of antebellum homes in the deep south. Nearby attractions include city of New Orleans, Superdome, New Orleans French Quarter, Riverwalk, IMAX Theatre, National Cemetery, historic battlefield, zoo, aquarium, Audubon Park, streetcars.

## NEW ORLEANS COAST GUARD INTEGRATED SUPPORT COMMAND (LA10R2)
4640 Urquhart Street
New Orleans, LA 70117-4698

**TELEPHONE NUMBER INFORMATION:** Main installation number: C-504-942-3020.

**LOCATION:** From I-10 go south on Elysian Fields Avenue, left on Claiborne Avenue, right on Poland Street, left on Urquhart Street to main gate. USMRA: Page 79 (H-6,7), page 90 (E-3). NMC: New Orleans, in city limits.

**GENERAL INFORMATION:** Provides industrial and repair support to primarily the Eighth CG District. Host Command to many tenants, including CG Group New Orleans, CG Station and CG Aids to Navigation Team NOLA, and others.

**TEMPORARY MILITARY LODGING:** None. See Jackson Barracks listing.

**RV, CAMPING/FAMCAMP:** None. See New Orleans NSA listing, Magnolia Shade RV Park.

**SPACE-A:** None. See New Orleans NAS listing.

**LOGISTICAL SUPPORT:**  Exchange-942-4537

**ADMINISTRATIVE SUPPORT:**  CDO/OOD-942-3020

**HEALTH & WELFARE:**  Medical
  Emergency-911
  Information-942-3021

**REST & RECREATION:** None. See Jackson Barracks/Louisiana National Guard Base listing.

**ATTRACTIONS:** City of New Orleans, Superdome, Jefferson Downs Racetrack, Audubon Park, New Orleans Zoo, Bayou Segnette State Park.

## NEW ORLEANS NAVAL AIR STATION/ JOINT RESERVE BASE (LA11R2)
400 Russell Avenue
New Orleans, LA 70143-5012

**TELEPHONE NUMBER INFORMATION:** Main installation numbers: C-504-678-3253, D-312-678-3253.

**LOCATION:** Take I-10 to US-90 Business West, cross the Crescent City Connection Bridge to the Westbank Expressway. Exit at Lafayette Street. Make a left turn at the traffic light. Keep straight on Belle Chasse Hwy LA-23. Go through a tunnel. At the traffic light after the tunnel, make a left turn to go in the back gate or stay on Hwy 23 (Belle Chasse Hwy) about 7-9 miles to go in the main gate. Clearly marked. USMRA: Page 79 (H-7), page 90 (F-6). NMC: New Orleans, 10 miles north.

**GENERAL INFORMATION:** Navy Fighter, Logistics, and Patrol Aircraft Squadrons, Coast Guard Air Station, Air Force Reserve and ANG units, U.S. Customs Service and Marine Air Group Det 42.

**TEMPORARY MILITARY LODGING:** Lodging office, Building 21 (Olson Avenue) and Building 40 (Rinard Avenue), 24 hours daily, C-504-678-3841, D-312-678-3841. Fax: C-504-678-9745. All ranks. DV/VIP C-504-678-3260, 06+, Navy Lodge: C-800-NAVY INN.

**RV, CAMPING/FAMCAMP:** Campground on base, year round, C-504-678-3448, 17 camper spaces with full hookups, two camping trailers, one mobile home, 10 tent spaces.

**SPACE-A:** Pax Term/Lounge, Building 1, 0700-2300 hours daily, C-504-678-3213, D-312-678-3213, Fax: C-504-678-3156, D-312-678-3156, Rec: C-504-678-3103, D-312-678-3103, flights to CONUS, OCONUS and overseas.

**LOGISTICAL SUPPORT:**

| | |
|---|---|
| Bank-678-3527 | Barber Shop-678-3510 |
| Beauty Shop-678-3511 | Child Care-678-3654 |
| Conv Store-678-3506 | Dry Cleaner-678-3510 |
| Exchange-678-3510 | Gas Station-678-3506 |
| Package Store-678-3510 | Postal Service-678-3204 |
| SATO-678-3625 | Snack Bar-678-3514 |

**ADMINISTRATIVE SUPPORT:**

| | |
|---|---|
| CDO/OOD-678-3253 | Fire Dept-678-3105 |
| Legal-678-3266 | Locator-678-3253 |
| Police-678-3827 | Public Affairs-678-3260 |

**HEALTH & WELFARE:**

| | |
|---|---|
| Chapel-678-3525 | Medical-678-3660/1 |
| Retiree Services-678-2134 | TRICARE-678-2676 |

**REST & RECREATION:**

| | |
|---|---|
| Auto Hobby Shop-678-3448 | Bowling-678-3514 |
| Clubs | Gym-678-3230 |
|   Com-678-3509 | Golf Course-678-3453 |
|   EM-678-3509 | ITT-678-3695 |
|   NCO-678-3509 | MWR-678-3231 |
|   O-678-3844 | Outdoor Rec-678-3230 |

**ATTRACTIONS:** New Orleans French Quarter, Mississippi River, New Orleans Zoo, Aquarium, Swamp Tours, River Boat Casinos.

# NEW ORLEANS NAVAL SUPPORT ACTIVITY (LA06R2)

2300 General Meyer Avenue
New Orleans, LA 70142-5007

**TELEPHONE NUMBER INFORMATION:** Main installation numbers: C-504-678-5011, D-312-678-5011.

**LOCATION:** On the west bank of the Mississippi River. From I-10 east, take Mississippi River Bridge to the west bank. Take Gen. DeGaulle east exit after passing over bridge and turn left at Shirley Drive, which leads to NSA. USMRA: Page 90 (E,F-3,4). NMC: New Orleans, in city.

**GENERAL INFORMATION:** Headquarters for both the Naval and Marine Corps Reserve.

**TEMPORARY MILITARY LODGING:** Navy Lodge, Building 702, 0700-2000 daily, C-504-366-3266; Fax: C-504-362-3752. Consolidated Billeting C-504-678-2220, D-312-678-2220, Fax: C-504-678-2781. All ranks.

**RV, CAMPING/FAMCAMP:** Magnolia Shade RV Park on base, year round, C-504-678-2527/2285, D-312-678-2527/2285, 16 camper spaces with W&E hookups.

**SPACE-A:** None. See New Orleans NAS listing.

**LOGISTICAL SUPPORT:**

| | |
|---|---|
| Child Care-678-2450 | Commissary-678-2182 |
| Exchange-678-2702 | Gas Station-678-2747 |
| Package Store-678-2749 | SATO-678-2330 |

**ADMINISTRATIVE SUPPORT:**

| | |
|---|---|
| CDO/OOD-678-2655 | Locator-678-5011 |
| Legal-678-2520 | Police-678-2570 |
| Public Affairs-678-2540 | |

**HEALTH & WELFARE:**

| | |
|---|---|
| CHAMPUS-678-2675 | Chapel-678-2244 |
| Family Services-678-2647 | Medical |
| Retiree Services-678-2134 |   Central Appts-1-800-700-8603 |
| |   Clinic-678-2480 |
| |   Emergency-911 |

**REST & RECREATION:**

| | |
|---|---|
| Bowling-ext 2204 | Cnsolidated Club 678-2218 |
| Courts-ext 2527 | Hobby Shops-ext 2207 |
| ITT-678-2208 | MWR-678-2269 |
| Rec Equipment-ext 2527 | Swimming-ext 2654 |

**ATTRACTIONS:** New Orleans French Quarter, Bourbon Street, sports, New Orleans Zoo, River Boat Cruises, Aquarium, Superdome.

# TOLEDO BEND RECREATION SITE (LA04R2)

1310 Army Recreation Road
Florien, LA 71429-5000

**TELEPHONE NUMBER INFORMATION:** Main installation numbers: C-18-565-4235, C-1-888-718-9088. Police for recreation site, C-318-531-6825.

**LOCATION:** Off post. Take US-171 north from Leesville, west on LA-111 at Anacoco, bear right onto LA-392. North on LA-191, left at Army Travel Camp sign. USMRA: Page 79 (B-4). NMI: Fort Polk, 45 miles southeast. NMC: Alexandria, 60 miles northeast.

**GENERAL INFORMATION:** Operated by Fort Polk, off base, year round. Military personnel active, reservists, retired, DoD and NAF civilians. Reservations: Toledo Bend Recreation Site, 1310 Army Recreation Road, Florien, LA 71429-5000. C-1-888-718-9088. For information only, C-318-565-4235. Fort Polk also operates Alligator Lake Recreation Site on LA-469 just north of North Fort. It covers approximately 20 acres along a man-made lake. Ample space for picnicking and all sorts of sports. Lake itself offers paddle boating and some good fishing. C-318-531-5332.

**RV, CAMPING/FAMCAMP:**

| | |
|---|---|
| Mobile Homes-12 | Camper Spaces-15 |
| Tent Spaces-unlimited | |

**ATTRACTIONS:** Toledo Bend is the largest man-made lake in the South and fifth largest in the country. Excellent fishing and swimming area. Hodges Gardens and Fort Jesup offer sightseeing opportunities.

*For detailed information about this off-base recreation facility, as well as on-base recreation facilities, golf courses and marinas, consult Military Living's Military RV, Camping and Outdoor Recreation Around the World.*

# TWIN LAKES RECREATION AREA (LA12R2)

Camp Beauregard
Pineville, LA 71360-3737

**TELEPHONE NUMBER INFORMATION:** Main installation numbers: C-318-640-2080, D-312-435-5600.

**LOCATION:** Seven miles from Camp Beauregard. Off US-165, east to LA-116, four miles. NMC: Alexandria, six miles south.

**GENERAL INFORMATION:** Operated by Camp Beauregard, off base, year round. Military personnel active, reservists, retired. Reservations: 1111 F Street, Camp Beauregard, LA 71360-3737. C-318-641-8302/8269. For information on recreation area, C-318-641-3355/65, C-318-640-2080, ext 269.

**RV, CAMPING/FAMCAMP:**

| | |
|---|---|
| Mobile Homes-3 | Camper Spaces-4 |
| Tent Spaces-10 | |

**ATTRACTIONS:** Lakes for fishing, boating.

*For detailed information about this off-base recreation facility, as well as on-base recreation facilities, golf courses and marinas, consult Military Living's Military RV, Camping and Outdoor Recreation Around the World.*

# MAINE

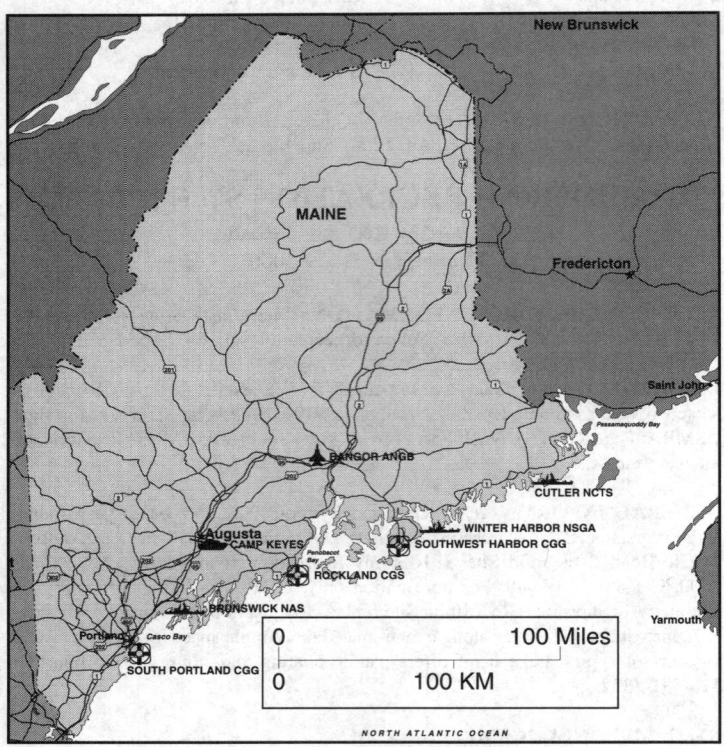

## BANGOR AIR NATIONAL GUARD BASE (ME10R1)

103 Maineiac Avenue, Suite 505
Bangor, ME 04401-3099

**TELEPHONE NUMBER INFORMATION:** Main installation numbers: C-207-990-7700 (ask for extensions), D-312-698-7700.

**LOCATION:** Located in Bangor city limits. Northbound from I-95 take exit 47, Ohio Street, drive west two blocks and turn left, one block to right turn on Union Street (ME-222), past Bangor IAP, turn left on Griffin Road; entrance is 300 yards on right. USMRA: Page 18 (E-6,7). NMC: Bangor, in city limits.

**GENERAL INFORMATION:** Air National Guard Air Refueling Wing with KC-135E aircraft, Over-the-Horizon Backscatter Radar Operations Center.

**TEMPORARY MILITARY LODGING:** The Army National Guard operates the Pine Tree Inn, 24 hours daily, C-207-942-2081, D-312-698-7700. Located at 22 Cleveland Avenue on Bangor IAP adjacent to Bangor ANG Base. All ranks.

**RV, CAMPING/FAMCAMP:** None. See Winter Harbor NSGA listing.

**SPACE-A:** Pax Term, Building 491, 0730-1600 Mon-Fri, C-207-990-7212, D-312-698-7212. Sign up for Space-A done only in person. Flights to CONUS and overseas.

**LOGISTICAL SUPPORT:**

| | |
|---|---|
| Child Care-941-0466 | Commissary-990-7751 |
| Exchange-990-7233 | SATO-ext 355 |

**ADMINISTRATIVE SUPPORT:** Public Affairs-990-7228

**HEALTH & WELFARE:**

| | |
|---|---|
| CHAMPUS-ext 458 | Retiree Services-ext 458 |

**REST & RECREATION:** None. See Winter Harbor NSGA listing.

**ATTRACTIONS:** Lobster and other seafood, Penobscot Marine Museum in Searsport, Acadia National Park, Bar Harbor, Mt Desert Island, beaches, and boating.

## BRUNSWICK NAVAL AIR STATION (ME07R1)

551 Fitch Avenue
Box 32
Brunswick Naval Air Station, ME 04011-5000

**TELEPHONE NUMBER INFORMATION:** Main installation numbers: C-207-921-1110, D-312-476-1110.

**LOCATION:** From I-95 north, exit Coastal Route 1 north. Take Route 1 four miles to Cooks Corner. Turn right to main gate of Brunswick NAS. USMRA: Page 18 (C-9). NMC: Portland, 30 miles southwest.

**GENERAL INFORMATION:** Home to over 5,000 military personnel and six maritime patrol squadrons flying P-3 aircraft. The last active duty military airfield in the northeast.

**TEMPORARY MILITARY LODGING:** Lodging office, Building 512, Sewall Road, 24 hours daily, C-207-921-2245, D-312-476-2245, Fax: C-207-921-2472. Navy Lodge, Topsham Annex, 0730-2200 daily, C-207-921-2206. Note: located seven miles from base. Call for directions. All ranks. DV/VIP C-207-921-2206/1-800-NAVY-INN.

**RV, CAMPING/FAMCAMP:** None. See Winter Harbor NSGA listing.

**SPACE-A:** Pax Term/Lounge, Building 200, 24 hours daily, C-207-921-2682/2692, D-312-476-2682. Fax: C-207-921-2152, D-312-476-2152, limited flights to CONUS and overseas.

**LOGISTICAL SUPPORT:**

| | |
|---|---|
| Barber Shop-921-2346 | Cafeteria-921-2455 |
| Child Care-921-2610 | Commissary-921-2971* |
| Conv Store-921-2182 | Credit Union-729-1831 |
| Dry Cleaner-729-9253 | Fast Food-921-2121 |
| Exchange-921-2387 | Postal Service-921-2518 |
| | *Located at Topsham Annex. |

**ADMINISTRATIVE SUPPORT:**

| | |
|---|---|
| CDO/NCO-921-2214 | Legal-921-2331 |
| Locator-921-1110 | Police-921-2585 |

**HEALTH & WELFARE:**

| | |
|---|---|
| CHAMPUS-921-2901 | Chapel-921-2231/2223 |
| Family Services-921-2273 | Medical |
| Retiree Services-921-2609 | Central Appts-921-2243 |
| | Emergency-921-2610 |

**REST & RECREATION:**

| | |
|---|---|
| Arts & Crafts-ext 2168 | Auto Hobby Shop-ext 2488 |
| Bowling-ext 2145 | EM Club-921-2121 |
| Golf Course-ext 2155 | Rec Equip-ext 2738 |
| Ski Shop-ext 2488 | |

**ATTRACTIONS:** The last active-duty DoD airfield in the northeast is located on the coast of Maine, with skiing two hours north. Lobsters and other seafood. Maine Maritime Museum in Bath, Summer Music Theater in Brunswick. L.L. Bean eight minutes south.

## CAMP KEYES (ME12R1)

HQ MAINE NG, Building 7
Augusta, ME 04333-0033

**TELEPHONE NUMBER INFORMATION:** Main installation numbers: C-207-626-4390, D-312-476-4390. E-mail: youngstr@me-arng.ngb.army.mil WEB: www.ngb.dtic.mil

**LOCATION:** From I-95 north or south, take the Western Avenue Exit 30. Follow signs east to Augusta Airport, continue past airport, veer right onto Winthrop Street. Camp Keyes entrance is on right. USMRA: Page 18 (C-8). NMC: Bath.

**GENERAL INFORMATION:** State of Maine DoD, Veterans and Emergency Management; Maine Army National Guard, Regional Training Institute; Maine Military Museum.

**TEMPORARY MILITARY LODGING:** BOQ-207-626-4218

**RV, CAMPING/FAMCAMP:** None. See Winter Harbor NSGA listing.

**SPACE-A:** None. See Brunswick NAS listing.

**LOGISTICAL SUPPORT:**                   Exchange-626-4213

**ADMINISTRATIVE SUPPORT:**
Legal-626-4328                            Police (Security)-626-4214

**HEALTH & WELFARE:** None. See Brunswick NAS listing.

**OTHER FACILITIES AVAILABLE:** Carlson Wagonlit Travel, combined club, snack bar.

**ATTRACTIONS:** Maine Military Museum.

## CUTLER NAVAL COMPUTER & TELECOMMUNICATIONS STATION (ME08R1)
HC 69, Box 1198
Cutler, ME 04626-9603

**TELEPHONE NUMBER INFORMATION:** Main installation numbers: C-207-259-8203, D-312-476-7203. E-mail: erobinson@nctscut.navy.com

**LOCATION:** From I-95 take Alt US-1 to Ellsworth, ME, US-1 east to East Machias, right (east) on ME-191 to base at Cutler. USMRA: Page 18 (G,H-7). NMC: Bangor, 100 miles west.

**GENERAL INFORMATION:** The world's most powerful VLF transmitter. Provides fleet communications.

**TEMPORARY MILITARY LODGING:** BEQ: C-207-259-8202.

**RV, CAMPING/FAMCAMP:** Sprague's Neck on base, year round, C-207-259-8285, D-312-476-8285, one log cabin (running water and indoor sanitary facilities, 15 May-15 September), 10 camper spaces without hookups.

**SPACE-A:** None. See Bangor ANGB listing.

**LOGISTICAL SUPPORT:**
Cafeteria-259-8277                        Commissary-259-8270/8389
Exchange-259-8244                         Snack Bar-259-8277

**ADMINISTRATIVE SUPPORT:**
CDO/OOD-259-8226                          Fire Dept-259-8260
Locator-259-8203                          Police-259-8267

**HEALTH & WELFARE:**
CHAMPUS-259-8219/09                       Chapel-259-8388
Medical
   Central Appts-259-8209/219
   Emergency, after hours-ext 226

**REST & RECREATION:**
Bowling-ext 275                           Consol-259-8277
Hobby Shop-ext 285                        ITT-259-8201
MWR 259-8284                              Rec Services-259-8284

**ATTRACTIONS:** Skiing, hiking.

## ROCKLAND COAST GUARD STATION (ME14R1)
54 Tillson Avenue
Rockland, ME 04841-3498

**TELEPHONE NUMBER INFORMATION:** Main installation numbers: C-207-596-6667.

**LOCATION:** Route 1 north into Rockland, go past Trade Winds Hotel, take a right at next stop sign onto Tillson Avenue. Follow road to Coast Guard Station. USMRA: Page 18 (D-8). NMC: Rockland, in city limits.

**GENERAL INFORMATION:** Part of the First District, U.S. Coast Guard.

**LOGISTICAL SUPPORT:**                   Exchange-594-7731

**ATTRACTIONS:** Maine Lobster Festival, whale watching.

## SOUTH PORTLAND COAST GUARD GROUP (ME11R1)
41 Mussey Street
South Portland, ME 04106-0007

**TELEPHONE NUMBER INFORMATION:** Main installation number: C-207-767-0320.

**LOCATION:** Exit I-95 east to I-295 north, exit I-295 #1 south to Broadway, east to South Portland. Watch for signs to the base. USMRA: Page 18 (B,C-9). NMC: South Portland, in city limits.

**GENERAL INFORMATION:** Industrial Base/SAR Station.

**TEMPORARY MILITARY LODGING:** None. See Brunswick NAS listing.

**RV, CAMPING/FAMCAMP:** None. See Winter Harbor NSGA listing.

**SPACE-A:** None. See Brunswick NAS listing.

**LOGISTICAL SUPPORT:**
Exchange-842-9197                         Package Store-842-9197
Dining-767-0374

**ADMINISTRATIVE SUPPORT:**
CDO-767-0303                              Housing Office-767-0390
Locator-767-0320                          Public Affairs-767-0310

**HEALTH & WELFARE:**                     Medical-767-0339

**REST & RECREATION:**
Consol Club-767-0374                      MWR-767-0311

**ATTRACTIONS:** City of Portland.

## SOUTHWEST HARBOR COAST GUARD GROUP (ME15R1)
Clark Point Road, P.O. Box 5000
Southwest Harbor, ME 04679-5000

**TELEPHONE NUMBER INFORMATION:** Main installation numbers: C-207-244-4213.

**GENERAL INFORMATION:** Part of First District, U.S. Coast Guard.

**LOCATION:** Take Route 1-A south to Ellsworth, Route 3 south to Mount Desert Island, Route 102 to downtown Southwest Harbor, second left onto Clark Point Road to end. USMRA: Page 18 (E,F-8).

**LOGISTICAL SUPPORT:**                   Shoppette 244-5670

**HEALTH & WELFARE:**                     Medical (Corpsman)-244-4267

**ATTRACTIONS:** Historic seafaring town, scenic harbor.

## WINTER HARBOR NAVAL SECURITY GROUP ACTIVITY (ME09R1)

10 Fabbri Green, Suite 10
Winter Harbor, ME 04693-7001

**TELEPHONE NUMBER INFORMATION:** Main installation numbers: C-207-963-5534/5535, (ask for extensions) D-312-476-9287.

**LOCATION:** From Ellsworth, take US-1 north to ME-186 east to Acadia National Park. Naval Security Station on Schoodic Point in the park. USMRA: Page 18 (F-8). NMC: Bangor, 45 miles northwest.

**GENERAL INFORMATION:** Provides communications security and performs other communications activities for Navy units.

**TEMPORARY MILITARY LODGING:** Lodging office, Building 84, 0730-2230 daily, C-207-963-5534 ext-223, D-312-476-9223. All ranks.

**RV, CAMPING/FAMCAMP:** Winter Harbor Recreation Area on base, 15 April-15 October, C-207-963-5537, D-312-476-9287/9288; 14 camp sites. Besides these, 6 duplex cabins, 5 full-size mobile homes for rent year-round.

**SPACE-A:** None. See Bangor ANG Base listing.

**LOGISTICAL SUPPORT:**

| | |
|---|---|
| Child Care-ext 265 | Commissary-ext 259 |
| Conv Store-ext 254 | Exchange-ext 254 |
| Gas Station-963-7391 | |

**ADMINISTRATIVE SUPPORT:**

| | |
|---|---|
| CDO/OOD-963-5535 | Fire Dept-ext 229 |
| Legal-ext 210 | Locator-963-5534 |
| Police-ext 225 | Public Affairs-ext 224 |
| Quarter Deck-963-5535 | |

**HEALTH & WELFARE:**

| | |
|---|---|
| CHAMPUS-ext 297 | Chapel-ext 279 |
| Medical-963-7206 or 963-5534 ext 297 | |

**REST & RECREATION:**

| | |
|---|---|
| Auto Hobby Shop-963-5537 ext 234 | Bowling-963-5537 ext 225 |
| Club (all ranks)-ext 283/4 | Fitness Center-963-5537 |
| MWR-963-5537/5534 | Rec Equipment-963-5537 |
| Recreation-ext 287 | |

**ATTRACTIONS:** Boating and fishing, hiking, swimming, golfing, fall foliage, downhill and cross-country skiing, fresh seafood, August blueberry harvest.

# MARYLAND

*Note: As of 1 May 1997, Maryland's telephone system went to a 10-digit dialing system. Regardless of the originating location, all phone calls must include the area code.*

## ABERDEEN PROVING GROUND (MD11R1)

US Army Test & Evaluation Command
ATTN: STEAP-CO
Aberdeen Proving Ground, MD 21005-5001

**TELEPHONE NUMBER INFORMATION:** Main installation numbers: C-410-278-1110/5201, D-312-298-1110/5201. E-mail: amstepa@apg-9.apg. army.mil. WEB: www.apg.army.mil

**LOCATION:** Aberdeen Area: From I-95, take exit 85 to MD-22 east for two miles to main gate. Edgewood Area: From I-95 take exit 77 to MD-24 east for two miles to main gate. Also from US-40 right (if coming from Baltimore) on MD-755 (Edgewood Road), then right on US-24 to main gate. USMRA: Page 42 (G-2,3). NMC: Baltimore, 23 miles southwest.

**GENERAL INFORMATION:** U.S. Army Test & Evaluation Command, Army Research Laboratory, U.S. Army Ordnance Center & School, School of Military Packaging Technology, Army Environmental Center, 203rd Military Intelligence Battalion, U.S. Army Center for Health Promotion and Preventive Medicine, Army Materiel Systems Analysis Activity, Chemical and Biological Defense Command, 389th Army Band, Aberdeen Test Center, Northeast Regional Civilian Personnel Operations Center.

**TEMPORARY MILITARY LODGING:** Aberdeen or Edgewood Area: Lodging office, Building 2207, Bel Air Street, 24 hours daily, C-410-278-5148/9, D-312-298-5148/9. All ranks.

**RV, CAMPING/FAMCAMP:** Skipper's Point Recreational Area on post, year round, C-410-278-5201, D-312-298-5201, six camper spaces without hookups, 15 tent spaces.

**SPACE-A:** None. See Andrews AFB listing.

**LOGISTICAL SUPPORT:**

| | |
|---|---|
| Bank-272-6907 | Barber Shop-272-7886 |
| Beauty Shop-272-6396 | Carlson Wagonlit Travel-273-1184 or |
| Child Care-278-9832 |  1-800-296-3074 |
| Child Dev Center-278-5748 | Class Six-272-1681 |
| Commissary-278-3926 | Credit Union-272-4000 |
| Dining Facilities-278-2164/2059 | Dry Cleaner-272-5215 |
| Education Office-278-3385 | Exchange-272-6828 |
| Postal Service-272-5462 | Shoppette-272-1681 |

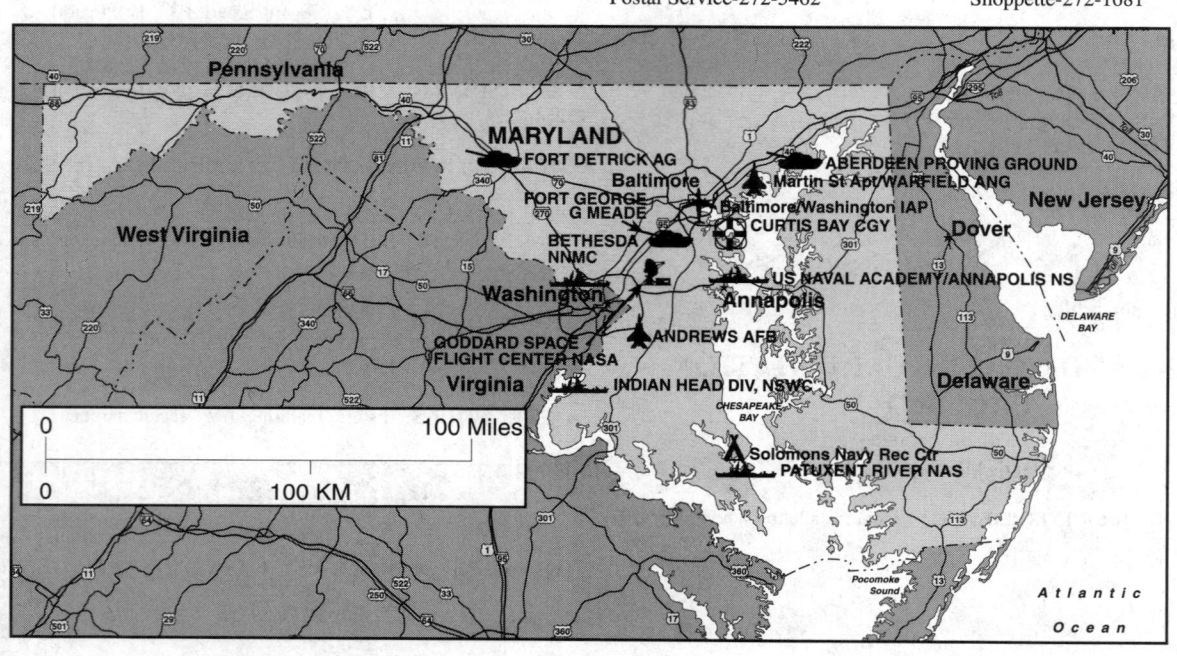

**ADMINISTRATIVE SUPPORT:**

Fire Dept-278-3601
Legal-278-4200
Pass/ID Office-278-4299
Public Affairs-278-1142

Housing Office-278-2814
Locator-306-1403
Police-306-0550
SDO-278-4500

**HEALTH & WELFARE:**

American Red Cross-278-2087
Army Emergency Relief-278-2508
Chapel-278-4333
Family Services-278-3137
Retiree Services-278-4331/2649
TRICARE-278-1719
Veterinary Services-278-4604/4575

ACS-278-7478
CHAMPUS-278-1719
Dental-278-1796
Medical
  Central Appts-278-1720
  Clinic-278-1752
  Emergency-911

**REST & RECREATION:**

Arts & Crafts-278-2759
Bowling-278-4794
Golf Course-278-4794/9994
Gym-278-5616
ITR-278-4011
MWR-278-7134
Theater-278-3351

Auto Hobby Shop-278-2884
Consolidated Club-278-3062
Fitness Center-278-9725
Indoor Rec-278-2621
Library-278-3417
Outdoor Rec-278-4124
Youth Services-278-4995

## EDGEWOOD AREA

U.S. Army Soldier and Biological Chemical Compound
Bldg E5101, Room 219
5183 Blackhawk Road
Aberdeen PG, MD 21010-5424

**TELEPHONE NUMBER INFORMATION:** Main numbers: C-410-278-5201, D-312-298-1110. WEB: www.apg.army.mil

**LOCATION:** From I-95, take exit 77 to MD-24 east for two miles to main gate. Also, from US-40 right (if coming from Baltimore) on MD 755 (Edgewood Road) then right on US-24 to main gate. USMRA: Page 42 (G-2,3). NMC: Baltimore, 23 miles southwest.

**LOGISTICAL SUPPORT:**

Barber Shop-676-8160
Credit Union-676-5700
Postal Service-676-1243

Child Dev Center-436-2692
Education Office-436-2166

**ADMINISTRATIVE SUPPORT:**     Pass/ID Office-278-3360

**HEALTH & WELFARE:**

Army Community Service-436-3362
Dental-436-3481

Chapel-436-4109
Medical-436-3001

**REST & RECREATION:**

Arts & Crafts-436-2153
Fitness Center-436-7135
Gym-436-3375
Library-436-3589
Youth Services-436-2862

Consolidated Club-436-5400
Golf Course-436-2213
Indoor Rec-436-2713
MWR-436-2713

**OTHER FACILITIES AVAILABLE:** Hunting and fishing programs, boat docks, Spesutie Island and Gunpowder Neck boating activities, swimming pools, parks and picnic areas, RV storage lots, instructional classes, flying activity and saddle activity.

**ATTRACTIONS:** Ordnance Museum. Baltimore a short drive away, one of the world's largest ports. Fort McHenry, where Francis Scott Key composed the "Star Spangled Banner."

# ANDREWS AIR FORCE BASE (MD02R1)

1535 Command Drive
Andrews Air Force Base, MD 20762-5000

**TELEPHONE NUMBER INFORMATION:** Main installation numbers: C-301-981-1110, D-312-858-1110. WEB: www.andrews.af.mil

**LOCATION:** From I-95 north (east portion of Capital Beltway, I-495) take exit 9; first traffic light after leaving exit ramp turn left. At next traffic light turn right into main gate of AFB. Also, from I-395 north, exit South Capitol Street, cross Anacostia River bear left to Suitland Pkwy east, exit at Morningside on Suitland Road east to main gate of AFB. From I-495 south, take exit 9; turn right at stop sign, turn right at next light onto Allentown Road; turn left into main gate on Suitland Road. USMRA: Page 42 (E-5), Page 55 (I,J-6,7). NMC: Washington, D.C., 10 miles northwest.

**GENERAL INFORMATION:** Air Mobility Command Base. 89th Airlift Wing and support units, 459th Airlift Wing (AFRES), D.C. Air National Guard, Air National Guard Readiness Center, Naval Air Facility (USN), and Marine Aircraft Group-49 Detachment A.

**TEMPORARY MILITARY LODGING:** Lodging, The Gateway Inn, Building 1375, Arkansas Road, 24 hours daily, C-301-981-4614, D-312-858-4614, Fax: C-301-981-7997. All ranks. DV/VIP: C-301-981-4525, D-312-858-4525, 06+.

**RV, CAMPING/FAMCAMP:** FAMCAMP on base, year round, C-301-981-4109/5663, DSN-858-4109/5663; 29 camper spaces with full hookups.

**SPACE-A:** Pax Term/Lounge, Building 1245, 0600-2200 hours daily, C-301-981-1854/3526, D-312-858-1854/3526, Fax: C-301-981-4241, D-312-858-4241. Flights to CONUS locations.

**LOGISTICAL SUPPORT:**

Bank-735-8100
Beauty Shop-735-1988
Car Rental-568-7900
Child Dev Center-981-3035
Credit Union-702-5500
Dry Cleaner-568-7492
Exchange-568-1500
Laundry-568-2546
SATO-
  Personal-817-2911
  Official-981-5362

Barber Shop-420-9383
Cafeteria-568-2381
Child Care-981-6927
Commissary-981-7105
Dining Facilities-981-6661/6548
Education Office-981-6377
Gas Station-735-0868
Postal Service-981-3539
Shoppette-568-2364
Snack Bar-568-2357
Visitor Center-981-0689

**ADMINISTRATIVE SUPPORT:**

Fire Dept-981-4985
Legal-981-2042
Pass/ID Office-981-4640
Public Affairs-981-4424

Housing Office-981-5516
Locator-981-1110
Police-981-2001

**HEALTH & WELFARE:**

AF Aid-981-7088
Chapel-981-2111
Family Services-981-7087
TRICARE-888-999-5195
Veterinary Services-981-2084

American Red Cross-981-6008
Dental-240-857-2696
Medical
  Central Appts-240-981-7511
  Clinic-240-981-6823/5
  Emergency-240-981-9911
  Health Benefits-240-981-5615
  Hospital-240-981-5911

**REST & RECREATION:**

Auto Hobby Shop-981-3917
Clubs
  E M-568-3100
  O-981-5091
Library-981-6454
Tennis Center-981-7101
Youth Center-981-5636

Bowling-981-3335
Fitness Center-981-7101
Golf Course-981-6300
ITT-981-4413
Outdoor Rec-981-4109/5663
Theater-981-6641

**ATTRACTIONS:** Aerial gateway to Washington, D.C., home of Air Force One, the President's aircraft. Monuments, White House, parks, and museums.

# BALTIMORE/WASHINGTON INTERNATIONAL AIRPORT (MD24R1)

Det 1, 305 APS/TR (AMC), P.O. Box 8613
Baltimore, MD 21240-0613

**TELEPHONE NUMBER INFORMATION:** Main installation numbers: C-410-918-6900, D-312-243-6900. WEB: www.bwiairport.com

**LOCATION:** From I-95 north or south, take the BWI exit 47 east, I-95 and airport. Also I-295 north or south exit 2 east, I-195 and airport. USMRA: Page 49 (A,B-4,5). NMC: Baltimore, five miles north.

**TEMPORARY MILITARY LODGING:** None, see Aberdeen Proving Ground or Curtis Bay Coast Guard Yard.

**SPACE-A:** C-410-918-6900, D-312-243-6900, Fax:410-918-6932.

**LOGISTICAL SUPPORT:**
Car Rental-Avis-410-859-1680
 Alamo-410-850-5011
 Hertz-410-850-7400

**ADMINISTRATIVE SUPPORT:** Police (Security) 410-859-7044/45

**ATTRACTIONS:** Baltimore Orioles (Major League Baseball), Baltimore Ravens (National Football League), Inner Harbor, Baltimore Aquarium.

# BETHESDA NATIONAL NAVAL MEDICAL CENTER (MD06R1)

8901 Wisconsin Avenue
Bethesda, MD 20889-5600

**TELEPHONE NUMBER INFORMATION:** Main installation numbers: C-301-295-4611, D-312-295-4611.

**LOCATION:** From VA: Take I-495 north to Wisconsin Avenue exit. Stay in left lane through two lights to NNMC entrance on left. From MD: Take I-95 south to I-495 west to Connecticut Avenue exit. Stay in center lane to light, turn left onto Connecticut Avenue. At next light turn right onto Jones Bridge Road, right on Wisconsin Avenue, right at next light into NNMC. USMRA: Page 55 (D,E-1). NMC: Washington, D.C., one mile southeast.

**GENERAL INFORMATION:** The Navy's largest and most advanced medical center, Uniformed Services University of the Health Sciences.

**TEMPORARY MILITARY LODGING:** BEQ/BOQ/DV/VIP 0800-1630 daily, C-301-295-5855/1111. D-312-295-0321/0307. Navy Lodge, Building 52, 0800-2200 daily, C-301-654-1795, for reservations call 1-800-NAVY-INN, Fax: C-301-295-5955. All ranks.

**RV, CAMPING/FAMCAMP:** None. See Andrews AFB listing.

**SPACE-A:** None. See Andrews AFB listing.

**LOGISTICAL SUPPORT:**

| | |
|---|---|
| Barber Shop-295-6390 | Beauty Shop-530-1624 |
| Cafeteria-295-5367 | Child Care-295-0167/5475 |
| Child Dev Center-295-0167/5475 | Conv Store-295-6129 |
| Credit Union-295-5555 | Dry Cleaner-295-6358 |
| Education Office-295-1150 | Exchange-295-0871/6362 |
| Gas Station-295-2665 | Package Store-295-6382 |
| Postal Service-295-0162 | SATO-295-5101 |
| Shoppette-295-2665 | |

**ADMINISTRATIVE SUPPORT:**

| | |
|---|---|
| CDO-295-4611 | Fire Dept-295-0043 |
| Housing Office-295-1138 | Legal-295-6052 |
| Locator-703-614-3158 | Pass/ID Office-295-1246/7 |
| Police-295-1246 | Public Affairs-295-5727 |

**HEALTH & WELFARE:**

| | |
|---|---|
| American Red Cross-295-1538 | CHAMPUS-295-5143/5144 |
| Chapel-295-1510 | Dental |
| Family Services-Anacostia | Central Appts-295-4339 |
|  202-433-6289 | Information-295-1126 |
| Medical | Navy-MC Relief-295-1207 |
|  Information-295-4611 | |
|  Sick Call-295-1093 | |

**REST & RECREATION:**

| | |
|---|---|
| Bowling-295-2034/2060 | Combined Club-652-6318 |
| Fitness Center-295-0030/31/32 | MWR-295-0030/31/32 |
| ITT-656-5154 | |

**OTHER FACILITIES AVAILABLE:** Library, marina.

**ATTRACTIONS:** National Zoo in nearby Rock Creek Park. Wisconsin Avenue S ends in the Georgetown section of Washington, D.C. Washington National Cathedral is off Wisconsin Avenue at Massachusetts Avenue.

# CURTIS BAY COAST GUARD YARD (MD01R1)

2401 Hawkins Point Road
Baltimore, MD 21226-1797

**TELEPHONE NUMBER INFORMATION:** Main installation number: C-410-789-1600.

**LOCATION:** Take I-695 east or west to exit 1, bear to your right, right on Hawkins Point Road, left into Coast Guard Yard. USMRA: Page 42 (F-3), page 49 (C-4). NMC: Baltimor, two miles north.

**GENERAL INFORMATION:** The Coast Guard's only shipbuilding and repair facility. Curtis Bay Station, CG Activities Baltimore, CG Engineering Logistics Center, two homeported ships.

**TEMPORARY MILITARY LODGING:** No central lodging office, CGES office, Building 28A (BOQ), C-410-636-7373; Transient Family Lodging, Guest Housing Manager, C-410-636-4187, 0900-1500 Mon-Fri, other hours, OOD/JOOD, Building 33, C-410-636-7493. All ranks. Space available.

**RV, CAMPING/FAMCAMP:** None. See Aberdeen Proving Ground listing, Skippers Point Rec Area.

**SPACE-A:** None. See Martin State Airport/Warfield ANG listing.

**LOGISTICAL SUPPORT:**

| | |
|---|---|
| Barber Shop-636-4156 | Credit Union-789-5420 |
| Exchange-636-4198 | Snack Bar-636-7382 |

**ADMINISTRATIVE SUPPORT:**

| | |
|---|---|
| Legal-636-7250 | OOD/JOOD-636-7766 |
| Police-636-3692 | |

**HEALTH & WELFARE:**

| | |
|---|---|
| CHAMPUS-636-3144 | Chapel-636-7715 |
| Family Services-636-3159 | Medical-636-3144 |

**REST & RECREATION:**

| | |
|---|---|
| Auto Hobby Shop-636-3785 | Bowling-636-3968 |
| Consol Club-636-7690 | Marina-636-2656 |
| MWR-636-4194 | Rec Center-636-7494 |
| Services-636-7494 | Swimming-636-7494 |

**ATTRACTIONS:** Oriole Park at Camden Yards, Inner Harbor (Aquarium, Science Center, Baltimore Zoo) maritime and streetcar museums, Baltimore Arena, Fort McHenry, World Trade Center.

# FORT DETRICK ARMY GARRISON (MD07R1)

810 Schreider Street
Fort Detrick, MD 21702-5000

**TELEPHONE NUMBER INFORMATION:** Main installation numbers: C-301-619-8000, D-312-343-8000. WEB: www.armymedicine.army.mil/detrick

**LOCATION:** From Washington, D.C., take I-270 north to US-15 north. From Baltimore take I-70 west to US-15 north. From US-15 north, in Frederick, exit Seventh Street to post. Clearly marked. USMRA: Page 42 (D-2). NMC: Baltimore, 50 miles east, and Washington, D.C., 50 miles southeast.

**GENERAL INFORMATION:** U.S. Army Medical Research and Materiel Command, U.S. Army Medical Research Institute of Infectious Diseases, 1110th Signal Battalion Telecommunications Center, Quad-Service Medical Logistics.

**TEMPORARY MILITARY LODGING:** Lodging office, Building 810, Schreider Street, 0745-1630 Mon-Fri, C-301-619-2154, D-312-343-2154. All ranks. DV/VIP C-301-619-7114.

**RV, CAMPING/FAMCAMP:** None. See Aberdeen Proving Ground listing, Skippers Point Rec Area.

**SPACE-A:** None. See Andrews AFB listing.

**LOGISTICAL SUPPORT:**

| | |
|---|---|
| Child Care-619-3300 | Commissary-619-2521 |
| Cafeteria-846-1750 | Dining-619-2274 |
| Exchange-619-2262 | Gas Station-662-7777 |
| Travel-631-2073 | |

**ADMINISTRATIVE SUPPORT:**

| | |
|---|---|
| Fire Dept-619-7318 | Legal-619-2221 |
| Locator-619-8000/1110 | Police-619-7114 |
| Public Affairs-619-2018 | SDO/NCO-619-7114 |

**HEALTH & WELFARE:**

| | |
|---|---|
| ACS-619-2197 | CHAMPUS-619-7175 |
| Chapel-619-7371 | Family Services-619-2197 |
| Medical-619-7175 | |

**REST & RECREATION:**

| | |
|---|---|
| Arts & Crafts-ext 2920 | Auto Hobby Shop-ext 2759 |
| Bowling-ext 2816 | Community Center-ext 2823 |
| Driving Range-ext 2964 | Field House/Gym-ext 2498 |
| Fishing-ext 7114 | Fitness Center-ext 2374 |
| Library-ext 7510 | MWR 619-2711 |
| Recreation-ext. 2711 | Skeet/3D Archery Range-ext 2823 |
| Swimming-ext 2374 | Tennis-ext 2498 |
| Youth Center-ext 2901 | |

**ATTRACTIONS:** Baltimore, Washington, and Gettysburg are easy drives. Near snow ski resorts. Quaint shops and excellent restaurants in Historic Frederick.

# FORT GEORGE G. MEADE (MD08R1)

ATTN: ANME-PA
Building 2837 Ernie Pyle Street
Fort George G. Meade, MD 20755-5025

**TELEPHONE NUMBER INFORMATION:** Main installation numbers: C-301-677-6261, D-312-923-6261. WEB: www.ftmeade.army.mil

**LOCATION:** From north: I-95 south to Baltimore. Take I-695 west (Baltimore-Washington Pkwy) around Baltimore. Take Fort Meade exit (Rt 175 east).Two miles, turn right at Mapes Road. From south: I-295 Baltimore-Washington Pkwy north. Exit at Rt 198 (Ft. Meade). Turn right on 32 east. Exit onto Rt 175 (Odenton). Turn left. At third traffic light, turn left onto Mapes Road. From east: (Annapolis) Rt 50 west, take I-97 north to Rt 32 west. Follow Rt 32 to Rt 175. Follow sign to Ft. Meade (bear right). At second traffic light, turn left onto Mapes Road. From west: (Howard County and I-95) Follow Rt 32 south. Exit on Rt 175 (Ft Meade/Odenton). Turn left. At third traffic light, turn left onto Mapes Road. Clearly marked. USMRA: Page 42 (E,F-4). NMC: Baltimore, 15 miles north.

**GENERAL INFORMATION:** Headquarters First Army (North), National Security Agency, 694th Intelligence Group, Naval Security Group Activities, Defense Information School, Army Field Band, Defense Courier Service, 1st Rctg Bde (NE), 902nd MI Grp, 704th MI Bde.

**TEMPORARY MILITARY LODGING:** Lodging office, Building 4707, Ruffner Road, Brett Hall, 24 hours daily, C-301-677-6529/5884, D-312-923-6529/5884. Fax: C-301-677-4704, D-312-923-4704.

**RV, CAMPING/FAMCAMP:** Building 2724, Ernie Pyle Street, 0700-1630. C-301-677-3810/3825, D-312-923-3810-3825. Fax: C-301-677-5616, D-312-923-5616.

**SPACE-A:** None. See Andrews AFB listing.

**LOGISTICAL SUPPORT:** *Note: All numbers with 677 prefix are Area Code 301. All other prefixes are Area Code 410.*

| | |
|---|---|
| Bank-551-5300 | Barber Shop-551-2053 |
| Beauty Shop-674-2262 | Carlson Wagonlit Travel-674-7325 |
| Car Rental-912-1804 | Child Care-677-7712 |
| Child Dev Center-677-5201/6002 | Class Six-674-7170 |
| Commissary-677-7463 | Conv Store-674-7170/6026 |
| Credit Union-551-5800 | Dining Facilities-677-0864 |
| Dry Cleaner-519-0003 | Education Office-677-6842/6421 |
| Exchange-674-7170 | Gas Station-672-3238 |
| Leisure Travel Office-677-7354 | Postal Service-551-0848/677-4660 |
| SATO-677-6477/3869 | Shoppette 872-1183 |

**ADMINISTRATIVE SUPPORT:**

| | |
|---|---|
| CPAC-677-6526 | Fire Dept-674-2117 |
| Housing Office-677-3106 | Legal-677-9504/9536 |
| Locator | Pass/ID Office-677-6031/32 |
|   Army-677-4547 | Police-677-6622 |
|   Navy-677-0217 | Public Affairs-677-1361 |
|   AF-677-0295 | SDO-677-4805 |
|   Marines-677-0266 | |

**HEALTH & WELFARE:**

| | |
|---|---|
| American Red Cross-677-2141 | ACS-677-5590/3418 |
| CHAMPUS-677-8982 | Chapel-677-7959/5673 |
| Dental-677-7903/8960/6078 | Emergency Relief-677-5662 |
| Family Services-677-6113/3586 | Medical |
| Navy-MC Relief-677-0219 |   Central Appts-677-8151 |
| Retiree Services-677-7433/7685 |   Health Benefits-677-8982 |
| TRICARE-677-8675 |   Information-677-8392 |
| Veterinary Services-677-1300 | |

**REST & RECREATION:**

| | |
|---|---|
| Arts & Crafts-677-7809 | Auto Hobby Shop-677-5542 |
| Bowling-677-5541 | Golf Course-677-5326 |
| Gym-677-3716/3042 | ITT-677-7354 |
| Library-677-5522 | MWR-677-2988 |
| O Club-677-5298 | Outdoor Rec-677-3810 |
| Theater-677-4620 | Wood Hobby Shop-677-7809 |
| Youth Center-677-1437 | Youth Services-677-1437 |

**ATTRACTIONS:** Museum on post, horse races at Laurel.

# GODDARD SPACE FLIGHT CENTER NASA (MD23R1)

Visitor Center, Greenbelt, MD 20771

**TELEPHONE NUMBER INFORMATION:** Main installation numbers: C-301-286-8981. WEB: www.gsfc.nasa.gov

**LOCATION:** From Washington, D.C.: take Rt 295 north (Baltimore-Washington Pkwy) to Greenbelt Road (Rt 193). Take Greenbelt Road east for about two miles. Main gate will be on left at the first traffic light after Cipriano Road. Visitors not on NASA business should continue on to the next traffic light, turn left onto Soil Conservation Road, take next left to Visitor Center. From Baltimore: Rt 295 south to Beltsville Agricultural Research Center. Exit at Powder Mill Road, follow signs. USMRA: Page 42 (E-4).

**GENERAL INFORMATION:** NASA research and development center.

**LOGISTICAL SUPPORT:**      Visitor Center-286-8981

**ATTRACTIONS:** Tours and exhibits.

# INDIAN HEAD DIVISION, NAVAL SURFACE WARFARE CENTER (MD04R1)

101 Strauss Avenue
Indian Head, MD 20640-5000

**TELEPHONE NUMBER INFORMATION:** Main installation numbers: C-301-743-4000, D-312-354-4000.

**LOCATION:** Take I-495 (Capital Beltway) east, exit to MD-210 south for 25 miles to station. USMRA: Page 42 (D-5,6). NMC: Washington, D.C., 25 miles north.

**GENERAL INFORMATION:** Naval Explosive Ordnance Disposal Technology Center.

**TEMPORARY MILITARY LODGING:** BEQ/BOQ, Building 901, C-301-743-4845, D-312-354-4845. Fax: C-301-743-4486.

**RV, CAMPING/FAMCAMP:** None. See Patuxent River NAS listing, Goose Creek/West Basin Rec Area.

**SPACE-A:** None. See Andrews AFB listing.

**LOGISTICAL SUPPORT:**

| | |
|---|---|
| Child Care-743-4458 | Exchange-743-4851 |
| SATO-743-7116 | |

**ADMINISTRATIVE SUPPORT:**

| | |
|---|---|
| CDO/OOD-743-4845 | Fire Dept-743-4370 |
| Legal-743-6668 | Locator-743-4000 |
| Police-743-4381 | SDO/NCO-743-4438 |

**HEALTH & WELFARE:**

| | |
|---|---|
| CHAMPUS-743-4601 | Chapel-743-3183 |
| Family Services-743-5180 | Medical-743-4601 |

**REST & RECREATION:**

| | |
|---|---|
| Auto Hobby Shop-ext 6314 | Bowling-ext 4761 |
| Combined Club-743-4648 | Golf Course-743-4662 |
| Gym-ext 4850 | ITT-743-4875 |
| Library-ext 4747 | MWR 743-4850 |
| Outdoor Rec-ext 4850/4761 | Racquetball-ext 1396 |
| Weight Room-ext 1396/4661 | |

**ATTRACTIONS:** New amphitheater alongside the Potomac River has summer concerts and special events. The Potomac River and Washington, D.C., 28 miles north.

# MARTIN STATE AIRPORT/WARFIELD AIR NATIONAL GUARD (MD21R1)

Building 1110, 2701 Eastern Boulevard
Baltimore, MD 21220-2899

**TELEPHONE NUMBER INFORMATION:** Main installation numbers: C-410-918-6210, D-312-243-6210.

**LOCATION:** From US-40 east, exit to MD-702 east and continue east to MD-150. Follow signs to airport. USMRA: Page 42 (F,G-3). NMC: Baltimore, eight miles southwest.

**GENERAL INFORMATION:** Home of 175th Wing, Air National Guard.

**SPACE-A:** Information: C-410-918-6381, D-312-243-6381; Rec: C-410-918-6551, D-312-243-6551.

**LOGISTICAL SUPPORT**       Exchange-918-6557

**ATTRACTIONS:** Baltimore Orioles (Major League Baseball), Baltimore Ravens (National Football League), Inner Harbor, Baltimore Aquarium.

# PATUXENT RIVER NAVAL AIR STATION (MD09R1)

Building 440
Patuxent River, MD 20670-5409

**TELEPHONE NUMBER INFORMATION:** Main installation numbers: C-301-342-3000/1000, D-312-342-3000. WEB: www.nawcad.navy.mil/pax

**LOCATION:** From I-95 (east portion of Capital Beltway, I-495) take exit 7-A to Branch Avenue (MD-5) south. Follow MD-5 until it becomes MD-235 near Oraville, on to Lexington Park, and the NAS. Main gate is on MD-235 and MD-246 (Cedar Point Road). USMRA: Page 42 (F-6,7). NMC: Washington, D.C., 65 miles northwest.

**GENERAL INFORMATION:** Naval Air Warfare Center Aircraft Division and Naval Air Station.

**TEMPORARY MILITARY LODGING:** Lodging Office C-301-863-9343, D-312-342-3601, BOQ C-301-863-9343, DV/VIP C-301-342-1108, Navy Lodge C-301-737-2400, 1-800-NAVY-INN. Housing Welcome Center Building 2371, C-301-342-3847, D-312-342-3847 All ranks.

**RV, CAMPING/FAMCAMP:** Goose Creek/West Basin Recreation Area on base, February-November, C-301-342-3508, D-312-342-3508, Fax: C-301-342-3232, 14 camper spaces with W&E hookups, 46 camper/tent spaces without hookups.

**SPACE-A:** Pax Term/Lounge, Building 103, 24 hours daily, C-301-342-3836/7, D-312-342-3836/7, C- 301-342-5961. Flights to CONUS locations.

**LOGISTICAL SUPPORT:**

| | |
|---|---|
| Child Care-342-7636 | Commissary-342-3789 |
| Conv Store-342-8715 | Exchange-863-8814 |
| Gas Station-342-5828 | Package Store-342-9315 |
| SATO-342-1051 ext 115 | Snack Bar-342-5608 |
| Theater-342-3572 | Visitor Center-342-3231 |

**ADMINISTRATIVE SUPPORT:**

| | |
|---|---|
| CDO/OOD-342-1095 | Command Post-342-1418 |
| Fire Dept-342-3333 | Legal-342-7643 |
| Locator-342-3000 | Police-342-3277 |
| Public Affairs-342-7512 | |

**HEALTH & WELFARE:**

| | |
|---|---|
| CHAMPUS-342-1457 | Chapel-342-3812 |
| Family Services-342-4911 | Medical |
| Navy-MC Relief Society-342-4739 | Central Appts-342-1506 |
| Retiree Services-342-4911 | Emergency-342-1422 |
| Veterinary Services-342-4213 | |

**REST & RECREATION:**

| | |
|---|---|
| Arts & Crafts-ext 3160 | Auto Hobby Shop-342-3507 |
| Bowling-342-3994 | Clubs |
| Golf Course-342-3597 | Consol-342-3940 |
| Gym-342-3559 | CPO-342-3657/3685 |
| ITT-342-3508 | EM-342-3657/3685 |
| Library-342-1927 | O-342-3656 |
| Marina-342-3573 | MWR-342-3510 |
| Rec equipment-342-3519 | Recreation-342-3510/3521 |
| Stables-342-3296 | Swimming-342-5960/4225 |
| Theater-342-3572 | Wood Hobby Shop-342- 3569 |
| Youth Center-342-1694 | |

**ATTRACTIONS:** Calvert Cliffs Nuclear Power Plant Museum, Calvert Marine Museum, Naval Air Test & Evaluation Museum, Potomac River, St. Clement's Island Museum, St. Mary's City, Sotterley Plantation, Cecil's Mill, Point Lookout State Park, Seafood Festivals.

# SOLOMONS NAVY RECREATION CENTER (MD05R1)

P.O. Box 147
Solomons, MD 20688-0147

**TELEPHONE NUMBER INFORMATION:** Main installation numbers: C-410-326-1260, DC Metro: 1-800-NAVY-230. Security-326-2436.

**LOCATION:** In southern Maryland where the Patuxent River meets the Chesapeake Bay. From US-301 take MD-4 southeast to Solomons; or take MD-5 southeast to MD-235, then MD-4 northeast to Solomons. USMRA: Page 42 (F-6). NMC: Washington, D.C., 65 miles northwest. NMI: Patuxent River NAS, 10 miles south.

**GENERAL INFORMATION:** Operated/managed by the Navy, on base year round. Military personnel active, retired, reserve and DoD civilians. Reservations (required): For specific information contact C-410-326-5203/4; D.C., Maryland and Virginia: 800-NAVY-230. Fax: C-410-326-4280.

**RV, CAMPING/FAMCAMP:**
Apartments, Bungalows, Log Cabins
Cottages-19 cottages handicap accessible    Camper spaces-146
Camper/tent spaces-56                       Group tent spaces-15

**ATTRACTIONS:** Local points of interest include Calvert Marine Museum, Cliffs of Calvert, Oyster Fleet, St. Mary's City, Battle Creek Cypress Swamp, Naval Air Test & Evaluation Museum, area festivals, Point Lookout State Park, Solomons Island area and many other historical sites. Excellent area for crabbing, fishing, sailing and boating.

*For detailed information about this off-base recreation facility, as well as on-base recreation facilities, golf courses and marinas, consult Military Living's Military RV, Camping and Outdoor Recreation Around the World.*

# UNITED STATES NAVAL ACADEMY/ ANNAPOLIS NAVAL STATION (MD10R1)

330 Kinkaid Road
Annapolis, MD 21402-5071

**TELEPHONE NUMBER INFORMATION:** Main installation numbers: C-410-293-1000, D-312-281-1000. WEB: www.nadn.navy.mil

**LOCATION:** The USNA and Annapolis NS are separated by the Severn River. From Washington, D.C.: Take US-50 east, exit 27 to MD Rt 450 to Annapolis. Go 1.5 miles to traffic light. Proceed straight over Naval Academy Bridge to reach USNA or turn left at the light (Rt 648) to go to Naval Station. From BWI Airport: Take 170 east to Annapolis. Turn right on Hammonds Ferry Road. Turn left on Dorsey Road, go into right lane. Take entrance ramp onto I-97 south to US-50 east. On US-50 take exit 27 to MD Rt 450. Go 1.5 miles to first light. Cross over the Naval Academy Bridge to reach the Naval Academy or make a left at this light (Route 648) to go to the Annapolis Naval Station. USMRA: Page 42 (F-4), page 48 (D,E,F,G-1,2,3). NMC: Annapolis, within city limits.

**GENERAL INFORMATION:** Navy education facility for officers and support personnel.

**TEMPORARY MILITARY LODGING:** BOQ, Building 2, 0730-1600 daily, C-410-293-3906, D-312-281-3906, Fax: C-410-293-2444, D-312-281-2444. Navy Lodge - 1-800-NAVY-INN.

**RV, CAMPING/FAMCAMP:** FAMCAMP on base, year round. Address, MWR Department, Bennion Road, Annapolis, MD 21402-5058, Mon-Fri 0645-2200, Sat 0900-2100, Sun 1200-2100, C-410-293-9200, D-312-281-9200, 14 camper spaces with W&E hookups.

**SPACE-A:** None. See Andrews AFB listing.

**LOGISTICAL SUPPORT:**

| | |
|---|---|
| Barber Shop-757-0005 | Beauty Shop-757-3101 |
| Cafeteria-757-8383 | Child Care-293-9390 |
| Commissary-293-2494 | Conv Store-757-2120 |
| Credit Union-266-1167/757-0700 | Dry Cleaner-757-0005 |
| Exchange-757-0005 | Gas Station-349-0226 |
| Package Store-293-3232 | Postal Service-293-3787 |
| SATO-268-7203 | Visitor Center-263-6933 |
| Uniform Shop 757-0005 | |

**ADMINISTRATIVE SUPPORT:**

| | |
|---|---|
| CDO/OOD-295-4737 | Fire Dept-293-3333 |
| Housing Office-293-9738 | Legal-293-9025 |
| Locator-293-2385 | OOD-293-2701 |
| Pass/ID Office-293-5762 | Police-293-9300 |
| Public Affairs-293-2291 | Quarter Deck-293-2385/9068 |

**HEALTH & WELFARE:**

| | |
|---|---|
| CHAMPUS-293-2276 | Chapel-293-1100/9018 |
| Dental | Family Services-293-2641 |
| Central Appts-293-3788 | Medical |
| Clinic-293-3921 | Central Appts-293-2061 |
| N-MC Relief-293-9220 | Clinic-293-1758/4400 |
| Retiree Services-293-2641 | Health Benefits-293-2276 |
| TRICARE 1-888-999-5195 | Information-293-1330 |
| Veterinary Services-677-1300 | |

**REST & RECREATION:**

| | |
|---|---|
| Auto Hobby Shop-293-3859 | Fitness Center-293-9200 |
| Golf Course-757-2022 | ITT-293-9200 |
| Library-293-9380 | Marinas-293-3731/2058 |
| MWR-293-9200/9201 | O Club-293-2611 |
| Outdoor Rec-293-9200 | Rec Center-ext 2518/3691 |
| Swimming-ext 2082/3033 | Theater-293-9200 |
| Youth Center-293-4997 | |

**ATTRACTIONS:** Walking tour of the Naval Academy, museum, tour of historic Annapolis, city dock area, and the Maryland Capitol building.

# MASSACHUSETTS

## BOSTON COAST GUARD INTEGRATED SUPPORT COMMAND (MA12R1)

427 Commercial Street
Boston, MA 02109-1027

**TELEPHONE NUMBER INFORMATION:** Main installation number: C-617-223-3257.

**LOCATION:** From the south on MA-93 or I-90 (Massachusetts Turnpike), exit at Atlantic Avenue (which becomes Commercial Street), follow for one mile. Center is on the right. Or from the north on I-93 take Charlestown/Sommerville exit, cross Charlestown Bridge, take first left onto Commercial Street. Center is on the left. USMRA: Page 24 (E-4,5). NMC: Boston, in city limits.

**GENERAL INFORMATION:** Logistic support for major cutters homeported here. Tenant Commands include Marine Safety Office, Group Boston, Naval Engineering Support Unit, Electronic Systems Support Unit.

**TEMPORARY MILITARY LODGING:** MAA office, Building 4, 427 Commercial Street, 0730-1500 Mon-Fri, C-617-223-3171. Cuttyhunk Island Rec Facility off base on Cuttyhunk Island, year round, two apartments. See Cuttyhunk Island Rec Facility listing for more information.

**RV, CAMPING/FAMCAMP:** None. See Fourth Cliff Rec Area listing.

**SPACE-A:** None. See Hanscom AFB listing.

**LOGISTICAL SUPPORT:**
Exchange-223-3133/67      Galley-223-3267

**ADMINISTRATIVE SUPPORT:**      CDO/OOD-223-3313

**HEALTH & WELFARE:**
CHAMPUS-223-3250      Chapel-223-3164
Medical
  Clinic-223-3250
  Hospital-782-3400

**REST & RECREATION:**
Consolidated Club-223-3265      Gym-ext 3125
Rec Equipment-ext 3125

**ATTRACTIONS:** City of Boston: Fenway Park, JFK Library and Museum, Blue Hills Reservation, Prospect Hill Ski Area, many universities, Aquarium, Franklin Park Zoo, "Boston Pops," Museum of Science, Celtics, Bruins, Patriots, Red Sox.

# CAMP EDWARDS (MA14R1)

Building 3468
Camp Edwards, MA 02542-5003

**TELEPHONE NUMBER INFORMATION:** Main installation numbers: C-508-968-5887.

**LOCATION:** Off MA-28 (MacArthur Boulevard) at the base of Cape Cod. From I-495 east, exit 3 to MA-28 south to camp, east of MA-28. USMRA: Page 17 (M-6,7). NMC: Boston, 70 miles northwest.

**GENERAL INFORMATION:** Massachusetts National Guard runs this multi-service training and support facility.

**TEMPORARY MILITARY LODGING:** Call C-508-968-5916.

**RV, CAMPING/FAMCAMP:** None. See Otis ANGB listing.

**SPACE-A:** None. See Hanscom AFB listing.

**LOGISTICAL SUPPORT:**      Exchange-772-4825

**ADMINISTRATIVE SUPPORT:** None. See Otis ANGB listing.

**HEALTH & WELFARE:** None. See Otis ANGB listing.

**OTHER FACILITIES AVAILABLE:** Gas station, golf course, shoppette.

**ATTRACTIONS:** On western part of Cape Cod, near Plymouth and other historic towns. Beaches and water sports.

# CUTTYHUNK ISLAND RECREATIONAL HOUSING FACILITY (MA04R1)

Commander (APS), ISC
427 Commercial Street
Boston, MA 02109-5000

**TELEPHONE NUMBER INFORMATION:** Main installation numbers: C-617-223-8047/8375.

**LOCATION:** Off base. On Cuttyhunk Island. From I-195 or MA-6 at New Bedford, south to State Pier (near Elm Street). Transportation to the island is via Cuttyhunk Boat Lines M/V ALERT (508-992-1432). USMRA: Page 17 (L-8). NMI: Newport Naval Station, RI, 35 miles southwest of New Bedford. NMC: New Bedford.

**GENERAL INFORMATION:** Operated by the U.S. Coast Guard, off base, Memorial Day through Labor Day. Military personnel active, reservists, retired, DOT Coast Guard civilian employees, 100% DAVs. Reservations (required, by application only): Commander (APS), ISC, 427 Commercial Street, Boston, MA 02109-5000. C-617-223-3181. Fax: C-617-223-3182.

**RV, CAMPING/FAMCAMP:**      Apartments-2

**ATTRACTIONS:** The dwelling site, a former Coast Guard lifeboat station, is located 14 miles south off the coast of New Bedford and just west of Martha's Vineyard.

*For detailed information about this off-base recreation facility, as well as on-base recreation facilities, golf courses and marinas, consult Military Living's Military RV, Camping and Outdoor Recreation Around the World.*

# DEVENS RESERVE FORCES TRAINING AREA (MA09R1)

ATTN: AFRTC-FMD-CO
Building 679, Quebec Street
Devens, MA 01433-5010

**TELEPHONE NUMBER INFORMATION:** Main installation numbers: C-978-796-2107, D-312-256-2107.

**LOCATION:** Take Route 2 (west from Route 495, or east from Leominster) to Devens/Jackson Road exit, to end of Jackson Road, right onto Givry, left onto MacArthur, take MacArthur to a right turn onto 10th Mountain Division Road. USMRA: Page 17 (I-2,3). NMC: Boston, 35 miles northwest.

**GENERAL INFORMATION:** Army training installation.

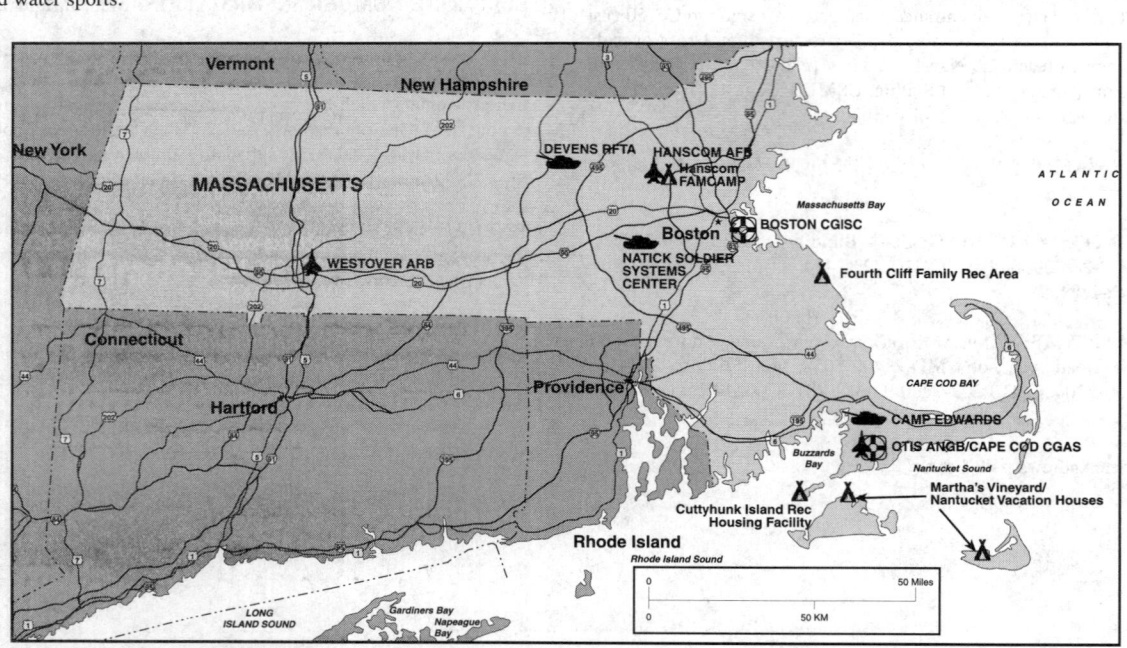

**TEMPORARY MILITARY LODGING:** C-796-2113/3951.

**RV, CAMPING/FAMCAMP:** None. See Hanscom Famcamp listing.

**SPACE-A:** None. See Hanscom AFB listing.

**LOGISTICAL SUPPORT:**
Bank-772-5451                          Class VI-772-7409
Commissary-796-3125                    Credit Union-772-5451
Dining-796-3074                        Education Center-796-2354
Exchange-796-2065

**ADMINISTRATIVE SUPPORT:**
Locator-796-7954                       Pass/ID Office796-2130
Police-772-7200

**HEALTH & WELFARE:**
ACS-796-2107/3023                      Medical-796-2577
*Clinic open May to September only.*

**REST & RECREATION:**                 Fitness Center-772-8826

**ATTRACTIONS:** One hour from Boston.

# FOURTH CLIFF FAMILY RECREATION AREA (MA02R1)

348 Central Avenue
P.O. Box 479
Humarock, MA 02047-5000

**TELEPHONE NUMBER INFORMATION:** Main installation numbers: C-781-377-4441, D-312-478-4441. Police for rec area, C-781-545-1212 (local police).

**LOCATION:** Off base. I-95 or I-93 to MA-3, approximately ten miles south of Boston, south to exit 12, MA-139 east to Marshfield. Go straight, through the traffic lights, for 1.5 miles to Furnace Street, turn left. Continue to T- intersection, left on Ferry Street. From Ferry Street to Sea Street, right over South River Bridge, left on Central Avenue, bear left at fork. (Do not go straight up hill on Cliff Road.) Proceed to gate. USMRA: Page 17 (M-4). NMC: Boston, 30 miles north. NMI: Hanscom AFB, 55 miles northwest.

**GENERAL INFORMATION:** Rec area is 56-acre seaside resort situated high on a cliff on the tip of a small peninsula overlooking the Atlantic Ocean on one side and scenic North River on the other. Operated by Hanscom Air Force Base, off base.16 units: Memorial Day-Columbus Day; 13 units: year round; self-contained trailers can be accommodated year round. Military personnel active, retired, 100% DAV, reserve, and DoD civilians. Check in at Fourth Cliff Recreation Hall, Building 7, 1200 daily, check out 1100. Call desk clerk at 781-837-6785 (before 1400 on weekdays and 1000 on Sundays and holidays) to make arrangements for other hours to check in or out and for off-season hours. No checking in after 2300. Reservations: Required on credit card or with one night's deposit. Reservation procedure based on status of sponsor. C-781-837-9269, C-1-800-468-9547 (0900-1630 Mon-Fri).

**TEMPORARY MILITARY LODGING:**
Cottage-1                              Townhouse-2
Chalets-11                             Cabins (in season only)-2

**RV, CAMPING/FAMCAMP:**
Camper spaces-11                       Primitive tent spaces

**ATTRACTIONS:** Easy access to Boston, Cape Cod, Martha's Vineyard, Nantucket Islands and a host of recreational activities.

*For detailed information about this off-base recreation facility, as well as other recreation facilities, golf courses, marinas and temporary military lodging, consult Military Living's Military RV, Camping and Outdoor Recreation Around the World or Military Living's Temporary Military Lodging Around the World.*

# HANSCOM AIR FORCE BASE (MA06R1)

Electronics Systems Center/Public Affairs
9 Eglin Street
Hanscom Air Force Base, MA 01731-2118

**TELEPHONE NUMBER INFORMATION:** Main installation numbers: C-781-377-4441, D-312-478-4441.

**LOCATION:** From I-95 south take exit 30 B (MA-2A) west for two miles then turn right at the Hanscom Field Sign. From I-95 north take exit 31B, keep to right, follow signs to base, two miles. USMRA: Page 17 (J-3), page 24 (A-2). NMC: Boston, 20 miles southeast.

**GENERAL INFORMATION:** Air Force Materiel Command Base. Hq, Electronics Systems Center.

**TEMPORARY MILITARY LODGING:** Lodging office, Building 1427, 24 hours daily, C-781-377-2112, D-312-478-2112. Fax: C-781-377-4961. All ranks. DV/VIP 781-377-5151, 07+.

**RV, CAMPING/FAMCAMP:** FAMCAMP off base, year round, C-781-377-4670, D-312-478-4670, Fax-781-377-4919, 35 camper spaces with full hookups, 21 camper spaces with W&E, 10 tent spaces. Operates Fourth Cliff Rec Area off base, 55 miles southeast of post. See Fourth Cliff Rec Area listing for more information.

**SPACE-A:** Pax Term, Building 1714, Mon-Fri: 0730-1600, C-781-377-1143, D-312-478-1143, (Daily flight recording C-781-377-3333, D-312-478-3333). Fax: C-781-377-2383, flights to Andrews AFB, MD and other East Coast locations. Uses runways of Lawrence G. Hanscom Field adjoining the base.

**LOGISTICAL SUPPORT:**
Barber Shop-377-5127                   Beauty Shop-274-6634
Cafeteria-377-2189                     Child Care-377-2858
Commissary-377-2544                    Conv Store-274-3675
Dry Cleaner-377-5139                   Exchange-377-5258
Gas Station-377-5155                   Laundry-274-8581
Package Store-377-3675                 Postal Service-377-2242
SATO-377-2631                          Snack Bar-377-2395

**ADMINISTRATIVE SUPPORT:**
Legal-377-2362                         Locator-377-5111/4441
Police-377-4357/2314                   Public Affairs-377-5191
SDO/NCO-377-5144

**HEALTH & WELFARE:**
CHAMPUS-377-4701                       Chapel-377-3538
Family Services-377-3436               Medical
Retiree Services-377-2476                Central Appts-377-4706
                                         Emergency-377-2333

**REST & RECREATION:**
Activity Schedule-ext 2687             Auto Hobby Shop-ext 2612
Bowling-ext 2237                       Clubs
Gym-ext 3435/3639                        Aero-ext 5160
ITT-377-3262                             NCO-377-2123
Library-ext 2177                         O-377-5740
Rec Center-ext 2610                    Services-ext 2610
Rec Equipment-ext 3348                 Rec Services-ext 3901
Swimming-ext 2455                      Theater-377-5200

**ATTRACTIONS:** The Bedford flag-"Oldest flag in America." Concord, North Bridge, Lexington, historic sites and taverns.

Find out more about Military Living online at
# www.militaryliving.com

# HANSCOM FAMCAMP (MA08R1)
66 SVS, 20 Schilling Circle
Hanscom AFB, MA 01731-1807

**TELEPHONE NUMBER INFORMATION:** Main installation numbers: C-781-377-4670, D-312-478-4670. Police for FAMCAMP: (Base) C-781-377-2314/5, (Bedford) C-781-275-1212.

**LOCATION:** Off base. From I-95, exit 31B to MA-4/225, west for a quarter mile to west on Hartwell Avenue, right on McGuire Road to end. USMRA: Page 17 (J-3), page 24 (A-2). NMI: Hanscom AFB, two miles west. NMC: Boston, 20 miles southeast.

**GENERAL INFORMATION:** Operated by Hanscom AFB, off base, open 1 May-31 October. Military personnel active, reservists, retired, DoD civilians at Hanscom AFB. First come, first serve: call C-781-377-4670, D-312-478-4670. Fax: C-781-377-4919, D-312-478-4919. For information off-season, C-781-377-3348.

**RV, CAMPING/FAMCAMP:**

Camper Spaces-56                  Tent Spaces-10

**ATTRACTIONS:** Near Concord Bridge (site of the shot heard round the world) and other Revolutionary War historical sites. Easy drive to Boston and the cultural and social world of the city known as the Hub of the Universe.

*For detailed information about this off-base recreation facility, as well as on-base recreation facilities, golf courses and marinas, consult Military Living's Military RV, Camping and Outdoor Recreation Around the World.*

# MARTHA'S VINEYARD/ NANTUCKET VACATION HOUSES (MA17R1)
USCG Air Station Cape Cod
Air Station Cape Cod, MA 02542-5024

**TELEPHONE NUMBER INFORMATION:** Main installation numbers: C-508-968-6447.
WEB: www.uscg.mil/d1/units/ascapecod/mwr.htm#Vineyard

**LOCATION:** Off base. One house on Nantucket, three houses on Martha's Vineyard. Island accessible via ferry from West Yarmouth, Cape Cod. USMRA (edition year 2000): Page 17 (M-8, O-9). NMI: Otis ANG/Cape Cod CGAS. NMC: Boston, 80 miles northwest.

**GENERAL INFORMATION:** Operated by Cape Cod Coast Guard Air Station, off base, year round. Military personnel active, reservists, retired, auxiliary personnel of Armed Forces, DoT civilian employees of CG, uniformed personnel of PHS and NOAA when assigned to CG. Reservations:
Commanding Officer, Attn: MWR-Morale House Reservations, USCG Air Station Cape Cod, Air Station Cape Cod, MA 02542-5024. Call C-508-968-6447, Fax: 508-968-6443.

**TEMPORARY MILITARY LODGING:**
Nantucket House (1)-sleeps 12
Martha's Vineyard Houses (2)-each sleeps 12
West Chop Lighthouse (1)-VIP guesthouse, sleeps 8

**ATTRACTIONS:** Martha's Vineyard and Nantucket–wonderful island communities with great beaches, nature preserves, historical sights and museums, fishing, boating.
*For detailed information about this off-base lodging facility, as well as other on- and off-base facilities, consult Military Living's Temporary Military Lodging Around the World.*

# NATICK SOLDIER SYSTEMS CENTER (MA11R1)
15 Kansas Street
Natick, MA 01760-5012

**TELEPHONE NUMBER INFORMATION:** Main installation numbers: C-508-233-4001, D-312-256-4001 E-mail: amsscpa@natick-emh2.army.mil WEB: www.natick.army.mil

**LOCATION:** Exit from I-90 (Massachusetts Turnpike), exit 13, Natick to MA-30 east to MA-27 south. Or exit MA-9 west for six miles to MA-27 south. Watch for signs to the Center's main entrance off Kansas Street. USMRA: Page 17 (J-4). NMC: Boston, 25 miles east.

**GENERAL INFORMATION:** Natick is a U.S. Army AMC Research, Development and Engineering Center and is responsible for food, clothing, shelters and parachute systems.

**TEMPORARY MILITARY LODGING:** None. See Hanscom AFB listing.

**RV, CAMPING/FAMCAMP:** None. See Hanscom AFB listing.

**SPACE-A:** None. See Hanscom AFB listing.

**LOGISTICAL SUPPORT:**

| | |
|---|---|
| Dining-233-4063 | Exchange-233-4794 |
| SATO-233-4299 | |

**ADMINISTRATIVE SUPPORT:**

| | |
|---|---|
| Legal 233-4322 | Locator-233-4001 |
| Police-233-4201 | |

**HEALTH & WELFARE:**

| | |
|---|---|
| ACS-233-4798 | Family Services-233-4798 |
| Medical-233-4155 | |

**REST & RECREATION:**

| | |
|---|---|
| Clubs | MWR-233-4960 |
|   NCO-233-4559 | Sailing-ext 4960 |
|   O-233-4791 | |

**OTHER FACILITIES AVAILABLE:** Auto hobby shop, weight room, rec services, swimming.

**ATTRACTIONS:** Cities of Boston and Cambridge, Boston National Historical Park, *USS Constitution* and Museum, and many other historical parks, sites and museums.

# OTIS AIR NATIONAL GUARD BASE/ CAPE COD COAST GUARD AIR STATION (MA07R1)
102 Fighter Wing (ANG)
158 Reilly Street
Otis Air National Guard Base, MA 02542-5028

**TELEPHONE NUMBER INFORMATION:** Main installation numbers: C-508-968-1000, D-557-1000. WEB: www.uscg.mil/d1/units/ascapecod/

**LOCATION:** South of Plymouth, from MA-28 north or south take MA Military Reservation exit, south on Connley Avenue approximately two miles to Bourne Gate. USMRA: Page 17 (M-7). NMC: Boston, 50 miles northwest.

**GENERAL INFORMATION:** Air Force Air National Guard, Army National Guard, Coast Guard Air Station, Marines, Dept of Agriculture.

**TEMPORARY MILITARY LODGING:** Temporary quarters, Building 5204, C-508-968-6461. Coast Guard also operates four houses on Martha's Vineyard and Nantucket Island. C-508-968-6447. See Martha's Vineyard/Nantucket Vacation Houses listing for more information.

**RV, CAMPING/FAMCAMP:** Cape Cod Vacation Apartments on base, year round, 12 townhouse apartments, 18 suites, two single rooms, C-508-968-6461.

**SPACE-A:** None. See Hanscom AFB listing.

**LOGISTICAL SUPPORT:**

| | |
|---|---|
| Beauty Shop-563-6535 | Car Rental-968-1700 |
| Child Care-968-6450 | Commissary-968-6662 |
| Conv Store-564-6153 | Dry Cleaners-563-5412 |
| Exchange-563-2495 | Galley-968-6425 |
| Gas Station-564-5486 | Grocery Annex-563-2756 |
| Package Store-564-5486 | Post Office-563-7336 |

**ADMINISTRATIVE SUPPORT:**
Commander
102d Air National Guard-968-4106
Army National Guard-968-5885
CG Air Station-968-6300
Marines-968-7169

**HEALTH & WELFARE:**
CHAMPUS-968-6570
Dental-968-6703
Chapel-968-6341
Medical-Appts-968-6582

**REST & RECREATION:**
Auto Hobby Shop-968-6516
Clubs-Consol-968-6448
Gym-968-5985
MWR-968-6448
Theater-968-6452
Youth Center-968-6451
Bowling-968-6448
Golf Course (9 hole)-968-6453
Library-968-6456
Rec Equipment-968-6448
Wood Hobby Shop-968-6405

**OTHER FACILITIES AVAILABLE:** Tennis, stables, racquetball, consignment shop 968-6682.

**ATTRACTIONS:** Beautiful Cape Cod, near Plymouth and other historic towns. Beaches and water sports.

## WESTOVER AIR RESERVE BASE (MA03R1)
439 Airlift Wing (AFRC)
Westover Air Reserve Base, MA 01022-5000

**TELEPHONE NUMBER INFORMATION:** Main installation numbers: C-413-557-1110, D-312-589-1110.
WEB: www.afrc.af.mil/units/439aw/default.htm

**LOCATION:** From Boston take I-90 west (Massachusetts Turnpike) to exit 5 in Chicopee; bear right after toll booth to traffic light; take a left onto Memorial Drive (Route 33) and follow signs to Westover ARB. USMRA: Page 16 (F-4). NMC: Springfield, eight miles south.

**GENERAL INFORMATION:** Air Force Reserve Base. 439th Airlift Wing, Army Reserve, Navy Reserve, Marine Corps Reserve, and Air Force Reserve units.

**TEMPORARY MILITARY LODGING:** Lodging office: Flyers Inn, Building 2201, Outer Drive. (VOQ) C-413-557-2700, D-312-589-2700, 24 hours daily. SDO, 557-3557. All ranks. DV/VIP Bldg. 2200. C-413-557-3478.

**RV, CAMPING/FAMCAMP:** None. See Hanscom AFB listing.

**SPACE-A:** Very limited. Pax Term, Building 7075, Base Ops, 0700-2300 daily, C-413-557-2622, D-312-589-2622, flight information C 413-557-2549, D-312-589-2549, flight sign-up C-413-557-2622, Fax: 557-3147. Flights to CONUS and OCONUS locations on transient aircraft.

**LOGISTICAL SUPPORT:**
Gas Station-593-3288
Snack Bar-557-3896
Shoppette-593-3288

**ADMINISTRATIVE SUPPORT:**
Fire Dept-557-3818
Locator-557-3874
Public Affairs-557-2020
Legal-557-3513
Police-557-3557
SDO/NCO-557-3571

**HEALTH & WELFARE:**
CHAMPUS-557-3918
Medical-557-3565
Chapel-557-3031
Retiree Services-557-3918

**REST & RECREATION:**
Bowling-ext 3010
Gym-ext 3958
Consol Club-593-5531
MWR-557-3958

**ATTRACTIONS:** Springfield, Mt Tom Snow Ski Resort, Holyoke. Basketball Hall of Fame in Springfield, Air Museum (Bradley Field, CT) and Military Museum (Danbury, CT).

# MICHIGAN

## ALPENA COMBAT READINESS TRAINING CENTER (MI16R2)
5884 A Street
Alpena, MI 49707-8125

**TELEPHONE NUMBER INFORMATION:** Main installation numbers: C-517-354-6291, D-312-741-3210.

**LOCATION:** Five miles west of Alpena on MI-32, (north side of MI-32). USMRA: Page 66 (F-4). NMC: Alpena, five miles west.

**GENERAL INFORMATION:** Air National Guard Training Base.

**TEMPORARY MILITARY LODGING:** None. See Camp Grayling MTC listing.

**RV, CAMPING/FAMCAMP:** None. See Camp Grayling MTC listing.

**SPACE-A:** Building 10, C-517-354-6305, D-312-741-3305.

**LOGISTICAL SUPPORT:**
Car Rental-354-3222
SATO-354-6290
Exchange-354-6272

**ADMINISTRATIVE SUPPORT:**    Police-354-6210

**HEALTH & WELFARE:** None. See Traverse City CGAS listing.

**REST & RECREATION:** None. See Camp Grayling Maneuver Training Center listing.

**ATTRACTIONS:** Lake Huron shore, fishing, hunting, and camping.

## CAMP GRAYLING MANEUVER TRAINING CENTER (MI10R2)
ATTN: PAO Hq. Bldg. 117
Grayling, MI 49739-0001

**TELEPHONE NUMBER INFORMATION:** Main installation numbers: C-517-344-6100. D-312-623-6100, Fax: C-517-348-3855, D-312-623-3855.
E-mail: paomtc@mi-arng.ngb.army.mil

**LOCATION:** Located three miles west of city of Grayling, just off of I-75. From gate at the end of Michigan highway M-93. USMRA: Page 66 (D-5). NMC: Grayling, three miles east.

**GENERAL INFORMATION:** Guard and reserve training center with approximately 147,000 acres of prime infantry, tank, helicopter, artillery, mortar and A/G training area. Largest National Guard Training Center with up-to-date techology and ranges for all weapon systems. New MPRC, MLRS range, air-to-ground bombing range, small arms to artillery ranges, water-borne operations areas, air field with two 5,000 foot runways and miles of maneuver training areas.

**TEMPORARY MILITARY LODGING:** Lodging office, Chargeable Quarters Building 560, C-517-344-6202, D-312-623-1202, Fax: C-517-344-6110. O Club Cottages C-517-348-9033, Fax: 517-348-6110.
**RV, CAMPING/FAMCAMP:** Camp Grayling Trailer Park on post, 15 May-15 Sep, C-517-348-7621 ext 3225, Fax: C-517-348-9033, 70 camper spaces with full hookups, 10 tent spaces. O-Club Campground C-517-348-9033, Fax:517-344-6110.

**SPACE-A:** None. See Alpena Combat Readiness Training Center listing.

**LOGISTICAL SUPPORT:**
Cafeteria-348-3662 ext 3286
Dining (summer only)-344-6200
Laundry (summer only)-348-4781
Snack Bar/Fast Food (summer only)
(Next to Pax Term)
Class VI-348-9033
Exchange-348-4781
Postal Svc (summer only)-344-6100

**ADMINISTRATIVE SUPPORT:**
Fire Dept. (Apr-Sept)-344-6183
Locator-344-6100
Police (Security)-344-6147/6100

Housing Office-344-6202
Pass/ID Office-344-6996/6115
Public Affairs-344-6107

**HEALTH AND WELFARE:**
Chapel-344-6202

Medical (May-Aug for Troops in Training)-348-4781

**REST & RECREATION:**
Clubs
EM-ext 3229
NCO-344-6100
O-348-9033

**ATTRACTIONS:** Lake Margrethe, boat launch and beach area, nearby. Huron National Forest, Lake Michigan, Lake Huron, skiing, water recreation. Hartick Pines State Park; Kirtland Warbler Nesting Area; Mackinaw area 90 miles north, Canada 130 miles north, Traverse City 55 miles west.

## DETROIT COAST GUARD GROUP (MI13R2)

110 Mount Elliott Avenue
Detroit, MI 48207-4380

**TELEPHONE NUMBER INFORMATION:** Main installation number: C-313-568-9525.

**LOCATION:** From 94 east or west, take the Mt Elliott exit and travel east. The base is located at 110 Mt Elliot Avenue, before Jefferson east. USMRA: Page 70 (E-4). NMC: Detroit, in city limits.

**GENERAL INFORMATION:** Host unit for Group Detroit Offices, Aids to Navigation Detroit, Marine Safety Office Detroit, USCGG Bristol Bay, and the entire Coast Guard Team (Reserves and auxiliary).

**TEMPORARY MILITARY LODGING:** None. See Selfridge ANGB listing.

**RV, CAMPING/FAMCAMP:** None. Nearest facility is over 100 miles away.

**SPACE-A:** None. See Selfridge ANGB listing.

**LOGISTICAL SUPPORT:** Exchange-259-6217

**ADMINISTRATIVE SUPPORT:** None. See Selfridge ANGB listing.

**HEALTH & WELFARE:**
CHAMPUS-568-9526

Medical-568-9526/7

**REST & RECREATION:** None. See Selfridge ANGB listing.

**ATTRACTIONS:** Pontiac Silverdome (Lions), the Palace (Pistons), Joe Louis Arena.

## GRAND HAVEN COAST GUARD GROUP (MI06R2)

650 Harbor Avenue
Grand Haven, MI 49417-1762

**TELEPHONE NUMBER INFORMATION:** Main installation number: C-616-850-2500.

**LOCATION:** From I-96 east, to US-31 south in Grand Haven, west on Jackson Street and follow it along the waterfront to the Group Office. From US-31 North, go west on Franklin Street to Harbor Drive, turn left and follow the road to the Group Office. USMRA: Page 66 (B-8). NMC: Muskegon, 12 miles north.

**GENERAL INFORMATION:** The center of Coast Guard operations for the western shore of Lake Michigan from Michigan City, IN to Frankfort, MI.

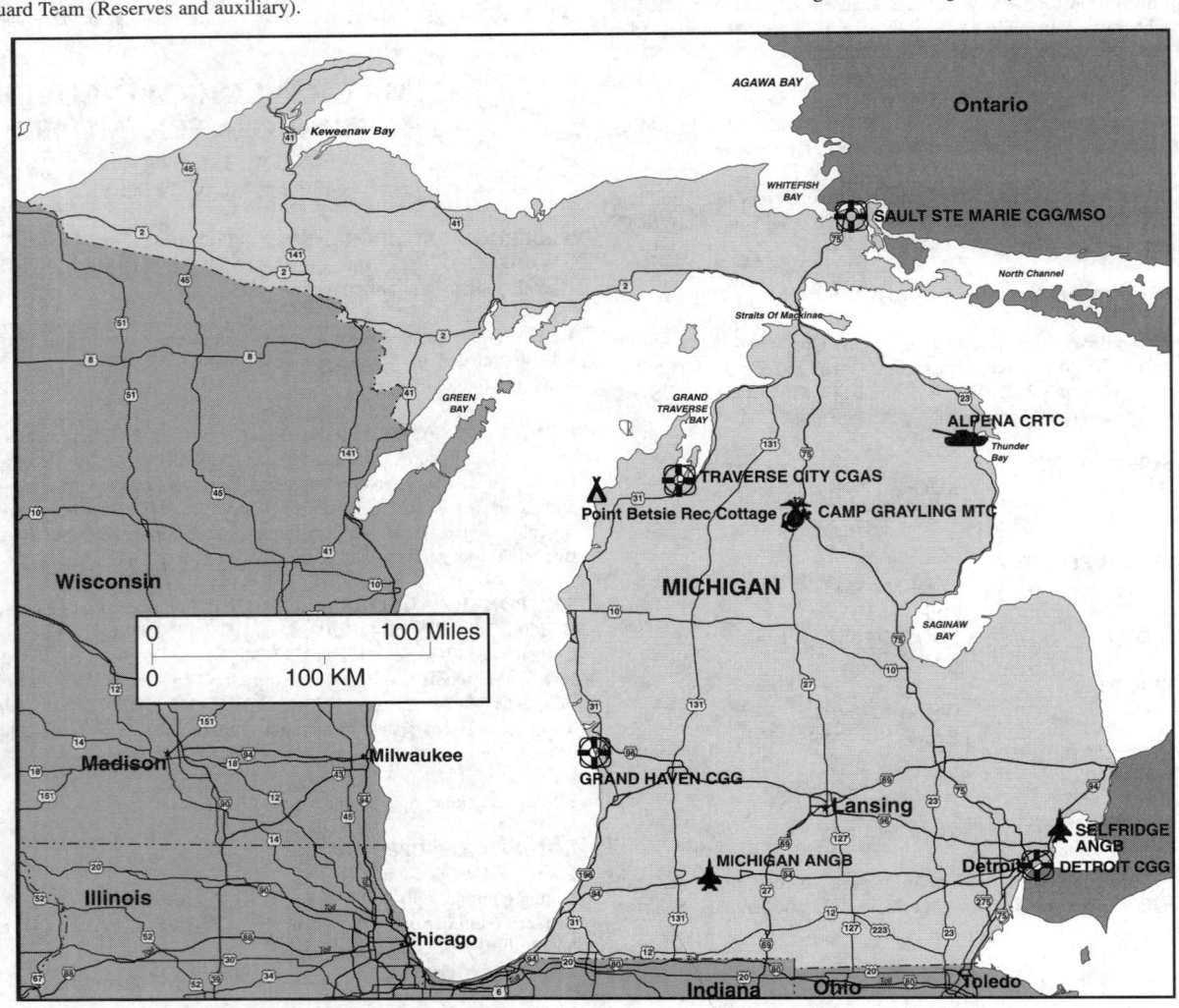

**TEMPORARY MILITARY LODGING:** None. See Camp Grayling MTC listing.

**RV, CAMPING/FAMCAMP:** Operates Point Betsie Recreation Cottage in Frankfort.

**SPACE-A:** None. See Selfridge ANGB listing.

**LOGISTICAL SUPPORT:**
Exchange-846-0490                 Package Store-846-0490

**ADMINISTRATIVE SUPPORT:**
CDO/OOD-847-4501                 Admin (Gen)-847-4517

**HEALTH & WELFARE:**
CHAMPUS-847-4520                 Family Services-847-4503

**REST & RECREATION:** Downhill skiing, cross country skiing, ice skating, boating, fishing, golf, beaches, indoor swimming, tennis courts, YMCA programs, trap/skeet shooting, bicycling, canoeing.

**ATTRACTIONS:** Grand Haven State Park, world's largest musical fountain, Annual Coast Guard Anniversary Festival (city has been recognized by Congress as Coast Guard City, USA).

## MICHIGAN AIR NATIONAL GUARD BASE (MI12R2)

110 Fighter Wing, 3545 Mustang Avenue
Battle Creek, MI 49015-5509

**TELEPHONE NUMBER INFORMATION:** Main installation numbers: C-616-969-3210, D-312-580-3210.

**LOCATION:** From I-94 to Helmer Road (exit 95), exit north; dead end at Dickman Road, left 1.5 miles to gate. USMRA: Page 66 (D-9). NMC: Battlecreek, three miles northeast.

**GENERAL INFORMATION:** Home of 110 Fighter Wing. Facilities extremely limited.

**LOGISTICAL SUPPORT:**                 Shoppette-969-3372

**REST & RECREATION:**                 Combined Club-969-3374

**ATTRACTIONS:** Area parks, forest, museums, Cereal City.

## POINT BETSIE RECREATION COTTAGE (MI04R2)

Morale Officer, USCG Group
650 Harbor Drive, Grand Haven, MI 49417-5000

**TELEPHONE NUMBER INFORMATION:** Main installation numbers: C-616-850-2510.

**LOCATION:** Off base. One hundred fifty miles north of Grand Rapids, take US-131 north to Highway 115 west into Frankfort, go north on M-22 for four miles to Point Betsie Road, cottage is at the end of Point Betsie Road. Recreation cottage is five miles north on MI-22. USMRA: Page 66 (C-5). NMI: Traverse City Air Station, 45 miles east. NMC: Traverse City, 45 miles east.

**GENERAL INFORMATION:** Operated by Grand Haven Coast Guard Group, off base, year round. Military personnel active, reservists, retired, CG civilian employees. Reservations: Required by phone 90 days in advance for Coast Guard, 60 days for others. Address for information and advance payment: Morale Officer, USCG Group, 650 Harbor Drive, Grand Haven, MI 49417-5000. C-616-850-2510.

**RV, CAMPING/FAMCAMP:**                 Cottage-sleeps seven

**ATTRACTIONS:** Located in northwest Michigan on eastern shores of Lake Michigan south of Sleeping Bear Dunes National Lakeshore. Crystal Lake and Betsie Bay resorts nearby.

*For detailed information about this off-base recreation facility, as well as on-base recreation facilities, golf courses and marinas, consult Military Living's Military RV, Camping and Outdoor Recreation Around the World.*

## SAULT STE. MARIE COAST GUARD GROUP/MARINE SAFETY OFFICE (MI15R2)

337 Water Street
Sault Ste. Marie, MI 49783-9501

**TELEPHONE NUMBER INFORMATION:** Main installation number: C-906-635-3217. E-mail: admin/grusault01@cgsmtp.uscg.mil

**LOCATION:** Take I-75 north to exit 392, merge onto I-75 Business Spur/Ashmun Street. Follow Ashmun Street until it ends at St. Mary's River. Turn right on Water Street; base is three blocks on left. USMRA: Page 66 (E-1,2). NMC: Detroit, 350 miles south.

**GENERAL INFORMATION:** Vessel Traffic Safety Search Rescue Group, Group Sault Radio telecommunications, Captain of the Port-marine safety, environmental pollution, general administration, ID card issuing activity, ATON/STA small boat stations.

**TEMPORARY MILITARY LODGING:** None. Nearest facility is more than 100 miles away.

**RV, CAMPING/FAMCAMP:** None. Nearest facility is more than 100 miles away.

**SPACE-A:** None. See Alpena CRTC listing.

**LOGISTICAL SUPPORT:**
Cafeteria-635-3267                 Exchange-635-3275

**ADMINISTRATIVE SUPPORT:**
Housing Office-635-3236           OOD-635-3228
Pass/ID Office-635-3301           Public Affairs-635-3310
Quarterdeck-635-3229              SDO/NCO-635-3233

**HEALTH & WELFARE:**
CHAMPUS-635-3225                 Dental 635-3226
Medical-635-3226                 Health Benefits Advisor 635-3225
TRICARE 635-3225

**REST & RECREATION:** None. Nearest facility is more than 100 miles away.

**ATTRACTIONS:** Hunting and fishing.

## SELFRIDGE AIR NATIONAL GUARD BASE (MI01R2)

29423 George Avenue
Selfridge Air National Guard Base, MI 48045-5029

**TELEPHONE NUMBER INFORMATION:** Main installation numbers: C-810-307-4011, D-312-273-4011.

**LOCATION:** Take I-94 north from Detroit to Selfridge exit 240, then east on MI-59 to main gate of base. USMRA: Page 66 (G-9), page 70 (G-1). NMC: Detroit, 10 miles southwest.

**GENERAL INFORMATION:** Air National Guard units, Reserve units of Air Force, Navy, Marine Corps and Army. Coast Guard Air Station Detroit.

**TEMPORARY MILITARY LODGING:** Lodging office, Building 410, George Avenue, 24 hours daily, C-810-307-4062, D-312-273-4062. DV/VIP C-810-307-4062. All ranks.

**RV, CAMPING/FAMCAMP:** New Famcamp, with 48 sites. Call C-810-307-5499.

**SPACE-A:** Information: C-810-307-5322, D-312-273-5322.

**LOGISTICAL SUPPORT:**

| | |
|---|---|
| Barber Shop-468-8009 | Child Care-307-4711 |
| Commissary-307-5570 | Conv Store-307-4256 |
| Credit Union-307-4744 | Dry Cleaner-954-9134 |
| Exchange-307-5789/465-0960 | Gas Station-307-4256 |
| Package Store-307-5072 | Postal Service-307-4123 |
| SATO-307-7651 | Snack Bar-307-6062 |

**ADMINISTRATIVE SUPPORT:**

| | |
|---|---|
| Locator-307-4021 | Police-307-4673 |
| SDO/NCO-307-4011 | |

**HEALTH & WELFARE:**

| | |
|---|---|
| Army Relief-307-4514 | CHAMPUS-307-5261 |
| Chapel-307-4020 | Family Services-307-5903 |
| Medical | |
|   Central Appts-307-4650 | |
|   Emergency-911 or 307-5000 | |

**REST & RECREATION:**

| | |
|---|---|
| Arts & Crafts-ext 5155 | Auto Hobby Shop-ext 4535 |
| Bowling-ext 5941 | Golf Course-ext 4344 |
| O Club-307-4785 | Outdoor Rec-ext 4344 |
| Picnic Area 463-3070 | Rec Center-ext 4524/4564 |
| Swimming/Tennis-ext 5765 | Wood Hobby Shop-ext 4535 |
| Youth Services-ext 4524/4564 | |

**OTHER FACILITIES AVAILABLE:** Selfridge Outdoor Rec Area, on base, April-September, C-810-307-5499, D-312-273-5499, marina only, no camping.

**ATTRACTIONS:** Air Museum, Detroit, Canadian cities of Windsor, Sarnia and Lake St. Clair (40 minutes away).

## TRAVERSE CITY COAST GUARD AIR STATION (MI07R2)

1175 Airport Access Road
Traverse City, MI 49686-3586

**TELEPHONE NUMBER INFORMATION:** Main installation number: C-616-922-8300.

**LOCATION:** Located across from Cherry Capital Airport. From US-31 north go south on Airport Access Road. Air Station will be on left. USMRA: Page 66 (C-5). NMC: Traverse City, in city limits.

**GENERAL INFORMATION:** A large rescue air station covering the northern and western Great Lakes area. Many activities for retirees and families year round in the area.

**TEMPORARY MILITARY LODGING:** None. See Camp Grayling MTC listing, C-517-348-3661, D-312-722-3661, Fax: C-517-348-3844.

**RV, CAMPING/FAMCAMP:** None. See Grand Haven CGG listing, Point Betsie Rec Cottage.

**SPACE-A:** None. See Alpena CRTC.

**LOGISTICAL SUPPORT:**

| | |
|---|---|
| Dining Facilities-922-8311 | Education Office-922-8278 |
| Exchange-922-8330 | |

**ADMINISTRATIVE SUPPORT:**

| | |
|---|---|
| Housing Office-922-8217 | Pass/ID Office-922-8228 |
| OOD-922-8216 | Operations-922-8211 |
| Public Affairs-922-8230 | |

**HEALTH & WELFARE:**

| | |
|---|---|
| CHAMPUS-922-8281 | Dental-922-8282 |
| Medical-922-8282 | |

**REST & RECREATION:** None. See Camp Grayling MTC listing.

**ATTRACTIONS:** All seasons recreational tourism, fresh water lakes, local golf courses, ski areas nearby. Sleeping Bear Dunes National Lakeshore, Peshawbetown Indian Village, Old Mission Lighthouse, Manistee National Forest.

# MINNESOTA

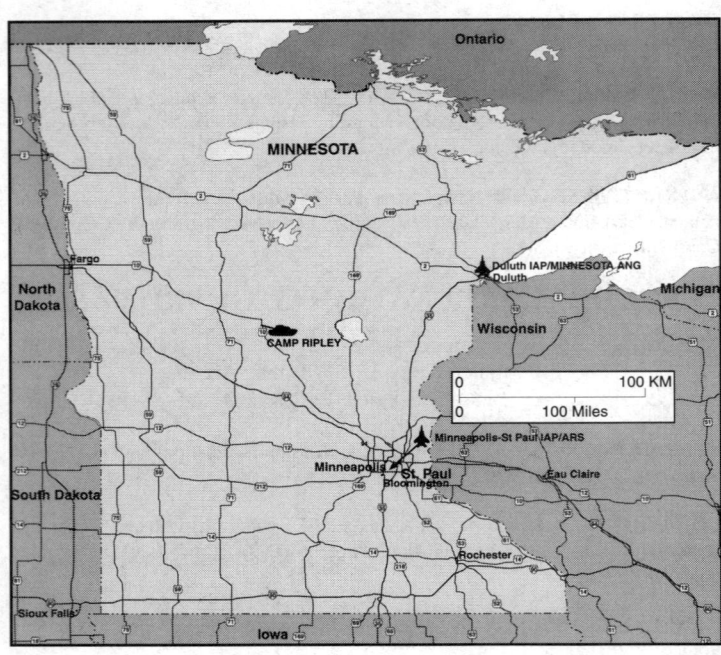

## CAMP RIPLEY (MN02R2)

P.O. Box 150
Little Falls, MN 56345-5000

**TELEPHONE NUMBER INFORMATION:** Main installation number: C-320-632-7000, D-312-871-7000.

**LOCATION:** West of Hwy 371, 12 miles south of Brainerd, west of Mille Lacs Lake, in central Minnesota. USMRA: Page 80 (C,D-6). NMC: Little Falls, seven miles south.

**TEMPORARY MILITARY LODGING:** BOQ when available. C-320-632-7378, D-312-871-7378.

**RV, CAMPING/FAMCAMP:** None. Nearest facility is more than 100 miles away.

**SPACE-A:** None. See Minneapolis-St Paul IAP/ARS listing.

**LOGISTICAL SUPPORT:**

| | |
|---|---|
| Exchange-632-7382 | SATO-632-7465 |
| Snack Bar-632-7412 | |

**ADMINISTRATIVE SUPPORT:**    Police-632-7665

**HEALTH & WELFARE:**    Family Services-632-7296

**REST & RECREATION:**    Clubs
                                 NCO-632-7255
                                 O-632-7239

**ATTRACTIONS:** Hunting, fishing and camping, military museum, Mississippi Headwaters, Charles Lindberg home.

## DULUTH INTERNATIONAL AIRPORT/MINNESOTA AIR NATIONAL GUARD (MN03R2)

4680 Viper Street
Duluth, MN 55811-6031

**TELEPHONE NUMBER INFORMATION:** Main installation numbers: C-218-727-6886, D-312-825-7210.

**LOCATION:** From I-35 to Midway Road to Hwy 53 turn right, five miles to left on Airport Road. USMRA: Page 80 (F-5). NMC: Duluth, in city limits.

**GENERAL INFORMATION:** Home of the 148th Fighter Wing.

**TEMPORARY MILITARY LODGING:** None. See Minneapolis/St. Paul IAP/ARS listing.

**RV, CAMPING/FAMCAMP:** None. Nearest facility is more than 100 miles away.

**SPACE-A:** None. See Minneapolis/St. Paul IAP/ARS listing.

**LOGISTICAL SUPPORT:**          Exchange-727-8365

**ADMINISTRATIVE SUPPORT:**
Pass/ID Office-723-7212          Police (Security)-723-7442
Public Affairs-723-7227

**HEALTH & WELFARE:**            Med-Clinic-723-7225

**REST & RECREATION:** None. See Minneapolis/St. Paul IAP/ARS listing.

**ATTRACTIONS:** Nearby museums, casinos, skiing, waterfront activities.

## MINNEAPOLIS-ST PAUL INTERNATIONAL AIRPORT/AIR RESERVE STATION (MN01R2)

760 Military Highway
Minneapolis, MN 55450-2000

**TELEPHONE NUMBER INFORMATION:** Main installation numbers: C-612-713-1110, D-312-783-1110.

**LOCATION:** From I-35 west or MN-55 south to crosstown MN-62, exit at 34th Avenue and entrance. Or I-495 east to exit 1A on MN-5 and entrance west to airport. USMRA: Page 89 (C-3,4). NMC: Minneapolis-St Paul, in city limits.

**GENERAL INFORMATION:** Air Reserve Station, co-located Air Force Reserve Wing, and ANG 133 Airlift Wing, Navy, Marine Corps and other reserve units. US Customs Service airport.

**TEMPORARY MILITARY LODGING:** Lodging office, Building 711, 0700-2200 hours Mon-Fri, 0630-1700 Sat, C-612-713-1978, D-312-783-1978. All ranks.

**RV, CAMPING/FAMCAMP:** None. Nearest facility is more than 100 miles away.

**SPACE-A:** Base Ops, Building 821, 0730-1600 daily, C-612-713-2461/2474, D-312-783-2461/2474, Rec: C-612-713-2450, D-312-783-2450. Flights to CONUS and OCONUS locations, mostly training flights on weekends.

**LOGISTICAL SUPPORT:**
Exchange-726-9023                Omega Travel-726-1995

**ADMINISTRATIVE SUPPORT:**
Police-713-1102                  Public Affairs-713-1217/2517

**HEALTH & WELFARE:**            Family Services-713-1516

**REST & RECREATION:**
Clubs                            Recreation-713-1128
  NCO-713-1655
  O-713-3678

**ATTRACTIONS:** Minneapolis-St Paul (Twin Cities) on the Mississippi, and Minnesota Rivers and the Mall of America. Many lakes within the cities with walking and bicycling trails.

# MISSISSIPPI

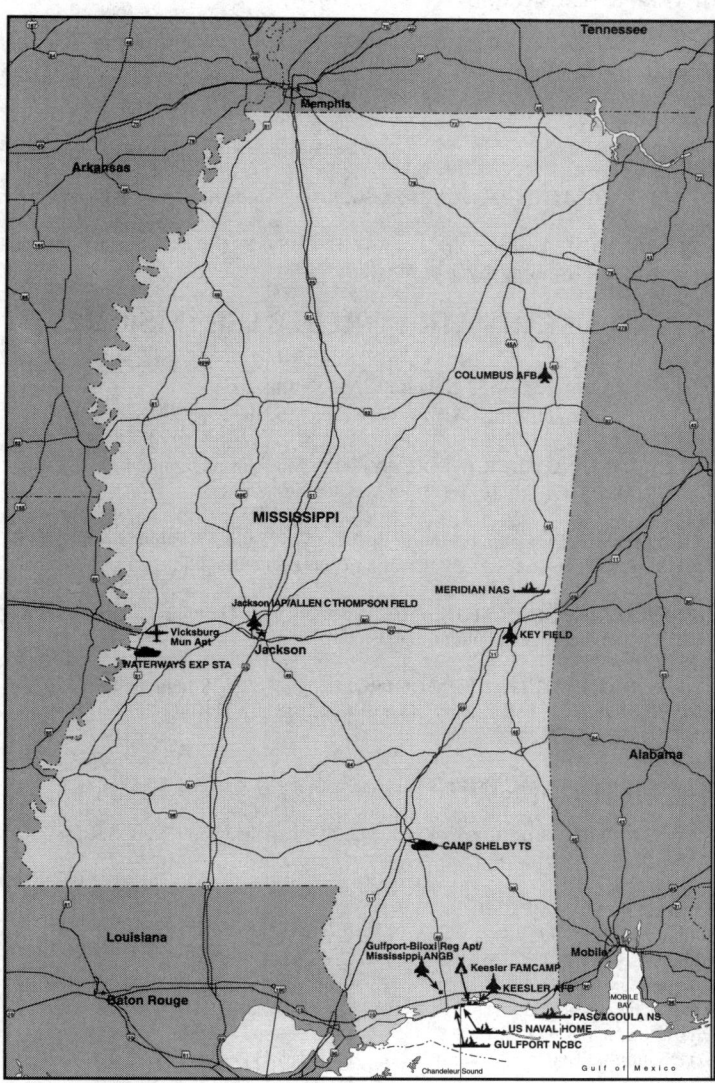

## CAMP SHELBY TRAINING SITE (MS07R2)

1001 Lee Avenue
Camp Shelby, MS 39407-5500

**TELEPHONE NUMBER INFORMATION:** Main installation numbers: C-601-558-2000, D-312-921-2000. WEB: www.campshelby.net

**LOCATION:** From Hattiesburg take US-49 south, or take US-98 east from Hattiesburg to MS-29 south, which bisects the training site. Follow signs. USMRA: Page 43 (F-8). NMC: Hattiesburg, 10 miles north.

**GENERAL INFORMATION:** Training Site Headquarters, Regional School Support Detachment, Mississippi Military Academy.

**TEMPORARY MILITARY LODGING:** Building 6606, 0730-1600 daily, C-601-558-2540, D-312-921-2540. All ranks.

**RV, CAMPING/FAMCAMP:** Lake Walker Family Campground on post, year round, C-601-558-2397, D-312-921-2397, eight cabins and 25 camper spaces with full hookups.

**SPACE-A:** None. See Meridian NAS listing.

**LOGISTICAL SUPPORT:**          Exchange-558-2349

**ADMINISTRATIVE SUPPORT:**      Locator-558-2000

**HEALTH & WELFARE:**
Chapel-558-2378                  Medical-558-2805

**REST & RECREATION:**
Clubs                            Museum-558-2757
  NCO-558-2427         Rec Center-ext 2397
  O-558-2749           Services-ext 2397

**OTHER FACILITIES AVAILABLE:** Swimming, softball, tennis, and basketball.

**ATTRACTIONS:** Kamper Park and Zoo, Hattiesburg Historical Society, Paul B. Johnson State Park, Armed Forces Museum.

## COLUMBUS AIR FORCE BASE (MS01R2)

14th FTW/Public Affairs
555 Seventh Sreet, Suite 203
Columbus Air Force Base, MS 39710-5000

**TELEPHONE NUMBER INFORMATION:** Main installation numbers: C-662-434-7322, D-312-742-1110. WEB: www.columbus.af.mil

**LOCATION:** From Columbus north on US-45, five miles north and west of US-45. USMRA: Page 43 (G-3). NMC: Columbus, 10 miles south.

**GENERAL INFORMATION:** Air Education and Training Command Base, Specialized undergraduate pilot training.

**TEMPORARY MILITARY LODGING:** Lodging office, Magnolia Inn, Building 956, B Street, 24 hours daily, C-662-434-2548, D-312-742-2548. All ranks. DV/VIP 662-434-7024.

**RV, CAMPING/FAMCAMP:** None. Nearest facility is over 100 miles away.

**SPACE-A:** Information: C-662-434-2862/7322. Unscheduled flights. See Meridian NAS listing.

**LOGISTICAL SUPPORT:**
Barber Shop-434-9958             Beauty Shop-434-6717
Child Care-434-2479              Class VI-434-6026
Commissary-434-7103             Conv Store-434-6026
Credit Union-434-7060            Dry Cleaner-434-6029
Education Center-434-2562        Exchange-434-6013
Gas Station-434-6026             Laundry-434-6029
Postal Svc-434-2959              SATO-434-2669
Snack Bar-434-2426               Travel Office-434-7858

**ADMINISTRATIVE SUPPORT:**
Fire Dept-434-2263               Housing Office-434-7276
Legal-434-7030                   Locator-434-7322
Pass/ID Office-434-7133          Police-434-7128
Public Affairs-434-7068          SDO/NCO-434-7020

**HEALTH & WELFARE:**
Air Force Aid Society 434-2790   CHAMPUS-434-2137
Chapel-434-2500                  Dental-Appointments 434-225
Family Services-434-2790         Retiree Services-434-2790
Medical                          TRICARE 434-5348
  Central Appts-434-2273   Veterinary Services-434-2281
  Emergency-911
  Health Benefits Advisor-434-2283

**REST & RECREATION:**
Arts & Crafts-434-7835           Auto Hobby Shop-434-7842
Bowling-434-2426                 Community Center-434-7858
Clubs                            Fitness Center-434-2772
  NCO-434-7927          Golf Course-434-7932
  O-434-2489            Gym-434-2722
Library-434-2934                 ITT-434-7858

Outdoor Rec-434-4-2507           Rec Equipment-434-2507
Services-434-7437/2316           Skills Development Center-434-7836
Theater-434-2932                 Wood Hobby Shop-434-7837
Youth Center-434-2504

**ATTRACTIONS:** Period historic homes, Columbus, and northeast Mississippi.

## GULFPORT-BILOXI REGIONAL AIRPORT/MISSISSIPPI AIR NATIONAL GUARD BASE (MS11R2)

Combat Readiness Training Center
4715 Hewes Avenue, Building 1
Gulfport, MS 39507-4324

**TELEPHONE NUMBER INFORMATION:** Main installation numbers: C-228-214-6200, D-312-363-8002. WEB: 172aw.ang.af.mil/crtc

**LOCATION:** Take US-49 south to Gulfport. Cross I-10 and exit east to airport. Follow signs to airport. USMRA: Page 43 (F-10). NMC: New Orleans, LA, 70 miles west.

**GENERAL INFORMATION:** Air National Guard training center.

**TEMPORARY MILITARY LODGING:** Call C-214-6165. Also, see Keesler AFB listing.

**RV, CAMPING/FAMCAMP:** None. See Keesler AFB listing.

**SPACE-A:** None. See Keesler AFB listing.

**LOGISTICAL SUPPORT:**           Exchange-214-6200

**ADMINISTRATIVE SUPPORT:**       Police (Security)-214-6148

**HEALTH & WELFARE:**             Medical-214-6014

**REST & RECREATION:** None. See Keesler AFB listing.

**ATTRACTIONS:** Seabee Museum, Gulf Coast, beaches, and water sports. Cities of Mobile and New Orleans, short drives.

## GULFPORT NAVAL CONSTRUCTION BATTALION CENTER (MS03R2)

5200 Construction Battalion Center 2nd Street
Gulfport, MS 39501-5001

**TELEPHONE NUMBER INFORMATION:** Main installation numbers: C-228-871-2555, D-312-868-2555.

**LOCATION:** Take US-49 south to Gulfport and west to Center off 28th Street West. From US-90 exit to Broad Avenue. From I-10 exit to US-49 south. USMRA: Page 43 (F-10). NMC: New Orleans, 70 miles west.

**GENERAL INFORMATION:** Naval Construction Training Center, 20th Naval Construction Regiment and Construction Battalions.

**TEMPORARY MILITARY LODGING:** Lodging office, 0700-1600 daily. Building 314 BOQ, C-228-871-2505, 1-800-628-9466, D-312-868-2505. Building 317 BEQ, C-228-871-2506, D-312-868-2505. Navy Lodge, C-228-377-3160. DV/VIP C-228-865-2202, D-312-363-2205, Fax: C-228-871-2130.

**RV, CAMPING/FAMCAMP:** RV Park opening in August 1999. C-871-2231. Also see Keesler AFB listing.

**SPACE-A:** None. See Keesler AFB listing.

**LOGISTICAL SUPPORT:**
Child Care-871-2323              Commissary-871-2040
Conv Store-863-4506             Exchange-871-2619
Gas Station-864-5527             Package Store-864-5527
SATO-864-9219                    Visitor Center-871-3164

**ADMINISTRATIVE SUPPORT:**

| | |
|---|---|
| CDO 871-2555 | Fire Dept-871-2333 |
| Housing Office-871-2586 | Legal-871-2626 |
| Locator-871-2555 | OOD-871-2555 |
| Police-871-2433 | Public Affairs-871-2393 |
| Quarter Deck-871-2555 | |

**HEALTH & WELFARE:**

| | |
|---|---|
| Chapel-871-2454 | Family Services-871-2581 |
| Medical | Retiree Services-871-3000 x 35 |
| Central appts-1-800-700-8603 | TRICARE-871-2821 |
| Emergency-871-2444 | |

**REST & RECREATION:**

| | |
|---|---|
| Auto Hobby Shop-871-2804 | Clubs |
| Gym-871-2668 | Anchors & Eagles-871-3311 |
| Golf Course-871-2494 | Stingers-871-3153 |
| ITT-871-2231 | Library-871-2409 |
| MWR-871-2538 | Racquetball-ext 2668 |
| Recreation-871-3153 | Youth Center-871-2251 |

**ATTRACTIONS:** Seabee Museum, Gulf Coast, beaches, and water sports. Cities of Mobile and New Orleans, short drives.

## JACKSON INTERNATIONAL AIRPORT/ ALLEN C. THOMPSON FIELD (MS09R2)

172nd AW
141 Military Drive, Building 129
Jackson, MS 39208-8881

**TELEPHONE NUMBER INFORMATION:** Main installation numbers: C-601-939-3633, D-312-731-9210. WEB: 172aw.ang.af.mil

**LOCATION:** Off I-20 east or west and US-80. From I-20 exit 52 north to IAP. Clearly marked. USMRA: Page 43 (D-6). NMC: Jackson, five miles west.

**GENERAL INFORMATION:** Mississippi Air National Guard, 172nd Airlift Group.

**TEMPORARY MILITARY LODGING:** None. See Meridian NAS listing.

**RV, CAMPING/FAMCAMP:** None. Nearest facility is more than 100 miles away.

**SPACE-A:** Pax Term Info, C-601-936-8761, D-312-731-9761, Fax: C-601-936-8634.

**LOGISTICAL SUPPORT:**     Exchange-932-3930

**ADMINISTRATIVE SUPPORT:**     Public Affairs-936-8311

**HEALTH & WELFARE:**     Medical-936-8351

**REST & RECREATION:**     Combined Club-936-8468

**ATTRACTIONS:** Historic Homes, Vicksburg National Battlefield Park 30 miles west.

## KEESLER AIR FORCE BASE (MS02R2)

720 Chappie James Avenue, Room 106
Keesler Air Force Base, MS 39534-2603

**TELEPHONE NUMBER INFORMATION:** Main installation numbers: C-228-377-1110, D-312-597-1110. WEB: www.keesler.af.mil

**LOCATION:** From I-10 exit 46 south on I-110 to base, west of I-110. From US-90, north on White Avenue to main gate. USMRA: Page 43 (F-10). NMC: Biloxi, in city limits.

**GENERAL INFORMATION:** Air Education and Training Command Base, Training Wing, USAF Medical Center, and AFRES units.

**TEMPORARY MILITARY LODGING:** Lodging office, Larcher Boulevard, 24 hours daily Building 2101, Muse Manor, 0715-1600 Mon-Fri, C-228-377-2631/3663, All ranks.

**RV, CAMPING/FAMCAMP:** Keesler FAMCAMP on base, year round, C-228-377-3160, D-312-597-3160, 40 camper spaces.

**SPACE-A:** Pax Term/Lounge, Building 0233, 0600-2300 daily, C-228-377-4538, D-312-597-4538, flights to CONUS locations.

**LOGISTICAL SUPPORT:**

| | |
|---|---|
| Bank-374-4285 | Barber Shop-377-2221/3200 |
| Car Rental-436-9248 | Child Dev Center-377-3324/2211 |
| Class Six-432-2367 | Commissary-377-2830 |
| Credit Union-385-5583 | Dry Cleaner-374-6994/6996 |
| Education Office-377-2323 | Exchange-435-2216 |
| Gas Station-432-2404 | Laundry-374-6994/6996 |
| Postal Service-377-2289 | SATO-377-2230 |
| Shoppette-432-2367 | Visitor Center-377-3844 |

**ADMINISTRATIVE SUPPORT:**

| | |
|---|---|
| Fire Dept-377-3441 | Housing Office-377-3014 |
| Legal-377-3510 | Locator-377-3988 |
| Pass/ID Office-377-3893 | Police-377-2878 |
| Public Affairs-377-2783 | Quarter Deck-377-9067 |
| SDO/NCO-377-1110 | |

**HEALTH & WELFARE:**

| | |
|---|---|
| AF Aid-377-2179 | American Red Cross-377-3030 |
| CHAMPUS-377-6001 | Chapel-377-8633 |
| Dental | Family Services-377-4293 |
| Central Appts-377-4510 | Medical |
| General-377-5130 | Central Appts-377-2530 |
| Retiree Services-377-3871 | Emergency-911 or 377-0500 |
| TRICARE-377-7685 | Information-377-6550 |

**REST & RECREATION:**

| | |
|---|---|
| Arts & Crafts-377-2821 | Auto Hobby Shop-377-3872 |
| Bowling-377-2817 | Clubs |
| Community Center-377-3708 | NCO-377-3439 |
| Golf Course-377-3832 | O-377-2219 |
| Gym-377-4385/2907 | Library-377-2181 |
| Marinas-377-3160 | Outdoor Rec-377-3160 |
| Theater-377-4281 | Wood Hobby Shop-377-3078 |
| Youth Center-377-3349 | |

**ATTRACTIONS:** Gulf Coast beaches, seafood, Pensacola, FL, New Orleans, LA, and Mobile, AL, all within easy driving distance.

## KEESLER FAMCAMP (MS05R2)

Outdoor Recreation
81 SVS/SVRO
625 Marina Drive
Keesler AFB, MS 39534-2623

**TELEPHONE NUMBER INFORMATION:** Main installation numbers: C-228-377-3186, D-312-597-1110. Police for FAMCAMP, C-228-377-3040.

**LOCATION:** Off base. From I-10 take I-110 south to US-90 west approximately 5.5 miles to Beauvoir Road (before Coliseum), right 1.5 miles to Pass Road, right 1 mile to Jim Money Road, left to Thrower Park Housing, right on Annex Road .25 miles. FAMCAMP is five miles west of gate 7. USMRA: Page 43 (F-10). NMC: Biloxi, two miles east.

**GENERAL INFORMATION:** Operated by Keesler AFB, off base, year round. Military personnel active, reservists, retired, DoD civilians. No advance reservations. Address: Outdoor Recreation, 81 SVS/SVRO, 625 Marina Drive, Keesler AFB, MS 39534-2623. C-228-377-3160/3186/0002, D-312-597-3160/3186/0002.

**RV, CAMPING/FAMCAMP:**     Camper Spaces-40

**ATTRACTIONS:** Mississippi Gulf Coast holds a wealth of history. In Biloxi, tours are available daily at Beauvoir, the home of Jefferson Davis. The marina is located off Ploesti Drive on Back Bay and offers a park, boating and fishing. Numerous large casinos line the beach in Biloxi and Gulfport.

*For detailed information about this off-base recreation facility, as well as on-base recreation facilities, golf courses and marinas, consult Military Living's Military RV, Camping and Outdoor Recreation Around the World.*

# KEY FIELD (MS13R2)

186th ARW
6255 M Street
Meridian, MS 39307-7112

**TELEPHONE NUMBER INFORMATION:** Main installation numbers: C-601-484-9000, D-312-778-9210. WEB: 186arw.ang.af.mil

**LOCATION:** From I-20 west, take US-45 south, Air National Guard signs clearly marked. Field is east of US-45. USMRA: Page 43 (F-6). NMC: Meridian, within the city limits.

**GENERAL INFORMATION:** Mississippi Air National Guard, 186 Air Refueling Wing.

**TEMPORARY MILITARY LODGING:** None. See Meridian NAS listing.

**RV, CAMPING/FAMCAMP:** None. Nearest facility is more than 100 miles away.

**SPACE-A:** Very limited, C-601-484-9730, D-312-778-9730. Fax: C-484-9470, D-312-778-9470

**LOGISTICAL SUPPORT:**               Exchange-485-3072

**ADMINISTRATIVE SUPPORT:** None. See Meridian NAS listing.

**HEALTH & WELFARE:**               Medical-484-9206

**REST & RECREATION:** None. See Meridian NAS listing.

**ATTRACTIONS:** Historic Homes, Vicksburg National Battlefield Park 120 miles west.

# MERIDIAN NAVAL AIR STATION (MS04R2)

1155 Rosenbaum Avenue, Suite 13
Meridian Naval Air Station, MS 39309-5003

**TELEPHONE NUMBER INFORMATION:** Main installation numbers: C-601-679-2211, D-312-637-2211.

**LOCATION:** Take MS-39 north from Meridian, for 12 miles to four-lane access road. Clearly marked. Right for three miles to NAS main gate. USMRA: Page 43 (G-6). NMC: Meridian, 15 miles southwest.

**GENERAL INFORMATION:** Naval Air Training Wing, Naval Technical Training Center, Marine Aviation Training Support Group and Regional Counterdrug Training Academy.

**TEMPORARY MILITARY LODGING:** Lodging office, 24 hours daily. Building 218 (CBQ), Fuller Road, BEQ C-601-679-2186, D-312-637-2186, Fax: C-601-679-2745.

**RV, CAMPING/FAMCAMP:** None. Nearest facility is more than 100 miles away.

**SPACE-A:** Pax Terminal, Building 1, 1400-0300 Mon-Thu, 1400-2200 Fri, C-601-679-2505, D-312-637-2505, Fax: C-601-679-2036, D-312-637-2036 Flights to CONUS destinations via Admin Aircraft.

**LOGISTICAL SUPPORT:**

| | |
|---|---|
| Bank-679-2585 | Barber Shop-679-2641 |
| Beauty Shop-679-8411 | Book Store-679-2568 |
| Cafeteria-679-2681 | Child Care-679-2362 |
| Child Dev Center-679-2652 | Commissary-679-2554 |
| Conv Store-679-2568 | Credit Union-693-8569 |

| | |
|---|---|
| Dining Facilities-679-2634 | Dry Cleaner-679-3430 |
| Education Office-679-2671 | Exchange-679-8461 |
| Fast Food-679-2650 | Gas Station-679-8553 |
| Laundry-679-3430 | Package Store-679-2653 |
| Postal Service-679-2580 | SATO-679-2346 |
| Snack Bar-679-2505 | |

**ADMINISTRATIVE SUPPORT:**

| | |
|---|---|
| CDO-679-2958 | Fire Dept-679-2336 |
| Housing Office-679-2555 | Legal-679-2590 |
| Locator-679-2301 | Pass/ID Office-679-2302 |
| Police-679-2601 | Public Affairs-679-2602 |
| Quarter Deck-679-2528 | |

**HEALTH & WELFARE:**

| | |
|---|---|
| American Red Cross-679-2679 | Chapel-679-2139 |
| Dental | Family Services-679-2360 |
| Central Appts-679-2633 | Medical-679-2633 |
| Clinic-679-2633 | Navy-MC Relief-679-2504 |
| Emergency-679-2633 | |

**REST & RECREATION:**

| | |
|---|---|
| Auto Hobby Shop-679-2609 | Bowling-679-2651 |
| Fitness Center-679-2379 | Golf Course-679-2526 |
| Gym-679-2379 | ITT-679-2636 |
| Library-679-2623 | MWR-679-2109 |
| Outdoor Rec-679-2731 | Rec Center-679-2640 |
| Swimming-ext 3470/3402 | Wood Hobby Shop-679-2609 |
| Youth Center-679-2687 | |

**ATTRACTIONS:** Lake Okatibbee, 10 miles west, Jimmie Rodgers Museum, Monument and annual music festival in Meridian, Meridian Breakmen Professional Baseball Club (Independent-Big South League), Meridian Little Theatre, Meridian Art Museum, Meridian Symphony Orchestra, Mississippi State Games, Dunn's Falls water park, 11 miles south.

# PASCAGOULA NAVAL STATION (MS06R2)

Building 10
Pascagoula, MS 39595-5000

**TELEPHONE NUMBER INFORMATION:** Main installation numbers: C-228-761-2140, D-312-358-2140. E-mail: pao@ns-pascogoula.navy.mil

**LOCATION:** From I-10 east, exit 69, four miles south to Highway 90, four miles west to Ingalls Access Road, one mile to Naval Station Causeway, three miles to the gate. USMRA: Page 43 (G-10). NMC: Mobile, Alabama, 30 miles east. NMI: Kesler, 30 miles west.

**GENERAL INFORMATION:** Shore Intermediate Maintenance Activity, Fleet Industrial Supply Center Detachment, Branch Medical Clinic, Branch Dental Clinic, U.S. Coast Guard Station.

**TEMPORARY MILITARY LODGING:** A 154-person combined Bachelor Quarters is sometimes used as temporary lodging. C-228-761-2182, D-312-358-2182. Also see Keesler AFB listing.

**RV, CAMPING/FAMCAMP:** None. See Keesler AFB listing.

**SPACE-A:** None. See Keesler AFB listing.

**LOGISTICAL SUPPORT:**

| | |
|---|---|
| Barber Shop-761-5460 | Beauty Shop-761-5460 |
| Book Store Nex-761-5133 | Convenience Store Nex-761-5133 |
| Credit Union-761-5658 | Education Center-761-5888 |
| Exchange-761-5133 | Snack Bar 761-5800 |

**ADMINISTRATIVE SUPPORT:**

| | |
|---|---|
| CDO-761-2020 | Fire Dept-761-2027 |
| Housing Office-377-2421 | Legal-761-2372 |
| Locator-761-2017 | OOD-761-2183 |
| Pass/ID Office-761-2017 | Police (Security)-761-2020 |
| Quarter Deck-761-2183 | |

**HEALTH & WELFARE:**
CHAMPUS-761-2365
Dental-761-2395
Medical-761-2222
  Central Appointments-1-800-700-8603
  Emergency-761-3333
  Health Benefits Advisor-761-2215

Chapel-761-2010
Family Services-761-4281
TRICARE-761-2365

**REST & RECREATION:**
ITT-761-2432
Fitness Center-761-2107

MWR-761-2184
Gym-761-2107

**OTHER FACILITIES AVAILABLE:** Ball fields, Tennis Courts, Cyber Cafe, USO.

**ATTRACTIONS:** Gulf Islands National Seashore, Sheppard State Park and beautiful beaches.

## UNITED STATES NAVAL HOME (MS08R2)

1800 Beach Drive
Gulfport, MS 39507-1597

**TELEPHONE NUMBER INFORMATION:** Main installation numbers: C-1-800-332-3527, C-228-897-4000. WEB: www.afrh.com/index.html

**LOCATION:** From I-10, exit Hwy 49 south, take Hwy 90 east. After Cowan Road (approximately four miles), take second left onto Beach Drive, one block to gate. USMRA: Page 43 (F-10).

**GENERAL INFORMATION:** Retirement home for Naval personnel.

**LOGISTICAL SUPPORT:**    Shoppette-897-4000

**ATTRACTIONS:** Seabee Museum, Gulf Coast, beaches, and water sports. Cities of Mobile and New Orleans, short drives.

## VICKSBURG MUNICIPAL AIRPORT (MS12R2)

Reserve Center, 386th Transportation Co., 1000 Lee Street
Vicksburg, MS 39180-9616

**TELEPHONE NUMBER INFORMATION:** Main installation numbers: C-601-636-4925.

**LOCATION:** Take US-61 south from I-20 east or west for six miles, exit west to airport. USMRA: Page 43 (C-6). NMC: Vicksburg, six miles north.

**SPACE-A:** Call C-601-636-4925 for information.

**ATTRACTIONS:** City of Vicksburg: historic tours, National Military Park, toy soldiers museum, houses of the Old South, and riverboat casino gambling.

## WATERWAYS EXPERIMENT STATION (MS10R2)

3909 Halls Ferry Road
Vicksburg, MS 39180-5000

**TELEPHONE NUMBER INFORMATION:** Main installation number: C-601-636-3111. WEB: www.wes.army.mil

**LOCATION:** From I-20, exit 1-C, one mile south on Halls Ferry Road. USMRA: Page 43 (C-6). NMC: Vicksburg, five miles west.

**TEMPORARY MILITARY LODGING:** None. Nearest facility is more than 100 miles away.

**RV, CAMPING/FAMCAMP:** None. Nearest facility is more than 100 miles away.

**SPACE-A:** None. See Vicksburg Municipal Airport listing or Jackson IAP listings.

**LOGISTICAL SUPPORT:**
Cafeteria-634-2560

Exchange-634-2136

**ADMINISTRATIVE SUPPORT:**    SDO/NCO-634-2513

**HEALTH AND WELFARE:**    CHAMPUS-634-5790

**REST & RECREATION:** Fitness Center on base.

**ATTRACTIONS:** Visitors facility, self-guided tours. City of Vicksburg: historic tours, National Military Park, toy soldiers museum, houses of the Old South, and riverboat casino gambling.

# MISSOURI

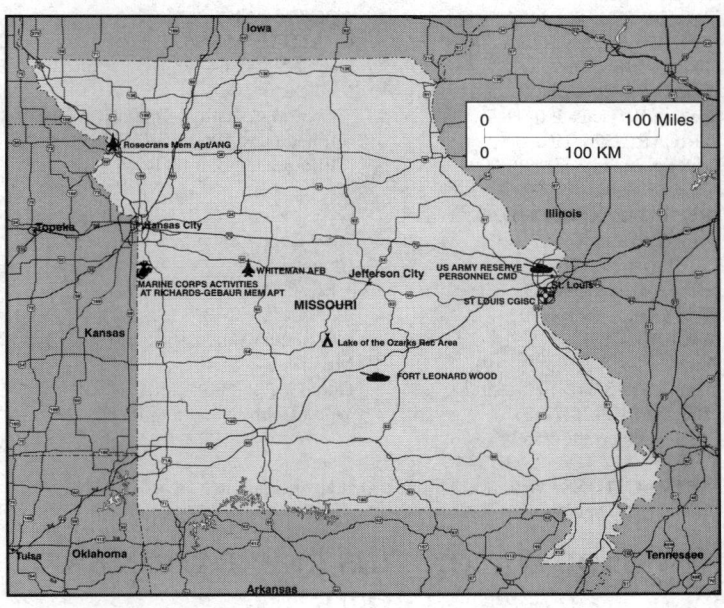

## FORT LEONARD WOOD (MO03R2)

US Army Engineering Center & Fort Leonard Wood
ATTN: ATZT-GC
Hoge Hall, Building 3200
Fort Leonard Wood, MO 65473-5000

**TELEPHONE NUMBER INFORMATION:** Main installation numbers: C-573-596-0131, D-312-581-0110. WEB: wood.army.mil

**LOCATION:** Two miles south of I-44 exit 161 south, adjacent to St. Robert & Waynesville, at Fort Leonard Wood exit. USMRA: Page 81 (E-6). NMC: Springfield, 85 miles southwest.

**GENERAL INFORMATION:** Basic training installation and Army, Navy, Marines, Air Force Training Center for Engineer Corps, military police and chemical defense personnel.

**TEMPORARY MILITARY LODGING:** Lodging office, Building 470, Missouri Avenue, 24 hours daily, C-573-596-0999, or 1-800-677-8356.

**RV, CAMPING/FAMCAMP:** Operates Lake of the Ozarks Recreation Area off post, 60 miles northwest of post. See Lake of the Ozarks Recreation Area listing for more information.

**SPACE-A:** Waynesville Regional Airport at Forney Field (WRAFF), Base Ops, 24 hours daily, C-573-596-0165/4819, D-312-581-0165, Fax: C-573-596-0166, D-312-581-0166. Flights to CONUS.

**LOGISTICAL SUPPORT:**

Bank-329-2000/3151
Beauty Shop-329-2212
Cafeteria-329-3601
Carlson Wagonlit Travel-329-3231
Child Dev Center-596-0197

Barber Shop-329-3655
Book Store-329-6034
Car Rental-329-6688
Child Care-596-1028
Class Six-329-6333

Commissary-596-0689
Credit Union-329-3151
Dry Cleaner-329-3490
Gas Station-329-3373
Shoppette-329-2777/6200
Visitor Center-596-8015

Conv Store-329-2777
Dining Facilities-596-6533
Exchange-329-2200
Postal Service-329-2717
Snack Bar-329-5677

**ADMINISTRATIVE SUPPORT:**
Fire Dept-596-0965
Legal-596-0629
Pass/ID Office-596-0744
Public Affairs-563-4015

Housing Office-596-0965
Locator-596-0677
Police-596-6141
SDO-563-6126

**HEALTH & WELFARE:**
American Red Cross-329-3334
Army Emergency Relief-596-0186
Chapel-596-0309
Family Services-596-0195
Retiree Services-596-0947
TRICARE-596-0552
Veterinary Services-596-0094

ACS-596-0186
CHAMPUS-596-9427
Dental-596-0364
Medical
  Central Appts-596-1490
  Emergency-596-0456/2157
  Information-596-0094

**REST & RECREATION:**
Arts & Crafts-596-0242
Bowling-596-1498
Fitness Center-596-4359
Golf Course-596-4770
Gym-596-4359
Library-563-4113
MWR-329-3300
Theater-596-1267/2531
Youth Center-596-2559

Auto Hobby Shop-596-0243
Clubs
  EM-329-6000
  NCO-329-6533
  O-329-6500
Marinas-346-5640
Outdoor Rec-596-4223
Wood Hobby Shop-596-0242

**ATTRACTIONS:** Near Lake of the Ozarks recreational areas and U.S. Army Engineer Museum.

# LAKE OF THE OZARKS RECREATION AREA (MO01R2)
Route 1, Box 380
Linn Creek, MO 65052-5000

**TELEPHONE NUMBER INFORMATION:** Main installation numbers: C-573-596-0131, D-312-581-0110. Police for rec area, C-573-346-3693.

**LOCATION:** Located on Grand Glaze Arm of the Lake of the Ozarks in the center of a State Wildlife Refuge. From I-70 take US-63 south to Jefferson City, then take US-54 to Linn Creek area; left at State Road A for six miles to Freedom, left on Lake Road A-33 about five miles. From I-44 northeast of Springfield, MO-7 northwest to Richland; right on State Road A and travel about 20 miles to Freedom; right on Lake Road A-33 about five miles. USMRA: Page 81 (D-6). NMC: Jefferson City, 40 miles northeast.

**GENERAL INFORMATION:** Situated on 360-acre reserve with excellent fishing and beautiful scenery. Operated by Fort Leonard Wood, off season early April to end of October (full season Memorial Day weekend to Labor Day weekend). Military personnel active, retired, NG, Reserve, DoD and NAF employees. Check in at Rental Office, Building 528, after 1500, check out everyday. Reservations: Required by phone or in person at the Lake of the Ozarks Recreation Area office, Building 528 (3 March-23 May, 0900-1700 Mon-Wed; 24 May-1 September, 0900-1700 Mon-Fri). No mail reservations. C-573-346-5640.

**TEMPORARY MILITARY LODGING:**
Duplexes-2
Mobile homes-27
Cabins-3

**RV, CAMPING/FAMCAMP:**
Camper spaces-16
Camper/tent spaces-21

**ATTRACTIONS:** Nearby attractions include Osage Beach, Ozark Caverns, musical shows, theme park, water slides, helicopter rides, etc. Historical and recreational points of interest surround the area.

*For detailed information about this off-base recreation facility, as well as other recreation facilities, golf courses, marinas and temporary military lodging, consult Military Living's Military RV, Camping and Outdoor Recreation Around the World or Military Living's Temporary Military Lodging Around the World.*

# MARINE CORPS ACTIVITIES AT RICHARDS-GEBAUR MEMORIAL AIRPORT (MO02R2)
15424 Andrews Road
Kansas City, MO 64147-1219

**TELEPHONE NUMBER INFORMATION:** Main installation number: C-816-843-3800.

**LOCATION:** From US-71 north or south, take 155th Street exit west to Andrews Road, left on Andrews Road. Between Grandview & Belton. USMRA: Page 81 (B-5), page 89 (B-5). NMC: Kansas City, 17 miles north.

**GENERAL INFORMATION:** Marine Corps Support Activity, Marine Corps Reserve Support Command, 24th Marine Regiment, 9th Marine Corps District.

**TEMPORARY MILITARY LODGING:** Lodging office, 15820 Elmwood, Kansas City, MO 64147. 0630-2345 Mon-Fri, 0730-2345 Sat-Sun, C-816-843-3850/3851, D-312-894-3850/3851, Fax: C-816-843-3857, D-312-894-3857.

**RV, CAMPING/FAMCAMP:** None. See Lake of the Ozarks Rec Area listing.

**SPACE-A:** None. See Rosecrans Memorial Airport/ANG listing.

**LOGISTICAL SUPPORT:**
Barber Shop (part-time)-843-3713
Exchange-331-2019
Credit Union-331-6600
SATO-843-3404/6

**ADMINISTRATIVE SUPPORT:**
Housing Office-843-3866/3863
Public Affairs-843-3051
Pass/ID Office-843-3816

**HEALTH & WELFARE:**
CHAMPUS-843-3900 (9th MCD)
Dental-843-3670/1/2
Health Benefits-843-3816
843-3816 (MCSA)
Family Services-843-3650
TRICARE-843-3667/6

**REST & RECREATION:**
Consol Club-843-3840/1
MWR-843-3870/1

**ATTRACTIONS:** Kansas City, the city of fountains. Harry S. Truman Library and home in Independence, a short drive away; KC Royals, KC Blades and KC Chiefs pro sports teams; Worlds of Fun; Oceans of Fun; Swope Park Zoo; Starlight (outdoor theater); Plaza Shopping (and Christmas lighting); Hallmark Crown Center.

# ROSECRANS MEMORIAL AIRPORT/ AIR NATIONAL GUARD (MO07R2)
705 Memorial Drive
St Joseph, MO 64503-9307

**TELEPHONE NUMBER INFORMATION:** Main installation numbers: C-816-236-3300. D-312-956-3300.

**LOCATION:** From US-36 east or west exit west of I-229 on MO-238. Straight 1.5 miles to airport entrance. USMRA: Page 81 (B-3). NMC: St. Joseph, four miles southeast. NMI: Fort Leavenworth, KS, 28 miles south.

**GENERAL INFORMATION:** Home of the 139th Airlift Wing. All support facilities of a regional airport.

**TEMPORARY MILITARY LODGING:** None. See Fort Leavenworth listing.

**RV, CAMPING/FAMCAMP:** None. Nearest facility is more than 100 miles away.

**SPACE-A:** Information: C- 816-236-3260, D-312-956-3260. Rec. C-816-236-3472, D-312-956-3472. Fax: C-816-236-3239, D-312-956-3239

**LOGISTICAL SUPPORT:**      Cafeteria-364-0319

**HEALTH & WELFARE:** None. See Fort Leavenworth listing.

**ATTRACTIONS:** In St. Joseph, Poly Express museums, Jesse James' home, National Military Heritage Museum and St. Joseph River Boat Casino.

## ST. LOUIS COAST GUARD INTEGRATED SUPPORT COMMAND (MO05R2)
1222 Spruce Street
St Louis, MO 63103-5000

**TELEPHONE NUMBER INFORMATION:** Main installation number: C-314-539-3900, ext 350.

**LOCATION:** Take I-70/44 west, exit I-55 to Bircher Boulevard south. USMRA: Page 81 (G-5), page 91 (B-3,4). NMC: St. Louis, in city limits.

**GENERAL INFORMATION:** Three WLR Class Buoy Tenders, two Reserve Units.

**TEMPORARY MILITARY LODGING:** None. See Scott AFB, IL listing.

**RV, CAMPING/FAMCAMP:** None. See Lake of the Ozarks Rec Area listing.

**SPACE-A:** None. See Scott AFB, IL listing.

**LOGISTICAL SUPPORT:**
Carlson Wagonlit Travel-421-0500          Exchange-845-2467/9303

**ADMINISTRATIVE SUPPORT:**      Locator-832-5941

**HEALTH & WELFARE:**      AF Aid-618-256-1110

**REST & RECREATION:**      EM Club-832-5021

**ATTRACTIONS:** St. Louis, Gateway Arch, *USS Inaugural* Minesweeper, planetarium, Ulysses S. Grant's farm.

## UNITED STATES ARMY RESERVE PERSONNEL COMMAND (MO10R2)
Building 101, 9700 Page Boulevard
St Louis, MO 63132-5000

**TELEPHONE NUMBER INFORMATION:** Main installation numbers: C-314-427-8188.

**LOCATION:** From I-70 west, take Page exit, turn right, at third light, take left into Federal Records Branch. USMRA: Page 91 (A-2). NMC: St. Louis, in city limits.

**GENERAL INFORMATION:** Career management and training for Reserve personnel, also manages Standby Reserve and Retired Reserve.

**LOGISTICAL SUPPORT:**      Exchange-427-8188

## WHITEMAN AIR FORCE BASE (MO04R2)
509 Spirit Boulevard, Suite 111
Whiteman Air Force Base, MO 65305-5097

**TELEPHONE NUMBER INFORMATION:** Main installation numbers: C-660-687-1110, D-312-975-1110. E-mail: 509bwpa@whiteman.af.mil
WEB: www.whiteman.af.mil

**LOCATION:** From I-70 east exit 49 south to US-13 south to US-50 east for ten miles, Hwy 23 (south) which leads to base, south of US-50 and east of MO-23. USMRA: Page 81 (C-5). NMC: Kansas City, 60 miles northeast.

**GENERAL INFORMATION:** Air Combat Command Base. 509th Bomb Wing and Air Force Reserve 442nd Fighter Wing, and the Missouri Army National Guard.

**TEMPORARY MILITARY LODGING:** Lodging office, Building 3200, Spirit Boulevard, 24 hours daily, C-660-687-1844, D-312-975-1844, Fax: C-660-687-3052. DV/VIP C-660-687-7144.

**RV, CAMPING/FAMCAMP:** None. See Lake of the Ozarks Rec Area listing.

**SPACE-A:** Base Ops, C-660-687-3101, D-312-975-3101, flights to CONUS locations.

**LOGISTICAL SUPPORT:**

| | |
|---|---|
| Bank-563-2002 | Barber Shop-563-5888 |
| Beauty Shop-563-3003 | Child Care-687-1180 |
| Child Dev-Center-687-5588 | Class VI-563-5445 |
| Commissary-687-5655 | Conv Store-563-5445 |
| Credit Union-563-3084 | Dining Facilities-687-5476 |
| Dry Cleaner-563-2536 | Education Center-687-5750 |
| Exchange-563-3003 | Food Court-563-3167 |
| Gas Station-563-5445 | Laundry-563-2536 |
| Postal Service-687-5097 | Shoppette-563-5445 |
| Travel Office-563-4120 | Visitor Center-687-2833 |

**ADMINISTRATIVE SUPPORT:**

| | |
|---|---|
| Fire Dept-911 | Housing Office-687-7171 |
| Legal-687-6809 | Locator-687-1841 |
| Pass/ID Office 687-6406 | Police-687-3700 |
| Public Affairs 687-6123 | |

**HEALTH & WELFARE:**

| | |
|---|---|
| Chapel-687-3652 | Dental-Central Appts-687-2201 |
| Family Services-687-3660 | Emergency-687-2188 |
| Medical-Central Appts-563-9100 | TRICARE-1-888-TRI-WEST |
| Emergency-687-2188 | Veterinary Services-687-2667 |

**REST & RECREATION:**

| | |
|---|---|
| Arts & Crafts-687-6492 | Auto Hobby Shop-687-5689 |
| Bowling-687-5114 | Combined Club-563-2273 |
| Community Center-687-5617 | Fitness Center-687-5496 |
| Golf Course-687-5573 | Indoor Recreation-687-6492 |
| Library-687-5614 | MWR-687-5617 |
| Swimming-ext 5502 | Outdoor Recreation-687-5567 |
| Theater-687-5110 | The Club-563-2273 |
| Youth Center-687-3196 | Youth Services-687-3199 |

**ATTRACTIONS:** Outdoor sports, Lake of the Ozarks region, Kansas City.

# MONTANA

## FORT HARRISON SITE (MT07R3)
P.O. Box 4789, Building 40
Helena, MT 59604-4789

**TELEPHONE NUMBER INFORMATION:** Main installation numbers: C-406-841-3000.

**LOCATION:** I-15 to Helena at the Capital exit to Avon (US0-12), toward Elliston. Two miles out of Helena, sign Camp Stan Stevens/Fort Harrison on right to gate, north of US-12. USMRA: Page 99 (D-5). NMC: Helena, two miles east.

**GENERAL INFORMATION:** Exchange site, VA regional office and medical facility.

**LOGISTICAL SUPPORT:**      Exchange-444-7910

**ATTRACTIONS:** State capital, national forests.

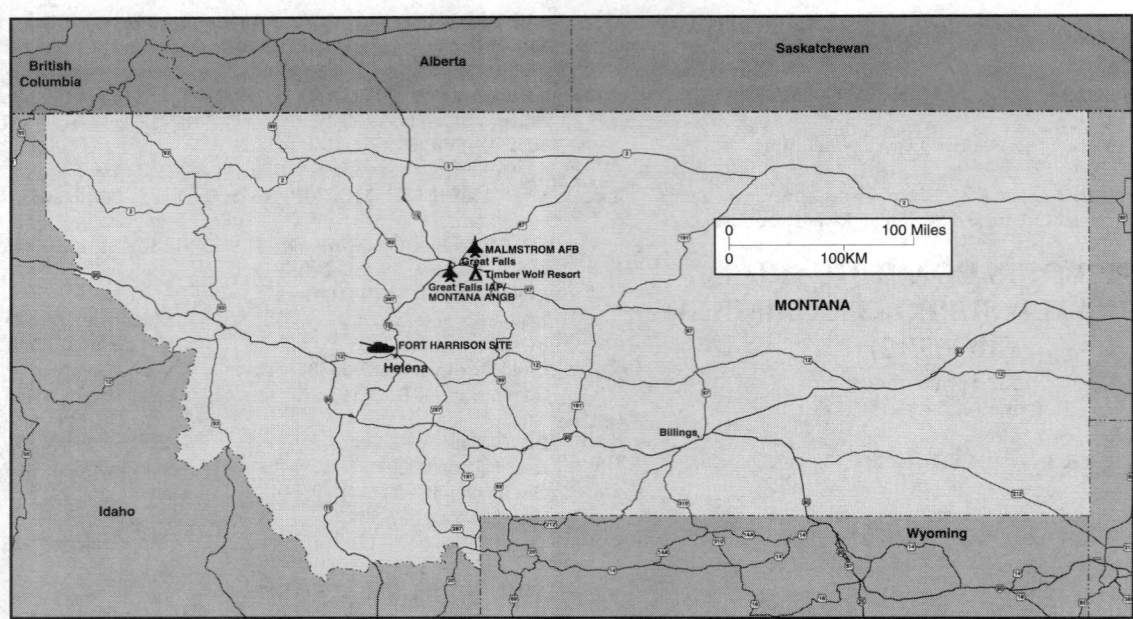

# GREAT FALLS INTERNATIONAL AIRPORT/ MONTANA AIR NATIONAL GUARD BASE (MT06R3)

120th Fighter Wing
2800 Airport Avenue B
Great Falls, MT 59404-5570

**TELEPHONE NUMBER INFORMATION:** Main installation numbers: C-406-791-6220, D-312-279-2220, Fax: C-406-791-6488.

**LOCATION:** Great Falls International Airport exit 277 is off I-15, and is one mile south of the 10th Avenue south exit. USMRA: Page 99 (D-4). NMC: Great Falls, one mile.

**GENERAL INFORMATION:** Montana Air National Guard, 120th Fighter Wing.

**TEMPORARY MILITARY LODGING**: None. See Malmstrom AFB listing.

**RV, CAMPING/FAMCAMP:** None. See Malmstrom AFB listing.

**SPACE-A:** 406-453-7613

**LOGISTICAL SUPPORT:**

| | |
|---|---|
| Credit Union-ext 2306 | Dining Facilities-ext 2259 |
| Exchange-791-6299 | Shoppette-ext 2299 |
| Snack Bar-791-6224 | Travel Office-ext 6277 |

**ADMINISTRATIVE SUPPORT:**

| | |
|---|---|
| Fire Dept-ext 2232 | Legal-ext 2180 |
| Pass/ID Office-ext 2337 | Police-ext 2336 |
| Public Affairs-ext 2228 | |

**HEALTH & WELFARE:** Chapel-ext 2300

**REST & RECREATION:** None. See Malmstrom AFB listing.

**ATTRACTIONS:** C.M. Russel Museum, Paris Gibson Art Gallery, Malmstrom Aircraft Museum, Heritage Park, Giant Springs State Park.

# MALMSTROM AIR FORCE BASE (MT03R3)

341st Space Wing, 21, 77th Street North
Malmstrom Air Force Base, MT 59402-5000

**TELEPHONE NUMBER INFORMATION:** Main installation numbers: C-406-731-1110, D-312-632-1110. E-mail: wollardc@malmstrom.af.mil
WEB: www.malmstrom.af.mil

**LOCATION:** From I-15 take 10th Avenue South, exit 278 to Malmstrom AFB. From the east take Malmstrom exit off US-87/89. Clearly marked. USMRA: Page 99 (D,E-4). NMC: Great Falls, one mile west.

**GENERAL INFORMATION:** Air Force Space Command Base and 341st Missile Wing (AFSPC); 819th Red Horse Squadron (Air Combat Command).

**TEMPORARY MILITARY LODGING:** Lodging office, Malmstrom Inn, Building 1860, 24 hours daily C-406-727-8600; D-632-3394.

**RV, CAMPING/FAMCAMP:** FAMCAMP on base, May-October, C-406-731-3263, D-312-632-3263, 25 camper spaces with full hookups, five camper/tent spaces without hookups. Timber Wolf Resort off base, see separate listing.

**SPACE-A:** None. Nearest facility is more than 100 miles away.

**LOGISTICAL SUPPORT:**

| | |
|---|---|
| Barber Shop-761-8131 | Beauty Shop-452-2552 |
| Cafeteria-731-4607 | Child Care-731-2377 |
| Child Dev. Center-731-2417 | Class VI-761-8004 |
| Commissary-452-6993 | Conv Store-761-8004 |
| Credit Union-761-8300 | Dry Cleaner-453-1031 |
| Education Center-731-3531 | Exchange-761-8004 |
| Gas Station-761-7333 | Postal Service-454-0716 |
| Snack Bar-761-7480 | Travel-731-2934 |
| Visitor Center-731-3892 | |

**ADMINISTRATIVE SUPPORT:**

| | |
|---|---|
| Fire Dept-731-1911 | Housing Office-731-3660 |
| Legal-731-2878 | Locator-731-4121/727-3895 |
| Pass/ID Office-731-3246 | Police-731-3827 |
| Public Affairs-731-4044 | |

**HEALTH & WELFARE:**

| | |
|---|---|
| Air Force Aid Society-731-4900 | Chapel-731-3721 |
| Dental-Central Appts-731-2846 | Family Services-731-4900 |
| Medical-Clinic-731-3701 | Medical-Information-731-3424 |
| Central Appointments-454-8240 | Retiree Services-452-9988 |
| Emergency-731-1911 | CHAMPUS-731-4396 |
| TRICARE-1-888-874-9378/454-8240 | Veterinary Services-731-6295 |

**REST & RECREATION:**

| | |
|---|---|
| Arts & Crafts-731-3691 | Auto Hobby Shop-731-3777 |
| Bowling-731-2695/2494 | Club Malmstrom-761-6430 |
| Community Center-731-4633 | Fitness Center-731-3621 |
| Library-731-4638 | Gym-731-3621 |
| Outdoor Rec-731-3263 | Sports Arena-ext 3621 |
| Theater-731-3236 | Wood Hobby Shop-731-3232 |
| Youth Center-731-4634 | |

**ATTRACTIONS:** Big Sky Country, snow skiing, wildlife, rafting, hunting, Canadian fishing trips, Lewis and Clark Interpretive Center and Charles Russell Museum.

## TIMBER WOLF RESORT (MT09R3)

341 SVS/SVRO
Outdoor Recreation
Malmstrom AFB, MT 59402-6863

**TELEPHONE NUMBER INFORMATION:** Main installation numbers: C-406-387-9653 or toll free C-877-846-9653.

**LOCATION:** Off base. From I-15 north of Great Falls and Conrad, take Route 44 west past Valier to Hwy 89 north to Browning. From Browning, take Hwy 2 to Hungry Horse. Camp is on left. USMRA: Page 99 (D-3). NMC: Great Falls, one mile west.

**GENERAL INFORMATION:** Operated by Malmstrom AFB, off base, May-September. For more information contact 341 SVS/SV RO, Outdoor Recreation, Malmstrom AFB, MT 59402-6863. C-406-387-9653 or toll free C-877-846-9653.

**RV, CAMPING/FAMCAMP:** Trailers-3

**ATTRACTIONS:** Big Sky Country, snow skiing, wildlife, rafting, hunting, Canadian fishing trips.

*For detailed information about this off-base recreation facility, as well as on-base recreation facilities, golf courses and marinas, consult Military Living's Military RV, Camping and Outdoor Recreation Around the World.*

# NEBRASKA

## CAMP ASHLAND (NE03R3)

Bldg. 508, 220 County Road "A"
Ashland, NE 68003-9801

**TELEPHONE NUMBER INFORMATION:** Main installation numbers: C-402-944-2110.

**LOCATION:** From I-80 north or south, exit 432 east, Highway 31, north one quarter mile to Highway 5, east four and a half miles to Highway 53 north, one half mile to Camp. USMRA: Page 82 (I-5). NMC: Omaha, 25 miles northeast.

**GENERAL INFORMATION:** Army National Guard training site. Regional Training Institute-Nebraska.

**TEMPORARY MILITARY LODGING:** Call C-402-944-2479 ext. 200.

**RV, CAMPING/FAMCAMP:** Call C-402-944-2110.

**SPACE-A:** None. See Offutt AFB listing.

**LOGISTICAL SUPPORT:**                Shoppette-944-2750

**ADMINISTRATIVE SUPPORT:**         Public Affairs-471-7352

**HEALTH & WELFARE:** None. See Offutt AFB listing.

**REST & RECREATION:** None. See Offutt AFB listing.

**ATTRACTIONS:** Strategic Air Command Museum, Mahoney State Park, Henry Doorly Zoo, fishing, swimming, boating on nearby Platte River.

## LINCOLN MUNICIPAL AIRPORT/NEBRASKA AIR NATIONAL GUARD BASE (NE05R3)

155 Air Refueling Wing
2420 West Butler Avenue
Lincoln, NE 68524-1897

**TELEPHONE NUMBER INFORMATION:** Main installation numbers: C-402-458-1110, D-312-946-1110.

**LOCATION:** Adjacent to Lincoln Municipal Airport, right on I-80. From I-80 east or west, exit 399 west to airport. USMRA: Page 82 (I-5). NMC: Lincoln, two miles southeast.

**GENERAL INFORMATION:** Home of the 155th Air Refueling Wing, Air National Guard.

**TEMPORARY MILITARY LODGING:** None. See Offutt AFB listing.

**RV, CAMPING/FAMCAMP:** None. See Offutt AFB listing.

**SPACE-A:** Pax terminal C-402-458-1291, D-312-946-1291; Fax: C-402-458-1272, D-312-946-1272-

**LOGISTICAL SUPPORT:**                Exchange-474-3454

**ADMINISTRATIVE SUPPORT:**
Fire Dept-458-1500                      Legal-458-1122
Police-458-1563                          SDO/NCO-458-1266

**HEALTH & WELFARE:**                  Chapel-458-1121

**REST & RECREATION:**                 Consol Club-458-1125

**OTHER FACILITIES AVAILABLE:** Running track, softball diamond.

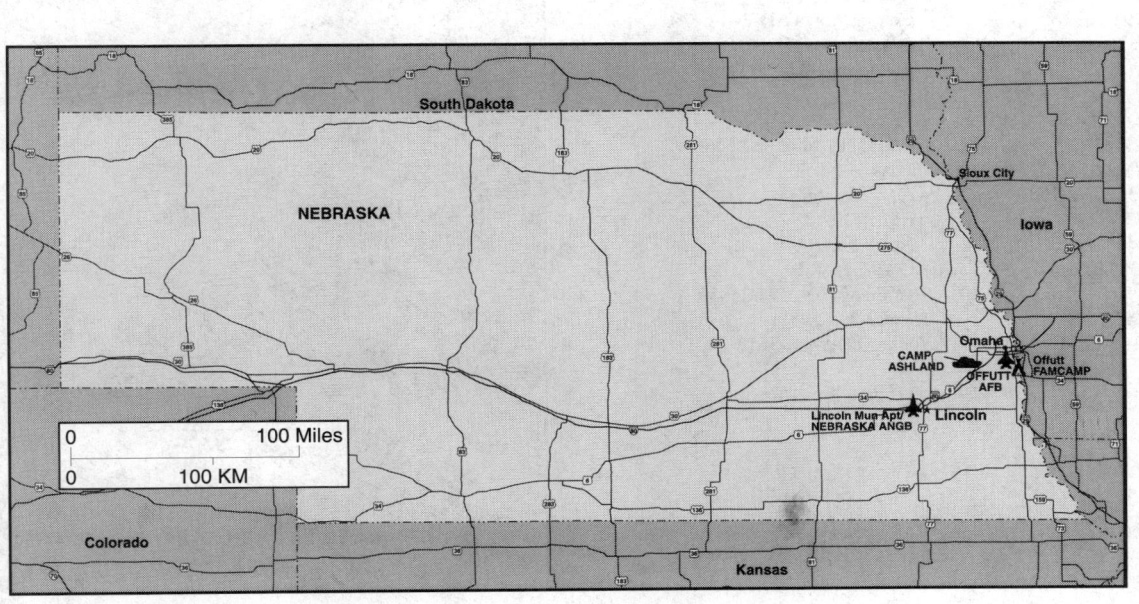

**ATTRACTIONS**: Home of state government, University of Nebraska, Elephant Hall at University of Nebraska, Nebraska State Historical Society Museum, and Lincoln Children's Zoo. Many fine restaurants, hotels/motels and area lakes with camping. "The Clean City."

## OFFUTT AIR FORCE BASE (NE02R3)
906 SAC Boulevard, Suite 1
Offutt Air Force Base, NE 68113-3206

**TELEPHONE NUMBER INFORMATION**: Main installation numbers: C-402-294-1110, D-312-271-1110.

**LOCATION**: From I-80 east or west, exit to US-75 south to AFB exit, 6.5 miles south of I-80/US-75 interchange, on east side of US-75. USMRA: Page 82 (I,J-5). NMC: Omaha, eight miles north.

**GENERAL INFORMATION**: Air Combat Command Base. 55th Wing, Headquarters U.S. STRATCOM, Air Force Weather Agency, and other support units.

**TEMPORARY MILITARY LODGING**: Lodging office, Building 44, Grants Pass Street, 24 hours daily, C-402-294-3671/9000, D-312-271-9000, Fax: C-294-3199, D-312-271-3199. All ranks. DV/VIP C-402-294-4212, D-312-271-4212.

**RV, CAMPING/FAMCAMP**: FAMCAMP on base, year round, C-402-294-2108, D-312-271-2108, 10 camper spaces with full hookups.

**SPACE-A**: Pax Term/Lounge, Building T-47, 0500-2100 Mon-Fri, 0700-1900 Sat-Sun, C-402-294-7111/8510, D-312-271-7111/8510, Recording: C-402-294-6235, D-312-271-6235. Fax: C-402-294-4070, D-312-271-4070. Flights to CONUS and OCONUS locations.

**LOGISTICAL SUPPORT:**

| | |
|---|---|
| Bank-291-1400 | Barber Shop-291-8521 |
| Beauty Shop-292-1520 | Cafeteria-291-9596 |
| Car Rental-292-9676 | Child Care-294-2203 |
| Class VI-292-7097 | Commissary-294-5920/6783 |
| Conv Store-292-0218 | Credit Union-292-8000 |
| Dining-294-3980 | Dry Cleaner-292-1232 |
| Education Office-294-5716 | Exchange-291-9100 |
| Food Court-291-9596 | Fast Food-292-6769 |
| Gas Station-291-8743 | Postal Service-294-3523 |
| Shoppette-291-9100 | |

**ADMINISTRATIVE SUPPORT:**

| | |
|---|---|
| Legal-294-3732 | Locator-294-5125 |
| Pass/ID Office-294-3932 | Police-294-6110 |

**HEALTH & WELFARE:**

| | |
|---|---|
| Chapel-294-6244/6051 | |
| Family Services-294-3111 | CHAMPUS-294-7424 |
| Retiree Services-294-7693 | Medical |
| TRICARE-293-6500 |   Central Appts AD-294-6477 |
| |   Dependents-292-5510 |
| |   Emergency-294-7334 |

**REST & RECREATION:**

| | |
|---|---|
| Arts & Crafts-ext 3872 | Auto Hobby Shop-ext 5564 |
| Bowling-ext 2514 | Clubs |
| Golf Course-ext 3362/292-1680 |   Aero-ext 3503 |
| Gym-ext 5904 |   EM-292-6785 |
| Library-ext 2533 |   NCO-292-1600 |
| Photo Hobby-ext 3872 |   O-292-1560 |
| MWR-294-4719 | Swimming-ext 2274/3593/6466 |
| Rec Center-ext 6247 | Theater-294-5951 |
| Wood Hobby Shop-ext 3318 | Youth Center-ext 5152 |

**ATTRACTIONS**: City of Omaha, Old Market area, Boys Town.

## OFFUTT FAMCAMP (NE01R3)
Outdoor Recreation
FAMCAMP, 55 SVS/SVRO
109 Grant Circle, Suite 101
Offutt AFB, NE 68113-2084

**TELEPHONE NUMBER INFORMATION**: Main installation numbers: C-402-294-1110, D-312-271-1110. Police for FAMCAMP, C-402-294-6110.

**LOCATION**: Off base. From I-80 in Omaha, take US-75 south to Bellevue. East on Mission Avenue (NE-370), through town, right on Hancock Street for 1.5 miles, left to base lake and FAMCAMP. USMRA: Page 82 (J-5). NMC: Omaha, eight miles north.

**GENERAL INFORMATION**: Operated by Offutt AFB, off base, year round. Military personnel active, reservist, retired, DoD civilians. Reservations: Outdoor Recreation, FAMCAMP, 55 SVS/SVRO, 109 Grant Circle, Suite 101, Offutt AFB, NE 68113-2084. C-402-294-2108, D-312-271-2108.

**RV, CAMPING/FAMCAMP:**
Camper Spaces-10                Tent Spaces-Wilderness

**ATTRACTIONS**: Open farm country, nearby Omaha.

*For detailed information about this off-base recreation facility, as well as on-base recreation facilities, golf courses and marinas, consult Military Living's Military RV, Camping and Outdoor Recreation Around the World.*

*Note: A new facility is scheduled for completion in mid-summer 1999 consisting of 30 units with E (110V/30/50A)/S/W hookups.*

# NEVADA

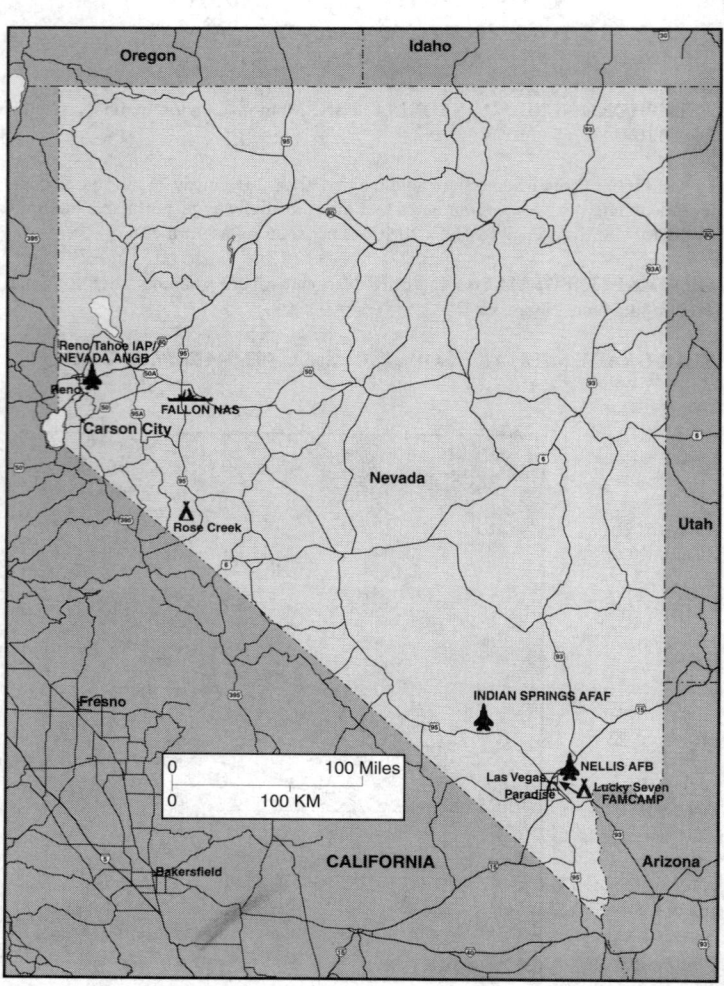

# FALLON NAVAL AIR STATION (NV02R4)

4755 Pasture Road
Fallon Naval Air Station, NV 89496-5000

**TELEPHONE NUMBER INFORMATION**: Main installation numbers: C-775-426-5161, D-312-890-2110. WEB: www.fallon.navy.mil

**LOCATION**: From Reno take I-80 east or west to Fernley (exit 48). Go to stop light and turn left (southeast) onto US Highway alternate 50 to Fallon. Once through Fallon, turn right on Crook Road, then left on Wildes Road, then right on Pasture Road to main gate. USMRA: Page 113 (C-4). NMC: Reno, 72 miles west.

**GENERAL INFORMATION**: Naval Strike & Air Warfare Center, Construction Battalion Unit 416, Strike Fighter Wing Detachment, VFC-13, Naval Air Station.

**TEMPORARY MILITARY LODGING**: Lodging office, 24 hours daily, BOQ C-775-428-3003, BEQ C-775-426-2515, D-312-890-2515. All ranks. DV/VIP C-775-428-2859, Fax: C-775-426-2408. Navy Lodge: C-775-428-2704 or 1-800-NAVY INN. Fax: C-775-423-3720.

**RV, CAMPING/FAMCAMP:** Fallon RV Park and Recreation Area on base, year round, C-775-426-2598, D-312-890-2598, 16 camper spaces with W&E hookups.

**SPACE-A:** Pax Term, hangar 7, Call for hours, C-775-426-3415, D-312-890-3415, flights to CONUS and OCONUS locations.

**LOGISTICAL SUPPORT:**

| | |
|---|---|
| Barber Shop-426-2547 | Beauty Shop-426-2547 |
| Cafeteria-426-2501 | Car Rental-426-2592 |
| Child Care-423-5808 | Child Dev Center-423-5808 |
| Commissary-426-3420 | Credit Union-426-2500 |
| Dining Facilities-426-2520 | Dry Cleaner-426-2484 |
| Exchange-426-2400 | Gas Station-426-2853 |
| Laundry-426-2484 | Postal Service-426-2738 |
| Snack Bar-426-3660 | Travel Office-426-2865 |

**ADMINISTRATIVE SUPPORT:**

| | |
|---|---|
| CDO-426-2715 | Fire Dept-911 |
| Housing Office-426-2788 | Legal-426-2711 |
| Locator-426-5161 | Pass/ID Office-426-2856 |
| Police-426-2853 (non emergency) | Public Affairs-426-2880 |

**HEALTH & WELFARE:**

| | |
|---|---|
| CHAMPUS-426-3102 | Chapel-426-2813 |
| Dental-426-3333 | Family Services-426-3333 |
| Medical | Navy-MC Relief-426-2739 |
|   Central Appts-426-3110 | |
|   Emergency-911 | |
|   Health Benefits-426-3102 | |

**REST & RECREATION:**

| | |
|---|---|
| Auto Hobby Shop-ext 2575 | Bowling-ext 2451 |
| Clubs | Fitness Center-ext 2251 |
|   CPO-ext 2483 | Gym-ext 2949 |
|   EM-ext 2445 | ITT-ext 2865 |
|   O-ext 2841/2625 | Library-ext 2599 |
| MWR-ext 2819 | Outdoor Rec-ext 2437/2279 |
| Theater-ext 2580 | Youth Center-423-4004 |

**ATTRACTIONS:** Reno, Carson City, Virginia City, and Lake Tahoe nearby.

# INDIAN SPRINGS AIR FORCE AUXILIARY FIELD (NV03R4)

3770 Duffer Drive
Indian Springs, NV 89018-5000

**TELEPHONE NUMBER INFORMATION**: Main installation numbers: C-775-652-0201, D-312-682-0201.

**LOCATION**: Off US-95, 47 miles northwest of Nellis Air Force Base. On the north side of US-95, take Indian Springs exit north. USMRA: Page 113 (F-8). NMC: Las Vegas, 45 miles southeast.

**GENERAL INFORMATION:** [...] airfield for Nellis AFB.

**TEMPORARY MILITA[...]**

**RV, CAMPING/FAM[...]** CAMP.

**SPACE-A:** None. Se[...]

**LOGISTICAL SUPPORT[...]**

**ADMINISTRATIVE SUPPORT: [...]**

**HEALTH & WELFARE:** [...]

**REST & RECREATION**: None. See Nellis AFB [...]

**ATTRACTIONS**: Desert area, Tolyabe National Forest a[...] south of US-95, nearby.

# LUCKY SEVEN FAMCAMP (NV04[...]

4907 Famcamp Drive
Las Vegas, NV 89115-5000

**TELEPHONE NUMBER INFORMATION:** Main installation numbers: C-702-643-3060. Police for FAMCAMP, C-702-652-2311. E-mail: famcamp@sus99.nellis.af.mil

**LOCATION:** Off base. From I-15 north of Las Vegas, exit east on Craig Road 48 west to Las Vegas Blvd North (NV-604), left onto Range Road (directly across from Nellis North Gate). Also from US-93/95 (Boulder Highway) in Las Vegas, go north on Nellis Blvd approximately eight miles, continue north on Las Vegas Blvd N (NV-604). From both routes, continue to North Gate, turn left onto Range Road directly across from gate. USMRA: Page 113 (G-9). NMC: Las Vegas, eight miles southwest.

**GENERAL INFORMATION:** Operated by Nellis AFB, off base, year round. Military personnel active, reservists, retired, DoD civilians, guests. Reservations (accepted up to 60 days in advance): 4907 FAMCAMP Drive, Las Vegas, NV 89115-5000. Phone-C-702-643-3060.

**RV, CAMPING/FAMCAMP:**

| | |
|---|---|
| Camper Spaces-48 | Tent Spaces-2 |

**ATTRACTIONS:** Located in desert Southwest with mountains on one side and Lake Mead National Recreation Area on the other. Easy drive to Grand Canyon. Las Vegas attractions nearby.

*For detailed information about this off-base recreation facility, as well as on-base recreation facilities, golf courses and marinas, consult Military Living's Military RV, Camping and Outdoor Recreation Around the World.*

# NELLIS AIR FORCE BASE (NV01R4)

4370 N Washington Boulevard
Nellis Air Force Base, NV 89191-5000

**TELEPHONE NUMBER INFORMATION:** Main installation numbers: C-702-652-1110, D-312-682-1110. WEB: www.nellis.af.mil

**LOCATION:** Off I-15. Also accessible from US-93/95. Exit 48 east on Craig Road to north on Las Vegas Blvd to main gate on right. Clearly marked. USMRA: Page 113 (G-9). NMC: Las Vegas, eight miles southwest.

**GENERAL INFORMATION:** Air Combat Command Base. Air Warfare Center, Combat Fighter units. USAF Air Demonstration Squadron, "The Thunderbirds."

**TEMPORARY MILITARY LODGING:** Lodging office, Building 780, 5990 Fitzgerald Boulevard, Nellis AFB NV 89191-6514, 24 hours daily, C-702-643-2710, D-312-682-2711. All ranks. DV/VIP C-702-652-2987.

**RV, CAMPING/FAMCAMP:** Lucky Seven FAMCAMP off base, year round, C-702-643-3060.

**SPACE-A:** Pax Term/Lounge, [...]
89191-7224, 0730-1630 daily, [...]
C-702-652-1561, flights to C[...]

**LOGISTICAL SUPPOR[...]**
Bank-651-8228
Beauty Shop-644-5558
Child Care-652-4241
Commissary-643-69[...]
Credit Union-457-[...]
Exchange-644-2[...]
Gas Station-643[...]
Postal Service[...]
Visitor Center[...]

**ADMINIS[...]**
Fire Dep[...]
Legal-6[...]
Pass/I[...]
Public[...]

...Building 1044, 6255 Depot Road, Nellis AFB NV
...C-702-652-2562/6099, D-312-682-2562/6099, Fax:
...ONUS locations.

### ...:

| | |
|---|---|
| | Barber Shop-643-9556 |
| | Car Rental-644-5567 |
| ...50 | Child Dev Center-652-4241 |
| ...000 | Conv Store-644-6375 |
| ...44 | Education Office-652-5280 |
| ...1686 | Fast Food-644-3374 |
| ...652-4679 | Package Store-643-3526 |
| ...652-3216 | SATO-644-5400 |

### ...RATIVE SUPPORT:

| | |
|---|---|
| ...-652-9630 | Housing Office-652-1840 |
| ...52-9188 | Locator-652-8134 |
| ...D Office-652-1845 | Police-652-2311 |
| ...c Affairs-652-2750 | SDO/NCO-652-2638 |

### ...ALTH & WELFARE:

| | |
|---|---|
| Chapel-652-2950 | Family Services-652-6070 |
| Medical | Retiree Services-652-8712 |
|   Central Appts-653-2778 | TRICARE-653-2500 |
|   Emergency-653-2343 | |
|   Health Benefits-653-2500 | |
|   Hospital-653-2260 | |

### REST & RECREATION:

| | |
|---|---|
| Arts & Crafts-ext 4021 | Auto Hobby Shop-ext 2284 |
| Bowling-ext 2170 | Clubs |
| Fitness Center-ext 6433 |   EM-652-9733 |
| Golf Course-652-2602 |   O-652-9188 |
| Gym-652-4891 | Library-ext 9210 |
| Theater-652-5020 | Youth Center-ext 5015 |

**ATTRACTIONS:** Las Vegas, Lake Mead National Recreation Area, Mt. Charleston, Hoover Dam, Red Rock Canyon, Spring Mountain Ranch, Valley of Fire, beautiful deserts.

## RENO/TAHOE INTERNATIONAL AIRPORT/ NEVADA AIR NATIONAL GUARD BASE (NV06R4)
### 1776 National Guard Way
### Reno, NV 89502-5000

**TELEPHONE NUMBER INFORMATION:** Main installation numbers: C-775-788-4500, D-312-830-4500.

**LOCATION:** Reno/Tahoe International Airport exit 64/65 east off I-395. Co-located with the IAP. USMRA: Page 113 (B-4). NMC: Reno, within city limits.

**GENERAL INFORMATION:** Air National Guard activities, Airlift Wing.

**TEMPORARY MILITARY LODGING:** None. See Fallon NAS listing.

**RV, CAMPING/FAMCAMP:** None. See Fallon NAS listing, Fallon RV Park and Rec Area.

**SPACE-A:** None. See Fallon NAS listing.

**LOGISTICAL SUPPORT:**    SATO-788-4667

**ADMINISTRATIVE SUPPORT:**
Police-788-4549    SDO/NCO-788-4550

**HEALTH & WELFARE:**
CHAMPUS-788-4510    Medical-786-7200
Chapel serving all faiths one weekend per month (during Guard drills).

**REST & RECREATION:**    Combined Club-788-4570

**ATTRACTIONS:** Lake Tahoe, skiing. casinos, gambling, fishing, historic sites, Virginia City, Pyramid Lake.

## ROSE CREEK (NV07R4)
### Fallon Naval Air Station
### Fallon NAS, NV 89496-5000

**TELEPHONE NUMBER INFORMATION:** Main installation numbers: C-775-426-5162, D-312-830-2110.

**LOCATION:** Off base. Area is located 70 miles south of bse off US-95 northwest of Hawthorne at Mount Grant, west of US-95. NMC: Reno, 75 miles northwest.

**GENERAL INFORMATION:** Operated by Fallon NAS, off base, May-October. Military personnel active, reservists, retired, DoD civilians. Reservations: MWR Department, Pony Express Outfitters, Fallon Naval Air Station, NV 89496-5000. C-775-426-2598/2279, D-312-830-2598/2279.

**RV, CAMPING/FAMCAMP:**    Cabin

**ATTRACTIONS:** Outdoor activities, good fishing.

*For detailed information about this off-base recreation facility, as well as on-base recreation facilities, golf courses and marinas, consult Military Living's Military RV, Camping and Outdoor Recreation Around the World.*

# NEW HAMPSHIRE

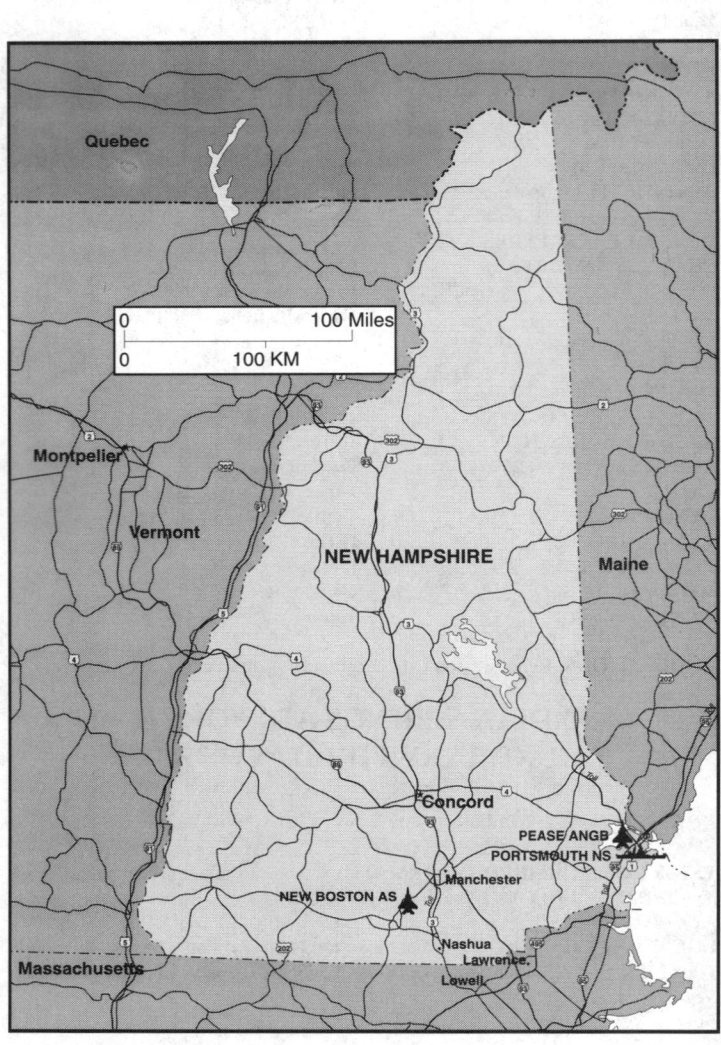

## NEW BOSTON AIR STATION (NH04R1)

23rd Space Operations Squadron
317 Chestnut Hill Road
Amherst, NH 03031-1514

**TELEPHONE NUMBER INFORMATION:** Main installation number: C-603-471-2000, D-312-489-2000.

**LOCATION:** From I-93 north, take I-293 west to Route 101 south west to Route 114 north. Take a left on New Boston Road, drive approximately 7-8 miles and New Boston Air Station is on your right. USMRA: Page 23 (F-10). NMC: Manchester, eight miles northeast. NMI: Hanscom AFB, 50 miles south.

**TEMPORARY MILITARY LODGING:** None. See Hanscom AFB, MA listing, C-617-377-2112, D-312-478-2112.

**RV, CAMPING/FAMCAMP:** New Boston Recreation Area on base, June-September, C-603-471-2234, D-312-489-2452/2234, three mobile homes, 12 camper spaces with W&E hookups, 42 camper/tent spaces without hookups. *Note: Camping area has been temporarily closed, with no date set to re-open. Call ahead for information.*

**SPACE-A**: None. See Hanscom AFB, MA listing.

**LOGISTICAL SUPPORT:**      Postal Service-471-2210

**ADMINISTRATIVE SUPPORT:**

| | |
|---|---|
| Fire Dept-471-2471 | Locator-471-2210 |
| Pass/ID Office-471-2379 | Police-471-2203 |
| Public Affairs-471-2211 | |

**HEALTH & WELFARE:** None. See Hanscom AFB, MA listing.

**REST & RECREATION:**

| | |
|---|---|
| Auto Hobby Shop-471-2469 | Combined Club-471-2452 |
| MWR-471-2452/2234 | Outdoor Rec-471-2452/2234 |

**ATTRACTIONS:** Snow skiing, hiking.

## PEASE AIR NATIONAL GUARD BASE (NH01R1)

157th Air Refueling Wing
302 Newington Street
Pease ANGB, NH 03803-0157

**TELEPHONE NUMBER INFORMATION:** Main installation numbers: C-603-430-2453, D-312-852-2453.

**LOCATION:** From I-95 north to Spaulding Turnpike NH-3 northwest exit 1, then follow signs. Base is at intersection of Spaulding Turnpike and Gosling Road. USMRA: Page 23 (H-9). NMC: Portsmouth, three miles northeast.

**GENERAL INFORMATION:** 157th Air Refueling Wing, New Hampshire Air National Guard.

**TEMPORARY MILITARY LODGING:** None. See Portsmouth Naval Shipyard listing.

**RV, CAMPING/FAMCAMP:** None. See New Boston AS listing.

**SPACE-A:** Pax Term/Lounge, Building 257, information: C-603-430-3323, D-312-852-3323, Fax: C-430-3335, D-852-3335. Flights to CONUS, OCONUS and overseas.

**LOGISTICAL SUPPORT:**

| | |
|---|---|
| Bank-436-0537 | Barber Shop-436-2903 |
| Exchange-436-0302 | |

**ADMINISTRATIVE SUPPORT:**      Public Affairs-430-3413

**HEALTH & WELFARE:** None. See Portsmouth NS listing.

**REST & RECREATION:** None. See Portsmouth NS listing.

**ATTRACTIONS:** City of Portsmouth, harbor, beaches; skiing in White Mountains is a one hour drive.

## PORTSMOUTH NAVAL SHIPYARD (NH02R1)

ATTN: Code 800, Bldg 86
Portsmouth Naval Shipyard, NH 03804-5000

**TELEPHONE NUMBER INFORMATION:** Main installation numbers: C-207-438-1000, D-312-684-1000.

**LOCATION:** From I-95 north, cross Piscataqua River Bridge into Maine. Take exit 2 to US-236 to US-1 south to US-203, left onto Walker Street to Gate 1. From I-95 south, take exit 2, follow above directions. Located on an island on Piscataqua River between Portsmouth and Kittery, ME. USMRA: Page 23 (H-9). NMC: Portsmouth, in city limits.

**GENERAL INFORMATION:** A Naval Shipyard and Repair Facility.

**TEMPORARY MILITARY LODGING:** Helmsman Inn, C-207-438-1513/2015, Fax-207-438-3580.

**RV, CAMPING/FAMCAMP:** None. See New Boston AS listing.

**SPACE-A**: None. See Pease ANGB listing.

**LOGISTICAL SUPPORT:**

| | |
|---|---|
| Child Care-438-3804 | Commissary-438-5532 |
| Exchange-438-2341 | Pizza Parlor-438-3536 |
| Visitor Center-438-3550 | |

**ADMINISTRATIVE SUPPORT:**

| | |
|---|---|
| Legal-438-2703 | Locator-438-1000 |
| OOD-438-1900 | Police-438-1901 |
| Public Affairs-438-1525 | Emergency-438-2444 |
| SDO/NCO-438-2200 | |

**HEALTH & WELFARE:**

| | |
|---|---|
| CHAMPUS-438-3862 | Chapel-438-1970 |
| Medical | |
|   Central Appts-438-1799 | |
|   Emergency-438-4940 | |

**REST & RECREATION:**

| | |
|---|---|
| Auto Hobby Shop-438-2981 | Bowling-438-2404 |
| Clubs | Fitness Center-438-2402 |
|   Consol-438-2269 | Gym-438-2360 |
|   O-438-2269 | ITT-438-2351 |
| Library-438-2769 | Marina-438-1583 |
| MWR-438-1583 | Rec Equipment-438-1514 |
| Tennis-438-2404 | Wood Hobby Shop-438-1820 |

**ATTRACTIONS:** Beaches, snow skiing nearby.

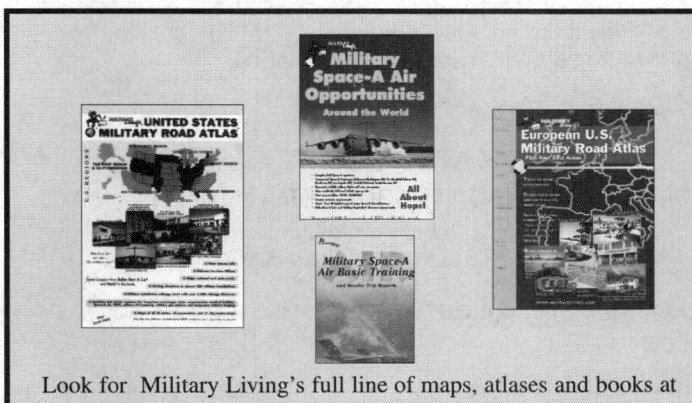

# NEW JERSEY

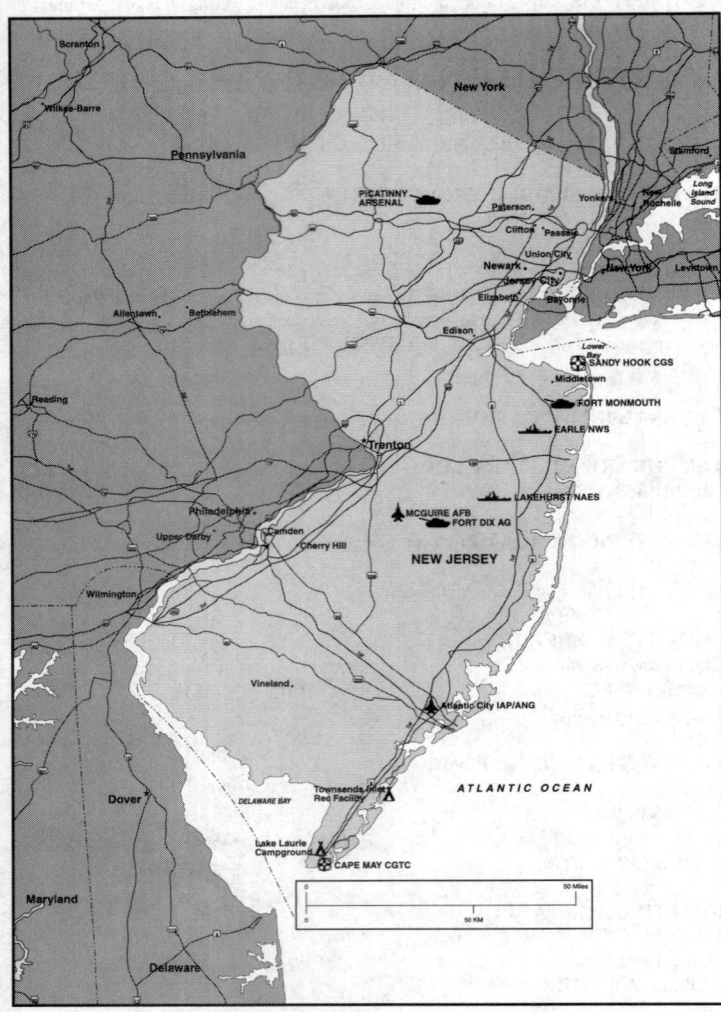

## ATLANTIC CITY INTERNATIONAL AIRPORT/AIR NATIONAL GUARD (NJ16R1)

177th FW, 400 Langley Road
Egg Harbor Township, NJ 08234-9500

**TELEPHONE NUMBER INFORMATION:** Main installation numbers: C-609-645-6000, D-312-455-6000.

**LOCATION:** Take Atlantic City Expressway to exit 12 east, go east, follow signs to airport. USMRA: Page 19 (E-8). NMC: Atlantic City, in city limits.

**GENERAL INFORMATION:** 177th Fighter Wing, Air National Guard.

**LOGISTICAL SUPPORT:**            Exchange-485-5115

**ATTRACTIONS:** Nearby Atlantic City.

## CAPE MAY COAST GUARD TRAINING CENTER (NJ13R1)

1 Munro Avenue
Cape May, NJ 08204-5002

**TELEPHONE NUMBER INFORMATION:** Main installation number: C-609-898-6900.

**LOCATION:** Take Garden State Parkway or US-9 to Cape May. In Cape May, take Pittsburgh Avenue to Pennsylvania Avenue to main gate of Center. USMRA: Page 19 (D-10). NMC: Atlantic City, 45 miles northeast.

**GENERAL INFORMATION:** Coast Guard Training Center for Recruits, Center, Cape May Air Station, several Coast Guard ships.

**TEMPORARY MILITARY LODGING:** Housing office, 0800-1630 hours daily, C-609-898-6922. All ranks.

**RV, CAMPING/FAMCAMP:** None. See Townsends Inlet Rec Facility.

**SPACE-A:** None. See McGuire AFB listing.

**LOGISTICAL SUPPORT:**

| | |
|---|---|
| Child Care-898-6922 | Commissary-898-6940 |
| Exchange-898-6940 | Package Store-898-6940 |
| SATO-884-3197 | Visitor Center-898-6922 |

**ADMINISTRATIVE SUPPORT:**

| | |
|---|---|
| Legal-898-6902 | Locator-898-6900 |
| Police-898-6225 | Public Affairs-898-6969 |
| SDO/NCO-898-6915 | |

**HEALTH & WELFARE:**

| | |
|---|---|
| CHAMPUS-898-6966 | Chapel-898-6974 |
| Family Services-898-6925 | Medical |
| | Central Appts-898-6959 |
| | Emergency-898-6959 |

**REST & RECREATION:**

| | |
|---|---|
| Clubs | Gym-ext 6973 |
| Com-898-6937 | ITT-898-6989 |
| CPO-898-6344 | MWR-898-6922 |
| Recreation-898-6922 | Swimming-ext 6973 |
| Theater-898-6922 | |

**ATTRACTIONS:** Beaches, Atlantic City Resort. Auto/Passenger ferry from Cape May to Lewes, DE, operates year round.

## EARLE NAVAL WEAPONS STATION (NJ11R1)

201 State Highway, 34 South
Colts Neck, NJ 07722-5007

**TELEPHONE NUMBER INFORMATION:** Main installation numbers: C-732-866-2000, D-312-449-2000.

**LOCATION:** From New Jersey Turnpike (I-95), exit 8 to NJ-33, east through Freehold to NJ-34, north to main gate. Or exit Garden State Parkway to NJ-33, west to NJ-34, north to Station. USMRA: Page 19 (F,G-5). NMC: Newark, 50 miles north.

**GENERAL INFORMATION:** Naval Ammunition, Storage and Trans-shipment site with loading facilities near Sandy Hook at Leonardo.

**TEMPORARY MILITARY LODGING:** Very limited in bachelor-type quarters. Officers C-732-866-2167, EM C-732-866-2121, Fax: C-732-866-1068.

**RV, CAMPING/FAMCAMP:** None. See Fort Dix AG listing, Brindle Lake Travel Camp.

**SPACE-A:** None. See McGuire AFB listing.

**LOGISTICAL SUPPORT:**

| | |
|---|---|
| Child Care-866-2518 | Exchange-866-2349 |
| Package Store-866-2417 | |

**ADMINISTRATIVE SUPPORT:**

| | |
|---|---|
| CDO/OOD-866-2500 | Fire Dept-866-2260 |
| Legal-866-2066 | Police-866-2069 |
| Public Affairs-866-2171 | SDO/NCO-866-2500 |

**HEALTH & WELFARE:**

| | |
|---|---|
| CHAMPUS-866-2303 | Chapel-866-2405 |
| Family Services-866-2115 | Medical-866-2300 |
| Retiree Services-866-2115 | |

**REST & RECREATION**:
Auto Hobby Shop-866-2105
Clubs
  All Hands-866-2438
  Consol-866-2002
Library-866-2167
Recreation-866-2351
Youth Activities-866-2148

Bowling-866-2394
Gym-866-2119
Hobby Shops-866-2105
ITT-866-2167
MWR-866-2350
Special Services-ext 2350/2389

**ATTRACTIONS:** The New Jersey Shore nearby. New York City, Atlantic City, Six Flags Great Adventure Theme Park.

## FORT DIX ARMY GARRISON (NJ03R1)
ATTN: AFZT-PAZ
Fort Dix, NJ 08640-5075

**TELEPHONE NUMBER INFORMATION:** Main installation numbers: C-609-562-1011, D-312-944-1011.

**LOCATION:** From NJ Turnpike (I-95), exit 7, right onto NJ-206, short distance left on NJ-68, continue to General Circle and main gate. USMRA: Page 19 (E,F-6). NMC: Trenton, 17 miles northwest.

**GENERAL INFORMATION:** Regional Reserve Training Center.

**TEMPORARY MILITARY LODGING:** Doughboy Inn, Building 5255, Maryland Avenue & First Street, 24 hours daily, C-609-723-5579, D-312-440-5579. All ranks. DV/VIP C-609-562-5059/6293.

**RV, CAMPING/FAMCAMP:** Brindle Lake Travel Camp on post, year round, C-609-562-6667, D-312-944-6667, Fax: C-609-562-2354; 10 spaces without hookups.

**SPACE-A:** None. See McGuire AFB listing.

**LOGISTICAL SUPPORT:**
Bank-723-7235
Beauty Shop-723-7377
Child Dev Center-723-1009
Commissary-724-4154
Credit Union-723-4415
Education Office-562-5001
Gas Station-723-0464
Postal Service-723-2089
Shoppette-723-2980

Barber Shop-723-5190
Car Rental-723-4419
Class Six-723-5488
Conv Store-723-2980
Dry Cleaner-723-0300
Exchange-723-6100
Laundry-723-6446
SATO-723-3426

**ADMINISTRATIVE SUPPORT:**
Fire Dept-562-3351
Legal-562-3290
Pass/ID Office-562-2177
Public Affairs-562-4035

Housing Office-562-2575
Locator-562-6051
Police-562-6001

**HEALTH & WELFARE:**
American Red Cross-562-2258
Army Emergency Relief-562-4245
Medical
  Central Appts-888-999-5195
  Health Benefits Advisor-562-9080
  Information-562-9501

ACS-562-2767
Chapel-562-2020
Retiree Services-562-9689
TRICARE-562-9283
Veterinary Services-562-4992

**REST & RECREATION:**
Arts & Crafts-562-5691
Bowling-562-6895
Fitness Center-562-3961
Golf Course-562-5443
ITT-724-4271
Library-652-3587
Outdoor Rec-562-6667
Theater-562-3986

Auto Hobby Shop-562-6762
Clubs
  Club Dix-723-3272
  NCO-562-5598
  Rod/Gun-652-4676
MWR-562-6772
Swimming-562-2863
Youth Services-562-2819

**ATTRACTIONS:** Atlantic City and Philadelphia, short drives.

## FORT MONMOUTH (NJ05R1)
ATTN: PAO/AMSEL-IO
Fort Monmouth, NJ 07703-5016

**TELEPHONE NUMBER INFORMATION:** Main installation numbers: C-732-532-9000, D-312-992-9000.

**LOCATION:** Take New Jersey Turnpike to Garden State Parkway, exit 105 for Eatontown, NJ-35 north to main gate. USMRA: Page 19 (G-5). NMC: New Brunswick, 23 miles northwest.

**GENERAL INFORMATION:** Army Communications-Electronics Command, other supporting electronics organizations, U.S. Military Academy Preparatory School.

**TEMPORARY MILITARY LODGING:** Lodging office, Building 270, Allen & Barton Avenue, 0745-2400 daily, C-732-532-1635/1092, D-312-992-1635. All ranks. DV/VIP C-732-532-1635.

**RV, CAMPING/FAMCAMP:** None. See Fort Dix AG listing, Brindle Lake Travel Camp.

**SPACE-A:** None. See McGuire AFB listing.

**LOGISTICAL SUPPORT:**
Barber Shop-542-4545
Cafeteria-532-1542
Class Six-542-1617
Conv Store-542-5353
Dining Facilities-532-0311
Gas Station-542-7417
Travel Office-532-3545

Beauty Shop-532-3552
Child Care-532-8069
Commissary-532-1260
Credit Union-542-7417
Exchange-542-7235
Postal Service-389-3496
Visitor Center-532-6078

**ADMINISTRATIVE SUPPORT:**
Fire Dept-532-1365
Legal-532-4371
Ombudsman-532-6078
Public Affairs-532-1258

Housing Office-532-5510
Locator-532-1492
Police-532-1112
SDO/NCO-532-1112

**HEALTH & WELFARE:**
ACS-532-2076
Chapel-532-2066
Family Services-532-3584
Retiree Services-532-4673
TRICARE-532-1341
Veterinary Services-532-2406

CHAMPUS-532-3203
Dental-Clinic-532-7060
Medical-
  Clinic-532-1764
  Emergency-532-3851

**REST & RECREATION:**
Auto Hobby Shop-532-3301
Clubs
  All Hands-532-3892
  EM-532-3892
  O-532-4520
Marina-532-4079
Outdoor Rec-532-2374
Youth Services-532-2202

Bowling-532-2805
Community Center-532-2041
Fitness Center-532-5803
Golf Course-532-4307
Library-532-3172
MWR-532-9604
Swimming-532-3275

**ATTRACTIONS:** New Jersey beaches nearby, Monmouth Park Racetrack, New York City, Atlantic City.

## LAKEHURST NAVAL AIR ENGINEERING STATION (NJ08R1)
Code 75000B/150-2
Highway 547
Lakehurst, NJ 08733-5041

**TELEPHONE NUMBER INFORMATION:** Main installation numbers: C-732-323-2011, D-312-624-1110. WEB: www.lakehurst.navy.mil

**LOCATION:** Take the Garden State Parkway south to NJ-70, west to junction of NJ-547, turn right and proceed one mile to base. USMRA: Page 19 (F-6). NMC: Trenton, 30 miles northwest.

**GENERAL INFORMATION:** Naval Air Warfare Center Aircraft Division, Naval Air Engineering Station.

**TEMPORARY MILITARY LODGING:** Lodging office, Building 480-481, 24 hours daily, BEQ/BOQ/DV/VIP C-732-323-2266, D-312-624-2266, Fax: C-732-323-2269. All ranks.

**RV, CAMPING/FAMCAMP:** None. See Fort Dix AG listing, Brindle Lake Travel Camp.

**SPACE-A:** Pax Terminal C-732-323-2438, D-312-624-2438, Fax: C-732-323-5316, D-312-624-5316.

**LOGISTICAL SUPPORT:**

| | |
|---|---|
| Child Care-323-2406/2034 | Commissary-323-2516 |
| Conv Store-323-2909 | Exchange-323-7680/7683 |
| Galley-323-2554 | |

**ADMINISTRATIVE SUPPORT:**

| | |
|---|---|
| COM-323-2340 | Legal-323-2571/2170 |
| Pass/ID Office-323-2693 | Police-323-2457/2332 |
| Public Affairs-323-2620 | |

**HEALTH & WELFARE:**

| | |
|---|---|
| Chapel-323-2272/2539 | Family Services-323-1223/4 |
| Medical-323-1223/4 | |

**REST & RECREATION:**

| | |
|---|---|
| Auto Hobby Shop-ext 2468 | Bowling-ext 2027 |
| Golf Course-ext 7483 | Gym-ext 2468 |
| Picnic Area-ext 2468 | Rec Equipment-ext 2468 |
| Swimming-ext 2468 | |

**ATTRACTIONS:** Atlantic City, New Jersey beaches, Six Flags Great Adventure Theme Park, Manhattan, Philadelphia.

## LAKE LAURIE CAMPGROUND (NJ14R1)
Willow Grove Naval Air Station
Willow Grove, PA 19090-5010

**TELEPHONE NUMBER INFORMATION:** Main installation numbers: C-215-443-1000, D-312-991-1000.

**LOCATION:** Off base. In Cape May, NJ. Campground entrance is on US-9, two miles north of junction with end of Garden State Parkway. USMRA: Page 19 (D-10). NMI: Cape May Coast Guard Training Center, 5 miles southeast. NMC: Vineland, approximately 50 miles northwest.

**GENERAL INFORMATION:** Operated by Willow Grove NAS, off base, mid-May through mid-September. Military personnel active, reservists, retired, civilian employees of Willow Grove NAS. Reservations (required, in person only): Willow Grove NAS ITT Office, Bldg 2, Willow Grove, PA. For information only: Recreation Services, Bldg 2, Willow Grove Naval Air Station, PA 19090-5010. C-215-443-6082, D-312-991-6082.

**RV, CAMPING/FAMCAMP:**            Campers-2

**ATTRACTIONS:** This well-planned recreation area is located at Lake Laurie in southern New Jersey close to beaches.

*For detailed information about this off-base recreation facility, as well as on-base recreation facilities, golf courses and marinas, consult Military Living's Military RV, Camping and Outdoor Recreation Around the World.*

## McGUIRE AIR FORCE BASE (NJ09R1)
2901 Falcon Lane
McGuire Air Force Base, NJ 08641-50002

**TELEPHONE NUMBER INFORMATION:** Main installation numbers: C-609-724-1100, D-312-440-1110. WEB: www.mcguire.af.mil

**LOCATION:** From New Jersey Turnpike (I-95), exit 7 to NJ-206 south to Route 68 south, then to Route 537, turn left. Take Route 537 northeast to intersection (traffic light) of Routes 545 and 680, turn right. Take Route 680 to base's main gate, about two miles. Clearly marked. USMRA: Page 19 (E-6). NMC: Trenton, 18 miles northwest. NMI: Fort Dix, adjacent.

**GENERAL INFORMATION:** Air Mobility Command base. Air Mobility Wing, East Coast Mobility Center, ANG and AFRES units.

**TEMPORARY MILITARY LODGING:** All American Inn: C-609-723-4730, D-312-440-3974. Reservations: C-609-724-3336/3337, D312-440-3336/3337. All ranks. DV/VIP C-609-724-2405.

**RV, CAMPING/FAMCAMP:** None. See Fort Dix AG listing, Brindle Lake Travel Camp.

**SPACE-A:** Pax Term/Lounge, Building 1706, C-609-724-5023, D-312-440-5023, Recording: C-1-800-569-8284. Fax: C-609-724-4621. Flights to CONUS and overseas.

**LOGISTICAL SUPPORT:**

| | |
|---|---|
| Car Rental-723-4419 | Child Care-724-2966 |
| Commissary-724-4155 | Conv Store-723-3933 |
| Exchange-723-6100 | Gas Station-724-4608 |
| Package Store-724-3888 | SATO-724-3131 |
| Visitor Center-724-3154 | |

**ADMINISTRATIVE SUPPORT:**

| | |
|---|---|
| Legal-724-4601 | Locator-724-1100 |
| Police-724-2001 | Public Affairs-724-2104 |
| SDO/NCO-724-3935 | |

**HEALTH & WELFARE:**

| | |
|---|---|
| Chapel-724-3811 | Family Services-724-3294 |
| Medical- | |
|   Health Benefits Advisor-562-9082/3 | Retiree Services-724-2459 |
|   Information-562-9200 | TRICARE-562-9319 |

**REST & RECREATION:**

| | |
|---|---|
| Clubs | |
|   NCO-724-23963153 | Fitness Center-724-4645 |
|   O-724-3296 | Golf Course-724-2169 |
| ITT-724-4271 | MWR-724-3737 |
| Outdoor Recreation-724-4271 | Youth Center-724-20505437 |

**ATTRACTIONS:** New Jersey Shore, Atlantic City and Philadelphia nearby.

## PICATINNY ARSENAL (NJ01R1)
US Army Tank-Automotive and Armaments Command
Armaments, Research, Development and Engineering Center
Building 1
Picatinny Arsenal, NJ 07806-5000

**TELEPHONE NUMBER INFORMATION:** Main installation numbers: C-973-724-4021, C-1-800-831-2759, D-312-880-4021.
WEB: www.pica.army.mil

**LOCATION:** From I-80 west, exit 34-B to Route 15 north, follow signs to Center, one mile north. From I-80 east, exit 34 to Route 15, follow signs to Center. USMRA: Page 19 (E-2). NMC: Newark, 30 miles east.

**GENERAL INFORMATION:** U.S. Army Tank-automotive and Armaments Command Armament Research, Development and Engineering Center located at Picatinny Arsenal.

**TEMPORARY MILITARY LODGING:** Lodging office, Building 3359, Lower Belt Road, 0800-1630 Mon-Fri, C-973-724-2633/3506, D-312-880-2633/3506. All ranks. DV/VIP ext 7026.

**RV, CAMPING/FAMCAMP:** Lake Denmark Rec Area on post, late June-September, C-973-724-4484, D-312-880-4484, 12 mobile homes, three camper spaces with W&E hookups, 15 camper spaces without hookups, and 16 tent spaces.

**SPACE-A:** None. See Philadelphia IAP/ARS, PA.

**LOGISTICAL SUPPORT:**

Barber Shop-724-7157
Beauty Shop-724-7157
Cafeteria-734-5649
Child Care-724-4994
Commissary-724-2918
Credit Union-724-5532
Exchange-724-2518
SATO-724-0525
Snack Bar-724-2405

**ADMINISTRATIVE SUPPORT:**

Fire Dept-724-4544
Legal-724-6598
Locator-724-2852
Police-724-6666
Public Affairs-724-6364

**HEALTH & WELFARE:**

CHAMPUS-724-2113
Chapel-724-4139
Family Services-724-4939
Medical
 Central Appts-724-2113
 Emergency-724-4611

**REST & RECREATION:**

Arts & Crafts-ext 4014
Clubs
Equipment Rental-ext 4016
 O-989-2460
Golf Course-724-4430
 Rod/Gun-ext 2598
Gymnasium-724-4835
 Ski-ext 4014
ITR-724-4186
Recreation-724-4186

**ATTRACTIONS:** Lake Country, skiing, New York City nearby.

## SANDY HOOK COAST GUARD STATION (NJ17R1)

20 Crispin Road
Sandy Hook, NJ 07732-4999

**TELEPHONE NUMBER INFORMATION:** Main installation numbers: C-732-872-3428. WEB: www.uscg.mil/d1/units/actny/stashook

**LOCATION:** From Garden State Parkway to exit 117, take Route 36 south 15 miles. Take first right after drawbridge onto Sandy Hook, Gateway National Park. Go straight six miles, follow signs for Coast Guard. USMRA: Page 19 (G-4). NMI: Fort Monmouth, 15 miles northeast.

**GENERAL INFORMATION:** Part of the Coast Guard First District, maintains canine training facility.

**TEMPORARY MILITARY LODGING:** None. See Fort Monmouth listing.

**RV, CAMPING/FAMCAMP:** None. See Fort Dix AG listing, Brindle Lake Travel Camp.

**SPACE-A:** None. See Lakehurst NAES listing.

**LOGISTICAL SUPPORT:**
Exchange-872-3478

**HEALTH & WELFARE:**
Medical-Clinic-872-3444

**REST & RECREATION:**
Consol Club-872-3457

**ATTRACTIONS:** Beaches, fishing.

## TOWNSENDS INLET RECREATION FACILITY (NJ20R1)

8101 Landis Avenue
Sea Isle City, NJ 08243-5000

**TELEPHONE NUMBER INFORMATION:** Main installation numbers: C-609-263-2361.

**LOCATION:** Off base. Old Coast lifesaving station in Sea Isle City, NJ. Two blocks from beach. From Garden State Pkwy exit to JN-625 east. USMRA: Page 19 (E-10). NMC: Atlantic City, 25 miles north.

**GENERAL INFORMATION:** Operated by Atlantic City Coast Guard Group, off base, open from 1 April-30 October. Military personnel active, reservists, retired.

Reservations (required): Townsends Inlet Recreation Facility, 8101 Landis Avenue, Sea Isle City, NJ 08243-5000. C-609-263-2361.

**RV, CAMPING/FAMCAMP:** Beach House-4 apartments

**ATTRACTIONS:** Located in southern New Jersey midway between Cape May and Atlantic City, this Victorian house is one block from the ocean and two blocks from the bay.

*For detailed information about this off-base recreation facility, as well as on-base recreation facilities, golf courses and marinas, consult Military Living's Military RV, Camping and Outdoor Recreation Around the World.*

# NEW MEXICO

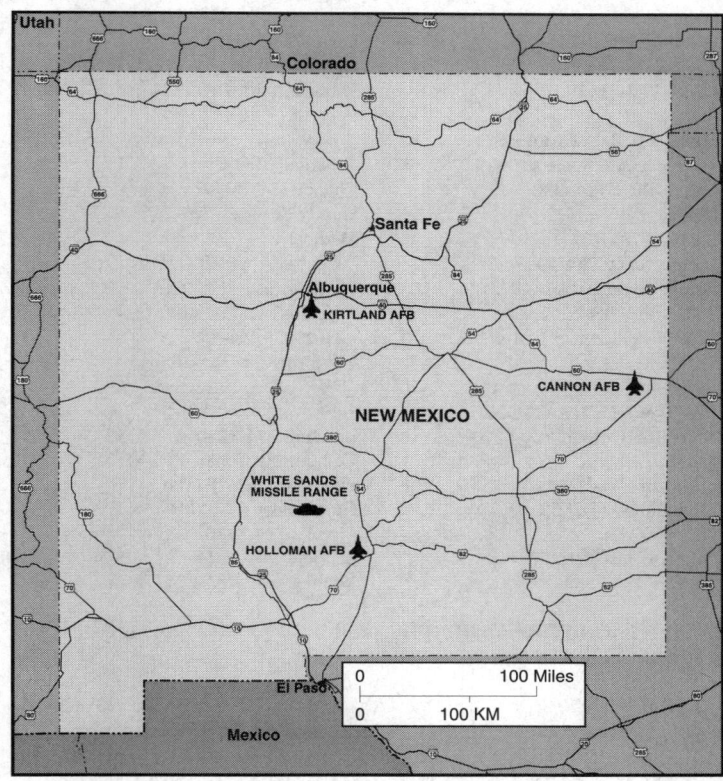

## CANNON AIR FORCE BASE (NM02R3)

100 S DL Ingram Boulevard, Suite 204
Cannon Air Force Base, NM 88103-5219

**TELEPHONE NUMBER INFORMATION:** Main installation numbers: C-505-784-3311, D-312-681-1110. WEB: www.cannon.af.mil

**LOCATION:** From Clovis, near the Texas border, west on US-60/84 for seven miles to AFB south of US-60/84. From NM-467 north or south enter the Portales gate. USMRA: Page 114 (H-5). NMC: Clovis, seven miles east.

**GENERAL INFORMATION:** Home of the 27th Fighter Wing, "America's Go-To Wing." An Air Combat Command installation. Base provides superior air combat power through F-16 operations.

**TEMPORARY MILITARY LODGING:** Lodging office, Caprock Inn, Building 1801, 401 S Olympic Boulevard, 24 hours daily, C-505-784-2935, D-312-681-2935, Fax: C-505-784-4833, D-312-681-4833. All ranks. DV/VIP C-505-784-2727. Advance reservations C-505-784-2935, Fax: C-505-784-4833.

**RV, CAMPING/FAMCAMP:** None. Nearest facility is more than 100 miles away.

**SPACE-A:** Extremely limited Space-A. Base Operations/Lounge, Building 135, 0700-2300 Mon-Fri, 0800-1600 weekends, closed holidays, C-505-784-2802, D-

312-681-2802, Fax: C-505-681-4658, D-312-681-4658. Flights to CONUS. Extremely limited.

**LOGISTICAL SUPPORT:**

| | |
|---|---|
| Bank-784-2500 | Child Dev Center-784-2704/6259 |
| Commissary-784-4331 | Credit Union-791-3353 |
| Dining Facility | Dry Cleaner-784-5347/3723 |
|   Pecos Trail-784-2420 | Education Office-784-4184 |
| Exchange-784-2141 | Gas Station-784-3421/5177 |
| Package Store-784-5766 | SATO-784-2304 |
| Shoppette-784-5766 | Snack Bar |
| Travel Office-784-2304 |   Bowling Alley-784-2280 |
| Visitor Center-784-2400 |   Golf Course-784-2312/2800 |
| |   Sports Lounge-784-2448 |

**ADMINISTRATIVE SUPPORT:**

| | |
|---|---|
| Command Post-784-2253/2256 | Fire Dept-784-2577 |
| Housing Office-784-2982 | Legal-784-2211 |
| Locator-784-4636 | Pass/ID Office-784-4621/2094 |
| Police-784-4111 | Public Affairs-784-4131 |

**HEALTH & WELFARE:**

| | |
|---|---|
| Air Force Aid Society-784-4228 | American Red Cross-784-2023 |
| CHAMPUS-784-4085 | Chapel-784-2507/2508 |
| Dental | Family Services-784-2452 |
|   Clinic-784-4041 | Medical |
|   Emergency-784-4033 |   Central Appts-784-2778 |
| Retiree Services-784-4865 |   Emergency-784-4033 |
| TRICARE-784-6251 |   Health Benefits Advisor-784-4085 |
| Veterinary Services-784-4098 |   Hospital-784-4582 |
| |   Information-784-4636 |

**REST & RECREATION:**

| | |
|---|---|
| Auto Hobby Shop-784-2170 | Bowling-784-2280 |
| Clubs | Community Center-784-4455 |
|   Endzone-784-2448 | Fitness Center-784-2466 |
|   Landing-784-2853 | Golf Course-784-2800 |
| ITT-784-2536 | Library-784-2786 |
| Outdoor Rec-784-2773 | Services-784-2374 |
| Theater-784-2582 | Youth Center-784-2747 |

**OTHER FACILITIES AVAILABLE:** Barber shop, beauty shop, commissary, postal service and hospital.

**ATTRACTIONS:** Blackwater Draw Archeological Site and Museum, Billy the Kid's Grave and Museum, Hillcrest Park Zoo and Ned Houk Memorial Park.

# HOLLOMAN AIR FORCE BASE (NM05R3)
490 First Street, Suite 2800
Holloman Air Force Base, NM 88330-8287

**TELEPHONE NUMBER INFORMATION:** Main installation numbers: C-505-475-6511, D-312-867-6511.

**LOCATION:** Exit US-70, eight miles southwest of Alamogordo. Route to AFB north of US-70 is clearly marked. USMRA: Page 114 (D,E-7). NMC: Las Cruces, 50 miles southwest.

**GENERAL INFORMATION:** Air Combat Command Base. Headquarters Fighter Wing, and many support activities.

**TEMPORARY MILITARY LODGING:** Billeting Office, Building 583, W New Mexico Avenue, 24 hours daily, C-505-475-3311/3468/3880, D-312-867-3311/3468/3880. Fax: C-475-7753, D-867-7753. All ranks. DV/VIP C-505-475-5573/5574.

**RV, CAMPING/FAMCAMP:** FAMCAMP on base, year round, C-505-475-5369, D-312-867-5369, 12 camper spaces with full hookups.

**SPACE-A:** Pax Term/Lounge, Building 571, 24 hours daily, C-505-475-5411, D-312-867-5411. Fax: C-505-475-7627, D-312-867-7627. Limited flights to CONUS locations.

**LOGISTICAL SUPPORT:**

| | |
|---|---|
| Cafeteria-479-2698 | Child Care-475-7505 |
| Commissary-475-5127 | Conv Store-479-2381 |
| Exchange-479-6164 | Gas Station-479-6004 |
| Package Store-479-2201 | SATO-475-3245 |
| Shoppette-479-2381 | Snack Bar-479-2779 |
| Visitor Center-475-5920 | |

**ADMINISTRATIVE SUPPORT:**

| | |
|---|---|
| Legal-475-7216 | Locator-475-7510 |
| Police-475-7171 | Public Affairs-475-5406 |
| SDO/NCO-475-7575 | |

**HEALTH & WELFARE:**

| | |
|---|---|
| CHAMPUS-475-7700 | Chapel-475-7211/7024 |
| Dental-475-3742 | Family Services-475-3944 |
| Medical-475-3260 | |
|   Appointment-475-2778 | |
|   Emergency-475-3268 | |

**REST & RECREATION:**

| | |
|---|---|
| Arts & Crafts-475-3970 | Auto Hobby Shop-475-7438 |
| Bowling-ext 7378 | Clubs |
| Consol Hobby-ext 3760 |   Aero-475-3752 |
| Fitness Center-ext 3229 |   NCO-475-3226 |
| Golf Course-ext 3574 |   O-475-3611 |
| Library-ext 3939 | Rec Equipment-ext 7328 |
| Rec Supply-ext 5369 | Stables-ext 3848 |
| Swimming-ext 3639 | Theater-475-3286 |
| Youth Center-ext 3753 | |

**ATTRACTIONS:** Sierra Blanca ski area. El Paso TX and Ciudad Juarez, Mexico easy drive south. International Space Hall of Fame and White Sands National Monument in Alamogordo; horse racing, Ruidoso; Carlsbad Caverns, Whites City.

# KIRTLAND AIR FORCE BASE (NM03R3)
377 Air Base Wing
2000 Wyoming Boulevard SE
Kirtland Air Force Base, NM 87117-5606

**TELEPHONE NUMBER INFORMATION:** Main installation numbers: C-505-846-0011, D-312-246-0011. WEB: www.kirtland.af.mil

**LOCATION:** From I-40 east or west exit on Wyoming Boulevard, south for two miles to Wyoming gate to AFB. USMRA: Page 114, (D-4). NMC: Albuquerque, one mile northwest.

**GENERAL INFORMATION:** Air Force Materiel Command Base. Air Force Operational Test and Evaluation Center, Air Force Research Laboratory, Albuquerque Operations Defense Threat Reduction Agency, 150th Fighter Wing (Air National Guard), Department of Energy, Sandia National Laboratories and 200 associate units.

**TEMPORARY MILITARY LODGING:** Lodging office, Building 22016, Club Drive, 24 hours daily, C-505-846-9652, D-312-246-9652, Fax: C-505-846-4142. All ranks. DV/VIP C-505-846-4119.

**RV, CAMPING/FAMCAMP:** Kirtland FAMCAMP, on base year round, C-505-846-0337, D-312-246-0337, Fax: C-505-846-7084, D-312-246-7084, 0800-1600 hours. Twenty-nine camper spaces with full hookups, 29 camper spaces, no hookups.

**SPACE-A:** Pax Term/Lounge, Building 333, 0715-1600 Mon-Fri, C-505-846-6184, D-312-246-6184, Fax: C-505-846-6185. Recorded flight information, C-505-846-0785, flights to CONUS locations.

**LOGISTICAL SUPPORT:**

| | |
|---|---|
| Barber Shop-266-5181 | Beauty Shop-266-6430 |
| Child Care-846-1103 | Commissary-846-9588 |
| Conv Store-265-7552 | Credit Union-254-4369 |
| Dining Facility-846-8048 | Dry Cleaner-266-8116 |
| Education Center-846-8955 | Exchange-846-9642 |

Gas Station-265-9093/7552
Postal Service-846-0560

Package Store-265-7301
Rogers Travel
  military-846-7171
  leisure-846-2914

**ADMINISTRATIVE SUPPORT:**

Fire Dept-846-8069
Legal-846-4217
Pass/ID Office-846-6429
Public Affairs-846-5991

Housing Office-846-8217
Locator-846-0011
Police-846-7913

**HEALTH & WELFARE:**

Air Force Aid Society-846-0741
Dental-846-3027
Medical
  Central Appts-846-3200
  Emergency-846-3730

Chapel-846-5691
Family Services-846-6359
Retiree Services-846-1536
TRICARE-260-2960
Veterinary Services-846-4276

**REST & RECREATION:**

Arts & Crafts-846-1070
Bowling-846-1156
Community Center-846-2059
Fitness Center
  East-846-1102
  West-846-1068
Golf Course-846-1169
Library-846-1071
Theater-846-SHOW(7649)
Youth Center-853-KIDS (5437)

Auto Hobby Shop-846-1104
Clubs
  CPO-265-6791
  O-846-5165
  NCO-846-1467
  Sandia Skeet-846-0196
ITT-846-2924
Outdoor Rec-846-1499
Wood Hobby Shop-846-1861

**ATTRACTIONS:** National Atomic Museum, Albuquerque, world's longest free span tram, Old Town–founded in 1706, variety of Indian Pueblos, Albuquerque International Hot Air Balloon Fiesta each October, State Fair each September –"fourth largest in U.S.," ski resorts, Santa Fe, Indian cliff dwellings and pueblos, Santa Fe Opera.

## WHITE SANDS MISSILE RANGE (NM04R3)

Building 122 Augusta Street
White Sands Missile Range, NM 88002-5047

**TELEPHONE NUMBER INFORMATION:** Main installation numbers: C-505-678-2121, D-312-258-2121. WEB: www.wsmr.army.mil

**LOCATION:** From US-70 north or south, 18 miles south of Alamogordo, follow signs to Visitors Center and White Sands Missile Range, north of US-70. Clearly marked. USMRA: Page 114 (D-6,7,8). NMC: El Paso, TX, 45 miles south.

**GENERAL INFORMATION:** Army Test and Evaluation Command, Navy, Air Force, NASA, and other tenants and support activities.

**TEMPORARY MILITARY LODGING:** Billeting Office, Mon-Thu, 0700-1630; Alternate Fri: 0700-1530, C-505-678-4559, D-312-258-4559. All ranks. DV/VIP C-505-678-1028.

**RV, CAMPING/FAMCAMP:** Volunteer Park Travel Camp Site on post, year round, C-505-678-1713, D-312-258-1713; eight camper spaces with full hookups.

**SPACE-A:** None. See the Fort Bliss, TX listing.

**LOGISTICAL SUPPORT:**

Cafeteria-678-2081
Child Care-678-7882
Conv Store-678-2072
Gas Station-678-4877
SATO-678-4778

Carlson Wagonlit Travel-678-4778
Commissary-678-2358
Exchange-678-2072
Package Store-678-2072

**ADMINISTRATIVE SUPPORT:**

Fire Dept-117
Locator-678-1630
Public Affairs-678-1134

Legal-678-1263
Police-678-1234
SDO/NCO-678-2031

**HEALTH & WELFARE:**

ACS-678-6767
Chapel-678-2615/2031
Medical-678-5411
  Emergency-678-2882
  Information-678-5416

TRICARE-678-0300
Family Services-678-6767

**REST & RECREATION:**

Arts & Crafts-ext 5321
Bowling-ext 3465
Golf Course-ext 1759
ITR-678-4134
Museum/Gift Shop-ext 8829
Rec Center-ext 4134
Swimming-ext 3870

Auto Hobby Shop-ext 5800
Community Club-678-2057
Gym-ext 3374
Library-ext 5820
MWR-678-1256
Rec Equipment-ext 1713
Theater-678-2483

**ATTRACTIONS:** White Sands National Monument and Space Center.

# NEW YORK

## BUFFALO COAST GUARD GROUP (NY27R1)

1 Fuhrman Boulevard
Buffalo, NY 14203-3189

**TELEPHONE NUMBER INFORMATION:** Main installation number: C-716-843-9503. E-mail: comms/grubuffalo@cgsmtp.uscg.gov.mil
WEB: www.uscg.mil/d9/grubuff/webpage.html

**LOCATION:** From Route 5 (Fuhrmann Blvd) Skyway toward Buffalo. Take exit marked Buffalo Coast Guard west to CGG. USMRA: Page 20 (D-6). NMC: Buffalo, in city limits.

**GENERAL INFORMATION:** Operational Commander for ten stations in Ohio, Pennsylvania and New York.

**TEMPORARY MILITARY LODGING:** None. See Niagara Falls ARS listing.

**RV, CAMPING/FAMCAMP:** None. Nearest facility is more than 100 miles away.

**SPACE-A:** None. See Niagara Falls ARS listing.

**LOGISTICAL SUPPORT:**    Shoppette-856-8143

**ADMINISTRATIVE SUPPORT:**    CDO/OOD-843-9527

**HEALTH & WELFARE:**    Benefits Advisor-843-9515

**REST & RECREATION:** None. See Niagara Falls ARS listing.

**ATTRACTIONS:** Niagara Falls.

## CAMP SMITH (NY26R1)

Building 501
Peekskill, NY 10566-5000

**TELEPHONE NUMBER INFORMATION:** Main installation numbers: C-914-734-7397. WEB: www.dmna.state.ny.us/map/cp-smith.html

**LOCATION:** From US-9 north or south at Peekskill, take US-6 2 miles northwest to base. USMRA: Page 28 (D,E-5,6). NMC: New York City, 50 miles south.

**GENERAL INFORMATION:** HQ 1st Battalion 53rd Troop Command. Tenants include DEA, FBI, 106th Regimental Training Institute, 199th Army Band. Collective training area, supply and maintenance activities for NYARNG, ChalleNGe program for Youth.

**TEMPORARY MILITARY LODGING:** Billeting: C-914-734-7395.

**RV, CAMPING/FAMCAMP:** None. See Round Pond Recreation Area listing.

**SPACE-A:** None. See Stewart ANGB listing.

**LOGISTICAL SUPPORT:** None. See U.S. Military Academy, West Point listing.

**ADMINISTRATIVE SUPPORT:**              Locator-734-7397

**HEALTH & WELFARE:**              Chapel-734-7931

**REST & RECREATION:**
EM Club-734-7966              Gym-734-7966

**ATTRACTIONS:** Great scenery, Anthony's Nose, Manitou Mountain, the old copper mine, remains of Revolutionary forts.
*Note: At press time, restructuring was taking place.*

# FORT DRUM (NY06R1)

10th Mountain Division (Light Infantry)
ATTN: AFZS-PAO
Fort Drum, NY 13602-5000

**TELEPHONE NUMBER INFORMATION:** Main installation numbers: C-315-772-6011, D-312-341-6011. E-mail: afzs-pac@drum-emh4.army.mil WEB: www.drum.army.mil

**LOCATION:** From I-81 north or south take exit 48 (north of Watertown) east, and follow signs to Fort Drum. USMRA: Page 21 (J-3). NMC: Watertown, eight miles southwest.

**GENERAL INFORMATION:** Home for the 10th Mountain Division (Light Infantry), and the largest reserve component training and mobilization center in the northeastern United States.

**TEMPORARY MILITARY LODGING:** Lodging office, Building T-2227, 24 hours daily, C-315-772-5435, D-312-341-5435. All ranks. DV/VIP C-315-772-5010. Also, the Inn at Fort Drum at 4205 Po Valley Road, C-315-773-7777.

**RV, CAMPING/FAMCAMP:** Remington Pond Recreational Area, on post, April 1-October-15, C-315-772-5169, D-312-341-5169. Six camper/tent spaces with no hookups.

**SPACE-A:** Wheeler-Sack Army Airfield, Building P-2065, 0700-1730 hours, C-315-772-5681, D-312-341-5681. Limited flights via executive aircraft to primarily east coast CONUS locations.

**LOGISTICAL SUPPORT:**

| | |
|---|---|
| Bank-772-7881/773-0155 | Barber shop-772-3498 |
| Beauty shop-772-4422 | Cafeteria-772-5164 |
| Car Care Center-773-8025/6 | Carlson Wagonlit Travel-772-8066/7 |
| Child Care-772-7105/8672 | Class Six-772-6989 |
| Commissary-772-7457 | Conv Store-773-4149 |
| Credit Union-772-5244 | Dining Facilities-772-3295 |
| Dry Cleaner-772-4977 | Food Court-773-0065 |
| Education Office | Exchange-773-0061 |
| 772-6878 | Laundry-772-4977 |
| 772-3286 | Postal Service-772-5220 |
| Shoppette-773-1005 | Travel Office-772-5750 |

**ADMINISTRATIVE SUPPORT:**

| | |
|---|---|
| Fire Dept-772-4131 | Housing Office-772-5435 |
| Legal-772-5261 | Locator-772-5869/9183 |
| Pass/ID Office-772-5149 | Police-772-5156/7 |
| Public Affairs-772-5461 | SDO/SNCO-772-5647/8 |

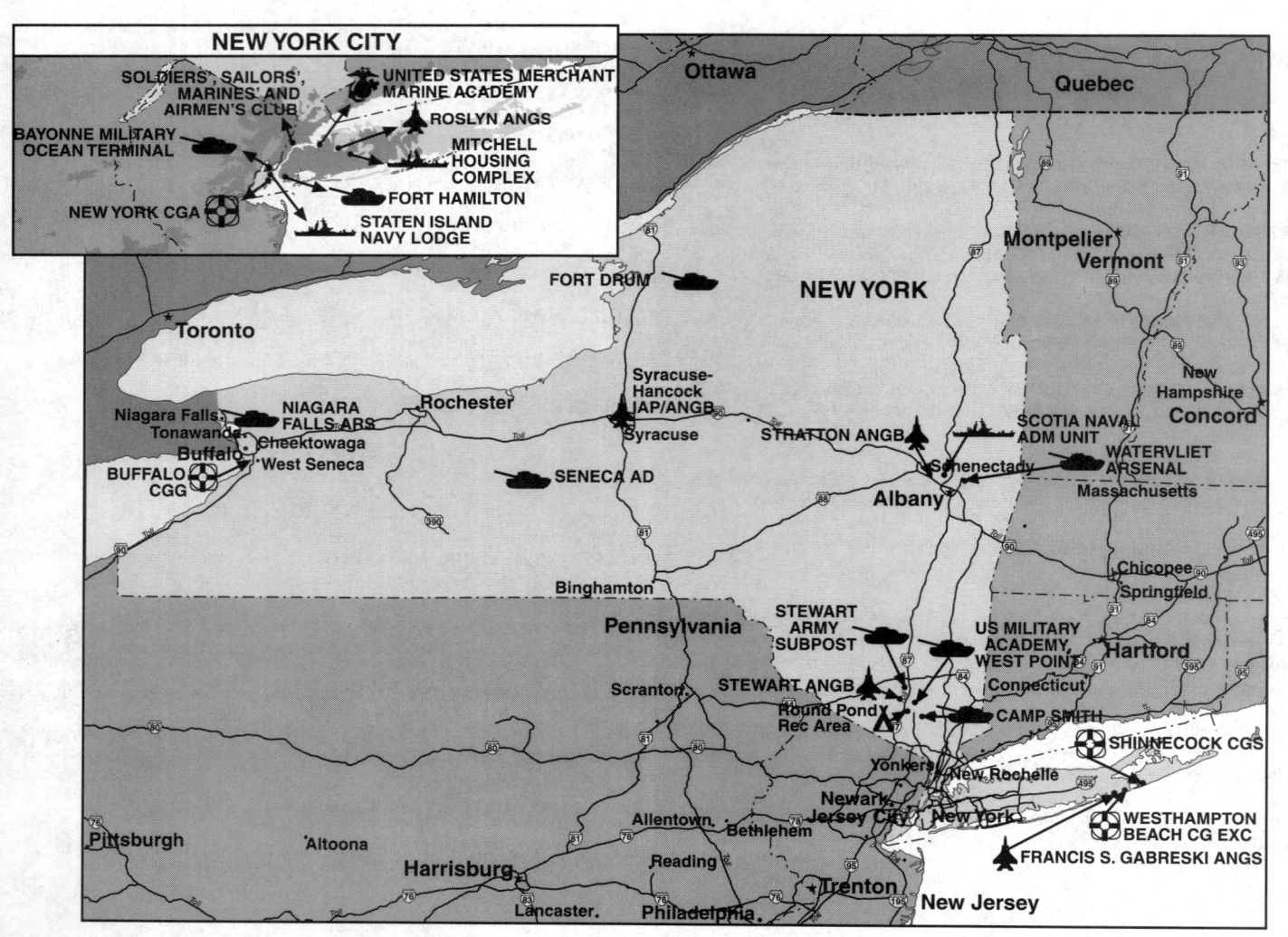

**HEALTH & WELFARE:**

American Red Cross-772-6561

Army Emergency Relief-772-6560

Chapel-772-5591

Family Services-772-6799

Medical

   Central Appts-772-8162

   Specialty Clinic-772-4350

   Emergency-911 or 772-5236

   Health Benefits-772-4855

   Information-722-8175

ACS-772-7618

CHAMPUS-772-5111

Dental

   Central Appts-772-8891

   Clinic-772-4614

   Emergency-772-5236

Retiree Services-772-6434

TRICARE-772-4312

Veterinary Services-772-4265

**REST & RECREATION:**

Arts & Crafts-772-6857/5606

Bowling-772-6601

Fitness Center-772-4806

Gym-772-9670

Indoor Rec-772-6857/5606

ITR-772-8222/3

Library-772-5929

MWR-772-5001

Outdoor Rec-772-5169

Youth Center-772-6717

Auto Hobby Shop-772-5785/7902

Clubs

   Benway's Tavern-772-2736

   Christie's-772-2734

   Commons-772-6222

   Pennants-773-8003

   Spinners-773-8005

   Winner's Circle-772-7673

Wood Hobby Shop-772-5606/6857

Youth Services-772-6719

**ATTRACTIONS:** Sackets Harbor Battlefield (site of War of 1812 battle), Thousand Islands and St. Lawrence River, New York Finger Lakes, Lake Ontario, Adirondack Park and Lake Placid and Canada (Toronto, Kingston, Montreal and Ottawa) nearby.

## FORT HAMILTON (NY02R1)

US Army Garrison, Fort Hamilton

ATTN: ANFH-PA

114 White Avenue, Suite 243

Brooklyn, NY 11252-5700

**TELEPHONE NUMBER INFORMATION:** Main installation numbers: C-718-630-4101, D-312-232-4101.
*Ten digit dialing required for local calls.*

**LOCATION:** From Belt Parkway exit 2 (Fort Hamilton Parkway) to 100th Street, right to Fort Hamilton Parkway, right to main gate. USMRA: Page 26 (D-7). NMC: New York, in city limits.

**GENERAL INFORMATION:** New York Area Command providing facilities and support for Army and DoD activities in the New York City metro area. Tenant Organizations: NY MEPS, NYC Recruiting Battalion, 8th Medical Brigade, North Atlantic Division Corps of Engineers.

**TEMPORARY MILITARY LODGING:** Lodging office, Building 109, 0800-1630 hours daily, C-718-630-4052/4937, D-312-232-4502/4937. All ranks. DV/VIP C-716-630-4052.

**RV, CAMPING/FAMCAMP:** None. See USMA, West Point listing, Round Pond Rec Area.

**SPACE-A:** None. See Stewart IAP/ANGB.

**LOGISTICAL SUPPORT:**

Carlson Wagonlit Travel-730-2706

Class VI-748-3440

Convenience Store-748-3440

Exchange-748-3440

Gas Station-680-2773

Snack Bar-748-3440

Child Care-630-4040

Commissary-630-4591

Education Center-630-4715

Fast Food-748-4876

SATO-230-2706

Visitor Center-630-4349

**ADMINISTRATIVE SUPPORT:**

Legal-630-4024

Protocol-630-4436

Police-630-4456

Public Affairs-630-4721

**HEALTH & WELFARE:**

ACS-630-4754

Family Services-630-4332

Chapel-630-4969

Medical-630-4129

Retiree Services-630-4930

TRICARE-630-4754/4129

Central Appts-630-4268

Emergency-630-4555

Hospital-390-6000

**REST & RECREATION:**

Arts & Crafts-ext 4942

Bowling-630-4440

Fitness Center-630-4793

Museum-630-4349

Rec Center-630-4476

Theater-748-3440

Auto Hobby Shop-630-4150

Community Club-630-4903

Library-630- 4875

MWR-630-4778/4433

Sports-630-4793

Youth Activities-630-4123

**ATTRACTIONS:** Historic fort, New York City nearby, Harbor Defense Museum.

## FRANCIS S. GABRESKI AIR NATIONAL GUARD STATION (NY25R1)

150 Old Riverhead Road

Westhampton Beach, NY 11978-1201

**TELEPHONE NUMBER INFORMATION:** Main installation numbers: C-516-288-7400, D-312-456-7400. WEB: www.infoshop.com/106rescue

**LOCATION:** On Long Island, one mile south of NY-27 (Sunrise Highway), exit 63 onto Old Riverhead Road. USMRA: Page 20 (F-2). NMC: Westhampton Beach, in city limits.

**GENERAL INFORMATION:** Home of the 106th Rescue Wing, Air National Guard.

**TEMPORARY MILITARY LODGING:** None. Nearest facility is more than 100 miles away. Military rates available at surrounding commercial motels.

**RV, CAMPING/FAMCAMP:** None. Nearest facility is more than 100 miles away.

**SPACE-A:** Pax Term, Building 369, Monday through Friday 0730-1600, C-516-288-7362, D-312-456-7362.

**LOGISTICAL SUPPORT:**

Exchange-288-7557

Package Store-288-7557

**ADMINISTRATIVE SUPPORT:**

CDO/OOD-288-7416

Legal-288-7587

Police-288-7478

Fire Dept-288-7534

Pass/ID Office-288-7571

Public Affairs-288-7400

**HEALTH & WELFARE:**

Chapel-288-7566

Medical-288-7447

**REST & RECREATION:**

Combined Club-288-7481

**ATTRACTIONS:** Beaches nearby, gateway to the Hamptons. New York City, with its many attractions, is just 70 miles east.

## MITCHEL HOUSING COMPLEX (NY21R1)

82B Mitchel Avenue

East Meadow, NY 11554-5000

**TELEPHONE NUMBER INFORMATION:** Main installation numbers: C-516-483-3405. E-mail: mhousing@aol.com

**LOCATION:** From north: Northern State Pkwy to Meadowbrook Pkwy (exit 29B) south to right at Merrick Avenue, right on Front Street, left at Mitchel Avenue. From south: Verrazano Bridge to east on Belt Pkwy, stay left to Southern State Pkwy to Meadowbrook Pkwy (exit 2) north to exit M3 (Stewart Avenue) west on Stewart to left at second light. At next light turn left at Garden City Center Bldg. Go one block, turn right. Mitchel Field is on the left, West Road. USMRA: Page 26 (I,J-4). NMC: New York City, 27 miles west.

**GENERAL INFORMATION:** Mitchel Field and Mitchel Manor Housing Areas with supporting facilities. The two areas are approximately five miles apart on Long Island, New York. It is a joint services community (Army, Air Force, Navy, Marines and Coast Guard): Mostly recruiters assigned throughout the New York area.

**TEMPORARY MILITARY LODGING:** None. See Fort Hamilton listing.

**RV, CAMPING/FAMCAMP:** None. Nearest facility is more than 100 miles away.

**SPACE-A:** None. See Suffolk County ANGB/Francis S. Gabreski ANGS listing.

**LOGISTICAL SUPPORT:**
Child Care-483-3106                    Class Six-222-1293/4
Commissary-222-0880                    Exchange-222-1293

**ADMINISTRATIVE SUPPORT:**
Housing Office-486-2022                Police-222-1285
SDO/NCO-222-1285

**HEALTH & WELFARE:**
CHAMPUS-222-0228                       Family Services-486-1922
Medical-222-0228                       Retiree Services-222-1282

**REST & RECREATION:**
Community Center-ext 0282              Fitness Center-483-3016
Gym-222-0340                           MWR-483-3106
Rec Equipment-ext 1611                 Swimming Pool-222-0340
Theater-222-1610                       Youth Services-483-3106

**ATTRACTIONS:** New York City Cradle of Aviation Museum on base (hangar 384), Nassau Veterans Memorial Coliseum, Jones Beach State Park, New York City and Garden City's Children's Museum. Departure site for Charles Lindbergh's first nonstop, solo transatlantic flight.

# NEW YORK COAST GUARD ACTIVITIES
## (NY01R1)
Commander
212 Coast Guard Drive
Fort Wadsworth
Staten Island, NY 10305-5000

**TELEPHONE NUMBER INFORMATION:** Main installation numbers: C-718-354-4037. WEB: www.uscg.mil/d1/units/actny
*Ten digit dialing required for local calls.*

**LOCATION:** Take I-95 north or south to exit 13 east to Goethals Bridge (I-278 east) to Staten Island. Last exit before Verrazano Bridge, (Lily Pond Avenue). At light go left onto School Road, follow School Road to next light, go right onto Bay Street to main gate. USMRA: Page 26 (D-5). NMC: New York City.

**GENERAL INFORMATION:** Coast Guard Activities New York. Co-located with Gateway National Park, Fort Wadsworth, NY.

**TEMPORARY MILITARY LODGING:** CG Guest House, 204 Molony Drive, Staten Island. Call Mon-Fri 0900-1500. C-718-354-4407; Fax: 718-354-4402. Navy Lodge: Ft. Wadsworth, NY 10305, C-718-420-0413; Fax: 718-816-0830.

**RV, CAMPING/FAMCAMP:** None. Nearest facility is more than 100 miles away.

**SPACE-A:** None. See McGuire AFB, NJ listing.

**LOGISTICAL SUPPORT:**
Dining-354-4360                        Exchange-815-6519

**ADMINISTRATIVE SUPPORT:**
Housing office-718-354-4401            Pass/ID Office-354-4037
Police (Security)-354-4398             Public Affairs-212-668-7114

**HEALTH & WELFARE:**
Chapel-354-4421
                                       Medical Information-354-4414

**REST & RECREATION:**
Fitness Center-390-1760                Gym-354-4407
ITT-354-4407                           MWR-354-4407

**ATTRACTIONS:** New York City.

# NIAGARA FALLS AIR RESERVE STATION
## (NY12R1)
914th AW/Public Affairs
2720 Kirkbridge Drive
Niagara Falls ARS, NY 14304-5001

**TELEPHONE NUMBER INFORMATION:** Main installation numbers: C-716-236-2000, D-312-238-3011.

**LOCATION:** Take I-190 north or south to Niagara Falls, exit 23 Porter Packard Road east. Turn right onto Porter Road (Route 182) east and stay on it past five traffic lights until it becomes Lockport Road. After one mile on Lockport, turn right at main gate. USMRA: Page 20 (D-6). NMC: Niagara Falls, six miles west.

**GENERAL INFORMATION:** 914th Airlift Wing (AFRES), 107th Air Refueling Group (NYANG).

**TEMPORARY MILITARY LODGING:** Bldg. 312, 10780 Kinross Street, 0700-2300 daily, C-716-236-2014, D-312-238-2014, Fax: C-716-236-6348, D-312-238-6348. All ranks. DV/VIP C-716-236-2136/2139.

**RV, CAMPING/FAMCAMP:** None. Nearest facility is more than 100 miles away.

**SPACE-A:** Pax Term/Lounge, Building 807, 0715-1600 Mon-Fri, C-716-236-2475, D-312-238-2475, Fax: C-716-236-2380, D-312-238-2380. Flights to CONUS and overseas via AFRES aircraft.

**LOGISTICAL SUPPORT:**
Bank-236-2085                          Class Six-236-2100
Credit Union-236-2085                  Dining-236-2027
Exchange-236-2100                      Snack Bar-236-2329
Travel Office-236-6392

**ADMINISTRATIVE SUPPORT:**
Fire Dept-236-2086                     Legal-236-2133
Pass/ID Office-236-2197/2280           Police-236-2280
Public Affairs-236-2136/7

**HEALTH & WELFARE:**
Chapel-236-2382                        Family Services-236-2097
Medical-236-2301                       Retiree Services-236-2389

**REST & RECREATION:**
Bowling-236-2329                       Consolidated Club-236-2027
Fitness Center-236-2101

**ATTRACTIONS:** Greater Buffalo, Niagara Falls, Canada and Festival of Lights.

# ROSLYN AIR NATIONAL GUARD STATION
## (NY31R1)
209 Harbor Hill Road
Roslyn, NY 11576-2345
*Scheduled to close 1999*

**TELEPHONE NUMBER INFORMATION:** Main installation numbers: C-516-299-5229. WEB: www.ngb.dtic.mil

**LOCATION:** From Meadowbrook State Parkway take 39 north exit onto Glen Cove. At third light turn left onto Harbor Hill Road. Go half a mile; base is on right. USMRA: Page 26 (I-4). NMC: New york (Manhattan), 16 miles east.

**GENERAL INFORMATION:** Home of the 213 Engineer Installation Squadron and 274 Combat Communications Squadron.

**LOGISTICAL SUPPORT:**                Shoppette-299-5310/625-6946

**ATTRACTIONS:** New York City.

## ROUND POND RECREATION AREA (NY04R1)

DCFA-CRD/Round Pond, Bldg 681
West Point, NY 10996-5000

**TELEPHONE NUMBER INFORMATION:** Main installation numbers: C-914-938-4011, D-312-688-1110. Police for recreation area, C-914-938-3333.

**LOCATION:** Off post. Three miles west of West Point on NY-293. Exit 16 from I-87, follow US-6 east to NY-293, continue east to recreation area. USMRA: Page 21 (M,N-10) and page 28 (D-3,4). NMI: U.S. Military Academy, West Point, three miles east. NMC: New York City, 50 miles southeast.

**GENERAL INFORMATION:** Operated by United States Military Academy, West Point, off base, open from 15 April-15 October. Military personnel active, reservists, retired, DoD civilians. Reservations (required): DCFA-CRD/Round Pond, Bldg 681, West Point, NY 10996-5000. C-914-938-2503, D-312-688-2503 0700-1800 hours. Fax: C-914-446-5503.

**RV, CAMPING/FAMCAMP:**

| | |
|---|---|
| Cabin-1 | Camper Spaces-26 |
| Tent Spaces-26 | |
| Lake Frederick Area, six miles from Round Pond: A-Frames-10 | |

**ATTRACTIONS:** Located on Academy property in rocky, wooded area near old Ramapo mines. Delightful place with natural spring-fed pond.

*For detailed information about this off-base recreation facility, as well as on-base recreation facilities, golf courses and marinas, consult Military Living's Military RV, Camping and Outdoor Recreation Around the World.*

## SCOTIA NAVAL ADMINISTRATION UNIT (NY32R1)

1 Amsterdam Road
Scotia, NY 12302-9460

**TELEPHONE NUMBER INFORMATION:** Main installation numbers: C-518-395-3600.

**LOCATION:** Take I-87 north and exit 9 to NY-146 west. Continue to Glenridge Road to Maple Avenue, left to Air National Guard Road and main gate. USMRA: Page 21 (M,N-6). NMC: Schenectady, three miles west.

**GENERAL INFORMATION:** Support for Naval Nuclear Power Training Unit.

**TEMPORARY MILITARY LODGING:** None. Nearest facility is more than 100 miles away.

**RV, CAMPING/FAMCAMP:** None. Nearest facility is more than 100 miles away.

**SPACE-A:** None. See Stratton ANGB listing.

**LOGISTICAL SUPPORT:**

| | |
|---|---|
| Child Care-584-3579 | Commissary-370-5935 |
| Exchange-377-6440 | Travel Office-382-0476 |

**ADMINISTRATIVE SUPPORT:** Police (Security)-370-3346

**HEALTH & WELFARE:**

| | |
|---|---|
| Dental-Clinic-885-3782/3 | Medical-885-4011/2/3 |
| Navy-MC Relief-583-2900 | |

**REST & RECREATION:**

| | |
|---|---|
| Community Center-581-0046 | MWR: 370-4022 |
| Outdoor Recreation-885-5138 | |

**ATTRACTIONS:** Area of great scenic beauty, boating, skiing, fishing, hiking, Albany, museums, caverns, Baseball Hall of Fame.

## SENECA ARMY DEPOT ACTIVITY (NY03R1)

ATTN: SIOSE-CO
5786 State Route 96
Romulus, NY 14541-5001
*Scheduled to close Sept 2000*

**TELEPHONE NUMBER INFORMATION:** Main installation numbers: C-607-869-1110, D-312-489-5110.

**LOCATION:** From I-90 east or west, exit 42 south on Route 14 for one mile to east, then south on Route 96 for 16 miles and front gate, on west side of Route 96 in town of Romulus. USMRA: Page 20 (H-7). NMC: Geneva, 12 miles north, Rochester, 55 miles northwest.

**GENERAL INFORMATION:** U.S. Coast Guard LORAN-C Transmitting Station; U.S. Army Test, Maintenance, and Diagnostic Equipment Support Operations; Defense Reutilization and Marketing Office-Romulus Branch; U.S. Army Health Clinic.

**TEMPORARY MILITARY LODGING:** None. See Niagara Falls ARS listing.

**RV, CAMPING/FAMCAMP:** None. Nearest facility is more than 100 miles away.

**SPACE-A:** None. See Niagara Falls ARS listing.

**LOGISTICAL SUPPORT:** Police-869-1366

**ADMINISTRATIVE SUPPORT:**

| | |
|---|---|
| Locator-869-1110 | Pass/ID Office-869-1202 |
| Police (Security)-869-1228 | Public Affairs-869-1235 |

**HEALTH & WELFARE:**

| | |
|---|---|
| CHAMPUS-869-1243 | |
| Family Services-869-1744 | TRICARE-869-1747 |

**REST & RECREATION:** None. See Niagara Falls ARS listing.

**ATTRACTIONS:** Finger Lakes region of NY, wineries and Womens' Rights National Park.

## SHINNECOCK COAST GUARD STATION (NY30R1)

Foster Avenue
Hampton Bays, NY 11946-3298

**TELEPHONE NUMBER INFORMATION:** Main installation numbers: C-516-728-0343.

**LOCATION:** From 27 north take Hampton Bays exit 65 south, get in left lane and take left at diner. At second light, turn right on Ponquoque Avenue, left on Shinnecock Road for half a mile, then right on Foster. Coast Guard Station is half mile on left. USMRA: Page 20 (G-2). NMC: Islip, 80 miles west.

**GENERAL INFORMATION:** Part of U.S. Coast Guard First District.

**LOGISTICAL SUPPORT:** Exchange-728-4350

**ATTRACTIONS:** Beaches, boating, fishing.

## SOLDIERS', SAILORS', MARINES' & AIRMEN'S CLUB (NY17R1)

283 Lexington Avenue
New York, NY 10016-3540

**TELEPHONE NUMBER INFORMATION:** Main installation numbers: Reservations C-1-800-678-8443; Fax: C-212-683-4374. WEB: www.ssmaclub.org
*Ten digit dialing required for local calls.*

**LOCATION**: Midtown Manhattan, on Lexington Avenue between 36th (one way eastbound) and 37th Streets (one way westbound); five blocks from Grand Central Terminal at 42nd Street and Lexington Avenue. USMRA: Page 26 (E-4). NMC: New York, in city limits.

**AUTHOR'S NOTE**: The Soldiers', Sailors', Marines' and Airmen's Club is a tax exempt, not-for-profit organization founded in 1919 to serve the needs of service personnel while visiting New York City. **This club is not U.S. Military/Government lodging.**

**OFFICE**: Check in and out at the lobby desk, 24 hours daily. Check in 1430 hours, check out 1030 hours. Call the numbers listed above for reservations and information on lodging and related club activities.

**OTHER INFORMATION**: Facilities include lounges, library and canteen with TV. The USO of Metropolitan New York is now located at the Soldiers', Sailors', Marines' and Airmen's Club and offers its services to all Uniformed Services ID holders.

## STATEN ISLAND NAVY LODGE (NY07R1)
Building 408 N Path Road
Staten Island, NY 10305-5000

**TELEPHONE NUMBER INFORMATION**: Main installation numbers: C-718-442-0413, Fax: 718-816-0830.

**LOCATION**: Take I-95 north or south to exit 13 east to Goethals Bridge (I-278 east) to Staten Island. Last exit before Verrazano Bridge, (Lily Pond Avenue). At light go left onto School Road, follow School Road to next light, go right onto Bay Street to main gate. USMRA: Page 26 (C-7). NMC: New York City, in city limits.

**GENERAL INFORMATION**: Fifty units, open to all ranks active, reservists, retired, DoD civilians.

**TEMPORARY MILITARY LODGING**: Navy Lodge C-718-442-0413, C-1-800-NAVY-INN, Fax: 718-816-0830.

**ATTRACTIONS**: New York City, Staten Island sights.

*For more detailed information about this and other military lodging facilities, refer to Military Living's Temporary Military Lodging Around the World.*

## STEWART AIR NATIONAL GUARD BASE (NY24R1)
218 Militia Way
Newburg, NY 12550-5043

**TELEPHONE NUMBER INFORMATION**: Main installation numbers: C-914-563-2285/6, D-312-636-2285/6. WEB: www-105aw.ang.af.mil

**LOCATION**: From I-84 or I-87 take exit 17 Union Avenue south to Route 17-K west for three miles. Follow signs to Stewart ANG Base, colocated with Stewart IAP. USMRA: Page 21 (M-10). NMC: New York Ciyt, 60 miles south.

**GENERAL INFORMATION**: Home of the 105th Airlift Wing, Air National Guard. Tenants include USMC.

**TEMPORARY MILITARY LODGING**: None. See USMA West Point listing.

**RV, CAMPING/FAMCAMP**: None. See Round Pond Recreation Area listing.

**SPACE-A**: Information: C-914-563-2226, D-312-636-2226, Fax: C-914-563-2228, D-312-636-2228.

**LOGISTICAL SUPPORT:**

| | |
|---|---|
| Credit Union-564-7860 | Dry Cleaner-563-3481 |
| Exchange-564-7601 | Shoppette-564-7600 |

**ADMINISTRATIVE SUPPORT:**          Public Affairs-563-2031/2040

**HEALTH & WELFARE**:

| | |
|---|---|
| Chapel-564-3310 | Dental-563-3438 |
| Medical-563-2113 | |

**REST & RECREATION:**          Group Tours-563-2007

**ATTRACTIONS:** New York City.

## STEWART ARMY SUBPOST (NY09R1)
United States Military Academy West Point
P.O. Box 9000
New Windsor, NY 12553-9000

**TELEPHONE NUMBER INFORMATION**: Main installation numbers: C-914-563-3323, D-312-688-1110.

**LOCATION**: From I-87 take Newburgh exit east to Union Avenue, south to NY-207 west. Follow signs to Stewart Airport and Subpost. USMRA: Page 21 (M-10). NMC: New York City, 60 miles south.

**GENERAL INFORMATION**: Support activity for U.S. Military Academy, West Point. In the process of divestiture from West Point. Facility availability and phone numbers subject to change as reorganization takes place.

**TEMPORARY MILITARY LODGING**: None. See USMA West Point listing for Five Star Inn info.

**RV, CAMPING/FAMCAMP**: None. See Round Pond Recreation Area listing.

**SPACE-A**: None. See Stewart IAP/ANGB listing.

**LOGISTICAL SUPPORT:**

| | |
|---|---|
| Barber Shop-567-0150 | Child Dev Center-563-3522 |
| Commissary-938-3663 | Conv Store-564-7601 |
| Credit Union-564-7860 | Dry Cleaner-563-3481 |
| Exchange-564-7600 | Laundry-563-3481 |

**ADMINISTRATIVE SUPPORT:**

Fire Dept-564-7033

Police-567-6031

Public Affairs (West Point)-938-3808

**HEALTH & WELFARE:**

ACS-563-3257

Chapel-564-3310

Dental-563-3438

Family Services-563-3485

Medical-563-2113

Navy-MC Relief-563-3203

**REST & RECREATION:**

Arts & Crafts-563-3584

Auto Hobby Shop-563-3420

Bowling-563-3447

Clubs

Gym-563-3565

    Community-564-6661

Library-563-3501

    Wings-564-7590

MWR-563-3485

Youth Services-563-3544

**ATTRACTIONS:** Historic USMA, West Point, and Hudson River Valley.

## STRATTON AIR NATIONAL GUARD BASE (NY23R1)

109th Airlift Wing, 1 Air National Guard Road
Stratton ANGB, Scotia, NY 12302-9460

**TELEPHONE NUMBER INFORMATION:** Main installation numbers: C-518-344-2300, D-312-974-9300.

**LOCATION:** From I-87 north or south, exit 89 to NY-146 west (Mechanicville Road). Continue on, as it changes to Glenridge Road, to Maple Avenue, left (south) onto Air National Guard Road and gate. USMRA: Page 21 (M,N-6). NMC: Schenectaday, three miles south.

**GENERAL INFORMATION:** Home of the 109th Airlift Wing, Air National Guard. All the support facilities of a regional airport.

**SPACE-A:** Information: C-518-344-2300, D-312-974-9300, Fax: C-518-344-2520, D-312-974-9520.

**ATTRACTIONS:** Saratoga Racecourse, 25 miles away. Saratoga Performing Arts Center, 24 miles away. Downtown Albany (State Capital), 20 miles away.

## SYRACUSE-HANCOCK INTERNATIONAL AIRPORT/AIR NATIONAL GUARD BASE (NY10R1)

174th FW, 6001 E Malloy Road
Syracuse, NY 13211-7099

**TELEPHONE NUMBER INFORMATION:** Main installation numbers: C-1-800-982-3696.

**LOCATION:** From I-81 north or south, take exit 27 north of Syracuse, east to IAP/ANGB. Clearly marked. USMRA: Page 21 (I-6). NMC: Syracuse, in city limits.

**GENERAL INFORMATION:** Home of the 174th Fighter Wing, Air National Guard.

**LOGISTICAL SUPPORT:**

Exchange-454-6440

**REST & RECREATION:**

Consol Club-454-6200

**ATTRACTIONS:** Syracuse has many museums; nearby are numerous lakes, parks, and Erie Canal.

## UNITED STATES MERCHANT MARINE ACADEMY (NY22R1)

Steamboat Road
Kings Point, NY 11024-1699

**TELEPHONE NUMBER INFORMATION:** Main installation numbers: C-516-773-5000. Emergency-ext 5911. WEB: www.usmma.edu

**LOCATION:** Take the Long Island Expressway to exit 33 north. Follow Community Drive north to East Shore Road, Hicks Lane (road changes names) to Middle Neck Road. Right onto Middle Neck Road to Steamboat Road. USMRA: Page 26 (H-3). NMC: New York City, in city limits.

**GENERAL INFORMATION:** Federal Academy operated by the Maritime Administration of the U.S. Department of Transportation.

**TEMPORARY MILITARY LODGING:** None. See Fort Hamilton listing.

**RV, CAMPING/FAMCAMP:** None. See Round Pond Recreation Area.

**SPACE-A:** None. See Francis S. Gabreski ANGS listing.

**LOGISTICAL SUPPORT:**

Bank-829-3937

Barber Shop-773-5738

Book Store-773-5296

Cafeteria-773-5557

Commissary-773-5372

Convenience Store-773-5616

Dining-773-5411

Education Center-773-5120

Postal Service-773-5298

**ADMINISTRATIVE SUPPORT:**

Police-773-5303

Public Affairs-773-5527

**HEALTH & WELFARE:** None. See Fort Hamilton listing.

**REST & RECREATION:**

O Club-773-5411

Library-773-5501

Gym-773-5454

Museum-773-5515

**ATTRACTIONS:** Waterfront activities, cultural events, The Schulyer Otis Bland Memorial Library and the American Merchant Marine Museum.

## UNITED STATES MILITARY ACADEMY, WEST POINT (NY16R1)

Building 600, Room A
West Point, NY 10996-5000

**TELEPHONE NUMBER INFORMATION:** Main installation numbers: C-914-938-4011, D-312-688-1110.

**LOCATION:** Off I-87 north or south or US-9 west. From I-81 take exit 16 west on Route 6 east to 9 west, north to main gate. Clearly marked. USMRA: Page 28 (C,D-3,4). NMC: New York City, 50 miles south.

**GENERAL INFORMATION:** Military Educational Institution, Corps of Cadets and support units.

**TEMPORARY MILITARY LODGING:** Hotel Thayer, Building 674, 24 hours daily, C-914-446-4731, D-312-688-2632 or 1-800-247-5047. All ranks. DV/VIP C-914-938-4315/4316, Five Star Inn C-800-GO ARMY1, C-914-446-1028/1034, D-312-688-6816. *Note: Lodging may not be available, due to ongoing renovations.*

**RV, CAMPING/FAMCAMP:** Lake Frederick Campgrounds, on base, 1 April-15 October, 18 campsites and 10 A-frame cabins. C-914-938-2503, D-312-688-2503. Nearby, off base, see Round Pond Recreation Area listing.

**SPACE-A:** None. See Stewart IAP/ANGB.

**LOGISTICAL SUPPORT:**

Barber Shop-446-6727

Child Care-938-4523

Commissary-938-2512

Conv Store-938-3035

Credit Union-446-4946

Education Center-938-3762

Exchange-446-5406

Fast Food-446-5755/5448

Gas Station-446-5556

SATO-446-6400

Visitor Center-938-2638

**ADMINISTRATIVE SUPPORT:**

Legal-938-3205

Locator-938-4412

Police-938-3333

Public Affairs-938-2006

SDO/NCO-938-3500

**HEALTH & WELFARE:**
ACS-938-2519
CHAMPUS-938-4838
Family Services-938-2023
Retiree Services-938-4217
TRICARE-888-999-5195

American Red Cross-938-4100
Chapel-938-2003
Medical-938-5169
  Emergency-938-4004
  Information-938-5169

**REST & RECREATION:**
Arts & Crafts-ext 4812/2074
Clubs
  Com-938-5120
  West Point-938-5120
Library-ext 2974
Rec Center-ext 3601/2070
Rental-ext 2503
Swimming-ext 2946/5158
Theater-938-4159

Bowling-ext 2140
Golf Course-ext 2435
Gym-ext 2338
ITR-938-2070
Lodge-ext 4335
Rec Office-ext 3809/4455
Ski Slope-ext 3726
Tate Skating Rink-ext 2991
Youth Center-ext 3208

**ATTRACTIONS:** Tours of historic USMA, West Point. Hudson River Valley.
*Note: At press time, West Point was undergoing much renovation.*

## WATERVLIET ARSENAL (NY19R1)
ATTN: SIOWV-CO
Building 10
Watervliet, NY 12189-4050

**TELEPHONE NUMBER INFORMATION:** Main installation numbers: C-518-266-5111, D-312-974-6111. WEB: www.wva.army.mil

**LOCATION:** From I-87 north or south, exit 23, take I-787 north to Route 387 west 0.5 miles to Route 32 north (2nd Avenue) 1.5 miles to Arsenal on west side of Route 32; or from I-81 north or south, exit 6 east on Route 2 (18th Street), go 3.5 miles to Route 32 south (2nd Avenue) for 1 mile to Arsenal on west side of Route 32. USMRA: Page 21 (N-7). NMC: Albany, six miles south.

**GENERAL INFORMATION:** Watervliet is an Army R&D and artillery/cannon production facility. Oldest continually active arsenal in the US.

**TEMPORARY MILITARY LODGING:** None. See Westover ARB, MA listing.

**RV, CAMPING/FAMCAMP:** None. Nearest facility is more than 100 miles away

**SPACE-A:** None. See Stewart IAP/ANGB listing.

**LOGISTICAL SUPPORT:**
Bank-266-5171
Convenience Store-266-5371
Exchange-266-5371

Cafeteria-266-5473
Dining-266-5971

**ADMINISTRATIVE SUPPORT:**
Legal-266-5298
Public Affairs-266-5418

Police-266-4334

**HEALTH & WELFARE:**
ACS-266-5103
Medical-266-4195

Family Services-266-5920
MWR-266-5424

**REST & RECREATION:**          Com Club-266-5971

**OTHER FACILITIES AVAILABLE:** Pitch and Putt Golf Course, tennis, swimming, racquetball court, health facility.

**ATTRACTIONS:** Albany (New York's Capital), Rivers Park (Industrial Heritage Tour), Saratoga Race Track, Saratoga Performing Arts Center, State Museum, Peebles Island State Park, Watervliet Arsenal Museum.

## WESTHAMPTON BEACH
## COAST GUARD EXCHANGE (NY33R1)
Bldg 222, Main Road, Suffolk County Airport
Westhampton Beach, NY 11978-5000

**TELEPHONE NUMBER INFORMATION:** Main installation numbers: C-516-288-7557.

**LOCATION:** On Long Island, east 1 mile south of NY-27 (Sunrise Hwy). Exit 63 south onto Old Riverhead Road (Route 31 south) to entrance. USMRA: Page 20 (F-2). NMC: Southampton, 12 miles east.

**LOGISTICAL SUPPORT:**          Exchange-288-7557

**ATTRACTIONS:** Beaches nearby, gateway to the Hamptons. New York City, with its many attractions, is just 70 miles east.

# NORTH CAROLINA

## CAMP LEJEUNE MARINE CORPS BASE (NC10R1)

Box 20004
Camp Lejeune Marine Corps Base, NC 28542-0004

**TELEPHONE NUMBER INFORMATION:** Main installation numbers: C-910-451-1113, D-312-751-1113.

**LOCATION:** Main gate is six miles east of junction of US-17 and NC-24, off NC-24. USMRA: Page 45 (L,M-5). NMC: Jacksonville, three miles northwest.

**GENERAL INFORMATION:** USMC Forces Atlantic, II MEF, 2nd Marine Division, 2nd Force Service Support Group.

**TEMPORARY MILITARY LODGING:** Lodging office, Building 2617, 24 hours daily, C-910-451-1385, D-312-751-1385. Hostess House, C-910-451-3041. DV/VIP C-910-451-2523.

**RV, CAMPING/FAMCAMP:** Onslow Beach Campsites and Rec Area, on base, year round, C-910-450-7473/7502, D-312-751-7473/7502.

**SPACE-A:** None. See Cherry Point MCAS listing.

**LOGISTICAL SUPPORT:**

| | |
|---|---|
| Bank-451-5877 | Credit Union-451-2492 |
| Commissary-451-2172 | Dining Facilities 451-1567 |
| Conv Store-451-5491 | Food Court-451-5776 |
| Exchange-451-5030 | Mess Halls-451-1567 |
| Gas Station-451-2443 | Omega Travel-451-3788 |
| SATO-451-2192/5889 | Visitor Center-451-2197 |

**ADMINISTRATIVE SUPPORT:**

| | |
|---|---|
| CDO-451-2414/3031 | Legal-451-1903 |
| Locator-451-3074 | Police-451-2555 |
| Public Affairs-451-5655 | SDO/NCO-451-2528 |

**HEALTH & WELFARE:**

| | |
|---|---|
| CHAMPUS-451-4150 | Chapel-451-5775/5646/5342 |
| Family Services-451-3212 | Medical-451-4300 |
| Retiree Services-451-5927 | |

**REST & RECREATION:**

| | |
|---|---|
| Clubs | Golf Course-451-5445 |
| CPO-451-2839 | ITT-451-5380 |
| EM-451-2872 | MWR-451-2425 |
| O-451-2465 | Marina-450-7386 |
| SNCO-451-2839 | Recreation-451-2108 |
| Theater-451-1759 | |

**ATTRACTIONS:** Raleigh, NC, state capital, 116 miles northeast. Wilmington, 45 miles south. Both offer many museums, historical areas and gardens. Beaches on base.

## CAPE HATTERAS COAST GUARD GROUP (NC09R1)

P.O. Box 604
Old Lighthouse Road
Buxton, NC 27920-0604

**TELEPHONE NUMBER INFORMATION:** Main installation number: C-252-995-6408. E-mail: gruchops@pinn.net WEB: www.uscg.mil/d5/group/capehatteras

**LOCATION:** From US-158 south or US-64 east, take NC-12 south to Buxton (approximately 50 miles south of Nags Head). East on Old Lighthouse Road, one half mile to base. USMRA: Page 45 (P-3). NMC: Elizabeth City, 110 miles northwest.

**GENERAL INFORMATION:** Coast Guard Group.

**TEMPORARY MILITARY LODGING:** Recreational Quarters, C-252-995-3676, Fax: C-252-995-6428. Six units that sleep four, one suite that sleeps six and one suite that sleeps seven.

**RV, CAMPING/FAMCAMP:** None. See Cherry Point MCAS listing.

**SPACE-A:** None. See Cherry Point MCAS listing.

**LOGISTICAL SUPPORT:**

| | |
|---|---|
| Class VI-995-6455 | Convenience Store-995-6455 |
| Dining Facilities-995-6421 | Exchange-995-6431 |
| Gas Station-995-6455 | |

**ADMINISTRATIVE SUPPORT:**

| | |
|---|---|
| Housing Service-995-6458 | OOD-995-6408 |
| Public Affairs-995-6416 | |

**HEALTH & WELFARE:** Medical-995-6427

**REST & RECREATION:** Fitness Center available

**OTHER FACILITIES AVAILABLE:** Gas station.

**ATTRACTIONS:** Within walking distance of the historic Cape Hatteras Lighthouse. Excellent beaches, fishing, and wind surfing.

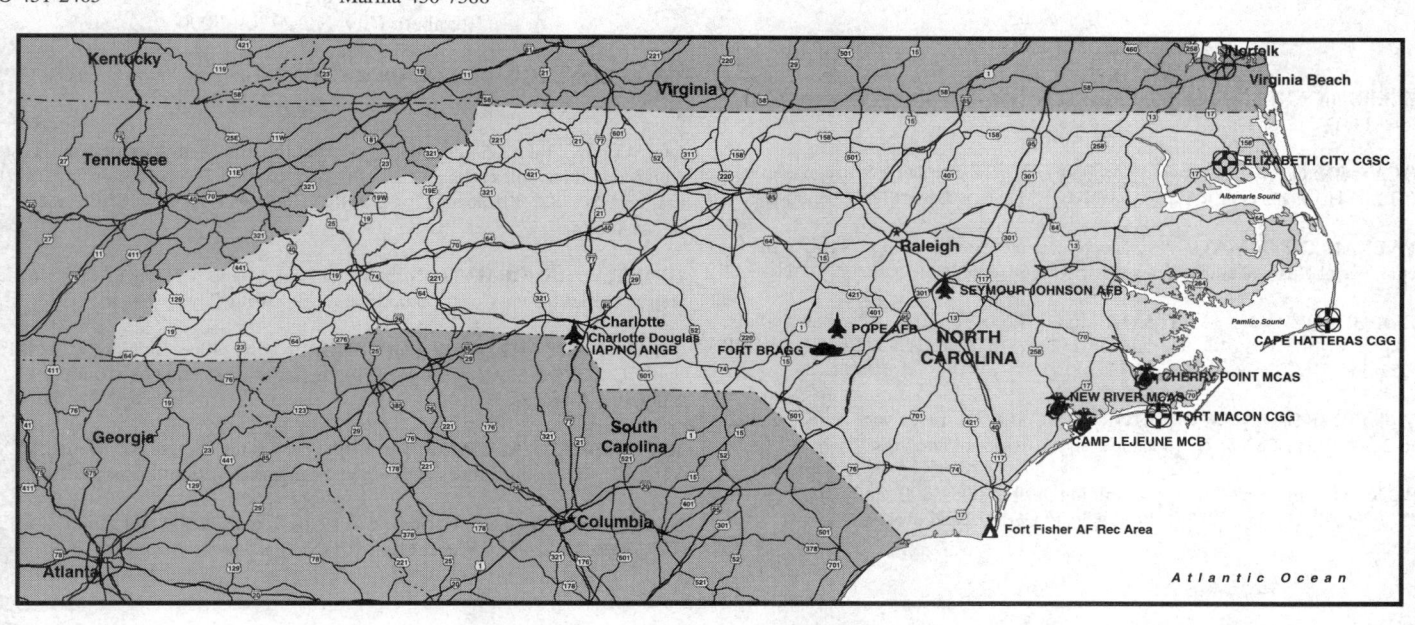

# CHARLOTTE DOUGLAS INTERNATIONAL AIRPORT/NORTH CAROLINA AIR NATIONAL GUARD BASE (NC20R1)

5225 Morris Field Drive
Charlotte, NC 28208-5797

**TELEPHONE NUMBER INFORMATION:** Main installation numbers: C-704-391-4100, D-312-583-9210.

**LOCATION:** From I-77 north or south take exit 6 A/B to Billy Graham Parkway (US-521) north to Morris Field Drive (3.5 miles), turn left. Base is on your right. From I-85 take Billy Graham Parkway Exit 33 south to Morris Field Drive, turn right. USMRA: Page 44 (G-4). NMC: Charlotte, three miles east.

**GENERAL INFORMATION:** Headquarters of the North Carolina Air National Guard.

**TEMPORARY MILITARY LODGING:** None. See Fort Bragg listing.

**RV, CAMPING/FAMCAMP:** None. See Fort Bragg listing, Smith Lake Army Travel Campground.

**SPACE-A:** Base Operations C-704-391-4148, D-312-583-9177, Fax: C-704-391-4322. Unscheduled flights to CONUS and overseas.

**LOGISTICAL SUPPORT:**
Cafeteria-391-4256/583-4256
SATO-391-4163
Dining-391-4256/583-4266

**ADMINISTRATIVE SUPPORT:**
Fire Department-391-4206
Pass/ID Office-391-4217
Public Affairs-391-4141
Legal-391-4260
Police-391-4152

**HEALTH & WELFARE:**
Chapel-391-4179
Medical Clinic-391-4350
Dental Clinic-391-4311

**REST & RECREATION:**
Clubs
  EM-391-4426
  O-391-4427
Fitness Center-391-4830

**ATTRACTIONS:** City of Charlotte, NC, Carowinds Amusement Park, Carolina Panthers Football.

# CHERRY POINT MARINE CORPS AIR STATION (NC02R1)

PSC Box 8003
Cherry Point, NC 28533-0003

**TELEPHONE NUMBER INFORMATION:** Main installation numbers: C-252-466-2811, D-312-582-1110.

**LOCATION:** On NC-101 between New Bern and Morehead City. US-70 connects with NC-101 at Havelock. USMRA: Page 45 (N-4). NMC: New Bern, 17 miles northwest.

**GENERAL INFORMATION:** Second Marine Aircraft Wing, Naval Aviation Depot, Naval Hospital and Defense Distribution Depot.

**TEMPORARY MILITARY LODGING:** Lodging office, 24 hours daily, Building 3673 (EM), 24 hours daily, C-252-464-0000, D-312-582-0000. DV/VIP C-252-466-5169, 24 hours daily.

**RV, CAMPING/FAMCAMP:** MWR FAMCAMP on base, year round, C-252-466-2197, D-312-582-2197, 15 camper spaces with full hookups.

**SPACE-A:** Pax Term/Lounge, Building 199, 0600-2300 daily, C-252-466-3232/2379, D-312-582-3232/2379. Flights to CONUS and overseas.

**LOGISTICAL SUPPORT:**
Bank-447-2077
Beauty Shop-447-1857
Child Care-466-3783
Conv Store-447-7041
Credit Union-447-0691
Dry Cleaner-447-2130
Exchange-447-7041
Laundry-447-2603
Postal Service-466-2496
Shoppette-447-4233
Visitor Center-466-5921
Barber Shop-447-7041
Cafeteria-466-4381
Child Dev Center-446-3782
Commissary-447-2061
Dining Facilities-466-4209
Education Office-466-3500
Gas Station-447-2402
Package Store-447-7041
Snack Bar-447-7041
Travel Office-466-5813

**ADMINISTRATIVE SUPPORT:**
Fire Dept-466-2241
Housing Office-466-3602
Locator-466-2109/2811
Police-466-4366
SDO/NCO-466-2848
CDO/OOD-466-5236/4388
Legal-466-2310
Pass/ID Office-466-4687
Public Affairs-466-4241

**HEALTH & WELFARE:**
American Red Cross-466-3641
Chapel-466-4000
Family Services-466-4401
Medical
  Central Appts-800-931-9501
  Emergency-466-0255/0256
  Health Benefits-466-0122
  Information-466-0266
CHAMPUS-466-0122
Dental
  Central Appts-466-0400
  Clinic-466-0438
Navy-MC Relief-466-2031
Retiree Services-466-4401
Veterinary services-466-2166

**REST & RECREATION:**
Arts & Crafts-ext 3965
Boat Docks-ext 5812
Clubs
  O-447-2395
  SNCO-466-5301
Indoor Rec-466-4232
Library-ext 3552
MWR-466-2431
Picnic Area-ext 2197
Swimming-ext 2277/2168
Wood Hobby Shop-466-3965
Auto Hobby Shop-466-2352
Bowling-ext 3910
Fitness Center-466-2713
Golf Course-466-3044
Gym-466-2566
ITT-466-2197
Marinas-466-2762
Outdoor Rec-466-2197
Recreation-466-4232/2197
Theater-466-3850/3884
Youth Center-466-3861

**ATTRACTIONS:** Outer Banks of NC, hunting, fishing, swimming, beaches and outdoor recreation of all types. New Bern, first colonial capital of NC, 17 miles north. Morehead City, 19 miles southeast, is a large commercial fishing port.

# ELIZABETH CITY COAST GUARD SUPPORT CENTER (NC03R1)

Building 47
Elizabeth City, NC 27909-5000

**TELEPHONE NUMBER INFORMATION:** Main installation numbers: C-252-335-6379.

**LOCATION:** Take I-64 east to US-17 south to Elizabeth City, left on Halstead Boulevard, three miles to main gate of Center; or from I-95 north or south, exit 176 east on US 158 to Elizabeth City. USMRA: Page 45 (O-1). NMC: Elizabeth City, in city limits.

**GENERAL INFORMATION:** Air Station, Aviation Technical Training and Repair Center for the Coast Guard, Station Elizabeth City.

**TEMPORARY MILITARY LODGING:** Lodging office, Building 5, 0800-1630 daily, C-252-335-6397. Six two-bedroom trailers, reservations required, C-252-335-6397. All ranks.

**RV, CAMPING/FAMCAMP:** Weeksville Campsites on base, year round, C-252-335-6397, six mobile homes and four camper spaces with full hookups.

**SPACE-A:** Coast Guard Air Station, Air Ops Center, 0800-1600 Mon-Fri, C-252-335-6333, D-312-935-1520, flights to CONUS and overseas.

## LOGISTICAL SUPPORT:

| | |
|---|---|
| Bank-335-6237 | Barber Shop-335-6403 |
| Beauty Shop-335-6382 | Cafeteria-335-6389 |
| Conv Store-335-6187 | Credit Union-338-1681 |
| Dining Facilities-335-6281 | Dry Cleaner-335-6207 |
| Education Office-335-6370 | Exchange-335-6207 |
| Gas Station-335-6187 | Laundry-335-6207 |
| Package Store-335-6187 | SATO-(AAA)335-6321/2855 |
| Snack Bar-335-6389 | |

## ADMINISTRATIVE SUPPORT:

| | |
|---|---|
| Fire Dept-335-6257 | OOD-335-6130 |
| Pass/ID Office-335-6379 | Police-335-6398 |
| Public Affairs- 335-6540 | |

## HEALTH & WELFARE:

| | |
|---|---|
| CHAMPUS-335-6460 | |
| Dental-335-6375 | Chapel-335-6202 |
| | Medical |
| | Central Appts-335-6460 |
| | Emergency-335-6460 |
| | Clinic-335-6460 |

## REST & RECREATION:

| | |
|---|---|
| Clubs | Gym-335-6397 |
| EM-335-6389 | MWR-335-6397 |
| Consol-335-6301 | |
| O-335-6226 | |

**OTHER FACILITIES AVAILABLE:** Auto hobby, boat ramp, gym, swimming pool (April-September, weekends only), racquet ball and tennis.

**ATTRACTIONS:** Outer Banks of North Carolina, fresh seafood, beaches.

## FORT BRAGG (NC05R1)

XVIII Airborne Corps & Fort Bragg
ATTN: AGZA-GC
Building I-1326
Fort Bragg, NC 28307-5000

**TELEPHONE NUMBER INFORMATION:** Main installation numbers: C-910-396-0011, D-312-236-0011. WEB: www.bragg.army.mil

**LOCATION:** From I-95 north or south, exit 52 to NC-24 west for 15 miles. NC-24 runs through Post as Bragg Boulevard. From US-401 (Fayetteville Bypass) exit to All American Expressway, west five miles to Fort. USMRA: Page 45 (I,J-4). NMC: Fayetteville, 10 miles southeast.

**GENERAL INFORMATION:** XVIII Airborne Corps, 82nd Airborne Division, U.S. Army Special Operations Command, Field Artillery Brigade, Corps Support Command, Joint Special Operations Command, other support units.

**TEMPORARY MILITARY LODGING:** Lodging office, Building D-3601 (Moon Hall), Room 101, 24 hours daily, C-910-436-2211, D-312-236-5575. All ranks. DV/VIP C-910-436-2804.

**RV, CAMPING/FAMCAMP:** Smith Lake Army Travel Campground on Post, year round, C-910-396-5979, D-312-236-5979, on post, year round, 13 camper spaces with full hookups, 11 camper spaces with W/E hookups.

**SPACE-A:** None. See Pope AFB, NC listing.

## LOGISTICAL SUPPORT:

| | |
|---|---|
| Car Rental-888-374-6466/436-5200 | Class VI-436-0404 |
| Child Care-396-6979 | Commissary-396-2428 |
| Conv Store-436-0800/4600 | Credit Union-864-2232 |
| Exchange-436-4888 | Gas Station-497-3985 |
| SATO-436-5808 | Visitor Center-396-2815 |

## ADMINISTRATIVE SUPPORT:

| | |
|---|---|
| Fire Dept-396-1504 | Legal-396-1445 |
| Locator-396-1461 | Public Affairs-396-5600 |
| Police-396-0391 | SDO/NCO-396-6100 |

## HEALTH & WELFARE

| | |
|---|---|
| ACS-396-8682 | CHAMPUS-432-4424/2741 |
| Chapel-396-1121 | Family Services-396-6316 |
| Medical | Retiree Services-396-5304 |
| Central Appts-432-1351 | |
| Emergency-432-0301/2 | |
| Information-907-6000 | |

## REST & RECREATION:

| | |
|---|---|
| Auto Hobby Shop | Bowling |
| -ext 4397 | 436-1432 |
| 432-5696 | 497-3428 |
| 497-1257 | Clubs |
| Field House/Swimming | EM-436-3200 |
| -ext 4468/2231 | Green Beret Parachute-436-4056 |
| 432-6489/3573 | NCO-436-4200 |
| 432-6493/1712 | O-436-0111 |
| 432-1031 | Rod/Gun-436-3323 |
| Golf Course | Sport Parachute-436-5858 |
| 436-3811 | ITT-396-8687 |
| 497-1752 | Library-ext 3526 |
| 436-3390 | MWR-396-2077 |
| Music Center-ext 4373 | Recreation-396-2077 |
| Rec Equipment-ext 1065/1340 | Stables-497-1257 |
| Theater-436-5323 | Youth Center-ext 1278 |

**ATTRACTIONS:** Pinehurst Resort is nearby. JFK Special Warfare Museum and 82nd Airborne Division Museum on Post.

## FORT FISHER AIR FORCE RECREATION AREA (NC13R1)

118 River Front Road
Kure Beach, NC 28449-5000

**TELEPHONE NUMBER INFORMATION:** Main installation numbers: C-910-458-6723, D-312-488-8781. E-mail:ffafra@wilmington.net WEB: www.ftfisher-milrec.com

**LOCATION:** Fort Fisher is located on Pleasure Island between Cape Fear River and Atlantic Ocean. On US-421 south of Wilmington, NC, go through Carolina and Kure Beaches to Fort Fisher AF Rec Area, on the east side of US-421. USMRA: Page 45 (L-6). NMC: Wilmington, NC, 20 miles north. NMI: Camp Lejeune, 65 miles northeast.

**GENERAL INFORMATION:** Operated by Seymour Johnson Air Force Base, off base, year round. Military personnel active, retired, reserve, NG, DoD civilians. Check in 1600 at Reception Center, check out 1100. Reservations: Accepted with advance payment or confirmation with major credit card. May be made up to 90 days in advance for active duty Air Force; up to 85 days for all other active duty; up to 75 days for retired military; up to 60 days for all others. C-910-458-6546/6549. Reservations for groups are welcomed during non-peak use periods.

## TEMPORARY MILITARY LODGING:

| | |
|---|---|
| Beach cottages-22 | Executive cottage-4 |
| Mobile home-6 | River Marsh landing exec suites-2 |
| Executive rooms-6 | Lodge suites13 |
| Lodge rooms-27 | |

## RV, CAMPING/FAMCAMP:

| | |
|---|---|
| Camper spaces-16 | Tent spaces-20 |

## LOGISTICAL SUPPORT:

| | |
|---|---|
| Convenience Store-458-6549/6 | Dining-458-6549/6 |

**ATTRACTIONS:** Numerous local attractions: North Carolina Aquarium at Fort Fisher; parks, fishing and museums nearby.

*For detailed information about this off-base recreation facility, as well as other recreation facilities, golf courses, marinas and temporary military lodging, consult Military Living's Military RV, Camping and Outdoor Recreation Around the World or Military Living's Temporary Military Lodging Around the World.*

# FORT MACON COAST GUARD GROUP
## (NC18R1)
2301 East Fort Macon Road
Atlantic Beach, NC 28512-0237

**TELEPHONE NUMBER INFORMATION:** Main installation numbers: C-252-247-4598, D-312-247-4598.

**LOCATION:** Take US-70 southeast to Atlantic Beach/Morehead City Bridge. Left at traffic light in Atlantic Beach onto NC-58 (Fort Macon Road). Proceed east to entrance at end of road on left. USMRA: Page 45 (N-5). NMC: New Bern, 30 miles northwest.

**GENERAL INFORMATION:** Homeport of USCGC's *Primrose, Block Island, Staten Island, Gentian,* and *ANT Primrose.*

**TEMPORARY MILITARY LODGING:** None. See Camp Lejeune listing.

**RV, CAMPING/FAMCAMP:** None. See Cherry Point MCAS listing.

**SPACE-A:** None. See Cherry Point MCAS listing.

**LOGISTICAL SUPPORT:**

| | |
|---|---|
| Cafeteria-247-8390 | Dining Facilities-240-8390 |
| Exchange-247-9442 | Postal Service-247-9442 |

**ADMINISTRATIVE SUPPORT:**

| | |
|---|---|
| CDO/OOD-247-4598/4570/4698 | Locator-247-4590 |
| Pass/ID Office-247-4594 | Public Affairs-247-4571 |
| SDO/NCO-247-4598 | |

**HEALTH & WELFARE:**

| | |
|---|---|
| CHAMPUS-247-4551 | Medical-247-4551 |
| TRICARE-247-4551 | |

**REST & RECREATION:**     Rec Equipment-ext 4598

**OTHER FACILITIES AVAILABLE:** Housing office, package store.

**ATTRACTIONS:** Resort town of Atlantic Beach, beaches, fishing, Fort Macon State Park, Cape Lookout National Seashore.

# NEW RIVER MARINE CORPS AIR STATION
## (NC06R1)
PSC Box 21002
Jacksonville, NC 28545-1002

**TELEPHONE NUMBER INFORMATION:** Main installation numbers: C-910-451-1113/1115, D-312-750-1113/1115.
WEB: www.lejeune.usmc.mil/mcasnr/index.htm

**LOCATION:** Off US-17 north or south, two miles south of Jacksonville, on east side of US-17. Clearly marked. USMRA: Page 45 (L,M-5). NMC: Jacksonville, two miles northeast.

**GENERAL INFORMATION:** Marine Aircraft Groups, Marine Air Traffic Control Squadron, and Marine Wing Support Squadron, Headquarters Squadron.

**TEMPORARY MILITARY LODGING:** Lodging office, Building 705, duty hours, C-910-450-5020, D-312-750-6621. Fax: C-910-450-6969. All ranks.

**RV, CAMPING/FAMCAMP:** Marina on base, year round, C-910-450-6578, D-312-750-6578. Six camper spaces without hookups.

**SPACE-A:** Information: C-910-450-6316, D-312-750-6316. Limited. Helicopters primarily. See Cherry Point MCAS listing.

**LOGISTICAL SUPPORT:**

| | |
|---|---|
| Bank-450-2492 | Barber Shop-450-0593 |
| Child Care-450-6712 | Commissary-450-6395 |
| Credit Union-450-2492 | Conv Store-450-0539 |
| Exchange-450-0539 | Gas Station-450-6092 |
| Package Store-450-0539 | Postal Service-450-6397 |
| Travel Office-450-6363 | |

**ADMINISTRATIVE SUPPORT:**

| | |
|---|---|
| CDO/OOD-450-6305 | Fire Dept-450-6620 |
| Legal-450-6160 | Locator-450-6568 |
| Police-450-6111 | Public Affairs-450-6196 |

**HEALTH & WELFARE:**

| | |
|---|---|
| CHAMPUS-450-4152 | Chapel-450-6866 |
| Family Services-450-6110 | Medical/Emergency-450-6511 |
| Navy-MC Relief-450-6431 | |

**REST & RECREATION:**

| | |
|---|---|
| Arts & Crafts-ext 6711 | Auto Hobby Shop -ext 6709 |
| Bowling-ext 6582 | Ceramics-ext 6711 |
| Clubs | Gym-ext 6714 |
|   EM-450-0589 | Library-450-6715 |
|   O-450-6409 | Marina-ext 6578 |
| MWR-450-6573 | Recreation-450-6410 |
| Rec Equipment-ext 6387 | Swimming-ext 6436 |
| Theater-450-6292 | Wood Hobby Shop-ext 6690 |

**ATTRACTIONS:** Great North Carolina beaches. Cape Lookout National Seashore to the northeast.

# POPE AIR FORCE BASE (NC01R1)
259 Maynard Street
Pope Air Force Base, NC 28308-2391

**TELEPHONE NUMBER INFORMATION:** Main installation numbers: C-910-394-1110, D-312-424-1110. E-mail:43aw.pa@pope.af.mil
WEB: www.pope.af.mil

**LOCATION:** Take I-95, exit to NC-87/24 west. Follow signs northwest for 15 miles to Pope AFB and Fort Bragg. USMRA: Page 45 (J-4). NMC: Fayetteville, 12 miles southeast.

**GENERAL INFORMATION:** Transferred to Air Mobility Command Base April 1997. 23rd Wing. 624th Air Mobility Support Group; 23rd Aeromedical Evacuation Squadron; 21st Special Tactics Squadron (AFSOC); 3rd Aerial Port Squadron.

**TEMPORARY MILITARY LODGING:** Lodging office, Carolina Inn, 302 Ethridge Street, 24 hours daily, C-910-394-4131, D-312-424-4131. Fax: C-910-394-4912. All ranks. DV/VIP C-910-394-4739.

**RV, CAMPING/FAMCAMP:** None. See Fort Bragg listing, Smith Lake Army Travel Campground.

**SPACE-A:** Pax Term/Lounge, 1427 Surveyor Street, 24 hours daily, C-910-394-6527, D-312-424-6527. Fax: C-910-394-6526, D-312-424-6526. Flights to CONUS and OCONUS locations.

**LOGISTICAL SUPPORT:**

| | |
|---|---|
| Bank-436-7370 | Barber Shop-497-6045 |
| Cafeteria-394-4377 | Carlson Wagonlit Travel-436-1888 |
| Child Dev Center-394-4323 | Class VI-394-2492 |
| Commissary-497-6777 | Credit Union-800-247-5626 |
| Dining-394-4377 | Dry Cleaner-394-4166 |
| Education Center-394-4692 | Exchange-436-4888 |
| Gas Station-497-6615 | Laundry-436-4166 |
| Postal Service-394-2828 | SATO-436-4700 |
| Shoppette-394-2492 | Snack Bar-394-2377 |
| Travel Office-436-1185 | Visitor Center-394-4569 |

**ADMINISTRATIVE SUPPORT:**

| | |
|---|---|
| Fire Dept-394-2464 | Housing Office-394-4867 |
| Legal-394-2341 | Locator-394-4822 |
| Pass & ID-394-2694 | Police-394-2800 |
| Public Affairs-394-4184 | |

**HEALTH & WELFARE:**

AFAS-394-2538
Dental Clinic-394-2283
Medical-
  Appointments-1-800-931-9501
  Health Benefits Advisor-394-1230

Chapel-394-2677
Family Services-394-2538
Retiree Services-394-1950
TRICARE-394-1230
Veterinary Services-396-9120

**REST & RECREATION:**

Arts & Crafts-394-4192
Bowling-394-2891
Consol Club-394-4031
Golf Course-394-2324
ITT-394-4478
Outdoor Recreation-394-2360
Services-394-6284
Woody Hobby Shop-394-5049

Auto Hobby Shop-394-2293
Community Center-394-2779
Fitness Center-394-2671
Gym-394-2671
Library-394-2791
MWR-394-2145
Theater-394-2679
Youth Center-394-4512

**ATTRACTIONS:** Raleigh, Durham, and Chapel Hill Triangle are easy drives. Myrtle Beach, SC is two-and-a-half hours southeast. Mountains three hours west. Several parks, including Pope Air Park. Great hunting and fishing areas.

# SEYMOUR JOHNSON AIR FORCE BASE (NC11R1)

1510 Wright Brothers Avenue
Seymour Johnson Air Force Base, NC 27531-2468

**TELEPHONE NUMBER INFORMATION:** Main installation numbers: C-919-722-5400, D-312-722-1110.

**LOCATION:** From US-70 Bypass east or west, take Seymour Johnson AFB exit east onto Berkeley Boulevard to main gate. Clearly marked. USMRA: Page 45 (L-3). NMC: Raleigh, 50 miles west.

**GENERAL INFORMATION:** Air Combat Command Base.

**TEMPORARY MILITARY LODGING:** Lodging office, Building 3804, 24 hours daily, Wright Brothers Avenue, C-919-722-0385, D-312-722-0385 All ranks.

**RV, CAMPING/FAMCAMP:** FAMCAMP on base, year round, C-919-722-1104, D-312-722-1104, eight camper spaces with full hookups. Also operates Fort Fisher Air Force Recreation Area off base. See Fisher Air Force Recreation Area listing for more information.

**SPACE-A:** Building 4012, 0800-1600 Mon-Fri, C-919-722-4170/4171, D-312-722-4170/4171. Fax: C-919-722-4162. Flights to CONUS and overseas.

**LOGISTICAL SUPPORT:**

Child Care-722-1199
Exchange-735-8511
Package Store-734-2948
Welcome Center-722-1343

Commissary-722-0319
Gas Station-734-7358
Shoppette-735-9364

**ADMINISTRATIVE SUPPORT:**

Legal-722-5322
Police-722-1211

Locator-722-1175
Public Affairs-722-0027

**HEALTH & WELFARE:**

TRICARE-800-931-9501
Family Services-722-1117
Retiree Services-722-1119

Chapel-722-0315
Healthcare Info-1-800-213-5453

**REST & RECREATION:**

Arts & Crafts-722-0412
Bowling-722-0350
Community Center-722-0339
Golf Course-722-0394
Gym-722-0408
Outdoor Rec-722-1104

Auto Hobby Shop-722-1309
Clubs
  EM-734-2993
  O-735-8547
  NCO-734-2993
Theater-722-0359

**ATTRACTIONS:** NC Research Triangle of Raleigh, Durham and Chapel Hill.

# NORTH DAKOTA

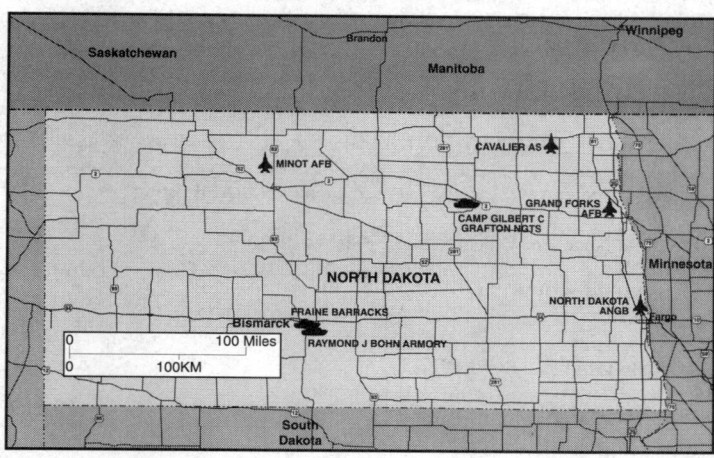

# CAMP GILBERT C. GRAFTON NATIONAL GUARD TRAINING SITE (ND03R3)

4417 Highway 20
Devils Lake, ND 58301-9000

**TELEPHONE NUMBER INFORMATION:** Main installation numbers: C-701-662-0200.

**LOCATION:** From the intersection of US Hwy 2 east or west and ND Hwy 20 in Devils Lake, turn south. Drive approximately 5 miles south. Main gate will be on the west (right hand) side of the highway. USMRA: Page 83 (G-3). NMC: Devils Lake, five miles north.

**GENERAL INFORMATION:** Army National Guard Training Site for National Guard Reserve and Active Duty units. Home to the 136th Quarter Master Battalion, 3662nd Maintenance Company and the 164th Regional Training Institute, which conducts engineer courses year-round.

**TEMPORARY MILITARY LODGING:** Billeting, C-701-662-0239, Fax: C-701-662-0597, 0700-1600 hours Mon-Thu, 0600-2300 hours Fri-Sun. Nineteen double wide trailers for retirees and military members in non-duty status.

**RV, CAMPING/FAMCAMP:** None. See Grand Forks AFB listing.

**SPACE-A:** None. See Grand Forks AFB listing.

**LOGISTICAL SUPPORT:**

Exchange-662-0314
Snack Bar-662-0285 (Lunch only Mon-Fri)

Shoppette-662-0314

**ADMINISTRATIVE SUPPORT:**

Locator-662-0200

Police-662-5323

**HEALTH & WELFARE:**

Medical-662-5323

**REST & RECREATION:**

Consol Club-662-0221

Indoor Rec-662-0285

**OTHER FACILITIES AVAILABLE:** Barber shop, boat rental and golf course.

**ATTRACTIONS:** Base has shoreline with Devils Lake, an excellent site for hunting and fishing. Casino located within five minutes of base.

# CAVALIER AIR STATION (ND08R3)

HCR 3, Box 260, Building 830
Cavalier AS, ND 58220-9314

**TELEPHONE NUMBER INFORMATION:** Main installation numbers: C-701-993-3292, D-312-330-3292.

**LOCATION:** North or south on I-29. Take Highway 5 west, Cavalier exit. Go west 18 miles to town of Cavalier, through town continuing west on Highway 5 another 16 miles to site, on left (south) side of road. USMRA: Page 83 (I-2). NMC: Grand Forks, 75 miles south.

**GENERAL INFORMATION:** 10th Space Warning Squadron.

**TEMPORARY MILITARY LODGING:** None. See Grand Forks listing.

**RV, CAMPING/FAMCAMP:** None. See Grand Forks AFB listing.

**SPACE-A:** None. See Grand Forks AFB listing.

**LOGISTICAL SUPPORT:**
Exchange-993-3224                    Snack Bar-993-3228

**ADMINISTRATIVE SUPPORT:**
Fire Dept-993-3671                   Police-993-3365
SDO/NCO-993-3292

**HEALTH & WELFARE:** None. See Grand Forks AFB listing.

**REST & RECREATION:**
Bowling-ext 3229                     Gym-ext 3376
MWR-ext 3201                         Recreation-ext 3201

**ATTRACTIONS:** Icelandic State Park, Pembina gorge, and Frost Fire mountain. The Red River Valley is one of the most fertile areas of the Midwest. Very good fishing, hunting, skiing and camping. Close to major cultural center in Winnipeg.

## FRAINE BARRACKS (ND06R3)
Joint HQ, North Dakota National Guard
Fraine Barracks, P.O. Box 5511
Bismarck, ND 58506-5511

**TELEPHONE NUMBER INFORMATION:** Main installation numbers: C-701-224-5101, D-312-344-5101.

**LOCATION:** From I-94 east or west, take Business Loop exit River Road, located just north of Memorial Bridge, follow signs. USMRA: Page 83 (E-5,6). NMC: Bismarck, two miles.

**GENERAL INFORMATION:** Home of the North Dakota Army National Guard.

**TEMPORARY MILITARY LODGING:** None. See Minot AFB listing.

**RV, CAMPING/FAMCAMP:** None. See Minot AFB listing.

**SPACE-A:** None. See Minot AFB listing.

**LOGISTICAL SUPPORT:**
Exchange-224-5119/5168               SATO-224-8615

**ADMINISTRATIVE SUPPORT:**
Legal-224-5194                       Public Affairs-224-5106

**HEALTH & WELFARE:**                 Retiree Services-224-5134

**REST & RECREATION:** None. See Minot AFB listing.

**ATTRACTIONS:** Missouri River, many national and state parks.

## GRAND FORKS AIR FORCE BASE (ND04R3)
319 ARW/PA
450 G Street, Bldg. 306, Rm 416
Grand Forks Air Force Base, ND 58205-6015

**TELEPHONE NUMBER INFORMATION:** Main installation numbers: C-701-747-3000, D-312-362-3000. E-mail: pawebadmin@grandforks.af.mil WEB: www.grandforks.af.mil

**LOCATION:** From I-29 north or south, take US-2 west exit for 14 miles to Grand Forks, County Road B-3 (Emeraldo/Air Base) north one mile to AFB on east (right) side of road. USMRA: Page 83 (I-3). NMC: Grand Forks, 15 miles east.

**GENERAL INFORMATION:** Air Mobility Command Base. 319th Air Refueling Wing 319th Operations Group; 319th Logistics Group; 319th Support Group.

**TEMPORARY MILITARY LODGING:** Billeting, 24 hours daily, C-701-747-7051/7050, D-312-362-7050/7051. Fax: C-701-747-3069. All ranks. DV/VIP C-701-747-5055; D-362-5055.

**RV, CAMPING/FAMCAMP:** FAMCAMP, on base, 1 May-1 October, C-701-747-3688, D-312-362-3688 (Bldg. 129); 21 camper spaces with full hookups.

**SPACE-A:** Pax Term/Lounge, Base Operations, Building 528, 24 hours daily, C-701-747-4409, D-312-362-4409. Fax: C-701-747-3169, D-312-362-3169. Flights to CONUS, OCONUS and overseas.

**LOGISTICAL SUPPORT:**
Bank-594-4433                        Barber Shop-594-2124
Beauty Shop-594-4531                 Child Dev Center-747-3042
Class Six-594-5206                   Commissary-747-3083
Credit Union-594-5515                Dining-747-3276
Dry Cleaner-594-2331                 Education Center-747-3316
Exchange-594-5542                    Gas Station-594-5951
Laundry-594-2331                     Postal Service-747-3339
SATO-747-3484                        Shoppette-594-5684/3191
Fast Food-594-8581                   Travel Office-594-5141
Visitor Center-747-4283

**ADMINISTRATIVE SUPPORT:**
Community Services-747-3112          Fire Dept-747-6304
Housing Office-747-3032/3030         Legal-747-3606
Locator-747-3344                     Pass/ID Office-747-6170
Police-747-3600                      Public Affairs-747-5023

**HEALTH & WELFARE:**
AFAS-747-6437                        CHAMPUS-747-5323
Chapel-747-5673                      Dental Clinic-747-5393
Family Services-747-3240             Emergency-594-3000
Medical-594-3000                     TRICARE-594-3000
Veterinary Services-747-3375

**REST & RECREATION:**
Arts & Crafts-747-3482               Auto Hobby Shop-747-3394
Bowling-747-3050                     Clubs
Community Center-747-3112            EM-747-3392
Fitness Center-747-3389             O-747-3131/594-5576
Golf Course-747-4279                 Library-747-3046
MWR-747-3220/3260                    Outdoor Recreation-747-3688/3672
Rec Center-747-3112                  Theater-747-3101
Woody Hobby Shop-747-3402            Youth Center-747-3151

**ATTRACTIONS:** Outdoor sports and recreation. Devils Lake, 75 miles west on Highway 2; Canada is 150 miles north of the base on I-29.

## MINOT AIR FORCE BASE (ND02R3)
201 Summit Drive, Unit 4
Minot Air Force Base, ND 58705-5000

**TELEPHONE NUMBER INFORMATION:** Main installation numbers: C-701-723-1110, D-312-453-1110. WEB: www.minot.af.mil

**LOCATION:** On US-83 north or south, 13 miles north of Minot. USMRA: Page 83 (D-2). NMC: Minot, 13 miles south.

**GENERAL INFORMATION:** Air Combat Command Base, 5th Bomb Wing (B-52) host; 91st Missile Wing (Minuteman III) Associate Wing.

**TEMPORARY MILITARY LODGING:** Lodging office, Building 173. C-701-723-2184, D-312-453-2184, Fax: C-701-723-1844, D-312-453-1844, 24 hours. All ranks. DV/VIP C-701-723-3474.

**RV, CAMPING/FAMCAMP:** 315 Bomber Boulevard, Building 510/511On base, 15 May-15 October, C-701-723-3648, D-312-453-3648. Fax: C-701-723-2175, first-come, first-served basis. Six camper spaces with W & E hookups.

**SPACE-A:** Pax Term/Lounge, Building 746, Base Ops, 24 hours daily, C-701-723-1854/2347/2348/, D-312-453-1854/2347/2348. Fax: C-701-723-3637, D-312-453-3637. Flights to CONUS and overseas.

**LOGISTICAL SUPPORT:**

| | |
|---|---|
| Bank-727-4523 | Barber Shop-727-4868 |
| Beauty Shop-727-9799 | Cafeteria-727-4462 |
| Child Dev Center-723-3750 | Child Care-723-3750 |
| Class Six-727-4973 | Commissary-723-4559 |
| Conv Store-727-4973 | Credit Union-727-6111 |
| Dining Facilities-723-2359 | Dry Cleaner-727-6800 |
| Education Office-723-2772 | Exchange-727-4717 |
| Gas Station-727-4876 | SATO-723-5575 |
| Shoppette-727-4973 | Visitor Center-723-3093 |

**ADMINISTRATIVE SUPPORT:**

| | |
|---|---|
| Fire Dept-723-2461 | Housing Office-723-4660 |
| Legal-723-3026 | Locator-723-1841 |
| Pass/ID Office-723-4066 | Police-723-3096 |
| Public Affairs-723-6212 | SDO/NCO-723-3102 |

**HEALTH & WELFARE:**

| | |
|---|---|
| Air Force Aid Society-723-2865 | American Red Cross-723-1855 |
| Chapel-723-2456 | Dental-727-5558 |
| Family Services-723-6605 | Medical-Emergency-723-5633 |
| Retiree Services-723-4365 | TRICARE-727-8400 |
| Veterinary Services-723-6449 | |

**REST & RECREATION:**

| | |
|---|---|
| Arts & Crafts-ext 3640 | Auto Hobby Shop-ext 2127 |
| Bowling-ext 2610 | Clubs |
| Community Center-ext 4670 | NCO-727-6156 |
| Golf Course-ext 3164 | O-723-3731 |
| Gym-ext 4915 | Library-ext 3344 |
| Outdoor Rec-727-5141 | Swimming (Summer only)-ext 4724 |
| Theater-723-3802 | Youth Center-723-2838 |

**ATTRACTIONS:** Trestle Valley Ski Area, outdoor recreation. Canada easy drive north via US-83.

## NORTH DAKOTA AIR NATIONAL GUARD BASE (ND07R3)

119th Fighter Wing
1400 28th Avenue N
Fargo, ND 58102-1031

**TELEPHONE NUMBER INFORMATION:** Main installation numbers: C-701-241-7241, D-312-362-8011. WEB: rrnet.com/hooligan

**LOCATION:** From I-29 north or south to 19th Avenue exit east to University Drive North to Hector Field on left. The base is located at the intersection of University Drive and 28th Avenue North. USMRA: Page 83 (J-5). NMC: Fargo, in city limits.

**GENERAL INFORMATION:** Air National Guard Base.

**TEMPORARY MILITARY LODGING:** None. See Grand Forks listing.

**RV, CAMPING/FAMCAMP:** None. See Grand Forks AFB listing.

**SPACE-A:** None. See Grand Forks AFB listing.

**LOGISTICAL SUPPORT:**

| | |
|---|---|
| Credit Union-232-0828 | SATO-241-7370 |
| Shoppette-241-7184 | |

**ADMINISTRATIVE SUPPORT:**

| | |
|---|---|
| Fire Dept-241-7220 | Legal-241-7156 |

| | |
|---|---|
| Pass/ID Office-241-7288 | Police-241-7287 |
| Public Affairs-241-7205 | |

**HEALTH & WELFARE:**
Family Services-241-7248. See Grand Forks AFB listing.

**REST & RECREATION:** None. See Grand Forks AFB listing.

**ATTRACTIONS:** Bonanzaville USA Historic Village & Museum, Hjemkomst Heritage Interpretive Center and the Fargo Dome.

## RAYMOND J. BOHN ARMORY (ND09R3)

P.O. Box 5511, 4200 East Divide Avenue
Bismarck, ND 58506-5511

**TELEPHONE NUMBER INFORMATION:** Main installation numbers: C-701-224-5105, D-312-344-5105.

**LOCATION:** From I-94 east or west exit 161 (Centennial Road), follow signs. USMRA: Page 83 (E-5,6.) NMC: Bismarck, two miles.

**GENERAL INFORMATION:** North Dakota Army National Guard site.

**TEMPORARY MILITARY LODGING:** None. See Minot AFB listing.

**RV, CAMPING/FAMCAMP:** None. See Minot AFB listing.

**SPACE-A:** None. See Minot AFB listing.

**LOGISTICAL SUPPORT:**

| | |
|---|---|
| Exchange-223-8808 | SATO-224-8615 |

**ADMINISTRATIVE SUPPORT:** None. See listing under Grand Forks AFB.

**HEALTH & WELFARE:** None. See Minot AFB listing.

**REST & RECREATION:** Five golf courses - all within close distance.

**ATTRACTIONS:** Meriweathers River Boat along Missouri River; Dakota Zoo, Seratoma Park and Custer House, 1.5 miles south of Mandan on Hwy 1806.

# OHIO

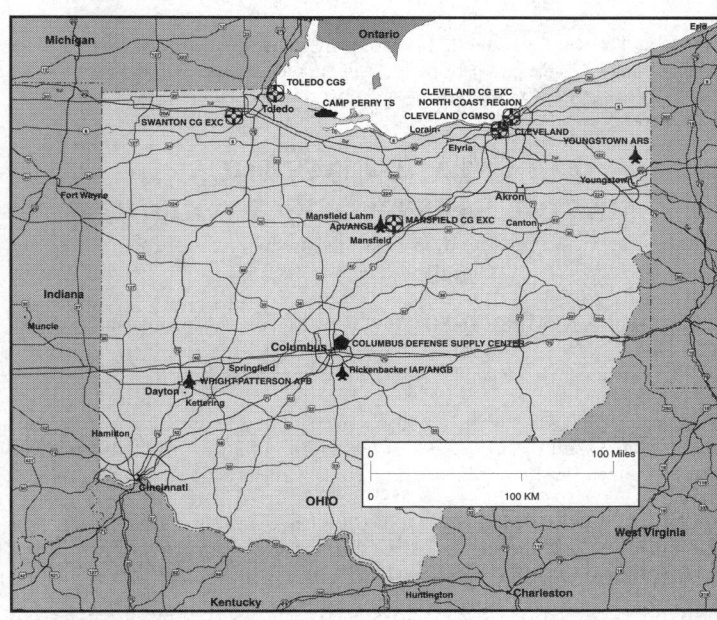

## CAMP PERRY TRAINING SITE (OH06R2)

1000 Lawrence Road, Building 600
Port Clinton, OH 43452-9578

**TELEPHONE NUMBER INFORMATION:** Main installation numbers: C-614-336-6280.

**LOCATION:** On Lake Erie, just north of State Route 2; 6 miles west of Port Clinton. USMRA: Page 67 (D-3). NMC: Toledo. NMI: Wright-Patterson AFB.

**GENERAL INFORMATION:** Home of the National Rifle and Pistol Matches.

**TEMPORARY MILITARY LODGING:** Camp Perry Clubhouse, Bldg.600, 1000 Lawrence Road, C-614-336-6214; Fax: 614-336-6238.

**RV, CAMPING/FAMCAMP:** None. See Wright-Patterson AFB listing.

**SPACE-A:** None. See Wright-Patterson AFB listing.

**LOGISTICAL SUPPORT:**
Class VI-419-635-0101                Exchange-635-0101 (Seasonal)

**ADMINISTRATIVE SUPPORT:** None. See Wright-Patterson AFB listing.

**HEALTH & WELFARE:** None. See Wright-Patterson AFB listing.

**REST & RECREATION:** None. See Wright-Patterson AFB listing.

**ATTRACTIONS:** Cedar Point is 25 miles east (Amusement Park). Toledo Zoo. Toledo Museum 40 miles west. Rutherford B. Hayes Presidential Home 20 miles south.

## CLEVELAND COAST GUARD EXCHANGE NORTH COAST REGION (OH08R2)

13920 West Parkway Road
Cleveland, OH 44135-5000

**TELEPHONE NUMBER INFORMATION:** Main installation numbers: C-216-671-3267/3500.

**LOCATION:** From I-71 north or south, exit to 150th Street, go 1 mile, turn left (west) on Puritas to second light (.5 mile), turn right, second drive on left. USMRA: Page 67 (F-3). NMC: Cleveland, in city limits.

**LOGISTICAL SUPPORT:**                Exchange-671-3267/3500

**ATTRACTIONS:** Rock and Roll Hall of Fame and Museum, Great Lakes Science Center. Major League baseball, soccer, and basketball teams, Great Lakes, NASA Lewis Research Center, West Side Market, world-class symphony orchestra, ballet and opera.

## CLEVELAND COAST GUARD MARINE SAFETY OFFICE (OH07R2)

1055 East 9th Street
Cleveland, OH 44114-1092

**TELEPHONE NUMBER INFORMATION:** Main installation numbers: C-216-522-4404.
WEB: www.uscg.mil/mlclant/Isc_Cleveland/ischomepage.html

**LOCATION:** Take I-71 north or I-90 east to OH-2 west. Exit at East 9th Street and travel north toward Lake Erie on East 9th Street. From I-77 north, also exit onto East 9th Street. USMRA: Page 67 (F-3). NMC: Cleveland, in city limits.

**GENERAL INFORMATION:** ISC Cleveland, *USCG Cutter Neah Bay*, Electronics Support Detachment, USCG Station Cleveland Harbor, Coast Guard Club and Coast Guard Exchange Satellite.

**TEMPORARY MILITARY LODGING:** None. See Camp Perry Training Site listing.

**RV, CAMPING/FAMCAMP:** None. Nearest facility is more than 100 miles away.

**SPACE-A:** None. See Wright-Patterson AFB listing.

**LOGISTICAL SUPPORT:**
Exchange*-671-3267/3500                Package Store-687-1756

* The Exchange is about a 10 minute drive from CGMSO at 13920 West Parkway Drive, C-216-671-3267/3500. It has exchange items and some uniform items for the five armed services.

**ADMINISTRATIVE SUPPORT:**                Public Affairs-522-4404

**HEALTH & WELFARE:**
CHAMPUS-522-73925                Hospital-281-2500
Medical-363-2353

**REST & RECREATION:**                Coast Guard Club-687-1755

**ATTRACTIONS:** Rock and Roll Hall of Fame and Museum, Great Lakes Science Center. Major League baseball, soccer, and basketball teams, Great Lakes, NASA Lewis Research Center, West Side Market, world-class symphony orchestra, ballet and opera.

## COLUMBUS DEFENSE SUPPLY CENTER (OH05R2)

P.O. Box 3990
3990 East Broad Street
Columbus, OH 43216-5000

**TELEPHONE NUMBER INFORMATION:** Main installation numbers: C-614-692-3131, D-312-850-3131.

**LOCATION:** From I-270 (Beltway) take exit 39 to Broad Street west, main gate on north side of street. USMRA: Page 67 (D-6). NMC: Columbus, in city limits.

**GENERAL INFORMATION:** Logistical Support for construction supplies, weapons systems, and equipment for DoD.

**TEMPORARY MILITARY LODGING:** Limited facility near O Club, C-614-692-4758. Advance reservations required.

**RV, CAMPING/FAMCAMP:** None. See Wright-Patterson AFB listing.

**SPACE-A:** None. See Wright-Patterson AFB listing.

**LOGISTICAL SUPPORT:**
Cafeteria-692-1423                Exchange-231-0976
Dry Cleaner-239-9553                SATO-692-1447

**ADMINISTRATIVE SUPPORT:**
CDO/OOD-692-2166                Fire Dept-692-2111
Legal-692-3284                Locator-692-3131
Police-692-3722                Public Affairs-692-2328

**HEALTH & WELFARE:**
CHAMPUS-692-2227                Medical-692-2227
Retiree Services-692-4165

**REST & RECREATION:**
Fitness Center-692-3084                Golf Course-692-2075
ITR-692-1111                MWR-692-2011
O Club-239-2694/0482                Recreation-692-3084
RV/Camping-692-1111                Swimming-692-3084

**ATTRACTIONS:** State Fairgrounds, Ohio Historical Center, Franklin Park Conservatory, Ohio State University, Center of Science and Industry, Palace Theatre, German Village, Brewery District, and Columbus Museum of Art.

## MANSFIELD COAST GUARD EXCHANGE
### (OH15R2)
2100 Harrington Memorial Road, Box C
Mansfield, OH 44903-5000

**TELEPHONE NUMBER INFORMATION:** Main installation numbers: C-419-526-5358.

**LOCATION:** From 13 north, turn left (west) on Harrington Memorial Road for two miles on south side of traffic circle. USMRA: Page (E-4,5). NMC: Mansfield, in city limits.

**GENERAL INFORMATION:** Exchange branch, Ninth District U.S. Coast Guard.

**LOGISTICAL SUPPORT:**                    Exchange-526-5358

**ATTRACTIONS:** Mid-Ohio Sports Car Course, Kingwood Center, Mohican State Park.

## MANSFIELD LAHM AIRPORT/
## AIR NATIONAL GUARD (OH10R2)
179 Airlift Wing
1947 Harrington Memorial Road
Mansfield, OH 44903-0179

**TELEPHONE NUMBER INFORMATION:** Main installation numbers: C-419-521-0124. WEB: www.179aw.ang.af.mil

**LOCATION:** From I-71, take US-30 east or west exit to Route 13 north for one mile. Turn left (west) on Harrington Memorial Road to airport. USMRA: Page 67 (E-4,5). NMC: Mansfield, 3 miles south.

**GENERAL INFORMATION:** Home of 179th Airlift Wing, Ohio Air National Guard. The Mansfield CG Exchange is nearby.

**SPACE-A:** Information: C-419-521-0124, D-312-696-6488. Flights via C-130H aircraft to CONUS, OCONUS and foreign country locations.

**ATTRACTIONS:** Mid-Ohio Sports Car Course, Kingwood Center, Mohican State Park.

## RICKENBACKER INTERNATIONAL AIRPORT/
## AIR NATIONAL GUARD BASE (OH02R2)
7556 South Perimeter Road
Rickenbacker ANGB, OH 43217-5910

**TELEPHONE NUMBER INFORMATION:** Main installation numbers: C-614-492-4223/4468, D-312-950-4223.

**LOCATION:** From I-270 south take Alum Creek Road exit 49 south to Rickenbacker IAP. Also accessible off US-23 south onto OH 317 east. Clearly marked. USMRA: Page 67 (D-7). NMC: Columbus, 13 miles southeast. NMI: Wright-Patterson AFB, 73 miles west.

**GENERAL INFORMATION:** Home of 121st Air Refueling Wing, 164th Weather Flight, Ohio Air National Guard. Port of entry and U.S. Customs Service Airport.

**TEMPORARY MILITARY LODGING:** Lodging Office: C-614-692-4758, D-314-850-4758, Fax: C-614-692-3390, D-312-850-3390. DV/VIP: C-614-692-2167, D-312-850-2167.

**RV, CAMPING/FAMCAMP:** None. See Wright-Patterson AFB listing.

**SPACE-A:** Information: C-614-492-4595, D-312-950-4595. Fax: C-614-492-3580, D-312-950-3580. Flights to CONUS, OCONUS and foreign country locations via KC-135 R aircraft.

**LOGISTICAL SUPPORT:** None. See Columbus Defense Supply Center listing.

**ADMINISTRATIVE SUPPORT:**        Police-492-4321

**HEALTH & WELFARE:** None. See Columbus Defense Supply Center listing.

**REST & RECREATION:** None. See Columbus Defense Supply Center listing.

**ATTRACTIONS:** Nearby Columbus offers State Fairgrounds, Ohio Historical Center, Franklin Park Conservatory, Ohio State University, Center of Science and Industry, Palace Theatre, German Village, Brewery District, and Columbus Museum of Art.

## SWANTON COAST GUARD EXCHANGE
### (OH13R2)
180 Fighter Wing
2660 S Eber Road
Swanton, OH 43558-5000

**TELEPHONE NUMBER INFORMATION:** Main installation numbers: C-419-867-9939.

**LOCATION:** From HWY 80/90 east or west, take exit 52, take overpass. Turn right on Eber Road, go 1.5 miles, turn right at 180th National Guard. USMRA: Page 67 (B,C-3). NMC: Toledo, 10 miles northeast.

**GENERAL INFORMATION:** Home of the 180th Fighter Wing, Ohio Air National Guard.

**LOGISTICAL SUPPORT:**                    Exchange-867-9939

**ADMINISTRATIVE SUPPORT:**        Police-868-4099

**ATTRACTIONS:** Nearby Toledo, Cedar Point Amusement Park, Lake Erie.

## TOLEDO COAST GUARD STATION (OH14R2)
Bay View Park, 3900 N Summit Street
Toledo, OH 43611-5000

**TELEPHONE NUMBER INFORMATION:** Main installation numbers: C-419-729-2034.

**LOCATION:** From I- 75 north or south, go east on Ottawa River Road, turn right on Summit Street, turn left on Bayview Park to Coast Guard Station. USMRA: Page 67 (C-3). NMC: Toledo, in city limits. NMI: Selfridge AFB, 50 miles.

**GENERAL INFORMATION:** Part of the Ninth District U.S. Coast Guard.

**LOGISTICAL SUPPORT:**                    Exchange-729-5911

**ADMINISTRATIVE SUPPORT:**        OOD-729-2034

**ATTRACTIONS:** Toledo with its many sights, Lake Erie, nearby Cedar Point Amusement Park.

## WRIGHT-PATTERSON AIR FORCE BASE
### (OH01R2)
1865 Fourth Street, Suite 15
Wright-Patterson Air Force Base, OH 45433-5542

**TELEPHONE NUMBER INFORMATION:** Main installation numbers: C-937-257-1110, D-312-787-1110. E-mail: ascpa@wpafb.af.mil WEB: www.wpafb.af.mil

**LOCATION:** South of I-70, off I-675 at Fairborn. Also access from OH-4 north or south. AFB clearly marked. USMRA: Page 67 (B-7). NMC: Dayton, 10 miles southwest.

**GENERAL INFORMATION:** Air Force Materiel Command Base. Air Force Institute of Technology, USAF Medical Center, Aeronautical Systems Center and National Air Intelligence Center, 88th Air Base Wing and Crew Systems Directorate of Armstrong Laboratory, 445th Airlift Wing (Reserve).

**TEMPORARY MILITARY LODGING:** Lodging office, Building 825, Schlatter Drive & Childlaw Road, 24 hours daily, C-937-257-3451, D-312-787-3451. All ranks. DV/VIP C-937-257-3110.

**RV, CAMPING/FAMCAMP:** FAMCAMP, on base, year round, C-513-257-9889, D-312-787-9889, 16-20 camper spaces with W/E hookups (no water in winter).

**SPACE-A:** Pax Term/Lounge, Building 206, Area C, Skeel Avenue, 0600-1800 Mon-Fri, other days 0800-1600. C-937-257-7741, D-312-787-7741. Fax: C-513-476-1580. Flights to CONUS and OCONUS locations.

**LOGISTICAL SUPPORT:**

| | |
|---|---|
| Bank-443-6340/50 | Barber Shop-879-5171 |
| Beauty Shop-879-5281 | Book Store-255-6063 |
| Car Rental-879-0023 | CJ Travel-257-7670 |
| Child Care-257-0366 | Child Dev Center-257-2173 |
| Commissary-257-7420 | Class VI-257-3705 |
| Credit Union-429-3340 | Dining-257-7895 |
| Dry Cleaner-879-3072 | Education Center-257-6585 |
| Exchange-879-5730 | Gas Station-252-8934/878-7260 |
| Postal Service-257-4458 | Snack Bar-879-4317 |
| Travel Office-257-7670 | Visitor Center-257-6264 |

**ADMINISTRATIVE SUPPORT:**

| | |
|---|---|
| Fire Dept-257-3033 | Housing Office-257-6547 |
| Legal-257-6142 | Locator-257-3231 |
| Pass/ID Office-257-6506 | Police-257-6516 |
| Public Affairs-255-2725 | |

**HEALTH & WELFARE:**

| | |
|---|---|
| Air Force Aid Society-257-3592 | CHAMPUS-257-9166 |
| Chapel-257-7941 | Dental Clinic-257-8761 |
| Family Services-257-6934 | Emergency-257-2969 |
| Medical-257-2969 | Retiree Services-257-3221 |
|   Information-257-0837 | Veterinary Services-257-6853 |
|   Health Benefits Advisor-800-941-4501 | |
|   Hospital-257-0837 | |

**REST & RECREATION:**

| | |
|---|---|
| Arts & Crafts-257-7025 | Auto Hobby Shop-257-3310 |
| Bowling-257-7796 | Clubs |
| Fishing/Hunting-257-9889 |   Aero-257-7714 |
| Fitness Center-255-1960 |   NCO-257-7292 |
| Golf-257-7961/4130 |   O-257-9762 |
| Gym-257-3607/7444 | Library-257-4815 |
| MWR-257-4346 | Outdoor Rec-257-9889 |
| Swimming-257-2977 | Services-257-4697 |
| Theater-257-4697 | Woody Hobby Shop-257-7025 |
| Youth Center-255-5053 | |

**OTHER INFORMATION:** Annual Air Force Marathon held here the first Saturday in September closest to the Air Force birthday.

**ATTRACTIONS:** Air Force Museum on base. Wright Brothers Memorial, Dayton. Other aviation attractions in Dayton area.

## YOUNGSTOWN AIR RESERVE STATION (OH11R2)

ATTN: 910 AW/PA
3976 King Graves Road, Unit 12
Vienna, OH 44473-5912

**TELEPHONE NUMBER INFORMATION:** Main installation numbers: C-330-609-1000 or 1-800-278-7046 (press 2, then 1000), D-312-346-1000.

**LOCATION:** From OH-11 north or south, exit to King Graves Road Hwy 82 east to Hwy 193 north at signs pointing to base, main gate left (west) one mile. Base is clearly marked. USMRA: Page 67 (H-3). NMC: Youngstown, three miles south.

**GENERAL INFORMATION:** Provides service to neighboring Youngstown Municipal Airport and support to transient U.S. government aircraft. Military support available for transient aircrews and government/military personnel on orders to ARB.

**TEMPORARY MILITARY LODGING:** Eagles Nest Inn, C-330-609-1268, D-312-346-1268, Fax: C-330-609-1120, D-312-346-1120.

**RV, CAMPING/FAMCAMP:** None. Nearest facility is more than 100 miles away.

**SPACE-A:** Pax Term, C-330-609-1082, D-312-346-1082, Fax: C-330-609-1371, D-312-346-1371.

**LOGISTICAL SUPPORT:**

| | |
|---|---|
| Bank-609-1235 | Dining-609-1234 |
| Exchange-609-1393 | |

**ADMINISTRATIVE SUPPORT:**

| | |
|---|---|
| Fire Dept-609-1117 | Legal-609-1292 |
| Police-609-1277 | Public Affairs-609-1236 |

**HEALTH & WELFARE:**

| | |
|---|---|
| Chapel-609-1393 | Family Readiness-609-1201 |

**REST & RECREATION:**

| | |
|---|---|
| Consol Club-609-1295 | MWR-609-1295 |

**ATTRACTIONS:** Geauga Lake amusement park and Sea World.

# OKLAHOMA

## ALTUS AIR FORCE BASE (OK02R3)

100 Inez Boulevard
Altus Air Force Base, OK 73523-5047

**TELEPHONE NUMBER INFORMATION:** Main installation numbers: C-580-482-8100, D-312-866-1110. WEB: www.lts.aetc.af.mil

**LOCATION:** From US-62 traveling west from Lawton, turn right (north) at first traffic light in Altus and follow the road to the main gate on Falcon Road. USMRA: Page 84 (E-5). NMC: Lawton, 56 miles east.

**GENERAL INFORMATION:** Air Education and Training Command Base. C-141, C-5, C-17 and KC-135 aircrew training missions. Worldwide Air Refueling and Airlifting Mission.

**TEMPORARY MILITARY LODGING:** Billeting Office, Building 82, 24 hours daily, C-580-481-7356, D-312-866-7356. All ranks. DV/VIP C-580-481-7044.

**RV, CAMPING/FAMCAMP:** FAMCAMP, on base, year round, C-580-481-6704, D-312-866-6704. Four camper spaces with full hookups, three camper spaces with E hookups.

**SPACE-A:** Pax Term/Lounge, Building 178, 0730-1630 hours Mon-Fri. C-580-481-6350/6428, D-312-866-6350/6428, Fax: C-580-481-5065. Flights to CONUS and overseas.

**LOGISTICAL SUPPORT:**

| | |
|---|---|
| Bank-481-7722 | Barber Shop-482-8221 |
| Beauty Shop-482-4051 | Child Dev. Center-481-7502 |
| Class VI-481-6276 | Commissary-481-5810 |
| Conv Store-481-7095 | Credit Union-481-7148 |
| Dining-481-7781 | Dry Cleaner-477-2213 |
| Education Center-481-6619 | Exchange-481-8733 |
| Gas Station-481-7002 | Laundry-477-2213 |
| Package Store-481-6276 | Postal Service-481-6364 |
| SATO-481-6466 | Shoppette-481-7095 |
| Snack Bar-482-3399/6420/6411 | Travel Office-481-6973 |

**ADMINISTRATIVE SUPPORT:**

| | |
|---|---|
| Fire Dept-481-6333 | Legal-481-7294 |
| Locator-481-7250 | Housing Office-481-7235 |

OOD-481-6313
Public Affairs-481-7700

Police-481-7444

**HEALTH & WELFARE:**
Air Force Aid Society-481-6761
Dental Clinic-481-5262
  Emergency-481-5222
Family Services-481-7460
TRICARE-481-5212

Chapel-481-7485/5222
Medical-Appointments-481-5235
  Central Appts-481-5970
Retiree Services-481-6776
Veterinary Services-481-5220

**REST & RECREATION:**
Arts & Crafts-481-7048
Bowling-481-6300
Community Center-481-6600
Fitness Center-481-7153
Golf Course-481-7207
Library-481-6225
Services-481-7731
Woody Hobby Shop-481-7331

Auto Hobby Shop-481-6326
Clubs
  EM-481-7034
  O-481-6224
Gym-481-7153
Outdoor Recreation-481-7416
Theater-481-7341
Youth Center-481-7904

**ATTRACTIONS:** Western prairie country. Lake Altus, 15 miles north. Outdoor sports.

## CAMP GRUBER (OK03R3)
P.O. Box 29
Building 154
Braggs, OK 74423-0029

**TELEPHONE NUMBER INFORMATION:** Main installation numbers: C-918-487-6001. Fax: C-918-487-6008.

**LOCATION:** From I-40 east or west, exit north at Webber Falls (exit 287), take US-64 east to Gore. From US-64 exit onto Hwy 10 north to Braggs. First entrance to camp after passing through Braggs. OR from north, take Hwy 62 east out of Muskogee, take Hwy 10 south to Braggs and Camp Gruber. USMRA: Page 84 (I-4). NMC: Muskogee, 12 miles north.

**GENERAL INFORMATION:** Camp Gruber is an Army National Guard Training Site.

**TEMPORARY MILITARY LODGING:** Lodging office, Building 120, on Southern France Road, between 3rd and 4th Street., 0700-1630 Mon-Fri, C-918-487-6065/6067, Fax: C-918-487-6135.

**RV, CAMPING/FAMCAMP:** Blackhawk Recreational Vehicle Park, on base year round, ATTN: Billeting Office, P.O. Box 29, C-918-487-6065, Fax: C-918-487-6135. Twelve camper spaces with W/S/E hookups.

**SPACE-A:** None. See Tinker AFB listing.

**LOGISTICAL SUPPORT:**
Class VI-487-5643

Exchange-487-5643

**ADMINISTRATIVE SUPPORT:**
Fire Dept-487-6071
Locator-487-6062
Public Affairs-487-6222

Housing Office-487-6065
Police-487-6021

**HEALTH & WELFARE:**
American Red Cross-682-1366

Medical-683-3261

**REST & RECREATION:**

Fitness Center-487-6065

**OTHER FACILITIES AVAILABLE:** Barber shop, convenience store, laundry, marinas, gas station, golf course, package store, postal service, shoppette, snack bar.

**ATTRACTIONS:** Located in western edge of Ozark Mountains. Rolling hills, lakes, fishing and water recreation, Native American culture, Cherokee Heritage Center, Trail of Tears dramatization, all short drives.

## FORT SILL (OK01R3)
US Army Field Artillery Center
ATTN: ATZR-CS
Building 455
Fort Sill, OK 73503-5001

**TELEPHONE NUMBER INFORMATION:** Main installation numbers: C-580-442-8111, D-312-639-7090.

**LOCATION:** From Lawton, take I-44 north to Key Gate exit. Clearly marked. USMRA: Page 84 (E,F-5.) NMC: Lawton, on the north border.

**GENERAL INFORMATION:** Headquarters, U.S. Army Field Artillery Center, U.S. Army Field Artillery School, Headquarters III Corps Artillery and support units.

**TEMPORARY MILITARY LODGING:** Billeting Office, Building 5676, Fergusson Road, 24 hours daily, C-580-442-5000/353-5007, D-312-639-5000, Fax: C-580-442-7033.

**RV, CAMPING/FAMCAMP:** DCA, ATTN: ATZR-PN, Fort Sill, OK 73503, 0700-1600 hours daily. C-580-442-4522, D-312-639-4522, Fax: C-580-442-2549.

**SPACE-A:** None. See Will Rogers World Airport/ANGB listing.

**LOGISTICAL SUPPORT:**
Bank-357-9880
Beauty Shop-353-6104
Car Rental-355-9010
Child Care-442-3927
Class Six-355-4088

Barber Shop-353-5788
Cafeteria-353-2557
Carlson Wagonlit Travel-357-6616
Child Dev. Center-442-2320
Commissary-442-3601

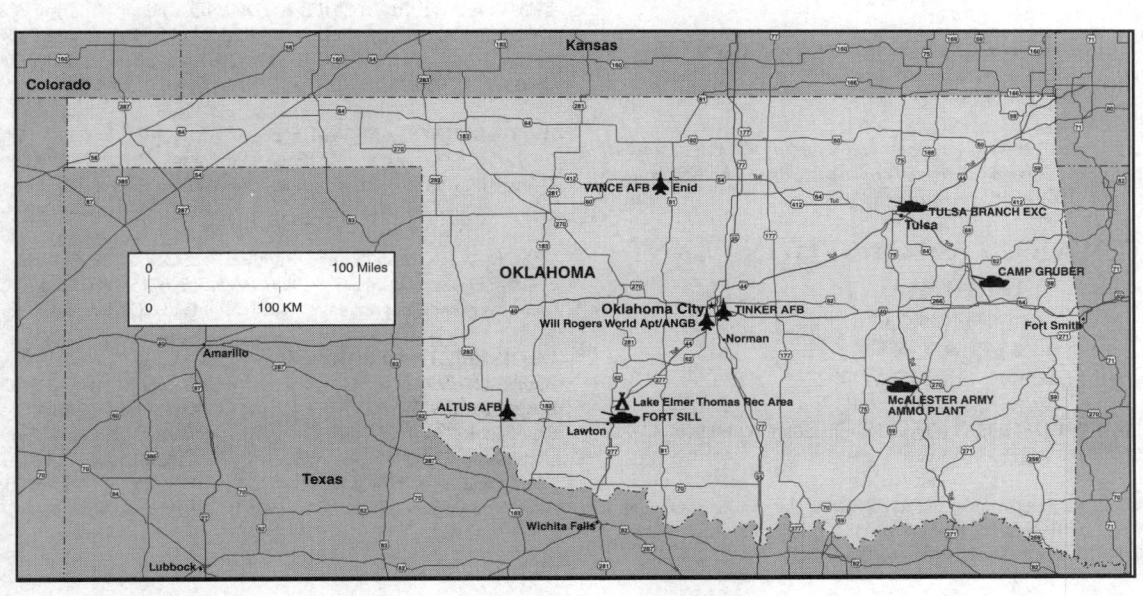

Credit Union-353-2124
Family Services-442-5018
Gas Station-357-0786
Postal Service-442-6172

Exchange-248-7506/2105/2120
Fast Food-353-4260
Laundry-248-2255/1223
Shoppette-357-7601

**ADMINISTRATIVE SUPPORT:**

Fire Dept-442-6010
Legal-442-2685
Pass/ID Office-442-5010
Public Affairs-442-4500

Housing Office-442-2813
Locator-442-3693
Police-442-2101
SDO/NCO-442-4912

**HEALTH & WELFARE:**

American Red Cross-442-2426/2586
Army Emergency Relief-442-2946
Chapel-442-3319/5001
Medical-458-2500/2800
  Emergency-458-2770/2033
TRICARE-458-2102

ACS-442-4337
CHAMPUS-458-2484
Dental-442-5223
  Emergency-442-5566/4263
Retiree Services-442-5963/4009
Veterinary Services-442-3416/4951

**REST & RECREATION:**

Arts & Crafts-442-4824/5687
Bowling-442-2882
Fitness Center-442-6652
Golf Course-442-2723
Gym-442-2740/4670
Library-442-3806
Outdoor Adventure Center-442-3342
Rec Center-442-5623
Theater-353-5623

Auto Hobby Shop-442-4147/2549
Clubs
  EM-355-3201/357-4380
  O-355-9113
ITR-442-6211
MWR-442-4522
Outdoor Rec-355-8270
Swimming-442-3482/4280/6390
Youth Services-442-6745

**ATTRACTIONS:** Geronimo's burial place in post's Apache Cemetery, Fort Sill Museum, Wichita Mountains Wildlife Refuge and Lake Latonka.

## LAKE ELMER THOMAS RECREATION AREA (OK14R3)

Fort Sill
Fort Sill, OK 73503-5100

**TELEPHONE NUMBER INFORMATION:** Main installation numbers: C-580-442-8111, D-312-639-7090.

**LOCATION:** Off post. Take I-44 north or south to Medicine Park exit (Hwy 49) west. Follow signs to LETRA. USMRA: Page 84 (E,F-5). NMI: Fort Sill, 12 miles southwest. NMC: Wichita Falls, TX, 64 miles southwest.

**GENERAL INFORMATION:** Operated by Fort Sill, off base, year round. Military personnel active, reservists, retired, DoD civilian employees. Reservations: MWR, Fort Sill, OK 73503-5100. C-580-442-5858/9.

**RV, CAMPING/FAMCAMP:**

Camper Spaces-62                    Tent Spaces-10

**ATTRACTIONS:** Located in the Wichita Mountains of southwestern Oklahoma, the recreation area offers a 360-acre lake and a wildlife refuge in the Wichita Mountains.

*For detailed information about this off-base recreation facility, as well as on-base recreation facilities, golf courses and marinas, consult Military Living's Military RV, Camping and Outdoor Recreation Around the World.*

## McALESTER ARMY AMMUNITION PLANT (OK09R3)

ATTN: SIOMC-CO
1 C Tree Road
McAlester, OK 74501-9002

**TELEPHONE NUMBER INFORMATION:** Main installation numbers: C-918-420-7490, D-312-420-7490.

**LOCATION:** Off Indian Nation Turnpike, west of US-69. The southeast Oklahoma area is mostly rolling pasture with timber-covered hills and creek bottoms. USMRA: Page 84 (I-5). NMC: Tulsa, 90 miles north.

**GENERAL INFORMATION:** Produces, stores, renovates, and issues ammunition, explosives, and ordnance items to all branches of the Armed Forces.

**TEMPORARY MILITARY LODGING:** None. See Tinker AFB listing, Indian Hills Inn.

**RV, CAMPING/FAMCAMP:** Murphy's Meadow on base, year round, C-918-420-7484/6673, D-312-956-7484/6673, 34 camper spaces.

**SPACE-A:** None. See Tinker AFB listing.

**LOGISTICAL SUPPORT:**

Bank-420-6377
Exchange-421-6388
Travel Office-420-6462

Child Care-421-2204
Snack Bar-421-2384

**ADMINISTRATIVE SUPPORT:**

Fire Dept-421-2221
Legal-420-6439
Public Affairs-421-2591

Housing Office-420-7480
Police-4220-6377
SDO/NCO-421-2642

**HEALTH & WELFARE:**

ACS-421-3490
CHAMPUS-421-2496
Medical-420-6495

American Red Cross-423-0481
Family Services-420-6204

**REST & RECREATION:**

Arts & Crafts-420-7484
Gym-420-7668
MWR-421-7262/420-7456

Bowling-420-2673Com Club-421-3587

Recreation-421-3262

**OTHER FACILITIES AVAILABLE:** Auto hobby shop, boat rental, library, pool, rec center, rec equipment, tennis and youth activities.

**ATTRACTIONS:** Lake Eufaula.

## TINKER AIR FORCE BASE (OK04R3)

3001 Staff Drive, Suite 1AG78A
Tinker Air Force Base, OK 73145-3010

**TELEPHONE NUMBER INFORMATION:** Main installation numbers: C-405-732-7321, D-312-884-1110. WEB: www.tinker.af.mil

**LOCATION:** Southeast Oklahoma City, off I-40. Use Tinker gate exit 157A off South Air Depot Boulevard. Clearly marked. USMRA: Page 84 (G-4). NMC: Oklahoma City, 12 miles northwest.

**GENERAL INFORMATION:** Air Force Materiel Command Base. Major Logistics Center for the Air Force. Navy Stratcom E-6 Wing. AWACS E-3 Sentry Wing. AFRES Tanker Wing.

**TEMPORARY MILITARY LODGING:** Indian Hills Inn, 72nd SPTG/SVML, 4002 Mitchell Avenue, Tinker AFB, OK 73145-8101. C-405-734-2822, D-312-884-2822. Fax: C-405-734-7426, D-312-884-7426, 24 hours daily. DV/VIP: Bldg. 3001, C-405-734-2000/3737.

**RV, CAMPING/FAMCAMP:** FAMCAMP, 72D SPTG/SV, 6120 Arnold, Tinker AFB, OK 73145-8101, off base, year round, C-405-734-3162, D-312-884-3162. Twenty-nine paved camper spaces with W/E and sewer hookups and five tent spaces without hookups.

**SPACE-A:** Pax Term/Lounge, Building 268, C-405-739-4339, D-312-339-4339. Fax: C-405-739-3826, D-312-339-3826, Mon-Fri 0715-1800 hours. Off schedule show times, weekends and holidays closed. Flights to CONUS and overseas locations.

**LOGISTICAL SUPPORT:**

Bank-732-2717
Beauty Shop-737-6509
Child Care-734-3116
Conv Store-733-3445
Dining Facilities-734-2918
Education Office-739-7408

Barber Shop-732-5032
Cafeteria-734-3884
Commissary-734-5965
Credit Union-734-7888
Dry Cleaner-734-5225
Exchange-734-3035

Gas Station-734-3040
Package Store-734-3466
SATO-739-5057
Snack Bar-739-0340

Laundry-737-5225
Postal Service-734-3578
Shoppette-733-3445
Travel Office-739-5057

**ADMINISTRATIVE SUPPORT:**

Fire Dept-734-7964
Legal-739-5811
Pass/ID Office-734-2605
Public Affairs-739-2026

Housing Office-734-2821
Locator-732-7321
Police-734-3737
Quarter Deck-739-3044

**HEALTH & WELFARE:**

Air Force Aid Society-739-2747
CHAMPUS-734-2615
Dental-736-2074
Medical
  Central Appts-734-2778
  Clinic-734-2778
  Emergency-736-2184/6
  Health Benefits-800-406-2832
  Hospital-734-8455

American Red Cross-734-3030
Chapel-734-2111
Family Services-739-2505
Retiree Services-739-7388
TRICARE-1-800-406-2832
Veterinary Services-734-5780

**REST & RECREATION:**

Arts & Crafts-734-5615
Boat Rental-734-2289
Clubs
  EMC-734-3435
  NCO-734-3435
  O-734-3418
737-4775
Theater-734-3400
Youth Center-734-7866

Auto Hobby Shop-734-5616
Bowling-734-3484
Fitness Center-734-3651
Golf Course-734-2909
Handball-734-5607
Outdoor Rec-734-3162Riding Club-
Swimming-734-5607
Wood Hobby Shop-734-5616

**ATTRACTIONS:** Oklahoma City (the capital), Kirkpatrick Planetarium, Oklahoma Air Space Museum, Omniplex Science Museum, National Cowboy Hall of Fame and Western Heritage Center, Oklahoma City Zoo, Remington Park Racetrack, Myriad Botanical Gardens, Frontier City Theme Park, arts and entertainment.

## TULSA BRANCH EXCHANGE (OK14R3)

4200 North 93rd East Avenue
Tulsa, OK 74115-1699

**TELEPHONE NUMBER INFORMATION:** Main installation numbers: C-918-833-7000.

**LOCATION:** From I-44 east or west, get on 244, merge into US-75 N. Take OK-11 west/36th Street north exit. Keep left at fork in ramp. Turn left onto OK-266. From East 46th Street north, take right on North 93rd East Avenue. USMRA: Page 84 (I-3). NMC: Tulsa, in city.

**GENERAL INFORMATION:** Near Tulsa International Airport and Tulsa Air National Guard Base.

**LOGISTICAL SUPPORT:**          Exchange-836-0921

**ATTRACTIONS:** Mohawk Park and the Tulsa Zoo, numerous lakes and golf courses, many museums, Tulsa Air and Space Center.

## VANCE AIR FORCE BASE (OK05R3)

246 Brown Parkway
Vance Air Force Base, OK 73705-5016

**TELEPHONE NUMBER INFORMATION:** Main installation numbers: C-580-213-5000, D-312-448-7110.

**LOCATION:** Off of US-81 south of Enid (on west side of US-81). Clearly marked. USMRA: Page 84 (F-3). NMC: Oklahoma City, 90 miles southeast.

**GENERAL INFORMATION:** Air Education and Training Command Base. Flying Training Wing, Undergraduate Pilot Training.

**TEMPORARY MILITARY LODGING:** Lodging office, Building 714, Williams Road, 24 hours daily, C-580-213-7358, D-312-448-7358. All ranks.

**RV, CAMPING/FAMCAMP:** None. See Altus AFB listing.

**SPACE-A:** Base Ops, C-580-213-2121/7424, D-312-448-2121/7424.

**LOGISTICAL SUPPORT:**

Bank-249-5921
Child Care-213-7310
Credit Union-213-7229
Gas Station-237-7445

Class VI-237-6765
Commissary-213-7788
Exchange-237-6765

**ADMINISTRATIVE SUPPORT:**

Legal-213-7404
Police-213-7127

Locator-213-7791/7358

**HEALTH & WELFARE:**

CHAMPUS-249-7746
Family Services-249-7322
Retiree Services-249-7421

Chapel-213-7711
Medical-213-7416
  Central Appts-237-7416
  Inpatient-734-6841
  Emergency-237-6117

**REST & RECREATION:**

Arts & Crafts-ext 7402
Bowling-213-7331
Gym-213-7830/7670
Youth Center-213-7474

Auto Hobby Shop-213-7508
Consol Club-213-7595
Library-213-7368

**ATTRACTIONS:** National Cowboy Hall of Fame, Kirkpatrick Planetarium, National Softball Hall of Fame, Humphrey Heritage Village/Museum of the Cherokee Strip, Railroad Museum of Oakland, Midgley Museum, Leonardo's Discovery Warehouse, George's Museum of Antique Cars, the Zoo, and Frontier City.

## WILL ROGERS WORLD AIRPORT/ AIR NATIONAL GUARD BASE (OK10R3)

137 Airlift Wing (ANG)
5624 Air Guard Drive
Oklahoma City, OK 73179-1090

**TELEPHONE NUMBER INFORMATION:** Main installation numbers: C-405-686-5210, D-312-940-5210.

**LOCATION:** From I-40 east or west, exit 144 south 2.5 miles to airport. USMRA: Page 84 (G-4). NMC: Oklahoma City, seven miles northeast.

**GENERAL INFORMATION:** Home of the 137th Airlift Wing.

**TEMPORARY MILITARY LODGING:** None. See Tinker AFB listing.

**RV, CAMPING/FAMCAMP:** None. See Tinker AFB listing.

**SPACE-A:** C-405-686-5550, D-312-940-5550. Hours: 0630-1700 Mon-Thu.

**LOGISTICAL SUPPORT:**          Dining facilities-686-5276

**ADMINISTRATIVE SUPPORT:**

Legal-686-5387
Police-686-5301

Pass/ID Office-686-5239
Public Affairs-686-5227

**HEALTH & WELFARE:**

Chapel-686-5334
Medical-Clinic-686-5245

Family Services-686-5328

**REST & RECREATION:**          NCO Club-686-5279

**ATTRACTIONS:** Oklahoma City, Cowboy Hall of Fame, the 45th Infantry Division Museum, The Oklahoma Zoological Park, Softball Hall of Fame.

# OREGON

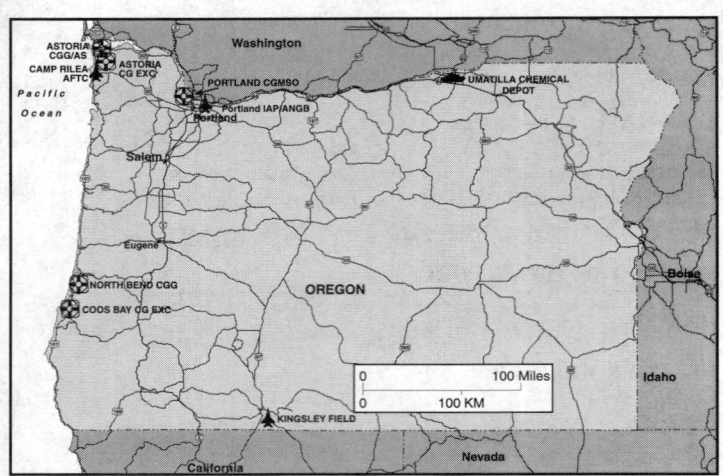

## ASTORIA COAST GUARD EXCHANGE (OR08R4)

1240 W Marine Drive
Astoria, OR 97103-5612

**TELEPHONE NUMBER INFORMATION:** Main installation numbers: C-503-861-3350.
**LOCATION:** From HWY 101/202 junction head southeast on Hwy 202 (also known as West Marine Drive) approximately one and a half miles. Exchange is the first right hand turn, clearly visible. USMRA: Page 100 (B-1).

**LOGISTICAL SUPPORT:**          Exchange-861-3350

**ADMINISTRATIVE SUPPORT:**          Public Affairs-325-0108

**ATTRACTIONS:** The Columbia River. Fort Stevens State Park, Saddle Mountain State Park, Fort. Canary State Park, Fort Columbia State Park, Cape Disappointment Lighthouse, North Head Lighthouse, Washington State, Saddle Mountain State Park, Clatsop Beach, Clatsop and Tillamook National Forests.

## ASTORIA COAST GUARD GROUP/ AIR STATION (OR05R4)

2185 SE, Airport Road, 12th Place
Warrenton, OR 97146-5000

**TELEPHONE NUMBER INFORMATION:** Main installation number: C-503-861-6105.

**LOCATION:** Take Hwy 30 from Portland west to Astoria. Go through Astoria and across the Young River Bridge. Follow signs, plainly marked. USMRA: Page 100 (B-1). NMC: Portland, 100 miles east.

**GENERAL INFORMATION:** Coast Guard Group is based in Astoria. The Coast Guard Air Station is based in Warrenton. It also covers the following outlying units: Gray's Harbor Lifeboat Station in Westport, WA; Tillamook Bay Lifeboat Station in Garibaldi, OR; Station Cape Disappointment, Ilwaco, WA; and USCG National Motor Lifeboat School in Ilwaco, WA.

**TEMPORARY MILITARY LODGING:** None. See Camp Rilea AFTC listing.

**RV, CAMPING/FAMCAMP:** None. See Camp Rilea AFTC listing.

**SPACE-A:** None. See Portland IAP/ANGB listing.

**LOGISTICAL SUPPORT:**
Barber Shop-861-6170                    Commissary-325-0108
Conv Store-861-3350                      Education Office-861-6231
Exchange-325-0108 ext 13               Gas Station-325-0108

**ADMINISTRATIVE SUPPORT:**
CDO/OOD-861-6211/2                    Housing Office-861-6193
Pass/ID Office-861-6130                   Public Affairs-861-6123

**HEALTH & WELFARE:**
Chapel-861-6225                            Dental-861-6240
Medical-861-6240

**REST & RECREATION:**
Fitness Center-861-6138                    Gym-861-6349
MWR-861-6237

**ATTRACTIONS:** The Columbia River. Fort Stevens State Park, Saddle Mountain State Park, Fort Canary State Park, Fort Columbia State Park, Cape Disappointment Lighthouse, North Head Lighthouse. Minutes from: Washington State, Saddle Mountain State Park, Clatsop Beach, Clatsop and Tillamook National Forests.

## CAMP RILEA ARMED FORCES TRAINING CENTER (OR07R4)

Route 2, Box 497-E
Warrenton, OR 97146-9711

**TELEPHONE NUMBER INFORMATION:** Main installation numbers: C-503-861-4000, D-312-355-3972.

**LOCATION:** From Portland, Oregon, take US-26 northwest to Oregon Coast, approximately 65 miles. When you reach US-101, proceed north 12 miles. Located between Seaside and Astoria. USMRA: Page 100 (B-1). NMC: Astoria, five miles north.

**GENERAL INFORMATION:** Oregon National Guard training site.

**TEMPORARY MILITARY LODGING:** C-861-1018/4052.

**LOGISTICAL SUPPORT:**          Shoppette-861-4231

**ATTRACTIONS:** The Columbia River. Fort Stevens State Park, Saddle Mountain State Park, Fort Canary State Park, Fort Columbia State Park, Cape Disappointment Lighthouse, North Head Lighthouse, Washington State, Saddle Mountain State Park, Clatsop Beach, Clatsop and Tillamook National Forests.

## COOS BAY COAST GUARD EXCHANGE (OR06R4)

1684 Ocean Boulevard
Coos Bay, OR 97420-5000

**TELEPHONE NUMBER INFORMATION:** Main installation numbers: C-541-888-5285.

**LOCATION:** North on Hwy 101, west on Central Avenue, which turns into Ocean Blvd. USMRA: Page 100 (A-6). NMC: Eugene, 85 miles northeast.

**LOGISTICAL SUPPORT:**          Exchange-888-5285

**ATTRACTIONS:** Scenic beaches, parks and lakes, water activities.

## KINGSLEY FIELD (OR03R4)

302 Vandenberg Drive, Suite 38
Klamath Falls, OR 97603-1925

**TELEPHONE NUMBER INFORMATION:** Main installation numbers: C-541-885-6350, D-312-830-6110. WEB: www.orklam.ang.af.mil

**LOCATION:** Take I-5 north or south through Medford to Hwy 140 east 5.5 miles to southside bypass. Go east approximately four and a half miles to the airport. USMRA: Page 100 (D-8). NMC: Medford, 80 miles west.

**GENERAL INFORMATION:** Home of the 173rd Fighter Wing, Air National Guard.

**TEMPORARY MILITARY LODGING:** Billeting Office, Kingsley Lodge, Building 208, McConnell Circle, 0800-1600 Mon-Fri (closed 1200-1300), C-541-885-6365.

**RV, CAMPING/FAMCAMP:** Kingsley Kampground on base. Five spaces. C-541-885-6198.

**SPACE-A:** Limited. C-541-885-6686, D-312-830-6686.

**LOGISTICAL SUPPORT:**

| | |
|---|---|
| Barber Shop-885-6370 | Class Six-885-6371 |
| Credit Union-885-6410 | Dry Cleaner-885-6371 |
| Exchange-885-6371 | |

**ADMINISTRATIVE SUPPORT:**

| | |
|---|---|
| Pass/ID Office-885-6142 | Police-885-6647 |

**HEALTH & WELFARE:**

| | |
|---|---|
| | Medical-885-6312 |

**REST & RECREATION:**

| | |
|---|---|
| | Consol Club-885-6484 |

**OTHER FACILITIES AVAILABLE:** Bank, fire department.

**ATTRACTIONS:** Crater Lake, Lava Beds, Oregon Caves, Freemont National Forest, Rogue River National Forest, Winema National Forest.

## NORTH BEND COAST GUARD GROUP (OR02R4)

2000 Connecticut Avenue
North Bend, OR 97459-2399

**TELEPHONE NUMBER INFORMATION:** Main installation numbers: C-541-756-9210/9220.

**LOCATION:** Take US-101 north or south to Virginia Avenue, west one mile to Connecticut, turn right (north), two blocks (follow signs). USMRA: Page 100 (A-5,6). NMC: Eugene, 80 miles northeast.

**GENERAL INFORMATION:** Part of the thirteenth district, U.S. Coast Guard.

**TEMPORARY MILITARY LODGING:** None. Nearest facility is more than 100 miles away.

**RV, CAMPING/FAMCAMP:** None. Nearest facility is more than 100 miles away.

**SPACE A:** None. See Portland IAP/ANGB listing.

**LOGISTICAL SUPPORT:** Exchange-888-5285

**ADMINISTRATIVE SUPPORT:**

| | |
|---|---|
| Public Affairs-756-9669 | SDO/NCO-756-9210 |

**HEALTH & WELFARE:**

| | |
|---|---|
| CHAMPUS-756-9234 | Family Services-756-9234 |
| Medical-756-9234 | |

**REST & RECREATION:** MWR-756-9282

**ATTRACTIONS:** Oregon Dunes National Recreation Area.

## PORTLAND COAST GUARD MARINE SAFETY OFFICE (OR04R4)

6767 N. Basin Avenue
Portland, OR 97217-3929

**TELEPHONE NUMBER INFORMATION:** Main installation numbers: C-503-240-9310.

**LOCATION:** From airport take 205 S. exit to I-84 W, and then I-5 N to exit 303 (Killingsworth/Swan Island). Follow signs to N. Basin Avenue for the USCG & Reserve Center. USMRA: Page 100 (C-2). NMC: Portland, in city limits.

**GENERAL INFORMATION:** Part of the thirteenth district, U.S. Coast Guard.

**LOGISTICAL SUPPORT:** Exchange-286-3510

**OTHER FACILITIES AVAILABLE:** Dining facilities.

**ATTRACTIONS:** Greater Portland area.

## PORTLAND INTERNATIONAL AIRPORT/ AIR NATIONAL GUARD BASE (OR01R4)

6801 NE Cornfoot Road
Portland, OR 97218-2797

**TELEPHONE NUMBER INFORMATION:** Main installation number: C-503-335-4000, D-312-638-4000. WEB: www.orport.ang.af.mil

**LOCATION:** Go south on I-205 to NE Airport Way exit, west on NE Airport Way to Alderwood, south on Alderwood to NE Cornfoot Road. Co-located with Portland International Airport. USMRA: Page 100 (C-2), page 103 (C-1). NMC: Portland, in city limits.

**GENERAL INFORMATION:** Oregon Air National Guard, 142nd Fighter Wing, 244th and 272nd Combat Communications Squadrons, 939th Rescue Wing and 304th Air Rescue Squadrons, Civil Air Patrol. Major tenant unit: 939th Rescue Wing (AFRES).

**TEMPORARY MILITARY LODGING:** None. See Camp Rilea AFTC listing.

**RV, CAMPING/FAMCAMP:** None. See Camp Rilea AFTC listing.

**SPACE-A:** Portland IAP/ANG Ops, 24 hours daily, C-503-335-4390/4421, D-312-638-4390. Fax: C-503-335-5098, transit aircraft.

**LOGISTICAL SUPPORT:**

| | |
|---|---|
| Barber Shop-287-4794 | Carlson Wagonlit Travel-335-4265 |
| Credit Union-335-4894 | Exchange-249-0997 |

**ADMINISTRATIVE SUPPORT:**

| | |
|---|---|
| Fire Dept-335-4889 | Pass/ID Office-335-5054 |
| Police-335-4221 | Public Affairs-335-4104 |

**HEALTH & WELFARE:**

| | |
|---|---|
| Chapel-335-4449 | CHAMPUS-335-4029 |
| Medical-335-4757 | Retiree Services-335-4945 |
| TRICARE-335-4029 | |

**REST & RECREATION:**

| | |
|---|---|
| Camping Equipment-335-4748 | Consol Club-335-5151 |
| Fitness Center-335-4176 | MWR-335-4176 |
| Rec Center 335-4748 | |

**ATTRACTIONS:** Greater Portland area.

## UMATILLA CHEMICAL DEPOT (OR08R4)

245-B East Main Street
Hermiston, OR 97838-9544

**TELEPHONE NUMBER INFORMATION:** Main installation numbers: C-541-564-8632/6424, D-312-790-8632.

**LOCATION:** Take I-84 east from Portland. At 177 mile marker, take exit 182 for Hermiston on north side of I-82. Follow signs. USMRA: Page 100 (G-2). NMC: Hermiston, five miles south.

**GENERAL INFORMATION:** Army chemical weapons storage facility.

**ADMINISTRATIVE SUPPORT:** Public Affairs-564-5312

**HEALTH & WELFARE:** Medical-564-5215

**REST & RECREATION:** MWR-564-5240

**ATTRACTIONS:** Nearby Blue Mountains, Columbia River, Umatilla River, and many parks, including Hat Rock, make this area great for water activities, fishing, hunting, skiing and camping.

# PENNSYLVANIA

## CARLISLE BARRACKS (PA08R1)

US Army War College, ATTN: ATZE-GC
122 Forbes Avenue
Carlisle, PA 17013-5050

**TELEPHONE NUMBER INFORMATION:** Main installation numbers: C-717-245-3131, D-312-242-3131. WEB: carlisle-www.army.mil

**LOCATION:** From I-81 north or south exit 17 to US-11, two miles southwest to Carlisle. Signs clearly marked to Carlisle Barracks and Army War College. USMRA: Page 22 (F-6). NMC: Harrisburg, 18 miles northeast.

**GENERAL INFORMATION:** U.S. Army War College and U.S. Army Military History Institute, Center for Strategic Leadership, Army Physical Fitness Center.

**TEMPORARY MILITARY LODGING:** Lodging office, Building 7, 0700-1800 Mon-Fri, 0800-1600 Sat-Sun and holidays, C-717-245-4245, D-312-242-4245. All other times C-717-245-4115. All ranks. DV/VIP C-717-245-4818.

**RV, CAMPING/FAMCAMP:** None. See Letterkenny Army Depot listing.

**SPACE-A:** None. See Fort Indiantown Gap listing, Muir Army Airfield.

**LOGISTICAL SUPPORT:**

| | |
|---|---|
| Barber Shop-249-4958 | Beauty Shop-258-4700 |
| Book Store-258-3326 | Carlson Wagonlit Travel-245-9891 |
| Child Care-245-3701 | Child Dev Center-245-3701 |
| Class Six-245-2275 | Commissary-245-3105 |
| Credit Union-243-3900 | Dry Cleaner-258-1856 |
| Education Office-245-3943 | Exchange-243-2463 |
| Postal Service-258-1930 | SATO-245-3158 |
| Snack Bar-245-4883 | |

**ADMINISTRATIVE SUPPORT:**

| | |
|---|---|
| Fire Dept-245-4419 | Housing Office-245-4017 |
| Legal-245-4940 | Locator-245-3131 |
| Police-245-4115 | Public Affairs-245-4101 |

SDO/NCO-245-4342

**HEALTH & WELFARE:**

| | |
|---|---|
| ACS-245-4357 | CHAMPUS-245-4112 |
| Chapel-245-3318 | Dental-245-4542 |
| Family Services-245-4357 | Medical |
| Retiree Services-245-4501 | Central Appts-245-3400 |
| Veterinary Services-245-3430 | Clinic-245-3915 |

**REST & RECREATION:**

| | |
|---|---|
| Arts & Crafts-245-3319 | Auto Hobby Shop-245-3319 |
| Bowling-245-4109 | Com Support Center-245-3215/3319 |
| Fitness Center-245-3228 | Golf Course-243-3262 |
| Gym | ITR-245-3309 |
| 245-3418 (Building 23) | Library |
| 245-4375 (Building 120) | 245-4300 (Building 122) |
| Outdoor Rec-245-4935 | 245-3718 (Building 46) |
| Sports Office-245-4343 | Theater-245-4108 |
| Wood Hobby Shop-245-3314 | Youth Center-245-3354 |
| Youth Services-245-3354 | |

**OTHER FACILITIES AVAILABLE:** Army Emergency Relief.

**ATTRACTIONS:** Hessian Powder Magazine Museum and Omar N. Bradley Museum; Amish Country and Gettysburg Battlefield nearby.

## CHARLES E. KELLY SUPPORT FACILITY (PA12R1)

6 Lobaugh Street
Oakdale, PA 15071-5000
*Scheduled to close July 2001*

**TELEPHONE NUMBER INFORMATION:** Main installation numbers: C-724-693-1844/5.

**LOCATION:** From I-279 east or west take I-79 south to Carnegie exit (exit 13). Bear right (left if coming from the south) on Noblestown Road and travel approximately two-and-a-half miles through town of Rennerdale. Follow signs. USMRA: Page 22 (A-6). NMC: Pittsburgh, 13 miles east.

**GENERAL INFORMATION:** Location of 99th Reserve Support Command. A local area Army Support Center.

**TEMPORARY MILITARY LODGING:** None. See Pittsburgh IAP/ARS listing.

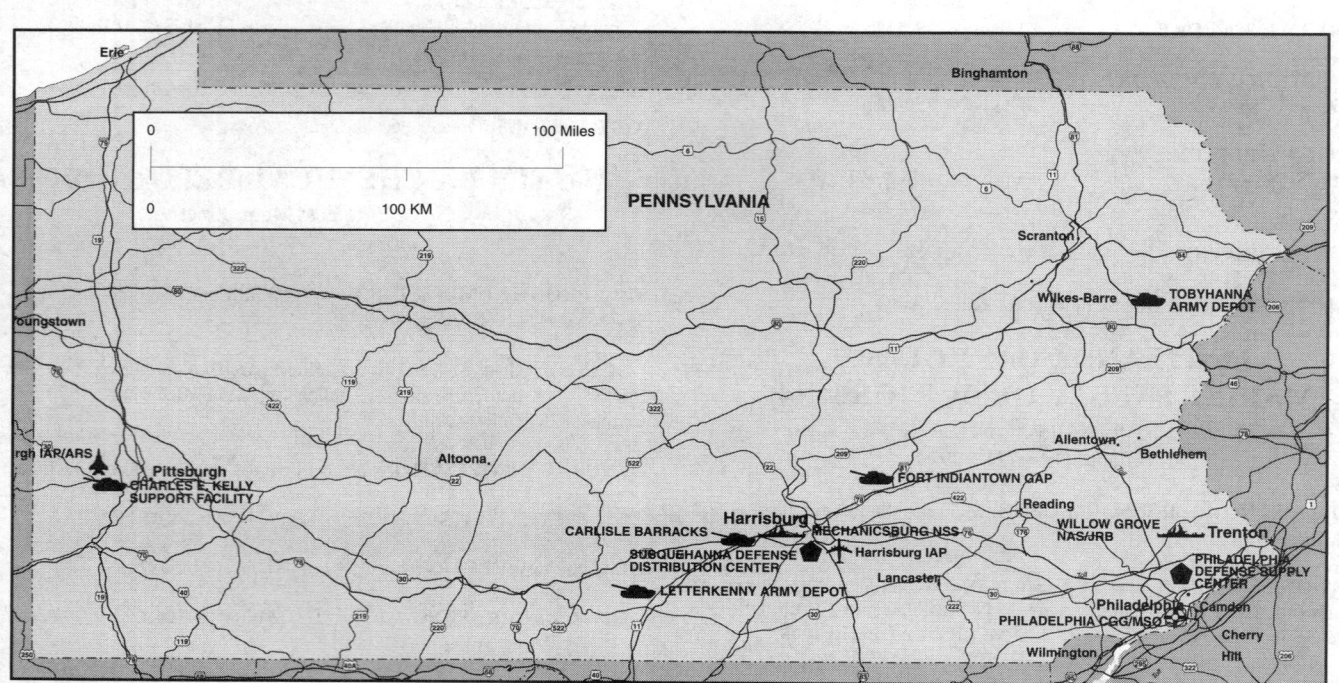

**RV, CAMPING/FAMCAMP:** None. Nearest facility is more than 100 miles away.

**SPACE-A:** None. See Baltimore/Washington IAP listing.

**LOGISTICAL SUPPORT:**

| | |
|---|---|
| Carlson Wagonlit Travel-693-8710/11 | Commissary-693-2471/2463 |
| Exchange-693-2434 | Four Seasons-693-2426 |
| Package Store-693-2436 | Snack Bar-693-2437 |

**ADMINISTRATIVE SUPPORT:**          Pass/ID Office-693-2475

**HEALTH & WELFARE:**

| | |
|---|---|
| CHAMPUS-693-2475/6 | Medical |
| Retiree Services-693-2186 | Emergency- 693-2476 |

**REST & RECREATION:**

| | |
|---|---|
| Community Center-695-1858 | Fitness Center-693-1860 |
| Recreation-693-1858/1860 | |

**ATTRACTIONS:** City of Pittsburgh, the Shops at Station Square, Carnegie Science Center, the Boardwalk, the Gateway Clipper Fleet boats and a magnificent view of the city atop Mount Washington. Pittsburgh Pirates baseball, Penguins hockey and Steelers football.

## FORT INDIANTOWN GAP (PA04R1)

1 Garrison Road, Bldg 11-7
Fort Indiantown Gap, PA 17003-5002

**TELEPHONE NUMBER INFORMATION:** Main installation numbers: C-717-861-2000, D-312-491-2000.

**LOCATION:** From I-81 north or south, take exit 29 B north on PA-934 to post. USMRA: Page 22 (G-6). NMC: Harrisonburg, 18 miles southwest.

**GENERAL INFORMATION:** Pennsylvania Department of Military and Veterans Affairs, Reserve Component training and area support. Pennsylvania National Guard assumed command of Fort Indiantown Gap in October of 1998.

**TEMPORARY MILITARY LODGING:** Lodging office, Building 11-9 Hours: 0800-1630 daily, C-717-861-2540, D-312-491-2540. All ranks. DV/VIP C-717-861-2540.

**RV, CAMPING/FAMCAMP:** None. See Letterkenny Army Depot listing

**SPACE-A:** Muir Army Airfield, C-717-861-2000, D-312-491-2000.

**LOGISTICAL SUPPORT:**

| | |
|---|---|
| Barber Shop-861-2853 | Class Six-861-2058 |
| Carlson Wagonlit Travel-865-1073 | Credit Union-865-6641 |
|  or 865-1068 | Exchange-861-2058 |
| Gas Station-865-6938 | Shoppette-865-6938 |
| Snack Bar-865-2044 | |

**ADMINISTRATIVE SUPPORT:**

| | |
|---|---|
| Fire Dept-861-2111 | Locator-861-2000 |
| Police-861-2727 | Public Affairs-861-8468 |

**HEALTH & WELFARE:**          Medical-861-2091

**REST & RECREATION:**

| | |
|---|---|
| Com Club-861-2450 | Gym 861-2860 |
| MWR-861-2060 | Swimming-861-2656 |

**ATTRACTIONS:** Hershey Amusement Park, Pennsylvania Dutch Country, Lebanon and origin of Lebanon Bologna.

## HARRISBURG INTERNATIONAL AIRPORT (PA14R1)

Middletown, PA 17057-5086

**TELEPHONE NUMBER INFORMATION:** Main installation numbers: C-717-948-2200.

**LOCATION:** From I-76 east or west exit 19 south on PA-230 (2nd Street) south to IAP on right. USMRA: Page 22 (G-6). NMC: Harrisburg, five miles northwest.

**GENERAL INFORMATION:** Home of 193rd Special Operations Wing, Air National Guard, C-130H.

**TEMPORARY MILITARY LODGING:** None. See Susquehanna Defense Distribution Region listing.

**RV, CAMPING/FAMCAMP:** None. See Letterkenny Army Depot listing.

**SPACE-A:** None. See Baltimore/Washington IAP listing.

**LOGISTICAL SUPPORT:**          Exchange-948-2415

**ADMINISTRATIVE SUPPORT:**          Public Affairs-717-948-2581

**HEALTH & WELFARE:**          Medical-948-2234

**REST & RECREATION:** None. See Susquehanna Defense Distribution Region listing.

**ATTRACTIONS:** Capital city of Harrisburg, museums, Susquehanna River.

## LETTERKENNY ARMY DEPOT (PA03R1)

ATTN: SIOLE-CO
1 Overcash Avenue
Chambersburg, PA 17201-4150
*This base is scheduled to downsize in October 2000.*

**TELEPHONE NUMBER INFORMATION:** Main installation numbers: C-717-267-8111, D-312-570-5110. E-mail: letterkenny-emh1.army.mil. WEB: www.letterkenny.army.mil

**LOCATION:** From I-81 north or south exit 8 to PA-997 north (left), enter depot at gate 6. USMRA: Page 22 (E-7). NMC: Harrisburg, 55 miles northeast.

**GENERAL INFORMATION:** Army Depot that maintains Army materiel and ammunition. DoD tactical missile maintenance center.

**TEMPORARY MILITARY LODGING:** Lodging office, Building 663, 0730-1615 Mon-Fri, C-717-267-8890, D-312-570-8890. All ranks.

**RV, CAMPING/FAMCAMP:** Army Travel Camp on post, 1 April-31 October, C-717-267-9494/9620, D-312-570-9494/9620, eight camper spaces, with W/E hookups.

**SPACE-A:** None. See Baltimore/Washington IAP listing.

**LOGISTICAL SUPPORT:**

| | |
|---|---|
| Barber Shop-267-8685 | Cafeteria-264-1321 |
| Carlson Wagonlit Travel-267-1316 | Child Care-267-8846 |
| Class Six-264-1713 | Credit Union-263-4444 |
| Exchange-264-1713 | Travel-267-1315 |

**ADMINISTRATIVE SUPPORT:**

| | |
|---|---|
| Fire Dept-267-9101 | Housing Office-267-8890 |
| Legal-267-9889 | Locator-267-8366 |
| Pass/ID Office-267-9754 | Police-267-8800 |
| Public Affairs-267-5102 | |

**HEALTH & WELFARE:**

| | |
|---|---|
| Medical-267-8416 | Retiree Services-267-9725 |

**REST & RECREATION:**

| | |
|---|---|
| Community Center-267-8478 | Com Club-267-8478 |
| Gym-ext 9383 | |

**ATTRACTIONS:** Gettysburg Battlefield, Hershey Park, Potomac C&O Canal, Carlisle Barracks and War College.

# MECHANICSBURG NAVAL SUPPORT STATION (PA07R1)

P.O. Box 2020
5450 Carlisle Pike
Mechanicsburg, PA 17055-0788

**TELEPHONE NUMBER INFORMATION:** Main installation numbers: C-717-605-2000, D-312-430-2000.

**LOCATION:** From I-83 north or south, exit 20 to US-11 west, four miles to Main Gate on left (south). Or from PA Turnpike (I-76) exit 16 (Carlisle) eight miles on PA 641 east to Naval Support Station. USMRA: Page 22 (F,G-6). NMC: Harrisburg, 10 miles northeast.

**GENERAL INFORMATION:** Logistics support activity for Naval ships parts.

**TEMPORARY MILITARY LODGING:** None. See Carlisle Barracks listing, C-717-245-4245, D-312-242-4245.

**RV, CAMPING/FAMCAMP:** None. See Letterkenny Army Depot listing, C-717-267-9494/9620, D-312-570-9494/9620.

**SPACE-A:** None. See Baltimore/Washington IAP listing.

**LOGISTICAL SUPPORT:**

| | |
|---|---|
| Barber Shop-605-4344 | Cafeteria-605-3537 |
| Child Dev Center-605-5683 | Credit Union-605-3596 |
| Exchange-605-2608 | Package Store-605-2608 |
| SATO-1-800-949-7286 | |

**ADMINISTRATIVE SUPPORT:**

| | |
|---|---|
| CDO-605-4444 | Fire Dept-605-3467 |
| Housing Office-605-2900 | Legal-605-2424 |
| Pass/ID Office-605-3795 | Police-605-3351 |
| Public Affairs-605-3338 | SDO/NCO-605-4444 |

**HEALTH & WELFARE:** Medical-605-3409/2636

**REST & RECREATION:**

| | |
|---|---|
| Auto Hobby Shop-605-4338 | Bowling-605-3948 |
| O Club-605-3505 | Fitness Center-605-3948 |
| Golf Course-605-1610 | Gym-605-3948 |
| MWR-605-1610 | |

**ATTRACTIONS:** Gettysburg National Battlefield Park and Pennsylvania State capital, Harrisburg.

# PHILADELPHIA COAST GUARD GROUP/ MARINE SAFETY OFFICE (PA19R1)

1 Washington Avenue
Philadelphia, PA 19147-4395

**TELEPHONE NUMBER INFORMATION:** Main installation number: C-215-271-4800, Fax: C-215-271-4919. E-mail: editor@msogruphilly.uscg.mil WEB: www.uscg.mil/d5/msophilly/index.html
*Ten digit dialing required for local calls.*

**LOCATION:** Exit 16 off I-95 to Columbus Blvd north to east on Washington Avenue. USMRA: Page 27 (D,E-6). NMC: Philadelphia, within city limits.

**TEMPORARY MILITARY LODGING:** None. See Willow Grove NAS/JRB listing.

**RV, CAMPING/FAMCAMP:** None. See Fort Dix AG, NJ listing, Brindle Lake Travel Camp.

**SPACE-A:** None. See McGuire AFB listing.

**LOGISTICAL SUPPORT:** Exchange-271-4921

**ADMINISTRATIVE SUPPORT:**

| | |
|---|---|
| CDO-271-4800 | Fire Dept-271-4927/4940 |
| OOD-271-4940 | Police-271-4971 |
| Public Affairs Office-271-4860 | |

**HEALTH & WELFARE:** Medical-271-4816

**OTHER FACILITIES AVAILABLE:** Fitness room, galley, outdoor baseball and weight room.

**ATTRACTIONS:** Independence Hall, Betsy Ross House, Liberty Bell Pavilion. Edgar Allen Poe National Historic Site. Museums, professional sports, tours.

# PHILADELPHIA DEFENSE SUPPLY CENTER (PA02R1)

700 Robbins Avenue
Philadelphia, PA 19111-5096

**TELEPHONE NUMBER INFORMATION:** Main installation numbers: C-215-737-2000, D-312-444-2000. E-mail: fjohnson@dpsc.dla.mil. WEB: www.dscp.dla.mil/index.htm
*Ten digit dialing required for local calls.*

**LOCATION:** From I-76 north or south exit 34 to US-1. Go four miles east to Oxford Avenue (Route 232). Turn left onto Oxford and follow for 1.3 miles to gate. Located in NAVICP compound. USMRA: Page 27 (E-3). NMC: Philadelphia, in city limits.

**GENERAL INFORMATION:** Provides defense personnel and their eligible dependents with $3 billion worth of food, clothing and textiles, medicines, and medical equipment.

**TEMPORARY MILITARY LODGING:** None. See Willow Grove NAS/JRB listing.

**RV, CAMPING/FAMCAMP:** None. See Fort Dix AG, NJ listing, Brindle Lake Travel Camp.

**SPACE-A:** None. See McGuire AFB listing.

**LOGISTICAL SUPPORT:**

| | |
|---|---|
| Cafeteria-737-3932 | Exchange-697-3703 |
| Snack Bar-737-3933 | Travel Office-467-5925 (official) |
| | 467-5945 (Leisure) |

**ADMINISTRATIVE SUPPORT:**

| | |
|---|---|
| CDO/OOD-737-2341 | Locator-737-2411 |
| Police-737-2220 | Public Affairs-737-2311 |

**HEALTH & WELFARE:** None. See Willow Grove NAS/JRB listing.

**REST & RECREATION:**

| | |
|---|---|
| Fitness Center-697-2069 | MWR-697-9092 |

**ATTRACTIONS:** Independence Hall, Betsy Ross House, Liberty Bell Pavilion. Edgar Allen Poe National Historic Site. Museums, professional sports, tours.

# PITTSBURGH INTERNATIONAL AIRPORT/ AIR RESERVE STATION (PA15R1)

911 Airlift Wing/PA
2475 Defense Avenue, Suite 227
Coraopolis, PA 15108-4403

**TELEPHONE NUMBER INFORMATION:** Main installation numbers: C-412-474-8000, D-312-277-8000.

**LOCATION:** Take I-279 west, which merges into PA-60 (Airport Parkway), then take exit 3 Business Route 60 to Thorn Run Interchange, follow signs to Air Reserve Station. USMRA: Page 22 (A-5,6). NMC: Pittsburgh, 15 miles southeast.

**TEMPORARY MILITARY LODGING:** 316 Defense Avenue, 0700-2400, C-412-474-8230, D-312-277-8230, Fax: C-412-474-8752, D-312-277-8752.

**RV, CAMPING/FAMCAMP:** None. Nearest facility is more than 100 miles away.

**SPACE-A:** Pax Term Building 419, 0730-1600, C-412-474-8163, D-312-277-8163, Fax: C-412-474-8156, D-312-277-8156.

**LOGISTICAL SUPPORT:**

| | |
|---|---|
| Credit Union-474-8208 | Education Office-474-8519 |
| Exchange-424-8207 | Snack Bar-474-8737 |
| Travel Office-474-8197 | |

**ADMINISTRATIVE SUPPORT:**

| | |
|---|---|
| Fire Dept-911 | Legal-474-8265 |
| Pass/ID Office-474-8274 | Police-474-8255 |
| Public Affairs-474-8750 | |

**HEALTH & WELFARE:**

| | |
|---|---|
| Chapel-474-8204 | Family Services-474-8544 |
| Retiree Services-474-8558 | |

**REST & RECREATION:**

| | |
|---|---|
| Consolidated Mess-474-8227 | Fitness Center-474-8245 |
| Gym-474-8245 | Services-474-8241 |

**ATTRACTIONS:** City of Pittsburgh, the Shops at Station Square, Carnegie Science Center, Carnegie Museum, the Boardwalk, the Gateway Clipper Fleetboats and a magnificent view of the city atop Mount Washington. Pittsburgh Pirates baseball, Penguins hockey, and Steelers football.

## SUSQUEHANNA DEFENSE DISTRIBUTION CENTER (PA06R1)

2001 Mission Drive
New Cumberland, PA 17070-5001

**TELEPHONE NUMBER INFORMATION:** Main installation numbers: C-717-770-6011, D-312-977-1110.

**LOCATION:** From I-83 north or south, exit 18 to PA-114 east for one mile to Old York Road, left three-quarters-of-a-mile to Ross Avenue, right for one mile to main gate of Center. USMRA: Page 22 (G-6). NMC: Harrisburg, seven miles northeast.

**GENERAL INFORMATION:** Defense Logistics Agency.

**TEMPORARY MILITARY LODGING:** Lodging office, Building 268, J Avenue, 0700-1700 hours daily, C-717-770-7035, D-312-977-7035. All ranks. DV/VIP C-717-770-7192.

**RV, CAMPING/FAMCAMP:** None. See Letterkenny Army Depot listing.

**SPACE-A:** None. See McGuire AFB listing.

**LOGISTICAL SUPPORT:**

| | |
|---|---|
| Bank-770-7539 | Cafeteria-770-7165/6973 |
| Carlson Wagon Travel-770-6668 | Child Care-770-7360 |
| Class VI-774-4066 | Commissary-770-6540 |
| Conv Store-774-4066 | Dining-770-7915 |
| Exchange-774-4066 | Gas Station-774-4066 |
| Snack Bar-770-5125 | |

**ADMINISTRATIVE SUPPORT:**

| | |
|---|---|
| Fire Dept-770-6632 | Legal-770-6310 |
| Locator-770-6770 | Police-770-6222 |
| Public Affairs-770-6223 | |

**HEALTH & WELFARE:**

| | |
|---|---|
| CHAMPUS-770-7281 | Family Services-770-6203 |
| Medical-782-7281 | |

**REST & RECREATION:**

| | |
|---|---|
| Auto Hobby Shop-ext 6664 | Bowling-770-7539 |
| Consol Club-770-7802 | Fitness Center-ext 6428 |
| Golf Course-770-5199 | Gym-ext 6428 |
| ITR-770-7670 | MWR-770-5072 |
| Outdoor Recreation-ext 7718 | Recreation-770-7718 |
| Rec Center-ext 7625 | Rec Equipment-ext 7625 |
| Swimming-ext 6476 | Youth Center-ext 4413 |

**ATTRACTIONS:** State Capitol in Harrisburg, Harley Davidson Plant (York, PA), Hershey Park, Gettysburg Battlefield, Pennsylvania Dutch Country.

## TOBYHANNA ARMY DEPOT (PA05R1)

ATTN: SIOTY-C
11 Hap Arnold Boulevard
Tobyhanna, PA 18466-5076

**TELEPHONE NUMBER INFORMATION:** Main installation numbers: C-570-895-7000, D-312-795-7000. E-mail: ktoolan@tobyhanna.army.mil
WEB: www.tobyhanna.army.mil

**LOCATION:** Take I-80 east or west to I-380 north, exit 7 to PA 507 and one mile to depot. USMRA: Page 22 (I-4). NMC: Scranton, 24 miles northwest.

**GENERAL INFORMATION:** The Defense Department's largest facility for the repair, overhaul and fabrication of communications-electronics systems and equipment, including radio, radar and satellite communications systems.

**TEMPORARY MILITARY LODGING:** Lodging office, Building 1001, Admin Loop, 0800-1630 daily, C-570-895-7970, D-312-795-7970. All ranks. DV/VIP C-570-895-6223.

**RV, CAMPING/FAMCAMP:** None. See Picatinny Arsenal, NJ listing, Lake Denmark Rec Area.

**SPACE-A:** Army flights C-570-895-7000. Also see McGuire AFB, NJ listing.

**LOGISTICAL SUPPORT:**

| | |
|---|---|
| Barber Shop-895-7695 | Cafeteria-895-7998 |
| Carlson Wagonlit Travel-894-8025 | Child Care-895-6148 |
| Child Dev Center-895-6148 | Class Six-895-7030 |
| Commissary-895-7246 | Credit Union-894-8325 |
| Dining Facilities-895-7998/7045 | Education Office-895-7697 |
| Exchange-895-7716/7030 | Gas Station-895-7401 |
| SATO-895-6318 | Snack Bar-895-7030 |

**ADMINISTRATIVE SUPPORT:**

| | |
|---|---|
| Fire Dept-895-7300 | Housing Office-895-7970 |
| Legal-895-7210 | Locator-895-7409 |
| Pass/ID Office-895-7409 | Police-895-7550 |
| Public Affairs-895-7308 | |

**HEALTH & WELFARE:**

| | |
|---|---|
| ACS-895-7069 | Army Emergency Relief-895-6128 |
| CHAMPUS-895-7225 | Chapel-895-7351 |
| Family Services-895-7069 | Medical-895-7225 |
| Retiree Services-895-7834 | Clinic-895-7121 |
| Veterinary Services-895-7950 | Emergency-911 |

**REST & RECREATION:**

| | |
|---|---|
| Arts & Crafts-895-7634 | Auto Hobby Shop-895-6609 |
| Com Club-895-7045 | Fitness Center-895-7583 |
| Gym-895-7583 | ITT-895-7584 |
| Library-895-7316 | MWR-895-7584 |
| Outdoor Rec-895-7092/7584 | Wood Hobby Shop-895-7650 |
| Youth Center-895-6156 | |

**ATTRACTIONS:** Located in the Pocono Mountains of northeastern Pennsylvania. The Poconos are a four-season tourist and resort area.

## WILLOW GROVE NAVAL AIR STATION/ JOINT RESERVE BASE (PA01R1)

Bldg. 2, MWR
Willow Grove, PA 19090-5000

**TELEPHONE NUMBER INFORMATION:** Main installation numbers: C-215-443-1000, D-312-991-1000.
*Ten digit dialing required for local calls.*

**LOCATION:** Six miles north of Philadelphia. Take PA Turnpike (I-76) to Willow Grove exit 27 north approximately three or four miles on PA-611 to NAS. USMRA: Page 22 (I,J-6). NMC: Philadelphia, eight miles south.

**GENERAL INFORMATION:** Naval Air Reserve Unit training.

**TEMPORARY MILITARY LODGING:** Lodging office, Building 609, 24 hours daily, C-215-442-5800/5801, D-312-991-5800/5801, Fax: C-215-442-5817. All ranks. DV/VIP 215-443-1776.

**RV, CAMPING/FAMCAMP:** Operates Lake Laurie Campground, NJ, C-215-443-6082, D-312-991-6082, two campers with full hookups.

**SPACE-A:** Pax Term/Lounge, Hangar 80, 0730-1600 Wed-Sun, C-215-433-6216, D-312-991-6216, Fax: C-215-443-6188, flights to CONUS and overseas.

**LOGISTICAL SUPPORT:**

| | |
|---|---|
| Bank-443-6025 | Barber Shop-443-6030 |
| Cafeteria-443-6282 | Child Care-443-6080 |
| Conv Store-443-6078 | Credit Union-443-6025 |
| Dining Facilities-443-6282 | Exchange-443-6028 |
| Package Store-443-6078 | Postal Service-443-6053 |
| Travel Office-443-6867 | Visitor Center-443-6033 |

**ADMINISTRATIVE SUPPORT:**

| | |
|---|---|
| CDO/OOD-443-6454 | Fire Dept-443-6198 |
| Housing Office-773-2114/6 | Legal-443-6056 |
| Locator-443-1000 | Pass/ID Office-443-1776 |
| Police-443-6067 | Public Affairs-443-1766 |
| Quarter Deck-443-6454 | SDO-443-6454 |

**HEALTH & WELFARE:**

| | |
|---|---|
| CHAMPUS-443-6351 | Chapel-443-6002 |
| Dental-443-6379 | Family Services-443-6033 |
| Medical | Navy-MC Relief-443-6024 |
|   Central Appts-443-6372/3 | Retiree Services-443-6033 |
|   Clinic-443-6360 | TRICARE-443-6351 |
|   Emergency-443-1600 | |
|   Health Benefits-443-6351 | |
|   Information-443-6360 | |

**REST & RECREATION:**

| | |
|---|---|
| Auto Hobby Shop-443-6087 | Bowling-443-6092 |
| Clubs | Fitness Center-443-6066 |
|   EM-443-6089 | Gym-443-6066 |
|   O-443-6081 | ITT-443-6082 |
| Library-443-6095 | MWR-443-6979 |
| Rec Equipment-443-6066 | Services-443-6082 |
| Swimming-443-6079 | |

**ATTRACTIONS:** New Jersey beaches are a one and a half hour drive; Pocono Mountain resorts, a one hour drive.

# RHODE ISLAND

## CARR POINT RECREATION AREA(RI04R1)

MWR Ticket Connection
656 Whipple Street
Newport, RI 02841-5000

**TELEPHONE NUMBER INFORMATION:** Main installation number: C-401-841-3116. Police for recreation area, C-401-841-3241.

**LOCATION:** Off base. From north and east, at the junction of Routes 24 and 114, take Route 114 south for 1.7 miles to Stringham Road. From south and west, take Route 95 to Route 138 east to Route 114 north. Follow Route 114 for 4.7 miles to Stringham Road. Follow Stringham for 2.3 miles to the turn into the facility. Clearly marked. USMRA: Page 17 (J-8). NMC: Providence, 30 miles northwest.

**GENERAL INFORMATION:** Operated by Newport NS, off base, Memorial Day weekend through Labor Day weekend. Military personnel active, reservists, retired, DoD civilians. Reservations: MWR Ticket Connection, 656 Whipple Street, Newport, RI 02841-5000. C-401-841-3116 0830-1700 hours. Fax: C-401-841-4500.

**RV, CAMPING/FAMCAMP:**        Camper Spaces-6

**ATTRACTIONS:** Located on Naragansett Bay. Summer resort area. Home of the Newport Jazz Festival, Ben & Jerry's Folk Festival, international boat shows and famous Newport mansions. Great public beaches and seafood restaurants nearby.

*For detailed information about this off-base recreation facility, as well as on-base recreation facilities, golf courses and marinas, consult Military Living's Military RV, Camping and Outdoor Recreation Around the World.*

## NEWPORT NAVAL STATION (RI01R1)

61 Capodanno Drive
Newport, RI 02841-1513

**TELEPHONE NUMBER INFORMATION:** Main installation numbers: C-401-841-2311, D-312-948-2311.

**LOCATION:** From US-1 exit to RI-138 east over Jamestown/Newport bridge (toll) to Newport. Follow signs north to Navy Base, gate 1. USMRA: Page 17 (J-8), page 25 (B,C-1,2,3). NMC: Newport, adjacent.

**GENERAL INFORMATION:** Naval War College, Surface Warfare Officers School, Naval Justice School, Naval Hospital, Naval Undersea Warfare Center, other training and support activities.

**TEMPORARY MILITARY LODGING:** Lodging office, 24 hours daily; Building 684 (Officers) C-401-841-3156; Building 447 (EM), C-401-841-4410. Navy Lodge, Building 685, 0700-2300 daily, C-401-849-4500. All ranks. DV/VIP C-401-841-3715, Fax: C-401-849-3906.

**RV, CAMPING/FAMCAMP:** Carr Point Recreation Area, off base, Memorial Day Weekend-30 September, 656 Whipple Street, C-401-841-3116. Fax: C-401-841-4500. Six sites with W & E hookups.

**SPACE-A:** None. See Quonset State Airport listing.

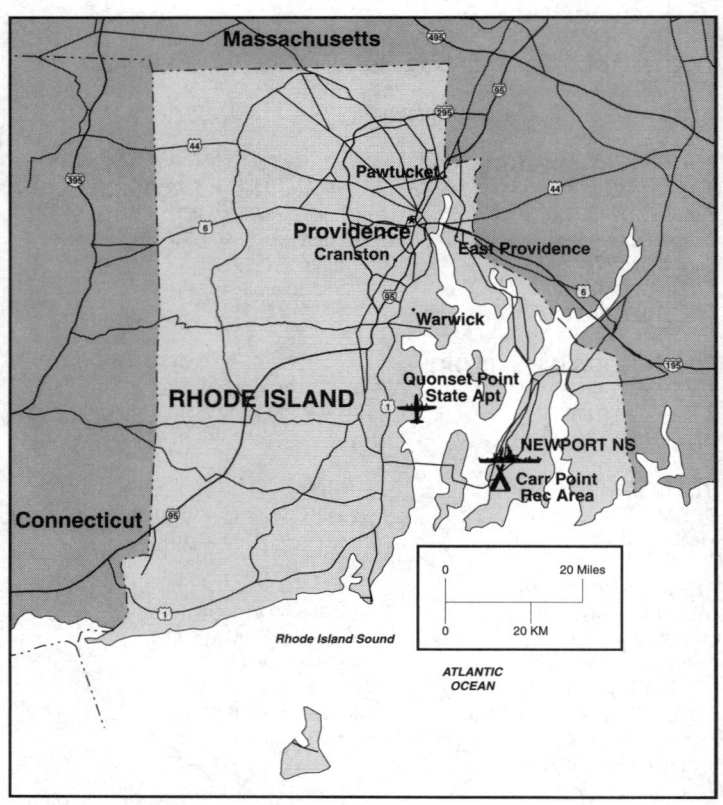

**LOGISTICAL SUPPORT:**

Bank-847-7062
Child Care-841-4562
Conv Store-846-2831
Gas Station-841-3192
SATO-841-3710

Cafeteria-841-4445
Commissary-841-2111
Exchange-841-1399
Package Store-846-3080
Snack Bar-846-7671/814

**ADMINISTRATIVE SUPPORT:**

Legal-841-3766
OOD-841-3456
Public Affairs-841-3538

Locator-841-3456
Police-841-3241/3242

**HEALTH & WELFARE:**

Chapel-841-2234
Medical-841-7100
  Emergency-841-2222

Family Services-841-2283
Retiree Services-841-4089
TRICARE-841-3216

**REST & RECREATION:**

Auto Hobby Shop-ext 3026
Gym-ext 3154
MWR-841-2643
ITT-841-3116
Rec Center-ext 4293
Rec Equipment-ext 2568
Yacht Club-ext 3283

Bowling-841-4293
Clubs
  CPO-841-2575
  EMC-841-3054
  O-846-2515
Swimming-ext 6628

**ATTRACTIONS:** Beaches, Newport Music Festivals, Tennis Hall of Fame, mansion tours.

# QUONSET POINT STATE AIRPORT (RI03R1)

1 Minuteman Way
North Kingstown, RI 02852-7502

**TELEPHONE NUMBER INFORMATION:** Main installation numbers: C-401-886-1420.

**LOCATION:** From US-1 exit to RI-403 south or I-95 north or south, exit 9 to RI-4 south to exit 7 on RI-403 southwest. Airport is clearly marked. USMRA: Page 17 (J-7). NMC: Providence, 20 miles north.

**GENERAL INFORMATION:** Home of the 143rd Air Wing, Air National Guard.

**SPACE-A:** C-401-886-1420.

**REST & RECREATION:**      NCO Club-886-1143

**ATTRACTIONS:** Nearby Providence, Newport, beaches, water activities.

# SOUTH CAROLINA

## BEAUFORT MARINE CORPS AIR STATION (SC01R1)

P.O. Box 55001, Geiger Boulevard
Beaufort Marine Corps Air Station, SC 29904-5001

**TELEPHONE NUMBER INFORMATION:** Main installation numbers: C-843-228-7100, D-312-335-7100.

**LOCATION:** From I-95 take Beaufort exit 33 to SC-21 southeast and follow signs. Sixteen miles to MCAS east of SC-21. Clearly marked. USMRA: Page 44 (G-9). NMC: Savannah, GA, 40 miles south.

**GENERAL INFORMATION:** Marine Aircraft Group, Marine Air Control Squadron, Marine Corps Support Squadron.

**TEMPORARY MILITARY LODGING:** BOQ, Building 431, 24 hours daily, C-843-228-7676, D-312-335-7676. All ranks. DV/VIP C-843-228-7158. DeTreville House C-843-228-1663.

**RV, CAMPING/FAMCAMP:** None. See Charleston AFB listing.

**SPACE-A:** Pax Term/Lounge, Building 860, 0700-2300 Mon-Fri, 1000-1800 Sat, 1200-2000 Sun, C-843-228-7143, D-312-335-7143. Fax: C-843-228-7221, flights to CONUS and OCONUS locations.

**LOGISTICAL SUPPORT:**

Barber Shop-228-6130
Cafeteria-228-7895
Conv Store-228-7615
Dry Cleaner-228-6107
Laundry-228-6107

Beauty Shop-228-6130
Child Care-228-7290
Credit Union-525-6300
Exchange-228-7627
Education Office-228-7754

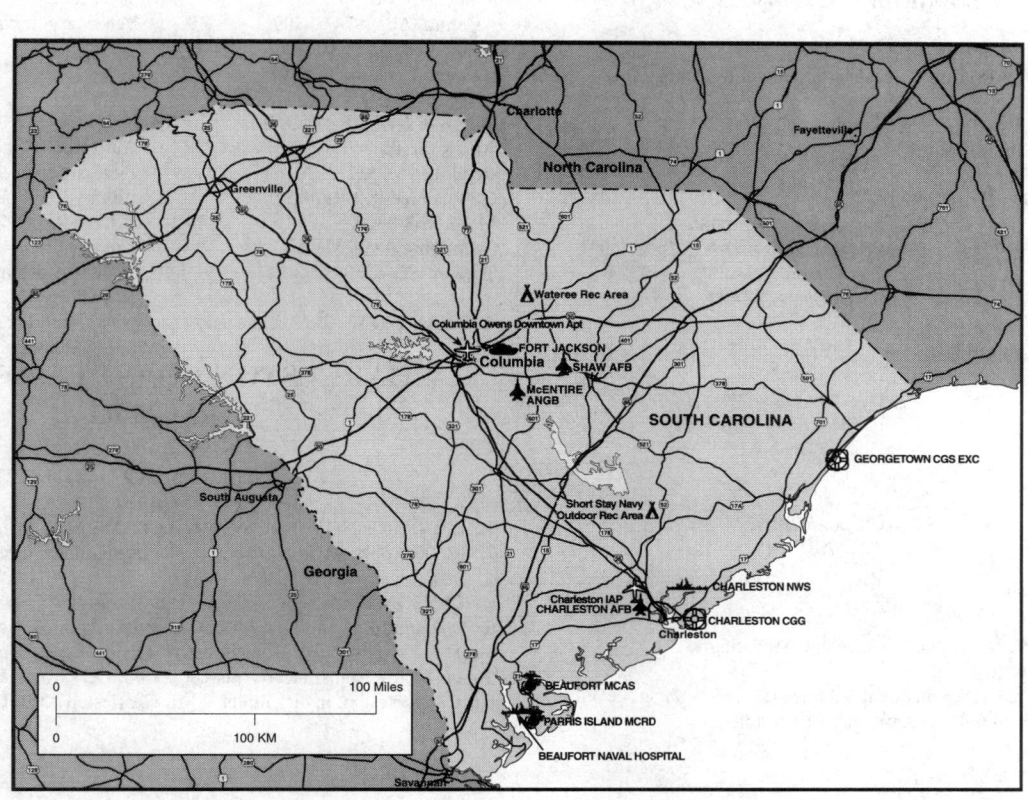

Gas Station-228-7727
Postal Service
   Mil-228-6053/7220
   US-228-7003

Package Store-228-7627
Snack Bar-228-7895
Shoppette-228-7751
Travel Office-228-7820

**ADMINISTRATIVE SUPPORT:**
Fire Dept-7293
Legal-228-7330
OOD-228-7017
Police-228-7373/7589
SDO-228-7121

Housing Office-228-7069
Locator-228-7100
Pass/ID Office-228-7750/7941
Public Affairs-228-7201

**HEALTH & WELFARE:**
CHAMPUS-525-5343/9415
Dental-228-7512
Medical-228-7424/7495
   Emergency-228-7311

Chapel-228-7775
Family Services-228-7353

**REST & RECREATION:**
Auto Hobby Shop-228-7586
Clubs
   NCO-228-7543/7726
   O-228-7541/7561
Marina-228-7472
MWR-228-7400
RV Rental-228-7472
Swimming-228-7524

Bowling-228-7106
Gym-228-7192
ITT-228-6375/6377/7340
Library-228-7682
   The Club-228-7534/7726
Picnic Area-228-6099
Stables-846-2644
Theater-228-7183

**ATTRACTIONS:** Beaches, seafood, period homes, Savannah, Charleston.

## BEAUFORT NAVAL HOSPITAL (SC07R1)

1 Pinckney Boulevard
Beaufort, SC 29902-6148

**TELEPHONE NUMBER INFORMATION:** Main installation numbers: C-843-525-5600, D-312-832-5600. E-mail: bfh1mtj@bfh10.med.navy.mil

**LOCATION:** From I-95 north or south, exit 33 south on SC-21 to Beaufort exit and follow signs. USMRA: Page 44 (G-9). NMC: Savannah, 40 miles south.

**GENERAL INFORMATION:** Serving Parris Island; Marine Corps Recruit Depot and Marine Corps Air Station, Beaufort.

**TEMPORARY MILITARY LODGING:** BEQ C-843-525-5418/9, D-312-832-5419, Fax: C-525-5320.

**RV, CAMPING/FAMCAMP:** None. See Charleston AFB listing, Shady Oaks Family Campground.

**SPACE-A:** None. See Beaufort MCAS listing.

**LOGISTICAL SUPPORT:**
Bank-525-5490
Child Care-525-5423
Exchange-525-5483
Mini Mart-525-5488

Barber Shop-525-5486
Convenience Store-525-5488
Gas Station-525-5488
Snack Bar-525-5489

**ADMINISTRATIVE SUPPORT:**
Fire Dept-525-5333
Housing-525-5431
Police (Security)-525-5317
OOD-525-5470

Legal-525-5309
Pass/ID Office-525-5364
Public Affairs-525-5433
Quarter Deck-525-5331

**HEALTH & WELFARE:**
Medical-Clinic-986-5230
   Emergency-525-5400
   Hospital-525-5331
   Information-525-5331

Chapel-525-5417
TRICARE-525-9415

**REST & RECREATION:** None. See Beaufort MCAS listing.

**ATTRACTIONS:** Fort Frederick – national historic site; Camp Shaw – Civil War site; beaches, seafood, period homes, Savannah, Charleston.

## CHARLESTON AIR FORCE BASE (SC06R1)

102 East Hill Boulevard, Room 223
Charleston Air Force Base, SC 29404-5154

**TELEPHONE NUMBER INFORMATION:** Main installation numbers: C-843-963-6000, D-312-673-1110.

**LOCATION:** From I-26 east or west, exit 211 to West Aviation Avenue to traffic light, continue through light to second light right, follow perimeter road around end of runway to gate 2 (Rivers Gate). USMRA: Page 44 (H-8,9). NMC: Charleston, 10 miles southeast.

**GENERAL INFORMATION:** Air Mobility Command Base. Active Duty Airlift Wing.

**TEMPORARY MILITARY LODGING:** Lodging office, Building 322, Simpson Street & Davis Drive, 24 hours daily, C-843-963-3806, (552-9900-room number after duty hours), D-312-673-3806, Fax: C-843-963-3394. All ranks.

**RV, CAMPING/FAMCAMP:** Shady Oaks Family Campground on base, year round, C-843-963-5270, D-312-673-5270, 23 camper spaces with W/E hookups.

**SPACE-A:** Pax Term/Lounge, Building 164, 0500-2300 daily, C-843-963-3083, D-312-673-3083, Rec: C-843-963-3082, Fax: C-843-963-3060. Flights to CONUS and overseas.

**LOGISTICAL SUPPORT:**
Child Care-963-4366
Exchange-552-5000
Package Store-767-4594
Travel-963-3091

Commissary-963-5709/5696
Gas Station-767-4594
Shoppette-767-4594

**ADMINISTRATIVE SUPPORT:**
Fire Dept-963-3118/3777
Legal-963-5502
Pass/ID Office-963-4514
Public Affairs-963-5537

Housing Office-963-3859
Locator-963-3282
Police-963-3600

**HEALTH & WELFARE:**
Air Force Aid Society-963-4414
Chapel-963-2536
Family services-963-4406
Medical-963-6750
   Central Appts-743-3709
   Emergency-743-7011
   Health Benefits-963-3971

American Red Cross-963-3377
Dental-963-6892
Retiree Services-963-2228
TRICARE-963-6706
Veterinary Services-963-4264

**REST & RECREATION:**
Arts & Crafts-963-4936
Bowling-963-3315
Golf Course-963-4174
MWR-963-3800
Swimming-963-5271
Theater-963-3333

Auto Hobby Shop-963-4942
Fitness Center-963-3347
Library-963-3320
O Club-963-3920
Tennis-963-3347
Youth Center-963-5684

**ATTRACTIONS:** Beautiful sandy beaches, period homes, gardens.

## CHARLESTON COAST GUARD GROUP (SC16R1)

196 Tradd Street
Charleston, SC 29401-1899

**TELEPHONE NUMBER INFORMATION:** Main installation numbers: C-843-724-7600. WEB: www.awod.com/gallery/uscg/index.html

**LOCATION:** From I-26 east, bear right (Route 17 toward Savannah). Stay in center lane and follow around to Lockwood Blvd. Follow Lockwood Blvd to Chisom Street, take right on Chisom Street to Tradd Street. Take another right on Tradd Street. Follow signs, clearly marked to the CG Group. USMRA: Page 44 (H-9). NMC: Charleston, in city limits. NMI: Charleston AFB, five miles.

**GENERAL INFORMATION:** Performs search-and-rescue operations.

**TEMPORARY MILITARY LODGING:** None. See Charleston AFB listing.

**RV, CAMPING/FAMCAMP:** None. See Charleston AFB listing, Shady Oaks Family Campground.

**SPACE-A:** None. See Charleston AFB listing.

**LOGISTICAL SUPPORT:**
Barber Shop-724-7608
Package Store-722-8817
Exchange-722-8817/8421

**ADMINISTRATIVE SUPPORT:**
CDO/OOD-724-7619/76
Housing Office-724-7635
Public Affairs-724-7628
Locator-724-7608
Pass/ID Office-724-7608

**HEALTH & WELFARE:**
CHAMPUS-724-7653
Medical-724-7653
Chaplain-724-7608

**REST & RECREATION:**
Clubs
EM-724-7674
NCO-724-7674

**ATTRACTIONS:** Charleston, one of America's most historic cities, features miles of beautiful, sandy beaches, gardens, fresh water lakes and great fishing.

# CHARLESTON INTERNATIONAL AIRPORT (SC15R1)

Suite 124, 5500 International Boulevard
Charleston, SC 29418-6924

**TELEPHONE NUMBER INFORMATION:** Main installation numbers: C-843-963-5794/5.

**LOCATION:** From I-26 take I-526 west one mile to airport exit. Turn right onto International Blvd, follow signs to airport. USMRA: Page 44 (H-9). NMC: Charleston, five miles southeast.

**GENERAL INFORMATION:** Commercial facilities in IAP. USO Lounge on ground floor under domestic baggage claim. See Charleston AFB listing.

**SPACE-A:** Information: C-843-963-5749/5795, D-312-673-5794/5795, Rec: C-843-963-5794. Fax: C-843-963-3845, D-312-673-3845.

**ATTRACTIONS:** Historic Charleston, beaches, period homes.

# CHARLESTON NAVAL WEAPONS STATION (SC11R1)

2316 Red Bank Road, Suite 100
Goose Creek, SC 29445-8601

**TELEPHONE NUMBER INFORMATION:** Main installation numbers: C-843-764-7901, D-312-794-7901.

**LOCATION:** From I-26 north or south, exit 205 south, east on US-78, to US-52 north, to SC-37 southeast (Red Bank Road) to main gate. USMRA: Page 44 (H-8,9). NMC: Charleston, 25 miles south.

**GENERAL INFORMATION:** Provides materiel and technical support for ammunition and assigned weapons and weapon systems. It operates an explosive ordnance out-loading facility. Manages Navy family housing for Charleston area.

**TEMPORARY MILITARY LODGING:** BEQ/BOQ C-843-764-7646. Also, see Charleston AFB listing, C-843-556-3806, D-312-673-3806.

**RV, CAMPING/FAMCAMP:** None. See Charleston AFB listing, Shady Oaks Family Campground.

**SPACE-A:** None. See Charleston AFB listing.

**LOGISTICAL SUPPORT:**
Child Care-764-7408
Exchange-764-7042
Package Store-764-7314
Commissary-764-7015
Gas Station-764-7573

**ADMINISTRATIVE SUPPORT:**
Police-764-7202

**HEALTH & WELFARE:**
Chapel-764-7222
Medical
  Clinic-764-7634
  Hospital-525-7000
Family Services-764-7294

**REST & RECREATION:**
Com Club-764-7797
ITT-764-7601
Outdoor Rec-761-8353
Gym/Fitness Center-764-7530
MWR-764-7601

**OTHER FACILITIES AVAILABLE:** Bowling, golf course, hunting/fishing, picnic area, racquetball, swimming and theater.

**ATTRACTIONS:** Historic Charleston (25 miles south), and scenic Myrtle Beach (100 miles northeast).

# COLUMBIA OWENS DOWNTOWN AIRPORT (SC19R1)

Midlands Aviation Corporation
1400 Jim Hamilton Blvd
Columbia, SC 29205-5000

**TELEPHONE NUMBER INFORMATION:** Main installation numbers: C-803-771-7915.

**LOCATION:** From I-20 east or west, exit US-1 (Two Notch Road) southwest, to south on Millwood Avenue to right (west) on Rosewood Drive to left (south) on South Holly Street and Airport. USMRA: Page 44 (F-6, 7). NMC: Columbia, in city limits.

**SPACE-A:** C-803-771-7915. Very limited flights. Call for destinations, routings, and schedules.

**ATTRACTIONS:** Capital city of Columbia, museums, Lake Murray, zoo.

# FORT JACKSON (SC09R1)

US Army Training Center & Fort Jackson
ATTN: ATZJ-GC
Percival Road
Fort Jackson, SC 29207-5060

**TELEPHONE NUMBER INFORMATION:** Main installation numbers: C-803-751-7511, D-312-734-1117. E-mail: pao@jackson-emhl.army.mil
WEB: jackson-www.army.mil

**LOCATION:** Exit from I-20 north of fort, or from US-76/378 at the main gate. From I-20 and I-77 interchange exit 16 take newly constructed Beltway south to Percival Road, right onto Percival Road to Gate 2.

**GENERAL INFORMATION:** Two Training Brigades for training recruits, one Combat Service Support Training (AIT) Brigade, Army Reception Station, and Reserve Command, U.S. Army Soldier Support Institute, U.S. Army Chaplain Center and School.

**TEMPORARY MILITARY LODGING:** Kennedy Hall, Building 2785, Semmes & Lee Road, 24 hours daily, C-803-751-6223/6149, D-312-734-6223/6149. Palmetto Lodge, Building 6000: C-803-751-5205/4429, D-312-734-5205/4429. All ranks. DV/VIP C-803-751-6618, D-312-734-5218.

**RV, CAMPING/FAMCAMP:** Weston Lake Recreation Area & Travel Camp on post, year round, C-803-751-5253, D-312-734-5253, 13 camper spaces with full hookups, five camper spaces with W/E, 10 tent spaces with W/E, seven cabins.

**SPACE-A:** None. See Charleston AFB listing.

**LOGISTICAL SUPPORT:**

| | |
|---|---|
| Child Care-751-6222/6221 | Class VI-787-3323 |
| Commissary-751-2789 | Conv Store-782-0590 |
| Exchange-787-1950 | Gas Station-782-1639 |
| Shoppette-790-4478 | Retiree Services-751-6715 |
| SDO/NCO-751-7611 | Snack Bar-751-4759 |
| Travel-782-5121 | Visitor Center-751-7576 |

**ADMINISTRATIVE SUPPORT:**

| | |
|---|---|
| Fire Dept-751-7217 | Housing Office-751-5306 |
| Legal-751-4287 | Locator-751-7671 |
| Pass/ID Office-751-6020 | Police-751-3113 |
| Public Affairs-751-6719 | SDO-751-7611 |

**HEALTH & WELFARE:**

| | |
|---|---|
| American Red Cross-751-4329 | ACS-751-5256 |
| Army Emergency Relief-751-4518 | CHAMPUS-751-2425 |
| Chapel-751-3121 | Dental-751-6625 |
| Family Services-751-5256 | Medical |
| Retiree Services-751-6652 | Clinic-751-4733 |
| TRICARE-751-CARE | Emergency-751-2169 |
| Veterinary Services-751-4390 | Hospital-751-2117 |
| | Information-751-5308 |

**REST & RECREATION:**

| | |
|---|---|
| Arts & Crafts-ext 6359 | Auto Hobby Shop-ext 5755 |
| Bowling-ext 4656 | Clubs |
| Fitness Center-751-5896 | NCO-782-1932 |
| Golf course-787-4344 | O-787-4906 |
| Gym-787-6258 | Riding-ext 6357 |
| Indoor Rec-751-4057 | ITT-751-6219 |
| Library-ext 5589 | Marinas-751-7865 |
| MWR-782-8876 | Outdoor Rec-ext 4948 |
| Picnic Area-ext 6606/4215 | Rec Center-ext 5743/4057 |
| Rec Equipment-ext 5481 | Rifle Range-ext 6954 |
| Swimming-ext 4796/7472/7084 | Theater-751-7488 |
| Wood Hobby Shop-751-3910 | Youth Center-751-6387 |
| Youth Services-751-5040 | |

**ATTRACTIONS:** Outdoor sports and recreation. Columbia, the state capital. Ernie Pyle Media Center located on Fort Jackson, a memorial to the slain World War II correspondent, Finance Corps Museum, Adjunct General Corps Museum. Museum traces South Carolina and Fort Jackson history.

## GEORGETOWN COAST GUARD STATION EXCHANGE (SC14R1)

355 Marina Drive
Georgetown, SC 29440-2412

**TELEPHONE NUMBER INFORMATION:** Main installation numbers: C-843-520-4116.

**LOCATION:** From US north or south 17 turn east onto Marina Drive. USMRA: Page 45 (J-7).

**LOGISTICAL SUPPORT:**      Exchange-520-4116

**ATTRACTIONS:** Historic Georgetown, coastal South Carolina.

## McENTIRE AIR NATIONAL GUARD BASE (SC18R1)

1325 South Carolina Road
Eastover, SC 29044-5017

**TELEPHONE NUMBER INFORMATION:** Main installation number: C-803-647-8301, D-312-583-8301.

**LOCATION:** On US-76/378 between Sumter and Columbia, north side of US-76/378. USMRA: Page 44 (G-6,7). NMC: Columbia, 15 miles west.

**GENERAL INFORMATION:** Home of the 169th Tactical Fighter Group, 240th Combat Communications Squadron.

**TEMPORARY MILITARY LODGING:** None. See Shaw Air Force Base listing.

**RV, CAMPING/FAMCAMP:** None. See Fort Jackson, Weston Lake Rec Area and Travel Camp listing.

**SPACE-A:** C-803-647-8301, D-312-583-8301. Fax: C-803-647-8479, D-312-583-8479.

**LOGISTICAL SUPPORT:**

| | |
|---|---|
| Credit Union-647-8212 | Exchange-647-8517 |

**ADMINISTRATIVE SUPPORT:**

| | |
|---|---|
| Fire Dept-647-8287 | Legal-647-8210 |
| Public Affairs-647-8208 | Police-647-8284 |

**HEALTH & WELFARE:**

| | |
|---|---|
| Chapel-647-8265 | Medical-647-8296 |

**REST & RECREATION:**
Clubs
  EM-647-8326
  NCO-647-8326
  O-647-8326

**ATTRACTIONS:** Charleston, Myrtle Beach 100 miles, Columbia: State Capital, State Fairgrounds, gardens, zoo.

## PARRIS ISLAND MARINE CORPS RECRUIT DEPOT (SC08R1)

Building 283, Boulevard De France
Parris Island, SC 29905-0059

**TELEPHONE NUMBER INFORMATION:** Main installation numbers: C-843-525-2111, D-312-832-2111.

**LOCATION:** From I-95 north or south, exit 33 to US-17 east to US-21 south to SC-280 to SC 802 south, which leads to the main gate of the depot. USMRA: Page 44 (G-10). NMC: Savannah, GA 43 miles southwest.

**GENERAL INFORMATION:** Recruit Depot for USMC male recruits east of Mississippi and all female recruits.

**TEMPORARY MILITARY LODGING:** Billeting, 24 hours daily, C-843-525-2976/3460, D-312-832-2976/3460: Building 200 (Hostess House), Building 254 (TLQ), Building 331 (BEQ), Building 289 (BOQ). All ranks. DV/VIP C-843-525-2594.

**RV, CAMPING/FAMCAMP:** None. See Charleston AFB listing, Shady Oaks Family Campground.

**SPACE-A:** None. See Beaufort MCAS listing.

**LOGISTICAL SUPPORT:** *Note: in order to access an extension for any of the following numbers, you must first dial 525-3302.*

| | |
|---|---|
| Bank-525-1161 | Barber Shop-525-3550 |
| Beauty Shop-525-3270 | Child Care-525-3514 |
| Commissary-525-2679 | Conv Store-ext 7351 |
| Credit Union-525-3801 | Dry Cleaner-ext 7320 |
| Exchange-525-3301 | Gas Station-ext 7351 |
| Package Store-525-3611 | Postal Service-525-2812 |
| SATO-525-2627 | Snack Bar-525-4578 |
| Travel Office-525-2410 | Visitor Center-525-3650 |

**ADMINISTRATIVE SUPPORT:**

| | |
|---|---|
| Fire Dept-525-3637 | Housing Office-525-2853 |
| Legal-525-2559 | Locator-525-3358 |
| Pass/ID Office-525-2478 | Police-525-2478 |
| Public Affairs-525-3276 | SDO-525-3712 |

**HEALTH & WELFARE:**

| | |
|---|---|
| CHAMPUS-525-5343 | Chapel-525-3533 |
| Dental-525-3725 | Family Services-228-3301 |
| Medical | Veterinary Services-525-3317 |

Clinic-525-2617
  Emergency-525-3351
  Hospital-525-5301

**REST & RECREATION:**

| | |
|---|---|
| Auto Hobby Shop-ext 7321 | Bowling-ext 7324 |
| Clubs | Ceramics Hobby Shop-ext 7322 |
|   Com-525-3302 | Fitness Center-ext 7360 |
|   E-ext 7367 | Golf Course-525-2240 |
|   SNCO-ext 7344 | ITT-525-3302 ext 7341 |
|   O-525-2905 | Library-ext 7327 |
|   Rod/Gun-525-3635 | Marinas-ext 7370 |
| MWR-525-3302 | Special Services-525-3301 |
| Swimming-ext 7339/6/7 | Theater-525-3302 ext 7325 |

**ATTRACTIONS:** Weekly recruit graduations at 9:15 AM most Fridays. Museum on base. Visitors Center Building 283.

# SHAW AIR FORCE BASE (SC10R1)

20 Fighter Wing/PA
517 Lance Avenue
Shaw Air Force Base, SC 29152-5000

**TELEPHONE NUMBER INFORMATION:** Main installation numbers: C-803-895-1110, D-312-965-1110. WEB: www.shaw.af.mil

**LOCATION:** Off US-76/378, eight miles west of Sumter, north side of US-76/378. Clearly marked. USMRA: Page 44 (H-6). NMC: Columbia, 35 miles west.

**GENERAL INFORMATION:** Air Combat Command. 9th Air Force Headquarters, 20th Fighter Wing.

**TEMPORARY MILITARY LODGING:** Lodging office, Building 464, 24 hours daily, C-803-895-3803, D-312-965-3803. Switchboard, C-803-895-3658, D-312-965-3803. All ranks. DV/VIP C-803-965-3210.

**RV, CAMPING/FAMCAMP:** New outdoor rec facility: Falcons Nest, on base, C-803-895-0449/50 D-312-965-0449. Operates Wateree Recreation Area off base, 39 miles west of post. See Wateree Recreation Area listing for more information.

**SPACE-A:** Information:C-803-895-1741/1738, D-312-965-1741/1738; Fax: C-843-895-1742, D-312-965-1742. Infrequent flights to CONUS locations.

**LOGISTICAL SUPPORT:**

| | |
|---|---|
| Bank-469-8600 | Child Care-895-2247 |
| Commissary-895-1281 | Conv Store-666-3467 |
| Dining-895-2930/2924 | Exchange-666-3481 |
| Gas Station-666-3140 | Package Store-666-3167 |
| SATO-895-1663 | Shoppette-895-3467/2701 |
| Visitor Center-895-5199 | |

**ADMINISTRATIVE SUPPORT:**

| | |
|---|---|
| CDO/OOD-895-3330 | Legal-895-1560 |
| Locator-895-2811 | Police-895-1073 |
| Public Affairs-895-2019 | |

**HEALTH & WELFARE:**

| | |
|---|---|
| Chapel-895-1106 | Family Services-895-1254 |
| Medical-895-2778 | Retiree Services-895-3036 |
| TRICARE-895-6228 | |

**REST & RECREATION:**

| | |
|---|---|
| Arts & Crafts-ext 2727 | Auto Hobby Shop-ext 6283 |
| Bowling-895-2731 | Clubs |
| Fitness Center-ext 2784 |   EM/NCO-666-3651 |
| Golf course-ext 1399 |   O-895-1316 |
| ITT-895-4774 | Library-ext 9810 |
| Rec Equip-ext 0449 | Rod/Gun Club-ext 0449 |
| Swimming-ext 1473 | Theater-ext 2199 |
| Youth Center-ext 2251 | |

**ATTRACTIONS:** Sumter Iris Gardens. Columbia is an easy drive. Myrtle Beach is a one-and-a-half hour drive. Outdoor sports and recreation.

# SHORT STAY NAVY OUTDOOR RECREATION AREA (SC02R1)

211 Short Stay Road
Moncks Corner, SC 29461-5000

**TELEPHONE NUMBER INFORMATION:** Main installation numbers: 1-800-447-2178, C-843-761-8353, 843-743-1366. E-mail: jtully@awod.com WEB: www.shortstay.com

**LOCATION:** Off Base. On Lake Moultrie five miles north of Moncks Corner. Take US-52 north from Charleston. Follow the signs. USMRA: Page 44 (H-8). NMI: Charleston Naval Station, 35 miles south. NMC: Charleston, 30 miles south.

**GENERAL INFORMATION:** Situated on a 55-acre peninsula at southern tip of Lake Moultrie. Excellent freshwater fishing. Family programs and activities during summer months. Open year round. Military personnel active, retired, reserve and DoD civilians. Check in 1500, check out 1100. Reservations: Short Stay, Navy Outdoor Recreation Area, 211 Short Stay Road, Moncks Corner, SC 29461-5000. C-1-800-447-2178, C-843-761-8353. Fax: C-843-761-4792.

**TEMPORARY MILITARY LODGING:**

| | |
|---|---|
| Villas-36 | Cabins-6 |
| Log cabins-5 | Conference Center & Pavilions |

**RV, CAMPING/FAMCAMP:**

| | |
|---|---|
| Waterfront RV/Camper spaces-13 | Wooded camper spaces-70 |
| Primitive camper/tent spaces-25 | |

**ATTRACTIONS:** Freshwater fishing, boating, sun and fun.

*For detailed information about this off-base recreation facility, as well as other recreation facilities, golf courses, marinas and temporary military lodging, consult Military Living's Military RV, Camping and Outdoor Recreation Around the World or Military Living's Temporary Military Lodging Around the World.*

# WATEREE RECREATION AREA (SC05R1)

2030 Baron Dekalb Road
Camden, SC 29020-5000

**TELEPHONE NUMBER INFORMATION:** Main installation numbers: C-803-895-1110, D-312-965-1110.

**LOCATION:** Off I-20, exit 98, take US-521/601 north to intersect SC Hwy 97 northwest for nine miles, then turn left for Lake Wateree access. USMRA: Page 44 (G-5). NMC: Columbia, 35 miles south. NMI: Shaw AFB, 39 miles east.

**GENERAL INFORMATION:** Operated by Shaw Air Force Base, off base year round. Military personnel active, retired, ANG, reserves and DoD civilians. Reservations: For cabins, available up to 60 days in advance for AD stationed at Shaw AFB. Reservation must be made in person. All others, up to 45 days in advance and by phone. Address: Outdoor Recreation, P.O. Box 52696, Shaw AFB, SC 29152-5000. For reservations: C-803-895-0449/0450, D-312-965-0449/0450 (Wateree Rec Area phone number is C-803-432-7976).

**TEMPORARY MILITARY LODGING:**
Cabins-13. All Cabins fully equipped, including TV/VCR, Satellite reception, linens, pots/pans/dishes/microwave/kitchen appliances. *Handicap accessible.

**RV, CAMPING/FAMCAMP:**

| | |
|---|---|
| Camper Spaces-13 | Tent spaces-unlimited |

Recreation Center: 3500sf facility with game room, restrooms and kitchen. Suitable for group conferences and parties. Catering available upon request with sufficient notification.

**ATTRACTIONS:** Peaceful, back to nature surroundings, fishing.

*For detailed information about this off-base recreation facility, as well as on-base recreation facilities, golf courses and marinas, consult Military Living's Military RV, Camping and Outdoor Recreation Around the World.*

# SOUTH DAKOTA

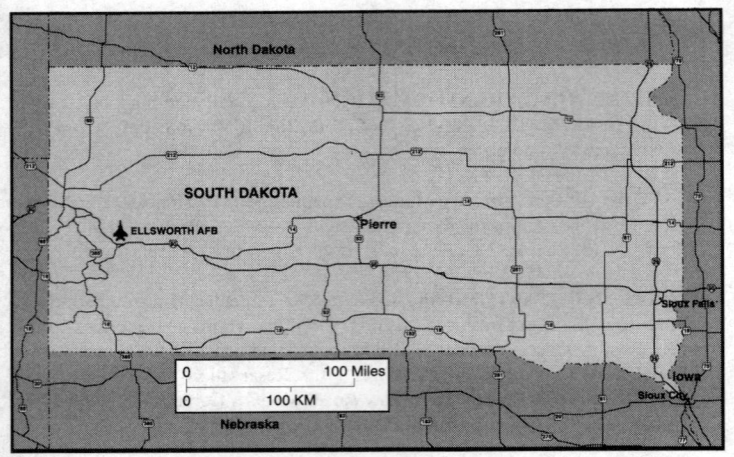

## ELLSWORTH AIR FORCE BASE (SD01R3)

1958 Scott Drive, Suite 1
Ellsworth Air Force Base, SD 57706-4710

**TELEPHONE NUMBER INFORMATION:** Main installation numbers: C-605-385-1000, D-312-675-1110. E-mail: 28bw/pa@ellsworth.af.mil
WEB: www.ellsworth.af.mil

**LOCATION:** Two miles north of I-90. Seven miles east of Rapid City. From I-90 take exit 66 north approximately two miles to gate. Clearly marked. USMRA: Page 85. (B-5). NMC: Rapid City, seven miles west.

**GENERAL INFORMATION:** Air Combat Command Base, 28th Bomb Wing, B-1B base.

**TEMPORARY MILITARY LODGING:** Billeting Office, Building 1103, Risner Drive, 24 hours daily, C-605-385-2844, D-312-675-2844: Fax: C-605-385-2718. All ranks. DV/VIP C-605-385-1052, D-312-675-1052.

**RV, CAMPING/FAMCAMP:** FAMCAMP on base, 15 May-15 October, C-605-385-2997/9, D-312-675-2997/9, 24 camper spaces with full hookups, 12 camper spaces with E hookups, 12 tent spaces.

**SPACE-A:** Pax Term/Lounge, Building 7510, 0700-1630 hours, C-605-385-1181, D-312-675-1181, Fax: C-605-385-2161, Medevac flights in twice each week.

**LOGISTICAL SUPPORT:**

| | |
|---|---|
| Cafeteria-923-1623 | Child Care-385-2488 |
| Class VI-923-6220 | Commissary-385-4364 |
| Conv Store-923-5231 | Credit Union-923-1405 |
| Dining-385-1625 | Exchange-923-4774 |
| Gas Station-923-1489 | Postal Service-385-6229 |
| SATO-923-1466 | Shoppette-923-5231 |
| Theater-385-1684/1685 | Visitor Center-385-2894 |

**ADMINISTRATIVE SUPPORT:**

| | |
|---|---|
| Legal-385-2329 | Locator-385-1379 |
| Police-385-4001 | Public Affairs-385-5056 |

**HEALTH & WELFARE:**

| | |
|---|---|
| CHAMPUS-385-3259 | |
| Family Services-385-1348 | Chapel-385-1597/7630 |
| Retiree Services-385-5050 | Medical-385-7630 |
| | Central Appts-385-3333 |

**REST & RECREATION:**

| | |
|---|---|
| Arts & Crafts 385-2899 | Auto Hobby Shop-ext 2900 |
| Bowling-385-2536 | Consolidated Club-385-1764 |
| Fitness Center-ext 2266 | Golf Course-923-4999 |
| Library-ext 1686 | MWR-385-1315 |
| Recreation-385-1613 | Rec Center-ext 1613 |
| Services-385-4321 | |

**ATTRACTIONS:** Air and Space Museum, and three small fishing lakes on base, Black Hills, Badlands, Deadwood (Casinos), Reptile Gardens, Museum of Geology, Mt Rushmore and Crazy Horse monuments nearby. An outdoor sports and recreation paradise.

# TENNESSEE

## ARNOLD AIR FORCE BASE (TN02R2)

100 Kindel Drive, Suite B213
Arnold Air Force Base, TN 37389-2213

**TELEPHONE NUMBER INFORMATION:** Main installation numbers: C-931-454-3000, D-312-340-5011.

**LOCATION:** From US-231 north of Huntsville, take TN-50/55 east to AEDC access highway in Tullahoma. From I-24 north or south take AEDC exit 117, four miles south of Manchester. Clearly marked. USMRA: Page 41 (I-9). NMC: Chattanooga, 65 miles southeast; Nashville, 65 miles northwest.

**GENERAL INFORMATION:** Air Force Materiel Command. Arnold Engineering Development Center, nation's largest complex of wind tunnels, altitude rocket test cells, space environment chambers, and other related R&D test and evaluation facilities.

**TEMPORARY MILITARY LODGING:** Lodging office, Building 3027, 0600-2200 Mon-Fri, 0700-1900 Sat, Sun and holidays. C-931-454-3099, D-312-340-3099. All ranks.

**RV, CAMPING/FAMCAMP:** FAMCAMP on base, 1 April-1 October, C-931-454-6084, D-312-340-6084, 26 camper spaces with W/E hookups, 57 tent spaces.

**SPACE-A:** None. See McGhee Tyson ANGB listing.

**LOGISTICAL SUPPORT:**

| | |
|---|---|
| Bank-454-7277 | Cafeteria-454-5732 |
| Class VI-454-7153 | Commissary-454-7249 |
| Exchange-454-7153 | Travel-454-4798/7804 |
| Visitor Center-454-5453 | |

**ADMINISTRATIVE SUPPORT:**

| | |
|---|---|
| Fire Dept-454-5648/3206 | Legal-454-7153/7814 |
| Locator-454-3000 | Police-454-5662 |
| Public Affairs-454-5586 | SDO/NCO-454-7752 |

**HEALTH & WELFARE:**

| | |
|---|---|
| CHAMPUS-454-5351 | Chapel-454-3470 |
| Medical-454-5351 | Retiree Services-454-4574 |

**REST & RECREATION:**

| | |
|---|---|
| All Ranks Club-454-3090 | Arts & Crafts-ext 6084 |
| NCO-454-3090 | Community Center-454-7710 |
| OC-454-3090 | Boat Rental-ext 6084 |
| Fitness Center-454-6440 | Golf Course-455-5870 |
| ITT-454-3128 | Marina-454-6084 |
| Sailing-454 6084 | Services-454-7424 |
| Tennis-ext 6084 | |

**ATTRACTIONS:** Chattanooga and Lookout Mountains are an easy drive southeast. Home of Grand Ole Opry, Opryland, Nashville.

## CHATTANOOGA ARMORY EXCHANGE (TN11R2)

1801 Holtz Claw Avenue
Chattanooga, TN 37404-5000

**TELEPHONE NUMBER INFORMATION:** Main installation numbers: C-423-265-8941.

**LOCATION:** From I-24 take Tennessee Temple University exit 180, right to 23rd Street, second light to right on Holtzclaw Avenue to gate. USMRA: Page 41 (J-10). NMC: Chattanooga, in city limits.

LOGISTICAL SUPPORT:                    Exchange-265-8941

ATTRACTIONS: Tennessee Aquarium, civil war sights, Lookout Mountain, Walnut Street Bridge, Ruby Falls.

## KINGSPORT SITE EXCHANGE (TN12R2)
4401 W Stone Drive
Kingsport, TN 37660-1050

TELEPHONE NUMBER INFORMATION: Main installation numbers: C-423-247-8721.

LOCATION: From I-81 north or south, exit 57 to I-181 north to Kingsport exit 55 west, Stone Drive, left on 11 west (Stone Drive) fifth light; exchange on left. USMRA: Page 41 (O-7). NMC: Kingsport, in city limits.

LOGISTICAL SUPPORT:                    Exchange-247-8721

ATTRACTIONS: Appalachian and Great Smoky Mountains, state parks, caves.

## MCGHEE TYSON AIR NATIONAL GUARD BASE (TN07R2)
134 Air Refueling Wing
134 Briscoe Drive
McGhee Tyson ANGB, TN 37777-6200

TELEPHONE NUMBER INFORMATION: Main installation numbers: C-865-985-3210, D-312-588-3210.

LOCATION: Exit north or south from US-129 onto Air Base Road. There is a large national guard sign at the exit. Proceed on Air Base Road approximately two miles to main gate. USMRA: Page 41 (L-8). NMC: Knoxville, 10 miles northeast.

GENERAL INFORMATION: Home of the 134th Air Refueling Wing, Air National Guard.

TEMPORARY MILITARY LODGING: C-865-985-3300.

RV, CAMPING/FAMCAMP: None. Nearest facility is over 100 miles away.

SPACE-A: Information: C-865-985-4404/4419, D-312-266-4404/4419; Rec: C-865-985-4403, D-312-266-4403. Fax: C-865-985-4397, D-312-266-4397.

LOGISTICAL SUPPORT:                    Exchange-985-3400

ADMINISTRATIVE SUPPORT: None. Nearest facility is over 100 miles away.

HEALTH & WELFARE:                    Dispensary-985-4277

ATTRACTIONS: Knoxville, Smoky Mountains.

## MEMPHIS INTERNATIONAL AIRPORT/ TENNESSEE AIR NATIONAL GUARD BASE (TN05R2)
2815 Democrat Road
Memphis, TN 38181-1510

TELEPHONE NUMBER INFORMATION: Main installation numbers: C-901-541-7111, D-312-966-8210.

LOCATION: From I-55 north or south, exit 5A (Brooks Road) east, two miles to IAP, left on Airways on Democrat Road, right to 164th Air National Guard Base (north side of IAP), go to Aerial Port building. USMRA: Page 40 (A-10). NMC: Memphis, in city limits.

GENERAL INFORMATION: Home of 164th Airlift Wing, Air National Guard.

TEMPORARY MILITARY LODGING: None. See Mid-South Naval Support Activity listing.

RV, CAMPING/FAMCAMP: None. See Mid-South Naval Support Activity listing.

SPACE-A: Information: C-901-541-7221, D-312-966-8221; Rec: C-901-541-7202, D-312-966-8202; Fax: C-901-541-7230, D-312-966-8230.

LOGISTICAL SUPPORT:                    Exchange-541-7232

ADMINISTRATIVE SUPPORT:                    Public Affairs-541-7133

HEALTH & WELFARE:                    Medical-541-7110

REST & RECREATION: None. See Mid-South Naval Support Activity listing.

ATTRACTIONS: Graceland, Peabody Hotel, Mud Island, Libertyland, The Orpheum, Overton Square, Memphis Zoo, and historic Beale Street–"Home of the Blues."

## MID-SOUTH NAVAL SUPPORT ACTIVITY (TN01R2)
5720 Integrity Drive
Millington, TN 38054-5045

TELEPHONE NUMBER INFORMATION: Main installation numbers: C-901-874-5111, D-312-882-5111.

LOCATION: From Memphis, take Route 51 north to Millington. Turn right (east) on Navy Road 205. Go approximately two miles to base entrance on north side of road. USMRA: Page 40 (B-9,10). NMC: Memphis, 20 miles southwest.

GENERAL INFORMATION: Support facility providing logistical support to approximately thirty tenant commands, including newly relocated Bureau of Naval Personnel and Navy Recruiting Command.

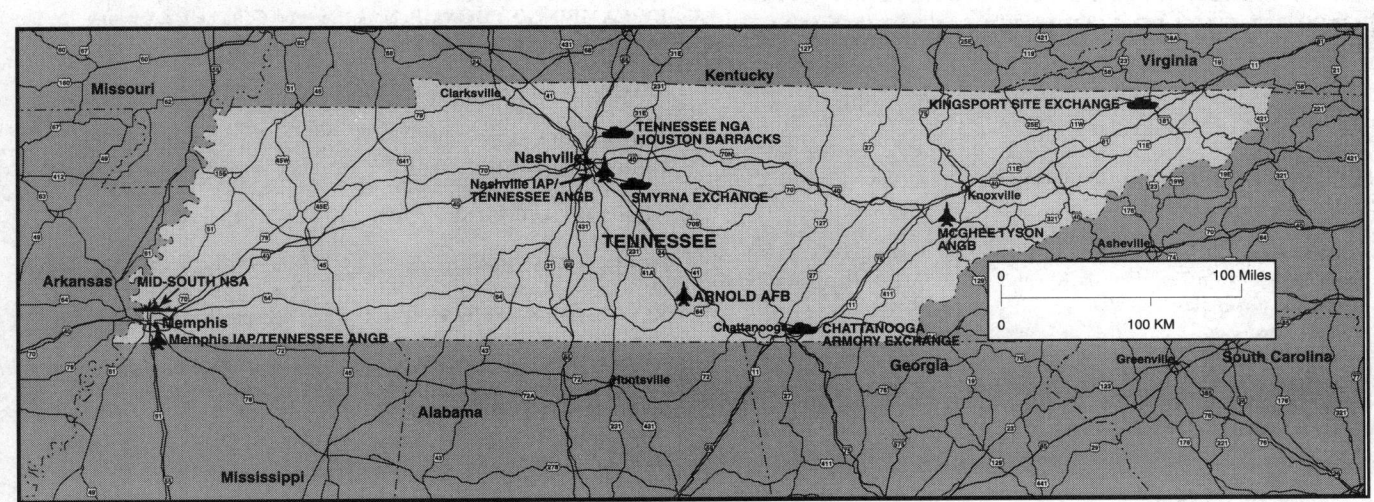

**TEMPORARY MILITARY LODGING:** All ranks: C-901-874-5459. Navy Lodge: C-1-800-NAVY-INN, Fax: C-901-873-1695.

**RV, CAMPING/FAMCAMP:** Navy Lake Recreational Area, on base, year round, MWR Dept, Mid-South NSA, 5720 Integrity Drive, Millington, TN 38054-5045, C-901-872-3656, Fax: C-901-874-5690. Twelve camper spaces with full hookups, some tent space.

**SPACE-A:** Limited. C-901-874-5111, D-312-966-5111.

**LOGISTICAL SUPPORT:**

| | |
|---|---|
| Barber Shop-872-2191 | Beauty Shop-873-4962 |
| Book Store-872-0139 | Child Dev Center-874-5745 |
| Commissary-874-5122 | Conv Store-872-1334 |
| Credit Union-873-2300 | Dining Facilities-874-5442 |
| Dry Cleaner-872-7985 | Education Office-874-5290 |
| Exchange-872-0139 | Family Services-874-5075 |
| Gas Station-872-2610 | Laundry-872-7259 |
| Package Store-872-1660 | Postal Service-874-5577 |
| SATO-872-0104 | Travel Office-874-5303 |

**ADMINISTRATIVE SUPPORT:**

| | |
|---|---|
| CDO/OOD-874-5509 | Fire Dept-874-5280 |
| Housing Office-874-5547 | Legal-874-5446 |
| Locator-874-5111 | Pass/ID Office-874-5537 |
| Police-874-5533 | Public Affairs-874-5761 |
| Quarter Deck-874-5509 | |

**HEALTH & WELFARE:**

| | |
|---|---|
| American Red Cross-874-5607 | Chapel-874-5341 |
| Dental Clinic-874-5060 | Family Services-874-7510 |
| Central Appts-874-5361 | Navy-MC Relief-872-7266 |
| Medical | Retiree Services-874-5195 |
| Central Appts-1-800-700-6101 | TRICARE-1-800-444-5445 |
| Clinic-874-6101 | Veterinary services-874-5858 |
| Health Benefits-874-6107/6111 | |
| Information-874-6100 | |

**REST & RECREATION:**

| | |
|---|---|
| Arts & Crafts-874-5507 | Auto Hobby Shop-874-5675 |
| Bowling-874-5779 | Clubs |
| Fitness Center-874-5497 | CPO-874-5442 |
| Golf course-874-5168 | EMC-874- 5442 |
| Gym-874-5383 5383 | ITT-874-5303 |
| Library-874-5683 | MWR-1-800-779-4252 |
| Outdoor Rec-874-5163 | Swimming-874-5187 |
| Tennis-874-5163 | Youth Center-874-5155 |

**OTHER INFORMATION:** Naval Personnel Research and Development Center to relocate to NAVSUPPACT Mid-South in Fall 1999.

**ATTRACTIONS:** Graceland, Peabody Hotel, Mud Island, Libertyland, the Orpheum, Overton Square, Memphis Zoo, and historic Beale Street–"Home of the Blues."

# NASHVILLE INTERNATIONAL AIRPORT/ TENNESSEE AIR NATIONAL GUARD BASE (TN06R2)

240 Knapp Boulevard
Nashville, TN 37217-2538

**TELEPHONE NUMBER INFORMATION:** Main installation numbers: C-615-399-6000/6532, D-312-778-6532.

**LOCATION:** From I-40 east to exit 216 B, from I-40 west to exit 216 south on Donelson Pike for two miles, right on Knapp Blvd. USMRA: Page 40 (G,H-8). NMC: Nashville, four miles northwest.

**GENERAL INFORMATION:** Home of the 118th Airlift Wing, Air National Guard.

**TEMPORARY MILITARY LODGING:** None. See Fort Campbell, KY listing.

**RV, CAMPING/FAMCAMP:** None. See Fort Campbell, KY listing.

**SPACE-A:** Information: C-615-399-5807, D-312-778-5807.

**LOGISTICAL SUPPORT:**  Exchange-399-5638

**ADMINISTRATIVE SUPPORT:**

| | |
|---|---|
| Pass/ID Office-399-5516 | Police-399-5854 |
| Public Affairs-399-5532 | |

**HEALTH & WELFARE:** None. See Fort Campbell, KY listing.

**REST & RECREATION:**  SATO-800-641-2968

**ATTRACTIONS:** General Jackson Steamboat, Music City Row, Music City Hall of Fame, and Ryman Auditorium.

# SMYRNA EXCHANGE (TN10R2)

Building 607, A Street
Smyrna, TN 37167-5000

**TELEPHONE NUMBER INFORMATION:** Main installation numbers: C-615-355-3616.

**LOCATION:** From I-24 north or south, take Sam Ridley Parkway exit to airport. Follow signs to airport. Take first left after golf course, go straight, first building on left past guard shack. USMRA: Page 40 (H-8). NMC: Smyrna, in city limits.

**GENERAL INFORMATION:** Located at the Grubbs Kyle Training Center.

**LOGISTICAL SUPPORT:**  Exchange-615-355-3616

**ATTRACTIONS:** Nearby Nashville's General Jackson Steamboat, Music City Row, Music City Hall of Fame, and Ryman Auditorium.

# TENNESSEE NATIONAL GUARD ARMORY, HOUSTON BARRACKS (TN09R2)

P.O. Box 41502
3041 Sidco Drive
Nashville, TN 37204-1502

**TELEPHONE NUMBER INFORMATION:** Main installation numbers: C-615-313-0662, D-312-683-0662. E-mail: paotn@tn-mgnet.army.mil. WEB: www.state.tn.us/military

**LOCATION:** Take I-65 south to Armory Drive exit. USMRA: Page 40 (G,H-8). NMC: Nashville, four miles northwest.

**GENERAL INFORMATION:** Headquarters Tennessee Army National Guard and Tennessee Air National Guard.

**TEMPORARY MILITARY LODGING:** None. See Fort Campbell, KY listing.

**RV, CAMPING/FAMCAMP:** None. See Fort Campbell, KY listing, Destiny Parks and Pavilions (Army Travel Camp).

**SPACE-A:** None. See Nashville IAP/Tennessee ANGB listing.

**LOGISTICAL SUPPORT:**

| | |
|---|---|
| Carlson Wagonlit Travel-313-0556 | Exchange-313-0531 |

**ADMINISTRATIVE SUPPORT:**  Legal-313-0659

**HEALTH & WELFARE:**  Family Services-313-0541

**REST & RECREATION:** None. See Fort Campbell, KY listing.

**ATTRACTIONS:** Opryland, Grand Ole Opry, The Hermitage (home of Andy Jackson) and "The District."

# TEXAS

## BIGGS ARMY AIRFIELD (TX45R3)

11210 CSM E Slewitzke Street
Biggs AAF, TX 79908-0053

**TELEPHONE NUMBER INFORMATION:** Main installation numbers: C-915-568-2121. D-312-978-0831.

**LOCATION:** From I-10 take exit 25 Airport Road to north. Airport Road will turn to the west. After first traffic light, look for gradual right turn below second traffic light. Heading north on Airport Road pass three traffic lights (not counting military crossing). Entrance to Biggs AAf is on right. Or from US-54 southbound, take Fred Wilson Drive exit. At first traffic light turn left (east) and continue to fifth traffic light, turn left into Biggs AAF. USMRA: Page 86 (B-6). NMC: El Paso, in city limits.

**GENERAL INFORMATION:** Part of Fort Bliss.

**TEMPORARY MILITARY LODGING:** Lodging Office: Bldg. 251, Club Road, C-915-568-4888, D-312-978-4888, Fax: C-915-568-7078, D-312-978-7078. The Inn at Fort Bliss, C-915-565-7777. All ranks. DV/VIP: Protocol Office: 915-568-5319.

**RV, CAMPING/FAMCAMP:** None. See Fort Bliss listing.

**SPACE-A:** Information: C-915-568-8097, D-312-978-8097.

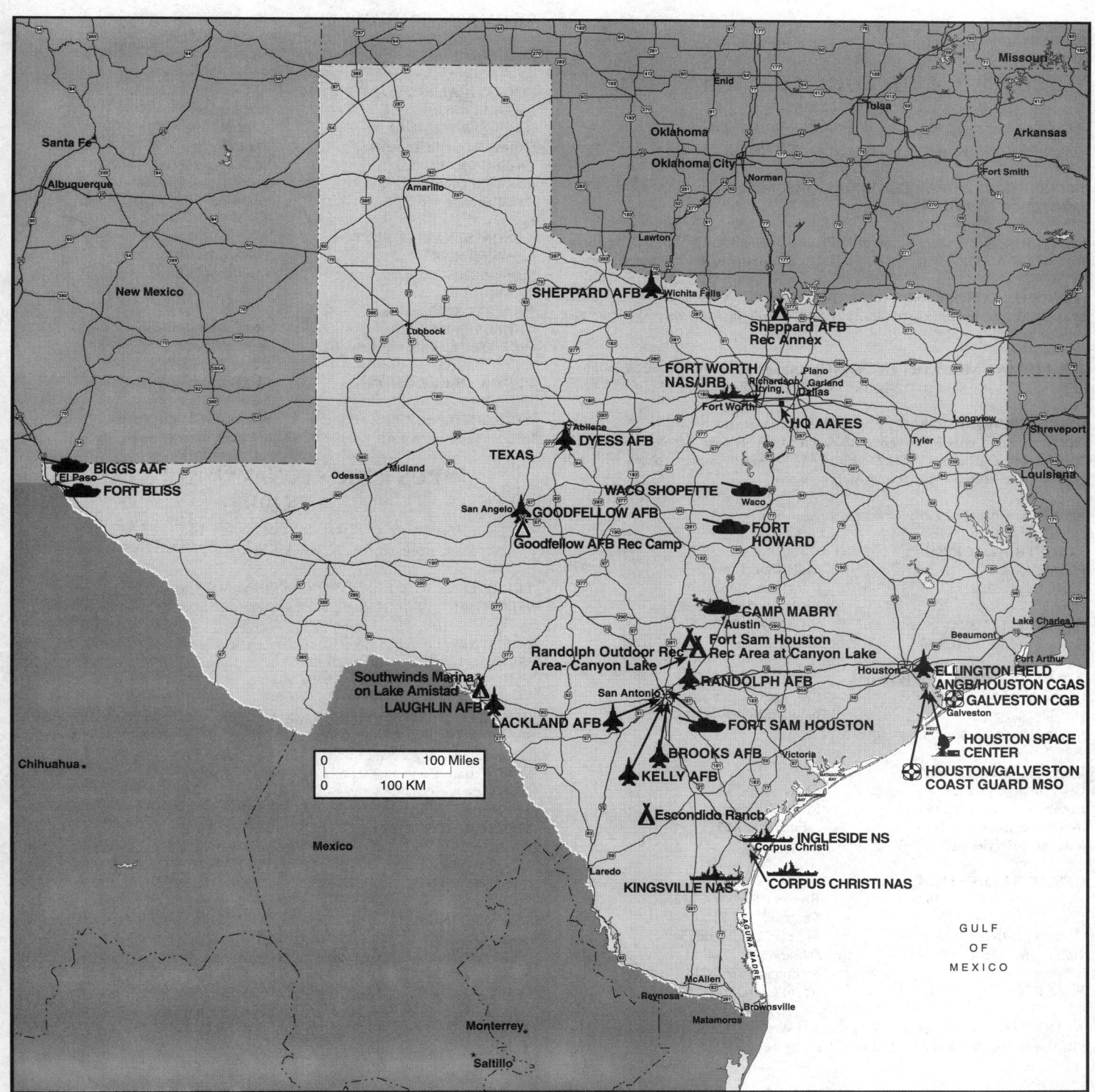

**LOGISTICAL SUPPORT:**

Bank-562-7778
Credit Union-562-1172
Exchange-562-9951
Postal Service-562-4036

Car Rental-779-2700/772-4255
Gas Station-562-8442
Laundry-568-5405
Shoppette-562-8442

**ADMINISTRATIVE SUPPORT:**

Police-568-2115

Public Affairs-568-8242/8088

**HEALTH & WELFARE:**

American Red Cross-568-5085/4898
Medical-567-2121

Chaplain-568-1519
Retirees Services-564-6100

**REST & RECREATION:**

NCO Club-562-5569

O Club-562-2040

**ATTRACTIONS:** Museums, Wilderness Park, Chamizal National Memorial, Rio Grande River, Tigua Indian Reservation and numerous golf courses.

# BROOKS AIR FORCE BASE (TX26R3)

311 HSW/PA
2510 Kennedy Circle, Bldg.150, Room 140
Brooks Air Force Base, TX 78235-5120

**TELEPHONE NUMBER INFORMATION:** Main installation numbers: C-210-536-1110, D-312-240-1110.

**LOCATION:** At the intersection of I-37 north or south and Military Drive (Loop 13) exit 135. USMRA: Page 91 (C-4). NMC: San Antonio, five miles northwest.

**GENERAL INFORMATION:** Air Force Materiel Command base. Human Systems Center, research laboratories, USAF School of Aerospace Medicine and support units.

**TEMPORARY MILITARY LODGING:** Lodging office, Building 214, 24 hours daily, C-210-536-1844, D-312-240-1844. All ranks. DV/VIP C-210-536 -3238.

**RV, CAMPING/FAMCAMP:** FAMCAMP on base, year round, 70 SVS/SVRO, ATTN: Lodging Office/Innkeeper, 2804 5th Street, Brooks Air Force Base, TX 78235-5000. C-210-536-1844, D-312-240-1844, seven camper spaces with full hookups, eight camper spaces with W/E hookups.

**SPACE-A:** None. See Kelly AFB listing.

**LOGISTICAL SUPPORT:**

Bank-531-4402
Commissary-536-2727
Dining-536-2383
Gas Station-532-2191
Snack Bar-536-2671/2140

Child Care-536-2736
Conv Store-533-9161
Exchange-533-9161
SATO-536-1800/3230
Visitor Center-531-9767

**ADMINISTRATIVE SUPPORT:**

Legal-536-3301
Police-536-2851
SDO/NCO-536-3278

Locator-536-1841
Public Affairs-536-3234

**HEALTH & WELFARE:**

CHAMPUS-536-2928
Family Services-536-2444
Retiree Services-536-2116
Veterinary Services-536-2723

Chapel-536-3824
Medical-536-1847
Emergency-911

**REST & RECREATION:**

Auto Hobby Shop-ext 2624
Consolidated Club-536-4158
Community Center-536-2847
Golf course-536-2636
Services-536-3691
Wood Hobby Shop-536-2120

Brooks Club-536-3782
Ceramics-536-2120
Fitness Center-536-2342
Library-536-2634
Swimming-536-3744
Youth Center-536-2515

**ATTRACTIONS:** Close to San Antonio, Sea World of Texas, museums, missions, the Alamo, San Antonio Zoo, Sea World, Fiesta Texas.

# CAMP MABRY (TX39R3)

2210 West 35th Street
Austin, TX 78763-5218

**TELEPHONE NUMBER INFORMATION:** Main installation numbers: C-512-465-5001, D-312-954-5001.

**LOCATION:** From Dallas take I-35 to Austin exit 236 B, right onto 38 1/2 Street exit (turns onto 35th Street West). Cross over Loop 1; installation is on the right. USMRA: Page 87 (K-5). NMC: Austin, in city limits.

**GENERAL INFORMATION:** Texas National Guard Headquarters.

**TEMPORARY MILITARY LODGING:** Lodging office, C-512-465-5500.

**RV, CAMPING/FAMCAMP:** None. See Randolph AFB listing.

**SPACE-A:** None. See Fort Hood listing for Robert Gray Army Airfield information.

**LOGISTICAL SUPPORT:**

Bank-453-6263
Beauty Shop-323-0762
Carlson Wagonlit Travel-452-5222
Credit Union-453-6263
Education Office-465-5515
Postal Service-465-5195

Barber Shop-454-6363
Cafeteria-706-6720
Class Six-465-5120
Dry Cleaner-371-1844
Exchange-465-5121
Snack Bar-706-6720

**ADMINISTRATIVE SUPPORT:**

Legal-465-5057
Public Affairs-465-5059

Police-465-5004
SDO-465-5001

**HEALTH & WELFARE:**

CHAMPUS-465-5239
Family Services-465-5000

Chapel-465-5069
Retiree Services-465-5090

**REST & RECREATION:**

Outdoor Rec-465-5001

**ATTRACTIONS:** The city of Austin's museums, live music, Barton Springs, nearby hill country, water activities at Highland Lakes, tours of nearby caverns.

# CORPUS CHRISTI NAVAL AIR STATION (TX10R3)

11001 D Street, Suite 143
Corpus Christi Naval Air Station, TX 78419-5021

**TELEPHONE NUMBER INFORMATION:** Main installation numbers: C-361-961-2811, D-312-861-1110. E-mail: nascc-pao-at-nas-cc@navdafgw.navy.mil.

**LOCATION:** From San Antonio, take Interstate 37 southeast to exit 4 A, Highway 358 southeast. Exit northwest for NAS after 12 miles. USMRA: Page 87 (K-8). NMC: Corpus Christi, 10 miles west.

**GENERAL INFORMATION:** Naval Air Training Command, Coast Guard Air Station, and Corpus Christi Army Depot, Tenant Commands, Training Squadrons 27, 38 and 31, Surveillance Support Center, Training Air Wing Four, Commander Mine Warfare Command, U.S. Coast Guard Group/Air Station, HM 15, Marine Corps Reserve Training Center, CNATRA.

**TEMPORARY MILITARY LODGING:** Lodging office, 24 hours daily, Building 1281, Ocean Drive C-361-961-2388/89, D-312-861-2388/89. Fax: C-361-961-3275. Navy Lodge, Building 1281, 0800-1800 Mon-Fri, 0900-1800 Sat-Sun, C-361-961-6361. All ranks. DV/VIP C-361-961-2388/89, Fax: C-361-961-3275.

**RV, CAMPING/FAMCAMP:** Shields Park NAS Recreation Area, on base year round, Outdoor Recreation, Building 39, Code 22, C-361-961-1293, 24 camper spaces with W/E, seven tent spaces with W hookups.

**SPACE-A:** Pax Term, Hangar 58, 0700-2300 Mon-Fri, C-361-961-2505, D-312-861-2505; Rec: C-361-961-3385; Fax: C-361-961-3774. Flights to CONUS locations.

**LOGISTICAL SUPPORT:**

| | |
|---|---|
| Barber Shop-961-7981 | Beauty Shop-961-7032 |
| Child Care-961-8702 | Child Dev Center-961-8702 |
| Commissary-961-2545 | Credit Union-961-7350 |
| Dry Cleaner-937-8942 | Education Office-961-7910 |
| Exchange-961-2166 | Gas Station-961-7910 |
| Package Store-961-2166 | Postal Service-961-2984 |
| SATO-937-8806 | Visitor Center-961-3722 |

**ADMINISTRATIVE SUPPORT:**

| | |
|---|---|
| CDO/OOD-961-2383 | |
| Housing Office-961-3336 | Fire Dept-961-3492 |
| Locator-961-3841 | Legal-961-3568 |
| Police-961-2282 | Pass/ID Office-961-2282 |
| | Public Affairs-961-2568/2674 |

**HEALTH & WELFARE:**

| | |
|---|---|
| American Red Cross-961-2180 | CHAMPUS-961-3238 |
| Chapel-961-3751 | Dental-961-2466 |
| Family Services-961-2372 | Central Appts-961-2485 |
| Medical-961-2994 | Clinic-961-3838 |
| Central Appts-961-3157 | Emergency-961-2688 |
| Emergency-961-3577 | Navy-MC Relief-961-3482 |
| Health Benefits-961-3238 | Retiree Services-961-3113 |
| Hospital-961-2688 | TRICARE-961-6610 |
| Veterinary Services-961-2031 | |

**REST & RECREATION:**

| | |
|---|---|
| Arts & Crafts-ext 3169 | Auto Hobby Shop-961-3470 |
| Bowling-961-3805 | Camping Equip-937-5071 |
| Fitness Center-961-3164 | Gym-961-2401 |
| Golf Course-961-3250 | Library-961-3574 |
| ITT-961-3637 | Marinas-937-5071 |
| MWR-961-2267 | O Club-961-2541 |
| Party House-ext 2444 | Picnic Area-ext 2444 |
| Skeet Range-937-5071 | Swimming-961-3256 |
| Theater-961-3488 | Youth Center-961-2355 |
| Youth Services-961-2355 | |

**ATTRACTIONS:** Bay and gulf water sports. Also, symphony, museums, and historical homes.

## DYESS AIR FORCE BASE (TX14R3)

466 Fifth Street, Suite 136
Dyess Air Force Base, TX 79607-1239

**TELEPHONE NUMBER INFORMATION:** Main installation numbers: C-915-696-3113, D-312-461-3113. WEB: www.dyess.af.mil

**LOCATION:** Turn left off of I-20/US-277 west onto Arnold Blvd. Main gate will be up three miles on the right. USMRA: Page 87 (I-3). NMC: Abilene, six miles northeast.

**GENERAL INFORMATION:** Air Combat Command Base and Air Mobility Command tenant unit, 7th Bomb Wing most tenant units, 7th Wing/317th Airlift Group and support units.

**TEMPORARY MILITARY LODGING:** Lodging office, 441 Fifth Street, Dyess Inn, 24 hours daily, C-915-696-2681, D-312-461-2681. Fax-C-915-696-2836. All ranks. DV/VIP C-915-696-5610.

**RV, CAMPING/FAMCAMP:** None. Nearest facility is more than 100 miles away.

**SPACE-A:** Pax Term/Lounge, 674 Alert Avenue, 24 hours daily, C-915-696-4505, D-312-461-4505. Fax: C-915-696-2943, D-312-461-2943. Flights to CONUS, OCONUS and foreign locations.

**LOGISTICAL SUPPORT:**

| | |
|---|---|
| Bank-690-6220 | Barber Shop-695-2089 |
| Beauty Shop-698-9257 | Cafeteria-692-7470 |
| Child Care-696-2839 | Commissary-696-2434 |
| Conv Store-698-1573 | Credit Union-692-9797 |
| Child Dev. Center-696-4337 | Class VI-696-3497 |

| | |
|---|---|
| Dining Facilities-696-2421 | Dry Cleaner-695-0231 |
| Education Center-696-5544 | Exchange-692-8996 |
| Fast Food-696-1171 | Gas Station-692-6721 |
| Postal Service-696-2655 | SATO-696-4743 |
| Shoppette-696-4771 | Snack Bar-698-1171 |
| Travel Office-696-2048 | Visitor Center-793-2198 |

**ADMINISTRATIVE SUPPORT:**

| | |
|---|---|
| Fire Dept-696-5224 | Housing Office-696-2150 |
| Legal-696-2232 | Locator-696-3098 |
| Pass/ID Office-696-3088 | Police (Security)-696-2432 |
| Public Affairs-696-2862 | |

**HEALTH & WELFARE:**

| | |
|---|---|
| Air Force Aid Society-696-5999 | CHAMPUS-696-2350 |
| Chapel-696-4224 | Dental-Clinic-696-2304 |
| Family Services-696-5996 | Central Appts-696-2305 |
| Medical-Central Appts-696-4667 | Emergency-696-3867 |
| Clinic-696-2334 | TRICARE-1-800-406-2832 |
| Emergency-696-2334 | Veterinary Services-696-3367 |
| Hospital-696-5459 | |

**REST & RECREATION:**

| | |
|---|---|
| Arts & Crafts-696-3379 | Auto Hobby Shop-696-4179 |
| Bowling-696-4166 | Clubs-Consol-696-4311 |
| Community Center-696-4305 | EM-696-4311 |
| Fitness Center-696-5919 | O-696-2405 |
| Golf Course-696-5067 | Gym-696-4306 |
| Library-696-2618 | Outdoor Recreation-696-2402 |
| Rec Center-696-4305 | Rec Equip-696-2402 |
| Services-696-2402 | Stables-696-3471 |
| Swimming-696-3346 | Theater-696-4320 |
| Youth Center-696-4797 | Youth Services-696-7363 |

**ATTRACTIONS:** Abilene, outdoor sports, Abilene Zoo, and Dyess Linear Air Park.

## ELLINGTON FIELD AIR NATIONAL GUARD BASE/HOUSTON COAST GUARD AIR STATION (TX41R3)

14657 Sneider Street
Houston, TX 77034-5586

**TELEPHONE NUMBER INFORMATION:** Main installation numbers: C-281-929-2110, D-312-954-2110.
*Ten digit dialing required for local calls.*

**LOCATION:** Take I-45 south from Houston exit 32 to Ellington Field. TX-1959, proceed 2.5 miles east of I-45 to base. USMRA: Page 89 (D-4,5). NMC: Houston, 15 miles northwest.

**GENERAL INFORMATION:** Home of the 147th Fighter Wing, Air National Guard, NASA Flight Operations, U.S. Coast Guard Station.

**TEMPORARY MILITARY LODGING:** None. See Camp Mabry listing.

**RV, CAMPING/FAMCAMP:** None. See Randolph Outdoor Recreation Area listing.

**SPACE-A:** C-281-929-2142, D-312-954-2142. Fax: C-281-929-2442, D-312-954-2442. Very limited flights available.

**LOGISTICAL SUPPORT:** Exchange-484-5892

**ADMINISTRATIVE SUPPORT:**

| | |
|---|---|
| Locator-281-929-2110 | Police-281-929-2041 |

**HEALTH & WELFARE:** None. See Corpus Christi NAS listing.

**REST & RECREATION:** None. See Corpus Christi NAS listing.

**ATTRACTIONS:** Six Flags Astroworld in Houston.

# ESCONDIDO RANCH (TX51R3)

Escondido Ranch, Attn: Reservations
P.O. Box 1810
Freer, TX 78357-1810

**TELEPHONE NUMBER INFORMATION:** Main installation numbers: C-512-516-6136, D-312-861-6136.

**LOCATION:** Off base. Located 23 miles northwest of Freer. USMRA: Page 87 (J-8). NMI: Kingsville NAS, 90 miles southeast. NMC: Corpus Christi, 80 miles east.

**GENERAL INFORMATION:** Off base. Located 23 miles northwest of Freer. From I-35 north or south, exit 38 east on TX-44 for 20 miles to signs for Ranch. USMRA: Page 87 (J-8). NMI: Kingsville NAS, 90 miles southeast. NMC: Corpus Christi, 80 miles east.

**RV, CAMPING/FAMCAMP:**

Cottages-1
Camper Spaces-12

Lodge-rooms-17
Tent Spaces-unlimited

**ATTRACTIONS:** Located on a hunting ranch in a remote desert area.

*For detailed information about this off-base recreation facility, as well as on-base recreation facilities, golf courses and marinas, consult Military Living's Military RV, Camping and Outdoor Recreation Around the World.*

# FORT BLISS (TX06R3)

US Army Air Defense Artillery Center and School
1733 Pleasonton Road, Building 15
Fort Bliss, TX 79916-6816

**TELEPHONE NUMBER INFORMATION:** Main installation numbers: C-915-568-2121, D-312-978-2121. E-mail: atzc-cgp@emh10.bliss.army.mil
WEB: www.bliss.army.mil

**LOCATION:** Take I-10 east or west to US-54 north, exit Fort Bliss/Forrest Road. USMRA: Page 86 (B,C-5,6). NMC: El Paso, within city limits.

**GENERAL INFORMATION:** Air Defense Artillery Center and School, Sergeants Major Academy, 11th Air Defense Artillery Brigade, 6th Air Defense Artillery Brigade, 108th Air Defense Artillery Brigade, 31st Air Defense Artillery Brigade, 35th Air Defense Artillery Brigade, Range Command, 1st Combined Arms Support Battalion, William Beaumont Army Medical Center, and other units.

**TEMPORARY MILITARY LODGING:** Lodging office, Fort Bliss Inn, 24 hours daily, C-915-565-7777, Fax: C-915-565-7778; Fort Bliss Billeting C-915-568-2703. All ranks. DV/VIP C-915-568-5319/5225. New YMCA Residence Center on William Beaumont Medical Center, C-915-562-8461.

**RV, CAMPING/FAMCAMP:** Fort Bliss RV Park, on post year round, Outdoor Recreation Branch, Building 1986, C-915-568-4693, D-312-978-4693/0106, Fax: C-915-568-2028, D-312-978-2028; 73 camper spaces with full hookups, eight tent spaces without hookups.

**SPACE-A:** Biggs Army Airfield, Building 11210, 0600-2200 Mon-Fri, 0800-1600 Sat-Sun, C-915-568-8097, D-312-978-8097. Limited CONUS flights.

**LOGISTICAL SUPPORT:**

| | |
|---|---|
| Barber Shop-562-2573 | Car Rental-562-5400 |
| Child Dev. Center-568-5709 | Class VI-566-8371 |
| Commissary-568-4022 | Conv Store-562-3774 |
| Education Center-568-7161 | Exchange-562-7200 |
| Gas Station-562-2353 | Postal Service-562-4036 |
| Shoppette-566-8371 | Travel-562-4488 |
| Visitor Center-568-2290 | |

**ADMINISTRATIVE SUPPORT:**

| | |
|---|---|
| Fire Dept-565-4100 | Housing Office-568-2538 |
| Legal-568-7141/6040 | Locator-568-1113 |
| Pass/ID Office-568-6210 | Police-568-2115 |
| Public Affairs-568-4505 | SDO-568-1501 |

**HEALTH & WELFARE:**

| | |
|---|---|
| ACS-568-3503 | Army Relief-568-7088 |
| CHAMPUS-569-2536 | Chapel-568-5992 |
| Dental-Clinic-568-1281 | Family Service-568-6291 |
| TRICARE-680-7600 | Medical-569-2450 |
| Retiree Services-568-2632 | Emergency-568-3194 |
| Veterinary Svc-569-2266 | |

**REST & RECREATION:**

| | |
|---|---|
| Auto Hobby Shop-568-7280 | Bowling-568-6272 |
| Clubs | Community Center-568-3503 |
| CC-568-3503 | Fitness Center-568-3264 |
| O-562-2040 | Golf Course-562-7255 |
| Rod & Gun-568-2983 | Indoor Rec-568-7431 |
| ITR-568-7506 | Library-568-2489 |
| MWR-568-3500 | Outdoor Rec-568-2869 |
| Theater-568-2516 | Youth Center-568-2908 |
| Youth Services-568-1958 | |

**ATTRACTIONS:** Four museums (Fort Bliss, Air Defense Artillery, and Non-commissioned Officer) on post, Carlsbad Caverns National Park, White Sands National Monument, Ciudad Juarez. El Paso Symphony and Tigua Indian Reservation.

# FORT HOOD (TX02R3)

HQ III Corps & Fort Hood
ATTN: AFZF-PO
Bldg 1001 Tank Destroyer Blvd
Fort Hood, TX 76544-5000

**TELEPHONE NUMBER INFORMATION:** Main installation numbers: C-254-287/288-1110, D-312-737/738-1110.

**LOCATION:** From I-35 north or south, exit to US-190 west, go twelve miles through Killeen. Main gate is clearly marked. USMRA: Page 87 (K-4,5). NMC: Killeen, at main entrance.

**GENERAL INFORMATION:** Armored Corps Headquarters, headquarters for 1st Cavalry Division and 4th Infantry Division (Mechanized), 13th Corps Support Command, 3rd Signal Brigade, 89th Military Police Brigade, 504th Military Intelligence Group, 3rd Air Support Group (AF), Medical Activity, Dental Activity, TEXCOM (Test Activity) and the 21st Cavalry Brigade (Air Combat).

**TEMPORARY MILITARY LODGING:** Lodging office, Building 36006, Wratten Drive, 24 hours daily, C-254-287-3067, D-312-738-3067, Fax: C-254-288-7604. DV/VIP C-254-287-5001.

**RV, CAMPING/FAMCAMP:** West Fort Hood Travel Camp on post year round, AFZF-CA-BOD-WFHTC, Building 70004, Clarke Road, P.O. Box K. Phone C-254-288-9926, D-312-738-9926; 64 camper spaces with full hookups, 20 tent spaces. Belton Lake Recreation Area on post year round, Business Operations Division, AFZF-CA-BOD-OR-BLORA, C-254-287-2523, D-312-737-2523; 10 cottages, 11 camper spaces with full hookups, 48 camper spaces with W/E hookups, 22 tent spaces with W/E hookups, 60 tent spaces without hookups.

**SPACE-A:** Robert Gray Army Airfield, Building 13, 0800-1700 Mon-Fri, C-254-288-9200, D-312-738-9200. Fax: C-254-288-1930. Occasional flights available within CONUS.

**LOGISTICAL SUPPORT:**

| | |
|---|---|
| Bank-532-2161 | Cafeteria-532-5779 |
| Car Rental-532-7333 | Class VI-532-5962 |
| Child Care-287-5448 | Commissary-287-5943 |
| Conv Store-532-3089 | Exchange-287-3228 |
| Gas Station-532-8464 | SATO-532-8955 |
| Shoppette-532-7353 | Snack Bar-532-5779 |
| Visitor Center-287-4936 | |

**ADMINISTRATIVE SUPPORT:**

| | |
|---|---|
| CDO/OOD-287-2520/2506 | Legal-287-3421 |
| Locator-287-2137 | Police-287-2176 |
| Public Affairs-287-0103 | SDO/NCO-287-2624 |

**HEALTH & WELFARE:**
ACS-287-3663
Chaplain-287-1625
Medical-288-8000
  Emergency-288-8113
  Central Appts-288-8888

Chapel-288-6548
Family Services-287-4031
Retiree Services-287-5210
TRICARE-532-0800

**REST & RECREATION:**
Archery-532-4552
Auto Hobby Shop-287-5551
Clubs
  Dirt Riders-532-4552
  EM-287-6737
  Hunt/Saddle-287-4552
  NCO-532-5816
  O-532-5329
  Rod/Gun-287-5847
  Sport Parachute-532-4552
Recreation-287-7803
Rec Equip-287-4126
Swimming/Beach-287-6644
Youth Activities-287-9833

Arts & Crafts-288-2417
Boat Rental-287-2249
Bowling-287-3424/2281
Golf Course-287-3466
Hunting/Fishing-287-5847
ITR-287-7310
Library-288-4921
Marina-287-2249
MWR-287-4339
Pool-287-4648
Rec Center-288-9828/0353
Skating Center-287-5623
Theater-287-2998

**ATTRACTIONS:** State capital, Austin. Hunting and fishing.

# FORT SAM HOUSTON (TX18R3)
ATTN: AFZG-CO
1212 Stanley Road, Building 124
Fort Sam Houston, TX 78234-5000

**TELEPHONE NUMBER INFORMATION:** Main installation number: C-210-221-1211. WEB: fshtx.army.mil/main1.htm

**LOCATION:** Accessible from I-410 or I-35. From I-35 north or south exit 159 A north to gate or New Braunfels Avenue. USMRA: Page 91 (C,D-2,3). NMC: San Antonio, in city limits.

**GENERAL INFORMATION:** Headquarters 5th Army, Headquarters 90th Army Reserve Command, Headquarters U.S. Army Medical Command, U.S. Army Medical Dept and School, Brooke Army Medical Center, U.S. Army Dental Command, U.S. Army Veterinary Command, 41st Combat Support Hospital, 147th Medical Logistics Battalion, 5th Recruiting Brigade.

**TEMPORARY MILITARY LODGING:** Lodging office, Building 592, Dickman Road, C-210-357-2705.

**RV, CAMPING/FAMCAMP:** Army Travel Camp C-210-221-5502. Operates Canyon Lake Army Recreation Area off post. C-1-888-882-9878.

**SPACE-A:** None. See Kelly AFB listing.

**LOGISTICAL SUPPORT:**
Carlson Wagonlit Travel-225-5261
Child Care-221-5002
Conv Store-225-0216
Exchange-225-5566
Snack Bar-228-9071

Class VI-225-3427
Commissary-221-5626
Dining-221-3021
Gas Station-228-9001

**ADMINISTRATIVE SUPPORT:**
Fire Dept-221-2727
Locator-221-3315
SDO/NCO-221-2810

Legal-221-2353
Police-221-0463

**HEALTH & WELFARE:**
ACS-221-2705
Medical-916-6141
  Central Appts-916-9900
  Emergency-221-6466

Chapel-221-5007
Retiree Services-221-6856
TRICARE-1-800-406-2832

**REST & RECREATION:**
Auto Hobby Shop-224-7046

Bowling-221-4740

Clubs
  NCO-224-2721
  O-224-4211
Hunting/Fishing-295-7577
Rec Center-221-4829
Swimming-221-4887/295-8861

Equipment Rental-221-5224
Fitness Center-221-1234
Golf Course-221-4388
Library-221-4702
Stables-224-7207

**ATTRACTIONS:** San Antonio, Botanical Gardens. Gulf Coast and Mexico nearby, Natural Bridge Caverns. Sea World, Fiesta Texas Amusement Park, Historic Fort Sam Houston, The Alamo, San Antonio Riverwalk.

# FORT SAM HOUSTON RECREATION AREA AT CANYON LAKE (TX29R3)
Canyon Lake, TX 78133-3535

**TELEPHONE NUMBER INFORMATION:** Main installation numbers: C-210-221-1211.

**LOCATION:** Take I-35 to Canyon Lake exit 191 west. Turn west onto FM 306, and drive approximately 16 miles to Canyon City. Continue another 1.5 miles past the blinking light in Canyon City to Jacob Creek Park Road. Turn left, and the recreation area will be on the right. USMRA: Page 87 (J-6). NMC: San Antonio, 48 miles south. NMI: Randolph AFB, 35 miles south.

**GENERAL INFORMATION:** Canyon Lake Recreation Area includes 300 feet of well-maintained sandy beach and 1/4-acre marina. Operated by Fort Sam Houston, off post year round. Military personnel active, retired, reserve, NG, DoD civilians and foreign military. Check in at office 1600-2000, check out 1200. Reservations: Required for mobile homes and cabanas; reservations may be made up to one year in advance. No advance reservations for camping areas and RV spots. Address: ITR, Building 124, Stanley Road, Fort Sam Houston, TX 78234-5000. C-1-888-882-9878 or 210-964-3318, D-312-471-3318, 0800-1630 Mon-Fri, 0800-1600 Sat.

**TEMPORARY MILITARY LODGING:** Mobile homes-32

**RV, CAMPING/FAMCAMP:**
Screened Shelters-10
Tent spaces-50

Camper spaces-32

**ATTRACTIONS:** Mild winter temperatures make this natural haven a year-round attraction for fishing, camping, boating and picnicking.

*For detailed information about this off-base recreation facility, as well as other recreation facilities, golf courses, marinas and temporary military lodging, consult Military Living's Military RV, Camping and Outdoor Recreation Around the World or Military Living's Temporary Military Lodging Around the World.*

# FORT WORTH NAVAL AIR STATION/ JOINT RESERVE BASE (TX21R3)
Commanding Officer, NAS/JRB
1510 Chennault Ave
Fort Worth, TX 76127-5000

**TELEPHONE NUMBER INFORMATION:** Main installation numbers: C-817-782-5000, D-312-739-1110.

**LOCATION:** On TX-183. From Fort Worth, west on I-30, exit at 78 north on TX 183, 1.5 miles to gate on left/north of TX-183. USMRA: Page 88 (A-3). NMC: Fort Worth, seven miles east.

**GENERAL INFORMATION:** Air Combat Command Base. Bomb Wing and AFRES units.

**TEMPORARY MILITARY LODGING:** Lodging office, Building 1324 Military Parkway, 24 hours daily, C-817-782-5393, Fax: C-817-782-5391. All ranks. DV/VIP C-817-782-7614.

**RV, CAMPING/FAMCAMP:** None. Nearest facility is over 100 miles away.

**SPACE-A:** Pax Term/Lounge, Building 1423, 0730-1630 Mon-Fri, C-817-782-6288, D-312-739-6288; Rec: C-782-6284, D-312-739-6284. Flights to CONUS, OCONUS and foreign locations.

**LOGISTICAL SUPPORT:**

| | |
|---|---|
| Bank-731-4211 | Cafeteria-782-7380Child Care-782-5753 |
| Conv Store-731-4187 | |
| Dining-738-7380 | Exchange-738-1943 |
| Gas Station-738-1002 | Package Store-738-0462 |
| SATO-782-5579 | Shoppette-731-4187 |
| Snack Bar-731-1943 | Visitor Center-782-5377 |

**ADMINISTRATIVE SUPPORT:**

| | |
|---|---|
| CDO-782-7153 | Legal-782-7595 |
| Locator-782-7082/5000 | Police-782-5200 |
| SDO/NCO-782-5555 | Quarter Deck-782-7153 |

**HEALTH & WELFARE:**

| | |
|---|---|
| CHAMPUS-782-4827 | Chapel-782-7301 |
| Family Services-782-5290 | Medical-782-5902 |
| Retiree Services-782-5661 | Central Appts-782-4500 |
| | Emergency-782-4050 |

**REST & RECREATION:**

| | |
|---|---|
| Arts & Crafts-ext 7114 | Auto Hobby Shop-ext 7114 |
| Bowling-ext 5505 | Clubs |
| Fitness Center-ext 7770 | EM-782-5293 |
| Golf course 738-8402 | O-782-5631 |
| Library-ext 5230 | Marina-ext 7972 |
| MWR-782-7744 | Rec Center-ext 7077 |
| Rec Equip-ext 7972 | Swimming-ext 7770/7869 |
| Tennis-ext 7770 | Theater-782-5450 |
| Youth Center-ext 5498 | |

**ATTRACTIONS:** Zoo, Fort Worth Botanic Gardens, Museum of Science and History. Dallas, Six Flags over Arlington and Ripley's Believe It or Not Wax Museum.

# GALVESTON COAST GUARD BASE (TX47R3)

P.O. Box 1912
End of Ferry Road, Galveston
TX 77553-1912

**TELEPHONE NUMBER INFORMATION:** Main installation numbers: C-409-766-5620/1 or 1-800-742-8917.

**LOCATION:** Take I-45 south to Island, changes to Broadway, at the seawall go northeast, follow signs to base. USMRA: Page 87 (N-6). NMC: Galveston, three miles south.

**GENERAL INFORMATION:** Part of Eighth District, U.S. Coast Guard.

**TEMPORARY MILITARY LODGING:** None. Nearest facility is more than 100 miles away.

**RV, CAMPING/FAMCAMP:** None. Nearest facility is more than 100 miles away.

**SPACE-A:** None. See Ellington ANGB/Houston CGAS listing.

**LOGISTICAL SUPPORT:**

| | |
|---|---|
| Dining-766-5663 | Exchange-766-4733 |

**ADMINISTRATIVE SUPPORT:**

| | |
|---|---|
| CDO/OOD-766-5677 | Public Affairs-766-5603 |

**HEALTH & WELFARE:**

| | |
|---|---|
| Chapel-766-5667 | Family Services-766-4751 |
| Medical-766-5661 | |

**REST & RECREATION:** None. Nearest facility is more than 100 miles away.

# GOODFELLOW AIR FORCE BASE (TX24R3)

184 Lancaster Avenue, Suite J
Goodfellow Air Force Base, TX 76908-4410

**TELEPHONE NUMBER INFORMATION:** Main installation numbers: C-915-654-3231, D-312-477-4000. E-mail: 17trw.ppa@mail.gdf.aetc.af.mil

**LOCATION:** Off US-87 or US-277. Clearly marked. USMRA: Page 86 (H-6,7). NMC: San Angelo, two miles southeast.

**GENERAL INFORMATION:** Air Education and Training Command.

**TEMPORARY MILITARY LODGING:** Lodging office, Building 3305, Kearney Boulevard, 24 hours daily, C-915-654-3332/3206, D-312-477-3332/3206. All ranks.

**RV, CAMPING/FAMCAMP:** Lake Nasworthy Recreation Camp off base, year round: Thu-Mon, 1950 S. Concho Drive, San Angelo, TX 76504-5000, C-915-944-1012, D-312-477-3217 (ask operator to ring 944-1012), 20 camper spaces with full hookups.

**SPACE-A:** None. See Dyess AFB listing.

**LOGISTICAL SUPPORT:**

| | |
|---|---|
| Bank-659-6922 | Barber Shop-653-8637 |
| Beauty Shop-655-5024 | Car Rental-655-6663 |
| Child Care-654-3241 | Child Dev Center-654-3240 |
| Class Six-654-3361 | Commissary-653-3357/8 |
| Credit Union-653-1465 | Dining Facilities-654-5131 |
| Dry Cleaner-653-1210 | Education Office-654-3317 |
| Exchange-655-3361 | Gas Station-655-5793 |
| Laundry-653-1210 | Postal Service-654-3466 |
| SATO-654-3328 | Shoppette-655-5794 |
| Travel Office-654-5139 | |

**ADMINISTRATIVE SUPPORT:**

| | |
|---|---|
| Fire Dept-654-3532 | Housing Office-654-3694 |
| Legal-654-3203 | Locator-654-3410 |
| Pass/ID Office-654-3264 | Police-654-3511 |
| Public Affairs-654-3876 | SDO/NCO-654-3044 |
| Quarter Deck-654-3668 | |

**HEALTH & WELFARE:**

| | |
|---|---|
| Air Force Aid Society-654-3263 | CHAMPUS-654-3276 |
| Chapel-654-3424 | Dental-654-3050 |
| Family Service-654-3893 | Medical-654-3135 |
| Retiree Services-654-5388 | TRICARE-481-3600 |
| Veterinary Services-654-3251 | |

**REST & RECREATION:**

| | |
|---|---|
| Arts & Crafts-654-3236 | Auto Hobby Shop-654-3233 |
| Bowling-654-3227 | Clubs |
| Community Center-654-3247 | Goodfellow-654-5327 |
| Fitness Center-654-3242 | Oasis-655-3256 |
| Gym-654-5127 | Library-654-3232 |
| Rec Center-ext 3247 | Theater-654-3206 |
| Wood Hobby Shop-654-5643 | Youth Center-654-3211 |

**ATTRACTIONS:** Lakes, Fort Concho and city of San Angelo.

# GOODFELLOW AIR FORCE BASE RECREATION CAMP (TX32R3)

1950 South Concho Drive
San Angelo, TX 76504-5000

**TELEPHONE NUMBER INFORMATION:** Main installation numbers: C-915-654-3231, D-312-477-4000.

**LOCATION:** Off base. From all directions, take Route 67 south (turns into Loop 306) south of the city of San Angelo to Knickerbocker Road (Ranch Road 584). Proceed south three miles. Turn left on South Concho (left turn is shortly after crossing Lake Nasworthy). Campground is on the left and marked by a sign. USMRA: Page 86 (H-7). NMI: Goodfellow AFB. NMC: San Angelo, 10 miles north.

**GENERAL INFORMATION:** Operated by Goodfellow AFB, off base, year round, Thursday-Monday. Military personnel active, reservists, retired, DoD civilians. No advance reservations. For info: 1950 S. Concho Drive, San Angelo, TX 76504-5000. C-915-944-1012, D-312-477-3217 (ask operator to ring 944-1012).

**RV, CAMPING/FAMCAMP:**

Camper Spaces-21                                        Tent Spaces-unlimited

**ATTRACTIONS:** Located on Lake Nasworthy in flat, open terrain with some trees and covered picnic areas.

*For detailed information about this off-base recreation facility, as well as on-base recreation facilities, golf courses and marinas, consult Military Living's Military RV, Camping and Outdoor Recreation Around the World.*

# HEADQUARTERS ARMY & AIR FORCE EXCHANGE SERVICE (TX11R3)

3911 South Walton Walker Boulevard
Dallas, TX 75236-1598

**TELEPHONE NUMBER INFORMATION:** Main installation numbers: C-214-312-2011, D-312-967-2011. WEB: www.aafes.com
*Ten digit dialing required for local calls.*

**LOCATION:** Take I-35 south to exit 423 to US-67, exit west at Loop 12, west to Walton Walker Blvd; enter at Exchange Service Drive. AAFES headquarters located at 3911. USMRA: Page 88 (F-4). NMC: Dallas, in city limits.

**LOGISTICAL SUPPORT:**                           Exchange-312-2011

**ATTRACTIONS:** Zoo, Fort Worth Botanic Gardens, Museum of Science and History. Dallas, Six Flags over Arlington and Ripley's Believe It or Not Wax Museum.

# HOUSTON/GALVESTON COAST GUARD MARINE SAFETY OFFICE (TX48R3)

9640 Clinton Drive
Galena Park, TX 77547-0446

**TELEPHONE NUMBER INFORMATION:** Main installation numbers: C-713-671-5100.
*Ten digit dialing required for local calls.*

**LOCATION:** From I-610 north take Clinton Drive exit east, make left at light and get in the right lane; go half a mile, turn right at Gate 8. USMRA: Page 89 (C-3). NMC: Houston, in city limits.

**GENERAL INFORMATION:** Part of the Eighth District, U.S. Coast Guard.

**LOGISTICAL SUPPORT:**
Dining-678-2245                                Exchange-678-4573

**ATTRACTIONS:** Six Flags Astroworld, Astrodome, zoo, many museums and activities in Houston.

# HOUSTON SPACE CENTER (TX52R3)

1601 NASA Road 1
Houston, TX 77058-5000

**TELEPHONE NUMBER INFORMATION:** Main installation numbers: C-281-483-0123. WEB: www.hern.org/space
*Ten digit dialing required for local calls.*

**LOCATION:** Follow signs on I-45 south from Houston, exit 26 east to Center. Clearly marked. USMRA: Page 87 (M-6). NMC: Houston, 20 miles north.

**GENERAL INFORMATION:** Official Visitors Center of NASA's Johnson Space Center, which is the home of astronaut training and Mission Control.

**LOGISTICAL SUPPORT:**                    Visitor Center-483-0123

**ATTRACTIONS:** Six Flags Astroworld, Astrodome, zoo, many museums and activities in Houston.

# INGLESIDE NAVAL STATION (TX30R3)

1455 Ticonderoga Road, Suite W123
Ingleside, TX 78362-5001

**TELEPHONE NUMBER INFORMATION:** Main installation numbers: C-361-776-4201, D-312-776-4201.

**LOCATION:** I-37 south to exit 1 A to US-181 northeast to Route 1069 east and Naval Station. USMRA: Page 87 (K,L-8). NMC: Corpus Christi, 37 miles south.

**GENERAL INFORMATION:** Navy's designated "Mine Warfare Center of Excellence," home port to 12 mine countermeasures ships (MCM), nine coastal mine hunters (MHC) and the Mine Countermeasures Command, Control and Support Ship, the *USS Inchon.*

**TEMPORARY MILITARY LODGING:** Lodging office, BEQ, C-361-776-4420, D-312-776-4420, Fax: C-361-776-4519.

**RV, CAMPING/FAMCAMP:** None. See Corpus Christi NAS listing.

**SPACE-A:** None. See Corpus Christi NAS listing.

**LOGISTICAL SUPPORT:**

| | |
|---|---|
| Barber Shop-776-4115 | Dining Facilities-776-4424 |
| Exchange-776-4100 | Postal Service-776-4256 |
| SATO-776-4216 | Snack Bar-776-4777 |

**ADMINISTRATIVE SUPPORT:**

| | |
|---|---|
| Fire Dept-776-4294 | Housing Office-776-4562 |
| Legal-776-4122 | Pass/ID Office-776-5854 |
| Police-776-4238 | Public Affairs-776-4206 |

**HEALTH & WELFARE:**

| | |
|---|---|
| Dental-776-4587 | Family Services-776-4551 |
| Central Appts-776-4581 | Medical-776-4580 |
| Clinic-776-4581 | Central Appts-776-4585 |
| Emergency-776-4581 | Health Benefits-776-4575 |
| Navy-MC Relief-776-4564 | Retiree Services-776-4551 |
| TRICARE-1-800-406-2823 | |

**REST & RECREATION:**

| | |
|---|---|
| Auto Hobby Shop-776-4299 | Fitness Center-776-4601 |
| Gym-776-4601 | ITT-776-4227 |
| Marinas-758-0350 | MWR-776-4631 |

**ATTRACTIONS:** Bay and gulf water sports. Also, symphony, museums, and historical homes.

# KELLY AIR FORCE BASE (TX03R3)

807 Buckner Drive, Suite 1
Kelly Air Force Base, TX 78241-5842
*Scheduled to close July 2001*

**TELEPHONE NUMBER INFORMATION:** Main installation numbers: C-210-925-1110, D-312-945-1110.

**LOCATION:** All of the following, I-10, I-35, I-37, I-410 intersect with US-90 in southwest San Antonio. From US-90 take either the Gen. Hudnell or Gen. McMullen exit and go south to AFB. USMRA: Page 91 (B-3,4). NMC: San Antonio, seven miles northeast.

**GENERAL INFORMATION:** Air Force Materiel Command Base. San Antonio Air Logistics Center, Air Intelligence Agency, Electronic Warfare Center, Air Force News Agency, AFRES and ANG units.

**TEMPORARY MILITARY LODGING:** Lodging office, Building 1650, 24 hours daily, C-210-925-1844/924-7201, D-312-945-1844. All ranks. DV/VIP 210-925-7678. (Protocol).

**RV, CAMPING/FAMCAMP:** On base, year round, C-210-925-5725. Thirty paved camper spaces with W/S/E hookups and many tent spaces without hookups.

**SPACE-A:** Pax Term/Lounge, Building 1614, 0700-1800 Mon-Fri, 0800-1600 Sat-Sun, C-210-925-8714/8715, D-312-945-8714/5; Rec: 210-925-1854, D-312-945-1854; Fax: C-210-925-2732, D-312-945-2732. Flights to CONUS, OCONUS and foreign locations.

**LOGISTICAL SUPPORT:**

| | |
|---|---|
| Cafeteria-925-4990 | Child Care-925-5747 |
| Commissary-925-5268 | Exchange-924-9247 |
| Gas Station-924-2960 | SATO-925-7371 |
| Visitor Center-925-5551 | |

**ADMINISTRATIVE SUPPORT:**

| | |
|---|---|
| Fire Dept-925-5526 | Legal-925-3095 |
| Locator-925-1841 | Police-925-6811 |
| Public Affairs-925-7951 | SDO/NCO-925-6906 |

**HEALTH & WELFARE:**

| | |
|---|---|
| CHAMPUS-925-0776 | Chapel-925-7874 |
| Family Services-925-4181 | Medical-925-6333 |
| Retiree Services-925-2984 | Emergency-925-4544 |
| | Appointments-925-1847 |

**REST & RECREATION:**

| | |
|---|---|
| Auto Craft Center-925-8346 | Bowling-925-5933/5480 |
| Golf Course-925-4006 | Clubs |
| Gym-925-4846 | NCO-924-8354 |
| ITT-925-4585 | O-924-8254 |
| MWR-925-7144 | Library-925-4116 |
| Pool-925-4846 | Services-925-7144 |
| Youth Center-925-8100 | |

**ATTRACTIONS:** The Alamo, River Walk, Tower of the Americas, San Antonio Zoo, Institute of Texas Cultures, McNay Art Museum, Six Flags Fiesta Texas and Sea World.

# KINGSVILLE NAVAL AIR STATION (TX22R3)
### 554 McCain Street, Suite 309
### Kingsville, TX 78363-5054

**TELEPHONE NUMBER INFORMATION:** Main installation numbers: C-361-516-6136, D-312-876-6136.

**LOCATION:** Off US-77 north or south, exit to TX-141 southeast to main gate. USMRA: Page 87 (K-9). NMC: Corpus Christi, 50 miles northeast.

**GENERAL INFORMATION:** Training Air Wing # 2, two squadrons, and support units.

**TEMPORARY MILITARY LODGING:** Lodging office, Building 3729, duty hours, C-361-516-6321/6309, D-312-876-6321/6309, Fax: C-361-516-6428. All ranks. DV/VIP C-361-516-6136/6321.

**RV, CAMPING/FAMCAMP:** Nasking Recreation FAMCAMP, on base year round, Outdoor Recreation, 3765 Nimitz Avenue, C-361-516-6443, D-312-876-6443, four campers for rent with W/E hookups, five camper spaces with W/E hookups, 10 camper spaces with W hookups.

**SPACE-A:** Very limited, C-361-516-6108, D-312-876-6108. Also see Corpus Christi NAS listing.

**LOGISTICAL SUPPORT:**

| | |
|---|---|
| Child Care-516-6176 | Commissary-516-6241 |
| Conv Store-516-6106 | Exchange-516-6361 |
| Gas Station-516-6106 | Package Store-516-6473 |

**ADMINISTRATIVE SUPPORT:**

| | |
|---|---|
| Legal-516-6426 | Police-516-6217 |

SDO/NCO-516-6136

**HEALTH & WELFARE:**

| | |
|---|---|
| CHAMPUS-516-6238 | Chapel-516-6331 |
| Family Services-516-6333 | Medical-516-6305 |
| Retiree Services-516-6333 | Central Appts-516-6342 |
| | Emergency-516-6911 |

**REST & RECREATION:**

| | |
|---|---|
| Arts & Crafts-ext 6171/2 | Auto Hobby Shop-ext 6171/2 |
| Bowling-ext 6171/2 | Clubs |
| Gym-ext 6171/2 | CPO-516-6121 |
| ITT-516-6449 | EM-516-6121 |
| Nautilus Center-ext 6171/2 | O-516-6121 |
| Picnic Area-ext 6171/2 | Swimming-ext 6171/2 |
| Tennis-ext 6171/2 | |

**ATTRACTIONS:** Gulf Coast, Corpus Christi, King Ranch, and fishing in Baffin Bay.

# LACKLAND AIR FORCE BASE (TX25R3)
### 1701 Kenly Avenue, Suite 220
### Lackland Air Force Base, TX 78236-5110

**TELEPHONE NUMBER INFORMATION:** Main installation numbers: C-210-671-1110, D-312-473-1110. E-mail: publicaf@lackland.af.mil WEB: www.lackland.af.mil/homepage

**LOCATION:** Lackland is located in the southwestern quadrant of the city. Take either IH-10 or I-35 to US-90 south. Loop 13 (Military Drive) bisects Lackland AFB. USMRA: Page 87 (J-6,7), page 91 (A,B-3). NMC: San Antonio, six miles northeast.

**GENERAL INFORMATION:** The "Gateway to the Airforce" Lackland hosts the 37th Training Wing (Basic Military and Technical Training), and is flanked by the 59th Medical Wing (Wilford Hall Medical Center), the Defense Language Institute, English Language Center, and the Inter-American Air Forces Academy.

**TEMPORARY MILITARY LODGING:** Lodging office: Gateway Inn, Building 10203, 24 hours daily, C-210-671-4270, D-312-473-4270, Fax: C-210-671-1447. All ranks. Bldg. 2435, DV/VIP C-210-671-3622, D-312-473-3622, Fax: C-210-671-2354.

**RV, CAMPING/FAMCAMP:** FAMCAMP on base, year round, C-210-671-3106, D-312-473-3106, 24 camper spaces with full hookups.

**SPACE-A:** None. See Kelly AFB listing.

**LOGISTICAL SUPPORT:**

| | |
|---|---|
| Bank-674-6266 | Barber Shop-673-5252 |
| Beauty Shop-674-1341 | Car Rental-670-4332 |
| Cafeteria-671-4047 | Child Care-671-3168 |
| Child Dev Center-671-3675 | Commissary-671-2830 |
| Conv Store-674-0848 | Credit Union-673-5610 |
| Dining-671-3784/670-1666 | Dry Cleaner-674-8943 |
| Education Center-671-2895 | Exchange-674-6465 |
| Gas Station-673-0848 | Laundry-674-8943 |
| Package Store-674-0848 | Postal Office-671-1058 |
| SATO-673-9057 | Shoppette-674-0848 |
| Snack Bar-671-4047 | Travel Office-671-3133 |
| Visitor Center-671-3024 | |

**ADMINISTRATIVE SUPPORT:**

| | |
|---|---|
| CDO/OOD-671-4225 | Command Post-671-4225 |
| Fire Dept-671-2921 | Housing Office-671-1840 |
| Legal-671-3361 | Locator-671-1841 |
| Pass/ID Office-671-3594 | Police-671-2018 |
| Public Affairs-671-2907 | |

**HEALTH & WELFARE:**

| | |
|---|---|
| American Red Cross-671-1855 | Air Force Aid Society-671-3722 |
| CHAMPUS-292-2832 | Chapel-671-4104 |
| Dental Clinic-292-6379 | Family Services-671-3722 |
| Central Appts-292-7251 | Health Benefits-1-800-406-2832 |

Emergency-292-7251
Medical Clinic-292-7100
  Central Appts-292-7177
  Emergency-292-7331
  Information-292-7100

Retiree Services-671-2728
TRICARE-292-4151
Veterinary Services-671-3354

**REST & RECREATION:**

| | |
|---|---|
| Arts & Crafts-671-2515 | |
| Bowling-671-2271 | Auto Hobby Shop-671-3549 |
| Community Center-671-2619 | Clubs |
| Fitness Center-671-2751 | NCO-645-7034 |
| Golf Course-671-3466 | O-645-7034 |
| Indoor Rec-671-3106 | Gym-671-2751 |
| Library-671-2678 | ITT-671-3133 |
| Outdoor Rec-671-3106 | MWR-671-3106 |
| Rec Equip-ext 3106 | Rec Center-671-2619 |
| Swimming-ext 3445 | Services-671-3395 |
| Youth Center-671-2388 | Theater-671-3985 |

**ATTRACTIONS:** City of San Antonio, Zoo, River Walk, The Alamo, El Mercado La Villita, Institute of Texan Cultures, Spanish Missions, McNay Art Institute, Sea World of Texas, Fiesta Texas.

# LAUGHLIN AIR FORCE BASE (TX05R3)

47FTW/PA
561 Liberty Drive, Suite 3
Laughlin Air Force Base, TX 78843-5230

**TELEPHONE NUMBER INFORMATION:** Main installation numbers: C-830-298-3511, D-312-732-1110.

**LOCATION:** Take US-90 west from San Antonio, 150 miles or US-277 south from San Angelo, 150 miles to Del Rio area, or exit I-10 east or west to US-277 south. The AFB is clearly marked off US-90. USMRA: Page 86 (H-9). NMC: Del Rio, six miles northwest.

**GENERAL INFORMATION:** Air Education and Training Command Base. Home of the 47th Flying Training Wing, Specialized Undergraduate Pilot Training.

**TEMPORARY MILITARY LODGING:** Lodging office, 416 Liberty Drive, 24 hours daily, C-830-298-5731, D-312-732-5731. All ranks. DV/VIP C-830-298-5041.

**RV, CAMPING/FAMCAMP:** FAMCAMP on base year round, Recreation Services, 47 SPTG/SVRO, 416 Liberty Drive, C-830-298-5474, D-312-732-5474, Fax: C-830-298-5554, D-312-732-5554, 15 camper spaces with full hookups. Also operates South Winds on Lake Amistad, off base year round. See Southwinds Marina listing for more details.

**SPACE-A:** Limited. Building 306, C-830-298-5308/5309, D-312-732-5308/5309.

**LOGISTICAL SUPPORT:**

| | |
|---|---|
| Bank-774-6861 | Barber Shop-298-3289 |
| Beauty Shop-298-0027 | Child Care-298-5419 |
| Child Dev Center-298-5419 | Class Six-298-3867 |
| Commissary-298-5821 | Conv Store-298-3867 |
| Credit Union-774-3503 | Dining Facilities-298-5295 |
| Education Center-298-5545 | Exchange-298-3627 |
| Gas Station-298-3867 | Postal Service-298-5417 |
| SATO-298-5205 | Shoppette-298-3867 |
| Snack Bar-298-3001 | |

**ADMINISTRATIVE SUPPORT:**

| | |
|---|---|
| CDO/OOD-298-5167 | Fire Dept-298-5034 |
| Housing Office-298-5904 | Legal-298-5172 |
| Locator-298-3511 | Pass/ID Office-298-5349 |
| Police-298-5100 | Public Affairs-298-5044 |
| SDO/NCO-298-5167 | |

**HEALTH & WELFARE:**

| | |
|---|---|
| Air Force Aid Society-298-5844 | American Red Cross-298-5125 |
| CHAMPUS-298-6350 | Chapel-298-5111 |
| Dental-298-6331 | Family Services-298-5620 |
| Medical Clinic-298-3578 | TRICARE-298-6350 |
| Central Appts-298-3578 | Veterinary Services-298-5500 |

Emergency-911
  Health Benefits-298-6350

**REST & RECREATION:**

| | |
|---|---|
| Auto Hobby Shop-298-5844 | Bowling-298-5526 |
| Clubs | Community Center-298-5474 |
| EM-298-5346 | Fitness Center-298-5326 |
| O-298-5134 | Golf-298-5451 |
| Library-298-5119 | Marina-775-5971 |
| Outdoor Rec-775-5971 | Services-298-5810 |
| Theater-298-5144 | Youth Services-298-5343 |
| Wood Hobby Shop-298-5153 | |

**ATTRACTIONS:** On the Mexican border at Ciudad Acuna, Mexico. Lake Amistad, Alamo Village.

# RANDOLPH AIR FORCE BASE (TX19R3)

1 Washington Circle, Suite 4
Randolph Air Force Base, TX 78150-4562

**TELEPHONE NUMBER INFORMATION:** Main installation numbers: C-210-652-1110, D-312-487-1110.

**LOCATION:** From I-35 north or south take exit 172 south on TX-1604 to AFB or I-10 exit 587 north on TX-1604 to AFB. USMRA: Page 91 (E-2). NMC: San Antonio, five miles southwest.

**GENERAL INFORMATION:** Air Education and Training Command Base. 12th Flying Training Wing, Headquarters Air Education and Training Command, Air Force Personnel Center, Air Force Recruiting Service, Headquarters 19th Air Force, Air Force Center for Quality and Management Innovation, Air Force Occupational Measurement Squadron, Air Force Services Agency, Air Force Security Assistance Training Squadron and support units.

**TEMPORARY MILITARY LODGING:** Lodging office, Building 118, 24 hours daily, C-210-652-1844, D-312-487-1844. All ranks. DV/VIP 652-4126.

**RV, CAMPING/FAMCAMP:** Randolph Off Base Recreation Area year round (marina closed Mon-Tue), Outdoor Recreation Resource Center, 415 B Street East, C-210-652-3702, six camper spaces with W/E hookups, 45 tent spaces without hookups, 11 primitive shelters with E hookups.

**SPACE-A:** Pax Term/Lounge, Hangar 7, east side, 0600-1800 Mon-Fri, Sat and Sun as required, C-210-652-1854/3725, D-312-487-1854/3725. Fax: C-210-652-5718, D-312-487-5718. Flights to CONUS locations.

**LOGISTICAL SUPPORT:**

| | |
|---|---|
| Bank-658-7427 | Child Care-652-4946 |
| Commissary-652-6545 | Dining-658-8976 |
| Exchange-652-2301 | Gas Station-658-1515 |
| Package Store-658-4544 | SATO-658-3585 |
| Shoppette-658-1717 | Snack Bar-659-5898 |
| Visitor Center-652-3939 | |

**ADMINISTRATIVE SUPPORT:**

| | |
|---|---|
| Legal-652-6781 | Locator-652-1841 |
| Police-652-5700 | Public Affairs-652-4410 |
| SDO/NCO-652-1859 | |

**HEALTH & WELFARE:**

| | |
|---|---|
| Chapel-652-6121/4659 | Family Services-652-3060 |
| Medical | Retiree Services-652-6880 |
| Central Appts-652-2273 | TRICARE-652-5524 |
| Clinic-652-4373 | |

**REST & RECREATION:**

| | |
|---|---|
| Art/Crafts-652-2788 | Auto Hobby Shop-652-2952 |
| Bowling-652-6271 | Clubs |
| Golf Course-652-4570 | EM-658-3557 |
| Gym 652-2955/5955 | Hunt/Saddle-652-2346 |
| ITT-652-2301 | O-658-7445 |
| Library 652-2617 | MWR Office-652-5971 |
| Rec Equip-652-3702 | Skeet Range-652-2064 |
| Theater-652-3278 | Youth Activities-652-3298 |

**ATTRACTIONS:** San Antonio, New Braunfels, Austin, and Canyon Lake. Rec areas are nearby.

# RANDOLPH OUTDOOR RECREATION AREA-CANYON LAKE (TX35R3)
781 Jacobs Creek Road
Canyon Lake, TX 78133-5000

**TELEPHONE NUMBER INFORMATION:** Main installation numbers: C-210-652-1110, D-312-487-1110. Police for recreation area, C-210-652-5510.

**LOCATION:** Off base. From I-35 north from San Antonio, through New Braunfels to Canyon Lake exit. Turn left on Farm Road 306, follow for 16 miles to Canyon City. Go another 1.5 miles past the blinking traffic light to Jacobs Creek Park Road. turn left. Clearly marked. USMRA: Page 87 (J,K-6). NMI: Randolph AFB, 43 miles southeast. NMC: San Antonio, 48 miles south.

**GENERAL INFORMATION:** Operated by Randolph AFB, off base, year round. Military personnel active, reservist, retired, DoD civilians at Randolph AFB. Reservations (all but tent spaces): 781 Jacobs Creek Road, Canyon Lake, TX 78133-5000. C-1-800-280-3466, C-830-964-4134. Marina, C-830-964-3804.

**RV, CAMPING/FAMCAMP:**

| | |
|---|---|
| Cabins-6 | Shelters-5 |
| Camper Spaces-10 | Tent Spaces-45 |
| Primitive-unlimited | Group Camping Area-2 |

**ATTRACTIONS:** Located on northeast end of Canyon Reservoir. There is a majestic view of the 8,240-acre lake and its 80-mile shoreline. Variety of water-oriented activities.

*For detailed information about this off-base recreation facility, as well as on-base recreation facilities, golf courses and marinas, consult Military Living's Military RV, Camping and Outdoor Recreation Around the World.*

# SHEPPARD AIR FORCE BASE (TX37R3)
82 TRW/PA
419 G Avenue, Suite 3
Sheppard Air Force Base, TX 76311-2943

**TELEPHONE NUMBER INFORMATION:** Main installation numbers: C-940-676-2511, D-312-736-2511.

**LOCATION:** Take US-281 north from Wichita Falls, exit to TX 325 which leads to main gate. Clearly marked. USMRA: Page 87 (J-1). NMC: Wichita Falls, five miles southwest.

**GENERAL INFORMATION:** Air Education and Training Command, 80th Flying Training Wing & support units. 82nd Training Wing, Logistics, Support, and Medical Groups. 782nd Training Group, 882nd Training Group, and 982nd Training Group.

**TEMPORARY MILITARY LODGING:** Lodging office, Building 1600, Avenue J, 24 hours daily, C-940-855-7370, D-312-736-2631 Fax: C-940-676-7434, D-312-736-7434. All ranks. DV/VIP C-940-855-2123.

**RV, CAMPING/FAMCAMP:** Operates Sheppard AFB Recreation Annex off base. See Sheppard AFB Recreation Annex listing for more information.

**SPACE-A:** Pax Term/Lounge, Building 1360, duty hours, C-940-676-2180/6474, D-312-736-2180/6474. Flights to CONUS locations.

**LOGISTICAL SUPPORT:**

| | |
|---|---|
| Bank-855-2321 | Barber Shop-855-2211 |
| Beauty Shop-855-2087 | Child Care-676-2038 |
| Child Dev Center-676-2038 | Commissary-676-7269 |
| Conv Store-855-4341 | Credit Union-720-8000 |
| Dining Facilities-676-2080 | Dry Cleaner-855-2880 |
| Education Office-676-5264 | Exchange-855-4318 |
| Gas Station-855-4341 | Laundry-855-2880 |
| Package Store-855-7295 | Postal Service-855-5641 |
| SATO-676-6398 | Snack Bar-855-4823 |

| | |
|---|---|
| Travel Office-676-4263 | Visitor Center-676-7441 |

**ADMINISTRATIVE SUPPORT:**

| | |
|---|---|
| Fire Dept-911 | Housing Office-676-1840 |
| Legal-676-6760 | Locator-676-1841 |
| Pass/ID Office-676-1853 | Police-676-6302 |
| Public Affairs-676-2732 | SDO/NCO-676-2621 |

**HEALTH & WELFARE:**

| | |
|---|---|
| Air Force Aid Society-676-4358 | American Red Cross-676-2308 |
| Chapel-676-4370 | Dental-676-1846 |
| Family Services-676-2300 | Medical-676-1847 |
| Retiree Services-676-5088 | TRICARE-676-1847 |
| Veterinary Services-676-6883 | |

**REST & RECREATION:**

| | |
|---|---|
| Arts & Crafts-676-2870 | Auto Hobby Shop-676-4110 |
| Bowling-676-7174 | Clubs |
| Community Center-676-3866 | EM-676-2083 |
| Fitness Center-676-6336 | NCO-676-6427 |
| Golf Course-676-6369 | O-676-6460 |
| Gym-676-6133 | ITT-676-2302 |
| Library-676-6152 | MWR-676-2745 |
| Outdoor Rec-676-4141 | Picnic Area-676-4141 |
| Rec Center-676-3866 | Services-676-2745 |
| Skeet/Trap Range-676-4141 | Swimming-676-6494 |
| Theater-676-4427 | Youth Center-676-5437 |

**ATTRACTIONS:** Wichita Falls and outdoor sports.

# SHEPPARD AIR FORCE BASE RECREATION ANNEX (TX16R3)
1030 Sheppard AFB Road
Whitesboro, TX 76273-5000

**TELEPHONE NUMBER INFORMATION:** Main installation numbers: C-903-523-4613, D-312-736-2511. Police-893-4388.

**LOCATION:** Located approximately 120 miles east of base at Wichita Falls, near the Texas/Oklahoma line. From US-82 east of Gainesville, take US-377 north approximately 11 miles (past Gordonville exit) to TX FM-901 and turn left. (Just prior to this exit is a green SAFB Annex sign.) Go two miles; turn right at SAFB Annex sign. Follow signs approximately five miles to recreation annex. Rec area is located on Texas side of Lake Texoma. USMRA: Page 87 (K-1,2). NMC: Dallas, 95 miles south.

**GENERAL INFORMATION:** Operated by Sheppard Air Force Base, off base year round. Military personnel active, retired, dependents, guard, reserve, federal civilian employees, retired federal employees, family members and sponsored guests. Check in at main lodge, 1500, check out 1300. Reservations: C-903-523-4613 (0800-1700 daily).

**TEMPORARY MILITARY LODGING:**

| | |
|---|---|
| Cabins-46 | Mobile home-1 |

**RV, CAMPING/FAMCAMP:**

| | |
|---|---|
| Camper spaces-24 | Tent spaces-many |

**ATTRACTIONS:** Great fishing, various water sports, sun and fun.

*For detailed information about this off-base recreation facility, as well as other recreation facilities, golf courses, and marinas, consult Military Living's Military RV, Camping and Outdoor Recreation Around the World.*

# SOUTHWINDS MARINA ON LAKE AMISTAD (TX34R3)
Laughlin Air Force Base
Laughlin AFB, TX 78843-5135

**TELEPHONE NUMBER INFORMATION:** Main installation numbers: C-830-298-3511, D-312-732-1110. Police for recreation area, C-911.

**LOCATION:** Off base. From US-90 northwest of Del Rio, take Amistad Dam Road (Spur 349) to Recreation area. USMRA: Page 86 (H-9). NMI: Laughlin AFB, 22.5 miles southeast. NMC: Del Rio, 12 miles southeast.

**GENERAL INFORMATION:** Operated by Laughlin AFB, off base, year round (16 April-15 October: 0800-2000 hours Thu-Sun, holidays. 16 October-15 April: 0800-1700 hours Sat-Sun, holidays). Military personnel active, reservists, retired, DoD and NAF civilians, others with Federal ID at discretion of commander. Reservations (required): HCR #3, Box 37J, Del Rio, TX 78840-5000. C-830-775-5971/7800. Fax: C-830-298-7800.

**RV, CAMPING/FAMCAMP:**

Cabins-2            Campers-6
Camper/Tent Spaces-5

**ATTRACTIONS:** Situated near Amistad Dam which serves as passageway to Mexico. Ideal fresh water recreation area and outstanding fishing. Many deer in the area. Good base for day trips into Mexico. Convenient to Ciudad Acuna, Mexico.

*For detailed information about this off-base recreation facility, as well as on-base recreation facilities, golf courses and marinas, consult Military Living's Military RV, Camping and Outdoor Recreation Around the World.*

## WACO SHOPPETTE (TX46R3)

1801 Exchange Parkway
Waco, TX 76712-5000

**TELEPHONE NUMBER INFORMATION:** Main installation numbers: C-254-666-8309.

**LOCATION:** In Waco, exit Hwy 6 west to Bagby Avenue, to AAFES Distribution Center. USMRA: Page 87 (K-4). NMC: Waco, in city limits.

**LOGISTICAL SUPPORT:**       Exchange-666-8309/8466

**ATTRACTIONS:** Dr Pepper Museum, historic Texas sights.

# UTAH

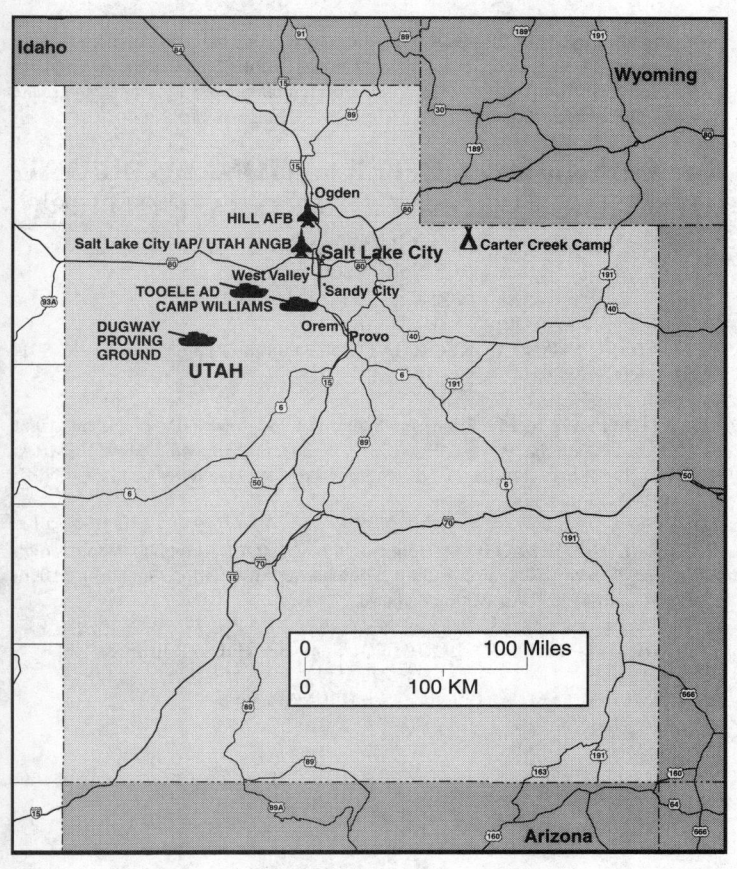

## CAMP W.G. WILLIAMS (UT11R4)

17800 South Camp Williams Road
Riverton, UT 84065-4999

**TELEPHONE NUMBER INFORMATION:** Main installation numbers: C-801-253-5455, D-312-766-5455.
WEB: www.nr.usu.edu/~tvn/campwil/campwil.html

**LOCATION:** From I-15 take exit 294 (Draper/Riverton UT-71). Turn left at UT-68, drive approximately seven miles, and Camp Williams is on the right. USMRA: Page 112 (D-4). NMC: Salt Lake City, 25 miles north.

**GENERAL INFORMATION:** Utah Regional Training Academy. Camp Williams is a National Guard training base.

**TEMPORARY MILITARY LODGING:** Lodging office, Building 802, 1000-1700 Mon-Fri, 1000-1400 Sat-Sun. C-801-253-5410, D-312-766-5410, Fax: C-801-253-9543.

**RV, CAMPING/FAMCAMP:** None. See Hill AFB listing.

**SPACE-A:** None. See Hill AFB listing.

**LOGISTICAL SUPPORT:**
Cafeteria-254-2819           Exchange-576-3815*

**ADMINISTRATIVE SUPPORT:**
Locator-253-5455           Police-253-5455

**HEALTH & WELFARE:**        Medical-576-3871*

**REST & RECREATION:**
Clubs           MWR-253-5401
   NCO-254-2819           Rec Equipment-253-5425
   O-254-7623

* Phone numbers will be changing. Call main installation number for further information.

**OTHER FACILITIES AVAILABLE:** Fitness center.

**ATTRACTIONS:** Salt Lake City: Temple Square, planetarium, Hogle Zoo, Trolley Square for shopping, Delta Center for pro sports. Close to skiing and hiking.

## CARTER CREEK CAMP (UT01R4)

Outdoor Recreation, Bldg 524
Hill AFB, UT 84056-5720

**TELEPHONE NUMBER INFORMATION:** Main installation numbers: C-801-777-7221, D-312-458-1110. Police for camp, C-801-777-3525.

**LOCATION:** Off base. From I-80 near Evanston, WY, take WY/UT-150 south 30 miles to Bear River Service Station, one tenth of a mile to east (left) on Mill Creek RS-7. Approximately four miles to camp on the right side of the road. USMRA: Page 112 (F-3). NMI: Hill AFB, 55 miles west. NMC: Salt Lake City, 105 miles southwest.

**GENERAL INFORMATION:** Operated by Hill AFB, off base, open weekend prior to 4 July through 31 October. Military personnel active, reservists, retired, DoD civilians at Hill AFB. Reservations (required): Outdoor Recreation, Bldg 524, Hill Air Force Base, UT 84056-5000. C-801-777-2225/9666 0800-1700 hours Mon-Fri.

**RV, CAMPING/FAMCAMP:**
Cabins-6           Trailers-3
Camper Spaces-3        Tent Spaces-3

**ATTRACTIONS:** The surroundings of Carter Creek are typical of the Uintah Mountains with lodgepole pines and quaking aspen, a perfect combination of sight and sound. Rustic campsite in mountains reaching heights of 13,500 feet. Fishing lakes and ponds nearby.

*For detailed information about this off-base recreation facility, as well as on-base recreation facilities, golf courses and marinas, consult Military Living's Military RV, Camping and Outdoor Recreation Around the World.*

# DUGWAY PROVING GROUND (UT04R4)

ATTN: STEDP-CO
Building 4142
Dugway Proving Ground, UT 84022-5000

**TELEPHONE NUMBER INFORMATION:** Main installation numbers: C-435-831-2151, D-312-789-2151. *Note: When calling from Salt Lake City the prefix is 522 instead of 831.*

**LOCATION:** Isolated, but can be reached from I-80. Take exit 77 south, UT-196, Skull Valley Road for 40 miles south to Dugway and entrance to Proving Ground. USMRA: Page 112 (B,C-4,5). NMC: Salt Lake City, 80 miles northeast.

**GENERAL INFORMATION:** Major command: Army Materiel, Test and Evaluation Command. Range and evaluation units.

**TEMPORARY MILITARY LODGING:** Lodging office, Building 5228, Valdez Circle, 0730-1845 Mon-Thu, 0700-1545 Fri. C-435-831-2333, D-312-789-2333. All ranks. DV/VIP C-435-831-2020.

**RV, CAMPING/FAMCAMP:** None. See Tooele Army Depot listing, Oquirrh Hills Travel Camp.

**SPACE-A:** None. See Salt Lake City IAP.

**LOGISTICAL SUPPORT:**

| | |
|---|---|
| Carson Wagonlit-831-2131 | Child Care-831-3345 |
| Commissary-831-2164 | Conv Store-831-4773 |
| Exchange-835-4773 | Gas Station-831-4773 |
| Package Store-831-4773 | |

**ADMINISTRATIVE SUPPORT:**

| | |
|---|---|
| Legal-831-3716 | Locator-831-3545/1110 |
| Police-831-2929 | SDO/NCO-831-3870 |

**HEALTH & WELFARE:**

| | |
|---|---|
| Chapel-831-2431 | Family Services-831-2278 |
| Medical-831-2222 | TRICARE-831-3313 |

**REST & RECREATION:**

| | |
|---|---|
| Bowling-831-2687 | Com Club-831-2901 |
| Fitness Center-831-2705 | Library-831-2178 |
| Outdoor Rec-831-2318 | Youth Center-831-2177 |

**ATTRACTIONS:** Great Salt Lake, Salt Lake City, historic Church of Jesus Christ of Latter Day Saints, museums, and skiing. Four national parks within a day's drive.

# HILL AIR FORCE BASE (UT02R4)

7981 Georgia Street
Hill Air Force Base, UT 84056-5824

**TELEPHONE NUMBER INFORMATION:** Main installation numbers: C-801-777-7221, D-312-777-7221 (Operator assistance), C-801-777-1411, D-312-777-1411.

**LOCATION:** Adjacent to I-15 between Ogden and Salt Lake City. From I-15, take exit 334, go north to UT-232 to south gate on South Gate Drive; or exit 338 to west gate. USMRA: Page 112 (D-3). NMI: Tooele Army Depot, 60 miles southwest. NMC: Ogden, eight miles north.

**GENERAL INFORMATION:** Air Force Materiel Command Base, Headquarters Ogden Air Logistics Center and 75th Air Base Wing. Provides engineering and logistics for F-16 Fighting Falcon and C-130 Hercules and Minuteman and Peacekeeper missiles, overhauls and repairs landing gear, brakes, struts and wheels for Air Force aircraft. Also, 388 FW (ACC) and 419 FW (AFRES), both flying F-16.

**TEMPORARY MILITARY LODGING:** Lodging office, Mountain View Inn, Building 146, D Ave, 24 hours daily, C-801-777-1844/0801, D-312-777-1844/0801, Fax: C-801-942-2014. All ranks. DV/VIP: C-801-777-5565.

**RV, CAMPING/FAMCAMP:** Carter Creek Camp, off base weekends prior to Jul 4-Oct 31, Outdoor Recreation, Building 402, C-801-777-2225/9666, six cabins, four trailers, four camper spaces with W/E hookups, three tent spaces. Hill FAMCAMP, on base year round, Outdoor Recreation, 75 Services, C-801-777-3250, D-312-777-3250.

**SPACE-A:** Pax Term/Lounge, Building 900, C-801-777-2887/3088, D-312-777-2887/3088. Fax: C-801-775-2677, D-312-775-2677. Flights to CONUS locations.

**LOGISTICAL SUPPORT:**

| | |
|---|---|
| Bank-773-8000 | Barber Shop-773-4602 |
| Beauty Shop-773-4076 | Car Rental-825-0080 |
| Child Dev Center-777-6321 | Class VI-777-2169 |
| Commissary-777-2300 | Credit Union-778-8705 |
| Dining-777-3428/8161 | Travel-777-4677 |
| Exchange-773-1207 | Gas Station-773-3600 |
| Postal Service-777-3507 | Restaurants-777-2043 |
| Shoppette-773-4673 | Visitor Center-777-7833/8631 |

**ADMINISTRATIVE SUPPORT:**

| | |
|---|---|
| Legal-777-6756 | Locator-777-1841 |
| Police-777-3056 | Public Affairs-777-5201 |

**HEALTH & WELFARE:**

| | |
|---|---|
| Chapel-777-2106 | Medical |
| Family Services-777-4681 |   Central Appts-728-2600 |
| Retiree Services-777-5735 |   Emergency-777-5285 |
| TRICARE-728-2600 |   Hospital-777-6298 |

**REST & RECREATION:**

| | |
|---|---|
| Arts & Crafts-777-2649 | Auto Hobby Shop-777-3476 |
| Bowling-777-6565 | Clubs |
| Community Center-777-3525 |   EM-777-3841 |
| Fitness Center-777-2762/8360 |   O-777-2809 |
| Golf Course-777-3272 | Library-777-3833 |
| Theater-777-2328 | Tickets & Tours-777-3525 |
| Outdoor Rec-777-9666 | Youth Center-777-2419 |

**ATTRACTIONS:** Hill Aerospace Museum, Great Salt Lake and Antelope Island, Bear River Bird Refuge and Golden Spike National Historic Site, Lagoon Amusement Park, nature trail, Dinosaur Park, Union Station, Temple Square, museums, Utah Jazz basketball, planetarium, zoo, Salt Lake City, snow skiing and Park City.

# SALT LAKE CITY INTERNATIONAL AIRPORT/ UTAH AIR NATIONAL GUARD BASE (UT10R4)

151 Air Refueling Wing
765 North 2200 West
Salt Lake City, UT 84116-5000

**TELEPHONE NUMBER INFORMATION:** Main installation numbers: C-801-595-2200, D-312-924-9200.

**LOCATION:** From I-215 north or south take exit 26, go west one block, turn right on McDonnell Douglas Way (2200 West). ANG is on the immediate left. USMRA: Page 112 (D-3), page 116 (B-2). NMC: Salt Lake City, five miles southeast. NMI: Hill AFB, 30 miles south.

**GENERAL INFORMATION:** Home of the 151st Air Refueling Wing, 169th Electronic Security Squadron, 130th Engineering Installation Squadron, 109th Tactical Control Fleet, Air National Guard.

**TEMPORARY MILITARY LODGING:** None. See Hill AFB listing.

**RV, CAMPING/FAMCAMP:** None. See Hill AFB listing.

**SPACE-A:** C-801-595-2274, D-312-924-9274; Rec: C-801-595-2415, D-312-924-9415; Fax: C-801-595-2271, D-312-924-9271.

**LOGISTICAL SUPPORT:**
Car Rental-575-2232                    Exchange-355-1923

**ADMINISTRATIVE SUPPORT:**    Police-595-2410

**HEALTH & WELFARE:**              Medical-595-2337

**REST & RECREATION:**           None. See Hill AFB listing.

**ATTRACTIONS:** Great Salt Lake, Salt Lake City, museums, and skiing. Four national parks within a day's drive.

## TOOELE ARMY DEPOT (UT05R4)
ATTN: SIOTE-CO
Building 1
Tooele, UT 84074-5008

**TELEPHONE NUMBER INFORMATION:** Main installation numbers: C-435-833-2211, D-312-790-2211.

**LOCATION:** From west I-80, exit 99 south, to UT-36 south for about 15 miles to main entrance on right (west) side of UT-36. USMRA: Page 112 (C-4). NMC: Salt Lake City, 40 miles northeast.

**GENERAL INFORMATION:** There are three main missions at Tooele Army Depot (TEAD), a subordinate of the Industrial Operations Command in Rock Island, Illinois. These include Ammunition Operations, Ammunition Equipment Design and Development and Rail Shop Maintenance and on-site support. Additionally the depot provides base operations support to various activities and tenants.

**TEMPORARY MILITARY LODGING:** Lodging office, Building 1, Hq Loop, 0630-1700 daily, C-435-833-2124, D-312-790-2124. All ranks.

**RV, CAMPING/FAMCAMP:** Oquirrh Hills Travel Camp on post, May-Oct, Community and Family Activities, Building 1011, C-435-833-3129, D-312-790-3129, 14 camper spaces with W/E hookups, eight tent spaces.

**SPACE-A:** None. See Hill AFB listing.

**LOGISTICAL SUPPORT:**
Bank-833-2991                          Exchange-833-2394
Package Store-833-2394              SATO-833-3251

**ADMINISTRATIVE SUPPORT:**
Fire Dept-833-2015                     Legal-833-2536
Locator-833-2094                       Police-833-2559
Public Affairs-833-2693               SDO/SNCO-833-2304

**HEALTH & WELFARE:**
ACS-833-2852                           CHAMPUS-1-800-842-4333
Family Services-833-2852            Medical-833-2572
Retiree Services-833-2249            Emergency-833-2666

**REST & RECREATION:**
Arts & Crafts-833-2940               Auto Hobby Shop-833-2873
Bowling-833-9922                       Com Club-833-2582
Gym-833-3189                           ITT-833-3129
MWR-833-2039                          Recreation-833-2039
Sports-833-2005                        Sports Rental-833-2107
Stables-833-3345                       Swimming-833-3189
Theater-833-2582

**ATTRACTIONS:** Salt Lake City nearby, Utah desert, and mountains are available for rock climbing, exploration, camping, motorcycling, hiking, and/or sightseeing.

# VERMONT

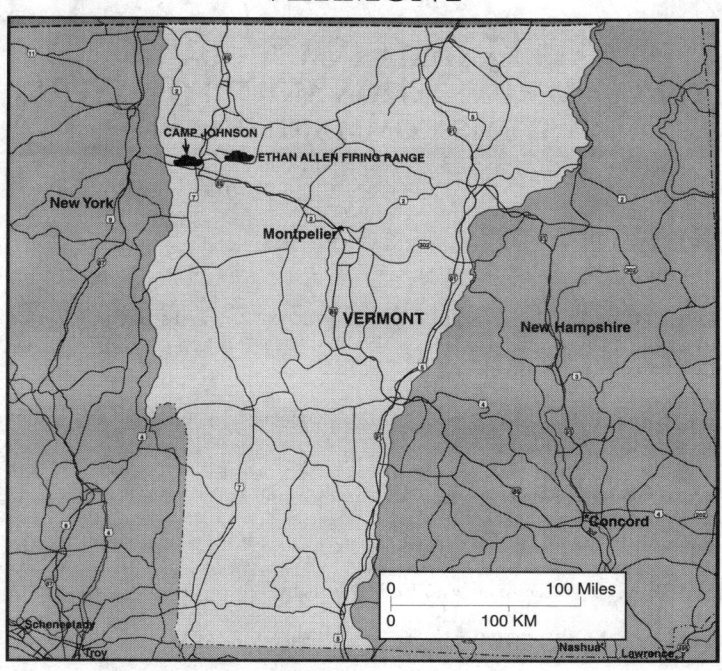

## CAMP JOHNSON (VT01R1)
Green Mountain Armory
Colchester, VT 05446-3006

**TELEPHONE NUMBER INFORMATION:** Main installation numbers: C-802-654-0000, D-312-636-3111. E-mail: mjohnson@vt.arng.ngb.army.mil WEB: www.vtng.com

**LOCATION:** From I-89 north or south, exit 15 east on VT-15 (College Pkwy), approximately two miles to entrance on left. USMRA: Page 23 (A-4).

**GENERAL INFORMATION:** Army National Guard and training site.

**LOGISTICAL SUPPORT:**          Shoppette-655-3030

**ATTRACTIONS:** Beautiful scenery, state parks, water activities at nearby Lake Champlain, city of Burlington.

## ETHAN ALLEN FIRING RANGE (VT02R1)
Rural Route 1, Box 57
Jericho, VT 05465-9706

**TELEPHONE NUMBER INFORMATION:** Main installation numbers: C-802-654-0000, D-312-636-3111. WEB: www.vtng.com

**LOCATION:** I-89 north or south to Route 15 east exit, north of Burlington about one and a half miles on left, just past St. Michael's College. USMRA: Page 23 (B-4). NMC: Burlington, Vermont.

**GENERAL INFORMATION:** Home of 86th BDE, 42ID (Mech); 158th Fighter Wing, 3/172 Mountain Infantry Battalion.

**TEMPORARY MILITARY LODGING:** Regional Training Institute, Lafayette Bldg. (Camp Johnson) C-802-654-0280, D-312-636-3280, Fax: 802-654-0164.

**LOGISTICAL SUPPORT:**
Exchange-899-2811*                   Carlson Wagonlit Travel-654-0219
Shoppette-655-3030
*Only open when units are in field for annual training - approximately eight to ten weeks a year.

**ADMINISTRATIVE SUPPORT:** Public Affairs-654-0246

**ATTRACTIONS:** Beautiful scenery, state parks, nearby Lake Champlain.

# VIRGINIA

## ALEXANDRIA COAST GUARD TELECOMMUNICATION AND INFORMATION SYSTEMS COMMAND (VA44R1)

7323 Telegraph Road
Alexandria, VA 22315-3940

**TELEPHONE NUMBER INFORMATION:** Main installation number: C-703-313-5400.

**LOCATION:** Take I-95/I-495 to Telegraph Road exit 2. Travel south on Telegraph Road four miles to base on left (east). USMRA: Page 47 (M-5). NMC: Washington, D.C. 15 miles northeast.

**GENERAL INFORMATION:** TISCOM, Ceremonial Honor Guard, Navigation Systems Center.

**TEMPORARY MILITARY LODGING:** None. See Fort Belvoir listing.

**RV, CAMPING/FAMCAMP:** None. See Quantico MCB listing, Lunga Park.

**SPACE-A:** None. See Andrews AFB, MD listing.

| | |
|---|---|
| **LOGISTICAL SUPPORT:** | Exchange-313-5992 |
| **ADMINISTRATIVE SUPPORT:** | Personnel-313-5431 |
| **HEALTH & WELFARE:** | Medical-313-5446 |

**REST & RECREATION:**

| | |
|---|---|
| Anchorage Club-313-5990 | Auto Hobby Shop-ext 5994 |
| Picnic Grounds-ext 5987 | Rec Equipment-ext 5797 |

**ATTRACTIONS:** Mount Vernon, Old Town Alexandria, Washington, D.C.

## ARMED FORCES HOSTESS ASSOCIATION (VA52R1)

Room 1A736 Pentagon
6604 Army Pentagon, Washington, D.C. 20310-6604

**TELEPHONE NUMBER INFORMATION:** Main installation numbers: C-703-697-3180/6857, D-312-227-6857, Fax: C-703-693-9510.

**LOCATION:** From I-395 north or south or Columbia Pike (VA-244) exit to South Parking. North Parking accessible from Boundary Channel Drive, exit from I-395 south. Visitor parking entrance is from Boundary Channel Drive and is paid parking. Bus, METRO, and taxi service from Concourse. USMRA: Page 54 (E-5). NMC: Washington, D.C., adjacent..

**GENERAL INFORMATION:** Volunteer association providing information about the area. Located in Pentagon. See Pentagon listing for support services.

## ARMED FORCES STAFF COLLEGE (VA48R1)

7800 Hampton Boulevard
Norfolk, VA 23511-1702

**TELEPHONE NUMBER INFORMATION:** Main installation numbers: C-757-444-0000, D-312-564-5150.

**LOCATION:** From I-64 east to I-564 to Terminal Boulevard. Armed Forces Staff College will be on the corner of Terminal and Hampton Boulevard. USMRA: Page 52 (F-6). NMC: Norfolk, in city limits. NMI: Norfolk Naval Base, two miles north.

**GENERAL INFORMATION:** Armed Forces Staff College.

**TEMPORARY MILITARY LODGING:** Building SC 407. C-757-444-0000, D-312-564-5311. Officers only.

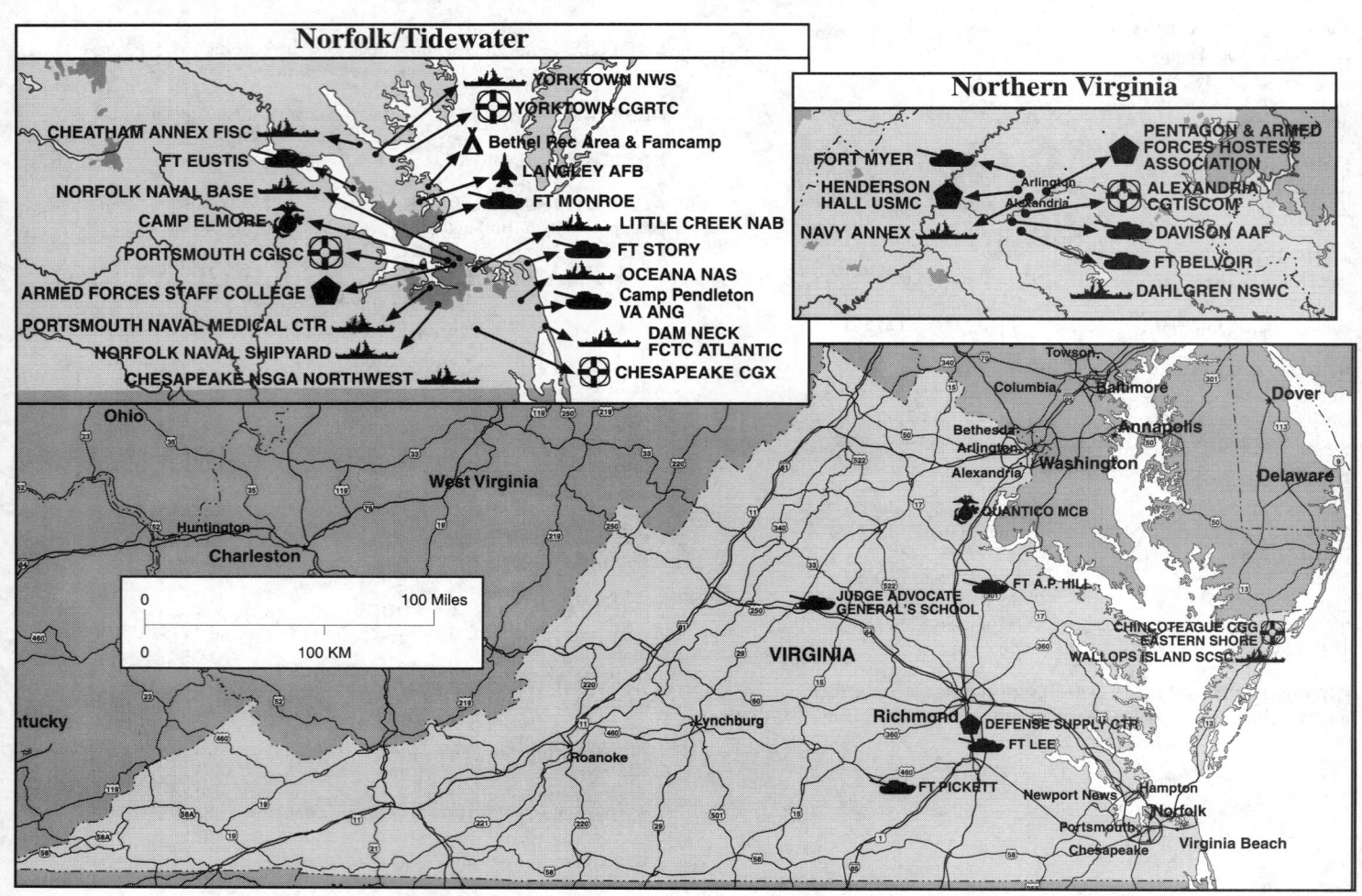

**RV, CAMPING/FAMCAMP:** None. See Little Creek NAB listing.

**SPACE-A:** None. See Norfolk NB listing, C-757-444-4118/4148/3947 or 445-6538, D-312-564-4118/4148/3947 or 565-6538; Fax: C-757-445-7501, D-312-565-7501.

**LOGISTICAL SUPPORT:**
Shoppette (Marianas Hall)-440-2070    Exchange-440-2000
   Snack Bar-423-4713

**ADMINISTRATIVE SUPPORT:**    Police-444-5255

**HEALTH & WELFARE:**
Chapel-444-5650    Family Services-444-5183

**REST & RECREATION:**
Fitness Center-ext 1198    Library-ext 5155
MWR-444-5327    O Club-423-4713
Rec Equip Rental-ext 5443    Youth Activities-ext 5443

**ATTRACTIONS:** Virginia Beach nearby, entertainment and restaurants.

## BETHEL RECREATION AREA PARK & FAMCAMP (VA22R1)
123 Saunders Road
Hampton, VA 23665-5000

**TELEPHONE NUMBER INFORMATION:** Main installation numbers: C-757-764-9990, D-312-574-1110.

**LOCATION:** From I-64 take exit 261A (Hampton Roads Center Pkwy). Go approximately 0.2 miles to a right on Big Bethel Road. For FAMCAMP go about 2.5 miles to Saunders Road (third light); turn left at 7-11 store. Entrance on right. For Bethel Park, instead of turning on Saunders Road, continue straight on Big Bethel Road for approximately 300 yards; park entrance will be on left before crossing bridge over reservoir. USMRA: Page 47 (N-9), page 52 (D-3). NMI: Langley AFB, five miles southeast. NMC: Hampton, seven miles south.

**GENERAL INFORMATION:** Operated by Langley AFB, off base. FAMCAMP is open February-December. The Park is closed October-April and the fishing area is closed December-January. The Park and fishing areas are open four days a week in summer and the fishing area is open on weekends only in the fall, winter and early spring. Military personnel active, reservists, retired, DoD civilians. Reservations (required for covered pavilions): C-757-764-7170. RV camping: Bethel Recreation Area - Park & FAMCAMP, 1 SVS/SVRO, 123 Saunders Road, Hampton, VA 23665-5000. C-757-766-3017 Park, C-757-766-7627 FAMCAMP. For information, C-757-764-7170/6510 Outdoor Recreation.

**RV, CAMPING/FAMCAMP:**
Camper Spaces-20    Tent Spaces-10

**ATTRACTIONS:** Situated in a beautiful lake setting at the border of York County and Hampton. Historical areas are nearby.

*For detailed information about this off-base recreation facility, as well as on-base recreation facilities, golf courses and marinas, consult Military Living's Military RV, Camping and Outdoor Recreation Around the World.*

## CAMP ELMORE (VA45R1)
1251 Yalu Street
Norfolk, VA 23515-4693

**TELEPHONE NUMBER INFORMATION:** Main installation numbers: C-757-423-1187, D-312-565-6672.

**LOCATION:** From I-64 east take I-564. Take Terminal Boulevard exit, at first light, right on Diven Stret, at left fork take Fechteler Street. Camp is 2.5 blocks on the right. USMRA: Page 52 (F-5,6). NMC: Norfolk, in city limits. NMI: Norfolk Naval Base, two miles north.

**GENERAL INFORMATION:** Marine Corps Exchange site.

**LOGISTICAL SUPPORT:**
Convenience Store-423-7165    Exchange-423-1187
Gas Station-423-1539

**ATTRACTIONS:** Hampton Roads Naval Museum, Gardens by the Sea, MacArthur Memorial, Williamsburg, nearby Virginia Beach, City of Norfolk and waterside downtown Norfolk.

## CAMP PENDLETON VIRGINIA ARMY NATIONAL GUARD (VA50R1)
P.O. Box 9
Virginia Beach, VA 23458-5000

**TELEPHONE NUMBER INFORMATION:** Main installation numbers: C-757-491-5140. Fax: C-757-491-5152.
**LOCATION:** Camp Pendleton is north of Dam Neck Fleet Combat Training Center, and south of Virginia Beach. Go south across the bridge from Virginia Beach on General Booth Blvd to Birdneck Road, turn left. Gate is on left. USMRA: Page 52 (J-7). NMC: Virginia Beach, in city limits.

**GENERAL INFORMATION:** Administered by Fort Pickett on what is now a state military reservation, cottages year round, trailers close in winter. Military personnel all ranks, leave or duty. Reservations: write Camp Pendleton Virginia Army National Guard, P.O. Box 9, Virginia Beach, VA 23458-5000 or call C-757-491-5140.

**TEMPORARY MILITARY LODGING:**
Cottages-5    Trailers-6

**ATTRACTIONS:** Situated one mile from the beach, nearby Virginia Beach activities.

*For detailed information about this lodging facility, as well as other lodging facilities, consult Military Living's Temporary Military Lodging Around the World.*

## CHEATHAM ANNEX FLEET AND INDUSTRIAL SUPPLY CENTER (VA02R1)
108 Sanda Avenue
Williamsburg, VA 23187-8792

**TELEPHONE NUMBER INFORMATION:** Main installation numbers: C-757-887-4000, D-312-953-4000.

**LOCATION:** From I-64 east or west take exit 242B northeast to US-199 east to main gate of Cheatham Annex. USMRA: Page 47 (N-8). NMC: Williamsburg, six miles west.

**GENERAL INFORMATION:** Annex of Norfolk Fleet and Industrial Supply Center, Depot activity for Naval supplies and other special programs.

**TEMPORARY MILITARY LODGING:** Lodging office, MWR, Building 284, 0700-1530 Mon-Fri, C-757-887-7224/7101, D-312-953-7224/7101. All ranks. DV/VIP C-757-887-7108.

**RV, CAMPING/FAMCAMP:** Recreation Cabins and RV Park, on base, year round, 108 Sanda Avenue, Williamsburg, VA 23185-8792, C-757-887-7224, D-312-953-7224. Nineteen camper spaces with full hookups, 12 cabins.

**SPACE-A:** None. See Norfolk NB listing.

**LOGISTICAL SUPPORT:**
Conv Store-887-3582    Exchange-887-3582
Gas Station-887-3582

**ADMINISTRATIVE SUPPORT:**
Police-887-7222    SDO/NCO-887-7222

**HEALTH & WELFARE:**    Medical-887-7222

**REST & RECREATION:**
Auto Hobby Shop-ext 7418
ITT-887-7101
Swimming-887-7102

Golf-887-7159/7101
MWR-887-7101
Services-887-7418

**ATTRACTIONS:** Historic Williamsburg, Jamestown, and Yorktown are nearby. Water Country USA, Busch Gardens, Mariners' Museum, and Virginia Living Museum within 30 minutes. Paramount's King's Dominion is 75 minutes away.

## CHESAPEAKE COAST GUARD EXCHANGE (VA49R1)
1430 Kristina Way
Chesapeake, VA 23326-1000

**TELEPHONE NUMBER INFORMATION:** Main installation numbers: C-757-523-6002.

**LOCATION:** From 64 east or west, take Greenbriar Parkway south, turn right onto Eden Way, right onto Kristina Way. USMRA: Page 52 (G-8). NMC: Norfolk, five miles north.

**LOGISTICAL SUPPORT:**          Exchange-523-6002

**ATTRACTIONS:** Casemate Museum at Fort Monroe, Portsmouth Naval Shipyard Museum, Mariners' Museum, Nauticus Marine Museum, and Busch Gardens and Williamsburg are nearby.

## CHESAPEAKE NAVAL SECURITY GROUP ACTIVITY, NORTHWEST (VA42R1)
1320 Northwest Boulevard, Suite 100
Chesapeake, VA 23322-4094

**TELEPHONE NUMBER INFORMATION:** Main installation numbers: C-757-421-8000, D-312-564-1336.

**LOCATION:** Five miles west of VA-168 at NC/VA border, turn right onto Ballahack Road and follow to base gate (a left on Relay Road). Located between Moyock, NC and Great Bridge, VA. USMRA: Page 47 (N,O-10). NMC: Norfolk, 35 miles north.

**GENERAL INFORMATION:** Naval Security Group and Communications Activity.

**TEMPORARY MILITARY LODGING:** BEQ/BOQ C-757-421-8282/8283, D-312-564-1336, DV/VIP C-757-421-8331, D-312-564-1336, Fax: C-757-421-8235.

**RV, CAMPING/FAMCAMP:** Stewart Campground, on base, 1 May-1 December, C-757-421-8264, Fax: C-757-421-8785. Eighteen camper spaces with E hookups.

**SPACE-A:** None. See Norfolk NB listing.

**LOGISTICAL SUPPORT:**
Barber Shop-421-8234
Conv Store-421-8254
Education Center-421-8217
Gas Station-421-8252
Postal Service-421-8259
Snack Bar-421-8250

Child Care-421-8266
Dining Facilities-421-8276
Exchange-421-8254
Package Store-421-8252
SATO-440-9530

**ADMINISTRATIVE SUPPORT:**
CDO/OOD-421-8000
Legal-421-8375
Public Affairs-421-8328

Fire Dept-421-8244
Police-421-8334

**HEALTH & WELFARE:**
American Red Cross-446-7700
Dental-421-8225
Medical-421-8220
TRICARE-1-800-931-9501

Chapel-421-8204
Family Services-421-8770
Navy-MC Relief-421-8204

**REST & RECREATION:**
Bowling Center-421-8267          Clubs-CPO-421-8290

Gym-421-8303
Fitness Center-421-8263
MWR-421-8260

EM-421-8250
O-421-8285
Swimming-421-8268

**ATTRACTIONS:** Casemate Museum at Fort Monroe, Portsmouth Naval Shipyard Museum, Mariners' Museum, Nauticus Marine Museum, and Busch Gardens and Williamsburg are nearby.

## CHINCOTEAGUE COAST GUARD GROUP - EASTERN SHORE (VA47R1)
3823 S Main Street
Chincoteague, VA 23336-1510

**TELEPHONE NUMBER INFORMATION:** Main installation numbers: C-757-336-2840.

**LOCATION:** From Washington, D.C. Beltway (I-495), turn right on Route 50 to Route 13. Turn onto Route 175 off Hwy 13. Take Route 175 to Chincoteague Island. After crossing bridge turn right at stop light. Go approximately one third of a mile and base will be on right. USMRA: Page 47 (P-7). NMC: Salisbury, MD.

**GENERAL INFORMATION:** Part of the Fifth District, U.S. Coast Guard.

**LOGISTICAL SUPPORT:**
Exchange-336-2848          Dining-336-2820

**ADMINISTRATIVE SUPPORT:**
CDO/OOD-336-2855
Pass/ID Office-336-2850/51

Housing Office-336-2897/2807
Public Affairs-336-2890

**ATTRACTIONS:** Chincoteague National Wildlife Refuge, Assateague Island, National Seashore, Kiptopeke State Park, VA; Shad Landing State Park, MD.

## DAHLGREN NAVAL SURFACE WARFARE CENTER (VA06R1)
17320 Dahlgren Road
Dahlgren, VA 22448-5100

**TELEPHONE NUMBER INFORMATION:** Main installation numbers: C-540-653-8291, D-312-249-8291.

**LOCATION:** From I-95 in Fredericksburg, east on VA-3 to VA-206 (17 miles), left at Arnold's Corner, east to Dahlgren (11 miles). Also US-301 south to VA-206, east to main gate of Center. USMRA: Page 47 (M-6). NMC: Washington, D.C., 38 miles north.

**GENERAL INFORMATION:** Naval Surface Weapons RDT&E Center.

**TEMPORARY MILITARY LODGING:** Lodging office, Building 960, 24 hours daily, C-540-653-7671, D-312-249-7671. All ranks. DV/VIP C-540-653-8153.

**RV, CAMPING/FAMCAMP:** None. See Fort A.P. Hill Recreation Facilities.

**SPACE-A:** None. See Andrews AFB, MD listing.

**LOGISTICAL SUPPORT:**
Cafeteria-653-3841
Commissary-653-7318
Gas Station-653-2050
SATO-653-0074

Child Care-653-4994
Exchange-663-2121
Gen Mess-653-8277
Snack Bar-653-2720

**ADMINISTRATIVE SUPPORT:**
Fire Dept-911
Locator-653-8216
Public Affairs-653-8153

Legal-653-7121
Police-653-8500
SDO/NCO-653-8531

**HEALTH & WELFARE:**
CHAMPUS-653-8241
Family Services-653-1839
Retiree Services-653-1839

Chapel-653-8297
Medical-653-8241

**REST & RECREATION:**

| | |
|---|---|
| Bowling-653-7327 | Clubs |
| Golf Course-653-3002 | EM-653-8785 |
| Gym-653-8580 | ITT-653-8785 |
| Library-653-7474 | MWR-653-7777 |
| Recreation-653-7777 | Rec Equip-653-8585 |
| Swimming-653-8088 | Tennis-653-8580 |
| Theater-653-7777 | |

**ATTRACTIONS:** Center is on the Potomac River. Washington, D.C., easy drive.

## DAM NECK FLEET COMBAT TRAINING CENTER, ATLANTIC (VA25R1)
### 1912 Regulus Avenue
### Virginia Beach, VA 23461-2098

**TELEPHONE NUMBER INFORMATION:** Main installation numbers: C-757-444-0000, D-312-433-0000. E-mail: fctclant.n1@smtp.cnet.navy.mil.

**LOCATION:** Route 44 East to exit 8 (Birdneck Road), turn right and follow to General Booth Blvd. Turn right and follow to Dam Neck Road. Turn left and follow to main gate. USMRA: Page 47 (O-9,10), page 52 (J-7,8). NMC: Virginia Beach, four miles north northwest.

**GENERAL INFORMATION:** Fleet Combat Training Center with major tenant commands. Navy and Marine Corps Intelligence Training Center, Naval Surface Warfare Center, Port Hueneme Division, East Coast Office, Naval Processing Facility and Tactical Training Group Atlantic.

**TEMPORARY MILITARY LODGING:** BEQ: C-757-492-6468, D-312-492-6468, Fax: C-757-492-6228; BOQ: C-757-492-7011. Navy Lodge: C-757-437-8100 or 1-800-NAVY-INN.

**RV, CAMPING/FAMCAMP:** Sea Mist Campground C-757-492-7545 or D-312-492-7545.

**SPACE-A:** None. See Oceana NAS listing.

**LOGISTICAL SUPPORT:**

| | |
|---|---|
| Child Dev Center-492-8683 | Conv Store-492-7749 |
| Exchange-492-6496 | Gas Station-492-7794 |

**ADMINISTRATIVE SUPPORT:**

| | |
|---|---|
| CDO-433-2366 | Housing Office-433-3101 |
| Locator-492-6000 | Police-433-2833 |

**HEALTH & WELFARE:**

| | |
|---|---|
| Chapel-492-6602 | Medical-314-7204 |

**REST & RECREATION:**

| | |
|---|---|
| Beaches-492-7028 | Bowling-492-6341 |
| Clubs- | Community Center-492-6233 |
|   Beach Club-492-6146 | Fitness Center-492-7185 |
|   EM-492-6146 | Golf-433-2866 |
|   O-492-8354 | MWR-492-6264 |
| Swimming-ext 6551 | |

**ATTRACTIONS:** Virginia Beach, water activities. Close to Norfolk, Williamsburg.

## DAVISON ARMY AIRFIELD (VA23R1)
### 6970 Britten Drive
### Fort Belvoir, VA 22060-5133

**TELEPHONE NUMBER INFORMATION:** Main installation numbers: C-703-806-7225, D-312-656-7225. WEB: www.belvoir.army.mil

**LOCATION:** From I-95 north and US-1 north or south take Fort Belvoir exits. Signs clearly mark support facilities. Gate is off Fairfax County Parkway on Britten Drive. USMRA: Page 47 (L,M-5). NMC: Washington, D.C., 10 miles northeast.

**GENERAL INFORMATION:** Part of Fort Belvoir. See Fort Belvoir listing for full support facilities.

**SPACE-A:** C-703-806-7224/7682, D-312-656-7224/7682. Fax: C-703-806-7538, D-312-656-7538.

**ATTRACTIONS:** Washington, D.C., Smithsonian Institution, Mount Vernon, Old Town Alexandria, Air & Space Museum, Arlington National Cemetery, and historic Georgetown.

## DEFENSE SUPPLY CENTER (VA30R1)
### 8000 Jefferson Davis Highway
### Richmond, VA 23297-5100

**TELEPHONE NUMBER INFORMATION:** Main installation numbers: C-804-279-3861, D-312-695-3861.

**LOCATION:** From I-95 north or south (Richmond-Petersburg Turnpike) exit 64 or 67 west to US-1/301. Clearly marked on west side of US-1/301, main gate Dwight Avenue. USMRA: Page 47 (L-8). NMC: Richmond, eight miles north.

**GENERAL INFORMATION:** A Defense Logistics Agency Field Level Activity.

**TEMPORARY MILITARY LODGING:** C-804-279-3371, D-312-695-4198, Fax: C-804-279-6419, D-312-695-6419.

**RV, CAMPING/FAMCAMP:** None. See Fort Pickett listing.

**SPACE-A:** None. See Langley AFB listing.

**LOGISTICAL SUPPORT:**

| | |
|---|---|
| Barber Shop-279-3553 | Cafeteria-271-9497 |
| Class VI-279-1498 | Conv Store-275-2654 |
| Child Care-279-6694 | Commissary-279-3904 |
| Exchange-279-2654 | Gas Station-279-1478 |
| Postal Service-279-3013 | Shoppette-279-3904 |
| Snack Bar-279-3572 | Travel Office-279-5774 |
| Visitor's Center-279-3139 | |

**ADMINISTRATIVE SUPPORT:**

| | |
|---|---|
| Fire Dept-279-3630 | Housing Office-279-5411 |
| Legal-279-4811 | Locator-279-3861 |
| OOD-279-3803 | Pass/ID Office-279-4888 |
| Police-279-4888 | Public Affairs-279-3139 |
| SDO/NCO-279-3805 | |

**HEALTH & WELFARE:**

| | |
|---|---|
| CHAMPUS-279-3821 | Medical-279-3821 |

**REST & RECREATION:**

| | |
|---|---|
| Fitness Center-279-4198 | Gym-279-4198 |
| Indoor Rec-279-4198 | O Club-279-3772 |
| Outdoor Rec-279-4198 | MWR-279-3371 |

**ATTRACTIONS:** Historic Richmond short drive north, Edgar Allen Poe Museum, First White House of the Confederacy. Museum of the Confederacy, Virginia Museum of Fine Arts, Science Museum of Virginia, St. John's Church, King's Dominion and Busch Gardens amusement parks, and various Civil War battlefields.

## FORT A.P. HILL (VA17R1)
### ATTN: AFKA-FHA-PA
### Bowling Green, VA 22427-5000

**TELEPHONE NUMBER INFORMATION:** Main installation numbers: C-804-633-8760, D-312-934-8760.

**LOCATION:** From I-95 north or south, take Bowling Green/Fort A.P. Hill exit 126. US-17 (bypass) east to VA-2 south to Bowling Green, take VA-301 northeast to main gate. Or take exit 104 from I-95 to VA-207 north to VA-301 north and to main gate. USMRA: Page 47 (L,M-6,7). NMC: Fredericksburg, 14 miles northwest.

**GENERAL INFORMATION:** Army Active, Reserve and ANG Training Center, Marine, Navy, Air Force Reserve Officer Training Corps, and other Civilian Organizations.

**TEMPORARY MILITARY LODGING:** Lodging office, Building P00179, 0800-1630 Sat-Thu, 0800-2300 Fri. C-804-633-8335, D-312-578-8335. All ranks. DV/VIP C-804-633-8205.

**RV, CAMPING/FAMCAMP:** A.P. Hill Recreation Facilities, on post year round, Commander, U.S. Army Garrison, ATTN: Morale Support Activities Division, C-804-633-8219, D-312-934-8219. The Lodge, four log cabins.

**SPACE-A:** Extremely limited. C-804-633-8335.

**LOGISTICAL SUPPORT:**

| | |
|---|---|
| Exchange-633-8690 | Snack Bar-633-8690 |

**ADMINISTRATIVE SUPPORT:**

| | |
|---|---|
| CDO/OOD-633-8206 | Fire Dept-633-8317 |
| Locator-633-8372 | Police-633-8425 |
| Public Affairs-633-8324/8120 | |

**HEALTH & WELFARE:**

| | |
|---|---|
| Chaplain-633-8311 | Family Services-633-8201 |
| Medical-633-8339 | |

**REST & RECREATION:**

| | |
|---|---|
| EM/Com Club-633-8378 | MWR-633-8219 |
| Recreation-633-8219 | |

**OTHER FACILITIES AVAILABLE:** Rec center, pool, hunting, skeet range, fishing, golf driving range.

**ATTRACTIONS:** Nearby historic Fredericksburg and Civil War battlefields.

# FORT BELVOIR (VA12R1)
ATTN: ANFB-GC
9820 Flagler, Suite 201
Fort Belvoir, VA 22060-5932

**TELEPHONE NUMBER INFORMATION:** Main installation numbers: C-703-545-6700, D-312-227-0101. E-mail: carrdona@belvoir.army.mil
WEB: www.belvoir.army.mil

**LOCATION:** From Washington, D.C., take I-95 South to Belvoir/Newington exit 166. Turn right, connect with the southern leg of Fairfax County Pkwy. Take Pkwy to the end at Richmond Highway. Turn left. At the first light, Tulley Gate is on right. At second light, Pence Gate (main entrance) is to the right. Visitor Center is just inside Pence Gate. USMRA: Page 47 (L,M-5), page 55 (B,C-8). NMC: Washington, D.C., 10 miles northeast. NMI: Fort Myer/Pentagon, 15 miles from base.

**GENERAL INFORMATION:** Defense Systems Management College, Defense Mapping School, Army Management Staff College and support units.

**TEMPORARY MILITARY LODGING:** Lodging office, Building 470, 24 hours daily, C-703-805-2333 or 1-800-295-9750, D-312-655-2333, Fax: C-703-805-3566. All ranks. DV/VIP C-703-805-2333.

**RV, CAMPING/FAMCAMP:** None. Large Rec area planned for the future. See Andrews Air Force Base, MD.

**SPACE-A:** Davison Army Airfield, Building 1327, 0730-1600 daily, C-703-806-7224/7682, D-312-656-7224/7682, Fax: C-703-806-7538. Flights to CONUS locations.

**LOGISTICAL SUPPORT:**

| | |
|---|---|
| Bank-838-3381 | Barber Shop-799-4975 |
| Beauty Shop-780-6600 | Car Rental-781-0480 |
| Carlson Wagonlit Travel-799-5680 | Child Care-806-4344/6540 |
| Class Six-806-6674 | Commissary-806-6371/6674 |
| Credit Union-551-0001/730-1800 | Conv Store-805-5155 |
| Dining Facilities-806-5198 | Dry Cleaner-780-0088 |
| Education Center-806-3113/4032 | Exchange-805-5800/01/02 |
| Food Court-806-5808 | Gas Station-806-4581 |
| Gas Station North-806-5488 | Laundry-781-9809 |
| SATO-799-5680/3400 | Snack Bar-805-3069 |
| Shoppette-805-5154 (South Post) | Visitor Center-805-4152 |
| North Post-806-5263 | |

**ADMINISTRATIVE SUPPORT:**

| | |
|---|---|
| Fire Dept-805-1107/781-1800 | Housing Office-805-2914 |
| Legal-805-4018/2857 | Locator-805-2043/3101 |
| Pass/ID Office-805-4429/3405 | Police (Security)-805-1104 |
| Public Affairs-805-5001 | SDO/NCO-805-3101 |

**HEALTH & WELFARE:**

| | |
|---|---|
| ACS-805-3436 | Army Emergency Relief-805-2277 |
| CHAMPUS-805-0166/0644 | Chapel-805-2742/4316/17 |
| Dental-Clinic-806-4392 | Family Services-805-2908 |
| Medical-Clinic-806-4586/805-0979 | Retiree Services-805-5571/1037 |
|   Central Appts-805-0612 | TRICARE-805-0058 |
|   Emergency-805-0510 | Veterinary Services-805-2368/4336 |
|   Hospital-805-0510 | |

**REST & RECREATION:**

| | |
|---|---|
| Arts & Crafts-806-4647 | Auto Hobby Shop-806-4655 |
| Bowling-805-3068 | Clubs-EM-780-0962 |
| Community Center-805-3714 |   NCO-780-0962 |
| Fitness Center-806-5369/3100 |   O-780-0930 |
| Golf Course-806-5878/4043 | Gym-806-3057/5369 |
| ITR-805-3715/16 | Library-806-3323 |
| Marina-805-3745 | MWR-805-2350 |
| Outdoor Recreation-805-3714 | Picnic Area-805-3781 |
| Rec Center-805-3714 | Rec Equip-805-2378 |
| Swimming-805-2620 | Tennis-805-2538 |
| Theater-806-5237 | Wildlife Refuge-806-4007 |
| Youth Center-805-4605 | |

**ATTRACTIONS:** Washington, D.C., Smithsonian Institution, Mount Vernon, Old Town Alexandria, Air & Space Museum, Arlington National Cemetery, and historic Georgetown.

# FORT EUSTIS (VA10R1)
ATTN: ATZF-GC
Building 213
Fort Eustis, VA 23604-5015

**TELEPHONE NUMBER INFORMATION:** Main installation numbers: C-757-878-1110, D-312-927-1110.

**LOCATION:** From I-64 east or west, exit 250A to VA-105, west to Fort Eustis. USMRA: Page 47 (N-9), page 52 (B,C-2,3). NMC: Newport News, 13 miles southwest.

**GENERAL INFORMATION:** Army Transportation Center.

**TEMPORARY MILITARY LODGING:** Lodging office, Building 2110, Pershing Avenue, 24 hours daily, C-757-878-5807, D-312-927-5807. All ranks. DV/VIP C-757-878-6030.

**RV, CAMPING/FAMCAMP:** None. See Langley AFB listing, Bethel Park Rec Area.

**SPACE-A:** None. See Langley AFB listing.

**LOGISTICAL SUPPORT:**

| | |
|---|---|
| Child Care-878-3794 | Commissary-878-5966 |
| Conv Store-887-0882 | Class VI-887-0882 |
| Credit Union-877-2444 | Dining-878-5346 |
| Exchange-887-0293 | Gas Station-887-0392 |
| Shoppette-887-0882 | Snack Bar-887-0494 |
| Travel-878-5577 | |

**ADMINISTRATIVE SUPPORT:**

| | |
|---|---|
| Fire Dept-878-4281 | Legal-878-2205 |
| Locator-878-5215 | Police-878-4554 |
| Public Affairs-878-4920 | SDO/NCO-878-5050 |

**HEALTH & WELFARE:**

ACS-878-3638
Chapel-878-1304/1317
Medical-314-7511
  Emergency-314-7675

CHAMPUS-878-7861
Family Services-878-3638
Retiree Services-878-2953
TRICARE-677-6000

**REST & RECREATION:**

Auto Hobby Shop-ext 5440
Clubs
  Consol-887-5700
  Flying-ext 3722
  Saddle-ext 2835
Library-ext 5017
MWR-878-3694/3285
Swimming-ext 5544
Theater-878-3436

Bowling-ext 5482
Go-Cart Track-ext 5883
Golf Course-878-2965
Gym-ext 4380
ITT-878-3694
Marina-ext 2610
Skeet Range-ext 5822
Tennis-ext 2097
Youth Activities-ext 4448

**ATTRACTIONS:** On the James River, historic Williamsburg nearby, Busch Gardens, Water Country USA, U.S. Transportation Museum (free), Mariners' Museum, Nauticus, and the Virginia Air & Space Center.

# FORT LEE (VA15R1)

USACASCOM & Fort Lee
ATTN: ATZM-G
1100 Lee Avenue
Fort Lee, VA 23801-1720

**TELEPHONE NUMBER INFORMATION:** Main installation numbers: C-804-765-3000, D-312-539-3000.

**LOCATION:** From I-95 north or south take Fort Lee/Hopewell exit 52 east, and follow VA-36 to main gate on right (south). USMRA: Page 47 (L-8). NMC: Petersburg, three miles west.

**GENERAL INFORMATION:** Combined Arms Support Command, Quartermaster Center and School, Defense Commissary Agency, Army Logistics Management College, Army Information Systems Software Development Center-Lee, and reserve units.

**TEMPORARY MILITARY LODGING:** Lodging office, Building P-8025, Mahone Avenue, 24 hours daily, C-804-733-4100, D-312-687-6698. All ranks.

**RV, CAMPING/FAMCAMP:** None. See Fort Pickett listing.

**SPACE-A:** None. See Langley AFB listing.

**LOGISTICAL SUPPORT:**

Bank-862-4785
Carlson Wagonlit Travel-733-1460
Commissary-765-2260
Dining-734-7471
Fast Food-733-3839
Package Store-861-3297
Snack Bar-734-6861

Cafeteria-861-6480
Child Care-765-3765
Conv Store-861-3297
Exchange-861-5970
Gas Station-861-6621
Shoppette-861-3297
Visitor Center-734-4547

**ADMINISTRATIVE SUPPORT:**

Fire Dept-734-7031
Locator-734-6855
Public Affairs-734-4547

Legal-765-1500
Police-734-7400
SDO/NCO-734-7993

**HEALTH & WELFARE:**

ACS-734-7955
Chapel-734-1187
Medical-734-9000
  Central Appts-765-3400/734-9166
  Emergency-734-9269

CHAMPUS-734-9448
Family Services-734-6388
Retiree Services-734-6973

**REST & RECREATION:**

Arts & Crafts-734-6858
Bowling-734-6860
Fitness Center-765-3070
Golf Course-734-1228
Gym-765-3635

Auto Hobby Shop-734-6859
Clubs
  Leisure-765-2651
  O-734-7545
  Rod/Gun-765-2210

Live Theater-734-6630/2611
Music Center-734-6623
Rec Equip-734-2212
Swimming-734-6747

MWR-724-7195
Recreation-765-2212
Riding Club-734-6396
Youth Center-765-3763

**ATTRACTIONS:** Quartermaster Museum, Petersburg National Battlefield Park, Colonial Williamsburg, Richmond's Virginia and Poe Museums and Monument Avenue; Petersburg's Blandford Church and Cemetery and Trapezium House, Colonial Heights' Lee Headquarters (Violet Bank), and Hopewell's Appomattox Manor.

# FORT MONROE (VA13R1)

ATTN: ATZG-CO
Headquarters, Building 77
Fort Monroe, VA 23651-6000

**TELEPHONE NUMBER INFORMATION:** Main installation numbers: C-757-727-2111, D-312-680-2111. WEB: www-tradoc.monroe.army.mil

**LOCATION:** From I-64 east or west, exit at 268 east and follow VA-143 to tour signs through Phoebus to fort. USMRA: Page 47 (N-9), page 52 (F-4). NMC: Hampton, one mile north.

**GENERAL INFORMATION:** Headquarters Army Training & Doctrine Command, U.S. Army Reserve Officers' Training Corps (ROTC) Cadet Command, Joint Warfighting Center, Mobility Concepts Agency, Naval Surface Weapons Center, Continental Army Band, and support units.

**TEMPORARY MILITARY LODGING:** Lodging office, Building 80, Ingalls Road, 0800-1645, Mon-Fri, C-757-727-2128, D-312-680-2128. All ranks.

**RV, CAMPING/FAMCAMP:** "The Colonies" Travel Park on post, year round, ATTN: MCECC, P.O. Box 51106, Fenwick Road, Fort Monroe, VA 23651-6144, C-757-727-2384, D-312-680-2384, 13 camper spaces with full hookups.

**SPACE-A:** None. See Langley AFB listing.

**LOGISTICAL SUPPORT:**

Bank-727-3495, 728-1272
Beauty Shop-722-3714
Carlson Wagonlit Travel-727-0427
Class Six-722-0794
Credit Union-722-1626
Dry Cleaner-723-9285
Exchange-722-0794
Snack Bar-722-0794

Barber Shop-722-3604
Car Rental-727-0427
Child Care-727-2855
Commissary-727-3326/4178
Dining Facilities-727-2334
Education Office-728-5853
Postal Service-722-6267
Travel Office-727-0427

**ADMINISTRATIVE SUPPORT:**

CDO-727-2238
Housing Office-727-2127/2129
Locator-727-2000
Police-727-2238
SDO/NCO-727-2256

Fire Dept-727-2422
Legal-727-3616
Pass/ID Office-727-3175/2960
Public Affairs-727-3205

**HEALTH & WELFARE:**

American Red Cross-764-2652
Army Emergency Relief-727-4132
Chapel-727-2611/4157
Family Services-727-3993
Retiree Services-727-2093
TRICARE-1-800-931-9501
Veterinary services-727-2623

ACS-727-3878
CHAMPUS-1-800-931-9501
Dental-314-8060
Medical
  Central Appts-1-800-931-9501
  Clinic-314-8023
  Emergency-727-2840
  Health Benefits-314-8023
  Information-727-3305

**REST & RECREATION:**

Arts & Crafts-727-2728
Bowling-727-2939
Fishing/Boating-727-4308
Gym-727-2783
Library-727-2909
MWR-727-3737
Services-727-2650
Theater-727-2793

Auto Hobby Shop 727-2311
Consol Club-727-2406
Fitness Center-727-3090
Indoor Rec-727-3302
Marinas-727-4308
Outdoor Rec-727-4305
Swimming-727-4181
Wood Hobby Shop-727-3594

Youth Center-727-3957      Youth Services-727-3957

**ATTRACTIONS:** Williamsburg, Jamestown, Norfolk, Casemate Museum.

## FORT MYER (VA24R1)
ATTN: ANMY-GC
204 Lee Avenue
Fort Myer, VA 22211-5050

**TELEPHONE NUMBER INFORMATION:** Main installation numbers: C-703-696-3250, D-312-426-3250. E-mail: Christensenn@fmmc.army.mil WEB: www.fmmc.army.mil

**LOCATION:** Adjacent to Arlington National Cemetery. Take Fort Myer exit US-258 south from Washington Blvd at 2nd Street, or enter from US-50 (Arlington Blvd) first gate. Also exit from Boundary Drive to 12th Street North entrance near the Iwo Jima Memorial. USMRA: Page 54 (E-5). NMC: Washington, D.C., one mile northeast.

**GENERAL INFORMATION:** Headquarters Command Fort Myer, Headquarters 3rd Infantry (Old Guard), Headquarters U.S. Army Band, and support units.

**TEMPORARY MILITARY LODGING:** Lodging office, Building T-49, Jackson Street, 24 hours daily, C-703-696-3576, D-312-426-3576. All ranks. DV/VIP C-703-696-7051.

**RV, CAMPING/FAMCAMP:** None. See Quantico MCB listing, Lunga Park.

**SPACE-A:** None. See Andrews AFB, MD listing.

**LOGISTICAL SUPPORT:**
| | |
|---|---|
| Child Care-696-3095 | Commissary-696-3674 |
| Consol Club-527-1300 | Exchange-522-4575 |
| Gas Station-522-2584 | Snack Bar-528-4855 |

**ADMINISTRATIVE SUPPORT:**
| | |
|---|---|
| Fire Dept-696-3483 | Legal-696-0761 |
| Locator-475-2005 | Police-696-3525 |
| Public Affairs-696-3944 | SDO/NCO-696-2974 |

**HEALTH & WELFARE:**
| | |
|---|---|
| ACS-696-3510 | CHAMPUS-696-3656 |
| Chapel-696-3532 | Medical-696-3476 |
| Retiree Services-696-5948 | |

**REST & RECREATION:**
| | |
|---|---|
| Arts & Crafts-696-3470 | Auto Hobby Shop-696-3387 |
| Bowling-528-4767 | Clubs |
| Community Center-696-3470 |   NCO-527-1300 |
| Fitness Center-696-7867 |   O-524-7000 |
| MWR-696-8864 | Library-696-3555 |
| Museum-696-6670 | Recreation-696-8849 |
| Swimming-696-1300 | Youth Activities-696-3728 |

**ATTRACTIONS:** Arlington National Cemetery, Tomb of the Unknown Soldier, barracks and activities of the Old Guard, Old Guard Museum, Iwo Jima Memorial, Netherlands Carillon, Washington, D.C.

## FORT PICKETT (VA16R1)
ATTN: VAFP-PA
Building 472, Military Road
Blackstone, VA 23824-9000

**TELEPHONE NUMBER INFORMATION:** Main installation numbers: C-804-292-2722, D-312-438-2722.

**LOCATION:** On US-460, one mile from Blackstone. From I-95 north or south, exit 27 north on VA-46 to Blackstone and gate. Clearly marked. USMRA: Page 47 (K-9). NMI: Fort Lee, 45 miles northeast. NMC: Petersburg, 40 miles northeast.

**GENERAL INFORMATION:** Provides and maintains maneuver and training areas that reflect current doctrine of the active and reserve components of the Army and other military services. Controlled and operated by the Virginia Army National Guard.

**TEMPORARY MILITARY LODGING:** Lodging office, Building T-469, Military Road, 0730-1600 duty days, C-804-292-2443, D-312-438-2443. All ranks.

**RV, CAMPING/FAMCAMP:** Pickett Travel Camp, on post year round, Commander, MTC, ATTN: VAFP-2 Building T-469, Military Road, Fort Pickett, Blackstone, VA 23824-9000, C-804-292-2443, D-312-438-2443, Fax: C-804-292-8617, 15 Pegram camper spaces with full hookups, six tent spaces.

**SPACE-A:** None. See Langley AFB listing.

**LOGISTICAL SUPPORT:**
| | |
|---|---|
| Barber Shop-292-2783 | Exchange-292-8680 |
| Gas Station-292-3491 | Package Store-292-8680 |

**ADMINISTRATIVE SUPPORT:**
| | |
|---|---|
| Fire Dept-292-2217 | Housing Office-292-2443 |
| Locator-292-2306 | Pass/ID Office-292-2306 |
| Police-292-8444 | |

**HEALTH & WELFARE:**
| | |
|---|---|
| CHAMPUS-292-2528 | Chapel-292-2601 |
| Medical-292-2528 | Retiree Services-292-2306 |

**REST & RECREATION:**
| | |
|---|---|
| Bowling-292-1182 | Com Club-292-2336 |
| Crafts-292-2616 | Gym-292-8626 |
| Hunting/Fishing-292-2618 | MWR-292-2613 |
| Outdoor Rec-292-2618 | Sports-292-8626 |
| Swimming-292-8538 | Theater-292-8466/298-0585 |

**OTHER FACILITIES AVAILABLE:** Racquetball courts.

**ATTRACTIONS:** Dollhouse Museum, Petersburg Civil War Battlefields, Appomattox Court House National Historic Park.

## FORT STORY (VA08R1)
ATTN: ATZF-FS
Building 300
Fort Story, VA 23459-5001

**TELEPHONE NUMBER INFORMATION:** Main installation numbers: C-757-422-7305, D-312-438-7305.

**LOCATION:** From the south exit of Chesapeake Bay Bridge Tunnel (US-13), east on US-60 (Atlantic Avenue) to Fort Story. Clearly marked. From I-64 take US-60 east. From VA-44 (Norfolk-VA Beach Expressway) exit US-58, turn left, North Atlantic Avenue (US-60) to 89th Street to Fort Story. USMRA: Page 47 (O-9), page 52 (I,J-5,6). NMC: Virginia Beach, three miles south.

**GENERAL INFORMATION:** Sub-Installation of Fort Eustis. Army Transportation Units, Test Activity, Army Logistics, and Over-the-Shore Training & Test Site.

**TEMPORARY MILITARY LODGING:** All ranks. DV/VIP, Fort Eustis, C-757-878-5206, D-312-927-5206/5207.

**RV, CAMPING/FAMCAMP:** Cape Henry Travel Camp, on post, year round, ATTN: Travel Camp, Fort Story, VA 23459-5034, C-757-422-7601, D-312-438-7601, 13 log cabins, three Kamping Kabins. Also Cape Henry Inn on post year round. Military personnel active, retired, reserve and DoD civilians. Reservations: C-757-422-8818. Fax: C-757-422-6397. Bungalows near Fort Story center, built in 1942, spacious; most have two TVs, screened-in front/back porches, most are close to the fishing beach, but no water view, ground level.

**SPACE-A:** None. See Norfolk NB listing.

**LOGISTICAL SUPPORT:**
| | |
|---|---|
| Barber Shop-422-7027 | Child Care-422-7413 |
| Child Dev Center-422-7413 | Class Six-422-7863 |
| Conv Store-428-7071 | Credit Union-425-0241 |
| Dry Cleaner-422-7622 | Exchange-422-7858 |

Gas Station-428-7071
Postal Service-422-7816
Snack Bar-422-7458
Visitor Center-425-0001

Mini Mall-425-0001
Shoppette-422-7071
Travel Office-422-7101 ext 240

**ADMINISTRATIVE SUPPORT:**

Fire Dept-422-7456
Legal-878-3031
Pass/ID Office-422-7834
Public Affairs-422-7755 ext.230

Housing Office-442-7510
Locator-422-7682
Police-422-7141
SDO/SNO-422-7101 ext. 227

**HEALTH & WELFARE:**

American Red Cross-462-7581
Army Emergency Relief-422-7311
Chapel-422-7552/7665
Medical-422-7822/7851
Veterinary Services-422-7734

ACS-422-7311
CHAMPUS-1-800-990-8272
Family Services-422-7311
TRICARE-1-800-990-8272

**REST & RECREATION:**

Auto Craft Shop-422-7713
Community Center-422-7558
Gym-422-7975/7052
ITT-422-7472
MWR-878-3102
Rec Center-ext 7472
Sports-422-7052
Theater-422-7555

Bowling-422-7458
Fort Story Club-425-6631
Indoor Rec-422-7472
Library-422-7548
Outdoor Rec-422-7601
Rec Equip-422-7472
Tennis-422-7975
Youth Center-422-7714

**ATTRACTIONS:** City of Virginia Beach and resort beaches nearby. See the Cross at Cape Henry (located on Fort Story), site of the first stop of English settlers in the USA, and the Old Cape Henry Lighthouse, a registered Historical Landmark.

# HENDERSON HALL USMC (VA21R1)

1555 South Southgate Road, Building 29
Arlington, VA 22214-5000

**TELEPHONE NUMBER INFORMATION:** Main installation numbers: C-703-694-1235, D-312-224-1235.

**LOCATION:** From Columbia Pike, VA-244, exit to South Orme Street, Sheraton National Hotel at corner, west to dead end, left to main gate. Also, from Memorial Drive (VA-27) exit to Columbia Pike, first traffic light right onto Southgate Road, enter gate straight ahead. USMRA: Page 54 (E-5). NMC: Washington, D.C., one mile northeast.

**GENERAL INFORMATION:** Headquarters Battalion USMC, HQMC and support units. Provides support to personnel at HQMC (Navy Annex across the street).

**TEMPORARY MILITARY LODGING:** None. See Fort Myer listing.

**RV, CAMPING/FAMCAMP:** None. See Andrews AFB, MD listing.

**SPACE-A:** None. See Andrews AFB, MD listing.

**LOGISTICAL SUPPORT:**

Child Care-607-7281
Exchange-979-8420

Conv Store-979-8420 ext 107
Package Store-979-8420

**ADMINISTRATIVE SUPPORT:**

Legal-614-3800
Police-614-2200
Relocation Assistance-614-7202

Pass/ID Office-614-2013
Public Affairs-614-8958
SDO/NCO-746-0950

**HEALTH & WELFARE:**

Chapel-614-9280
Medical-614-1229

Family Services-614-7200/01

**REST & RECREATION:**

EM Club-614-2125/5830
ITT-979-4011
Swimming-695-7691

Gym-607-8463
Rec Equip-687-2706

**ATTRACTIONS:** Adjacent to Arlington National Cemetery and Pentagon. Iwo Jima Memorial, Netherlands Carillon, Kennedy Center for the Performing Arts, Lincoln Memorial, Washington, D.C. with its many sights, museums and galleries.

# JUDGE ADVOCATE GENERAL'S SCHOOL (VA01R1)

600 Massie Road
Charlottesville, VA 22903-1781

**TELEPHONE NUMBER INFORMATION:** Main installation numbers: C-804-972-6300, D-312-934-6300.

**LOCATION:** On the grounds of the University of Virginia in Charlottesville. Take the 250 bypass off I-64 to the Baracks Road exit southeast. Take right at first light onto Milmont Street, first right onto Arlington Blvd, at the three-way stop sign turn right into the parking lot. USMRA: Page 47 (J-7). NMC: Charlottesville, in city limits.

**GENERAL INFORMATION:** Army Judge Advocate General's School.

**TEMPORARY MILITARY LODGING:** Lodging office, room 156, 0750-1650 Mon-Fri, C-804-972-6450.

**RV, CAMPING/FAMCAMP:** None. See Fort A.P. Hill listing.

**SPACE-A:** None. See Andrews AFB, MD listing.

**LOGISTICAL SUPPORT:**

Exchange-972-6324

Snack Bar-972-6324

**ADMINISTRATIVE SUPPORT:**

Housing Office-972-6334
Pass/ID Office-972-6300

Locator-972-6325
SDO-972-6300

**HEALTH & WELFARE:**

CHAMPUS-972-6336

**REST & RECREATION:** All the facilities of the University of Virginia, with special permission.

**ATTRACTIONS:** Historic University of Virginia, and city of Charlottesville.

# LANGLEY AIR FORCE BASE (VA07R1)

159 Sweeney Boulevard, Suite 100
Langley Air Force Base, VA 23665-2292

**TELEPHONE NUMBER INFORMATION:** Main installation numbers: C-757-764-9990, D-312-574-1110.

**LOCATION:** From I-64 east or west in Hampton take Armistead Avenue exit 205B northeast, keep right to stop light; right into LaSalle Avenue and enter AFB. USMRA: Page 47 (N-9). NMC: Hampton, one mile west.

**GENERAL INFORMATION:** Air Combat Command Base. Headquarters Air Combat Command, Headquarters Air Division Air Combat Command, 1st Fighter Wing, and support units.

**TEMPORARY MILITARY LODGING:** Lodging office, Building 75, Nealy Avenue, 24 hours daily, C-757-764-4667, D-312-574-4667. All ranks. DV/VIP C-757-764-3467.

**RV, CAMPING/FAMCAMP:** Bethel Park Rec Area, off base, 1235 Saunders Road, Hampton, VA 23666 C- 757-766-3017, D-312-574-7170. Camper spaces now available.

**SPACE-A:** Pax Term/Lounge, Building 371, 0600-1800 Mon-Fri. C-757-764-4311, D-312-574-4311. Fax: C-757-764-3722. Flights to CONUS locations.

**LOGISTICAL SUPPORT:**

Bank-873-7816
Beauty Shop-766-1283
Child Dev Center-764-3585
Commissary-766-1304
Credit Union-827-7200

Barber Shop-766-1805
Child Care-764-3449
Class Six-766-1330
Conv Store-766-1249
Dining Facilities-764-3694

Dry Cleaner-766-1287
Exchange-766-1253
Laundry-766-1288
SATO-766-5890
Travel Office-764-2292

Education Office-764-2962
Gas Station-766-1286
Postal Service-764-3136
Shoppette-766-1249
Visitor Center-764-4169

**ADMINISTRATIVE SUPPORT:**
Fire Dept-764-7717
Legal-764-3277
Pass/ID Office-764-7770
Public Affairs-764-2018

Housing Office-764-5048
Locator-764-5615
Police-764-2000

**HEALTH & WELFARE:**
Air Force Aid Society-764-3990
CHAMPUS-764-6987
Dental-764-7611
Medical
   Central Appts-677-6000
   Emergency-764-6801
   Health Benefits-764-6987
   Hospital-764-6833
   Information-764-6833

American Red Cross-764-2652
Chapel-764-7847
Family Services-764-3390
Retiree Services-764-7386
TRICARE-677-6000
Veterinary Services-764-5678

**REST & RECREATION:**
Arts & Crafts-764-4647
Bowling-7642433
Eagle Park-764-5792
Golf Course-764-4547
Gym-764-5791
ITT-764-2983
Library-865-2906
Marinas-764-7220
MWR-764-3999
Rec Center-764-7175
Services-764-7881
Theater-764-2580
Youth Center-764-2300

Auto Hobby Shop-764-4607
Clubs
   Flying-764-7486
   NCO-766-3550
   O-766-1361
   Rifle-764-2312
   Scuba-764-2312
   Skeet-764-3769
Outdoor Rec-764-7170
Rec Equip-764-4616
Swimming-764-5791
Wood Hobby Shop-764-3978
Youth Services-764-4343

**ATTRACTIONS:** Virginia Tidewater area, Norfolk nearby. Great fishing, beaches, and water sports.

## LITTLE CREEK NAVAL AMPHIBIOUS BASE (VA19R1)

2600 Tarawa Court, Suite 107
Norfolk, VA 23521-2438

**TELEPHONE NUMBER INFORMATION:** Main installation numbers: C-757-462-7000, C-757-462-7782, D-312-253-7000.

**LOCATION:** From I-64 north or south to exit US-60 to base. From Chesapeake Bay Bridge/Tunnel US-60 west to base. USMRA: Page 47 (N,O-9), page 52 (G,H-5,6). NMC: Norfolk, 11 miles southwest.

**GENERAL INFORMATION:** Expeditionary Warfare Training Group Atlantic, Special Warfare Group Atlantic, and homeport for approximately 30 ships.

**TEMPORARY MILITARY LODGING:** Lodging office, 24 hours daily, Building 3408 (BOQ) C-757-462-7522/3; Building 3601 (BEQ) C-757-462-7577/8601. Navy Lodge, Building 3531, C-757-464-6215. Fax: C-757-464-1194. All ranks. DV/VIP: C-757-462-5901, Fax: C-757-462-8635.

**RV, CAMPING/FAMCAMP:** MWR RV Park on base, year round, C-757-462-7282, D-312-253-7282, 45 camper spaces with W/E hookups, 6 tent spaces.

**SPACE-A:** None See Norfolk NAS listing.

**LOGISTICAL SUPPORT:**
Child Care-462-7868
Conv Store-462-3090
Exchange-462-3218
Gas Station-462-3119
Snack Bar-462-2663

Commissary-462-3561/2
Credit Union-480-1777
Galley-462-7546
SATO-462-2392

**ADMINISTRATIVE SUPPORT:**
Legal-462-7331
Police-462-7438
SDO/NCO-462-7385

Locator-462-7226
Public Affairs-462-7923

**HEALTH & WELFARE:**
CHAMPUS-462-8189
Family Services-462-7563

Chapel-462-7427/9
Medical-462-7850/7793
   Central Appts-462-1100
   Emergency-462-7850

**REST & RECREATION:**
Auto Hobby Shop-462-7339
Boats/Campers-462-7516
Clubs
   CPO-462-7789
   EM-462-7949
   O-460-1111
Library-462-7998
MWR Dir-462-7282
Rec Equip-462-7735
Tennis-462-8118

Ballet/Slimnastic Classes-462-7665
Bowling-462-7952
Ceramics Hobby-462-7998
Golf-462-8526
Gym-462-4821
ITT-462-7665
Marina-462-7516
Picnic Area-462-7369
Swimming-462-8139
Wood Hobby Shop-462-7605

**ATTRACTIONS:** Water sports, beaches, fishing, Norfolk, Virginia Beach.

## NAVY ANNEX & QUARTERS K (VA53R1)

Department of Navy, Chief of Naval Personnel
Washington, D.C. 20371-0500

**TELEPHONE NUMBER INFORMATION:** Main installation numbers: C-703-614-2000, D-313-224-2000.

**LOCATION:** In Arlington, VA, at Columbia Pike (VA-244) and Arlington Ridge Road (between Sheraton Hotel and Pentagon). USMRA: Page 54 (E-5). NMC: Washington, D.C., one mile east.

**GENERAL INFORMATION:** Chief of Naval personnel, department of Navy. Provides support to personnel at HQMC. For other support services see listing for Henderson Hall.

**LOGISTICAL SUPPORT:**
Barber Shop-614-2393
Credit Union-255-8030
Dry Cleaners-979-1813
Gas Station-979-3891

Convenience Store-979-3891
Cafeteria-892-0428
Florist-521-4058
Postal Service-614-2049

**HEALTH & WELFARE:**
Chapel-612-5630
Medical-614-2726

Dental-614-1229

**OTHER SUPPORT & FACILITIES AVAILABLE:** Pharmacy annex, uniform shop.

**ATTRACTIONS:** Across from Henderson Hall, adjacent to Arlington National Cemetery and Pentagon. Iwo Jima Memorial, Netherlands Carillon, Kennedy Center for the Performing Arts, Lincoln Memorial, Washington, D.C. with its many sights, museums and galleries.

## NORFOLK NAVAL BASE (VA18R1)

1530 Gilbert Street, Bldg. N-26, Suite 2200
Norfolk, VA 23511-5000

**TELEPHONE NUMBER INFORMATION:** Main installation numbers: C-757-444-0000, D-312-564-0000. E-mail: mpkessler@cmar.navy.mil WEB: cmar.navy.mil

**LOCATION:** From north take I-64 east, Naval Base exit 276 for I-564 northwest, follow signs. From south take I-64 exit I-564 northwest to Gate 3A. USMRA: Page 52 (F-5,6). NMC: Norfolk, in city limits.

**GENERAL INFORMATION:** CINC Atlantic Fleet, SACLANT (NATO), FMF Atlantic, Surface and Submarine Forces Atlantic, Air Forces Atlantic, Armed Forces Staff College, and the world's largest Naval Base comprised of Norfolk NAS, Norfolk Naval Station, Naval Computer and Telecommunications Area Master Station Atlantic, Fleet Industrial Supply Center, and Camp Elmore Marine Corps Base.

**TEMPORARY MILITARY LODGING:** Lodging office, Building R-63 (BEH), 0730-1600 Mon-Fri, C-757-444-4425, Fax: C-757-444-0797. Building A-128 (BOH), 24 hours daily, C-757-402-4444, Fax: C-757-445-9888. Navy Lodge, 24 hours daily, C-757-489-2656. All ranks. DV/VIP C-757-444-6323, Navy C-757-402-4401.

**RV, CAMPING/FAMCAMP:** None. See Little Creek NAB listing.

**SPACE-A:** Norfolk Naval Air Station, Naval Air Terminal, Code 053, 8449 Air Cargo Road, Bldg LP-84, Norfolk Naval Air Station, VA 23511-4497. C-757-444-4118/4148/3947 or 445-6538, D-312-564-4118/4148/3947 or 565-6538; Fax: C-757-445-7501, D-312-565-7501. AMC Terminal is three miles from Gate 4 off Patrol Road on A-Term Road, Bldg LP-84, flights to CONUS, OCONUS and foreign locations.

**LOGISTICAL SUPPORT:**
Bank-489-0037
Car Rental-855-1944
Commissary-423-8286
Dining-489-0422
Gas Station-440-2141/2269
SATO-440-0621
Visitor Center-444-7955
Cafeteria-423-8267
Child Care-444-3379
Conv Store-440-2321
Exchange-440-2214
Package Store-440-2119
Snack Bar-440-2114

**ADMINISTRATIVE SUPPORT:**
CDO/OOD-322-2866
Housing Office-445-4591/4694
Locator-444-0000
Public Affairs-322-2853
SDO/NCO-322-2866
Fire Dept-444-3333
Legal-444-4497
Police-444-2324
Quarter Deck-322-2866

**HEALTH & WELFARE:**
Chapel-444-7361
Medical-677-6291
  Central Appts-667-6000
  Emergency-677-6290
Veterinary Clinic-445-0922
Family Services-444-2102
Navy-MC Relief-423-8830
Retiree Services-444-2102
TRICARE-677-6000

**REST & RECREATION:**
Arts & Crafts-444-3846
Bowling-444-2178/4398
Fishing-444-4392
Golf Course-444-5572/5267
Gym-444-2276/4016
Indoor Pool-444-2134
Library-444-2888
Outdoor Rec-444-4388
Rec Equip-444-5448
Rec Park-444-2536
Theater-440-5304
Auto Hobby Shop-444-8159
Clubs
  CPO-444-2125
  EM-440-5483
  O-444-0773
ITT-444-6663
MWR-444-3670
Rec Center-444-0897
Rec Office-444-7218/2276
Sailing-444-2918
Youth Services-444-4033

**ATTRACTIONS:** Largest naval base in the world. Local attractions include: Hampton Roads Naval Museum, Gardens by the Sea, MacArthur Memorial, Williamsburg, City of Norfolk, and Waterside Downtown Norfolk.

## NORFOLK NAVAL SHIPYARD (VA26R1)
Code 1160, Building 5000
Portsmouth, VA 23709-5000

**TELEPHONE NUMBER INFORMATION:** Main installation numbers: C-757-396-3000, D-312-961-3000.

**LOCATION:** From I-264 in Portsmouth exit on 5 south on US-17 or on Effingham Street south to enter the Shipyard. USMRA: Page 52 (F-7). NMC: Portsmouth, in city limits.

**GENERAL INFORMATION:** World's largest shipyard devoted exclusively to warship repair work.

**TEMPORARY MILITARY LODGING:** Lodging office, 24 hours daily, Building 1504A, C-757-396-4449, D-312-961-4449, Fax: C-757-396-4968. All ranks. Chesapeake Inn, Building 1530, C-757-398-8500. DV/VIP C-757-396-8605.

**RV, CAMPING/FAMCAMP:** None. See Chesapeake NSGA, NW.

**SPACE-A:** None. See Norfolk NB listing.

**LOGISTICAL SUPPORT:**
Child Care-396-5863
Exchange-397-2220
Package Store-396-6100
Snack Bar-397-2220
Commissary-393-6309
Gas Station-397-4319
SATO-398-0636

**ADMINISTRATIVE SUPPORT:**
Legal-396-8625
Police-396-7266
SDO/NCO-396-3221
Locator-396-3000
Public Affairs-396-9550

**HEALTH & WELFARE:**
CHAMPUS-398-5100
Medical-468-1871
  Ambulance-396-3678
  Central Appts-396-3226
Chapel-396-5021
Retiree Services-396-4484

**REST & RECREATION:**
Athletic Facilities-396-3845/3835
Consol Club-396-5054
ITT-396-7539
MWR Office-396-3835
Swimming-396-3835
Bowling-396-3808/7051
Gym-396-3845
Library-444-1571
Pool Tables-396-3835

**ATTRACTIONS:** Virginia Beach nearby. Tidewater outdoor sports. Naval Shipyard Museum, Mariners' Museum, college sports, Triple-A baseball.

## OCEANA NAVAL AIR STATION (VA09R1)
1750 Tomcat Boulevard
Virginia Beach, VA 23460-2191

**TELEPHONE NUMBER INFORMATION:** Main installation numbers: C-757-444-0000, D-312-433-2000. E-mail: tsnead@series2000.com
WEB: oceana-navy.com

**LOCATION:** From I-64 east or west exit to Norfolk-Virginia Beach Expressway (VA-44 E), east on Virginia Beach Boulevard. Bordered by Oceana Boulevard (VA-615) and London Bridge Road. Also bordered by Potters and Harpers Roads. USMRA: Page 47 (O-9), page 52 (I,J-7). NMC: Virginia Beach, in city limits.

**GENERAL INFORMATION:** Home to all F-14 Tomcats and A-6 Intruders on the East Coast. Headquarters for Commander Fighter Wing, U.S. Atlantic Fleet, and Commander Attack Wing, U.S. Atlantic Fleet.

**TEMPORARY MILITARY LODGING:** Lodging office, Building 460, 24 hours daily, C-757-433-2574, D-312-423-3293. Fax: C-757-422-0173.

**RV, CAMPING/FAMCAMP:** None. See Chesapeake NSGA, NW.

**SPACE-A:** Pax Term/Lounge, Building 100, 24 hours daily, C-757-433-2903/2260, D-312-433-2903/2260. Fax: C-757-433-2711, D-312-433-2711. Unscheduled flights to CONUS locations.

**LOGISTICAL SUPPORT:**
Bank-473-2834
Child Care-433-3164
Commissary-428-2931
Credit Union-491-2354
Education Center-433-3129
Gas Station-425-4282
SATO-422-0487
Shoppette-425-4200
Barber-425-4255
Child Dev Center-433-3164
Conv Store-491-4267
Dining-425-4200
Exchange-425-4200
Package Store-433-2840
Snack Bar-425-4200

**ADMINISTRATIVE SUPPORT:**
Fire Dept-433-2407
Legal-433-2223
Pass/ID Office-433-3212
Public Affairs-433-3131
Housing Office-433-2195
Locator-433-2367
Police-433-2224
Q-Deck-433-2366

**HEALTH & WELFARE:**
CHAMPUS-433-3328
Family Services-433-2912
Chapel-433-2871
Medical-677-7000

Dental Clinic-314-7197
  Central Appts-314-7190
    Emergency-314-6516
Health Benefits Advisor-314-7129

Central Appts C-1-800-931-9501
  Emergency-433-2221
  Information-314-7135
Family Services-433-2912

**REST & RECREATION:**

Athletic/Rec Office-ext-2695
Bowling-433-2167
Fishing Boat/Campers-ext 3215
Fitness Center-433-2049
Golf-433-2588
Gym-433-2695
ITT-433-3301
MWR-433-2560-
Picnic Area-ext-3381
Skeet/Trap ext-2875
Stables-433-3266
Youth Center-433-3976

Auto Hobby Shop-ext-3403
Clubs
  EM-433-2112
  CPO-433-2637
  O-428-0036
Indoor Rec-433-2786
Library-433-2401
Outdoor Rec-433-2786
Rifle/Pistol ext-2875
Spec Services-ext-3381
Swimming Office-433-3285
Youth Services-433-3976

**ATTRACTIONS:** Virginia Beach, resort beaches, and entertainment nearby.

# PENTAGON (VA41R1)

Room 2E 765
Washington, D.C. 20301-5000

**TELEPHONE NUMBER INFORMATION:** Main installation numbers: C-703-545-6700, D-312-227-0101.

**LOCATION:** From I-395 north or south, exit to South Parking, or from Columbia Pike (VA-244) exit to South Parking. North Parking accessible from Boundary Channel Drive, exit from I-395 S. Visitor parking entrance is from Boundary Channel Drive and is paid parking. Due to tightened security, River and Mall entrances accessible only by walking from other parking areas. Bus, METRO, taxi from Concourse. Concourse and all entrances have directions posted to support facilities. USMRA: Page 54 (E-5), page 55 (B-4). NMC: Washington, D.C., adjacent.

**GENERAL INFORMATION:** Headquarters Department of Defense, Joint Chiefs of Staff and the military departments. The world's largest office building, 17.5 miles of corridors, employing about 27,000 people.

**TEMPORARY MILITARY LODGING:** None. See Fort Myer listing.

**RV, CAMPING/FAMCAMP:** None. See Quantico MCB listing, Lunga Park.

**SPACE-A:** None. See Andrews AFB, MD listing.

**LOGISTICAL SUPPORT:**

Bank-769-6040
Convenience Store-979-3891
Gas Station-979-3891
Snack Bar-695-2886

Carlson Wagonlit Travel 979-5500
Credit Union-683-7787
MCSS-695-7637

**ADMINISTRATIVE SUPPORT:**

Legal-USAF-695-2450
Legal-USN-695-1332

Legal-USA-697-3170

**HEALTH & WELFARE:**

CHAMPUS-695-3597
Medical
  Clinic AF-697-4598
  Clinic AR-697-6594
  Clinic-civ-697-0850

Chapel-695-3336

**REST & RECREATION:**

Athletic Center 521-5020
Library 695-5346
Rec Services
  USA-697-3816
  USAF 697-9866

ITT-AR-697-3816
MWR-695-5338
Ski Club 697-9866

**OTHER FACILITIES AVAILABLE:** Armed Forces Hostesses Association, Room 1A736, 697-6857/3180, volunteers, info on the area.

**ATTRACTIONS:** The Pentagon guided one-hour tour is an exciting tourist attraction (office on Concourse). Free tours leave approximately every 30 minutes, 695-1776. Great military art on the corridor walls and in Hall of Heroes (Medal of Honor winners).

# PORTSMOUTH COAST GUARD INTEGRATED SUPPORT COMMAND (VA43R1)

4000 Coast Guard Boulevard
Portsmouth, VA 23703-2199

**TELEPHONE NUMBER INFORMATION:** Main installation numbers: C-757-483-8586, D-312-483-8532.

**LOCATION:** From I-664 exit 9 take VA-164 east toward Portsmouth. Exit Cedar Lane, turn right. left at first intersection onto West Norfolk Road. Left on Coast Guard Blvd, to gate. USMRA: Page 47 (N-9), page 52 (E-6). NMC: Norfolk, eight miles southeast.

**TEMPORARY MILITARY LODGING:** None. See Norfolk NB listing, (BEH) C-757-444-2839, Fax: C-757-444-0797; (BOQ) C-757-402-4444, Fax: C-757-445-9888. Navy Lodge, C-757-489-2656. Reservations: C-1-800-NAVY-INN. DV/VIP, C-757-402-4401.

**RV, CAMPING/FAMCAMP:** None. See Little Creek NAB listing.

**SPACE-A:** None. See Norfolk NB listing.

**LOGISTICAL SUPPORT:**

Barber Shop-483-8614
Credit Union-483-6393
Dry Cleaner-483-8576
SATO-686-3010

Conv Store-483-8615
Dining Facilities-483-8539
Exchange-483-8615/8612

**ADMINISTRATIVE SUPPORT:**

CDO/OOD-483-8428
Public Affairs-483-4020

Police-483-8586

**HEALTH & WELFARE:**

CHAMPUS-483-8462
Medical-483-8596

Chapel-483-8699

**REST & RECREATION:**

All Hands Club-483-8535
Gym-483-8532
Recreation-483-8671

Auto Hobby Shop-483-8685
MWR-483-8532

**OTHER FACILITIES AVAILABLE:** Pool, tennis court.

**ATTRACTIONS:** Tours: Portsmouth Harbor, MacArthur Memorial, Naval Museums.

# PORTSMOUTH NAVAL MEDICAL CENTER (VA27R1)

620 John Paul Jones Circle
Portsmouth, VA 23708-5100

**TELEPHONE NUMBER INFORMATION:** Main installation numbers: C-757-398-5008, D-312-564-0111. WEB: www-nmcp.med.navy.mil

**LOCATION:** Off I-264 east or west in Portsmouth, take Effingham Street exit to medical center. USMRA: Page 52 (F-7). NMC: Norfolk, two miles north.

**GENERAL INFORMATION:** The oldest medical center in the Navy; providing continuous medical care since 1830. One of four major teaching hospitals in the Navy. Supports the entire Tidewater area. Undergoing major construction/renovation project through year 2003 to add parking garage, support facilities, BEQs, and large replacement hospital.

**TEMPORARY MILITARY LODGING:** BEQ: C-757-953-7756.

**RV, CAMPING/FAMCAMP:** None. See Little Creek NAB listing.

**SPACE-A:** None. See Norfolk NB listing.

**LOGISTICAL SUPPORT:**

| | |
|---|---|
| Barber Shop-397-2662 | Cafeteria-953-5564 |
| Credit Union-397-1123 | Education Center-953-7853 |
| Exchange-397-5858 | Package Store-397-5857 |
| SATO-398-0640 | Snack Bar-393-2761/399-5324 |

**ADMINISTRATIVE SUPPORT:**

| | |
|---|---|
| CDO/OOD-953-5008 | Fire Dept-953-5444 |
| Legal-953-5452 | Emergency-953-5777 |
| Pass/ID Office-953-6950 | Police-953-5225 |
| Public Affairs-953-7422 | Quarter Deck-953-5008 |

**HEALTH & WELFARE:**

| | |
|---|---|
| American Red Cross-953-5435 | CHAMPUS-953-2596/2600 |
| Chapel-953-5550 | Dental-953-2711 |
| Family Services-953-7801 | Medical-953-5064 |
| Navy-MC Relief-953-5956 | Central Appts-953-1100 |
| Retiree Services-953-7689 | Clinic-953-5692 |
| TRICARE-800-931-9501 | Emergency-953-1365 |

**REST & RECREATION:**

| | |
|---|---|
| Consolidated Club-953-5017 | Gym-953-7024 |
| Indoor Pool-953-5946 | Indoor Rec-953-5095 |
| ITT-953-5439 | Library-953-5384 |
| Marinas-953-5943 | MWR-953-5094 |
| Outdoor Rec-953-5095 | Rec Equipment-953-5855 |
| Theater-953-5858 | |

**ATTRACTIONS:** Tours: Portsmouth Harbor, MacArthur Memorial, Naval Museums.

# QUANTICO MARINE CORPS BASE (VA11R1)

Marine Corps Combat Development Command
Building 3250
Quantico, VA 22134-5000

**TELEPHONE NUMBER INFORMATION:** Main installation numbers: C-703-784-2121, D-312-278-2121.

**LOCATION:** From I-95 north or south, take exit 150-A (Quantico/Triangle) east. US-1 runs parallel to I-95 and is adjacent to the base. Directions to the base from I-95 and US-1 are clearly marked. USMRA: Page 47 (L-5,6). NMC: Washington, D.C., 30 miles north.

**GENERAL INFORMATION:** Home to the Marine Corps Combat Development Command and various tenant commands.

**TEMPORARY MILITARY LODGING:** Liversedge Hall (BOQ/BEQ/DV), C-703-784-3148/9, D-312-278-3148/9. Crossroads Inn, C-800-965-9511, C-703-630-4444.

**RV, CAMPING/FAMCAMP:** Lunga Park, c/o Recreational Branch, P.O. Box 186, on base, year round, C-703-784-5270, D-312-278-5270, 13 camper spaces with full hookups, six camper spaces with W/E hookups, 12 tent spaces.

**SPACE-A:** None. See Andrews AFB, MD listing.

**LOGISTICAL SUPPORT:**

| | |
|---|---|
| Bank-640-9220/9200 | Barber Shop-784-6497/7900/7501 |
| Beauty Shop-640-6600 | Child Care-784-2716/4322/4470 |
| Commissary-784-2476/2233 | Conv Store-640-6615 |
| Credit Union-640-7505/7181 | Dining Facilities-640-0965 |
| Dry Cleaner-640-6902 | Education Office-784-3308 |
| Exchange-640-8800 | Gas Station-221-3109/4553 |
| Package Store-221-4553 | Postal Service-784-4293 |
| Snack Bar-784-5943/5942 | Pro Travel Corp-784-7101 |
| Golf Course-784-2426 | Visitor Center-784-2506 |

**ADMINISTRATIVE SUPPORT:**

| | |
|---|---|
| CDO/OOD-784-2707 | Fire Dept-640-2224 |
| Housing Office-784-2711 | Legal-784-3122/3 |
| Locator-784-2048/9 | Police-784-2251/2/3 |
| Public Affairs-784-3341 | |

**HEALTH & WELFARE:**

| | |
|---|---|
| American Red Cross-784-3113 | CHAMPUS-784-2491 |
| Chapel-784-2131 | Dental |
| Family Services-784-2650/2659 | Central Appts-784-2802/3/4 |
| Medical | Clinic-784-2803 |
| Clinic-784-2708/2796 | Navy-MC Relief-640-7137 |
| Information-784-1699 | Retiree Services-784-2511 |
| Health Benefits Advisor | Veterinary Services-784-2770/9 |

**REST & RECREATION:**

| | |
|---|---|
| Auto Hobby Shop-784-2729 | Bowling-784-2210 |
| Clubs | Golf Course-784-2424/2463 |
| Aero-640-6596 | Gym-784-2003 |
| EM-784-4262/64 | ITT-784-6259 |
| O-784-2676 | Library-784-2240/2248 |
| Rifle/Pistol-640-6336 | Marinas-784-2359 |
| SNCO-784-2676 | MWR-784-3007 |
| Special Interest-784-3196 | Recreation-784-2014 |
| TBSO/Hawkins Bar-784-5238/5283 | Stables-784-2930 |
| Swimming-784-2973 | Theater-784-2638 |
| Youth Center-784-2249 | Youth Services-784-2305/2014 |

**ATTRACTIONS:** Borders Potomac River, near historic Fredericksburg, VA and Washington, D.C.

# WALLOPS ISLAND SURFACE COMBAT SYSTEMS CENTER (VA46R1)

Building R-30
Wallops Island, VA 23337-5000

**TELEPHONE NUMBER INFORMATION:** Main installation number: C-757-824-1979/1692. WEB: www.navy.mil/homepages/aegis

**LOCATION:** From the south: Take Chesapeake Bay Bridge/Tunnel north, stay on US Route 13 to Route 175 (a right at T's Corner) for five miles, a left at Route 798 (Ocean Deli). BQ facilities will be on right. From the north: Take Route 13 south, five miles over MD/VA line to Route 175, same directions as above. USMRA: Page 47 (P-7). NMC: Norfolk, VA, 100 miles south.

**GENERAL INFORMATION:** Aegis Combat Systems Center is a tenant of NASA, Goddard Space Flight Center, Wallops Flight Facility.

**TEMPORARY MILITARY LODGING:** Lodging office, Building R-20, Route 798. 24 hours daily, BEQ C-757-824-2064, BOQ C-757-824-2355, Fax: C-757-824-1764. All ranks.

**RV, CAMPING/FAMCAMP:** None. Nearest facility is more than 100 miles away.

**SPACE-A:** None. See Dover AFB, DE listing.

**LOGISTICAL SUPPORT:**

| | |
|---|---|
| Exchange-824-5434 | Galley-824-1009 |

**ADMINISTRATIVE SUPPORT:**

| | |
|---|---|
| CDO/OOD-824-2058 | Locator-824-2079 |
| Police-824-2037 | Public Affairs-824-1692 |

**HEALTH & WELFARE:**

| | |
|---|---|
| CHAMPUS-824-2130 | Medical-824-2130 |
| | Emergency-546-6400 |

**REST & RECREATION:**     MWR-824-1836

**ATTRACTIONS:** NASA/Wallops Visitor Center. Close to beaches, boating, fishing. Assateague and Chincoteague Island, with wild horse populations.

## YORKTOWN COAST GUARD RESERVE TRAINING CENTER (VA28R1)

Thayer Hall
Yorktown, VA 23690-5002

**TELEPHONE NUMBER INFORMATION:** Main installation numbers: C-757-898-3500, D-312-827-3500.

**LOCATION:** From I-64 east or west, exit 25-D east on VA-105, follow signs to Highway 17. Left on Highway 17, then right at second light onto Cook Road. Follow this until road ends, then take a right. This will lead to the base. USMRA: Page 47 (N-8,9), page 52 (D-1). NMC: Newport News, 15 miles southeast.

**GENERAL INFORMATION:** Coast Guard Training Schools.

**TEMPORARY MILITARY LODGING:** Lodging Office, C-757-898-2378, D-312-827-2378, Fax: C-757-890-0406. DV/VIP C-757-898-2212, D-312-827-2212.

**RV, CAMPING/FAMCAMP:** Yorktown CG Campground, on base, year round, C-757-898-2279. Nine camper spaces and five tent spaces available.

**SPACE-A:** None. See Langley AFB listing.

**LOGISTICAL SUPPORT:**

| | |
|---|---|
| Exchange-898-2153/2115 | Gas Station-898-2156 |
| Package Store-898-2156 | |

**ADMINISTRATIVE SUPPORT:**

| | |
|---|---|
| CDO/OOD-898-2354 | Legal-898-2374 |
| Locator-898-3500 | Police-898-3500 |

**HEALTH & WELFARE:**

| | |
|---|---|
| Chapel-898-2245 | Medical-898-2230 |

**REST & RECREATION:**

| | |
|---|---|
| Auto Hobby Shop-898-2279 | Clubs |
| Gym-898-2128 | EM-898-2141 |
| Library-898-2396 | O-898-2108/2286 |

**ATTRACTIONS:** Historic Yorktown, Jamestown, and Williamsburg nearby. Busch Gardens, Water Country USA.

## YORKTOWN NAVAL WEAPONS STATION (VA14R1)

P.O. Drawer 160
Yorktown, VA 23691-0160

**TELEPHONE NUMBER INFORMATION:** Main installation numbers: C-757-887-4000, D-312-953-4000.

**LOCATION:** From I-64 east, take exit 247 east, turn left. One half mile to Gate 3 and pass office. For Station Hq: Go past Gate 3, 0.8 mile to stoplight. Turn left on Route 238 (Yorktown Road) 2.3 miles to Gate 1 on left. Or from I-64 west: Take exit 247, turn right to stoplight. For pass office, turn left, 0.8 mile to Gate 3. For Station Hq: Go straight through stoplight on Route 238 (Yorktown Road), 2.3 miles to Gate 1 on left. USMRA: Page 47 (N-8), page 52 (B,C-1). NMC: Newport News, two miles southeast.

**GENERAL INFORMATION:** Naval Ordnance Center Atlantic Division and 23 Tenant Activities which include: Naval Ophthalmic Support and Training Activity; Navy Submarine Torpedo Facility; Mobile Mine Assembly Unit and the Second Fleet Anti-Terrorism Security Team.

**TEMPORARY MILITARY LODGING:** Lodging office, Building 704, 0800-1530 Mon-Fri, BEQ/BOQ/DV/VIP C-757-887-7621, D-312-953-7631, Fax: C-757-887-4340. All ranks.

**RV, CAMPING/FAMCAMP:** None. See Yorktown CGRTC listing.

**SPACE-A:** None. See Langley AFB listing.

**LOGISTICAL SUPPORT:**

| | |
|---|---|
| Child Care-887-4733 | Conv Store-887-2307 |
| Exchange-887-2307 | SATO-887-1422 |
| Snack Bar-887-4555 | |

**ADMINISTRATIVE SUPPORT:**

| | |
|---|---|
| CDO/OOD-887-4545 | Fire Dept-887-7343 |
| Legal-887-7641 | Police-887-7103 |
| Public Affairs-887-4939 | Q-Deck-887-4545 |
| SNO-887-7230 | |

**HEALTH & WELFARE:**

| | |
|---|---|
| Chapel-887-4711 | Family Services-887-4606 |
| Medical | |
| Central Appts-887-7255 | |
| Emergency-887-7404 | |

**REST & RECREATION:**

| | |
|---|---|
| Auto Hobby Shop-ext 7294 | Boats/Motors-ext 4601 |
| Bowling-ext 4207 | Clubs |
| Golf-ext 4323 | EM-887-4555 |
| Gym-847-7829/30 | O-887-4272 |
| ITT-887-4609 | MWR-887-4609 |
| Tickets-ext 4609 | Youth Center-ext 4824 |

**ATTRACTIONS:** Historic Yorktown, Jamestown and Williamsburg nearby, Busch Gardens, and Water Country USA.

# WASHINGTON

## BANGOR NAVAL SUBMARINE BASE (WA08R4)

1100 Hunley Road
Silverdale, WA 98315-1199

**TELEPHONE NUMBER INFORMATION:** Main installation numbers: C-360-396-6111, D-312-744-6111. WEB: www.bangor.navy.mil
*Ten digit dialing required for local calls.*

**LOCATION:** From SeaTac Airport, take I-5 south to Tacoma. take exit 132 for Bremerton and WA 16 north and go approximately 30 miles. After passing through small town of Gorst, go approximately five miles. Turn left at stoplight on WA 3 north. Go approximately seven miles, make a right at the exit for keyport and Bangor, follow left over freeway to main gate. USMRA: Page 103 (A-1,2). NMC: Bremerton, 12 miles south.

**GENERAL INFORMATION:** Ohio-class (TRIDENT) Submarines, Commander Submarine Group 9, Commander, Naval Base Seattle, Submarine Squadron 17, Trident Training Facility, Strategic Weapons Facility (Pacific), Trident Refit Facility, Marine Corps Security Force Company, Personnel Support Activity, Puget Sound.

**TEMPORARY MILITARY LODGING:** Lodging office, Building 2300, Scorpion Street, 24 hours daily, BEQ/BOQ/DV/VIP C-360-396-4046/6581, D-312-744-4046/6581, Fax: C-360-396-6032. BEQ: C-360-535-7000 ext 1000, D-312-744-4035; BOQ (Evergreen Lodge): C-360-535-7000 ext 1002, D-312-744-6581. Navy Lodge C-360-779-9100.

**RV, CAMPING/FAMCAMP:** None. See Whidbey Island NAS listing.

**SPACE-A:** None. See McChord AFB listing.

**LOGISTICAL SUPPORT:**

| | |
|---|---|
| Barber Shop-697-8737 | Beauty Shop-697-8738 |
| Child Care-779-4066 | Commissary-396-6025 |
| Conv Store-697-8727 | Credit Union-692-2710 |
| Dining Facilities-535-5931 | Exchange-697-8703 |
| Gas Station-697-8711 | Package Store-697-8727 |
| Post Office-396-6141 | SATO-779-1458 |
| Shoppette-697-9727 | Snack Bar-779-9907 |
| Travel Office-535-5912 | Visitor Center-396-4665 |

**ADMINISTRATIVE SUPPORT:**

| | |
|---|---|
| CDO/OOD-396-4800 | Fire Dept-396-4333 |
| Housing Office-396-4399 | Legal-396-6003 |

Locator-396-5733
Public Affairs-396-4843

Police-396-4312
SDO/NCO-396-4800

**HEALTH & WELFARE:**
CHAMPUS-396-4391
Dental-Clinic-315-4287
Family Services-396-4115
Navy-MC Relief-396-6704
Retiree Services-396-4115
TRICARE-475-0725

Chapel-396-6005
Family Hotline-396-6310
Medical
  Central Appts-396-4391
  Emergency-396-4222

**REST & RECREATION:**
Arts & Crafts-535-5919
Bowling-535-5917
Fitness Center-535-5909
Golf Course-779-4852
Gym-779-4852
ITT-535-5938
MWR-697-8000
Rec Center-779-3815
Theater-535-5923
Youth Activities-535-5915

Auto Hobby Shop-535-5921
Clubs
  CPO-535-7000- ext 8033
  EM-535-7000-ext 8039/ext 8047
  O-697-8033
Library-535-5918
Outdoor Rec-535-5919
Swimming-535-5941
Wood Hobby Shop-ext 2264

**ATTRACTIONS:** Kitsap and Olympic Peninsulas, Hood Canal, Puget Sound, Poulsbo, and the Seattle/Tacoma area.

# BREMERTON NAVAL STATION (WA11R4)

120 South Dewey Street
Bremerton, WA 98314-5020

**TELEPHONE NUMBER INFORMATION:** Main installation numbers: C-360-476-3711, D-312-439-3711.
*Ten digit dialing required for local calls.*

**LOCATION:** From Sea-Tac Airport follow signs for I-5 south; after taking I-5 south exit, go approximately 30 miles to exit 132, Highway 16, Bremerton and Gig Harbor. Follow Highway 16 approximately 34 miles to Highway 3N, take Highway 3N to Kitsap Way exit. Go right at stop sign, right onto Naval Avenue to 24-hour gate. One hour ferry ride from Seattle. USMRA: Page 101 (C-4), page 103 (A-3). NMC: Bremerton, in city limits.

**GENERAL INFORMATION:** Homeport support for one aircraft carrier and numerous other ships.

**TEMPORARY MILITARY LODGING:** Lodging office, Building 865, C-476-7660, BEQ C-360-475-3035, BOQ C-360-475-3030.

**RV, CAMPING/FAMCAMP:** None. See Whidbey Island NAS listing.

**SPACE-A:** None. See McChord AFB listing.

**LOGISTICAL SUPPORT:**
Bank-478-2240
Beauty Shop-478-5515
Child Care-476-1152
Commissary-405-1971
Credit Union-478-2241
Dry Cleaner-478-5522
Exchange-478-5544
Galley-476-2527
Package Store-478-5522
SATO-476-5417 (official)
  476-2044 (leisure)

Barber Shop-478-5513
Cafeteria-476-2527
Child Dev Center-476-1152
Conv Store-478-5540
Dining Facilities-476-1332
Education Office-476-4282
Fast Food-476-6719
Laundry-478-5522
Postal Service-478-5522
Shoppette-478-5527
Snack Bar-476-5756/5529

**ADMINISTRATIVE SUPPORT:**
CDO/OOD-476-2335
Housing Office-476-2363
Locator-476-7210
Police-476-2515
Quarter Deck-476-0126

Fire Dept-476-2796
Legal-476-2156
Pass/ID Office-476-4883
Public Affairs-476-7111

**HEALTH & WELFARE:**
American Red Cross-478-9341
CHAMPUS-478-9386
Dental-476-2211

ACS-377-0602
Chapel-476-2183
Family Services-476-5113

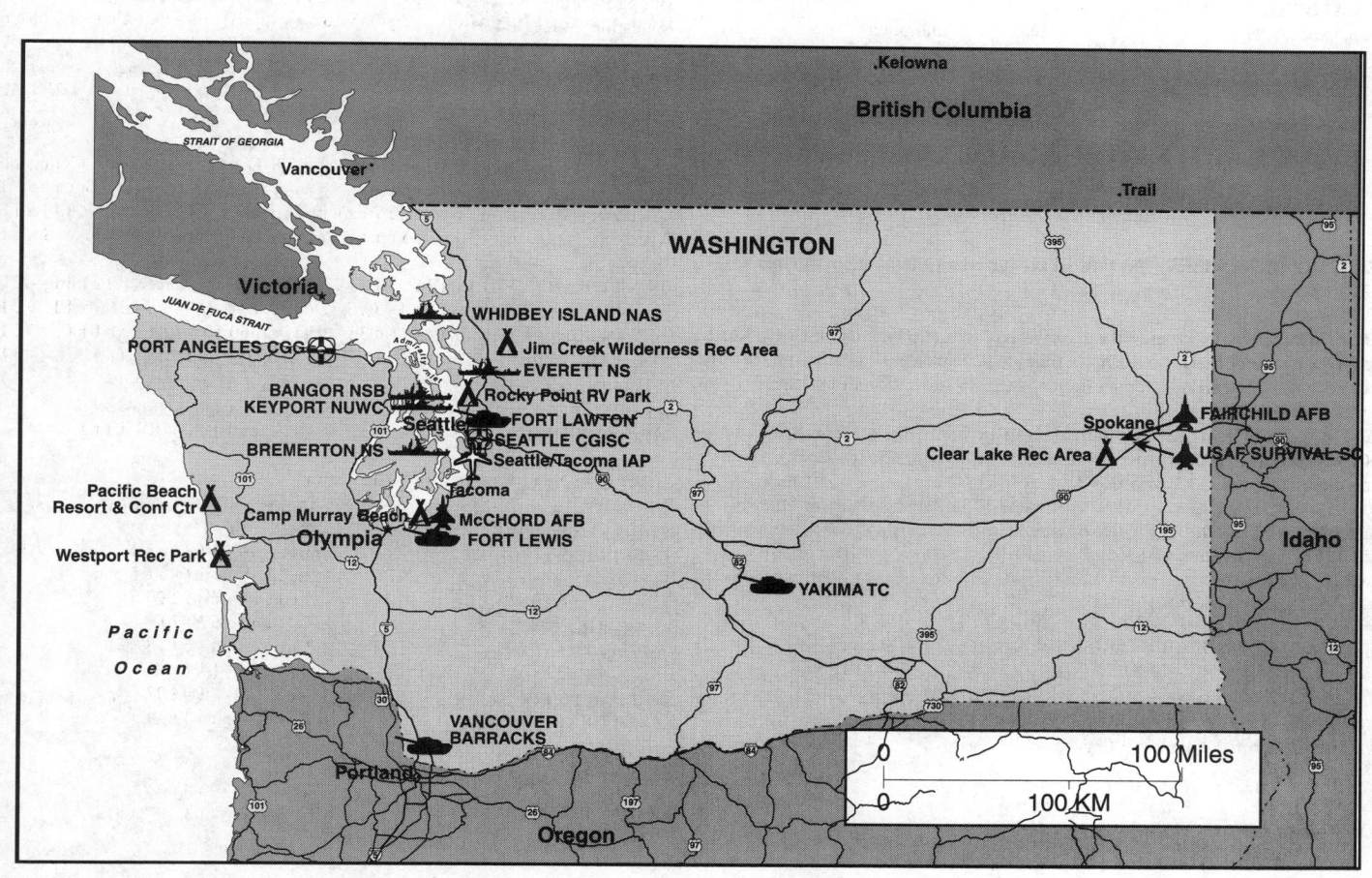

Medical-479-6600
  Central Appts-1-800-404-4506
  Emergency-478-9286
  Health Benefits-478-9201
  Hospital-479-6600
  Med Records-475-4608

Navy-MC Relief-377-0602
Retiree Services-476-5113
TRICARE-478-9651

**REST & RECREATION:**

Auto Hobby Shop-476-2778
Clubs
  CPO-476-3391
  EM-476-2546
  O-373-5014
MWR-476-8198
Wood Hobby Shop-476-2778
Youth Services-476-6405

Bowling-476-2190
Fitness Center-476-9416/9412
Gym-476-2231
ITT-476-7576
Library-476-3178
Outdoor Rec-476-3428
Youth Center-476-6405

**OTHER FACILITIES AVAILABLE:** Swimming, tennis, picnic area.

**ATTRACTIONS:** Puget Sound and Seattle/Tacoma area.

## CAMP MURRAY BEACH (WA21R4)
P.O. Box 92055
Tillicum, WA 98492-5000

**TELEPHONE NUMBER INFORMATION:** Main installation numbers: C-253-584-5411. Police for camp, C-253-512-7900.
*Ten digit dialing required for local calls.*

**LOCATION:** From I-5 south of Tacoma, take exit 122 west across railroad tracks, left through Camp Murray gate and follow signs to beach. USMRA: Page 101 (C-5). NMC: Tacoma, 10 miles north.

**GENERAL INFORMATION:** Operated by Camp Murray (no support facilities on post), year round. Military personnel active, reservists, retired. Reservations (recommended): Camp Murray Beach, P.O. Box 92055, Tillicum, WA 98492-5000. For more info call C-253-584-5411.

**RV, CAMPING/FAMCAMP:**
Camper spaces-24          Tent spaces-unlimited

**ATTRACTIONS:** Camp Murray is located on the southern end of Puget Sound in the Olympia Mountain region. Quiet, wooded site along American Lake.

## CLEAR LAKE RECREATION AREA (WA01R4)
S 14824 Clear Lake Road
Cheney, WA 99004-5000

**TELEPHONE NUMBER INFORMATION:** Main installation numbers: C-509-299-5129.

**LOCATION:** Off base. From I-90 east or west, take exit 264 north on Salnave Road (WA-902), right on Clear Lake Road, 0.5 miles to recreation area. USMRA: Page 101 (I-4). NMI: Fairchild AFB, 7.5 miles north. NMC: Spokane, 12 miles northeast.

**GENERAL INFORMATION:** Operated by Fairchild AFB, off base. Open mid-April to mid-June. Military personnel active, reservists, retired, DoD civilians. Reservations: Clear Lake Recreation Area, S 14824 Clear Lake Road, Cheney, WA 99004-5000. C-509-299-5129. Fax: C-509-247-5759. For information off-season, contact: 92 SVS/SVROE, 121 N Doolittle Avenue, Fairchild AFB, WA 99011-5000. C-509-247-5366, D-312-657-5366.

**RV, CAMPING/FAMCAMP:**
Cabins-3                  Yurts-1
Camper Spaces-27          Tent Spaces-10

**ATTRACTIONS:** Located on Clear Lake in a state where natural wildlife is a challenge and recreation an adventure, this 34-acre area is the perfect place for camping, water skiing, fishing and boating.

*For detailed information about this off-base recreation facility, as well as on-base recreation facilities, golf courses and marinas, consult Military Living's Military RV, Camping and Outdoor Recreation Around the World.*

## EVERETT NAVAL STATION (WA10R4)
2000 West Marine View Drive
Everett, WA 98207-5001

**TELEPHONE NUMBER INFORMATION:** Main installation numbers: C-425-304-3000, D-312-727-3000. E-mail: kitchens@everett.navy.mil
*Ten digit dialing required for local calls.*

**LOCATION:** Take I-5 north, exit 193 to Pacific Avenue. Turn right onto West Marine View Drive, base is on the left. To Smokey Point Family Support Complex (13910 45th Avenue NE, Marysville, WA 98271-5000), which is located about 11 miles north of the main base: From main base, take I-5 north, take exit 202, turn right. Turn left on State Street/Smokey Point Blvd. Turn right onto 136th Street. Turn left on 45th to Family Support Complex. USMRA: Page 101 (D-3), page 103 (C-2). NMC: Seattle, 25 miles south.

**GENERAL INFORMATION:** Support Activity for the Navy in the Seattle area. Most support facilities are located at Smokey Point Family Support Complex. See above for directions.

**TEMPORARY MILITARY LODGING:** BOQ C-425-304-4860, BEQ C-425-304-3111/3112. Navy Lodge at Smokey Point Family Support Complex: 1-800-NAVY-INN.

**RV, CAMPING/FAMCAMP:** Operates Pacific Beach Resort & Conference Center off base. See Pacific Beach Resort & Conference Center listing for more information. Also, see Jim Creek NRS listing.

**SPACE-A:** None. See McChord AFB listing.

**LOGISTICAL SUPPORT:**
Bank-304-4110
Beauty Shop-304-4965
Commissary-304-3411
Dining Facilities-304-3169
Education Office-304-3159
Package Store-527-7858
SATO-304-4001
Snack Bar-304-4450

Barber Shop-304-4968
Child Care-304-3640
Conv Store-304-4453
Dry Cleaner-304-4447
Exchange-
  Fleet-304-4455
  Smokey Point-304-4940

**ADMINISTRATIVE SUPPORT:**
CDO/OOD-304-3366
Housing Office-1-800-972-3372
Locator-304-3000
Police-304-3446
Quarter Deck-304-3366

Fire Dept-911
Legal-304-4551
Pass/ID Office-304-3260
Public Affairs-304-3201
SDO/NCO-304-3366

**HEALTH & WELFARE:**
American Red Cross-304-4476
Chapel-304-3342
Family Services-304-3367
Navy-MC Relief-304-3203
TRICARE-1-800-404-4506

CHAMPUS-304-4057
Dental-304-4092
Medical-304-4062
  Central Appts-800-404-4506

**REST & RECREATION:**
Arts & Crafts-304-3531
Com Club-304-3912
Gym-304-3912
ITT-304-3167
Marina-304-3918
Outdoor Rec-304-3125
Services-304-3167

Auto Hobby Shop-304-3583
Fitness Center-304-3912
Indoor Rec-304-3912
Library-304-3912
MWR-304-3912
Recreation-304-5967

**ATTRACTIONS:** Seattle and the Puget Sound area, hiking, camping, fishing and skiing.

# FAIRCHILD AIR FORCE BASE (WA02R4)
1 East Bong Street, Suite 103
Fairchild Air Force Base, WA 99011-5000

**TELEPHONE NUMBER INFORMATION:** Main installation numbers: C-509-247-1212, D-312-657-1110. WEB: www.fairchild.af.mil

**LOCATION:** Take US-2 exit from I-90 west of Spokane. Follow US-2 through Airway Heights, after two miles turn left to base main gate and visitors control center. USMRA: Page 101 (I-4). NMC: Spokane, 18 miles east.

**GENERAL INFORMATION:** Air Mobility Command, 92nd Air Refueling Wing, 141st ANG Air Refueling Wing, USAF Survival School, and support units.

**TEMPORARY MILITARY LODGING:** Lodging office, Fairchild Inn, 300 N. Short Street, 24 hours daily, C-509-247-5519; D-312-657-2307, Fax: 509-247-2307; Survival School, 1000 W. Survival Place, FAFB. C-509-244-3028, D-312-657-5127, Fax: C-509-247-5893. DV/VIP Bldg 2392, C-509-247-2127.

**RV, CAMPING/FAMCAMP:** On base, year round, C-509-247-2511/5366, D-312-657-2511, Fax: C-509-247-4495. Sixteen camper spaces with W/S/E hookups.

**SPACE-A:** Pax Term/Lounge, Building 1, 24 hours daily, C-509-247-5435, D-312-657-5435; Rec: C-509-247-4636, D-312-657-4636. Fax: C-509-247-4909, D-312-657-4909. Unscheduled flights to CONUS and overseas.

**LOGISTICAL SUPPORT:**

| | |
|---|---|
| Bank-353-5040 | Barber Shop-244-2848 |
| Beauty Shop-244-5380 | Cafeteria-247-5348 |
| Car Rental-747-8081 | Child Care-247-2403/2408 |
| Child Dev Center-247-2408 | Class VI-244-2601 |
| Commissary-244-5591 | Conv Store-244-5095 |
| Credit Union-244-9216 | Dining Facilities-247-7627 |
| Dry Cleaner-244-9786 | Education Center-247-2340 |
| Exchange-244-2832 | Fast Food-244-2680 |
| Gas Station-244-5095 | Laundry-244-9786 |
| Postal Service-244-5368 | Shoppette-244-5695 |
| Snack Bar-244-2022 | Travel Office-247-5059 |
| Visitor Center-247-5495 | |

**ADMINISTRATIVE SUPPORT:**

| | |
|---|---|
| CDO-247-4051 | Fire Dept-247-2537 |
| Housing Office-247-2341 | Legal-247-2838 |
| Locator-247-5875 | Pass/ID Office-247-5590 |
| Police-247-5493 | Public Affairs-247-5704 |

**HEALTH & WELFARE:**

| | |
|---|---|
| Air Force Aid Society247-2246 | CHAMPUS-247-2672 |
| Chapel-247-3408 | Dental |
| Family Services-247-5154 |   Central Appts-247-5829 |
| Health Benefits Advisor-247-2672 | Medical |
| Retiree Services-247-5359 |   Clinic-247-2131 |
| TRICARE-244-0732 |   Central Appts-247-2361 |
| Veterinary Services-247-2584 |   Emergency-247-5661 |

**REST & RECREATION:**

| | |
|---|---|
| Arts & Crafts-247-2810 | Auto Hobby Shop-247-2310 |
| Bowling-247-2422 | Clubs |
| Gym-247-2791 |   EMC-244-3622 |
| Library-247-5556 |   O-244-3622 |
| Community Center-247-5649 |   C C-247-2559 |
| Fitness Center-247-2791 |   MWR-247-2511 |
| Pool-247-2242 | Outdoor Rec-247-5366 |
| Rec Center-247-5649 | Services-247-2250 |
| Theater-244-5600 | Woody Hobby Shop-247-5189 |
| Youth Center-247-5601 | Youth Services-247-2422 |

**ATTRACTIONS:** Spokane, parks, EXPO site, theater, nightlife.

# FORT LAWTON (WA18R4)
4575 36th Avenue West
Fort Lawton, WA 98199-5000

**TELEPHONE NUMBER INFORMATION:** Main installation numbers: C-800-347-2735.
*Ten digit dialing required for local calls.*

**LOCATION:** I-5 north exit 45th Street west, (becomes Market Street) left on 15th, across Ballard Bridge, right on Emerson Street across railroad tracks, right on W. Government Way, to four-way stop, (Discovery Park). Just past stop, turn right on Texas Avenue to parking lot. USMRA: Page 101 (C-4), page 103 (B,C-2). NMC: Seattle, in city limits.

**GENERAL INFORMATION:** Regional Support Command, providing support for Reservists and their families.

**LOGISTICAL SUPPORT:**         Exchange-217-9213

**ADMINISTRATIVE SUPPORT:**      Public Affairs-281-3026

**HEALTH & WELFARE:**
Family Services-800-677-3980/206-281-3131
Retiree Services-281-3299

**ATTRACTIONS:** Naval Undersea Museum, nearby Seattle.

# FORT LEWIS (WA09R4)
I Corps & Fort Lewis
ATTN: AFZH-GC
Building 5025, Liggett Avenue
Fort Lewis, WA 98433-9500

**TELEPHONE NUMBER INFORMATION:** Main installation numbers: C-253-967-1110, D-312-357-1110. E-mail: dpca@lewis.army.mil WEB: www.lewis.army.mil
*Ten digit dialing required for local calls.*

**LOCATION:** On I-5 in north or south, exit 120 in Puget Sound area, 14 miles northeast of Olympia, 12 miles southwest of Tacoma. Clearly marked. USMRA: Page 101 (C-5), page 103 (A,B-7). NMC: Tacoma, 12 miles north.

**GENERAL INFORMATION:** I Corps Headquarters, and ROTC Region Headquarters.

**TEMPORARY MILITARY LODGING:** Lodging office, Building 2111, between Utah and Pendleton Streets, 24 hours daily, C-253-967-2815, D-312-357-2815. All ranks. Also, fully furnished log cabins (10) on American Lake, C-967-7744/5415.

**RV, CAMPING/FAMCAMP:** Travel Camp on post, year round, C-253-967-5415/7744, D-312-357-5415/7744, 48 camper spaces with full hookups, five tent sites.

**SPACE-A:** Gray Army Airfield, Building 3082, 0730-1700 Mon-Fri, C-253-967-6628/5998, D-312-357-6628/5998. Limited unscheduled flights.

**LOGISTICAL SUPPORT:**

| | |
|---|---|
| Bank-593-5219 | Barber Shop-964-9600 |
| Beauty Shop-964-3252 | Book Store-964-3749 |
| Car Rental-964-1331 | Carlson Wagonlit Travel-964-0424 |
| Child Care-967-3056 | Child Dev Center-967-3506 |
| Class Six-964-4128 | Commissary-967-3142 |
| Conv Store-964-5459 | Credit Union-964-3113 |
| Dining Facilities | Dry Cleaner-964-5872 |
|   Burger King-964-8998 | Education Office-967-7175 |
| Exchange-964-3161 | Gas Station-964-5459 |
| Laundry-964-1250 | Package Store-964-4128 |
| Postal Service-471-6133 | SATO-967-5099 |
| Shoppette-964-5459 | Visitor Center-967-4873 |

**ADMINISTRATIVE SUPPORT:**
Fire Dept-967-4479
Legal-967-0701
Pass/ID Office-967-5065
Public Affairs-967-0156

Housing Office-967-4512
Locator-967-6221
Police-967-3107
SDO/SNO-967-0015

**HEALTH & WELFARE:**
American Red Cross-967-7686
Army Emergency Relief-967-7166
Chapel-967-8489
Family Services-967-7166
Retiree Services-967-4424
Veterinary Services-967-6410

ACS-967-7166
CHAMPUS-968-2165
Dental-968-1240
Medical-964-7136
TRICARE-964-7136

**REST & RECREATION:**
Archery-ext 6263
Auto Hobby Shop-967-3728
Clubs
  EM-964-0473
  Flying-964-4932
  NCO-964-2555
  O-964-0331
  Parachute-ext 3906
  Riding-964-2318
Marina-967-2510
Outdoor Rec-967-7788
Rec Equip-967-5415
Swimming-ext 2490
Youth Center-967-4441

Arts & Crafts-967-5746
Bowling-967-6761
Fitness Center-967-3508
Golf Course-967-6522
Gym-967-4771
Handball-ext 3694
Hunting/Fishing-ext 6263
ITT-967-3085
Library-967-2824
MWR-967-5335
Rec Center-ext 2539
Stadium-ext 2912
Theater-967-5976
Youth Services-967-4441

**ATTRACTIONS:** Military Museum, Tacoma, Olympia and Seattle nearby.

## JIM CREEK WILDERNESS RECREATION AREA (WA07R4)

21027 Jim Creek Road
Arlington, WA 98223-8599

**TELEPHONE NUMBER INFORMATION:** Main installation numbers: C-425-304-5315/5363, D-312-727-5315/5363.
*Ten digit dialing required for local calls.*

**LOCATION:** Take I-5 to exit 208, east on SR 530 approximately three miles through Arlington, cross bridge, another four miles to Jim Creek Road, take right, follow to end of road approximately 7 miles. USMRA: Page 101 (D-3). NMC: Arlington, 14 miles. NMI: Everett NS, 35 miles south.

**TEMPORARY MILITARY LODGING:** Group Lodge-accommodates 70, kitchen, dining room, fireplace rooom, handicap restroom. C-425-304-5315, D-312-727-5315, Fax-C-425-304-5364.

**RV, CAMPING/FAMCAMP:** Jim Creek Regional Outdoor Recreation Area, on base year round, Outdoor Recreation Area, Jim Creek NRS (T), C-425-304-5315, D-312-727-5315, Fax: C-425-304-5364, four RV spaces with W/E/S hookups, 16 campsites, two group campsites, two log cabins, and one group picnic area.

**SPACE-A:** None. See McChord AFB listing.

**LOGISTICAL SUPPORT:**
MWR-304-5315

Visitor Center-304-5315/5363

**ADMINISTRATIVE SUPPORT:**

Police-304-5314

**HEALTH & WELFARE:** None. See Everett NS listing.

**REST & RECREATION:** None. See Everett NS listing.

**ATTRACTIONS:** Beautiful mountains and wilderness, lakes for fishing and boating, mountain bike/hiking trails.

## KEYPORT NAVAL UNDERSEA WARFARE CENTER (WA27R4)

610 Dowell Street
Keyport, WA 98345-7610

**TELEPHONE NUMBER INFORMATION:** Main installation numbers: C-360-396-5111. WEB: www.keyport.kpt.nuwc.navy.mil
*Ten digit dialing required for local calls.*

**LOCATION:** Approximately 15 miles north of Bremerton on WA-3, exits east to WA-308 and base clearly marked. USMRA: Page 103 (A-2). NMC: Bremerton, 14 miles south.

**GENERAL INFORMATION:** Fleet support site for undersea warfare systems.

**TEMPORARY MILITARY LODGING:** None. See Bremerton NS listing.

**RV, CAMPING/FAMCAMP:** None. See Bremerton NS listing.

**SPACE-A:** None. See Bremerton NS listing.

**LOGISTICAL SUPPORT:**
Credit Union-697-6903

Exchange-779-5189

**ADMINISTRATIVE SUPPORT:** None. See Bremerton NS listing.

**HEALTH & WELFARE:**

Medical-396-2561

**REST & RECREATION:** None. See Bremerton NS listing.

**ATTRACTIONS:** Naval Undersea Museum, nearby Seattle.

## McCHORD AIR FORCE BASE (WA05R4)

100 Main Street
McChord Air Force Base, WA 98438-1109

**TELEPHONE NUMBER INFORMATION:** Main installation numbers: C-253-512-1110, D-312-984-1110.
*Ten digit dialing required for local calls.*

**LOCATION:** From I-5 north or south, take exit 125 east onto Bridgeport Bay. One mile to main gate. Clearly marked. USMRA: Page 101 (C-5), page 103 (B-7). NMC: Tacoma, nine miles north.

**GENERAL INFORMATION:** Air Mobility Command Base. 62nd Airlift Wing, 446th AFRES units, 22nd Special Tactics Squadron, Western Air Defense Sector and other support activities.

**TEMPORARY MILITARY LODGING:** Lodging office, Building 166, Main Street, 24 hours daily, C-253-984-3591/92/93, D-312-984-3591/92/93; All ranks. DV/VIP C-253-984-3591.

**RV, CAMPING/FAMCAMP:** Holiday Park FAMCAMP on base year round, Holiday Park FAMCAMP, c/o Adventures Unlimited, 62 SVS/SVRO, Building 739, C-253-984-5488, 18 camper spaces with full hookups, 18 camper spaces with W/E, 20 camper spaces without hookups, 20 tent spaces.

**SPACE-A:** Pax Term/Lounge, Building 1179, 24 hours daily, C-253-512-4260/4259, D-312-982-4260/4259; Rec: C-235-512-4268, D-312-982-4268; Fax: C-253-512-3815, D-312-982-3815. Flights to CONUS and foreign locations.

**LOGISTICAL SUPPORT:**
Bank-581-9272
Beauty Shop-584-1595
Child Care-984-2958
Class VI-589-4807
Credit Union-584-5413
Dry Cleaner-584-7038

Barber Shop-588-2345
Cafeteria-984-2145
Child Dev Center-984-2958
Commissary-984-3285
Dining Facilities-984-2145
Education Office-984-5695

Exchange-582-9451
Postal Service-984-5198
Snack Bar-581-5145
Visitor Center-984-2119

Gas Station-584-4807
Shoppette-589-4807
Travel Office-984-3521

**ADMINISTRATIVE SUPPORT:**

Fire Dept-984-2603
Legal-984-5512
Pass/ID Office-984-2256
Public Affairs-984-5637

Housing Office-984-5514
Locator-984-1110
Police-984-5624

**HEALTH & WELFARE:**

Air Force Aid Society-984-2695
Chapel-984-5556
Family Services-984-2695
Retiree Services-984-3214
TRICARE-581-0818
Veterinary Services-984-3951

American Red Cross-984-5577
Dental-984-5505
Medical
 Central Appts-1-800-404-4506
 Emergency-984-5453
 Health Benefits-984-2476

**REST & RECREATION:**

Arts & Crafts-512-3726
Bowling-984-5954
Health & Wellness Center-984-2393
Gym-984-5666
Rec Equip-ext 2206
Tickets-ext 2206
Youth Center-984-2203

Auto Hobby Shop-512-4226
Combined Clubs-984-5581
Golf Course-984-4927
Library-984-3454
Swimming-984-2807
Wood Hobby Shop-512-3726

**ATTRACTIONS:** Tacoma and Puget Sound area, Seattle, 30 miles north and Cascade Mountains (Mt. Rainier).

# PACIFIC BEACH RESORT AND CONFERENCE CENTER (WA16R4)

P.O. Box O
108 First Street
Pacific Beach, WA 98571-1700

**TELEPHONE NUMBER INFORMATION:** Main installation numbers: C-1-800-626-4414, C-360-276-4414.
*Ten digit dialing required for local calls.*

**LOCATION:** From I-5 at Olympia, take exit 104 (Aberdeen/Port Angeles); west on US-8 and US-12 through Aberdeen to Hoquiam. Follow US-101 north approximately four miles to sign indicating Ocean Beaches; turn left and continue on Ocean Beach Road through Copalis Crossing, Carlisle and Aloha to Pacific Beach. Follow Main Street to entrance to Pacific Beach Recreation and Conference Center. Watch for signs to office. USMRA: Page 101 (A-4,5). NMC: Aberdeen, 25 miles southeast. NMI: Fort Lewis, 115 miles northeast.

**GENERAL INFORMATION:** Operated by Everett Naval Station off base year round. Military personnel active, retired, guard, reserve, DoD civilians and 100% DAV. Check in 1600-2000, check out 1100 (1300 for RV/tent spaces). Reservations: Recommended for RV park, studios and motel units; required for cabins and suites. C-1-800-626-4414, 360-276-4414, Fax: 360-276-4615 (Mon-Fri 0800-1600, Sat-Sun 0800-1600). For information, C-360-304-3122.

**TEMPORARY MILITARY LODGING:**

Beach houses-28
Studios-15

Suites-6
Family units-12

**RV, CAMPING/FAMCAMP:**

RV spaces-43

Camper/tent spaces-125

**ATTRACTIONS:** Rain forest, Quinalt Indian Reservation and Ocean Shores.

*For detailed information about this off-base recreation facility, as well as other recreation facilities, golf courses, marinas and temporary military lodging, consult Military Living's Military RV, Camping and Outdoor Recreation Around the World or Military Living's Temporary Military Lodging Around the World.*

# PORT ANGELES COAST GUARD GROUP/ AIR STATION (WA19R4)

Commander U.S. Coast Guard Group
Eniz Hook Road
Port Angeles, WA 98362-0159

**TELEPHONE NUMBER INFORMATION:** Main installation numbers: C-360-417-5805, D-312-744-6431.
*Ten digit dialing required for local calls.*

**LOCATION:** Take I-5 North to Tacoma, 16 north to Bremerton, 3 to Hood Canal Bridge, 104 to 101 west to Port Angeles and Air Station on north side of US-101. USMRA: Page 101 (B-3). NMC: Bremerton, 50 miles southeast.

**GENERAL INFORMATION:** Coast Guard Air Station and Group.

**TEMPORARY MILITARY LODGING:** None. See Whidbey Island NAS listing.

**RV, CAMPING/FAMCAMP:** None. See Pacific Beach Resort and Conference Center listing.

**SPACE-A:** None. See McChord AFB listing.

**LOGISTICAL SUPPORT:**

Barber Shop-457-2288

Exchange-457-2285

**ADMINISTRATIVE SUPPORT:**

Legal-457-2212
Housing Office-457-2219
Public Affairs-457-2228

Locator-457-2226
OOD-457-2226
SDO/NCO-457-2226

**HEALTH & WELFARE:**

CHAMPUS-457-2275
Medical-457-2275
 Central Appts-457-2777
 Emergency-457-8513

Dental-457-2275
Retiree Services-457-2275

**REST & RECREATION:**

Gym-ext 399

**ATTRACTIONS:** Olympic National Park, great hunting, fishing. hiking. Port Angeles only 18 miles south of Victoria, BC, and 87 miles west of Seattle (two hour drive with ferry ride).

# ROCKY POINT RV PARK (WA22R4)

Gallery Golf Course
3065 N Cowpens Road, Bldg 130
Whidbey Island Naval Air Station
Oak Harbor, WA 98278-1900

**TELEPHONE NUMBER INFORMATION:** Main installation numbers: C-360-257-2178. WEB: www.mwrwhidbey.com
*Ten digit dialing required for local calls.*

**LOCATION:** From I-5 north or south, exit 230 to WA-20 west. Turn onto Ault Field Road, follow to Clover Valley Road (do not bear right on Heller Road). Continue straight on Clover Valley, bear left at Golf Course Road. Sign in at the Pro Shop at the Gallery Golf Course on west side of WA-20. USMRA: Page 101 (D-4). NMC: Seattle, 60 miles southeast.

**GENERAL INFORMATION:** Operated by Whidbey Island NAS, off base, year round. Military personnel active, reservist, retired, DoD civilians with MWR User Card. No reservations. For info contact: Gallery Golf Course, 3065 N Cowpens Road, Whidbey Island Naval Air Station, Bldg 130, Oak Harbor, WA 98278-1900. C-360-257-2178, D-312-820-2178.

**RV, CAMPING/FAMCAMP:**

RV Spaces-23

**ATTRACTIONS:** RV park located within walking distance of local Gallery Golf Course. Sites with water view, and salt-water beach and picnic area nearby.

*For detailed information about this off-base recreation facility, as well as on-base recreation facilities, golf courses and marinas, consult Military Living's Military RV, Camping and Outdoor Recreation Around the World.*

## SEATTLE COAST GUARD INTEGRATED SUPPORT COMMAND (WA20R4)

1519 Alaskan Way, South
Seattle, WA 98134-1192

**TELEPHONE NUMBER INFORMATION:** Main installation number: C-206-217-6400.
*Ten digit dialing required for local calls.*

**LOCATION:** From I-5 north or south, take exit 164 (4th Avenue South, Kingdome). Stay right. At the light take right onto 4th Avenue South. take next right onto Royal Brougham Way. (Kingdome will be on your right.) Follow to the end, take left onto Alaskan Way South. Pier 36 will be on the right. Or, from the east, take I-90 west until it ends. Follow signs for Kingdome, then follow above directions. USMRA: Page 103 (C-3). NMC: Seattle, in city limits.

**GENERAL INFORMATION:** Coast Guard Cutters: Bayberry, Mariposa, Mellon, Midgett, Polar Sea, and Polar Star. Units: Naval Engineering Support Unit Seattle, Electronic Support Unit Seattle, Marine Safety Office Puget Sound, Vessel Traffic Service Puget Sound, Group Seattle, and Station Seattle.

**TEMPORARY MILITARY LODGING:** BEQ, 1519 Alaskan Way South, 0730-1600 daily, C-206-217-6410. Transient enlisted only (Active or Reserve in Drill Status).

**RV, CAMPING/FAMCAMP:** None. See Whidbey Island NAS listing.

**SPACE-A:** None. See McChord AFB listing.

**LOGISTICAL SUPPORT:**

| | |
|---|---|
| Barber Shop-622-1579 | Cafeteria-217-6416 |
| Dining Facilities-217-6417 | Exchange-587-0307 |
| Package Store-587-0307 | Visitor Center-217-6993 |

**ADMINISTRATIVE SUPPORT:**

| | |
|---|---|
| CDO-217-6410 | Housing Office-217-6480 |
| Legal-220-7110 | Pass/ID Office-217-6510 |
| Police-217-6990 | Public Affairs-217-6408 |
| SDO/NCO-217-6410 | |

**HEALTH & WELFARE:**

| | |
|---|---|
| CHAMPUS-217-6430 | Chaplain-217-6995 |
| Dental-217-6430 | Family Services-217-6999 |
| Medical-217-6430 | Retiree Services-217-6430 |
| TRICARE-217-6430 | |

**REST & RECREATION:**

| | |
|---|---|
| Fitness Center-217-6358 | Gym-217-6358 |
| MWR-217-6357 | Museum-217-6993 |
| Rec Center-ext 6410 | |

**ATTRACTIONS:** Space Needle, Pike Place Market, Seattle Zoo (Woodland Park), Puget Sound, Olympic and Mt. Rainier National Parks, Seattle King Dome, Seattle Aquarium, Museum of Flight, Boeing and Microsoft, Crystal Mountain, Mount Baker-Snoqualmie National Forest and Tillicum Village.

## SEATTLE/TACOMA INTERNATIONAL AIRPORT (WA28R4)

AMC Seattle Gateway
Main Terminal Sea Tac Airport
Seattle, WA 98158-5000

**TELEPHONE NUMBER INFORMATION:** Main installation numbers: C-206-444-9096.
*Ten digit dialing required for local calls.*

**LOCATION:** From I-5 take exit 152 west. Clearly marked. USMRA: Page 103 (C-4). NMC: Seattle, 15 miles north.

**GENERAL INFORMATION:** Called the "Gateway to the Orient," this is a Port of Entry and U.S. Customs Service airport. Flights to CONUS and OCONUS locations.

**TEMPORARY MILITARY LODGING:** None. See Everett NS or McChord AFB listings.

**RV, CAMPING/FAMCAMP:** None. See Everett NS listing.

**SPACE-A:** Information: C-206-444-9096 or C-1-877-863-1463, D-312-982-5555. Fax: C-253-512-5557, D-312-982-5557. Dual Sign-up with McChord AFB: Fax:C-253-984-5659, D-312-984-5659. AMC is located on the southside of the main terminal between American West and Asiana Airlines. See McChord AFB for support.

**LOGISTICAL SUPPORT:**

| | |
|---|---|
| Car Rental-433-0182 | Food Court-433-5622 |

**ADMINISTRATIVE SUPPORT:**       Public Affairs-206-444-9098

**HEALTH & WELFARE:** None. See McChord AFB listing.

**ATTRACTIONS:** Seattle and Puget Sound area.

## UNITED STATES AIR FORCE SURVIVAL SCHOOL (WA17R4)

336 TRG/CCE
811 W Los Angeles Avenue, Suite 101
Fairchild AFB, WA 99011-8648

**TELEPHONE NUMBER INFORMATION:** Main installation numbers: C-509-247-2691/2523, D-312-657-2691/2523. E-mail: jenkins@336server.fairchild.af.mil. WEB: www.fairchild.af.mil/336trg/index.htm

**LOCATION:** From Hwy 2 west of Fairchild AFB, first left after Rambo Road through main gate and visitors center. USMRA: Page 101 (I,J-4). NMC: Spokane, 15 miles west.

**GENERAL INFORMATION:** Home of the 336th Training Group.

**TEMPORARY MILITARY LODGING:** C-509-244-3028, D-312-657-5127, Fax: C-509-247-5893.

**RV, CAMPING/FAMCAMP:** See Fairchild AFB listing.

**SPACE-A:** See Fairchild AFB listing.

**LOGISTICAL SUPPORT:**

| | |
|---|---|
| Dining-247-5553 | Shoppette-244-9615 |

**ADMINISTRATIVE SUPPORT:** See Fairchild AFB listing.

**HEALTH & WELFARE:** See Fairchild AFB listing.

**REST & RECREATION:**

| | |
|---|---|
| Fitness Center-247-2991 | Library-247-2597 |

**ATTRACTIONS:** Spokane, parks, EXPO site, theater, nightlife.

## VANCOUVER BARRACKS (WA23R4)

Building 752, Hathaway Road
Vancouver, WA 98661-3826

**TELEPHONE NUMBER INFORMATION:** Main installation numbers: C-360-695-8749.
*Ten digit dialing required for local calls.*

**LOCATION:** Take I-5 north or south, exit 1C east on Mill Plain Blvd. Follow signs to Fort Vancouver and Officers' Row (first right after exit). USMRA: Page 101 (C-8). NMC: Vancouver, in city limits.

**GENERAL INFORMATION:** Reserve Command support.

**LOGISTICAL SUPPORT:**
Class VI-695-9000
Shoppette-285-1303

Exchange-695-8749/9000

**ATTRACTIONS:** Vancouver, Mt Saint Helens, fishing.

# WESTPORT RECREATION PARK (WA14R4)

Ocean Avenue
Grays Harbor USCG Station
1600 N. Nyrus Street, P.O. Box 568
Westport, WA 98595-0568

**TELEPHONE NUMBER INFORMATION:** Main installation numbers: C-360-268-0121.
*Ten digit dialing required for local calls.*

**LOCATION:** Off base. At Grays Harbor Lighthouse. Take US-12 to Aberdeen, southwest on WA-105 to Westport. Take first exit into Westport, approximately three miles to right turn, following signs to U.S. Coast Guard Station. USMRA: Page 101 (A-5). NMC: Olympia, 50 miles east.

**GENERAL INFORMATION:** Great salmon fishing from charter boats. Full range of support facilities available at Fort Lewis, 85 miles east. Operated by Grays Harbor CGS, off base, April-October. Military personnel active, retired, reservists and DoD civilians. For reservations call and ask for Petty Officer at C-360-268-0121. Reservations are accepted with deposit up to 90 days in advance for active duty, up to 60 days for others.

**RV, CAMPING/FAMCAMP:**
Camper spaces-6

Tent spaces-6

**ATTRACTIONS:** Beach activities, great salmon fishing.

*For detailed information about this recreation facility, as well as other on- and off-base recreation facilities, golf courses and marinas, consult Military Living's Military RV, Camping and Outdoor Recreation Around the World.*

# WHIDBEY ISLAND NAVAL AIR STATION (WA06R4)

3730 N Charles Porter Avenue, B-385, Room 219
Oak Harbor, WA 98278-5100

**TELEPHONE NUMBER INFORMATION:** Main installation numbers: C-360-257-2211, D-312-820-2211. WEB: www.naswi.navy.mil
*Ten digit dialing required for local calls.*

**LOCATION:** From I-5 north or south, exit 230, take WA-20 southwest to Whidbey Island, three miles west of WA-20 on Ault Field Road. USMRA: Page 101 (C-2,3). NMC: Seattle, 80 miles southeast.

**GENERAL INFORMATION:** Commander, Electronic Attack Wing, U.S. Pacific Fleet (COMVAQWINGPAC), Marine Aviation Training Support Group (MASTG), Naval Air Maintenance Training Group Detachment (NAMTRAGRUDET), Commander, Patrol Wing Ten, U.S. Pacific Fleet (COMPATWING-10).

**TEMPORARY MILITARY LODGING:** Lodging office: Buildings 973, McCormick Lodger, Midway Boulevard, C-360-257-2529. Navy Lodge, Building 2125 N Coral Sea Avenue, Oak Harbor, WA 98278, C-1-800-NAVY-INN, C-360-675-0633. DV/VIP C-360-257-2037. All ranks.

**RV, CAMPING/FAMCAMP:** Cliffside RV Park on base, year round. Outdoor Recreation Center, 1130 W Storm Lane, C-360-257-2434, D-312-820-2434; 20 camper spaces with W/E hookups, six tent spaces without hookups. Rocky Point RV Park, off base year round, Gallery Golf Course, 1130 W Storm Lane, C-360-257-2178, 23 RV spaces, self-contained, with no hookups.

**SPACE-A:** Pax Term/Lounge, Building 2734, 0730-1900 daily, C-360-257-2604, D-312-820-2604; Rec: C-360-257-2328, D-312-257-2328. Fax: C-360-257-1942, D-312-820-1942. Flights to CONUS locations.

**LOGISTICAL SUPPORT:**
Barber Shop-257-0511

Beauty Shop-257-0530

Cafeteria-257-5981
Child Dev Center-257-3302
Dining Facilities-257-2715
Education Office-257-2284
Fast Food-257-675-8598
Laundry-257-0522
Postal Service-257-2424
Snack Bar-675-8598
MWR Leisure Travel-679-3461

Child Care-257-3302
Commissary-257-3318
Dry Cleaner-257-0522
Exchange-257-0600
Gas Station-257-2829
Package Store-257-0564
SATO-679-4415
Travel Office-679-7432

**ADMINISTRATIVE SUPPORT:**
CDO/OOD-257-2631
Housing Office-257-3331
Locator-257-2631
Police-257-2406
Quarter Deck-257-2631

Fire Dept-257-2532
Legal-257-2126
Pass/ID Office-257-5620
Public Affairs-257-2286

**HEALTH & WELFARE:**
CHAMPUS-257-9542
Dental-257-2301
Medical-257-9500
Retiree Services-257-8054
Veterinary Services-257-2001

Chapel-257-2414
Family Services-257-2902
Navy-MC Relief-257-2728
TRICARE-675-0536

**REST & RECREATION:**
Auto Hobby Shop-257-2295
Clubs
　Archery-257-6427
　CPO-257-2891
　EM-257-2432
　Flying-679-4359
　O-257-2521
　Rod/Gun-ext 5539
Theater-257-5537
Youth Center-257-3150

Bowling-257-2074
Fitness Center-257-2420
Golf Course-257-2178
Gym-257-2420
Library-257-2432
Marina-257-3355
MWR-257-2432
Outdoor Rec-257-2434
Wood Hobby Shop-257-3603

**OTHER FACILITIES AVAILABLE:** American Red Cross, indoor rec, services.

**ATTRACTIONS:** Beautiful island setting, water activities, fishing, great seafood.

# YAKIMA TRAINING CENTER (WA24R4)

Building T-201, Yakima
WA 98901-9399

**TELEPHONE NUMBER INFORMATION:** Main installation numbers: C-509-577-3205, D-312-638-3205.

**LOCATION:** Take I-82 west from Yakima. Take exit 26 west to Yakima Training Center. Turn east at stop sign. USMRA: Page 101 (F-5,6). NMC: Yakima, six miles.

**GENERAL INFORMATION:** Subinstallation of Fort Lewis. Training center for Army Reserve and National Guard units.

**TEMPORARY MILITARY LODGING:** See Fort Lewis listing.

**RV, CAMPING/FAMCAMP:** See Fort Lewis listing.

**SPACE-A:** See Fort Lewis listing.

**LOGISTICAL SUPPORT:**

Exchange-577-3416/452-7356

**ADMINISTRATIVE SUPPORT:** See Fort Lewis listing.

**HEALTH & WELFARE:** See Fort Lewis listing.

**REST & RECREATION:**
Consol Club-577-3415
MWR-577-3271

Gym-577-3209
Rec-Equipment-577-3271

**ATTRACTIONS:** Military Museum, Tacoma, Olympia and Seattle nearby.

# WEST VIRGINIA

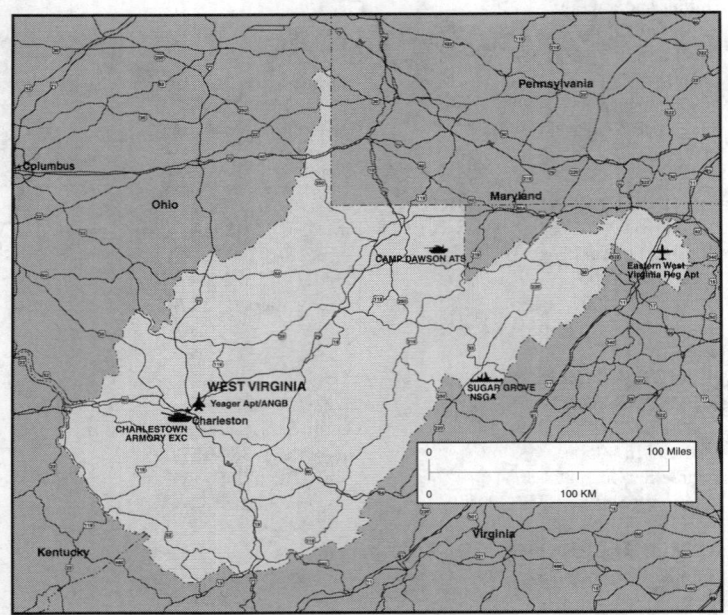

## CAMP DAWSON ARMY TRAINING SITE (WV03R1)

240 Army Road
Kingwood, WV 26537-1092

**TELEPHONE NUMBER INFORMATION:** Main installation numbers: C-304-329-4334, D-312-366-6552.

**LOCATION:** From I-68 east or west to Morgantown exit (Route 7 southeast), turn left at traffic light. Follow Route 7 through Kingwood. At bottom of hill, cross bridge, make a left, then another immediate left (under bridge) to Camp Dawson. USMRA: Page 46 (H-3). NMC: Morgantown, 24 miles northwest.

**GENERAL INFORMATION:** Regional Training Institute.

**TEMPORARY MILITARY LODGING:** Billeting: C-304-329-4420.

**RV, CAMPING/FAMCAMP:** None. Nearest facility is more than 100 miles away.

**SPACE-A:** None. See Yeager Airport/ANGB listing.

**LOGISTICAL SUPPORT:**
Exchange-329-4469                          Snack Bar-329-4383
Dining Facilities-329-4327/4384

**ADMINISTRATIVE SUPPORT:** None. Nearest facility is more than 100 miles away.

**HEALTH & WELFARE:**
Chapel-329-4388                            Medical-329-4314

**REST & RECREATION:**                     MWR-329-4458

**ATTRACTIONS:** Rafting, skiing, hunting.

## CHARLESTON ARMORY EXCHANGE (WV01R1)

1679 Coonskin Drive
Charleston, WV 25311-1085

**TELEPHONE NUMBER INFORMATION:** Main installation numbers: C-304-346-4957.

**LOCATION:** From I-64 east or west, exit Greenbriar left, third stoplight left to Coonskin Drive, top of hill. USMRA: Page 46 (E-6). NMC: Huntington 50 miles west.

**GENERAL INFORMATION:** Home of the 130th Airlift Wing.

**LOGISTICAL SUPPORT:**                     Exchange-346-4957

**ATTRACTIONS:** Capital city of Charleston, area offers good fishing, hunting.

## EASTERN WEST VIRGINIA REGIONAL AIRPORT (WV02R1)

167th Airlift Wing (ANG)
Martinsburg, WV 25401-0204

**TELEPHONE NUMBER INFORMATION:** Main installation numbers: C-304-262-5210, D-312-242-5210.

**LOCATION:** From I-81, take exit 12 east, right to Route 11, south for four miles, left to Paynes Ford Road. Go one mile, turn right at intersection. Airport is approximately half a mile away. USMRA: Page 47 (K-3,4). NMC: Hagerstown, MD, 15 miles north.

**GENERAL INFORMATION:** Home of the 167th Air National Guard Unit.

**TEMPORARY MILITARY LODGING:** None. See Fort Detrick, MD listing.

**RV, CAMPING/FAMCAMP:** None. See Quantico MCB, VA listing.

**SPACE-A:** C-304-262-5250. D-312-242-9250; Fax: C-304-262-5144, D-312-242-9144. Unscheduled flights to CONUS and OCONUS locations.

**LOGISTICAL SUPPORT:**
Credit Union-262-5262                      Education Office-262-5208
Exchange-262-5204                          Travel Office-262-5216

**ADMINISTRATIVE SUPPORT:**
Fire Dept-262-5277                         Pass/ID Office-262-5276
Police-262-5300

**HEALTH & WELFARE:**                       Medical-262-5244

**REST & RECREATION:**
Consol Club-262-5298                       Services-267-5174

**ATTRACTIONS:** Harpers Ferry National Park, Antietam Battlefield, Civil War Battlefields, malls and scenic Shenandoah Valley, 20 miles south.

## SUGAR GROVE NAVAL SECURITY GROUP ACTIVITY (WV04R1)

ATTN: PAO
Sugar Grove, WV 26815-9700

**TELEPHONE NUMBER INFORMATION:** Main installation numbers: C-304-249-6304, D-312-564-7276 ext 6304.

**LOCATION:** From I-81 in VA take Route 33 west from Harrisonburg, VA to Brandywine, WV. Turn left onto West Virginia Route 21 five miles south to NSGA Sugar Grove on the right. USMRA: Page 47 (I-6). NMC: Harrisonburg, VA, 36 miles east.

**GENERAL INFORMATION:** Naval Radio Station, Naval Security Group Detachment, Customer Service Desk, and branch medical clinic.

**TEMPORARY MILITARY LODGING:** Lodging office, Building 63, 0730-1600 daily, C-304-249-6309, D-312-564-7276, Fax: C-304-249-6307.

**RV, CAMPING/FAMCAMP:** Sugar Grove Cabins, on base, year round. C-304-249-6309.

**SPACE-A:** None. See Eastern West Virginia Regional Airport listing.

**LOGISTICAL SUPPORT:**
Barber Shop-249-6355                       Cafeteria-249-6362
Child Care-249-6309                        Exchange-249-6355
Education Office-249-6374

**ADMINISTRATIVE SUPPORT:**
CDO/OOD-249-6310
Police-249-6310

Fire Dept-249-6390
Public Affairs-249-6304

**HEALTH & WELFARE:**
CHAMPUS-249-6380
Medical-249-6380
  Emergency-249-6390
TRICARE-249-6380

Family Services-249-6354
Navy-MC Relief-249-6375
Retiree Services-249-6304

**REST & RECREATION:**
Auto Hobby Shop-249-6367
Community Center-249-6362
ITT-249-6360
Library-249-6360
MWR-249-6309
Outdoor Recreation-249-6367
Wood Hobby Shop-249-6367

Clubs
  CPO-249-6362
  EM-249-6362
  NCO-249-6362
  O-249-6362
  Theater-249-6362
  Youth Services-249-6309

**ATTRACTIONS:** Excellent hunting and fishing area.

## YEAGER AIRPORT/
## AIR NATIONAL GUARD BASE (WV05R1)

1679 Coonskin Drive, Bldg. 131
Charleston, WV 25311-5000

**TELEPHONE NUMBER INFORMATION:** Main installation numbers: C-304-341-6000, D-312-366-6210.

**LOCATION:** From I-77 north or south, take exit 99 north, Greenbrier Street, WV-114 to airport. USMRA: Page 46 (E-6). NMC: Charleston, four miles southwest.

**GENERAL INFORMATION:** Home of the 130th Airlift Wing, Air National Guard. All support of a regional airport.

**TEMPORARY MILITARY LODGING:** None. Nearest facility is more than 100 miles away.

**RV, CAMPING/FAMCAMP:** None. Nearest facility is more than 100 miles away.

**SPACE-A:** Information: C-304-341-6185, D-312-366-6185. Fax: C-304-341-6047, D-312-366-6047. Unscheduled flights to CONUS and OCONUS locations.

**LOGISTICAL SUPPORT:**
Car Rental-1-800-831-2847

Exchange-341-4957

**ADMINISTRATIVE SUPPORT:** None. Nearest facility is more than 100 miles away.

**HEALTH & WELFARE:**

Medical-341-6252

**REST & RECREATION:** None. Nearest facility is more than 100 miles away.

**ATTRACTIONS:** Capital city of Charleston, area offers good fishing, hunting.

# WISCONSIN

## FORT McCOY (WI02R2)

ATTN: AFRC-FM-CO
100 E Headquarters Road
Fort McCoy, Sparta, WI 54656-5263

**TELEPHONE NUMBER INFORMATION:** Main installation numbers: C-608-388-2222, D-312-280-1110. E-mail: tcc@mccoy-emhl.army.mil
WEB: www.mccoy.army.mil

**LOCATION:** From I-90/94, exit 143 west to WI-21 northeast to fort. Main gate on north side of WI-21. USMRA: Page 68 (C,D-7). NMC: La Crosse, 35 miles east.

**GENERAL INFORMATION:** Army Reserve Readiness Training Center, 2nd Brigade (Field Exercise) 85th Division, Readiness Group-McCoy, 88th Explosive

Ordnance Company, Wisconsin National Guard Mobilization and Training Equipment Site and Military Academy, Region E, Tradoc Regional Coordinating Element, Defense Automated Printing Agency, Naval Mobile Construction Battalion 25 (25-Seabees) and Army Corps of Engineers.

**TEMPORARY MILITARY LODGING:** Lodging office, Building 2168, 8th Street, 24 hours daily, C-608-388-2107, D-312-280-2107, Fax: C-608-388-3946. All ranks. DV/VIP C-608-388-3607, D-312-280-3607.

**RV, CAMPING/FAMCAMP:** Pine View Recreation Area, on post 18 April-30 November, DPCA, Bldg. 8053 1439. ATTN: Pine View Recreation Area, C-608-388-3517, D-312-280-3517, two duplexes, two cabins, 27 camper spaces with full hookups, 70 camper spaces with E hookup, 32 tent/camper spaces.

**SPACE-A:** C-608-388-5641, D-312-280-5641.

**LOGISTICAL SUPPORT:**
Barber Shop-388-3690
Cafeteria-269-4865
Child Care-388-2238
Class Six-269-4860/4134
Conv Store-269-5364
Dining Facilities-388-2642/3800
Dry Cleaners-269-5364/388-4134
Gas Station-269-5364/388-4134
Postal Service-388-3825
Shoppette-269-5364

Beauty Shop-388-3690
Car Rental-269-7692
Child Dev Center-388-2238/4124
Commissary-388-3542
Credit Union-269-4777
Education Center-338-3656/3967
Exchange-388-4134
Laundry-269-5364/388-4134
SATO-388-2370
Snack Bar-388-4968

**ADMINISTRATIVE SUPPORT:**
Fire Dept-388-2508
Legal-388-2165
Pass/ID Office-388-4563
Public Affairs-388-2407

Housing Office-388-2804
Locator-388-2222
Police-388-4116

**HEALTH & WELFARE:**
ACS-388-3505
CHAMPUS-388-2246
Dental
  Central Appts-372-1720 ext 6720
  Health Benefits-388-2246
TRICARE-388-2246

Army Emergency Relief-388-3505
Chapel-388-3528/4203
Family Services-388-2919
Medical-388-3025/3128
Retiree Services-388-3716
Veterinary Services-388-3208

**REST & RECREATION:**
Arts & Crafts-388-4353
Bowling-388-2065
Community Center-388-3213
Fitness Center-388-2625

Auto Hobby Shop-388-3015
Com Club-388-2065
Fishing/Hunting-ext 3337
Golf-(miniature) 388-3517

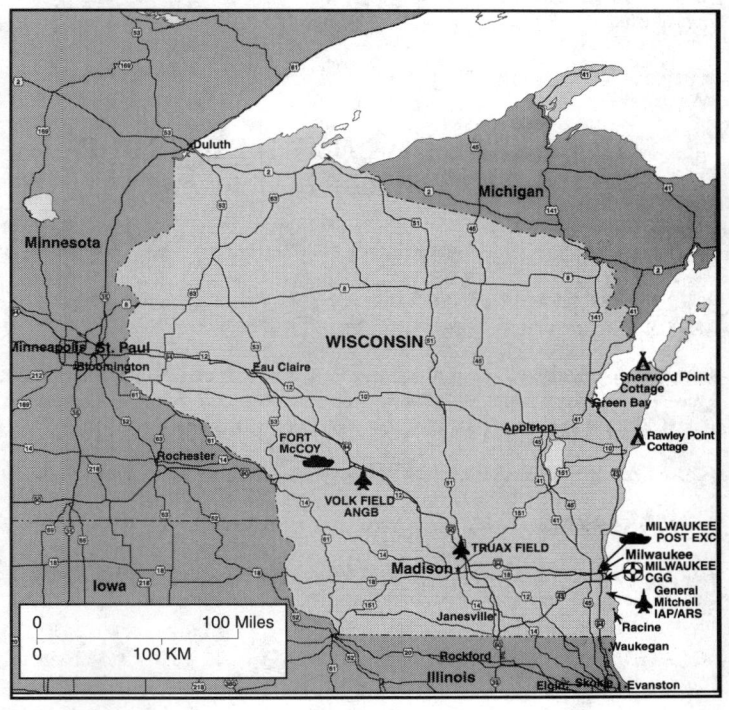

Gym-388-2625
Library-388-2410
Outdoor Rec-388-3360
Rec Equip-ext 2619
Tennis-ext 2290
Wood Hobby Shop-388-2516
Youth Center-388-4373

Indoor Rec-388-3213
MWR-388-4375
Rec Center-ext 3213
Swimming-ext 2290
Theater-388-4968
Youth Services-388-4373

**ATTRACTIONS:** History Center, Equipment Park, La Crosse, Sparta, and Tomah. Outdoor sports and recreation.

# GENERAL MITCHELL INTERNATIONAL AIRPORT/AIR RESERVE STATION (WI05R2)

300 East College Avenue
Milwaukee, WI 53207-6299

**TELEPHONE NUMBER INFORMATION:** Main installation numbers: C-414-482-5000 (AFRES), 414-747-4420 (ANG), D-312-950-5000 (AFRES), 312-550-8420 (ANG).

**LOCATION:** From I-94 north or south take the 318 east exit to 119 east and to the airport. Right onto Howell Avenue. Left on College Avenue, approximately two blocks to base entrance. USMRA: Page 68 (G-9). NMC: Milwaukee, three miles north.

**GENERAL INFORMATION:** Units at General Mitchell IAP include the 128th Air Refueling Group (ANG) and the 440th Airlift Wing (AFRES).

**TEMPORARY MILITARY LODGING:** None. See Great Lakes NTC, IL listing.

**RV, CAMPING/FAMCAMP:** None. See Milwaukee CGG listing, Rawley Point Cottage and Sherwood Point Cottage.

**SPACE-A:** Information: Bldg. 522. Very limited hours of operation. Rec: C-414-944-8732, D-312-580-8732. Flights via ANG KC-135R and AFRES C-130H aircraft to CONUS, OCONUS and foreign country locations.

**LOGISTICAL SUPPORT:**
Exchange-744-1207

SATO-482-5799

**ADMINISTRATIVE SUPPORT:**
Fire Dept-482-5000
Police-482-5375

Legal-482-5214
Public Affairs-482-5481

**HEALTH & WELFARE:**

Family Services-482-5424

**REST & RECREATION:**
Consol Club-482-5711

MWR-482-5706

**ATTRACTIONS:** City of Milwaukee, Summerfest, Wisconsin State Fairgrounds, Lake Michigan.

# MILWAUKEE COAST GUARD GROUP (WI06R2)

2420 South Lincoln Memorial Drive
Milwaukee, WI 53207-1997

**TELEPHONE NUMBER INFORMATION:** Main installation numbers: C-414-747-7100.

**LOCATION:** Take I-94 north or south to Milwaukee to exit 310, east on I-794. Proceed over Hoan Bridge on I-794 to stop sign. Turn left, office is one-quarter mile. USMRA: Page 68 (G-9). NMC: Milwaukee, in city limits.

**GENERAL INFORMATION:** USCG Group/Base, Marine Safety Office.

**TEMPORARY MILITARY LODGING:** None. See Great Lakes NTC, IL listing.

**RV, CAMPING/FAMCAMP:** None. Group operates two off-base cottages: Rawley Point Cottage and Sherwood Point Cottage. See separate listings for more information.

**SPACE-A:** None. See General Mitchell IAP/ARS listing.

**LOGISTICAL SUPPORT:**

Exchange-747-1466

**ADMINISTRATIVE SUPPORT:**

SDO/NCO-747-7266

**HEALTH & WELFARE:** None. See Great Lakes NTC, IL listing.

**REST & RECREATION:** None. None. See Great Lakes NTC, IL listing.

**ATTRACTIONS:** City of Milwaukee. Lake Michigan, lakefront festivals, recreational boating and charter fishing. Wisconsin farmland to the south, west, and north. All professional sports.

# MILWAUKEE POST EXCHANGE (WI10R2)

4828 W Silver Spring Drive
Building 304, Milwaukee, WI 53218-5000

**TELEPHONE NUMBER INFORMATION:** Main installation numbers: C-414-438-6219.

**LOCATION:** From I-43 exit 78 west on Silver Spring Drive, five miles, at 4828 west Silver Spring Drive. USMRA: Page 68 (G-8). NMC: Milwaukee, in city limits.

**LOGISTICAL SUPPORT:**

Exchange-438-6219

**ATTRACTIONS:** City of Milwaukee. Lake Michigan, lakefront festivals, recreational boating and charter fishing. Wisconsin farmland to the south, west, and north. All professional sports.

# RAWLEY POINT COTTAGE (WI04R2)

Commander, Group Milwaukee USCG
2420 South Lincoln Memorial Drive
Milwaukee, WI 53207-1997

**TELEPHONE NUMBER INFORMATION:** Main installation numbers: C-414-747-7185.

**LOCATION:** Off base. From I-43 north or south near Two Rivers take WI-310 east to north on WI-42 into the city. Right on 17th Street, cross drawbridge, right on east Street, four blocks to Two Rivers CG Station at 13 East Street. Cottage is located five miles north of CG Station. Directions to cottage will be sent when reservations are made. USMRA: Page 68 (G,H-7). NMC: Manitowoc, 10 miles south.

**GENERAL INFORMATION:** Operated by Milwaukee Coast Guard Group, off base, year round. Military personnel active, reservists, retired, DOT civilians, CG Auxiliary. Reservations (required): Commander, Group Milwaukee USCG, 2420 South Lincoln Memorial Drive, Milwaukee, WI 53207-1997. C-414-747-7185, 0700-1500 hours.

**RV, CAMPING/FAMCAMP:**
Townhouse-Two-bedroom apartment (2), sleeps eight.

**ATTRACTIONS:** Historical 115-year-old lighthouse overlooking Lake Michigan. Cottage is situated within 2800-acre Point Beach State Park. Twin cities of Two Rivers/Manitowoc are rich in festivals, fishing derbies and maritime events. Charter boats provide offshore fishing for lake trout and salmon.

*For detailed information about this off-base recreation facility, as well as on-base recreation facilities, golf courses and marinas, consult Military Living's Military RV, Camping and Outdoor Recreation Around the World.*

# SHERWOOD POINT COTTAGE (WI03R2)

Milwaukee Coast Guard Group
Milwaukee, WI 53207-1997

**TELEPHONE NUMBER INFORMATION:** Main installation numbers: C-414-747-7185.

**LOCATION:** Off base. From US-41 at Green Bay, take WI-57 north to Sturgeon Bay to 2501 Canal Road. To get to cottage take WI-42/57 south to County S, turn right on Duluth Street, left on Elm Street to County M, right to Potawatomi State

Park, turn left just before Fishing Hole Tavern. This is the access road to the Coast Guard lighthouse. Approximately nine miles from Elm and County M. USMRA: Page 68 (H-5). NMI: Fort McCoy, 190 miles southwest. NMC: Green Bay, 45 miles southwest.

**GENERAL INFORMATION:** Operated by Milwaukee Coast Guard Group, off base, year round. Military personnel active, reservists, retired, CG Auxiliary. Reservations (required): Commander, Coast Guard Group Morale Fund, 2420 South Lincoln Memorial Drive, Milwaukee, WI 53207-1997. C-414-747-7185 0700-1500 hours.

**RV, CAMPING/FAMCAMP:**
Cottage: One-bedroom (1), sleeps eight

**ATTRACTIONS:** Lighthouse situated on western shores of Lake Michigan. Beautiful cottage overlooking bay and wooded area. Near winter ski area.

*For detailed information about this off-base recreation facility, as well as on-base recreation facilities, golf courses and marinas, consult Military Living's Military RV, Camping and Outdoor Recreation Around the World.*

## TRUAX FIELD (WI07R2)
115 Fighter Wing
3110 Mitchell Street, Building 500
Madison, WI 53704-2591

**TELEPHONE NUMBER INFORMATION:** Main installation numbers: C-608-245-4300, D-312-724-8210.

**LOCATION:** From I-90/94 exit 135 west on Highway 151. North on US-51 for one and a half miles, take a left on Persdorf then a left on Mitchell Street, two blocks to front gate. USMRA: Page 68 (E-8). NMC: Madison, in city limits.

**GENERAL INFORMATION:** Home of the 115 Fighter Wing, Air National Guard.

**TEMPORARY MILITARY LODGING:** None. See Great Lakes NTC, IL listing.

**RV, CAMPING/FAMCAMP:** None. See Rawley Point Cottage and Sherwood Point Cottage listings.

**SPACE-A:** None. See General Mitchell IAP/ARS listing.

**LOGISTICAL SUPPORT:**
Credit Union-245-4599          Exchange-249-5229
SATO-245-4573

**ADMINISTRATIVE SUPPORT:**
Fire Dept-245-4340             Legal-245-4396
Pass/ID Office-245-4468        Police-245-4560
Public Affairs-245-4395

**HEALTH & WELFARE:**
Medical-245-4567               Retirees Services-242-3115

**REST & RECREATION:**          Com Club-249-6201

**ATTRACTIONS:** State Capital, state parks, University Wisconsin-Madison campus, State Guard headquarters, Milwaukee.

## VOLK FIELD AIR NATIONAL GUARD BASE (WI08R2)
Combat Readiness Training Center, 100 Independence Drive
Camp Douglas, WI 54618-5001

**TELEPHONE NUMBER INFORMATION:** Main installation numbers: C-608-427-1210, D-312-946-3210. E-mail: wivolk.ang.af.mil
WEB: www.volkfield.ang.af.mil

**LOCATION:** From Madison take I-90/94 northwest, 85 miles to Camp Douglas exit northeast. From Lacrosse, take I-90 east to I-94 south to Camp Douglas exit (55

miles). USMRA: Page 68 (D-7). NMI: Fort McCoy, 25 miles northwest. NMC: La Crosse, 55 miles west.

**GENERAL INFORMATION:** One of four ANG Combat Readiness Training Centers (CRTCs), manages 10,000 acres including Hardwood Air to Ground Range and 4,000 square miles of Airspace. WI National Guard Museum, Camp Williams adjacent to field, State of the art Air Combat Maneuvering and Instrumentation System, and also hosts units deployed for inspections, exercises and field training.

**TEMPORARY MILITARY LODGING:** None. See Fort McCoy listing.

**RV, CAMPING/FAMCAMP:** None. See Fort McCoy listing.

**SPACE-A:** Information: C-608-427-1205, D-312-946-3205. Fax: 608-427-1266. Flights via transient ANG aircraft.

**LOGISTICAL SUPPORT:**
Exchange-427-1274              SATO-388-2370
Snack Bar-427-1276

**ADMINISTRATIVE SUPPORT:**
Fire Dept-ext 317              Pass/ID Office-ext 245 or 236
Police-427-1236                Public Affairs- ext 202

**HEALTH & WELFARE:**          Consol Club-427-1276

**OTHER INFORMATION:** Full range of support facilities available at Fort McCoy.

**ATTRACTIONS:** Wisconsin Dells, 30 miles south.

# WYOMING

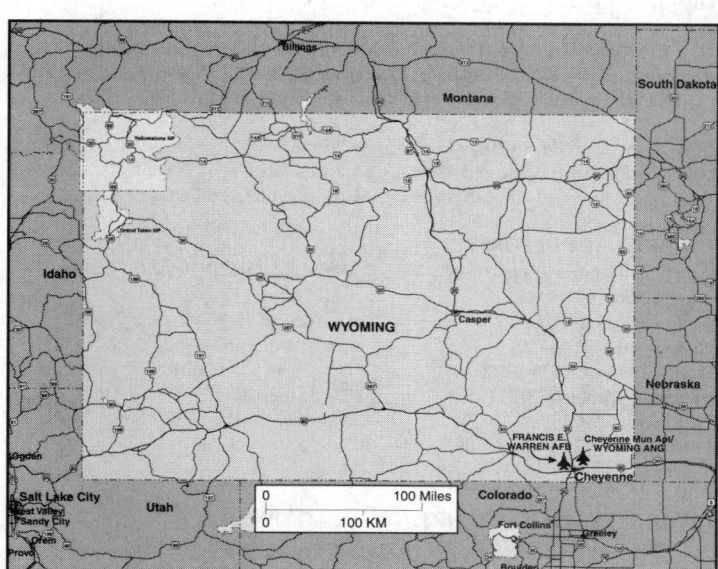

## CHEYENNE MUNICIPAL AIRPORT/WYOMING AIR NATIONAL GUARD BASE (WY04R3)
217 Dell Range Boulevard
Cheyenne, WY 82009-4799

**TELEPHONE NUMBER INFORMATION:** Main installation numbers: C-307-772-6132, D-312-943-6132.

**LOCATION:** From I-25 north or south, exit on Central Avenue exit 12 east to airport. Turn onto Yellowstone Road to first light. Turn onto Dell Range Blvd, first right into guard base. USMRA: Page 102 (I-8). NMC: Cheyenne, one mile south.

**GENERAL INFORMATION:** Full support of a regional airport. No military facilities. U.S. Customs Service airport.

**TEMPORARY MILITARY LODGING:** None. See F.E. Warren AFB listing.

**RV, CAMPING/FAMCAMP:** None. Nearest facility is more than 100 miles away.

**SPACE-A:** Information: Bldg-116, Mon-Fri 0730-1630. C-307-772-6347 ext. 71, C-1800-832-1957 ext. 71, D-312-943-6347. Fax: C-307-772-6000, D-312-943-6000.

**LOGISTICAL SUPPORT:** None. See F.E. Warren AFB listing.

**ADMINISTRATIVE SUPPORT:** None. See F.E. Warren AFB listing.

**HEALTH & WELFARE:** None. See F.E. Warren AFB listing.

**ATTRACTIONS:** Museums, cowboy crafts, rodeo, wildlife, Pine Bluffs.

## FRANCIS E. WARREN AIR FORCE BASE (WY01R4)
5305 Randall Avenue
Francis E. Warren Air Force Base, WY 82005-2266

**TELEPHONE NUMBER INFORMATION:** Main installation numbers: C-307-773-1110, D-312-481-1110.

**LOCATION:** Off I-25, exit 11 west on Randall Avenue; main gate two miles north of I-80. Clearly marked. USMRA: Page 102 (I-8). NMC: Cheyenne, adjacent to city.

**GENERAL INFORMATION:** Air Force Space Command base, 90th Missile Wing, 20th Air Force support units.

**TEMPORARY MILITARY LODGING:** Lodging Office: Crow Creek Inn, 7103 Randall Street, 24 hours daily, C-307-773-1844, D-312-481-1844. All ranks. DV/VIP C-307-773-2137/3052.

**RV, CAMPING/FAMCAMP:** FAMCAMP on base, year round, Outdoor Recreation, 7103 Randall Avenue. C-307-773-2988, D-312-481-2988; 40 camper spaces (W/E hookups May-September; no water in winter); 10 tent spaces.

**SPACE-A:** Limited. C-307-773-3275, D-312-481-3275. Operational support aircraft flights to Midwest and West Coast areas. MEDEVAC available. Also, see Cheyenne Municipal Airport/Wyoming Air National Guard listing.

**LOGISTICAL SUPPORT:**
American Express Travel-634-2948
Beauty Shop-634-7149
Child Dev Center-773-3221
Commissary-773-3509
Dining Facilities-778-8272
Education Center-773-2117
Fast Food-773-2399
Postal Service-773-2276/3409
Visitor Center-773-3694
Barber Shop-638-3046/773-3164
Child Care-773-2639
Class Six-773-3008
Credit Union-634-9685
Dry Cleaner-638-0311
Exchange-634-1593
Gas Station-634-7432
Shoppette-634-7432

**ADMINISTRATIVE SUPPORT:**
Fire Dept-773-2931
Legal-773-2256
Pass/ID Office-773-1853
Public Affairs-773-3381
Housing Office-773-1840
Locator-773-1841
Police-773-3501
SDO/NCO-773-3921

**HEALTH & WELFARE:**
Chapel-773-3434
Family Services-773-3739
Retiree Services-773-2309
TRICARE-772-4020
Dental-773-1846
Medical-Appts-772-4020
  Health Benefits Advisor-773-2620
  Hospital-773-2277
  Information-773-2277

**REST & RECREATION:**
Auto Hobby Shop-481-3869
Consol Club-773-3024/3048
Fitness Center-773-2304
Gym-773-2680
Library-773-3416
Bowling-773-2210
Community Center-773-2446
Golf Course-773-3556
ITT-773-2988
Outdoor Rec-773-2988

Rec Equip-773-2988
Swimming-773-3195
Youth Center-773-2564
Services-773-2858
Theater-773-2345

**ATTRACTIONS:** Cheyenne, historic Governor's Mansion, National First Day Cover Museum, State Capital.

## YELLOWSTONE COUNTRY TRAILERS GRAND TETON NATIONAL PARK (ID05R4)

*See under Yellowstone Country Trailers listing in Idaho.*

# UNITED STATES POSSESSIONS

# AMERICAN SAMOA

## PAGO PAGO INTERNATIONAL AIRPORT (AS01R8)
PPG/Pago Pago International Airport
P.O. Box 280
Pago Pago, American Samoa 96799-5000

**TELEPHONE NUMBER INFORMATION:** Main installation numbers: C-011-684-699-1515.

**LOCATION:** On the south coast of the Island of Tutuila in American Samoa. Approximately 2,630 miles southwest of Honolulu, HI, and 2,660 miles northeast of Christchurch, NZ. NMC: Village of Utulei, main U.S. Government offices, nine miles from IAP.

**SPACE-A:** C-685-699-1515, Fax: C-684-699-1515.

**LOGISTICAL SUPPORT:**          Exchange-699-2241

**ADMINISTRATIVE SUPPORT:**      Police-699-9101

**HEALTH & WELFARE:**
American Red Cross-633-6222      Medical-633-6222 (emergency)

**ATTRACTIONS:** Beaches, scenery, fishing.

# GUAM

## ANDERSEN AIR FORCE BASE (GU01R8)
Unit 14003, Box 25
APO AP 96543-4003

**TELEPHONE NUMBER INFORMATION:** Main installation numbers: C-671-366-1110, D-315-366-1110. WEB: www.andersen.af.mil/

**LOCATION:** On the north end of the island, accessible from Marine Drive, which extends the entire length of the island of Guam. USMRA: Page 130 (E,F-1,2). NMC: Agana, 15 miles south.

**GENERAL INFORMATION:** Pacific Air Forces. Air Base Wing, AMC Squadron and other support units.

**TEMPORARY MILITARY LODGING:** Lodging office, Building 27006, 4th & Caroline Streets, 24 hours daily, C-671-366-8201/8144, D-315-366-8201/8144. All ranks. DV/VIP C-671-651-4228.

**RV, CAMPING/FAMCAMP:** Outdoor Recreation Services, off base, year round, Guam Naval Activities MWR Office, PSC 455, Box 169, FPO 96540-4153. C-671-

564-1847/81, D-315-564-4153, Fax: C-671-564-1853. Camping is allowed on some beaches, no hookups, no fees.

**SPACE-A:** Pax Term/Lounge, Building 17002, 24 hours daily, C-671-366-5135/5165, D-315-366-5135/5165, Rec: C-671-366-2095, D-312-366-2095. Fax: C-671-366-3984. Flights to CONUS, OCONUS and foreign locations.

### LOGISTICAL SUPPORT:
Bank-653-8371
Car Rental-653-6945
Class VI-653-8143
Conv Store-653-8143
Exchange-653-1141
Gas Station-653-4677
Shoppette-653-8143/4
Visitor Center-366-4230
Cafeteria-362-3247
Child Care-362-6280
Commissary-366-2264
Dining-366-3648
Fast Food-653-0782
SATO-653-8945
Snack Bar-366-8283

### ADMINISTRATIVE SUPPORT:
Fire Dept-911 or 366-5268
Locator-366-3247
Public Affairs-366-4202
Legal-366-2937
Police-911 or 366-2913
SDO/NCO-366-2981

### HEALTH & WELFARE:
CHAMPUS-366-6547
Family Services-366-8136
Retiree Services-366-4315
Chapel-366-6139
Medical-366-2978
  Emergency-366-4267

### REST & RECREATION:
Arts & Crafts-366-5214
Bowling-366-2695
Fitness Center-366-6100
Golf Course-362-4653
Gym-366-6100
MWR-366-4221
Rec Equip-ext 5197
Theater-653-7450/1334
Auto Hobby Shop-366-1258
Consol Clubs
  366-6166
  653-9810/1
Library-366-4294
Recreation-366-2209
Services-653-5152
Youth Center-366-2137

**ATTRACTIONS:** Great beaches, scuba diving, snorkeling, and many other popular water sports.

## MARIANAS U.S. NAVAL FORCES (GU02R8)
Building 100, Johnson Road
PSC 455, Box 152
FPO AP 96540-1000

**TELEPHONE NUMBER INFORMATION:** Main installation numbers: C-671-355-1110, D-315-355-1110.

**LOCATION:** South on Marine Drive on west side of island, clearly marked. USMRA: Page 130 (C-3). NMC: Agana, 10 miles north.

**GENERAL INFORMATION:** Headquarters Commander U.S. Naval Forces Marianas; Naval Hospital; Camp Covington (Seabees); Naval Activities; Naval Pacific and Meterological Oceanography Center/Joint Typhoon Warning Center (NAVCMETOCCENT/JTWC); Marianas Section Coast Guard; Naval Computer & Telecommunications Area Master Station Western Pacific (NAVCAMS WESTPAC).

**TEMPORARY MILITARY LODGING:** Centralized lodging office, 24 hours daily, C-671-339-5259, D-315-339-5139, Fax: C-671-339-6250. All ranks.

**RV, CAMPING/FAMCAMP:** Outdoor Recreation Services, on base, year round, Guam Naval Activities MWR Office, PSC 455, Box 169, FPO AP 96540-4153, C-671-336-5197/4221, D-315-336-5197/4221.

**SPACE-A:** None. See Andersen AFB listing.

### LOGISTICAL SUPPORT:
Barber Shop-564-3131
Cafeteria-564-3124
Conv Store-564-3285
Dining Facilities-564-2263
Garage-564-3191
SATO-564-1636
Beauty Shop-564-3110
Commissary-339-5177
Credit Union-477-1055
Exchange-564-3177
Navy Campus-339-8291/2
Snack Bar-564-3124

### ADMINISTRATIVE SUPPORT:
Housing Office-333-2081
Locator-355-1110
SDO-349-5235
Legal-339-3155
Police (Security)-339-6312

### HEALTH & WELFARE:
Chapel-339-2126
Medical-344-9202
  Central Appts-344-9326/7
  Emergency-344-9314
  Hospital Info-344-9340
Family Services-333-2056/9
Navy-MC Relief-477-1881

### REST & RECREATION:
Beach-564-1823
Clubs
  CPO-564-1834/5
  O-472-4607/6/7
Library-564-1836
Rec Center-564-1847
Theater-564-1830
Bowling-564-1828
Golf-344-5838
Gym-564-1824
Hobby Complex-564-1826
MWR-564-1847
Swimming-564-1822

**ATTRACTIONS:** Great beaches, water sports, hiking, historical landmarks, miniature submarine tour, boat tours, Cocos Island.

# PACIFIC ISLANDS

## BUCHOLZ ARMY AIRFIELD (KWAJALEIN ATOLL) (KW01R8)
Kwajalein Missile Range, Attn: CSSD-KA-IS, P.O. Box 26
APO AP 96555-2526
*Note: Permission/Official Approval required to visit.*

**TELEPHONE NUMBER INFORMATION:** Main installation numbers: C-805-355-3452/2101, D-315-254-/3452/2101.

**LOCATION:** Republic of the Marshall Islands, NMC: Honolulu, HI. NMI: Hickam AFB, HI.

**GENERAL INFORMATION:** Support available: Open air passenger lounge, DV lounge, snack bar, combined club, limited bus service, transient hotel for official visitors only.

**SPACE-A:** Information: C-805-355-3452/2101, D-315-254-3452/2101, Fax: C-805-355-1215, D-315-254-1215.

**ATTRACTIONS:** Nice beaches and excellent scuba diving.

## JOHNSTON ATOLL (JO01R8)
FCDSWA Term Ops
JQ/AMC Rep, Johnston Atoll
APO, AP 96558-5000
*Note: Permission/Official Approval required to visit.*

**TELEPHONE NUMBER INFORMATION:** Main installation numbers: C-808-621-3044 ext 2252, D-315-441-2252.

**LOCATION:** Pacific Island located between Hawaii and Guam.

**GENERAL INFORMATION:** Other support facilities include chapel, dining hall, library, medical clinic, fitness center.

**SPACE-A:** Information: C-808-621-3044 ext 2252. D-315-441-2252, Fax: C-808-621-3044/2343, D-315-441-2343.

**LOGISTICAL SUPPORT:**          Exchange-621-3044 ext 2128

**ATTRACTIONS:** Beaches, sunshine.

# WAKE ISLAND ARMY AIRFIELD (WK01R8)
Terminal Building
Wake Island, HI 96898-5000

**TELEPHONE NUMBER INFORMATION:** Main installation numbers: C-808-424-2101, D-314-424-2101.

**LOCATION:** A U.S. island in the Mid-Pacific, 2300 air miles west of Hawaii. NMC: Honolulu, 2300 air miles southeast.

**GENERAL INFORMATION:** U.S. Army airfield.

**TEMPORARY MILITARY LODGING:** Lodging Office: Hours: 0800-1700 Mon-Sat, ext 424-2222. Very limited.

**SPACE-A:** Information: C-808-424-2210, D-315-424-2210. Fax: C-808-424-2190, D-315-424-2190. Base Ops 24 hours daily. All arrivals via air. Letter of approval from base commander required for all active duty/non-active duty visitors.

**LOGISTICAL SUPPORT:**
Bar-ext 424-2310
Exchange-424-2210 ext 310
Barber and laundry facilities available.
Cafeteria-424-2210 ext 486
Postal Service-424-2259

**ATTRACTIONS:** Tropical climate and nice beaches.

# PUERTO RICO

## BORINQUEN COAST GUARD AIR STATION (PR03R1)
ATTN: Special Services
Aguadilla, PR 00604-9999

**TELEPHONE NUMBER INFORMATION:** Main installation numbers: C-787-890-8400. WEB: home.coqui.net/firnhabe

**LOCATION:** At the old Ramey Air Force Base, north of Aguadilla. Take PR-22/2 west from San Juan or north from Mayaguez to PR-110 north of CGAS. Main gate is at the end of Wing Road, just past 5th Street. USMRA: Page 130 (B,C-2). NMC: San Juan, 65 miles east.

**GENERAL INFORMATION:** Coast Guard Air Station for the Puerto Rico area.

**TEMPORARY MILITARY LODGING:** Lodging office, La Plaza, Room 26. 0800-1600 Mon-Fri, C-787-890-8492. Fax: C-787-890-8400. All ranks. There are 14 guest houses and two VIP cottages. E-mail: mwrbqn@aol.com

**RV, CAMPING/FAMCAMP:** Recreation Area on base, year round, C-787-890-8492.

**SPACE-A:** Pax Term/Lounge, CG Hangar, 0730-1530 Mon-Fri, C-787-890-8423, weekends, C-787-890-8421. Unscheduled flights to Puerto Rico and CONUS.

**LOGISTICAL SUPPORT:**
Barber Shop-890-8484
Child Care-890-8494
Exchange-890-3127
SATO-890-8975
Beauty Shop-890-8400
Conv Store-890-8701
Package Store-890-8701
Shoppette-890-8701

**ADMINISTRATIVE SUPPORT:**
Housing Office-890-8470
OPS/OOD-890-8421
Locator-882-8400
Police-890-8472

**HEALTH & WELFARE:**
Red Cross-890-8400 ext 8807
Chapel-890-8486
CHAMPUS-ext 1500
Medical-890-8477

**REST & RECREATION:**
Clubs
CG-890-2581
CPO-8499
EM-890-8729
NCO-890-2581
Library-890-8497
MWR-890-8492
Swimming-890-8496
Theater-890-8495
Youth Center-890-2538

**OTHER FACILITIES AVAILABLE:** Fitness center, golf course, gym, indoor rec (racquetball), outdoor recreation (basketball, tennis, volleyball).

**ATTRACTIONS:** Local beaches and restaurants, excellent surfing during winter months, 18-hole golf course, excellent snorkeling and scuba diving, whale watching during migratory season.

## CAMP SANTIAGO TRAINING SITE (PR07R1)
P.O. Box 1166
Salinas, PR 00751-1166

**TELEPHONE NUMBER INFORMATION:** Main installation numbers: C-787-824-7400, Fax: C-787-824-7477.

**LOCATION:** Route 52 from San Juan to south area of Puerto Rico. Camp Santiago is at the town of Salinas, west of the exit of Route 52. USMRA: Page 130 (D,E-3). NMC: Ponce, 25 miles.

**GENERAL INFORMATION:** Puerto Rico National Guard, 201st Evac Hospital, Troop E 192nd Cavalry, and other units.

**TEMPORARY MILITARY LODGING:** None. See Fort Buchanan listing.

**RV, CAMPING/FAMCAMP:** None. See Borinquen CGAS listing.

**SPACE-A:** None. See Roosevelt Roads NS listing.

**LOGISTICAL SUPPORT:**
Cafeteria-824-7662
Package Store-824-2562
Exchange-824-4270

**ADMINISTRATIVE SUPPORT:** None. See Fort Buchanan listing.

**HEALTH & WELFARE:** None. See Fort Buchanan listing.

**REST & RECREATION:**
Clubs
EM-824-7662
O-824-7521

**ATTRACTIONS:** Beaches, fishing, nearby San Juan.

## FORT BUCHANAN (PR01R1)
Attn: SOF B-PO
Fort Buchanan, PR 00934-5065

**TELEPHONE NUMBER INFORMATION:** Main installation numbers: C-787-707-3400, D-313-740-1110. E-mail: pao@emh1.buchanan.army.mil

**LOCATION:** From Luis Munoz Marin IAP toward San Juan, exit Caguas/Bayamon to PR-18, exit Bayamon right to PR-22, 1.5 miles to fort on left. USMRA: Page 130 (E-2). NMC: San Juan, six miles southwest.

**GENERAL INFORMATION:** The major U.S. Army Post in Puerto Rico providing support to National Guard and Reserve units.

**TEMPORARY MILITARY LODGING:** Su Casa Guest House, Building 119, 0700-1600 daily, C-787-792-7977, D-313-740-3821. Fax: C-787-707-3939. All ranks. DV/VIP C-787-707-3240.

**RV, CAMPING/FAMCAMP:** None. See Borinquen CGAS listing.

LISTA DE ESPERA 80/90
CALL IN DEC 04

**SPACE-A:** None. See Roosevelt Roads NS listing.

**LOGISTICAL SUPPORT:**

| | |
|---|---|
| Carlson Wagonlit Travel-792-1720 | Child Care-707-3280 |
| Commissary-707-2078 | Conv Store-707-8046 |
| Credit Union-783-1620 | Education Office-707-3244 |
| Exchange-792-2066 | Food Court-792-4049 |
| Gas Station-792-4297 | Package Store-793-1984 Post Office- |
| 707-3390 | Travel Office-707-3544 |
| Visitor Center-707-3714 | |

**ADMINISTRATIVE SUPPORT:**

| | |
|---|---|
| CPO/OOD-707-3773 | Fire Dept-707-3917 |
| Legal-707-3345 | Locator-707-2424 |
| Pass/ID Office-707-3877 | Police-707-3337 |
| Public Affairs-707-3205 | |

**HEALTH & WELFARE:**

| | |
|---|---|
| ACS-707-3518/3292 | American Red Cross-707-3471 |
| CHAMPUS-707-3339 | Chapel-707-3904 |
| Dental Clinic-707-2040 | Family Services-707-3332 |
| Medical-Appts-277-2050/2051 | Retiree Services-707-3877 |
| Emergency-911 | Veterinary Services-277-2038 |
| Health Benefits Advisor-277-2054 | |

**REST & RECREATION:**

| | |
|---|---|
| Auto Hobby Shop-707-3972 | Bowling-707-3272/277-2695 |
| Ceramics-707-7172 | Community Club-277-2582 |
| Clubs | Golf Course-707-3980 |
| EM-707-3535 | Fitness Center-707-3767 |
| NCO-707-3535 | Library-707-3516 |
| O-707-3535 | MWR-707-3301 |
| Recreation-707-3301 | Rec Equip-707-3734 |
| Rec Services-707-2101 | Scuba-707-8280 |
| Swimming-707-3982 | Tennis/Racquetball Court-707-7134 |
| Wood Hobby Shop-707-8160 | Youth Services-707-3207/3787 |

**ATTRACTIONS:** San Juan is the oldest city under the American flag, with 16th-Century Spanish architecture and fortresses. Largest shopping center in the Caribbean, rain forest, beaches, luxury hotels and casinos, water sports, deep sea fishing, world's largest radio telescope.

# LUIS MUNOZ MARIN INTERNATIONAL AIRPORT/AIR NATIONAL GUARD BASE (PR09R1)

156 Fighter Wing ANG
San Juan, PR 00914-5000

**TELEPHONE NUMBER INFORMATION:** Main installation numbers: C-787-253-5100.

**LOCATION:** Leaving main terminal of airport, follow sign for town of Catalina. Pass two exits on right and watch for sign for Base Munoz. Go straight at light at McDonald's to base; about 5-10 minutes from airport. USMRA: Page 130 (E-2). NMC: San Juan, in city limits.

**GENERAL INFORMATION:** Home of the 156th Fighter Wing, Air National Guard.

**SPACE-A:** C-787-253-7629.

**LOGISTICAL SUPPORT:**　　　　Exchange-253-5103

**ATTRACTIONS:** San Juan is the oldest city under the American flag, with 16th-Century Spanish architecture and fortresses. Largest shopping center in the Caribbean, rain forest, beaches, luxury hotels and casinos, water sports, deep sea fishing, world's largest radio telescope.

# ROOSEVELT ROADS NAVAL STATION (PR02R1)

COMFAIR CARIB
Building 92202, Langley Drive
PSC 1008, Box 3001
FPO AA 34051-3591

**TELEPHONE NUMBER INFORMATION:** Main installation numbers: C-787-865-2000, D-313-831-2000, Fax: C-787-831-2000.

**LOCATION:** From Luis Munoz Marin IAP, San Juan left (east) onto PR-3 for 45 miles, sign on right indicating exit to Naval Station. USMRA: Page 130 (F-2,3). NMC: San Juan, 50 miles northwest.

**GENERAL INFORMATION:** Fleet Air Caribbean, Atlantic Fleet Weapons Training Facility, Fleet Composite Squadron Eight, Marine Corps Security Force Company, Naval Air Station, and support units.

**TEMPORARY MILITARY LODGING:** Lodging office, BEQ: C-787-865-6922; BOQ: C-787-865-6921/6900; Navy Lodge C-787-865-8282, Fax: C-787-865-8283.

**RV, CAMPING/FAMCAMP:** None. See Borinquen CGAS listing.

**SPACE-A:** Pax Term/Lounge, Air Ops Building, STOP 23, 0700-1600 Mon-Sat, Sun for flights only, C-787-865-4374, D-313-831-3393. Flights to CONUS, OCONUS and foreign locations.

**LOGISTICAL SUPPORT:**

| | |
|---|---|
| Bank-865-8360 | Barber Shop-865-3465 |
| Beauty Shop-865-3465 | Car Rental-865-4495 |
| Child Care-865-4699 | Child Dev Center-865-3599 |
| Commissary-865-4287 | Conv Store-865-4868 |
| Credit Union-865-8360 | Deli-865-3509/4045 |
| Dining Facilities-865-4138 | Dry Cleaner-865-3484 |
| Education Center-865-7133 | EXA Travel-865-2130/2150 |
| Exchange-865-4365 | Gas Station-865-3137 |
| Package Store-865-7140 | SATO-865-1539/1570 |

**ADMINISTRATIVE SUPPORT:**

| | |
|---|---|
| CDO/OOD-865-4311 | Fire Dept-865-3373 |
| Housing Office-865-4024 | Legal-865-4315 |
| Locator-865-2000 | Pass & ID Office-865-4108 |
| Police-865-4011 | Public Affairs-865-4409 |
| Q-Deck-865-4311 | SNO-865-5767 |

**HEALTH & WELFARE:**

| | |
|---|---|
| American Red Cross-865-3428 | CHAMPUS-865-8598 |
| Chapel-865-4326 | Dental-865-4090 |
| Family Services-865-3369 | Central Appts-865-4051 |
| Medical-865-5700 | Emergency-865-4090 |
| Clinic-865-5700 | Navy-MC Relief-865-3210 |
| Central Appts-865-5822 | Retiree Services-865-4091 |
| Emergency-865-5997 | Health Benefits Advisor-865-5913 |
| Information-865-5767 | TRICARE-865-5700 |
| Veterinary Services-865-3438 | |

**REST & RECREATION:**

| | |
|---|---|
| Auto Hobby Shop-865-4773 | Bowling-865-4524 |
| Beach-865-4865 | Clubs |
| Com Center-865-4854 | CPO-865-4965 |
| Fitness Center-865-4033 | EM-865-3302 |
| Golf Course-865-4831 | Flying-865-3023 |
| Gym-865-4486 | C C-865-3273 |
| ITT-865-4757 | NCO-865-3358 |
| Library-865-4353 | O-865-3342 |
| Outdoor Rec-865-4839/4565 | Marina-865-3297 |
| MWR-865-4758 | Stables-865-3345 |
| Swimming-865-4033 | Theater-865-4380 |
| Wood Hobby Shop-865-4839 | Yacht Club-865-4537 |
| Youth Center-865-4926 | |

**ATTRACTIONS:** El Yunque rain forest with waterfalls, hiking trails, and restaurants. Vieques Island with beaches, restaurants and guest houses, San Juan and old San Juan casino, hotels and shopping.

## SABANA SECA NAVAL SECURITY GROUP ACTIVITY (PR04R1)
PSC 1009, Bldg.2
FPO AA 34053-1000

**TELEPHONE NUMBER INFORMATION:** Main installation numbers: C-787-795-2399.

**LOCATION:** From Luis Munoz Marin IAP, take Route 26 west to Bayamon exit to PR-22 west to PR-886 north (Las Arenas exit) to base. Or take Interstate 22 west (toward Arecibo), get off exit La Arena. At the next intersection turn left; the base will be located on the left. USMRA: Page 130 (D,E-2). NMC: San Juan, 14 miles east.

**GENERAL INFORMATION:** Naval Security Group Activity for the Caribbean.

**TEMPORARY MILITARY LODGING:** None. See Fort Buchanan listing.

**RV, CAMPING/FAMCAMP:** None. See Borinquen CGAS listing.

**SPACE-A:** None. See Roosevelt Roads NS listing.

**LOGISTICAL SUPPORT:**
Barber Shop-261-8376
Dining Facilities-261-8417/8421
Gas Station-261-8403
Postal Service-261-8313
Travel Office-261-8313
Child Dev Center-261-8451
Education Office-261-8466/8
Mini-Mart-261-8367/9
Snack Bar-261-8429

**ADMINISTRATIVE SUPPORT:**
Fire Dept-784-8385
Legal-261-8398
Police-261-8395
Quarter Deck-261-8300
Housing Office-261-8330/8357
Pass/ID Office-261-8395
Public Affairs-261-8307

**HEALTH & WELFARE:**
Chapel-261-8386
Medical-795-8755
Dental-8384

**REST & RECREATION:**
Auto Hobby Shop-261-8372
Com Club-261-8425
Gym-261-8386
Library-261-8312
Bowling-261-8429
Fitness Center-261-8386
ITT-261-8313
MWR-261-8363

**ATTRACTIONS:** Great beaches, El Yunque Rain Forest, El Morro Fort and Casinos.

## SAN JUAN COAST GUARD BASE (PR05R1)
P.O. Box S-2029, Old San Juan Station
San Juan, PR 00902-2029

**TELEPHONE NUMBER INFORMATION:** Main installation numbers: C-787-729-6800.

**LOCATION:** From Luis Munoz Marin IAP take Castro Avenue, pass Condado Lagoon to Munoz Rivera, bear right to old San Juan and CGB gate. USMRA: Page 130 (E-2). NMC: San Juan, in city limits.

**GENERAL INFORMATION:** U.S. Coast Guard aids to navigation team and marine safety office.

**LOGISTICAL SUPPORT:**          Exchange-722-9497

**ADMINISTRATIVE SUPPORT:**     Public Affairs-729-6800 ext 121

**HEALTH & WELFARE:**           Medical 729-6800 ext 230

**ATTRACTIONS:** San Juan is the oldest city under the American flag, with 16th-Century Spanish architecture and fortresses. Largest shopping center in the Caribbean, rain forest, beaches, luxury hotels and casinos, water sports, deep sea fishing, world's largest radio telescope.

# U.S. VIRGIN ISLANDS

## ALEXANDER HAMILTON AIRPORT/ U.S. VIRGIN ISLANDS NATIONAL GUARD BASE (VI01R1)
Army Aviation Operating Facility
VI National Guard, P.O. Box 2270
Kingshill, St. Croix, VI 00851-2270

**TELEPHONE NUMBER INFORMATION:** C-340-778-2165.

**LOCATION:** On the south central coast coast of the island of St. Croix. USMRA: Page 130 (H-4). NMC: Christiansted, Virgin Islands, eight miles northeast.

**GENERAL INFORMATION:** There are no U.S. military facilities. All flights handled through Ops Division. Emergency, call office of the Adjutant General. C-340-712-7935.

**SPACE-A:** Information: Virgin Islands Army National Guard Hangar. C-340-778-2165. Fax: C-340-778-9261. Unscheduled frequent flights to Roosevelt Roads NS, Puerto Rico.

**LOGISTICAL SUPPORT:**
Car Rental-778-9355/1402          Exchange-773-6570

**ATTRACTIONS:** Fort Christian, Fort Fredrick, Whim Great House, Buc Island National Park, East End Castle, tropical beaches, water activities.

## CYRIL E. KING AIRPORT (VI02R1)
P.O. Box 301707
Charlotte Amalie, St. Thomas, VI 00803-5000

**TELEPHONE NUMBER INFORMATION:** C-340-774-5100.

**LOCATION:** From Jackson Drive, follow signs to airport. USMRA: Page 130 (G-2), NMC: Charlotte Amalie, across island.

**SPACE-A:** C-340-774-5100.

**ATTRACTIONS:** Tropical beaches, water activities.

# APPENDIX A
## GENERAL ABBREVIATIONS USED IN THIS BOOK

This appendix contains general abbreviations used in this book. Commonly understood abbreviations and standard abbreviations found in addresses have not been included in order to save space.

**A**

AACALA - Army Armament & Chemical Acquisition & Logistics Activity
AAF - Army Airfield
AAFES - Army Air Force Exchange Service
AC - Air Conditioning
ACS - Army Community Services
AD - Active Duty or Army Depot
Admin - Administration
AF - Air Force
AFAF - Air Force Auxiliary Field
AFB - Air Force Base
AFRC - Armed Forces Reserve Center
AFRC - Armed Forces Recreation Center
AFS - Air Force Station
AMC - Air Mobility Command
ANG - Air National Guard
ANGB - Air National Guard Base
ANGS - Air National Guard Station
APG - Army Proving Ground
APO-Army Post Office
Appts - Appointments
ARB - Air Reserve Base
ARD&EC - Armament, Research, Development and Engineering Center
ARNG - Army National Guard
ARS - Air Reserve Station
ARW - Air Refueling Wing
ASU - Arizona State University
ATC - Aviation Training Center
ATM - Automated Teller Machine
ATTN - Attention
AW - Airlift Wing

**B**

BEQ - Bachelor Enlisted Quarters
Bldg - Building
BOQ - Bachelor Officers' Quarters
BQ - Bachelors' Quarters
BRAC - Base Realignment and Closure
BX - Base Exchange

**C**

C - Commercial
CATV - Cable Television
CBQ - Combined Bachelors Quarters
CDO - Command Duty Officer
CEC - Combat Engineering Command
cf - cubic feet
CG - Coast Guard
CGAS - Coast Guard Air Station
CGB - Coast Guard Base
CGG - Coast Guard Group
CGISC-Coast Guard Integrated Support Command
CGMSO - Coast Guard Marine Safety Office
CGRTC-Coast Guard Reserve Training Center
Civ - Civilian
Com - Community/Combined
Conf - Conference
Consol - Consolidated
CONUS - Continental United States
Conv - Convenience
CPO - Chief Petty Officer
CRTC - Combat Readiness Training Center
CSS - Coastal Systems Station

**D**

D - Defense Switched Network
DAV - Disabled American Veteran
DDRW - Defense Distribution Region West
Dep - Dependent
Dept - Department
Det - Detachment
Dev - Development
Dir - Director
DoD - Department of Defense
DSN - Defense Switched Network
DV - Distinguished Visitors
DVQ - Distinguished Visitors' Quarters

**E**

E - Electric
EM - Enlisted Members
ER - Emergency Room
Ext - Extension

**F**

FAMCAMP - Family Campground
FCTC - Fleet Combat Training Center
FG - Fighter Group
FPO - Fleet Post Office
FW - Fighter Wing

**H**

Hq - Headquarters

**I**

I - Interstate
IAP - International Airport
ID - Identification
INF - Infantry
ISC - Integrated Support Command
ITR - Information, Ticketing and Registration
ITT - Information, Tickets and Tours

**M**

MC - Marine Corps
MCAS - Marine Corps Air Station
MCB - Marine Corps Base
MCLB - Marine Corps Logistics Base
MCRD - Marine Corps Recruiting Depot
Mil - Military
MSO- Marine Safety Office
MWR - Morale, Welfare and Recreation
Mt - Mount
MTC - Maneuver Training Center

**N**

NAB - Naval Air Base or Naval Amphibious Base
NAES - Naval Air Engineering Station
NAF - Naval Air Facility
NARS - Naval Air Reserve Station
NAS - Naval Air Station
NAWC - Naval Air Weapons Center
NAWS - Naval Air Weapons Station
NB - Naval Base
NCAA - National Collegiate Athletic Association
NCO - Noncommissioned Officers'
NCS - Naval Communications Station
NCTS - Naval Computer & Telecommunications Station
NETC - Naval Education Training Center
NG - National Guard
NGB - National Guard Base
NGTS - National Guard Training Site
NMC - Nearest Major City
NMI - Nearest Major Installation
NNMC - National Naval Medical Center

NRS - Naval Reserve Station
NS - Naval Station
NSA - Naval Support Activity
NSB - Naval Submarine Base
NSGA - Naval Security Group Activity
NSS - Naval Security Station or Naval Support Station
NSWC - Naval Surface Weapons Center
NTC - Naval Training Center
NTTC - Naval Technical Training Center
NWC - Naval Weapons Center
NWS - Naval Weapons Station

**O**

O - Officers'
OCONUS - Outside Continental United States
OD - Officer of the Day
OOD - Officer of the Day/on Deck/on Duty
Ops - Operations

**P**

PA - Public Affairs
PAO - Public Affairs Office
Pax - Passenger
PCS - Permanent Change of Station
PGA - Professional Golf Association
PX - Post Exchange

**R**

Rec - Recreation
RV - Recreational Vehicle
RVC - Recreational Vehicle Camping

**S**

S - Sewer
SATO - Scheduled Airlines Ticket Office
SDO - Staff Duty Officer
SNCO - Senior Noncommissioned Officer
Space-A - Space Available
SSC - Soldier Systems Center

**T**

TDY - Temporary Duty
Term - Terminal
TLQ - Temporary Living Quarters
TML - Temporary Military Lodging
TV - Television

**U**

USA - United States of America
USAF - United States Air Force
USCG - United States Coast Guard
USCGG - United States Coast Guard Group
USMA - United States Military Academy
USMC - United States Marine Corps
USMRA - United States Military Road Atlas
USN - United States Navy
USO - United Service Organizations
USS - United States Service

**V**

VCR - Video Cassette Recorder
VIP - Very Important Personnel
VOQ - Visiting Officers' Quarters

**W**

W - Water

# APPENDIX B
## DISCOVER AMERICA TOURISM OFFICES

**ALABAMA**
Bureau of Tourism and Travel
401 Adams Avenue, Suite 126
Montgomery, AL 36104
Ph: 800-252-2262 (For free vacation kit)
Ph: 334-242-4169, Fax: 334-242-4554
WEB: www.state.al.us

**ALASKA**
Division of Tourism
P.O. Box 110801, Juneau, AK 99811-0801
Ph: 800-76-ALASKA or 800-667-8489 (For free kit)
Ph: 907-465-2010, Fax: 907-465-2287
WEB: www.commerce.state.ak.us/tourism

**AMERICAN SAMOA** (HAWAII OFFICE)
American Samoa Government Office
Tourism Information
1427 Dillingham Boulevard, Suite 210
Honolulu, HI 96817
Ph: 808-847-1998, Fax: 808-845-3420

**AMERICAN SAMOA**
P.O. Box 2272, Apia Western Samoa
Ph: 685-20180/20878, Fax 685-20886

**ARIZONA**
Office of Tourism
2702 N. 3rd Street, Suite 4015, Phoenix, AZ 85004
Ph: 800-842-8257 or 888-520-3434 (For free travel kit)
Ph: 602-230-7733, Fax: 602-240-5475
WEB: www.arizonaguide.com

**ARKANSAS**
Tourism Office, 1 Capitol Mall
Department 7701, Little Rock, AR 72201
Ph: 800-NATURAL (For free travel kit)
Ph: 501-682-7777, Fax: 501-682-1364
WEB: www.arkansas.com

**CALIFORNIA**
California Division of Tourism
801 K Street, Suite 1600, Sacramento, CA 95814
Toll-Free: 800-462-2543 (For free travel kit)
Ph: 916-323-9882, Fax: 916-322-3402
E-mail: tmckenzie@commerce.ca.gov
WEB: gocalif.ca.gov

**Los Angeles Convention & Visitors Bureau**
633 W. Fifth Street, Suite 6000
Los Angeles, CA 90071
Ph: 213-624-7300

**San Diego Convention & Visitors Bureau**
401 B Street, Suite 1400, San Diego, CA 92101
Ph: 619-232-3101
WEB: www.sandiego.org

**COLORADO**
Travel and Tourism Authority
1127 Pennsylvania Street, Denver, CO 80203
Ph: 800-COLORADO (For free travel kit)
Ph: 303-296-3384, Fax: 303-296-2015
WEB: http://www.colorado.com

**CONNECTICUT**
Office of Tourism
505 Hudson Street, Hartford, CT 06106
Ph: 800-CT-BOUND (For Free Travel Kit)
Ph: 860-270-8081, Fax: 860-270-8077
WEB: www.state.ct.us/tourism

**DELAWARE**
Tourism Office
99 Kings Highway, Dover, DE 19901
Ph: 800-441-8846 (For free travel kit)
Ph: 302-739-4271, Fax: 302-739-5749
WEB: www.state.de.us/tourism/intro.htm

**FLORIDA**
Visit Florida
661 E. Jefferson Street, Suite 300
Tallahassee, FL 32301
Ph: 888-7FLAUSA (For free travel kit)
Ph: 850-488-5607, Fax: 850-224-2938
WEB: www.flausa.com

**GEORGIA**
Department of Industry, Trade and Tourism
285 Peachtree Center Avenue N.E.
Suites 1000 and 1100, Atlanta, GA 30303-1230
Ph: 800-VISIT-GA (For free kit)
Ph: 404-656-3590, Fax: 404-651-9063
WEB: www.georgia.org

**GUAM**
Guam Visitors Bureau
401 Pale San Vitores Road
Tumon, Guam 96911
Ph: 1-800-US-3-GUAM (For free travel kit)
Ph: 671-646-5278/79, Fax: 671-646-8861
Email: guam@avisoinc.com

**GUAM** (CALIFORNIA OFFICE)
Guam Visitors Bureau
1336-C Park Street, Alameda, CA 94501
Ph: 1-800-873-4826 (For free travel kit)
Ph: 510-865-0366, Fax: 510-865-5165
Email: guam@avisoinc.com

**HAWAII**
Hawaii Tourism Office
250 S. Hotel Street, 4th Floor
Honolulu, HI 96815
Toll-Free: 888-547-2612 (For free travel kit)
Ph: 808-586-2550, Fax: 808-586-2549
WEB: www.gohawaii.com

**HAWAII** (CALIFORNIA OFFICE)
Hawaii Visitors Bureau
180 Montgomery Street, Suite 2360
San Francisco, CA 94104
Ph: 800-353-5846 (For free travel kit)
Ph: 415-248-3800, Fax: 415-248-3808
WEB: www.gohawaii.com

**IDAHO**
Travel Council, 700 W. State Street
P.O. Box 83720, Boise, ID 83720-0093
Ph: 1-800-635-7820 or Ph: 800-VISIT ID (For free kit)
Ph: 208-334-2470, Fax: 208-334-2631
WEB: www.visitid.org

**ILLINOIS** (CHICAGO OFFICE)
Illinois Bureau of Tourism
J.R. Thompson Center, Suite 3-400
100 West Randolph, Chicago, IL 60601
Ph: 800-419-0667 (For free travel kit)
Ph: 312-814-7179, Fax: 312-814-2370
WEB: www.enjoyillinois.com

**ILLINOIS** (SPRINGFIELD OFFICE)
Illinois Bureau of Tourism
620 E. Adams Street, Springfield, IL 62701
1-800-2-CONNECT (For free travel kit)
Ph: 217-782-7500, Fax: 217-524-3701

**INDIANA**
Tourism Division
1 N. Capitol Avenue, Suite 700
Indianapolis, IN 46204-2288
Ph: 800-289-6646 or 1-800-291-8844
Ph: 317-232-8860, Fax: 317-233-6887
WEB: www.ai.org/tourism

**IOWA**
Division of Tourism
200 E. Grand Avenue, Des Moines, IA 50309
Ph: 800-345-IOWA (For free travel kit)
Ph: 1-800-528-5265 (Special Events Calendar)

Ph: 515-242-4705, Fax: 515-242-4749
WEB: www.state.ia.us

**KANSAS**
Travel and Tourism Division
700 S.W. Harrison Street, Suite 1300
Topeka, KS 66603-3712
Ph: 800-2-KANSAS (For free travel kit)
Ph: 785-296-7091, Fax: 785-296-6988
WEB: www.kansascommerce.com./0400travel.html

**KENTUCKY**
Department of Travel
2200 Capitol Plaza Tower, Suite 22
500 Mero Street, Frankfort, KY 40601
Ph: 800-225-TRIP (For travel kit)
Ph: 502-564-4930, Fax: 502-564-5695
WEB: www.kentuckytourism.com

**LOUISIANA**
Office of Tourism, Inquiry Department
P.O. Box 94291, Baton Rouge, LA 70802
Ph: 800-99-GUMBO (994-8626) (For free travel kit)
Ph: 504-342-8119, Fax: 504-342-8390
WEB: www.louisianatravel.com

**MAINE**
Office of Tourism
33 Stone Street, 59 State House Station
Augusta, ME 04333-0059
Ph: 800-533-9595 or 888-624-6345 (For free kit only)
Ph: 207-287-5711, Fax: 207-287-8070
WEB: www.visitmaine.com

**MARYLAND**
Office of Tourism Development
217 East Redwood Street, 9th Floor
Baltimore, MD 21202
Ph: 800-543-1036 (For vacation kits only)
Ph: 410-767-6273/6288, Fax: 410-333-6643
WEB: www.mdisfun.org

**MASSACHUSETTS**
Office of Travel and Tourism
State Transportation Building
10 Park Plaza, Suite 4510, Boston, MA 02116
Ph: 800-227-MASS (For vacation kit only)
Ph: 617-973-8500, Fax: 617-973-8525
E-mail: vacationinfo@state.ma.us
WEB: www.mass-vacation.com

**MICHIGAN**
Michigan Economic Development Corporation
Travel Michigan, 105 W. Allegan, 3rd Floor
P.O. Box 30226, Lansing, MI 48909-7726
Ph: 888-78-GREAT or 800-784-7328 (For free kit)
Ph: 517-335-1879, Fax: 517-373-0059
WEB: www.michigan.org

**MINNESOTA**
Office of Tourism
500 Metro Square, 121 East Seventh Place
St. Paul, MN 55101-2146
Ph: 800-657-3700 (For free travel kit)
Ph: 651-296-5029, Fax: 651-296-2800
WEB: www.exploreminnesota.com

**MISSISSIPPI**
Division of Tourism Development
P.O. Box 849, Jackson, MS 39205
Ph: 800-WARMEST or 800-340-3323 (For free kit)
Ph: 601-359-3297, Fax: 601-359-5757
WEB: www.mississippi.org

**MISSOURI**
Division of Tourism
P.O. Box 1055, Jefferson City, MO 65102
Ph: 800-877-1234 (for free vacation kit)
Ph: 573-751-3051, Fax: 573-751-5160
WEB: www.missouritourism.org

*Appendix B, continued*

**MONTANA**
Travel Montana, Department of Commerce
1424 Ninth Avenue, P.O. Box 200533
Helena, MT 59620-0533
Ph: 800-VISIT-MT or 1-800-847-4868 (for free kit)
Ph: 406-444-2654, Fax: 406-444-1800
WEB: www.visitmt.com

**NEBRASKA**
Nebraska Tourism Office
Department of Economic Development
P.O. Box 98907, Dept. 9 Int.
Lincoln, NE 68509-8907
Ph: 800-228-4307 ext. 926
Ph: 402-471-3796, Fax: 402-471-3026
WEB: www.visitnebraska.org

**NEVADA**
Nevada Commission on Tourism
401 N. Carson Street, Carson City, NV 89701
Ph: 800-NEVADA-8 or 800-237-0774 (For free travel kit)
Ph: 775-687-4322, Fax: 775-687-6779
WEB: www.travelnevada.com

**NEW HAMPSHIRE**
Office of Travel and Tourism Development
P.O. Box 1856
Concord, NH 03302-1856
Ph: 800-FUN-IN-NH (For free kit)
Ph: 603-271-2665, Fax: 603-271-6784
WEB: www.visitnh.gov

**NEW JERSEY**
Office of Travel and Tourism
20 W. State Street, P.O. Box 820
Trenton, NJ 08625
Ph: 800-JERSEY-7 (For free travel kit)
Ph: 609-292-2470, Fax: 609-633-7418
WEB: www.state.nj.us/travel

**NEW MEXICO**
NM Department of Tourism
Lamy Building, 491 Old Santa Fe Trail
P.O. Box 20002, Santa Fe, NM 87501
Ph:1-800-545-2040 (for consumer materials)
Ph: 800-545-2070 (for Department)
Ph: 505-827-7400, Fax: 505-827-7402
WEB: www.newmexico.org

**NEW YORK**
NY Division of Tourism
P.O. Box 2603, Albany, NY 12220-0603
Ph: 1-800-CALL-NYS (For free travel kit)
Ph: 1-800-I-LOVE-NY or
Ph: 518-474-4116, Fax: 518-486-6416
WEB: www.iloveny.state.ny.us

Albany County Convention and Visitors Bureau
25 Quackenbush Square, Albany, NY 12207
Toll-Free: 800-258-3582 (For free travel kit)
Phone: 518-434-1217, Fax: 518-434-0887
E-mail: accvb@albany.org
WEB: www: www.albany.org

**NORTH CAROLINA**
Division of Tourism, Film and Sport Development
301 N. Wilmington Street, Raleigh, NC 27626-0571
Ph: 800-VISIT-NC (For free travel kit)
Ph: 919-733-4151/4171, Fax: 919-733-8582
WEB: www.visitnc.com

**NORTH DAKOTA**
ND Tourism, Liberty Memorial Building
604 E. Boulevard Avenue
Bismarck, ND 58505-0825
Ph: 800-HELLO ND (For free travel kit)
Ph: 701-328-2525, Fax: 701-328-4878
WEB: www.ndtourism.com

**OHIO**
Ohio Division of Travel and Tourism
1714 Schrock Road
P.O. Box 29366, Columbus, OH 43229-0366

Ph: 800-743-2303 (For free kit)
Ph: 614-895-1931, Fax: 614-895-2977
WEB: www.ohiotourism.com

**OKLAHOMA**
Oklahoma Tourism & Recreation Department
15 N. Robinson, Suite 801 P.O. Box 60789
Oklahoma City, OK 73146-0789
Ph: 800-652-6552 (Information requests only)
Ph: 405-521-2406/2409, Fax: 405-521-3992
WEB: www.travelok.com

**OREGON**
Oregon Tourism Commission
775 Summer Street N.E., Salem, OR 97310
Ph: 800-547-7842 (For free travel kit)
Ph: 503-986-0000, Fax: 503-986-0001
WEB: www.traveloregon.com

**PENNSYLVANIA**
Office of Travel, Tourism and Film Promotion
404 Forum Building,  Harrisburg, PA 17120
Ph: 800-VISITPA, (For free visitors guide)
Ph: 717-787-5453, Fax: 717-787-0687
WEB: www.state.pa.us

**PUERTO RICO**
Puerto Rico Tourism Company
Old San Juan Station
P.O. Box 902-3960
San Juan, PR 00902-3960
Ph: 1-800-223-6530
Ph: 787-721-2400/2723, Fax: 787-721-3135

**PUERTO RICO:** (LA OFFICE)
Puerto Rico Tourism Company
3575 W. Cahuenga Boulevard, Suite 405
Los Angeles, CA 90068
Ph: 800-874-1230 (For free travel kit)
Ph: 323-874-5991, Fax: 323-874-7257
WEB: www.prtourism.com

**RHODE ISLAND**
RI Economic Development Corporation
Tourism Division
1 W. Exchange Street, Providence, RI 02903
Ph:1-800-55-2484 (For free travel kit)
Ph: 401-222-2601, Fax: 401-222-2102
WEB: www.visitrhodeisland.com

**SOUTH CAROLINA**
SC Department of Parks, Recreation and Tourism
1205 Pendleton Street, Suite 248
Columbia, SC 29201
Ph: 800-346-3634 (For free travel kit)
Ph: 803-734-0122/0129, Fax: 803-734-0133
WEB: www.travels.com

**SOUTH DAKOTA**
South Dakota Department of Tourism
Capitol Lake Plaza
711 East Wells Avenue, Pierre, SD 57501-5070
Ph: 800-S-DAKOTA (For free travel kit)
Ph: 605-773-3301/3391, Fax: 605-773-3256
WEB: www.travelsd.com

**TENNESSEE**
Department of Tourist Development
5th Floor, 320 6th Avenue N., Nashville, TN 37243
Ph: 800-GO2TENN (For free travel kit)
Ph: 615-741-2159/8299, Fax: 615-741-7225
WEB: www.state.tn.us/tourdev.com

**TEXAS**
Texas Department of Economic Development
Tourism Division
P.O. Box 12728, 1700 N. Congress
Austin, TX 78711-2728
Toll-Free: 800-888-8TEX (839) (For free kit)
Ph: 512-462-9191, Fax: 512-936-0088
WEB: www.traveltex.com

**U.S. VIRGIN ISLANDS**
U.S. Virgin Islands Division of Tourism
P.O. Box 6400, St. Thomas, USVI 00804

Toll-Free: 800-372-8784 (For free kit)
Phone: 340-774-8784, Fax: 340-773-5074
WEB: www.usvi.net

**U.S. VIRGIN ISLANDS:** (LA Office)
U.S. Virgin Islands Department of Tourism
3460 Wilshire Boulevard, Suite 412
Los Angeles, CA 90010
Ph: 800-372-USVI (For free travel kit)
Ph: 213-739-0138, Fax: 213-739-2005
WEB: www.usvi.net

**UTAH**
Utah Travel Council
Council Hall/Capitol Hill
300 N. State Street, Salt Lake City, UT 84114
Ph: 800-200-1160 (For free travel kit)
Ph: 801-538-1030/1467, Fax: 801-538-1399
WEB: www.utah.com

**VERMONT**
Department of Tourism and Marketing
6 Baldwin Street, Drawer 33
Montpelier, VT 05633-1301
Ph: 800-VERMONT or Fax: 800-833-9756
(For free travel kit only)
Ph: 802-828-3683, Fax: 802-828-3233
WEB: www.travel-vermont.com

**VIRGINIA**
Virginia Tourism Corporation
901 E. Byrd Street, 19th Floor
Richmond, VA 23219
Ph: 800-VISIT-VA or 800-932- 5827 (For free travel kit)
Ph. 804-786-4484, Fax: 804-786-1919
WEB: www.virginia.org

**WASHINGTON STATE**
Washington State Tourism
P.O. Box 42500, Olympia, WA 98504-2500
Ph: 800-544-1800 (For free travel kit)
Ph: 360-586-2088, Fax: 360-753-4470
WEB: www.tourism.wa.gov

**WASHINGTON, D.C.**
Convention and Visitors Association
1212 New York Avenue N.W., Suite 600
Washington, D.C. 20005-3992
Ph: 202-789-7000, Fax: 202-789-7037
WEB: www.washington.org

**WASHINGTON, D.C. OFFICE OF TOURISM**
717 14th Street NW # 1100
Washington, D.C. 20005
Ph:1-800-422-8644 or 202-727-4511

**WEST VIRGINIA**
Division of Tourism
2101 Washington Street E., Charleston, WV 25305
Ph: 1-800-225-5982 or (800) CALL WVA
(For free travel kit)
Ph: 304-558-2200, Fax: 304-558-2956
WEB: www.state.wv.us/tourism

**WISCONSIN**
Department of Tourism and Travel Information
201 W. Washington Avenue, P.O. Box 7976
Madison, WI 53707-7606
Ph: 800-432-TRIP (out of state)
Ph: 800-372-2737 (in state) (For free travel kit)
Ph: 608-266-2161, Fax: 608-264-6150
WEB: www.travelwisconsin.com

**WYOMING**
Wyoming Business Council Tourism Office
Division of Tourism
214 West 15th Street, Cheyenne, WY 82002
Ph: 800-225-5996 (For free travel kit)
Ph: 307-777-7777, Fax: 307-777-6904
WEB: www.wyomingtourism.org

# APPENDIX C
## UNITED SERVICE ORGANIZATIONS (USO) DIRECTORY

**CALIFORNIA**
**USO OF GREATER LOS ANGELES AREA, INC.**
Los Angeles International Airport Center
Phone: 310-642-0188
Robert S. Bernier, Executive Director
*(Please note: This center is open during limited hours only.)*

**USO AT TRAVIS AFB**
P.O. Box 1663
Travis AFB, CA 94535
Phone: 707-424-3316
Fax: 707-437-9430

**USO OF NORTHERN CALIFORNIA, INC.**
USO Suite, Lobby
Marine's Memorial Club
609 Sutter Street
San Francisco, CA 94102
Phone: 415-440-2110
Fax: 415-440-2115
650-761-4611 (Airport Office)
E-mail: uso-nca@worldnet.att.net
Cynthia Smith, Executive Director

**USO OF SAN DIEGO, INC.**
303 A Street
San Diego, California 92101-4216
Phone: 619-235-6503
Fax: 619-232-5520
E-mail: usosandiego@juno.com
Regan R. Wright, Executive Director

**COLORADO**
**USO OF PIKES PEAK REGION, INC.**
207 N. Nevada Avenue
P.O. Box 1694
Colorado Springs, Colorado 80901
Phone: 719-471-9790 ext 222/223
Fax: 719-471-1723
E-mail: uso@ppymca.org
Ted Rinebarger, Executive Director

**DELAWARE**
**USO DELAWARE, INC.**
500 Eagle Way
USO, East Wing
Dover AFB, Delaware 19902
Phone: 302-677-2491
302-677-2410
Fax: 302-677-2982
Lounge: 302-677-6905
E-mail: uso2@uscom.com
Joan Cote, Executive Director

**DISTRICT OF COLUMBIA**
**USO OF METROPOLITAN WASHINGTON, INC.**
204 Lee Avenue
Bldg. #59, Post Headquarters
Room B-9
Fort Myer, Virginia 22211
Phone: 703-696-2628
Fax: 703-696-2550
Elaine Rogers, President

**FLORIDA**
**USO OF CENTRAL FLORIDA, INC.**
P.O. Box 149472
Orlando, Florida 32814
Phone: 407-647-0407
Fax: 407-647-2563
Betty Wyman, Executive Director

**GREATER JACKSONVILLE AREA USO, INC.**
Building #1050
P.O. Box 108
NAS Jacksonville, Florida 32212
Phone: 904-778-2821
Fax: 904-772-5214
E-mail: usojax@cybermax.net
William H. Kennedy, Executive Director

**USO OF ST. AUGUSTINE AND ST. JOHNS COUNTIES, INC.**
American Legion Post 37
1 Anderson Circle
P.O. Box 4
St. Augustine, Florida 32084
William H. Kennedy (see above) – Point of Contact

**USO OF GREATER PENSACOLA AREA, INC.**
P.O. Box 4321
Pensacola, Florida 32507-0321
Phone: 904-455-1064
Fax: 904-455-1064 *(Please call beforehand.)*
E-mail: usopcola@gulf.net
James M. Petrovich, Executive Director

**GEORGIA**
**USO OF GEORGIA, INC.**
Hartsfield International Airport
P.O. Box 20963
Atlanta, Georgia 30320
Phone: 404-530-6770
Fax: 404-765-1794
Mary Louise Austin, President

**HAWAII**
**USO OF HAWAII, INC.**
Honolulu International Airport
300 Rodgers Boulevard #48
Honolulu, Hawaii 96819-1897
Phone: 808-836-3351
Fax: 808-833-2012
E-mail: usohawaii@juno.com
Connie Guenther, Executive Director

**ILLINOIS**
**USO OF ILLINOIS, INC.**
332 North Michigan Avenue
3rd Floor
Chicago, Illinois 60601
Phone: 312-781-0730
Fax: 312-781-0740
Charles E. Anderson, Executive Director

**INDIANA**
**USO OF INDIANAPOLIS, INC.**
Phone: 317-241-6070 (Airport Center)
Betty Crawford, Executive Director

**KENTUCKY**
**USO OF KENTUCKY, INC.**
P.O. Box 72626
Louisville, Kentucky 40272
Phone: 502-624-6800
502-361-1888 (Airport Center)
Fran Moore, Executive Director

**MASSACHUSETTS**
**USO OF NEW ENGLAND, INC.**
Building #8, 2nd Deck
427 Commercial Street
Boston, Massachusetts 02109-1027
Phone: 617-720-4949/4531
Fax: 617-720-0982
E-mail: usone@msn.com
Phil Cronin, Executive Director

**USO at Logan Airport**
Terminal C, Lower Level
Boston, Massachusetts
Phone: 617-880-8930

Send correspondence to the following address:
USO of New England
427 Commercial Street
Boston, MA 02109-1027
E-mail: usone@msn.com

**USO OF PIONEER VALLEY, INC.**
1820 Seawolf Avenue
Chicopee, Massachusetts 01022-1659
Phone: 413-593-6395
Fax: 413-593-6396
E-mail: pvuso@sprintmail.com
Sandy Wakefield, Executive Director

**MISSOURI**
**JAMES S. MCDONNELL USO, INC.**
P.O. Box 10367
Lambert St. Louis International Airport
St. Louis, Missouri 63145
Phone: 314-429-7702
Fax: 314-429-0506
E-mail: usostlouis@aol.com
Ginny M. Compton, Executive Director

**NEW YORK**
**USO OF METROPOLITAN NEW YORK, INC.**
283 Lexington Avenue
New York, New York 10016
Phone: 212-448-0455
Fax: 212-448-9297
E-mail: usonyc16@aol.com
Eugene V. Lombardo, Executive Director

**USO GENERAL DOUGLAS MACARTHUR MEMORIAL CENTER**
283 Lexington Avenue
New York, New York 10016
Phone: 212-448-0496
Fax: 212-448-9297
E-mail: usonyc16@aol.com
Hazel Cathers, Director
*Note: Please direct all tourism inquiries to this center.*

**USO COUNCIL OF WATERTOWN, INC.**
P.O. Box 912
Watertown, New York 13601
Phone: 315-782-3082
Mary Parry, Council President

**NORTH CAROLINA**
**USO COUNCIL OF JACKSONVILLE-CAMP LEJEUNE AREA, INC.**
9 Tallman Street
Jacksonville, North Carolina 28540
Phone: 910-455-3411
Fax: 910-455-1341
E-mail: uso@gibralter.com
Matthew B. Hardiman, Executive Director

**OHIO**
**USO OF CENTRAL OHIO, INC.**
Port Columbus International Airport
4600 East 17th Avenue, Room 102-A
Columbus, Ohio 43219
Phone: 614-231-7300
Jake Brewer, Executive Director

**USO OF NORTHERN OHIO, INC.**
9199 Market Place
Broadview Heights, Ohio 44147
Phone: 440-717-0999
Bernice O'Malley, Executive Director

**PENNSYLVANIA**
**USO OF PHILADELPHIA, INC.**
Airport Center
Philadelphia International Airport
Terminal D
Philadelphia, Pennsylvania 19153
Phone: 215-365-8889
Fax: 215-365-0249
E-mail: usophl@juno.com
Josephine Dagel, Executive Director

*Appendix C, continued*

## SOUTH CAROLINA
### USO OF CHARLESTON, INC.
5500 International Boulevard
Suite #120
Charleston, South Carolina 29418-6922
Phone: 803-883-3811
Michael B. Ralston, Executive Director

## TENNESSEE
### USO OF METROPOLITAN MEMPHIS & SHELBY COUNTY, INC.
7918 Church Street
P.O. Box 907
Millington, Tennessee 38083-0907
Phone: 901-872-7722
Fax: 901-872-7330
E-mail: mempuso@bigriver.net
Joyce Waters, Executive Director

## TEXAS
### USO OF SOUTH TEXAS, INC.
Building 3, Naval Air Station
Corpus Christi, Texas 78419
Phone at Ingleside: 512-776-4779
Fax: 512-776-4778 (*Manual fax -- please call beforehand.*)
E-mail: uso@interconnect.net
Don Rymer, Executive Director

### USO OF GREATER HOUSTON, INC.
P.O. Box 397
Houston, Texas 77001-0397
Phone: 713-313-1754
Fax: 713-528-2422
E-mail: mtcarr@nol.net
Michael Carr, Executive Director

### USO OF SAN ANTONIO AND CENTRAL TEXAS, INC.
420 East Commerce Street
San Antonio, Texas 78205
Phone: 210-227-9373
Fax: 210-299-4435
E-mail: alamouso@alamouso.org
Caryl Hill, Executive Director

## VIRGINIA
### USO OF HAMPTON ROADS, INC.
Coliseum Mall
1800 West Mercury Boulevard
Hampton, Virginia 23666
Phone: 757-827-1063
Fax: 757-838-9020
E-mail: usohamptrd@aol.com
Gail Young, Executive Director

## WASHINGTON
### USO OF THE PUGET SOUND AREA, INC.
Sea-Tac International Airport
Military Lounge Terminal, 2nd Floor
Seattle, Washington 98158
Phone: 206-246-1908 Sea-Tac Main Office
Fax: 206-246-1914
Phone: 206-433-5438 Sea-Tac Airport Center
Phone: 206-984-2400 McChord AFB Center
Ruth Hamblin, Executive Director

## WISCONSIN
### USO OF WISCONSIN-SOUTHEASTERN REGION, INC.
War Memorial Center
750 N. Lincoln Memorial Drive
Milwaukee, Wisconsin 53202
Phone: 414-271-3133
Kenneth R. Nowak, Executive Director

## U.S. VIRGIN ISLANDS
### USO OF ST. THOMAS
P.O. Box 2112
St. Thomas, U.S.V.I 00340
Phone: 340-704-1193
Fraser Drummond, Council President
*Open during Navy ship visits.*

### USO OF ST. CROIX
114 Market Street
St. Croix, U.S.V.I. 00841
Phone: 340-772-0922
Rodger Nickell, Council President
*Open during Navy ship visits.*

### USO OF ST. MAARTEN
Netherlands Antilles
Annie Sotomayor, Council President
*USO volunteers will be located at the city landing during Navy ship visits.*

### USO WORLD HEADQUARTERS
Washington Navy Yard
1008 Eberle Place SE, Suite 301
Washington, D.C. 20374-5096
Phone: 202-610-5700
Fax: 202-638-0901

# APPENDIX D
## RETIREMENT SERVICES OFFICES DIRECTORY

| STATE INSTALLATION | BRANCH | PHONE # |
|---|---|---|
| AL Fort Rucker | Army | 334-255-9124 |
| AL Maxwell Air Force Base | Air Force | 334-953-6725 or 263-1400 |
| AL Redstone Arsenal | Army | 205-842-7374 |
| AK Elmendorf Air Force Base | Air Force | 907-522-2337 or 5532 |
| AK Fort Richardson | Army | 907-384-3500 |
| AK Fort Wainwright | Army | 907-353-2102 |
| AZ Davis-Monthan Air Force Base | Air Force | 520-228-5100 |
| AZ Fort Huachuca | Army | 520-533-5733 |
| AZ Luke Air Force Base | Air Force | 602-856-6827 |
| AZ Phoenix | Navy | 602-484-7296 |
| AZ Tucson | Navy | 520-748-1013/4 |
| AR Little Rock Air Force Base | Air Force | 501-987-6095 |
| CA Barstow MCLB | Marine Corps | 760-577-6755 |
| CA Beale Air Force Base | Air Force | 916-634-2157 |
| CA China Lake Naval Air Weapons Station | Navy | 619-939-0978 |
| CA Edwards Air Force Base | Air Force | 805-277-4931 |
| CA Fort Irwin National Training Center | Army | 661-277-4931 |
| CA Lemoore Naval Air Station | Navy | 209-998-4042 |
| CA Los Angeles Air Force Base | Air Force | 310-363-5120 |
| CA March Air Reserve Base | Air Force | 909-655-4077/9 |
| CA McClellan Air Force Base | Air Force | 916-643-2207 or 4309 |
| CA Miramar Marine Corps Air Station | Marine Corps | 619-577-4103 |
| CA Monterey Naval Postgrad School | Navy | 831-242-5595 |
| CA Onizuka Air Station | Air Force | 415-603-8047 |
| CA Port Hueneme NCBC | Navy | 805-982-1023 |
| CA Presidio of San Francisco | Army | 415-561-3600 |
| CA San Diego (MCRD) | Marine Corps | 619-524-5301 |
| CA San Diego (Miramar) | Marine Corps | 619-537-4806 |
| CA San Diego (NS) | Navy | 619-556-7404 |
| CA San Francisco (NS) | Navy | 415-395-5176/89 |
| CA Travis Air Force Base | Air Force | 707-424-3904 |
| CA Twentynine Palms MC Air/Ground CC | Air/Army | 760-830-7550 |
| CA Vandenberg Air Force Base | Air Force | 805-734-8232 |
| CO Buckley Air National Guard Base | Air Force | 303-677-6693/4 |
| CO Fort Carson | Army | 719-526-5709 or 800-880-7876 |
| CO Peterson Air Force Base | Air Force | 719-556-7153 |
| CT New London Naval Submarine Base | Navy | 860-694-3284 |
| DE Dover Air Force Base | Air Force | 302-677-4612 |
| DC Bolling Air Force Base | Air Force | 202-767-5244 |
| DC Washington NSA- Anacostia Annex | Navy | 202-433-6150/42 |
| FL Eglin Air Force Base | Air Force | 850-882-5916 |
| FL Homestead Air Reserve Station | Air Force | 305-224-7580 |
| FL Hurlburt Field | Air Force | 850-884-5443 |
| FL Jacksonville Naval Air Station | Navy | 904-542-5783 |
| FL MacDill Air Force Base | Air Force | 813-828-2712 |
| FL Mayport Naval Station | Navy | 904-270-6600 |
| FL Orlando Naval Training Center | Navy | 407-646-4613 |
| FL Patrick Air Force Base | Air Force | 407-494-5463 |
| FL Pensacola (NAS) | Navy | 850-452-5990/1 |
| FL St. Petersburg CCG | Navy | 727-824-7504 |
| FL Tyndall Air Force Base | Air Force | 850-283-2737 |
| GA Atlanta Naval Air Station | Navy | 770-919-6735 |
| GA Fort Benning | Army | 706-545-2715 |
| GA Fort Gordon/US Army Signal Center | Army | 706-791-1942 |
| GA Fort McPherson | Army | 404-464-3219 |
| GA Fort Stewart | Army | 912-767-5013 |
| GA Kings Bay NSB | Navy | 912-942-4517 |
| GA Moody Air Force Base | Air Force | 912-257-3315 |
| GA Robins Air Force Base | Air Force | 912-926-2019 |
| GU Andersen AFB | Air Force | 671-366-4315 |
| HI Camp H.M. Smith MCB | Marine Corps | 808-471-3345 |
| HI Fort Shafter | Army | 808-655-1514 |
| HI Hickam Air Force Base | Air Force | 808-449-9896 |
| HI Kaneohe MCB | Marine Corps | 808-257-3135 |
| HI Pearl Harbor Naval Station | Navy | 808-471-3345 |
| HI Wheeler Army Airfield | Army | 808-438-2798 |
| ID Gowen Field | Air Force | 208-422-5817 |
| ID Mountain Home Air Force Base | Air Force | 208-828-4878 |
| IL Great Lakes NTC | Navy | 847-688-5434 ext 421 |
| IL Scott Air Force Base | Air Force | 618-256-5092 |
| IA Camp Dodge/Iowa NGB | Army | 515-252-4413 |
| IN Crane Division NSWC | Navy | 812-854-1222 |
| IN Fort Benjamin Harrison ARC | Army | 317-542-4364 |
| IN Grissom Air Reserve Base | Air Force | 765-688-8687 |
| KS Fort Leavenworth | Army | 913-684-2425/6 |
| KS Fort Riley | Army | 785-239-3320 |
| KS McConnell Air Force Base | Air Force | 316-652-3729 or 3829 |
| KY Fort Campbell | Army | 502-798-5280 |
| KY Fort Knox | Army | 502-624-1765 |
| LA Barksdale Air Force Base | Air Force | 318-456-5976 |
| LA Fort Polk JRTC | Army | 318-531-4515 |
| LA New Orleans NAS/JRB | Navy | 504-678-2134 |
| ME Brunswick Naval Air Station | Navy | 207-921-2609 |
| MD Aberdeen Proving Ground | Army | 410-278-7017 |
| MD Andrews Air Force Base | Air Force | 301-981-2726 or 2180 |
| MD Annapolis Naval Station | Navy | 410-293-2641 |
| MD Fort George G. Meade | Army | 301-677-7433 or 7685 |
| MD Patuxent River Naval Air Station | Navy | 301-342-4911 |
| MA Devens RFTA | Army | 978-796-2285 |
| MA Hanscom Air Force Base | Air Force | 781-377-2476 |
| MA Otis ANGB/Cape Cod CGAS | Air Force | 508-968-4175 |
| MA Westover Air Reserve Base | Air Force | 413-557-3918 or 3424 |
| MI Fort McCoy/Lower Selfridge ANGB | Air Force | 810-307-5580 |
| MI Detroit (Selfridge) | Navy | 810-307-5580 |
| MI Detroit | Navy | 313-824-4542 |
| MN Minneapolis | Navy | 612-725-5737 |
| MS Columbus Air Force Base | Air Force | 601-434-2780 |
| MS Gulfport NCBC | Navy | 228-871-3000 ext 35 |
| MS Keesler Air Force Base | Air Force | 228-377-3871 or 7309 |
| MO Fort Leonard Wood | Army | 573-596-0947 |
| MO St. Louis | Navy | 314-263-6443 |
| MO Whiteman Air Force Base | Air Force | 660-687-6457 |
| MT Malmstrom Air Force Base | Air Force | 406-731-3071 |
| NE Lincoln | Navy | 402-470-2142 |
| NE Offutt Air Force Base | Air Force | 402-294-2590 or 4566 |
| NV Fallon Naval Air Station | Navy | 702-426-3333 or 2317 |
| NV Nellis Air Force Base | Air Force | 702-652-6070 |
| NJ Earle Naval Weapons Station | Navy | 908-866-2585 |
| NJ Fort Dix Army Garrison | Army | 509-562-9689 |
| NJ Fort Monmouth | Army | 732-532-4673 |
| NJ Lakehurst NAES | Navy | 908-323-1224 |
| NJ McGuire Air Force Base | Air Force | 609-724-2459 |
| NM Cannon Air Force Base | Air Force | 505-784-4865 |
| NM Holloman Air Force Base | Air Force | 505-475-3140 |
| NM Kirtland Air Force Base | Air Force | 505-846-1536 |
| NY Amityville | Navy | 516-842-6620 |
| NY Fort Drum | Army | 315-772-6434 |
| NY Fort Hamilton | Army | 718-630-4930 |
| NY Niagara Falls Air Reserve Station | Air Force | 716-236-2389 |
| NY USMA, West Point | Army | 914-938-4217 |
| NY Watervliet Arsenal | Army | 518-266-5920 or 5169 |
| NC Camp Lejeune MCB | Navy | 910-451-5927 |
| NC Cherry Point MCAS | Marine Corps | 252-466-4401 |
| NC Fort Bragg | Army | 910-396-5304 |
| NC Pope Air Force Base | Air Force | 910-394-1950 |
| NC Seymour Johnson Air Force Base | Air Force | 919-722-1119 |

| STATE | INSTALLATION | BRANCH | PHONE # |
|-------|-------------|--------|---------|
| ND | Grand Forks Air Force Base | Air Force | 701-747-6197 |
| ND | Minot Air Force Base | Air Force | 701-723-6449 |
| OH | Defense Supply Center (Columbus) | Air Force | 614-692-4947 |
| OH | Wright-Patterson Air Force Base | Air Force | 937-257-3221 |
| OK | Altus Air Force Base | Air Force | 580-481-6776 |
| OK | Fort Sill | Army | 405-442-5963 |
| OK | McAlester AA Plant | Army | 918-421-7549 |
| OK | Tinker Air Force Base | Air Force | 405-739-7388 |
| OK | Vance Air Force Base | Air Force | 580-213-7421 |
| OR | Central Point | Navy | 503-772-2566 |
| OR | Eugene | Navy | 503-686-9266 |
| OR | Kingsley Field | Air Force | 541-885-6362 |
| OR | Portland | Navy | 503-335-4945 |
| PA | Carlisle Barracks | Army | 717-245-4501 |
| PA | Charles E. Kelly Support Center | Army | 412-777-1177 |
| PA | Pittsburgh IAP/ARP | Air Force | 412-474-8559 |
| PA | Tobyhanna Depot | Army | 570-895-7834 |
| PA | Willow Grove NAS/JRB | Navy | 215-443-6033 |
| PR | Fort Buchanan | Army | 787-273-3877 |
| PR | Roosevelt Roads Naval Station | Navy | 787-865-4091 |
| RI | Newport NS | Navy | 401-841-4089 |
| SC | Charleston Air Force Base | Air Force | 843-963-2228 |
| SC | Charleston NWS | Navy | 803-764-7294 |
| SC | Fort Jackson | Army | 803-751-6652 |
| SC | Shaw Air Force Base | Air Force | 803-668-3036 |
| SD | Ellsworth Air Force Base | Air Force | 605-385-5050 |
| TN | Arnold Air Force Base | Air Force | 931-454-4574 |
| TN | Mid-South NSA | Navy | 901-874-7510 |
| TX | Brooks Air Force Base | Air Force | 210-536-2116 |
| TX | Camp Mabry | Army | 512-465-5090 |
| TX | Corpus Christi Naval Air Station | Navy | 512-939-3113 |
| TX | Dyess Air Force Base | Air Force | 915-672-6897 or 674-1328 |
| TX | Fort Bliss | Army | 915-568-2632 |
| TX | Fort Hood | Army | 254-287-5210 or 800-403-6640 |
| TX | Fort Sam Houston | Army | 210-221-9004 |
| TX | Goodfellow Air Force Base | Air Force | 915-654-5388 |
| TX | Houston | Navy | 713-795-4109 |
| TX | Ingleside Naval Station | Navy | 361-776-4551 |
| TX | Kelly Air Force Base | Air Force | 210-925-2984/76 |
| TX | Kingsville Naval Air Station | Navy | 512-595-6105 |
| TX | Lackland Air Force Base | Air Force | 210-671-2728 |
| TX | Randolph Air Force Base | Air Force | 210-652-6880 |
| TX | San Antonio | Navy | 210-225-2997 |
| TX | Sheppard Air Force Base | Air Force | 940-676-5088 or 3381 |
| UT | Hill Air Force Base | Air Force | 801-775-5735 |
| UT | Utah Retiree Council | Army | 801-965-8773 |
| VA | Dahlgren NSWC | Navy | 540-653-1839 |
| VA | Fort Belvoir | Army | 703-805-2675 |
| VA | Fort Eustis | Army | 757-878-2953 |
| VA | Fort Lee | Army | 804-734-6973 |
| VA | Fort Monroe | Army | 757-727-2093 |
| VA | Fort Myer | Army | 703-696-5948 |
| VA | Fort Pickett Army Nat'l Guard MTC | Army | 804-292-2306 |
| VA | Langley Air Force Base | Air Force | 757-764-7386 |
| VA | Little Creek NAB | Navy | 757-464-8101 ext 306 |
| VA | Norfolk Naval Base | Navy | 804-444-2102 or 800-372-5463 |
| WA | Bangor Naval Submarine Base | Navy | 206-396-4115 or 800-562-3301 |
| WA | Bremerton Naval Station | Navy | 206-476-5113 800-643-4100 (WA only) |
| WA | Everett Naval Station | Navy | 206-304-3367 |
| WA | Fairchild Air Force Base | Air Force | 509-247-5359 |
| WA | Fort Lewis | Army | 253-967-5913 |
| WA | McChord Air Force Base | Air Force | 253-984-3214 |
| WA | Whidbey Island Naval Air Station | Navy | 206-257-8054 |
| WI | Fort McCoy | Army | 608-388-3716 |
| WI | Gen. Mitchell IAP/ARS | Air Force | 414-482-5207/8 |
| WI | Milwaukee | Navy | 414-744-9766 |
| WI | Truax Field | Air Force | 608-242-3115 |
| WY | Francis E. Warren Air Force Base | Air Force | 307-773-2309 |

# INDEX

# INDEX

# INDEX

# CENTRAL ORDER COUPON

P.O. Box 2347, Falls Church, VA 22042-0347
TEL: (703) 237-0203  FAX: (703) 237-2233

www.militaryliving.com
E-mail: militaryliving@aol.com

| Item # | Publications | ISBN / ISSN | Price | | QTY | Extended Amount |
|--------|-------------|-------------|-------|---|-----|-----------------|
| | **R&R Travel News™.** *The worldwide travel newsletter.* 6 issues/year 1 yr/$19.00 - 2 yrs/$29.00 - 3 yrs/$39.00 - 5 yrs/$59.00 by Standard Business Mail | 0740-5073 | ❏ new ❏ renewal | RR | | |
| 6 | **Assignment Washington Military Road Atlas.** | 0-914862-91-X | $12.25 | AW | | |
| 14 | **U.S. Military Installation Road Map.** (Folded) | 0-914862-80-4 | $8.65 | MAP US | | |
| 14A | (1 unfolded laminated wall map in a hard tube) | 0-914862-80-4 | $19.95 | | | |
| 14B | (2 unfolded laminated wall maps in a hard tube) | 0-914862-80-4 | $35.40 | | | |
| 15 | **COLLECTOR'S ITEM! Desert Shield Commemorative Maps.** (Folded) | 0-914862-27-8 | $8.20 | MAP DS | | |
| 15A | (2 unfolded wall maps in a hard tube) | 0-914862-27-8 | $19.00 | | | |
| 21 | **United States Military Road Atlas.** | 0-914862-83-9 | $20.25 | ATL | | |
| 26 | **Temporary Military Lodging Around the World.** | 0-914862-72-3 | $18.75 | TML | | |
| 27 | **Military RV, Camping & Outdoor Recreation Around the World Including Golf Courses and Marinas.** | 0-914862-74-X | $16.75 | RVC | | |
| | **MILITARY ROAD MAPS** | | | | | |
| 28A | **Alaska & Washington States -** (Folded) | 0-914862-75-8 | $8.15 | MAP AL | | |
| 28B | **California State -** (Folded) | 0-914862-76-6 | $8.15 | MAP CA | | |
| 28C | **Florida State & Puerto Rico -**(Folded) | 0-914862-77-4 | $8.15 | MAP FL | | |
| 28D | **Georgia, North & South Carolina States -** (Folded) | 0-914862-78-2 | $8.15 | MAP GA | | |
| 28E | **Hawaii State & Guam -** (Folded) | 0-914862-79-0 | $8.15 | MAP HI | | |
| 28G | **New Jersey & Pennsylvania States and New York City -** (Folded) | 0-914862-85-5 | $8.15 | MAP NJ | | |
| 28H | **Texas State -** (Folded) | 0-914862-86-3 | $8.15 | MAP TX | | |
| | Any Military State Wall Map (Unfolded Laminated, mix and match) | 1/$19.45, 2/$33.40 | | MAP ___ | | |
| 29 | **European U.S. Military Road Atlas, Plus Near East Areas** *All New Sept '99* | 0-914862-73-1 | $24.25 | ERA | | |
| 30 | **U.S. Forces Travel Guide to U.S. Military Installations.** New Nov. '99 | 0-914862-81-2 | $16.25 | TGA | | |
| 31 | **Military Space-A Air Opportunities Air Route Map** *All New May 2000* | 0-914862-88-X | | | | |
| | (folded) | | $12.95 | MAP SA | | |
| | (2 unfolded wall maps in a hard tube) | | $26.00 | MAP SA | | |
| 32 | **Military Space-A Air Opportunities Around the World.** | 0-914862-87-1 | $21.25 | SAB | | |
| 33 | **Military Space-A Air Basic Training.** | 0-914862-89-8 | $15.75 | BT | | |

**Virginia Addresses add 4.5% sales tax (Books, Maps, & Atlases only)**      **TOTAL $**

Mail order prices are for non- APO/FPO addresses within the U.S. APO/FPO addresses must add $4.00 **per order** for insurance and return receipt. Shipments to Canadian addresses must add an additional $2.50 **per item ordered** for additional postage, shipping, insurance and processing. We do not ship to overseas/international addresses other than U.S. Military Post Offices. Sorry, no billing. We're as close as your telephone...by using our Telephone Ordering Service. We honor American Express, MasterCard, Visa, and Discover. Call us at **703-237-0203** (Voice Mail after hours); FAX: 703-237-2233 or E-mail: milliving@aol.com and order today! Sorry, no collect calls. Or...fill out and mail the order coupon below. Order by internet on our secure web order. Web address– www.militaryliving.com

NAME:_____

STREET:_____

CITY/STATE/ZIP:_____

PHONE:_____ SIGNATURE:_____

Credit Card #_____ Card Expiration Date_____

Name/Address as it appears on credit card/credit card statement _____

The above credit card information is necessary for credit card verification and to obtain approval on your card. It will not be used for any other purpose.

Mail check/money order to Military Living Publications, P.O. Box 2347, Falls Church, VA 22042-0347
Save $$$s by purchasing any of our Books, Maps, and Atlases at your military exchange.
Prices are subject to change. **Please check here if we may ship and bill the difference** ❏

revised 06/21/200
This form may be duplicate

**ALL ORDERS SHIPPED BY 1ST CLASS/PRIORITY MAIL or UPS**

Travel Notes

# CENTRAL ORDER COUPON

P.O. Box 2347, Falls Church, VA 22042-0347
TEL: (703) 237-0203 FAX: (703) 237-2233

www.militaryliving.com
E-mail: militaryliving@aol.com

| Item # | Publications | ISBN / ISSN | Price | QTY | Extended Amount |
|---|---|---|---|---|---|
| | **R&R Travel News™.** *The worldwide travel newsletter.* 6 issues/year<br>1 yr/$19.00 - 2 yrs/$29.00 - 3 yrs/$39.00 - 5 yrs/$59.00 by Standard Business Mail | 0740-5073 | ❏ new<br>❏ renewal RR | | |
| 6 | **Assignment Washington Military Road Atlas.** | 0-914862-91-X | $12.25 AW | | |
| 14<br>14A<br>14B | **U.S. Military Installation Road Map.** (Folded)<br>(1 unfolded laminated wall map in a hard tube)<br>(2 unfolded laminated wall maps in a hard tube) | 0-914862-80-4<br>0-914862-80-4<br>0-914862-80-4 | $8.65 MAP US<br>$19.95<br>$35.40 | | |
| 15<br>15A | **COLLECTOR'S ITEM! Desert Shield Commemorative Maps.**<br>(Folded)<br>(2 unfolded wall maps in a hard tube) | 0-914862-27-8<br>0-914862-27-8 | $8.20 MAP DS<br>$19.00 | | |
| 21 | **United States Military Road Atlas.** | 0-914862-83-9 | $20.25 ATL | | |
| 26 | **Temporary Military Lodging Around the World.** | 0-914862-72-3 | $18.75 TML | | |
| 27 | **Military RV, Camping & Outdoor Recreation Around the World**<br>**Including Golf Courses and Marinas.** | 0-914862-74-X | $16.75 RVC | | |
| | **MILITARY ROAD MAPS** | | | | |
| 28A | **Alaska & Washington States -** (Folded) | 0-914862-75-8 | $8.15 MAP AL | | |
| 28B | **California State -** (Folded) | 0-914862-76-6 | $8.15 MAP CA | | |
| 28C | **Florida State & Puerto Rico -**(Folded) | 0-914862-77-4 | $8.15 MAP FL | | |
| 28D | **Georgia, North & South Carolina States -** (Folded) | 0-914862-78-2 | $8.15 MAP GA | | |
| 28E | **Hawaii State & Guam -** (Folded) | 0-914862-79-0 | $8.15 MAP HI | | |
| 28G | **New Jersey & Pennsylvania States and New York City -** (Folded) | 0-914862-85-5 | $8.15 MAP NJ | | |
| 28H | **Texas State -** (Folded) | 0-914862-86-3 | $8.15 MAP TX | | |
| | **Any Military State Wall Map** (Unfolded Laminated, mix and match) | 1/$19.45, 2/$33.40 MAP ___ | | | |
| 29 | **European U.S. Military Road Atlas,**<br>**Plus Near East Areas** *All New Sept '99* | 0-914862-73-1 | $24.25 ERA | | |
| 30 | **U.S. Forces Travel Guide to U.S. Military Installations.** New Nov. '99 | 0-914862-81-2 | $16.25 TGA | | |
| 31 | **Military Space-A Air Opportunities Air Route Map** *All New May 2000*<br>(folded)<br>(2 unfolded wall maps in a hard tube) | 0-914862-88-X | <br>$12.95 MAP SA<br>$26.00 MAP SA | | |
| 32 | **Military Space-A Air Opportunities Around the World.** | 0-914862-87-1 | $21.25 SAB | | |
| 33 | **Military Space-A Air Basic Training.** | 0-914862-89-8 | $15.75 BT | | |
| | | | | | |

**Virginia Addresses add 4.5% sales tax (Books, Maps, & Atlases only)**      **TOTAL $**

Mail order prices are for non- APO/FPO addresses within the U.S. APO/FPO addresses must add **$4.00 per order** for insurance and return receipt. Shipments to Canadian addresses must add an additional **$2.50 per item ordered** for additional postage, shipping, insurance and processing. We do not ship to overseas/international addresses other than U.S. Military Post Offices. Sorry, no billing. We're as close as your telephone...by using our Telephone Ordering Service. We honor American Express, MasterCard, Visa, and Discover. Call us at **703-237-0203** (Voice Mail after hours); FAX: 703-237-2233 or E-mail: milliving@aol.com and order today! Sorry, no collect calls. Or...fill out and mail the order coupon below. Order by internet on our secure web order. Web address– www.militaryliving.com

NAME:_____

STREET:_____

CITY/STATE/ZIP:_____

PHONE:_____ SIGNATURE:_____

Credit Card #_____Card Expiration Date_____

Name/Address as it appears on credit card/credit card statement _____

The above credit card information is necessary for credit card verification and to obtain approval on your card. It will not be used for any other purpose.

Mail check/money order to Military Living Publications, P.O. Box 2347, Falls Church, VA 22042-0347
Save $$$s by purchasing any of our Books, Maps, and Atlases at your military exchange.
Prices are subject to change. **Please check here if we may ship and bill the difference ❏**

**revised 06/21/2000**
This form may be duplicated

**ALL ORDERS SHIPPED BY 1ST CLASS/PRIORITY MAIL or UPS**